BRIEF CONTENTS

CONTENTS

PREFACE

Today's accountant operates in a rapidly changing business environment. Business operations and transactions are increasingly global, and entities must consider the sustainability and social consequences of their operations. The global financial crisis has highlighted the use of a range of financial derivatives, and the limited information provided about their use and value. Globalisation has led to international convergence of accounting practices, which in turn has led to substantial changes in those accounting practices. Global warming has resulted in the introduction of emissions trading schemes or carbon tax requirements in many jurisdictions. Each of these events has extended the boundaries of financial accounting. This textbook considers a broad range of these contemporary financial accounting issues.

It is not possible, in one textbook, to consider all the issues and influences on financial accounting. In this book we have selected issues to consider based on their contemporary relevance and significance. We examine the regulatory setting within which accounting operates from the context of the process of standard setting, and the *Conceptual Framework*. Within this framework one of the most controversial areas of accounting — measurement — is examined in detail. Alternative measurement choices are considered, with intangibles and sustainability reporting being examined in more detail as they are areas with unique measurement challenges. With the increasing use of fair value measurement, we present a comprehensive analysis of this measurement basis, including its application in specific contexts. The globalisation of business resulting in international convergence of accounting regulations is also evaluated, along with a discussion of the impact of a range of environmental and cultural factors that lead to diversity of international accounting practice. The impact of international accounting and tax issues on multinational enterprises is also considered.

Corporate failures and the recent global financial crisis have influenced financial accounting. This text examines the causes and consequences of corporate failure, factors used to predict failure, and the role of corporate governance. Corporate governance is examined elsewhere in the text in more detail, including its relationship with executive compensation and earnings management. Given the increasing importance of climate change, sustainability is an area of concern for society, government and business. We explore sustainability and the role of accounting, and consider accounting for emissions trading schemes.

Contemporary Issues in Accounting is suited to a wide range of courses, and is particularly relevant to advanced financial accounting subjects at both undergraduate and postgraduate level. Examining financial accounting issues from a range of perspectives is a particular strength of the book. In doing so it explores issues from a practical perspective, considering the range of issues and characteristics of a financial accounting problem or issue that poses a problem or challenge for contemporary accounting. Appropriate theories and research findings that can advance our understanding and provide guidance, insights or explanations are also examined. This encourages students to look beyond procedural 'debits and credits' and to appreciate the many influences on contemporary financial accounting decisions, and the role of financial accountants in business today.

Recognising the increasing demand for graduates with strong skills in communication, problem solving, critical thinking and judgement, and the need to provide assurance that graduates have developed these skills, Threshold Learning Outcomes for accounting bachelors and coursework masters degrees have been developed. This text supports the development of these learning outcomes by highlighting which skills are developed across the range of end-of-chapter activities and within chapter Contemporary Issue features.

We would like to offer our thanks to colleagues who provided valuable feedback that greatly contributed to the development of this text. In particular, our sincere thanks go to Ellie Chapple, Queensland University of Technology; Victoria Clout, University of New South Wales; Jesmin Islam, University of Canberra; Majella Percy, Griffith University; and Monte Wynder, University of the Sunshine Coast. Patricia Stanton would also like to thank Gregory Phillip, a PhD student and part-time lecturer at The University of Newcastle, for assisting with the development of chapter 14 on special reporting issues.

We also thank the highly professional editorial and management team at John Wiley & Sons for its hard work and dedication to the production of *Contemporary Issues in Accounting*, and its commitment to supporting quality accounting education. Finally, we thank our families for their continual support and patience throughout the writing of this text.

Michaela Rankin
Patricia Stanton
Susan McGowan
Kimberly Ferlauto
Matthew Tilling
February 2012

Michaela Rankin

Michaela Rankin, PhD (RMIT), MEc (UNE), GradCertHE (Monash), BBus (Hons) (USQ), CPA, is a senior lecturer in the Department of Accounting and Finance at Monash University, Melbourne. Prior to joining Monash, Michaela held positions at both RMIT University and the University of Southern Queensland, where she was awarded the Institute of Chartered Accountants in Australia Award for Teaching Excellence in 1998. She teaches financial accounting and accounting theory at both undergraduate and postgraduate levels. Michaela has a broad range of research interests including financial reporting and governance, executive compensation, the regulation and practice of sustainability reporting, carbon emissions disclosure, and accounting education. She has published widely in international journals including *Accounting, Auditing & Accountability Journal, British Accounting Review, Accounting & Finance, Higher Education Research and Development* and *Australian Accounting Review.*

Patricia Stanton

Patricia Stanton, PhD (Newcastle), BComm (Hons 1) (Newcastle), BA (Sydney) and DipEd (Sydney), is a senior lecturer in financial accounting at The University of Newcastle. She has published widely in international journals such as *Accounting, Auditing & Accountability Journal, Australian Accounting Review, Corporate Communications: An International Journal* and *Accounting History.* Two of her papers have won international best paper awards. Her current research interests are focused on the value of current reporting practices, and the implications of corporate failure for the accounting profession.

Susan McGowan

Susan McGowan, BAcc (SAIT), MCom (UniSA), and GradCertEd(HigherEd) (QUT), is currently a senior lecturer in the School of Commerce at the University of South Australia. Her research interests focus on accounting education and international accounting.

Kimberly Ferlauto

Kimberly Ferlauto, BComAcctg (UWS), MComAcctg (UWS), CPA, is an associate lecturer in accounting at the University of Western Sydney. She has been teaching accounting theory for many years at both an undergraduate and postgraduate level. Her focus when teaching theory is on understanding why we do what we do as accountants and application of accounting theory to current real world events. Other teaching interests include entrepreneurship and small business, accounting information systems and financial planning. Kimberly's main research interests include accounting measurement and social and environmental accounting.

Matthew Tilling

Matthew Tilling, BCom (Flinders), is a senior lecturer in accounting at the University of Notre Dame, Australia. He has taught a range of accounting topics to both undergraduates and postgraduates in over a decade of university teaching, with a primary focus on issues affecting large corporations. This academic focus has been complemented with the provision of extensive consulting and training services to a range of professional and corporate entities on a wide range of current accounting problems. He has also been involved with syllabus and exam design for high school accounting in Western Australia. Matthew has published articles on accounting education and social and environmental accounting in a range of international journals.

HOW TO USE THIS BOOK

Contemporary Issues in Accounting has been designed with you — the student — in mind. The design is our attempt to provide you with a book that both communicates the subject matter and facilitates learning. We have tried to accomplish these goals through the following elements.

LEARNING OBJECTIVES are clearly stated and linked to subsequent discussion in the chapter.

CONCEPTUAL MIND MAPS diagrammatically present the topics in the chapter and the interrelationship between them.

CONTEMPORARY ISSUE vignettes apply the accounting concepts and approaches presented in the chapter to actual events in business. Each vignette has a number of questions, linked to the Threshold Learning Outcomes for accounting. Completing these activities will help you to develop key competencies relevant to your studies in accounting.

THRESHOLD LEARNING OUTCOMES What are they? Threshold learning outcomes recognise the desirable graduate attributes and skills of communication, problem solving, critical thinking and judgement, and the need to provide assurance graduates have developed these skills. The text supports the development of these learning outcomes by highlighting which skills are developed across the range of end-of-chapter activities and in the Contemporary Issue features within the chapters.

Threshold learning outcomes for accounting

J Judgement

K Knowledge

AS Application Skills

CT Communication and Teamwork

SM Self-Management

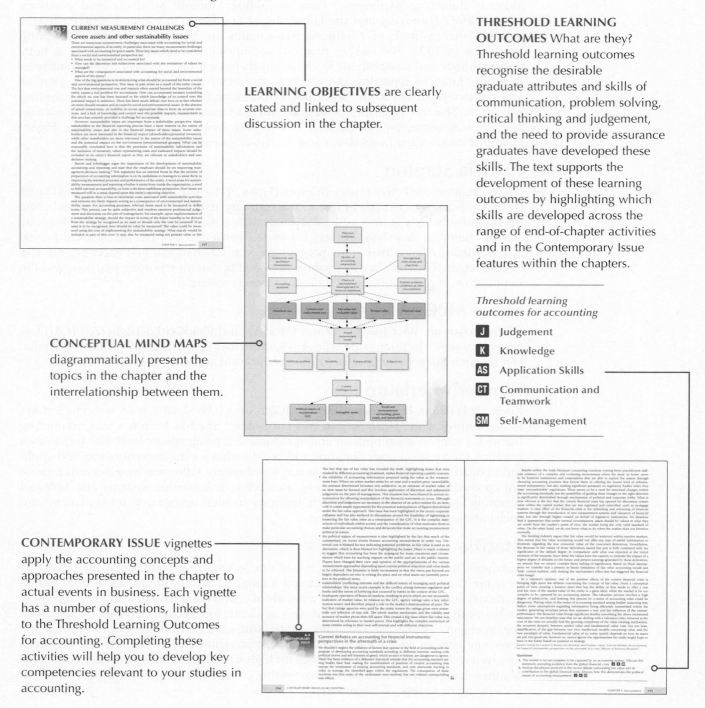

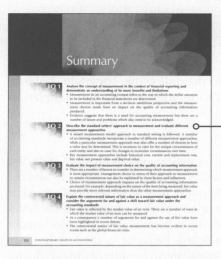

ADDITIONAL READINGS provides a list of current and relevant readings on the chapter topics.

The **SUMMARY** restates each learning objective and outlines the key knowledge associated with each learning objective.

APPLICATION QUESTIONS develop your conceptual understanding of the material presented in the chapter, and encourage considered comment. Each question is codified according to the appropriate Threshold Learning Outcome for Accounting.

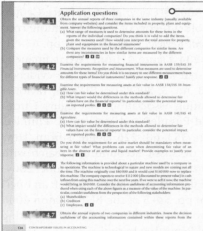

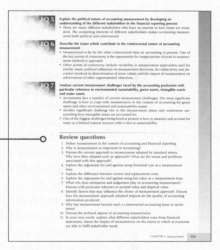

REVIEW QUESTIONS test your understanding of the material presented in the chapter, and encourage considered comment.

KEY TERMS are presented at the end of the book, and provide an invaluable resource for your learning.

CASE STUDIES encourage detailed evaluation of accounting models, concepts and policy choices and their application to contemporary issues. These challenging exercises are ideal for group discussion and build professional communication skills.

ACKNOWLEDGEMENTS

The authors and publisher would like to thank the following copyright holders, organisations and individuals for their permission to reproduce copyright material in this book.

Images

• Australian accounting standards © 2011 Australian Accounting Standards Board (AASB). The text, graphics and layout of this publication are protected by Australian copyright law and the comparable law of other countries. No part of the publication may be reproduced, stored or transmitted in any form or by any means without the prior written permission of the AASB except as permitted by law. For reproduction or publication permission should be sought in writing from the Australian Accounting Standards Board. Requests in the first instance should be addressed to the Administration Director, Australian Accounting Standards Board, PO Box 204, Collins Street West, Melbourne, Victoria, 8007 • Copyright Clearance Center: **146** from Donaldson, T & Preston, LE 1995, 'The stakeholder theory of the corporation: concepts, evidence and implications', *Academy of Management Review*, vol. 20, no. 1, pp. 65–91, with permission from the Academy of Management; **234** Figure 1 from 'What financial and non-financial information on intangibles is value-relevant? A review of the evidence' by Anne Wyatt, *Accounting and Business Research*, vol. 38, no. 3, 2008, pp. 217–56, Taylor & Francis Group www.informaworld • © American Accounting Association: **173** Figure 1 from 'Assurance on XBRL for financial reporting' by R. David Plumlee and Marlene A. Plumlee, *Accounting Horizons*, vol. 22, no. 3, September 2008, pp. 353–68; **226** Figure 1 from 'How do earnings numbers relate to stock returns? A review of classic accounting research with updated evidence' by Nichols and Wahlen, *Accounting Horizons*, vol. 18, no. 4, December 2004, pp. 263–86 • © Ernst & Young South Africa: **199** from 'Effective governance model: an operating framework', 2009, p. 3 • BHP Billiton: **316–7** from pp. 54–5 of the BHP Billiton 2006 full sustainability report. Reproduced with permission from BHP Billiton • Global Reporting Initiative: **324** Reproduced with permission from Global Reporting Initiative • © AGL Energy Ltd: **326** • © CIMA: **405** from 'Intangibles and the OFR' by Vivien Beattie and Sarah Jane Thomson, *Financial Management*, June 2005.

Text

• Australian accounting standards © 2011 Australian Accounting Standards Board (AASB). The text, graphics and layout of this publication are protected by Australian copyright law and the comparable law of other countries. No part of the publication may be reproduced, stored or transmitted in any form or by any means without the prior written permission of the AASB except as permitted by law. For reproduction or publication permission should be sought in writing from the Australian Accounting Standards Board. Requests in the first instance should be addressed to the Administration Director, Australian Accounting Standards Board, PO Box 204, Collins Street West, Melbourne, Victoria, 8007 • International financial reporting standards © 2011 IFRS Foundation. All rights reserved. No permission granted to reproduce or distribute. Reproduced by Rankin with the permission of the IFRS Foundation • Copyright Clearance Center: **13** Abstract for *Critical Perspectives on Accounting*, vol. 21, iss. 8, '"No accounting for these people": Shell in Ireland and accounting language' by Shiela Killian, November 2010, with permission from Elsevier; **13–14** Reprinted from the abstract for 'To tell the truth: A discussion of issues concerning truth and ethics in accounting' by Bayou, Reinstein & Williams, *Accounting, Organizations and Society*, vol. 36, no. 2, 2011, with permission from Elsevier; **141** Adapted from K Eisenhardt 1988, 'Agency — and institutional — theory explanations: The case of retail sales compensation', *Academy of Management Journal*, vol. 31, no. 3,

p. 491. Reproduced with permission; **228** from 'Economists and the global financial crisis' by J. E. King, *Global Change, Peace and Security*, vol. 21, iss. 3, October 2009, pp. 389–96, reprinted by permission of Taylor & Francis Group, http://www.informaworld.com; **407** from John Holland, 2006, 'Fund management, intellectual capital, intangibles and private disclosure', *Managerial Finance*, vol. 32, no. 4, pp. 313–14 © Emerald Group Publishing Limited all rights reserved • CPA Journal: **34** from 'The GAAP between public and private companies' by Mary-Jo Kranacher. Reprinted from *The CPA Journal*, June 2006, with permission from the New York State Society of Certified Public Accountants; **107–9** from 'The subprime lending crisis and reliable reporting' by Benjamin P. Foster and Trimbak Shastri. Reprinted from *The CPA Journal*, April 2010, with permission from the New York State Society of Certified Public Accountants • Incisive Media: **40–1** from 'No pain, no gain' by Veronica Poole, *Accountancy Age*, 9 September 2010. Reproduced with permission • ICAA: **54–6** 'What's new in water and carbon accounting' by Keryn Chalmers, Jayne Godfrey & Brad Potter, *Charter*, September 2009. vol. 80, iss. 8; pp. 20–2, reproduced with permission • Wright's Media: **56–7** 'Companies brace for powerful impact of lease accounting changes' by Beth Mattson–Teig, *National Real Estate Investor*, September 9, 2010. Copyrighted 2011. Penton Media, Inc. 82657:1111SH • Accountancy Ireland: **53–4** from 'Code of Ethics — IFAC issues revised code for professional Accountants' by Richard George, October 2005. Reproduced with permission • Copyright Agency Limited: **75–6** from 'Treasury chiefs revolt over budget rules' by Mark Davis, *The Australian Financial Review*, Fairfax Media, 3/4/06. Reproduced with permission; **138** from 'News resets top executive pay' by Neil Shoebridge, *The Australian Financial Review*, Fairfax Media, 5/8/10, p. 19. Reproduced with permission; **143–4** from 'The banks take much, but give less and less back' by Stuart Wilson, *The Age*, Fairfax Media, 9/4/09, p. 16. Reproduced with permission; **154** from 'Boral hoses down concerns over debt covenants' by Scott Rochfort, *The Sydney Morning Herald*, Fairfax Media, 21/1/09, p. 17. Reproduced with permission; **154–5** 'Pay backlash prompts shift to bonuses' by Patrick Durkin, *The Australian Financial Review*, Fairfax Media, 21/1/07, p. 3. Reproduced with permission; **169–70** from 'Be kind to shareholders' by Stuart Wilson, *The Australian*, News Limited, 9/6/06, p. 32. Reproduced with permission; **208–9** from 'Individuals must take responsibility' by Alex Malley, *The Age*, Fairfax Media, 23/6/10. Reproduced with permission; **240–1** 'Road to wealth may lie in marching out of step' by Ross Gittins, *The Sydney Morning Herald*, Fairfax Media, 30/9/06, p. 38. Reproduced with permission; **250** 'Women take more risks when investing: survey' by Anna Fenech, *The Weekend Australian*, News Limited, 22/7/06, p. 40. Reproduced with permission; **263** 'Earnings quality', *The Herald Sun*, Herald & Weekly Times, 6/10/07, p. 90. Reproduced with permission; **289** 'How to conjure up billions' by Jonathan Weil, *The Sydney Morning Herald*, Fairfax Media, 13/9/10. Reproduced with permission; **295–6** 'Serial floats and patent porkies' by Kate McClymont and Michael West, *The Sydney Morning Herald*, Fairfax Media, 4/1/11. Reproduced with permission; **336–7** from 'Super funds crucial in shift to green economy' by Derek Parker, *The Australian*, News Limited, 23/1/09. Reproduced with permission; 372–3/ From 'Not open and shut', *Hobart Mercury*, News Limited, 22/2/11, p. 12. Reproduced with permission; **379–80** 'ABC Learning 'reliant' on debt to cover cash shortfalls' by Danny John, *The Sydney Morning Herald*, Fairfax Media, 19/3/10, p. 5. Reproduced with permission • © John Wiley & Sons, Inc, **101–3** from 'Measurement in financial reporting' by G Whittington, *Abacus*, vol. 46, no. 1, pp. 104–6, March 2010; **258** Adapted from G Giroux 2004, 'Detecting earnings management', p. 3; **403–4** from 'R&D reporting biases and their consequences' by Lev, Sarath & Sougiannis, *Contemporary Accounting Research*, vol. 22, no. 4, pp. 981, 1018 • Matthew Egan: **125–7** 'Taking account of water' by Matthew Egan and Geoff Frost, *InTheBlack*, July 2009, pp. 51–2. • © Retail Merchandiser: **127–8** 'CMG Worldwide — Intangible assets' from *Retail Merchandiser*, May/June 2010, pp. 74–7 • American Marketing Association: **167** reprinted with permission from 'Customer equity: An integral part of financial reporting' by Wiesel, Skiera & Villanueva, *Journal of Marketing*, vol. 72, March 2002, pp. 1–14, published by the American Marketing Association • © Australian Securities and

Investments Commission: **179–81**. Reproduced with permission. • ASX: **193–4** © Copyright 2011 ASX Corporate Governance Council Association of Superannuation Funds of Australia Ltd, ACN 002 786 290, Australian Council of Superannuation Investors, Australian Financial Markets Association Limited ACN 119 827 904, Australian Institute of Company Directors ACN 008 484 197, Australian Institute of Superannuation Trustees ACN 123 284 275, Australasian Investor Relations Association Limited ACN 095 554 153, Australian Shareholders' Association Limited CAN 000 625 669, ASX Limited ABN 98 008 624 691 trading as Australian Securities Exchange, Business Council of Australia ACN 008 483 216, Chartered Secretaries Australia Ltd ACN 008 615 950, CPA Australia Ltd ACN 008 392 452, Financial Services Institute of Australasia ACN 066 027 389, Group of 100 Inc, The Institute of Actuaries of Australia ACN 000 423 656, The Institute of Chartered Accountants in Australia ARBN 084 642 571,The Institute of Internal Auditors — Australia ACN 001 797 557, Financial Services Council ACN 080 744 163, Law Council of Australia Limited ACN 005 260 622, National Institute of Accountants ACN 004 130 643, Property Council of Australia Limited ACN 008 474 422, Stockbrokers Association of Australia ACN 089 767 706. All rights reserved 2011 • OECD: **193–4** OECD (2004), OECD Principles of Corporate Governance 2004, OECD Publishing, http://dx.doi.org/10.1787/9789264015999-en • © KPMG LLP (United Kingdom): **200–1** from 'Audit committees to put risk management at the top of their agendas' dated 16 June 2008 • Sanjay Anandaram: **215–6** 'Critical questions of governance' by Sanjay Anandaram, 26/12/08, *Financial Express (India)*, reproduced with permission from Sanjay Anandaram • Sarah Anderson: **216–7** 'Reining in executive pay' by Sarah Anderson and Sam Pizzigati, *Los Angeles Times*, 19/9/10, p. B.9 • Ed Waitzer: **218–9** 'Limits to governance: Corporate reforms often have unintended consequences' © Ed Waitzer and Marshall Cohen, Financial Post, 8/12/10 • Crikey website: **248–9** 'Who needs credit ratings? They should be optional' by Adam Creighton, 23/8/11, sourced from www.crikey.com.au • New Zealand Institute of Chartered Accountants: **271** from 'The ethics of earnings management' by James Gaa and Paul Dunmore, *Chartered Accountants Journal*, September 2007, pp. 60–2. Reproduced with permission; **330–1** from 'Perfect timing for world's first carbon neutral winery' by Bruce Gilkison, *Chartered Accountants Journal*, May 2008, pp. 56–9. • CFO Publishing Corp.: **308–9** Article 'Former FDIC Chief: Fair value caused the crisis' by David M. Katz, 29 October 2008 © CFO.com • © PricewaterHouse Coopers UK: **332** Table from p. 27 of 'Trouble-Entry Accounting — Revisited', September 2007 • Christine Grimard: **335–6** from 'Turning the heat on' by Christine Grimard, *InTheBlack*, December 2009, pp. 19–20 • © Daily News (Sri Lanka): **350–1** from 'Adopting IFRS in Asian countries vital', dated 16 December 2009 • Deloitte — London: **352–3** from 'IFRS in your pocket 2011'. Reproduced with permission from Deloitte — London • Haymarket Direct: **397** 'Valuing the Rosetta Stone and other priceless assets' by Ray Jones, *Third Sector* — Haymarket ©, 13 April 2010, iss. 610, p. 21, reproduced with permission from Haymarket Business Publications • V. Balakrishnan: **360** 'Making the most of IFRS' by V. Balakrishnan, dated 9 September 2010, *Financial Express (India)*, reproduced with permission from V. Balakrishnan • © Singapore Press Holdings: **375** from Editorial 'Penalties, enforcement key to real reforms', 18/12/09, *The Business Times Singapore* • New Zealand Herald: **380** from 'Company failures soar by 40pc' by Maria Slade, 10/3/09, *The New Zealand Herald*, reproduced with permission • Fairfax New Zealand Limited: **405–6** from 'The sum of us' by Ruth Laugesen, *The Sunday Star Times*, Wellington, New Zealand, 22/9/02, p. C. 3. Reproduced with permission from Fairfax New Zealand Limited.

Every effort has been made to trace the ownership of copyright material. Information that will enable the publisher to rectify any error or omission in subsequent editions will be welcome. In such cases, please contact the Permissions Section of John Wiley & Sons Australia, Ltd who will arrange for the payment of the usual fee.

1

Contemporary issues in accounting

After studying this chapter, you should be able to:

1 define 'theory'

2 explain the role of theory in financial accounting

3 explain the differences between positive theories and normative theories

4 explain the reasons for evaluating and testing theories

5 describe the role of research in accounting

6 identify some of the research areas in accounting.

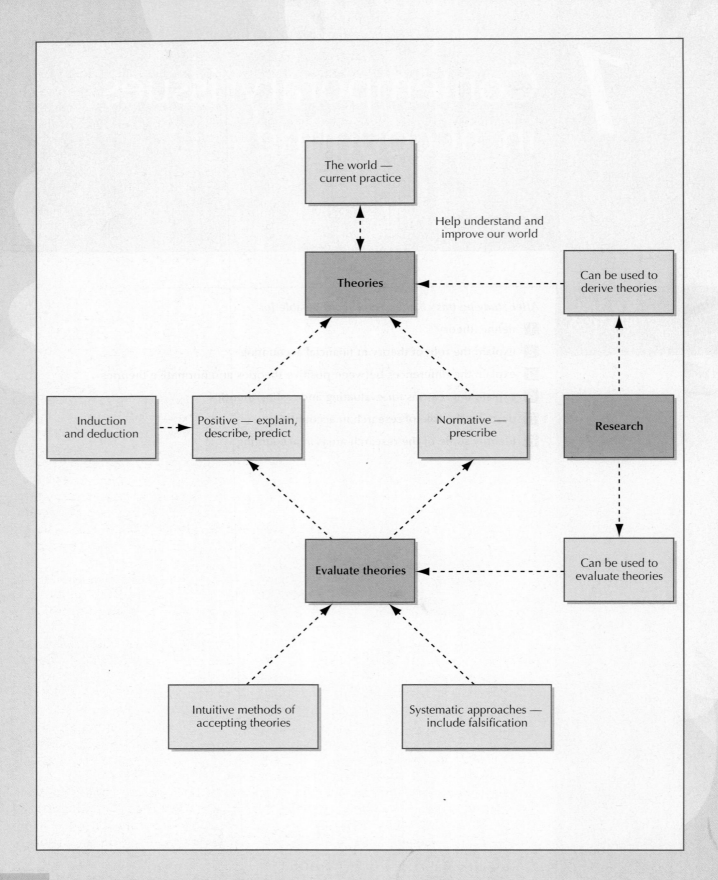

This text, as its title indicates, considers some of the contemporary issues in accounting. Its key focus is on issues in financial accounting. Financial accounting can be defined as the regular reporting of the financial position and performance of an entity through financial statements issued to external users. This definition is relatively straightforward but financial accounting is neither straightforward nor simple. As this text shows, the influences on financial accounting are many and complex, and often the application of financial accounting principles and practices in specific contexts brings unique challenges.

Some accounting students may question why there are issues or problems in accounting that are different from those in the past. After all, the basic building blocks of accounting — the debit and credit rules — have not changed for centuries. However, the world certainly has changed. Business activities and transactions are more varied and complicated, and, increasingly, more global; and social expectations and priorities are changing. There are now transactions and events that were never even thought of when accounting rules were created. For example:

- the subprime credit swaps associated with the global financial crisis
- special purpose entities connected to the Enron collapse
- emissions trading schemes introduced to address global warming concerns.

Accounting is often cited as the 'language of business' and financial accounting provides much of the public information about business (and non-business) entities that people rely on to make decisions. If the financial accounting information provided is not 'right', this can have significant adverse consequences; for not only shareholders, but also the public, the managers of businesses and accountants themselves. Even a brief look at business failures (such as Enron, WorldCom, HIH, One.Tel and the global financial crisis) confirms this.

Accounting regulation has also changed. Prior to the last decade, accounting standards (the 'rules' for financial statements) were largely determined on a country by country basis, varying substantially. Globalisation of business has changed this. There is now acceptance that a global and uniform set of accounting standards is required to ensure the quality of financial accounting. However, the implementation of international accounting standards is impacting on the substance and form of accounting requirements. Major participants, such as the European Union and the United States, are exerting their influence. For example:

- To facilitate the expected adoption by the United States of international accounting standards, reviews of, and changes to, a range of accounting standards and even the basic concepts (such as the definition of an asset) have been made or are in progress.
- In the global financial crisis, pressure by the European Union forced a change to international accounting standards to allow banks to reclassify assets retrospectively and thereby improve their reported financial position.

Regulation is also increasing; not only in financial accounting but in other areas where professional accountants play a significant role. Corporate failures, such as the Enron collapse and the more recent global financial crisis, have led not just to increased scrutiny of accounting requirements but to the introduction of further regulation. Corporate governance practices and earnings management have also come into greater focus with an expansion of the duties and roles of accountants.

The role of accountants has been changing over many years. The traditional 'book-keeping' role is in the past, with much of the mechanics of financial accounting undertaken by non-accountants facilitated by specifically designed accounting software. Professional accountants now require a skill set that emphasises problem-solving ability, lifelong learning and communication skills. A survey of chief financial officers expects that senior accountants will spend at least 40% of their time in the future on 'non-traditional' functions. Accountants will always be required to maintain stringent oversight of financial reporting, but in the coming years an increasing amount of their time will be devoted to providing strategic insight that helps support company initiatives.[1]

This shift in roles is reflected in the type of skills that employers of accounting graduates are seeking. A report by Hancock et al. into the changing skill set for professional accounting found that:

> Employers valued [an accounting graduate's] ability to relate concepts learned at university to new situations in the workplace, the ability to think for oneself, the ability to regard critically new information and situations. Theory learned at university needed to be applied to a range of new problems and contexts and the graduate who had this ability was in demand. Problem solving was strongly related to being able to apply theoretical knowledge learned at university to real-life situations encountered in the workplace. Employers valued highly the ability to apply knowledge from one workplace context or problem to another.[2]

So what does all this mean? First, accounting cannot be viewed as a static and uncontested set of technical rules. Deciding what is to be reported and how to report in financial accounting is a complicated matter influenced not only by political, financial and personal interests, but also by accounting not being an exact science. At times there are no 'black and white' rules and often alternative solutions may be offered to financial accounting problems and preferred solutions will change over time. It is likely that much of the specific technical content that you have been 'taught' at university will be out of date in a short period of time and in the workplace you will certainly encounter situations that you have not previously experienced. The dynamic nature of accounting needs to be appreciated. Second, the changing nature of accounting and the accounting profession provides both opportunities and challenges for future accountants. The changing roles allow accountants to broaden their impact and accountants are now part of the key decision-making teams within business and the global nature of both accounting and business provides further opportunities to individuals to pursue challenging and diverse careers. However, with these opportunities there is a responsibility for professional accountants to develop the skills to solve new problems and to keep up to date with the ever-changing financial accounting landscape.

The approach of this text

A brief review of the chapter titles for this text will reveal that some chapters discuss particular theories or research. For example, the next chapter examines the *Conceptual Framework for Financial Reporting*, which is a normative theory, and chapter 5 discusses particular theories in accounting. The remaining chapters focus on financial accounting in either specific contexts (such as its role in corporate governance) or in relation to particular issues (such as accounting for sustainability) and the distinct problems and approaches relevant to these contexts. The examination of many of these issues in financial accounting, you will observe, often involves the use or discussion of theories and research. An alternative approach could have been to write each chapter around a particular theory. The approach in this text, however, is based on the premise that whenever you examine a particular financial accounting problem or issue, you need to consider a range of factors including the nature of the issue and the characteristics that cause it to be problematic, whether there are any relevant theories that provide explanations, insights or guidance, and whether there is any related research. By considering particular issues or contexts, this text allows you to see the interrelationship between financial accounting issues, theories and research. For example:

- Agency theory is examined in chapter 5 to explain the components of executive packages and motivations for providing accounting information, but is also considered in chapter 7 with corporate governance and in chapter 9 in relation to earnings management.
- Stakeholder theory is outlined in chapter 5, but is also considered in chapter 6 when the products of financial accounting are considered, and the role of stakeholders in explaining why entities would provide disclosures about environmental performance is examined in chapter 11.

You can see that specific theories can be used when considering a range of issues and in various contexts in financial accounting and should be able to recognise that analysing financial accounting problems and issues has come a long way from the simple and unproblematic application of debit and credit rules.

Before you consider the individual topics, it is useful to have some understanding of the nature and types of theories, and related research, and how these are used in accounting to solve or identify problems.

ACCOUNTING THEORY

Accounting is often viewed as a 'practical' discipline and your earlier studies may have involved learning how to apply accounting rules (such as debits and credits), often using computerised accounting programs. There may seem to be little use for theory. This doubt about the relevance of theory is not limited to accounting students. Many people say that they do not need theories; that by definition theories are not practical or useful in the real world. However, theories are necessary for us to try to understand the world we live in. Theories provide a basis for decisions we make. Even though you may not yet have explicitly studied any accounting theories, you no doubt have used them. For example, when deciding whether to include an item in the financial statements, you may have applied the concepts of materiality and recognition criteria, such as relevance. These concepts are part of an accounting theory, referred to as the *Conceptual Framework*, which provides the basis for accounting standards. When choosing how to measure items in the financial statements (e.g. choosing between fair value and historical cost), you are applying measurement theory.

There is no simple definition of 'theory'. In different circumstances, it can mean different things. People often use the word to mean a guess or their thoughts on something, such as 'I have a theory about why my friend is always late'. Or it is used to suggest an unrealistic or impossible ideal, such as 'In theory, it should take one hour to get to work but the traffic always causes delays'. In this usage, a 'theory' is simply an opinion or explanation.

The following are dictionary definitions of what a theory is:

- a belief or principle that guides actions or behaviour (such as behavioural theories of positive reinforcement or theories in management about motivating employees)
- an idea or set of ideas that is intended to explain something (such as Darwin's theory of evolution)
- the set of principles on which a subject is based or of ideas that are suggested to explain a fact or event (such as economic theory or the theory of relativity)
- more generally, a conjecture or an opinion.

As these definitions show, theories can do different things: some describe and some explain what is happening. Some of these theories will also make predictions about what will happen. Other theories make suggestions or guide action (i.e. say what should happen). This text is not concerned with the 'opinions' that characterise the common usage of the term 'theory', but considers the more systematic theories. Accounting theory therefore means the following:

- 'A description, explanation or a prediction [of accounting practice] based on observations and/or logical reasoning'[3]
- 'Logical reasoning in the form of a set of broad principles that (1) provide a general framework of reference by which accounting practice can be evaluated and (2) guide the development of new practice and procedures'.[4]

Before looking at the different types of theories, the next section considers why it is important to consider and know about theory.

 **WHY THEORY IS NEEDED**

In some civilisations, there was initially a theory that the world was flat. However, this theory was replaced by a new theory that the Earth was round. Let us consider how this 'round Earth' theory may have developed and the impact it may have had on people's views and actions. People would have sat on the shore and watched boats sail off, and will have seen the boats disappearing as they neared the horizon but always hull first. Also, some stars disappeared from the sky if you travelled north or south. There may have been many individual observations of this happening. But without some explanation (some theory) about why the stars disappeared or why boats disappeared from view hull first, the observations were interesting but provided little useful information. Then a theory was formed that 'fitted' with the observations. If the world was round, then the stars disappearing as you travelled north or south or the boats disappearing hull first on the horizon would be explained. It would 'fit' with what people had seen. This helped people understand their world and would of course influence their views and actions: if you believed this theory, then you would certainly not be concerned about travelling too far out in a boat thinking you would fall off the edge of the world. It also allowed people to predict what would happen if you continued travelling in one direction — that is, you would end up where you began.

This example illustrates two different ways in which theories are useful:
- providing an explanation of what is happening
- helping us predict what will happen.

This example also demonstrates a further point. Just because there is a theory about something does not mean that the theory is correct. An important issue when learning about or using theory (including accounting theory) is to consider how the appropriateness of any particular theory can be assessed. We now know that the theory of the Earth being round is incorrect (it is not a true sphere), but to the people of the day, this theory was useful: it provided an explanation of how their world worked, so provided a basis for their actions and decisions.

Today, much of life is affected by theory. Only the end results of the application of theories are usually seen and the theories behind them may not be fully understood. However, theories are the driving force behind many of the things that affect our daily lives. For example:
- Governments make decisions about whether to increase or decrease taxes based on economic theories that explain and predict the impact rises or falls in tax will have on consumer behaviour, inflation, unemployment and national debt. These decisions

also take into account theories of social justice, which consider which groups in society should be helped or should bear the burden of higher taxes.

- There are theories about global warming and the impact of the use of resources on the environment. Some of these theories also make predictions about what will happen (such as the increase in temperatures to be expected and the impact this will have on climate in particular regions). Other theories suggest what should be done to reduce environmental damage. Our daily lives are witness to the result of these theories, reflected in recycling programs, reductions in certain chemicals in the petrol used in cars and in water restrictions.

These are only two examples but you should see that theory intrudes into our lives every day; from theories about the best way to treat diseases, to theories about the best way to teach university students, to mathematically based theories that underlie the building of bridges and tunnels. These examples also illustrate two further things about theories:

- There are also theories that do not explain what is happening in the world but, rather, provide solutions or ways to improve the world.
- There are often different theories on the same topic. There are many alternative theories about the impact of global warming and how best to prevent it. There are some theories that suggest that global warming is a natural cyclical event and that there is no need to do anything.

From this, you should see that theories are important. As noted, theories can do different things and in accounting there are many, some of which describe, explain or predict accounting practice and others that provide recommendations or suggestions about what accounting practice should be. Theories inform our everyday lives and provide important information that can be used in making decisions, such as whether to sail off into the horizon, or whether to recycle and reduce waste. Theories can provide the same benefits in accounting by:

- Describing and explaining current accounting practices. For example:
  - Capital market theory describes how share prices react to accounting information.
  - Researchers investigating financial reporting failures (such as Enron) have, after identifying factors that have contributed to these problems (e.g. lack of independence of auditors, rules-based accounting standards and share-based compensation payments), arrived at theories about why these failures have occurred.
- Predicting accounting practice. For example:
  - Agency or contracting theory, as well as explaining why managers may change the way in which they account (i.e. the accounting policies) for items in the financial statements, makes predictions about the accounting policies that will be chosen by managers in particular circumstances.
- Providing principles to take into account when taking action or making decisions. For example:
  - In management accounting courses you will have used theories of capital budgeting, which might involve calculating net present values of projects and payback periods, to help decide which projects to invest in.
  - A theory of asset recognition helps to determine when and how assets should be included in the financial statements.
- Helping to identify problems and deficiencies with current accounting practice and improve accounting practice. For example:
  - The conceptual framework for accounting, by providing the basic principles on which to base accounting standards (the more detailed reporting rules), can make accounting practice more consistent.

- Theories about how investors make decisions and what information they need and use can explain which accounting measures are most useful and suggest ways to improve the usefulness of financial statements (e.g. by increasing the use of fair values).
- Theories about corporate social responsibility can suggest that companies also need to provide information about environmental impacts of their activities.

LO 3 TYPES OF THEORIES

Theories are often placed into two categories:
- positive theories
- normative theories.

Each of these will be discussed in turn.

Positive theories

Positive theories are used to represent theories that are about the world as it is. They can:
- describe what is actually happening
- explain what is happening
- make predictions about what will happen.

Examples of positive theories are:
- theories of how contagious diseases are spread
- theories that explain why managers prefer or choose particular accounting methods or policies over others.

These theories are concerned with the world as it is and help to make sense of what is happening. If a positive theory makes a prediction about what is happening, or is expected to happen, this prediction is often framed as a **hypothesis**. This hypothesis can then be tested to help decide whether the theory is correct. Positive theories are often referred to as 'empirical' theories. 'Empirical' means 'derived from or guided by experience or experiment' (Macquarie dictionary) and positive theories involve observations of the world, directly or indirectly, as a basis for their descriptions or explanations and to test any predictions made. Most positive theories are developed from observation and by the process of induction and deduction.

Where positive theories come from

Let's consider a simple example of how a positive theory might be derived. A researcher observes a number of swans and notices that all swans she has seen are white. From this, the researcher arrives at the conclusion that it may be that all swans are white. This is a theory about swans. This process of moving from specific observations (particular instances) to a theory or conclusion is called **induction**.

After the theory has been developed, it needs to be tested, which involves making predictions (a hypothesis) about the characteristics (in this case the colour) of swans. This process of developing predictions from theories is known as **deduction**. The researcher would then test the theory by making further observations of swans to see whether the observations agreed with its prediction (i.e. the hypothesis from the theory). This process is depicted in figure 1.1.

You should see that in this instance all of the observations do not 'fit' with the hypothesis because one black swan has been found and so disprove the theory that 'all swans are white'. This process of beginning with limited observations, analysing them to derive a theory and then making predictions that are tested by further observations, is often referred to as the **scientific method**. It is how positive theories commonly emerge.

FIGURE 1.1 Scientific method

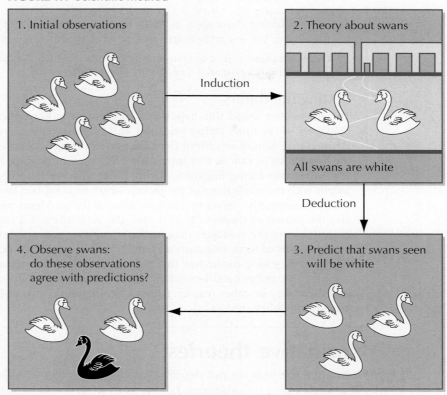

Figure 1.2 considers an example (based on Rivett)[5] of some positive research in accounting that illustrates a positive accounting theory and this approach.

FIGURE 1.2 Positive theory and accounting policy choice

Two accounting researchers, Hall and Stammerjohan,[6] arrived at a positive theory about influences on managers' choice of accounting policies and aimed to explain what accounting policy choices would be made by managers in particular circumstances.

This research considered the accounting policies of oil companies. You should know from your previous studies that managers often have a choice of accounting policies. For example, companies may value some assets at cost or fair value; depreciation is based on estimates of useful life of assets and probable resale value. In choosing different policies or methods managers can (without changing the actual and physical economic performance of the company) alter the financial statements significantly.

Initial observations

The researchers initially observed that in some companies in the oil industry, managers seemed to choose policies that reduced income or assets. This led the researchers to question the cause and one of the other observations they made was that oil companies were often involved in litigation (e.g. being sued for environmental damage from an oil tanker spill) and noticed that the damages awarded in these cases often seemed to be linked to the wealth of the company (in other words, 'richer' companies had to pay greater amounts in damages).

Conclusion: theory

Given these facts, the researchers theorised that where oil companies were being sued for damages, managers would choose accounting policies and methods to reduce profit and assets in an attempt to reduce the potential damages to be awarded. One of the

FIGURE 1.2 *(continued)*

choices available to managers in oil companies was how to report new discoveries or reserves of oil. The researchers arrived at several hypotheses, one of which was:

> [Oil] firms under-report reserves during periods in which they are defendants in litigation with high potential damages relative to other periods.

Testing the theory

The researchers tested this hypothesis by comparing how reserves were reported by managers of oil firms facing litigation and by those who were not. The researchers claimed that their observations of managers' reporting of reserves were consistent with the hypothesis — that is, that firms facing litigation under-reported reserves compared with those not facing litigation, so the policy choices made by managers were consistent with the predictions of the theory, which may explain those choices.

This example also serves to illustrate some of the problems with accounting research and the testing of theories. In this case, the researchers did not directly research the motivations of the managers making the accounting policies choices but inferred them from two sets of facts: litigation and under-reporting of reserves. The researchers theorised that they were connected: that the litigation caused the managers to under-report reserves. The researchers themselves identify as one of the limitations of the research that there may be other reasons (other than litigation) that influenced the managers' accounting policy choices.

Normative theories

Normative theories do not describe, explain or predict what is happening, but rather make suggestions or recommendations as to what *should* happen or what 'ought to be'. In other words, they prescribe. The prescriptions or recommendations of these theories aim to achieve some goal or objective. For example:

- There are theories about what should be done to reduce greenhouse gas emissions with the aim of reducing the rate of global warming and the environmental damage it results in.
- There are theories in accounting that propose that fair values should be used to measure assets in the financial statements with the aim to ensure that more relevant information is provided to users of financial statements.

This does not, however, mean that observations or facts about, say, current accounting practice are not considered in the development of normative theories. Indeed, it is often a result of considering positive theories and its related research that normative theories evolve.

Figure 1.3 provides an example of the evolution of a normative theory in relation to environmental damage.

FIGURE 1.3 Normative theories of environmental damage

Goal: what we are trying to achieve

People may believe that we should prevent further environmental damage. So the goal is to reduce the impact of our activities on the environment.

Premises

There may be evidence that one of the largest impacts on the environment comes from the generation of power. Research may confirm that using fossil fuels (such as coal) in power generation produces large amounts of greenhouse gases. There may be theories that suggest that greenhouse gases are a major cause of global warming and climate change and these damage the environment. There may be evidence that nuclear power generation results in much less production of greenhouse gases.

Conclusion: Prescription

Given the goal and the premises, it would be suggested that nuclear reactors should replace power generation facilities that rely on fossil fuels.

Do you think everyone would agree with this conclusion and prescription? The answer is no. Many people are opposed to nuclear reactors because of the potential for environmental damage from accidents and the radioactive waste products from this method of power generation. These concerns may require the addition of further premises to consider (such as there being evidence that waste products from nuclear power generation can cause environmental damage or the magnitude and nature of damage to the environment from potential accidents at nuclear power generation facilities). The inclusion of these premises may cause the conclusion and prescription to change.

Some of the normative accounting theories that suggested that fair values should be used came about by identification of problems with the measurements (mainly historical cost) being used in accounting, combined with research that indicates that many of the current accounting measures may have limited usefulness for users.

The nature of the conclusion of a normative theory is a prescription (it is a recommended course of action) and this factor needs to be considered when looking at how to test normative theories. The conclusion of a normative theory cannot be tested by seeing whether it actually happens: the theory is not saying this is what actually happens but what should happen.

LO 4   EVALUATING AND TESTING THEORIES

There are many theories, in some cases alternative theories, about the same topic or area. In financial accounting, for example, there are alternative theories about how items should be measured. Just because there is a theory about something does not mean that it is correct. So how can it be decided whether a theory should be accepted? How do people decide that they believe a particular theory is true? In practice, various ways are used to make judgements about theories. These range from simple (often intuitive) approaches, to more systematic and scientific approaches. People accept theories every day that they may not fully understand (such as theories of global warming, the theory of relativity and theories about how certain diseases are spread).

There are a number of reasons theories might be accepted without 'first hand' or direct knowledge, including the authority of the source of the theory, whether the theory makes sense and fits with personal experiences and beliefs, and whether other people accept the theory. If you are a researcher or professional in a particular discipline, it would be expected that more legitimate, independent and justifiable methods would be applied in assessing and evaluating theories. These would include examining the logical construction of the theory and considering evidence that confirmed or refuted the theory. It is generally accepted that theories cannot be proven true. This is because regardless of how many observations 'fit' or confirm a theory, it can never be certain that there are 'enough' (e.g. relating back to the swans example, how many observations of white swans would prove that the theory was true). A theory can, however, be proven incorrect by just one observation that does not fit with the theory (e.g. finding one black swan would establish that the theory that all swans are white is wrong). Therefore, the rational way to use observation to test a theory is not to try to find observations that confirm the theory but to search for instances that do not fit with the theory, which disprove it. This is referred to as falsification.

This book does not consider in further detail the specific ways in which theories are tested and you should refer to more detailed texts that specifically focus on accounting theories if you wish to consider this issue further. The testing and evaluation of theories will usually involve research, although this is not the only reason for the latter. The following sections consider accounting research because the specific issues in financial accounting this text goes on to consider all involve or are influenced by research.

LO 5 UNDERSTANDING THE ROLE OF RESEARCH

As outlined, an accounting theory is either a description, explanation or prediction of accounting practice or a set of principles with which to evaluate or guide practice. According to the Macquarie dictionary, research is the 'diligent and systematic enquiry or investigation into a subject in order to discover facts or principles'. Research is often repeated and adjusted, which means that later studies build on earlier ones, so that knowledge about a particular aspect of accounting is expanding.

Most research studies will not provide definitive answers to the problem examined, but, by searching over and over again, each study should contribute to our understanding of the issue.

Relationship between theory and research

The relationship between theory and research is complex. Empirical research is essentially concerned with observation; although this may not be observation of the 'real' world. For example, researchers may conduct experiments and use the results (observations). Research is not categorised in the same way as theories, as either positive or normative. Research is an activity that can be associated with both positive and normative theories. For example:

- Research may be conducted using an experiment in which the relative usefulness of historical cost and fair value measures are considered and it is found that better decisions are made using fair values. This may suggest a normative theory that fair value should be used as the measure for items in the financial statements.
- There may be a positive theory that explains the relationship between the accounting methods a manager chooses and the compensation package of the manager. This could predict that if a manager's bonus is related to the accounting profit, the manager will choose accounting methods that increase reported profits. Research could test whether this actually happens by examining the bonus plans of managers and the accounting choices they make.

As you can also see from these examples, research can come before a theory is formed or after it is formed.

You should note that positive and normative accounting theories are intertwined and accounting research and solving accounting problems will often consider and involve both types of theories. For example:

- There is positive research on conceptual framework projects (which is a normative theory) such as that undertaken by Ruth Hines (see additional readings), whose theory provides an alternative explanation for why conceptual frameworks are developed.
- When considering alternative measurements of assets, positive research can be used to inform whether existing measures are useful (e.g. through capital market research) or which measures would be preferred by management (e.g. through accounting policy choice research).

Because accounting is a human activity, the object of the accounting research extends beyond the economic events, the procedures for recording and the methods of reporting them, to the uses made of accounting products and the users and their interests in accounting information. That accounting is a human invention also means that research (and related theories) can be categorised in two ways, although these can overlap.

Research *of* or *about* accounting

Research *of* or *about* accounting considers the role of accounting itself (the 'bigger' picture) at the macro level and considers questions such as what is the role of accounting, is accounting information useful in investment decisions, should accountability or decision usefulness be the key goal of accounting, what impact does culture have on accounting, and what role has accounting played in the rise of capitalism or environmental degradation.

A developing research area here is critical accounting. Critical accounting aims to develop:

> A critical understanding of the role of accounting processes and practices and the accounting profession in the functioning of society and organisations with an intention to use that understanding to engage (where appropriate) in changing these processes, practices and the profession.[7]

The two abstracts in Contemporary Issue 1.1 represent examples of critical accounting research. You can see that this type of research considers the social context of accounting. Such research often challenges and questions the current state of accounting and in particular the relationships (and relative power or influence) of the participants.

1.1 CONTEMPORARY ISSUE

Abstracts from critical accounting research

Accounting lays claims to be the language of business: a clear, technical, unambiguous means of communication for decisions on investment and economic development. Accounting concepts have increasingly entered mainstream debate on issues affecting society at large. This makes the fairness and effectiveness of accounting as a mode of communication more important for social justice than ever before. In a contentious development, if the discussion is framed primarily in accounting terms, this may disenfranchise those parties to the dispute whose issues are not readily expressed in the common vocabulary of business. Their concerns may become invisible in the debate. If this happens, then accounting has failed as a means of communication, and that failure is non-neutral in that it favours those whose position is best supported by economic arguments.

This paper explores this phenomenon using the case of a dispute between Royal Dutch Shell and a local community in Ireland concerning a gas refinery located in an environmentally sensitive area. The issues in conflict are complex and at times intangible. I explore how the limitations of accounting as a language blinded the protagonists to an understanding of each other's concerns, marginalised the concerns of protestors from the public discourse, shifting power from objectors within the local community to those whose primary concern was the economic exploitation of natural resources. I argue that accounting failed as a mode of communication to progress a resolution of the dispute, and that this failure was both unnecessary, and systematic in its support of economic interests.

Source: Abstract by Sheila Killian, '"No accounting for these people": Shell in Ireland and accounting language', *Critical Perspectives on Accounting*.[8]

Such major scandals as the savings and loan failures in the late 1980s and 1990s, the Enron, Global Crossing, WorldCom and Tyco corporate scandals, Arthur Andersen's demise, and the current crisis of the financial system have all been linked directly or indirectly to false, misleading, or untruthful accounting. Thus, in a pragmatic sense the question of the veracity of accounting or what it could mean for accounting to be true seems to exist. The assertion of a false or misleading financial report implies some belief that there could exist a true or not-misleading report. Accounting standard setters have finessed this issue by agreeing that 'decision usefulness', not truth, is financial reporting's ultimate objective. Over time they have gravitated to a coherence notion of truth to provide rationales for accounting policy. The result has been a serious conflict between the content of financial accounting and the auditing of that content. In this paper we describe this conflict and its consequences and, relying on John McCumber's work, provide an argument about how accounting scholars and practitioners might begin to think more cogently about what a truthful type of corporate reporting might be. We suggest that accounting-standard setters have too narrowly construed what accounting's role in democratic society is and how the contradictions of current standard setting jeopardise the essential professional franchise of accountants, the audit function.

Source: Abstract by Mohamed E Bayou, Alan Reinstein & Paul F Williams, 'To tell the truth: A discussion of issues concerning truth and ethics in accounting', *Accounting, Organizations and Society.*[9]

Threshold learning outcomes for accounting

J Judgement

K Knowledge

AS Application Skills

CT Communication and Teamwork

SM Self-Management

Questions

1. In each of these abstracts the notion of true or fair accounting for financial statements is considered. Identify any requirements in accounting standards or corporations legislation that relate to the truth or fairness of financial statements or reports. **K**
2. Can you think of reasons why there could be claims that financial statements that are prepared in accordance with accounting standards are not true or fair? **J** **K** **SM**
3. The first extract states that current accounting 'may disenfranchise those parties to the dispute whose issues are not readily expressed in the common vocabulary of business'. What do you think the author means by 'the common vocabulary of business'? Given this, what type of issues may not be included in accounting reports or statements and how could their exclusion impact on decision making? **J** **AS**

Research *in* accounting

Research *in* accounting focuses at the more micro level on issues within accounting and considers questions such as: what measurements are being used, what measures should be used, what impact do changes in specific accounting policies have on share prices.

An analogy would be medicine. To research *about* or *of* medicine would be to consider what is the role of medicine. For example, should a holistic approach be taken, which considers lifestyle, cultural context, personal preferences and choices and so on, or should the role be to treat physical health only? Research *in* medicine would be at a more micro level, such as considering different approaches to treating a particular disease or impacts of particular drugs. Within both of these categories, there may be normative or positive theories and associated research.

LO 6 RESEARCH AREAS IN ACCOUNTING

Financial accounting has a wide range of theories and research. Examples of some are described in the following.

Capital market research

Ball and Brown[10] and Beaver[11] began the positive research stream known as capital market research, which investigated the use (and impact) of accounting information by capital markets. Given that a key role identified by normative researchers prior to this had been that accounting information should be useful to investors, this research provided descriptions and explanations of market behaviours and reactions to accounting information.

Accounting policy choice research

Another major school of accounting research is accounting policy choice research (this is often known simply as 'positive accounting theory' because of its domination of research for a significant period), which began with Watts and Zimmerman.[12] This research attempted to explain the motivations behind the accounting choices made by managers and its significant position continues. Agency (or contracting) theory, which underlies much of this research, is considered in chapter 5.

Accounting information processing research

Given that the objective of financial accounting is to provide information to aid decision making, this research investigates the use (and users) of information in the decision-making process, often using theories and models from psychology. One example here is the Brunswick Lens model, which can be used to examine how specific types of information are used in, for example, investment decisions by a particular user of financial accounting information (say an investor).

Critical accounting research

As discussed, critical accounting research considers the role of accounting in society and its social context. It can adopt a social welfare perspective or rely on philosophical perspectives and theories (e.g. those of Marx, Habermas or Foucault).

International accounting research

With increasing calls for more uniform accounting standards worldwide and effort towards harmonisation of financial accounting, this research area grew in the second half of the twentieth century. This has included research into differences in accounting practices and also considered contextual and cultural influences on financial accounting.

There are of course other areas of research (such as those specifically relating to auditing and accounting history). Research about an issue in accounting can involve many types of research and research areas. For example, the issue of environmental accounting and disclosures could involve the following research:

- documenting the environmental disclosures made by companies and evaluating the quality of these disclosures
- determining whether environmental disclosures have been used in decisions. This could involve information processing research and trying to identify how decision makers have used this information or could involve capital market research by examining market reactions to the disclosure of such information.
- examining the motivations behind companies' disclosure (or nondisclosure) of environmental information
- examining the impact that accounting's focus on measurable financial costs (rather than externalities such as environmental costs) has on environmental impacts made by companies, so taking a more critical approach.

OVERVIEW OF CHAPTERS IN THIS TEXT

This book examines issues related to financial accounting. Many of these involve consideration of associated theories and research, although the extent will vary. There are many issues in and influences on financial accounting and it is not possible to consider all of these in one book. So the text is selective and chooses issues to consider based on their significance, prevalence and contemporary relevance. The topics chosen should provide you with an understanding of a range of issues and influences confronting financial accounting that will help you recognise the implications and rationales behind some of the decisions, changes and developments in the accounting arena. The following is an overview of the chapters considered in this book.

Chapter 2: The *Conceptual Framework for Financial Reporting*

This is a normative theory that you should already be familiar with, at least in part, from your previous studies in accounting. Conceptual frameworks, which specify the purpose of financial reporting and the nature and qualities of information to be included in financial reports, have been dominant in the normative theories of accounting both locally and internationally for more than 20 years. The text looks at the theory itself, by looking at the *Conceptual Framework for Financial Reporting* (*Conceptual Framework*) issued by the International Accounting Standards Board, and recent developments to this as a result of the joint project by the international and United States accounting standards bodies to develop a common conceptual framework. The chapter also considers the alternative reasons and rationales for having such a normative theory as the *Conceptual Framework* and looks at some specific criticisms of these.

Chapter 3: Standard setting

This chapter examines the application of the conceptual framework in its practical form: accounting standards. It considers the process of setting accounting standards and examines the structure of this procedure in Australia in more detail. It also considers the benefits and disadvantages of rules- over principles-based standards and examines several theories of regulation that attempt to explain the purpose of standards in accounting. Finally, it examines the political nature of the standard-setting process, and looks briefly into the program to harmonise international standards.

Chapter 4: Measurement

This chapter considers one of the most controversial areas of accounting: measurement. A variety of measures are currently used in financial reporting. The *Conceptual Framework*, in its recognition criteria, requires that items reported in the financial statements be measured. However, the *Conceptual Framework* does not specify *how* the items are to be measured. This chapter considers the alternative measurement choices that are available and the factors to be considered in determining which measurement approach is most appropriate. It also identifies some specific areas, such as intangibles and sustainability reporting, that involve unique challenges in terms of measurement.

Chapter 5: Theories in accounting

While chapter 1 considers theory in general, chapter 5 is concerned with the role of theories in the specific context of accounting and how theories can be used to explain, understand or guide accounting practice. The distinction between positive and normative theories is outlined. Further, this chapter explains a number of dominant theories in accounting including agency theory, stakeholder theory and legitimacy theory and considers how these are applied to financial reporting issues.

Chapter 6: Products of the financial reporting process

The products of financial accounting include general purpose, special purpose and voluntary reporting practices. This chapter considers some of the ways these accounting products are manipulated (both legally and illegally) and undertakes an examination of the purpose of reported disclosures. It looks closely at the value of disclosures not required by law and the methods open to entities to manage their image through voluntary, non-regulated disclosure. It also examines some theories of management motivation, including some of the theories introduced in chapter 5, which attempt to explain why entities supply voluntary information in the first place.

Chapter 7: Corporate governance
Corporate governance is concerned with how companies are managed and controlled. Financial accounting plays a key role in ensuring good corporate governance, which this chapter discusses. There are positive theories of accounting that support the introduction of corporate governance practices and may provide explanations for some financial reporting problems (such as accounting policy choice research). The chapter also considers developments in corporate governance practices, including the role of accountants, resulting from the effects of the global financial crisis and the expansion of corporate governance principles beyond corporate entities. Furthermore, it briefly considers the role of ethics in corporate governance and accounting practices.

Chapter 8: Capital market research and accounting
Capital market research considers the relationship between security (share) prices and accounting information. Given that investors are often seen as the traditional users of accounting reports, it makes sense to see how much share prices reflect and are affected by accounting information. The research in this area considers such questions as whether the accounting information provided was useful and also examines the effect that changes in accounting policies have on share prices.

Chapter 9: Earnings management
The issue of earnings management, whether by accounting policy choice or other methods of manipulation, has been associated with a number of corporate scandals and collapses. This chapter examines the meaning and types of earnings management and how earnings management impacts on the quality of reported earnings. Further, it considers the roles of corporate governance and managerial compensation in this context.

Chapter 10: Fair value accounting
There has been an increasing use of fair value as the measurement basis for many items in financial statements and fair value is viewed as the preferred alternative by many to address the criticisms of the historical cost approach traditionally used in accounting. However, the determination of fair value in particular circumstances is problematic as it involves subjectivity and this can lead to possible manipulations, distortions and inconsistencies. With this in mind, this chapter outlines the application of fair value in specific contexts, considering the guidance and direction provided in the international accounting standard.

Chapter 11: Sustainability and environmental accounting
With the impact of climate change, sustainability is an increasing area of concern and interest for both society in general and for businesses. This chapter explores the meaning of sustainability and the role of accounting in sustainability reporting. It examines alternative reports that consider sustainability such as triple bottom line, integrated and environmental reporting practices. It also considers international guidelines that provide methods for comparing and analysing this kind of non-financial information and environmental management systems that support such reporting. The chapter concludes by examining in detail accounting for emissions trading schemes.

Chapter 12: International accounting
Business in the twenty-first century operates globally. Increased foreign investment and access to capital markets have opened countries that were previously closed. Accountants

and managers need to keep up to date with changing accounting and financial complexities when doing business on an international scale. The chapter introduces international accounting and highlights a range of issues that impact on financial reporting around the world.

Chapter 13: Corporate failure

Corporate failures often provide the impetus for scrutiny of financial reporting. This chapter focuses on corporate failures associated with the global financial crisis of 2008. While it concentrates on the causes and consequences of the global financial crisis, it also considers corporate failure more generally. It does this by examining the causes and costs associated with corporate failures, factors used to predict such failures, and the relationship between corporate governance and corporate failure. It also considers how regulation has responded to such events.

Chapter 14: Special reporting issues

The question of whether a simple item is an asset and how to include it in the financial statements would have been considered in introductory accounting courses. This chapter examines two types of items where recognition is more problematic and controversial: intangibles and heritage assets. With the knowledge economy and the acceptance that in many instances the value of a company is associated less with its physical assets and more with intangibles (such as brands and intellectual property), there are calls to include these intangible items in financial statements. The unique nature and the diverse range of heritage assets result in distinctive challenges in including such items in traditional financial statements. This chapter explains how the current definition of assets and recognition issues make reporting these items problematic.

Summary

Define 'theory'
- There is no one definition of theory because theories can do different things; they can describe, predict, explain and prescribe.
- Accounting theory in this text is defined as either a description, explanation or prediction of accounting practice or a set of principles on which to evaluate or guide practice.

Explain the role of theory in financial accounting
- In financial accounting, theories can help the understanding of current accounting practice and also provide the means to improve it by:
  - describing and explaining current accounting practice
  - providing principles on which to base actions and decisions in financial accounting
  - identifying problems and deficiencies with current accounting practice
  - providing suggestions for change.

Explain the differences between positive theories and normative theories
- Theories are often identified as positive or normative. Positive theories in accounting are theories about accounting practice as it is and may describe or explain what is currently happening or predict what will happen. Normative theories in accounting are not concerned with accounting as it is practised, but make prescriptions (recommendations) on how it should be practised.

Explain the reasons for evaluating and testing theories
- There are a number of reasons theories might be accepted without 'first hand' or direct knowledge. These include:
  - the authority of the source of the theory
  - whether the theory makes sense and fits with personal experiences and beliefs
  - whether other people accept the theory.
- A researcher or professional in a particular discipline would be expected to apply more legitimate, independent and justifiable methods in assessing and evaluating theories. These include:
  - examining the logical construction of the theory
  - considering evidence that confirms or refutes the theory.

Describe the role of research in accounting
- Research is an activity that involves investigation. Research can be used to test or to derive theories. Various types of research are undertaken in financial accounting, which contribute to knowledge of financial accounting issues and can also result in changes to financial accounting practice and developments.

- Research *of* or *about* accounting considers the role of accounting itself (the 'bigger' picture) at the macro level.
- Research *in* accounting focuses at the more micro level on issues within accounting.

Identify some of the research areas in accounting
- Some of the major research areas in accounting include:
  - capital market research
  - accounting policy choice research
  - accounting information processing research
  - critical accounting research
  - international accounting research.

Review questions

1. Define what is meant by 'theory' and explain how theory is useful. Do you think theory needs to be considered in financial accounting?
2. Explain what is meant by positive theory.
3. Explain what is meant by normative theory.
4. Explain what is meant by induction and deduction.
5. It has been stated that 'many people accept theories without justification'. Identify reasons people may accept theories. Provide examples of theories that you accept or believe although you may not have direct knowledge in the area.
6. Identify a positive theory (this can be about any area, e.g. global warming). Consider how you would test whether this theory was true. Do you think you could prove it?
7. What is your understanding of the term 'research'?
8. Explain the role of research and how this relates to theory.
9. Is the following statement correct: 'Empirical research is only related to positive theories.'?
10. Research can be classified in several ways. Outline them.

Additional readings

Gaffikin, MJR & Aitken, MJ 1982, *The development of accounting theory: significant contributors to accounting thought in the 20th century*, Garland Publishing, Inc., New York and London.

Godfrey, J, Hodgson, A, Tarca, A, Hamilton, J, & Holmes, S 2010, *Accounting theory*, 7th edn, John Wiley & Sons, Brisbane.

Hines, RD 1989, 'Financial accounting knowledge, conceptual framework projects and the social construction of the accounting profession', *Accounting, Auditing and Accountability Journal*, vol. 2, no. 2, pp. 72–92.

Magee, B 1974, 'Karl Popper: the world's greatest philosopher?' *Current Affairs Bulletin*, 1 January, pp. 14–23.

Previts, GJ & Merino, BD 1979, *A history of accounting in America*, Ronald Press, John Wiley & Sons, New York.

End notes

1. McDonald, P cited in Robert Half Management Resources 2009, *The evolution of the accountant*, press release, 18 August, http://rhmr.mediaroom.com.
2. Hancock, P, Howieson, B, Kavanagh, M, Kent, J, Tempone, I & Segal, N 2009, *Accounting for the future: more than numbers 2009*, vol. 1, p. 42. Support for the original work was provided by the Australian Learning and Teaching Council Ltd, an initiative of the Australian Government Department of Education, Employment and Workplace Relations.
3. Henderson, S, Pierson, G & Harris, K 2004, *Financial accounting theory*, Pearson Education Australia, Sydney, p. 4.
4. Hendrickson as cited in Godfrey, J, Hodgson, A, Tarca, A, Hamilton, J, & Holmes, S 2010, *Accounting theory*, 7th edn, John Wiley & Sons, Brisbane, p. 4.
5. Rivett, D 2000, *Issues in accounting theory study guide*, University of South Australia.
6. Hall, SC & Stammerjohan, WW 1997, 'Damages awards and earnings management in the oil industry', *The Accounting Review*, January, p. 47.
7. Laughlin, RC 1999, 'Critical accounting: nature, progress and prognosis', *Accounting, Auditing & Accountability Journal*, vol. 12, no. 1, pp. 73–8.
8. Killian, S 2010, '"No accounting for these people": Shell in Ireland and accounting language', *Critical Perspectives on Accounting*, vol. 21, iss. 8, pp. 711–23.
9. Bayou, ME, Reinstein, A & Williams, PF 2011, 'To tell the truth: A discussion of issues concerning truth and ethics in accounting', *Accounting, Organizations and Society*, vol. 36, iss. 2, pp. 109–24.
10. Ball, R & Brown, P 1968, 'An empirical evaluation of accounting income numbers', *Journal of Accounting Research*, vol. 6, no. 2, pp. 159–78.
11. Beaver, WH 1968, 'The information content of annual earnings announcements', *Journal of Accounting Research*, supplement, pp. 67–92.
12. Watts, R & Zimmerman, J 1978, 'Towards a positive theory of the determination of accounting standards', *The Accounting Review*, vol. 53, no. 1, pp. 112–34.

2 The *Conceptual Framework for Financial Reporting*

LEARNING OBJECTIVES

After studying this chapter, you should be able to:

1 explain what a conceptual framework is

2 understand the history, evolution of and current developments in the *Conceptual Framework for Financial Reporting*

3 outline the structure, approach and components of the *Conceptual Framework*

4 explain and evaluate the purpose, objective and underlying assumption of the *Conceptual Framework*

5 explain the qualitative characteristics of useful financial information in the *Conceptual Framework*

6 explain the elements of financial statements in the *Conceptual Framework*

7 explain the benefits of conceptual frameworks

8 explain and evaluate the problems and criticisms of conceptual frameworks, including the *Conceptual Framework*.

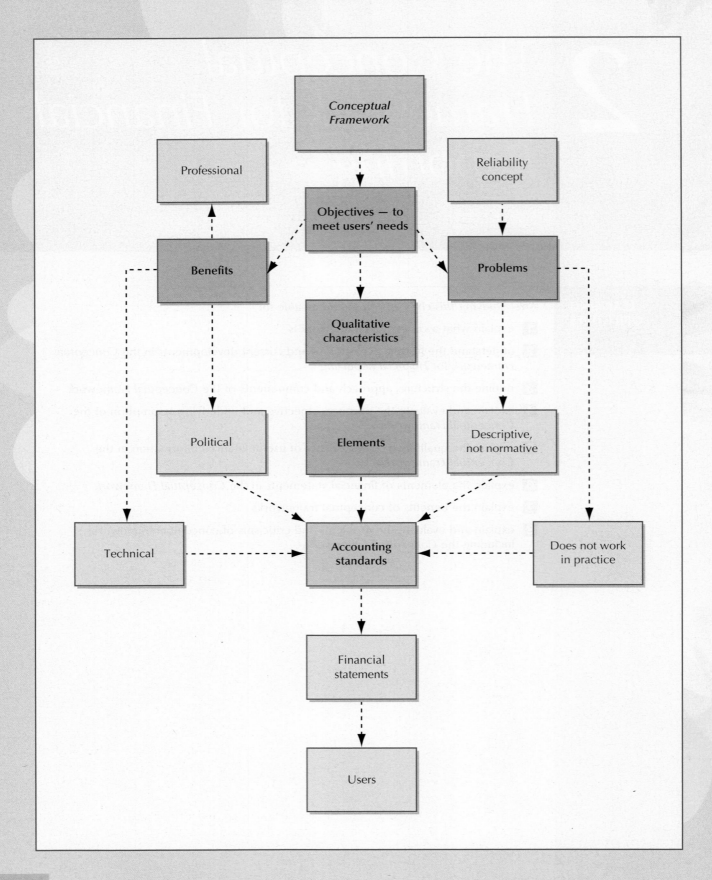

From your previous accounting studies, you will already be familiar with some parts of the *Conceptual Framework for Financial Reporting* (*Conceptual Framework*), although you may not have looked in detail at the *Conceptual Framework* itself. For example, the definitions of assets and liabilities that are in many of the accounting standards that you have studied will have come directly from an accounting conceptual framework. It is important to consider the *Conceptual Framework,* as influences on this, and changes, will significantly impact on the accounting standards that are used to direct financial reporting. Conceptual frameworks have been dominant internationally in the normative theories of accounting for the past 30 years. This chapter considers the *Conceptual Framework* developed by the International Accounting Standards Board (IASB). In addition, it looks at some of the reasons for having a conceptual framework in accounting, some of the criticisms of and problems with the current framework, and recent developments.

 # THE ROLE OF A CONCEPTUAL FRAMEWORK

A conceptual framework is a group of ideas or principles used to plan or decide something. It can be seen as a set of guiding principles — that is, those ideas or concepts that influence and direct decisions being made in a particular area.

Conceptual frameworks are not only found in accounting but are used in many areas to help establish specific guidelines, make decisions or solve problems. For example, your lecturers will use a set of principles relating to the purpose of professional education and principles of adult learning when deciding what assignments or other assessment tasks to set students.

Before examining the accounting conceptual framework in detail, this section looks at a simple example of how a *set of guiding principles* can be used to help influence and direct decisions.

Governments and judges need to set rules and make decisions about punishments or penalties to be applied when people are found guilty of a crime. In this simple example, the guiding principles (the underlying concepts) may be:
- All people should be treated fairly.
- The community's safety must be ensured.
- Punishments and penalties should reflect community values and expectations.

Any actual decisions about punishments and penalties to be imposed should be consistent because they should follow these guiding principles. Of course, the decisions would not necessarily all be identical. The guiding principles are very broad. Specific decisions could vary because of different interpretations. For example:
- Some people may interpret the first principle (that all people should be treated fairly) as saying that all should be treated identically. So, for example, any person who steals food from a shop should receive the same penalty or punishment. Others may interpret 'treat fairly' as requiring them to take into account the particular circumstances, so if it were a hungry child who stole the food, the penalty might be less.
- Values and expectations will vary from community to community, often because of cultural, religious and even economic influences. This can be seen in the different types of punishment imposed for the same crimes in various countries. One community may impose heavier penalties for a behaviour than do others. Also, community values and expectations may change over time.

Conceptual frameworks being made of broad principles is an advantage because it means that these principles can be used as a basis for making decisions across a wide range of situations or circumstances. However, the principles' breadth also has disadvantages — it is usual for more specific guidelines (consistent with the broader principles) to be established to ensure their clearer and more consistent application in particular circumstances. In accounting, these specific rules are found in the accounting standards and interpretations, and the *Conceptual Framework* contains the guidelines for accounting standards.

Conceptual framework theory

The *Conceptual Framework* is a normative theory. It prescribes the basic principles that are to be followed in preparing financial statements. So an **accounting conceptual framework** can be described as a coherent system of concepts, which are guidelines to the accounting standards used for financial reporting.

Normative theories are normally thought of as including terms such as 'should' or 'ought to'. The accounting conceptual framework studied here makes statements such as:

The objective of general purpose financial reporting is to . . .

An asset is a resource . . .

Information must be both relevant and faithfully represented if it is to be useful . . .

Although it does not use the terms 'should' or 'ought to', it is outlining the concepts that should be used in preparing financial statements.

How a conceptual framework differs from an accounting standard

As noted, the principles in the *Conceptual Framework* are general concepts. These are designed to provide guidance and apply to a wide range of decisions relating to the preparation of financial reports. Accounting standards provide *specific* requirements for a *particular* area of financial reporting. For example:
• The *Conceptual Framework* defines what an asset is and when it should be included in the financial statements.
• The accounting standard on inventory (e.g. AASB 102/IAS 2 *Inventories*) outlines the definition of what is considered inventory and what costs are included and also requires these assets to be measured at the lower of cost and net realisable value.

You should see that accounting standards apply to a much narrower area of financial reporting (in the example given, the accounting standard only applies to inventory and not to other assets) and include more detail, allowing less scope for different interpretations. Furthermore, accounting standards go beyond areas that the *Conceptual Framework* has considered. For example, the inventory standard requires that inventory be measured at the lower of cost and net realisable value, whereas the *Conceptual Framework* currently does not require any particular measures for assets. Another difference is that ordinarily accounting standards must be complied with (this varies between countries, but can be required by law or the professional accounting bodies). The principles in the accounting conceptual frameworks may not be mandatory (although it is often recommended that they are used for guidance) and if they conflict with a requirement of an accounting standard, the latter must be followed.[1] Figure 2.1 outlines the basic relationship between the *Conceptual Framework* and accounting standards and interpretations.

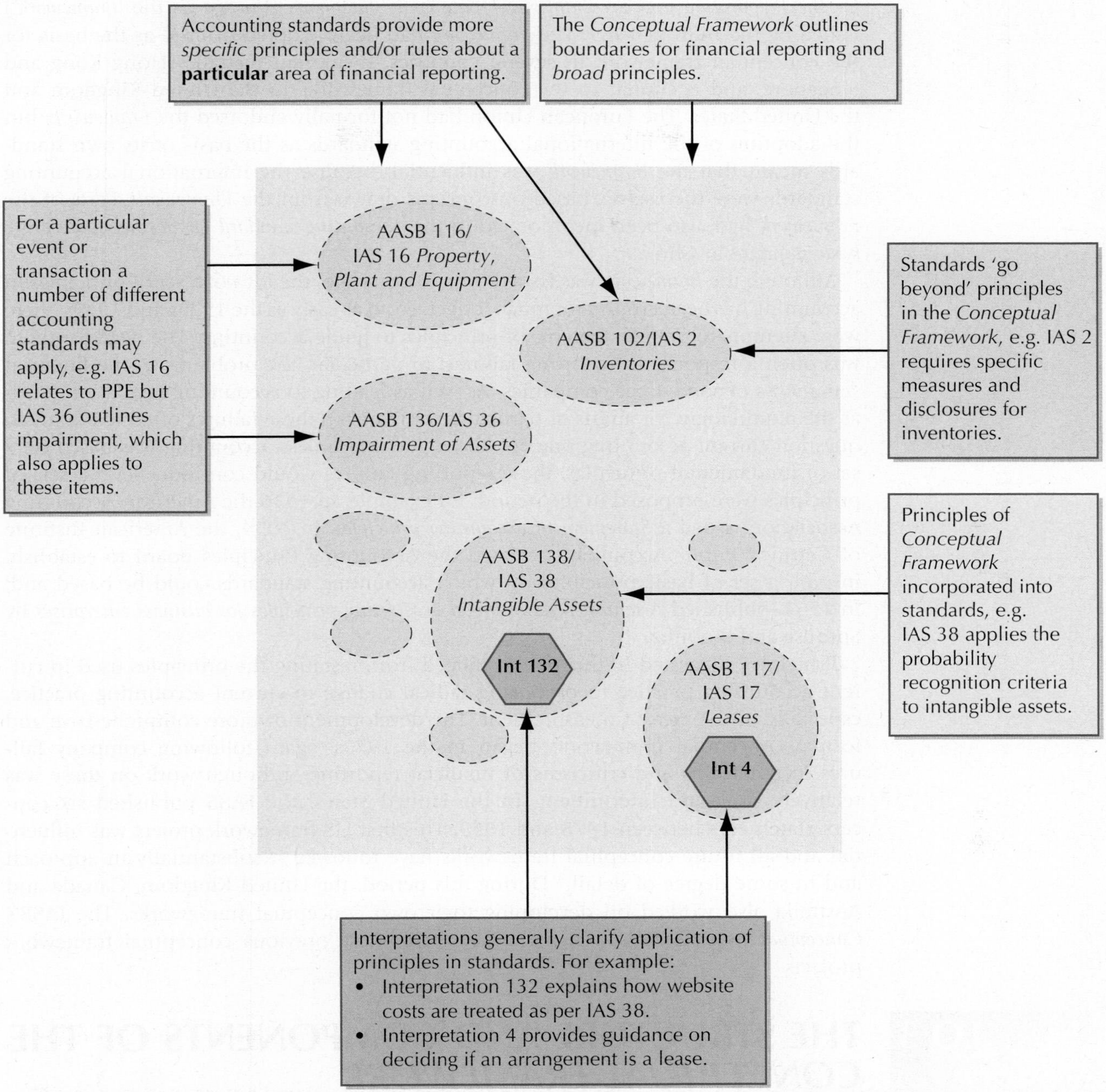
Accounting standards provide more specific principles and/or rules about a particular area of financial reporting.
The Conceptual Framework outlines boundaries for financial reporting and broad principles.
For a particular event or transaction a number of different accounting standards may apply, e.g. IAS 16 relates to PPE but IAS 36 outlines impairment, which also applies to these items.
AASB 116/ IAS 16 Property, Plant and Equipment
AASB 102/IAS 2 Inventories
AASB 136/IAS 36 Impairment of Assets
Standards 'go beyond' principles in the Conceptual Framework, e.g. IAS 2 requires specific measures and disclosures for inventories.
AASB 138/ IAS 38 Intangible Assets
Int 132
AASB 117/ IAS 17 Leases
Int 4
Principles of Conceptual Framework incorporated into standards, e.g. IAS 38 applies the probability recognition criteria to intangible assets.
Interpretations generally clarify application of principles in standards. For example:
• Interpretation 132 explains how website costs are treated as per IAS 38.
• Interpretation 4 provides guidance on deciding if an arrangement is a lease.

FIGURE 2.1 The relationship between the *Conceptual Framework* and accounting standards

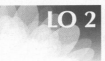

LO 2 HISTORY AND EVOLUTION OF THE *CONCEPTUAL FRAMEWORK*

The conceptual framework studied in this text is the *Conceptual Framework for Financial Reporting* (known as the '*Conceptual Framework*') issued by the IASB in 2010 as a result of a joint project between the IASB and the United States Financial Accounting Standards Board (FASB). The *Conceptual Framework* contains sections from the existing *Framework for the Preparation and Presentation of Financial Statements* (known as the 'Framework') issued by the IASB in 1989. The *Framework* had been adopted or used as the basis for the conceptual framework in several countries, including Australia, Hong Kong and Singapore, and is similar to the conceptual frameworks in the United Kingdom and the United States. The European Union had not formally endorsed the *Framework*, but the adoption of the international accounting standards as the basis of its own standards meant that the *Framework* was influential, because the international accounting standards were themselves based on concepts drawn from the *Framework*. Parts of the *Framework* had also been incorporated in the *Accounting standard for business enterprise: basic standard* in China.[2]

Although the *Framework* was issued over 20 years ago, the idea of a set of principles in accounting has been around for much longer. From as early as the 1920s and 1930s, there were attempts to draft statements of principles to guide accounting. The need for them was often a response to reporting failures; in particular, the problems in the financial statements of some large companies. As well as leading to accounting regulation (such as the requirement for audits of particular companies), these failures often led many to question current accounting practice and argue that unless accounting was based on a set of fundamental principles, these reporting failures would continue. Several sets of principles were proposed in the period; for example, in 1936 the American Accounting Association issued a *Statement of accounting principles*. In 1959, the American Institute of Certified Public Accountants created the Accounting Principles Board to establish, in part, a set of basic principles on which accounting standards could be based and, in 1962, published *A tentative set of broad accounting principles for business enterprises* by Sprouse and Moonitz.

Principles suggested in this period ranged from restating the principles used in current accounting practice to proposing radical change to current accounting practice, especially in the area of measurement. The development of more comprehensive and formal conceptual frameworks began in the 1970s, again following company failures in the 1960s and criticisms of financial reporting, although work on these was relatively slow and intermittent. In the United States, the FASB published six concept statements between 1978 and 1989. This first US framework project was influential and all future conceptual frameworks have followed it substantially in approach and in some degree of detail.[3] During this period, the United Kingdom, Canada and Australia also worked on developing their own conceptual frameworks. The IASB's *Conceptual Framework* is drawn directly from these previous conceptual framework projects.

LO 3 THE STRUCTURE AND COMPONENTS OF THE *CONCEPTUAL FRAMEWORK*

The *Conceptual Framework* can be seen as providing answers to questions that need to be considered when preparing financial statements such as:
- What is the purpose of financial statements?
- Who are they prepared for?
- What are the assumptions to be made when preparing financial statements?
- What type of information should be included?
- What are the elements that make up financial statements?
- When should the elements of financial statements be included?

Figure 2.2 provides an overview of the parts of the current *Conceptual Framework* in accounting.

Questions that the *Conceptual Framework* answers	Approach in the *Conceptual Framework**
What reports are we considering?	General purpose financial reports
Who are the financial reports for?	For a range of users who may provide resources (including current or potential investors, lenders, creditors)
Why report? What is the purpose of the financial reports?	The key objective is to meet the common information needs of the users for decision making.
What are the assumptions to be made when preparing financial reports?	There is one underlying assumption which is the going concern.
What type of information should be included?	To be useful to users, information must have the two fundamental qualitative characteristics of: • relevance • faithful representation. There are also desired enhancing characteristics of: • comparability • verifiability • timeliness • understandability. These are subject to the cost constraint.
What are the elements that make up financial statements?	Five elements are defined: • assets • liabilities • equity • income • expenses. The definitions identify the essential features of each element.
When should these elements be included?	There are two criteria required to be met before an element can be included in the financial statements. These are known as recognition criteria. These relate to: • probability • ability to measure reliably.

Questions that the *Conceptual Framework* does not answer	
What measurement basis should we use?	It is noted that different bases are used to measure (including historical cost, present value, current cost, realisable value). No particular measurement base is recommended.
What capital concept should be used?	It is noted that either a financial or physical capital concept can be used but none in particular is recommended.

FIGURE 2.2 Overview of the IASB *Conceptual Framework*

* This reflects the finalisation of Phase A of the joint project by the IASB and FASB.

Source: Adapted from Tim Sutton.[4]

The *Conceptual Framework* moves in what is essentially a series of steps or levels. It begins with principles that consider broader questions, such as those relating to objectives, and moves to more narrow and specific issues. The approach or answers to the broader (initial) questions provide direction and influence subsequent principles. For example, the decision about the nature of information included in financial reports (e.g. relevance and faithful representation) is influenced directly by the prior principle that financial reports are prepared to provide information for users to assist in decision making. The 'initial' principles determine and influence the principles included later in the *Conceptual Framework*, so that all parts are linked in a hierarchy.

Current developments

In 2004, the IASB and FASB began undertaking a project to develop a common conceptual framework. This has in part resulted from the decision by the FASB to adopt a principles-based (rather than rules-based) approach to standard setting. The project is being conducted in eight phases and as each phase is completed those related sections will be updated within the *Conceptual Framework*. A brief outline of each phase is provided below:

- Phase A relates to the objectives and qualitative characteristics. This phase was completed in September 2010. Figure 2.2 and the discussion of the objectives and qualitative characteristics in this chapter reflect the resulting changes.
- Phase B relates to elements and recognition. The objective of this phase is to reconsider (and revise if necessary) the definitions of assets and liabilities and the related recognition criteria concepts. No discussion paper has yet been issued.
- Phase C relates to measurement. This is perhaps one of the most controversial and important parts of this project and the objective is to provide guidance for choosing measurement bases for elements recognised in the financial statements. The current measurement section of the *Conceptual Framework* provides little guidance and simply identifies a limited range of different measurement bases, noting that the most common base is historical cost (paragraphs 4.54–4.56). The deliberations to date in the current project have identified a range of measurement bases and considered a number of approaches on a continuum: from providing a very basic list of possible measures and describing the advantages and disadvantages of these in terms of the qualitative characteristics, to providing a hierarchy of measures with very specific guidance for ranking and selecting between these, to prescribing a single measure for all items. The current consensus appears to be that this part should outline the relationship between the qualitative characteristics and alternative measures and provide guidance about when certain measures should be used at a conceptual level. However, recent discussions have indicated that a more restrictive approach, prescribing a hierarchy of measurement bases is finding support. No public discussion paper has yet been issued in relation to Phase C.
- Phase D relates to the reporting entity. This effectively determines the boundaries of financial reporting. An exposure draft chapter was issued in March 2010. This exposure draft's definition, discussed in further detail later in this chapter, is based on delineating the entity in terms of a 'circumscribed area of economic activities' and linking this to potential users of information. Responses to the exposure draft raised a number of issues (including requiring clarification of some terms and the role of the reporting entity concept itself) and will require reconsideration. Given other priorities, further work on this phase has been deferred.
- Phase E (presentation and disclosure) and Phase F (purpose and status) have not yet begun.
- Phase G relates to the application of the *Conceptual Framework* to not-for-profit entities and this phase has not yet begun. The existing *Framework* applied only to businesses entities and the current IASB/FASB project also gives priority to business entities with Phase G considered as a 'later' phase. The approach is to address the application of the *Conceptual Framework* to not-for-profit and public sector entities after the essential concepts have been determined and revised. This approach has its critics, arguing

that it will be more difficult to accommodate the issues and concerns of non-business entities unless adequate consideration is given throughout all phases of the project. The International Public Sector Accounting Standards Board (IPSASB) has been developing a conceptual framework for public sector entities and in December 2010 issued an exposure draft relating to the equivalents of Phases A, D and F and consultation papers relating to the equivalents of Phases B and C.

- Phase H relating to remaining issues will only commence after the previous seven phases are completed and only if other issues are identified that remain to be addressed.

As this summary indicates progress on this joint *Conceptual Framework* has been slow. The initial work program indicated that the entire framework would be finalised in 2010. However only one phase has been finalised and there is now no indication from the IASB/FASB when completion is expected, as their current priorities and resources are being expended on changes to a number of accounting standards to facilitate the convergence of the international and US accounting standards.

LO 4 PURPOSE, OBJECTIVE AND UNDERLYING ASSUMPTION OF THE *CONCEPTUAL FRAMEWORK*

The purposes of the *Conceptual Framework* are discussed under the section in this chapter relating to benefits of conceptual frameworks. Before looking at the objective of financial reporting as outlined in the *Conceptual Framework*, this section considers the *Conceptual Framework*'s scope.

Reporting focus

The *Conceptual Framework* states that it is concerned with **general purpose financial reports**. These can be defined as financial reports intended to meet the needs of users who are not in a position to require an entity to prepare reports tailored to their particular information needs. For example, if a person owns a few shares in a large company (in Australia, this could be the communications company, Telstra, or in Hong Kong, the transport provider, MTR), even though that shareholder is a part owner of the company, he or she could not ask the company for a report containing exactly the information he or she needs to decide whether he or she will continue to hold the shares in that company. The only information such small shareholders would have access to would be the annual reports that companies provide publicly. The financial report within an annual report is an example of a general purpose financial report.

The *Conceptual Framework* does not need to be applied in the preparation of *special* purpose financial reports, which are reports prepared to meet the needs of particular users. These normally contain specialised information designed for users who have the power to ask for the information they need. For example:

- Some lenders can require, as part of the terms for granting a loan, that reports be prepared with specific information.
- Taxation authorities can require specific reports.
- Management would require, and be able to obtain, more detailed reports.

Entity focus

While financial statements relate to a particular entity, there is no definition of a reporting entity in the *Conceptual Framework*. Paragraph 8 of the *Framework* stated:

> The *Framework* applies to the financial statements of all commercial, industrial and business reporting entities, whether in the public or the private sectors. A reporting

entity is an entity for which there are users who rely on the financial statements as their major source of financial information about the entity.

This paragraph has now been removed. Phase D of the current program to develop the *Conceptual Framework* is aimed at this aspect. As noted previously, completion of this phase has been delayed. The definition of a reporting entity proposed in the exposure draft was:

> A reporting entity is a circumscribed area of economic activities whose financial information has the potential to be useful to existing and potential equity investors, lenders, and other creditors who cannot directly obtain the information they need in making decisions about providing resources to the entity and in assessing whether the management and the governing board of that entity have made efficient and effective use of the resources provided.[5]

Rather than considering the legal form, a reporting entity is identified from a bounded set of economic events and transactions with a link to a group of users reliant on general purpose financial reports.

The *Conceptual Framework* is not aimed at financial reports prepared by not-for-profit entities. Some countries have made changes to the *Conceptual Framework* so that the principles also apply to them.

The *Conceptual Framework* does not set out which entities must actually prepare financial reports. Which entities must prepare general purpose financial reports (such as those included in annual reports) is decided by the specific laws and customs of particular countries. In its role as an international accounting body, the IASB does not have the authority to demand that particular entities prepare financial reports.

The objective of financial reporting

There are broadly two views of what should be the objective of financial reporting. These are:

- stewardship or accountability
- decision usefulness.

Stewardship or accountability focuses on the duty of the managers of an entity. They are entrusted with the resources of the entity. Stewardship (or accountability) requires the managers to provide a report to the providers of the resources to explain how well they have managed them. Historically, this was the main purpose of financial reports and accounting. Given the separation of managers and owners (such as shareholders), ensuring that managers provided 'an account' of their activities and how they managed the resources entrusted to them was considered the primary reason for financial reports.

> Stewardship is concerned with the accountability of the directors, or management board, of a business entity to its proprietors or owners. This is at the heart of the financial reporting process in many jurisdictions...[6]

Whereas the IASB *Framework* included accountability as a separate objective, the *Conceptual Framework* does not, giving primacy to the **decision usefulness** approach and states:

> The objective of general purpose financial reporting is to provide financial information about the reporting entity that is useful to existing and potential investors, lenders and other creditors in making decisions about providing resources to the entity. Those decisions involve buying, selling or holding equity and debt instruments, and providing or settling loans and other forms of credit.[7]

Under this objective, the financial statements should provide information that is useful to users in making decisions. This requires considering *how* information is used in decision making. In models of the decision process, information is needed to:

- *Help us predict what may happen in the future.* This does not mean, however, that financial statements necessarily provide forecasted or future-oriented information. However, the information provided should help users make these predictions.
- *Provide feedback on previous decisions.* Information can help in deciding whether past decisions, and the information used to make them, were correct, and can help in making better decisions in the future.

It is also assumed financial statements that provide information useful for decision making will also provide the information needed to assess accountability. As the *Conceptual Framework* states:

> Information about management's discharge of its responsibilities is also useful for decisions by existing investors, lenders and other creditors who have the right to vote on or otherwise influence management's actions.[8]

Thus, in the *Conceptual Framework*, accountability or stewardship is not considered a separate objective, but rather information about this is included as it is part of the information useful for users' decisions. However, this subsumption of accountability within decision making has been criticised.[9] As dissenting IASB board members stated:

> Stewardship may require more emphasis on related party transactions, and generally on past rather than future transactions or events, than would be required by the primary focus on future cash flows. Thus, stewardship and decision-usefulness for investors are parallel objectives which do not necessarily conflict, but which have different emphases.[10]

It should be noted that the IPSASB's proposed framework for public sector entities includes two objectives: decision usefulness and accountability.[11]

Users and their information needs

It is important to consider *who* the users are and what information they need, given that the purpose of financial statements is to provide them with useful information. The *Conceptual Framework* identifies a limited range of primary users of financial statements. They include:

- existing and potential investors
- lenders
- other creditors.

Compared to the *Framework*, which in addition to those listed above also included customers, employees, governments and their agencies and the public, this is a fairly limited set of users focused on those who provide financial resources to the entity. The *Conceptual Framework* accepts that financial reports may also be useful to others, but explicitly confirms that the information included is directed at the primary user groups and not alternative groups (paragraph OB10). The primacy of the investor is a common position taken in many of the accounting conceptual frameworks and reflects that historically these frameworks have been developed in countries where capital markets and the related protection of investors have been key influences on accounting developments and regulation.[12] However, the *Conceptual Framework* does not differentiate between the relative importance of those resource providers identified as the primary users.

Even with this restricted range of users, the *Conceptual Framework* acknowledges that not all their information needs can be met by general purpose financial statements. The aim is to provide information where users' needs overlap or are shared — that is, to meet the information needs that are *common* to these user groups and meet the needs of the maximum number of these primary users (paragraph OB8).

The information in financial reports is limited mainly to *financial* information. This is normally in the form of a statement of financial position, a statement of profit or loss and other comprehensive income, a statement of cash flows, a statement of changes in equity and associated notes. The *Conceptual Framework* explicitly states that these reports are not designed to show the value of a reporting entity (paragraph OB7).

The financial reports provide financial information about the *past* transactions and events of the entity. As noted, users will also need information about the future to help them make their decisions.

Some users will need and place importance on non-financial information. Many investors, for example, consider ethical issues (such as the nature of the product, the environmental impact of the entity or the entity's treatment of its employees) when making investment decisions. This type of information is not intended to be provided by the financial reports and would be part of the information needs that the *Conceptual Framework* acknowledges are not met by financial reports.

Contemporary Issue 2.1 considers some of the issues with users' information needs and how far these are met by current financial reports.

2.1 CONTEMPORARY ISSUE

The usefulness of financial reporting

This extract discusses the limitations of financial information and the relevance of non-financial information.

FASB Concepts Statement 2 states that, to be useful, financial information must be both relevant and reliable. Although much has been written about the importance of the reliability of financial information following the high-profile corporate scandals of Enron, WorldCom, and others, comparably little attention has been given to the relevance of the financial information presented. Because of the litigious nature of our society, many accountants prefer to provide more information, rather than less, sometimes without considering its relevance or usefulness.

So how do we determine what information is relevant? Simply put, relevant information enhances the user's ability to make an informed decision. Accordingly, relevant information is not limited to numbers. For example, if a technology company hires one of the best minds in the field, would that information be an important factor in making an informed decision about the company's future economic prospects? Or if a bioengineering company lost its most productive R&D scientist, might that information influence stakeholders' decisions?

In our knowledge-based society, many business entities derive much of their value from intangible assets; yet many intangibles, such as human capital, ideas, and innovations, are nowhere to be found on the balance sheet. The real value of these companies may not be accurately reflected in their financial reports. Although these economic resources may be difficult to quantify, to ignore them would not fairly represent the financial and business position of the company. Furthermore, assumptions and estimates in financial reporting will never be perfect, and there will always be some companies that go to great lengths to manipulate the numbers through aggressive, misleading, or even fraudulent application of the rules. If we're going to limit ourselves to counting beans, our value in the business reporting process won't be worth a hill of them.

Source: Extracts from Mary-Jo Kranacher, 'The GAAP between Public and Private Companies', *The CPA Journal*. Reprinted from *The CPA Journal*, June 2006, with permission from the New York State Society of Certified Public Accountants.[13]

Questions

1. Should information in the financial reports be limited to financial or numerical information? **J**
2. What are the difficulties or problems in requiring companies to provide non-financial information about, for example, human capital, intangibles, or innovations? **J** **K** **AS**

Underlying assumption

The *Conceptual Framework* requires the financial reports to be based on one underlying assumption, being the **going concern basis**. It states that 'the financial statements are normally prepared on the assumption that an entity is a going concern and will continue in operation for the foreseeable future' (paragraph 4.1).

The going concern assumption has a direct impact on both the recognition and measurement of items in the financial statements. If the entity is not expected to continue in business, then the economic benefits in particular items, such as prepaid insurance, would no longer be expected to be received, so they could not be recognised as assets. The reported values of assets would also need to be reconsidered. For example, if the business is to close, inventory may not realise its 'normal' selling price. Where the assumption that the entity is a going concern is inappropriate, this basis should not be used and this would need to be disclosed.

 LO 5

QUALITATIVE CHARACTERISTICS OF USEFUL FINANCIAL INFORMATION

Having decided that the role of financial reports is to provide information useful to users for making decisions, the *Conceptual Framework* then identifies the properties that financial information must have to be included in the financial reports. These properties are known as qualitative characteristics and the aim is to ensure that the information provided is of adequate quality to help users make decisions. The qualitative characteristics were revised in 2010 as part of Phase A of the current conceptual framework project by the IASB and FASB and there is now a hierarchy of qualitative characteristics: fundamental and enhancing. To be useful for decision making (and therefore appropriate to consider for inclusion in the financial reports), information *must* have both of the two fundamental characteristics. The enhancing characteristics are not essential, but can improve the usefulness of the information and also assist in making choices between information that has the fundamental characteristics.

Fundamental qualitative characteristics

The two fundamental qualitative characteristics are:

- relevance
- faithful representation.

Relevance

The **relevance** characteristic aims to ensure that only financial information that could make a difference in decisions is included. This fundamental qualitative characteristic outlines why the financial information is needed. It is linked directly to the purpose of financial reports — that is, to provide information useful to users in making decisions. Clearly, if the information cannot be used either to help make predictions or to provide feedback, it is not useful to users, so would not be relevant and should not be included in the financial reports. For these reasons, relevance is often the first 'test' applied to financial information although as noted later the other fundamental qualitative characteristic of faithful representation must also be met.

A related aspect of relevance is **materiality**. This is the quality of information if its omission or misstatement could influence the economic decision of users taken on the basis of the financial reports (paragraph QC11). As users' decisions are made in the context of a specific reporting entity the *Conceptual Framework* notes that materiality is entity-specific. In other words, the same information may be relevant for users of one entity but not for another. Some information is relevant because of what it is about — that is, its nature. For example, regardless of its size, information relating to loans to directors of the company may be considered material and important to users because of the position of directors in the company, even if these loans are relatively small. In other cases, it may be necessary to consider the size or amount of the item to determine whether it is material and so is relevant. For example, in a manufacturing company, specific information about individual expenses would not normally need to be provided, such as costs of postage, unless these items were large. Of course, for a mail order company, postage costs would be material in amount and also would be relevant because of the company's nature.

Faithful representation

The purpose of **faithful representation** is to make sure that users have confidence in and can 'trust' the financial information that is provided in financial reports and in the *Conceptual Framework* it replaces reliability as a qualitative characteristic. Faithful representation requires making sure that what is shown in the financial reports corresponds to the actual events and transactions that are being represented. Accounting standards often require us to consider the substance over form — that is, requiring items to be accounted for and presented in accordance with their substance and economic reality and not merely their legal form. For example, if a financial instrument is described in legal documents as a preference share, but the actual terms indicate that the instrument is in the nature of debt, it should be recognised as a liability.

Three characteristics or components need to be considered in determining the faithful representation of financial information.

Complete depiction

Users require *all* relevant information about an event or phenomena to be included in the financial reports, if these are to be useful for decision making. Good decisions cannot be made on the basis of incomplete information. The *Conceptual Framework* explains that a complete depiction is more than just including numbers and can require descriptions and explanations (paragraph QC13).

Neutrality

For information to be neutral, it must be free from bias (paragraph QC14). This component of faithful representation aims to ensure that there is no attempt to promote any particular view and that the financial reports provide an impartial description of the events and transactions.

Freedom from error

Clearly if there are errors in the information it is not a faithful representation. This does not imply however that the information is 'exact'. Many estimates are used in accounting and in hindsight many of these will be found to be incorrect or inaccurate. Providing these estimates are identified as such, and made on a reasonable basis, these would still meet the requirement for faithful representation (paragraph QC15).

Enhancing qualitative characteristics

The four enhancing qualitative characteristics are:
- comparability
- verifiability
- timeliness
- understandability.

Comparability

When comparing financial reports over time and between entities, users need to be able to determine the reasons for changes or differences. An important aspect of comparability is that it requires the accounting policies used in the preparation of the financial reports to be disclosed, so that users are able to understand whether changes or differences are caused by variations in accounting policies or actual economic conditions.

Comparability would generally be achieved with consistent measurement and presentation of items over time and between entities. However, this may not be possible or even desirable. The need to ensure comparability does not justify the use of a particular accounting policy if a more relevant or faithful representation of information could be provided with an alternative policy or measure.

Verifiability

Verifiability requires that the information can be supported or confirmed so that users are confident in relying on the information. Certain information can be verified directly (e.g. we can confirm the amount paid for an item from an invoice). In other cases, it may only be possible to verify information indirectly (e.g. where estimates are used, the calculations and assumptions could be disclosed and checked).

Timeliness

Users need information on a timely basis. Although delaying the issue of the financial reports may improve the quality of some information, it is likely to reduce its usefulness to users. For example, it may be that the entity has been found liable to pay damages, but the amount has not yet been decided by the courts. Waiting until it is decided would make the information more verifiable but the delay in issuing the financial reports would make them less useful overall. In this case, the issue of timeliness would override considerations of verifiability.

Understandability

Unless a person can understand information, they cannot use it. Understandability deals with this issue, but it does not require that the information be simplified so that anyone can understand it. The *Conceptual Framework* asserts that financial reports are prepared for users who have reasonable knowledge of business and economic activities and who will conduct a diligent review and analysis of the information.

Determining the relative importance of qualitative characteristics

The hierarchy requires that both of the fundamental qualitative characteristics are present for the financial information to be useful and therefore meet the objective of financial reporting. Ideally, the financial information should also have all of the enhancing qualitative characteristics. This may not always be possible in practice and there will often be a need to 'trade-off' to determine which should be given more importance. This is a matter of professional judgement and will depend on the particular circumstances. For example:

- Historical cost is often the most objective and understandable measure for assets. However, this may not be as relevant to users as other measures such as present value or fair value. In some cases, it may be decided that the other measures are not adequately verifiable, so historical cost is used. In other cases, it may be decided that relevance should override the reduction in the verifiability and/or understandability, so other measures are provided.
- Relevant information cannot be left out on the basis that it is very complex and may be difficult for some users to understand. This may require a reduction in understandability to ensure relevance.

Cost constraint on financial information

Although the *Conceptual Framework* states that information that is relevant and faithfully representative should be included in the financial reports, it acknowledges that cost is a constraint on the provision of information. This constraint relates to the general economic principle that the benefits of an action should outweigh the costs. The analysis for financial reporting would include the costs in preparing the reports and the benefits to users from better decisions. However, there are potentially more indirect costs and benefits that relate to the economic consequences of providing information. The concept of economic consequences is discussed later in this chapter. The *Conceptual Framework* recognises that this constraint is applied subjectively.

 LO 6 # THE ELEMENTS OF FINANCIAL STATEMENTS

The *Conceptual Framework* provides definitions for the five essential elements of the financial statements: assets, liabilities, equity, income and expenses.

The definitions for elements relating to the financial position are as follows.
An asset is defined in paragraph 4.4(a) of the *Conceptual Framework*:

> An asset is a resource controlled by the entity as a result of past events and from which future economic benefits are expected to flow to the entity.

A liability is defined in paragraph 4.4(b) of the *Conceptual Framework*:

> A liability is a present obligation of the entity arising from past events, the settlement of which is expected to result in an outflow from the entity of resources embodying economic benefits.

Equity is defined in paragraph 4.4(c) of the *Conceptual Framework*:

> Equity is the residual interest in the assets of the entity after deducting all its liabilities.

The definitions of the elements relating to financial performance are as follows:
Income is defined in paragraph 4.25(a) of the *Conceptual Framework*:

> Income is increases in economic benefits during the accounting period in the form of inflows or enhancements of assets or decreases of liabilities that result in increases in equity, other than those relating to contributions from equity participants.

Expenses are defined in paragraph 4.25(b) of the *Conceptual Framework*:

> Expenses are decreases in economic benefits during the accounting period in the form of outflows or depletions of assets or incurrences of liabilities that result in decreases in equity, other than those relating to distributions to equity participants.

These definitions do not refer to legal form but to economic benefits. This reflects the substance over form approach required by the *Conceptual Framework*. This has a significant impact on the financial statements. For example, a legal debt or obligation is not necessarily required for an item to meet the definition of liability, the obligation can be constructive; an item does not need to be owned by the entity for it to meet the definition of an asset, it can be leased. The *Conceptual Framework* also provides rules, known as recognition criteria, for deciding when these elements may actually be included in the financial statements.

The *Conceptual Framework* adopts what is known as the 'balance sheet' approach to defining the elements of the financial statements. This approach places most importance on the definitions of assets and liabilities. The other elements of financial statements (equity, income and expenses) are defined in terms of assets and liabilities. For example, the definition of an expense given in the *Conceptual Framework* includes a requirement to identify a decrease in economic benefits 'in the form of outflows or depletions of *assets* or incurrences of *liabilities*'. This means that before it can be determined whether an item is an expense, the definitions of assets or liabilities or both must be applied. The identification of balance sheet items (i.e. assets and liabilities) determines whether the definitions for the other items in the financial statements are met.

Recognition criteria

Having met the definition of a financial statement element, an item must meet two further tests, known as recognition criteria, before it can be recognised in the financial statements.

Recognition is defined in paragraph 4.37 of the *Conceptual Framework*:

> Recognition is the process of incorporating an item in the balance sheet or income statement . . . It involves depiction of the item in words and by a monetary amount and the inclusion of that amount in the balance sheet or income statement totals.

Paragraph 4.38 of the *Conceptual Framework* states that an item that meets the definition of an element should be recognised if:

(a) it is probable that any future economic benefit associated with the item will flow to or from the entity; and
(b) the item has a cost or value that can be measured with reliability.

Accordingly, the two tests for recognition of an element are probability and reliable measurement.

Probability

The probability test takes into account there being some uncertainty about many items in the financial statements. The probability recognition criteria are included in specific accounting standards which provide further guidance. For example, paragraph 23 of AASB 137/IAS 37 *Provisions, Contingent Liabilities and Contingent Assets* states that the probability criteria is met if 'the event is more likely than not to occur'. This would be interpreted as meaning more than 50% likelihood of occurrence.

Reliable measurement

To be included in the financial statements, the item needs to be measured to determine a monetary amount for that item. In many cases, measuring an item will require the use of estimates, but the use of estimates does not mean that a measure is unreliable. This test also requires *either* a cost *or* value to be able to be measured with reliability. If you cannot reliably measure the benefits, there may still be a cost (e.g. historic cost) that can be measured. Alternatively, simply because a particular item has no cost does not mean it cannot be measured with reliability.

Elements that meet both of the recognition criteria *should* be recognised; elements that do not meet both of the recognition criteria *cannot* be recognised, although information may be disclosed in notes to the statements (one example is contingent liabilities) where this is useful to users.

The outline above provides a summary of the definition and recognition criteria for elements of financial statements in the *Conceptual Framework*. Phase B of the joint conceptual framework project relates to these two aspects, but has not been finalised. However, the following should be noted:

- The use of terms such as 'control', 'expected' and 'probable' have already been identified as problematic and open to misinterpretation, so it is likely that these will be revised.
- An exposure draft on liabilities (ED/2010/1 *Measurement of Liabilities in IAS 37*) proposed to abolish the recognition criteria of probability for certain items. The completion of Phase B of the conceptual framework project is expected to be delayed given the potential revision of this aspect in IAS 37.
- Phase A replaced the previous qualitative characteristic of 'reliability' with 'faithful representation'. The recognition criteria discussed above still uses 'reliability'.

Contemporary Issue 2.2 illustrates how the application of the accounting definitions and recognition criteria of items can affect the financial statements.

2.2 CONTEMPORARY ISSUE

New lease accounting to have big impact

Background: In August 2010, the IASB issued an exposure draft proposing changes to the current standard on leases. This current standard requires a lease to be classified as either a finance or operating lease. Only finance leases are shown in the balance sheet with an asset (and a liability) to be recognised if the risks and benefits associated with ownership have been transferred. This approach has long been criticised as being inconsistent with the *Conceptual Framework*'s definition of an asset, which does not require ownership or a comparison to this. The exposure draft proposes that all leases be recognised in the balance sheet.

The new draft lease accounting standard is an overdue reality check for the corporate world but it also exposes the fault-lines in the standard-setting process.

No one can argue against the value of the standard. The existing rules mean that large amounts of liabilities are hidden **off balance sheet**. And that frankly cannot, particularly in a post-crisis world, be right. If the general public understood these things they would be shocked, in the same way that people going to the theatre to see 'Enron — The Play' were shocked.

The old rules were written a long time ago when we had very different ways of looking at the world. Investors now argue that disclosure is not a substitute for good accounting and that all assets and liabilities need to be on the balance sheet. Standard-setters now take a balance sheet view of life. And in this brave new world where we recognise more and more assets and liabilities on balance sheet, including many more intangibles, why would we not be recognising assets for leases that convey the rights to use the leased assets; and the corresponding liabilities to pay for that use? The proposed new rules reflect the way that the accounting world is moving and put all lease assets and liabilities on balance sheet.

The impact of the proposed standard should not be underestimated. Moving all those liabilities onto the balance sheet will inevitably have an effect. We will see lower asset turnover ratios, lower return on capital, and an increase in debt-to-equity ratios, which could have a knock-on effect on borrowing capital or compliance with banking covenants. The figures are vast. Some ball park calculations suggest that we are talking about an estimated ⌄

£94bn of leasing liabilities for the top 50 companies in the UK, and a mammoth $1.3 trillion (£843bn) for public companies in the US. There will be short-term pain but it will result in long-term gain as business realities are more clearly expressed in the financial reporting.

Source: Extract from Veronica Poole, 'No pain, no gain', *Accountancy Age*.[14]

Questions
1. Consider the definitions of an asset and liability in the *Conceptual Framework*. Would a 5-year lease for land meet these definitions? **J** **K**
2. The extract discusses the fact that these changes reflect the way in which accounting is moving — that is, towards putting all assets and liabilities on the balance sheet. What reasons could there be for this move? Given the identified impact on key company ratios, do you believe this approach is justified? **J**

LO 7 THE BENEFITS OF A CONCEPTUAL FRAMEWORK

It is claimed benefits may arise from a conceptual framework in accounting. These can be arranged into three categories:
- technical
- political
- professional.

Technical benefits

If you think of 'technical' improvements, you think of changes that make something work or function better. A key argument for a conceptual framework in accounting relates to technical benefits. As stated by Rutherford, the principal attraction of a conceptual framework in accounting:

> is argued to be the improvement in the quality of standards that would follow because they would rest on more solid ground; other less elevated, attractions include the contribution it can make to the technical consistency and speed of development of standards and the effectiveness with which standards can be defended.[15]

So the main benefit of having a conceptual framework is to improve accounting itself, to improve the practice of accounting and to provide a basis for answers to specific accounting questions and problems. It is stated that the *Conceptual Framework* does this in two ways:
- by providing a basis and guidance for those who set the specific accounting rules (such as accounting standards or interpretations)
- by helping individuals involved in preparing or auditing or using financial statements.

The role of a conceptual framework in setting accounting standards

For many years, accounting standards were set without a conceptual framework. This was referred to as a 'piecemeal' approach, because of the slowness of the process and because the rules within some standards were incompatible with those in others.

In the *Conceptual Framework* itself an important purpose is:

> to assist the Board in the development of future IFRSs and in its review of existing IFRSs.[16]

A conceptual framework provides a set of established and agreed principles. 'The key measure of the success of a standard is its acceptance. An important prerequisite for gaining acceptance is a language common to all parties involved. An agreed upon set of concepts and principles provides this language'.[17] Having a conceptual framework means that when determining the accounting rules or standards for specific events or transactions, the focus is on deciding how to apply the principles already in the conceptual framework. For example, when deciding on how to account for money spent on creating and maintaining websites, the issue considered is whether the costs should be recognised as an asset or expense, *given* the definitions and recognition criteria in the conceptual framework. This approach restricts the discussion on how to apply the principles in the conceptual framework to website costs. It also helps to ensure that the recognition of any assets, for example, is consistent with the recognition of assets in other circumstances. As Foster and Johnson state, a conceptual framework:

> provides a basic reasoning on which to consider the merits of alternatives. Although it does not provide all the answers, the framework narrows the range of alternatives by eliminating some that are inconsistent with it. It thereby contributes to greater efficiency in the standard setting process by avoiding the necessity of having to redebate fundamental issues such as 'what is an asset?' time and time again.[18]

Of course, using a conceptual framework as the basis for setting specific accounting rules does not mean there is no room for debate or disagreement. There may be different interpretations of the definition of assets or expenses in the conceptual framework. This problem with the current *Conceptual Framework* is considered later in this chapter. Also, in particular cases, standard setters may deliberately depart from the principles in the conceptual framework for other reasons (such as concerns over abuse of accounting requirements or political influences).

Benefits to preparers and users

Consider what would happen if you are preparing the financial reports but have a particular case for which there are no specific standards or rules. How do you decide how to account for it? One way is to go to the basic principles in the *Conceptual Framework* and use them as a guide to help you make your decision.

Also, standards based on a conceptual framework should be more easily understood and interpreted by users. This is because:
- Users can refer to the principles in the conceptual framework to understand the basis for the specific accounting rules.
- The accounting rules should be more consistent because they are based on the same underlying principles.

Political benefits

A further benefit of a conceptual framework is to prevent political interference in setting accounting standards. To understand this benefit, you need to be aware of the political nature of accounting. Many accounting students view accounting standards as boring and uncontroversial. However, remember that financial reports provide information on which people base their decisions. Therefore, if the information in these statements changes, it is likely that the decisions based on this information will also change.

Decisions made by users, such as where to invest or whether to continue to supply goods to a company, could change. Decisions by the management of the entity could also change. For example, when the accounting standard was introduced that required an asset and liability for finance leases to be included in financial statements, some companies stopped using finance leases. In the United States, when the accounting standard was introduced that required companies to include health benefits to be provided to employees as a liability, some companies ended these health benefit schemes to employees.[19] These decisions have a real economic impact and affect the wealth and welfare of particular individuals, entities and industries.

Political pressures and potential economic consequences

Of course, it is natural for people to try to look after their own interests and this leads to attempts to influence accounting requirements. For example, when the international accounting standard setters proposed that share-based payments made to employees be included as an expense in the financial statements, some argued that requiring recognition of these payments would have unfavourable economic impacts discouraging entities from introducing or continuing employee share-based share plans. This would in turn:

- disadvantage employees
- harm the economy because share option schemes are needed to attract employees
- harm young, innovative companies that did not have cash available to offer equivalent alternative payment
- place companies in countries that required these expenses to be recognised at a competitive disadvantage.

These potential impacts of changes in accounting standards are known as 'economic consequences'.

Political pressure takes the form of individuals or groups trying to influence the standard setters (by a range of methods including lobbying standard setters directly, as noted, or by lobbying governments; see Georgiou[20] for further examples) to make sure that the resulting accounting standards best meet their own preferences and do not result in unfavourable economic consequences that would 'disadvantage' them.

Political interference

A conceptual framework provides some defence against 'individual interests' and claims of economic consequences. Standard setters can argue the theoretical correctness of their decisions by referring to the principles in the conceptual framework.

It is more difficult for individuals to argue for their own preferred way of accounting for events if this is inconsistent with the principles in the *Conceptual Framework*. As Damant states, 'Individual standards cannot be attacked unless the principles on which they are based are attacked'.[21]

A conceptual framework cannot guarantee freedom from political interference. In some cases, proposed accounting standards have been either changed or not introduced because of political pressures.[22] In addition, there is still debate as to whether economic consequences should be considered when deciding on accounting standards. Some argue that the cost constraint within the *Conceptual Framework* itself justifies taking into account the economic consequences when deciding on accounting requirements.[23]

Professional benefits

An alternative reason for having a conceptual framework is the benefit it may provide to the accounting profession itself. The argument here is that conceptual frameworks exist not to improve accounting practice, but to protect the professional status of accounting and accountants.

This argument is based on the following line of reasoning:

- Professional status is valuable. People and groups that are members of professions generally have more influence and status, and receive higher rewards (payments) than do those who are seen as non-professionals.

- A profession has a unique body of knowledge; it has expertise in an area that other groups do not have.
- The historical 'knowledge base' of accounting is double-entry bookkeeping. However, this, at least in a simple form, is practised widely in the general community. Other problems with accounting's knowledge base cited include the influence of political pressure, accounting failures (e.g. Enron and WorldCom), and inconsistencies in standards.
- Because of the problems with the historical knowledge base of accounting, a conceptual framework has been developed to establish a unique body of knowledge of accounting.[24]

Although the accounting profession may state that the reason for conceptual frameworks is to improve accounting (i.e. to achieve the technical benefits discussed), the true reason is to provide the appearance of having a unique body of knowledge so that it can maintain its status as a profession and so that its members can gain the benefits of professional status.

However, others have questioned this theory and argue that:
- The professional status of accountants has been developed and maintained through 'social' actions of accounting bodies, such as creating barriers to entry to the profession, and legislation restricting certain activities (such as some auditing and taxation functions) to those with specialised qualifications.[25]
- The theory does not explain why some countries in which accounting rules are regulated by the government (such as China) have, at least in some way, adopted parts of the conceptual framework.[26]

 ## PROBLEMS WITH AND CRITICISMS OF THE *CONCEPTUAL FRAMEWORK*

Although benefits are claimed for having a conceptual framework in accounting, there are also some problems with and criticisms of the current *Conceptual Framework*. The criticisms are either:
- caused by the nature of a conceptual framework as a set of general guiding principles. These criticisms would apply to many conceptual frameworks, not only the accounting conceptual framework.
- related to specific parts of the current *Conceptual Framework*.

This chapter considers three main criticisms or problems with the current *Conceptual Framework*:
- that it is ambiguous and open to interpretation
- that it is too descriptive
- that the meaning of faithful representation or reliability is problematic.

You should remember some of the key benefits of the *Conceptual Framework* were to improve the quality of accounting rules by providing guidance, in the form of general principles, to standard setters and individuals. This would also help ensure consistency. However, some features of the *Conceptual Framework* suggest that these benefits may not occur.

The *Conceptual Framework* can be ambiguous

The principles in the *Conceptual Framework* are intended to provide a 'common language'. However, the principles and definitions in the *Conceptual Framework* are broad and individuals may interpret them differently. Much of the debate about some recent issues in financial reporting relates to the exact meanings of the definitions in the *Conceptual Framework*. For example, some have argued that share options to employees did not meet the definition of an expense. Although the international standard setters interpreted these options as meeting its definition of an expense, it noted:

> However, given that some people have arrived at a different interpretation of the Framework's expense definition, this suggests that the Framework is not clear.[27]

A common criticism of conceptual frameworks in general is that the principles are often too vague, leaving too much room for alternative interpretations. Therefore, the ability to provide practical guidance, and in particular consistent application of the principles, is limited.

Balancing the desired attributes of information

The *Conceptual Framework* lists enhancing qualitative characteristics for information and also identifies the cost constraint that impacts on the ability to provide information. These qualities and constraint require those deciding on the information to be included in the financial reports to balance or weight these issues. The *Conceptual Framework* provides no clear guidance on how to make these decisions, so the decisions will be subjective. Further, materiality, which is an entity-specific aspect of relevance (one of the fundamental qualitative characteristics) requires professional judgement.

Adjusting for deficiencies in the guidance

A major criticism of the *Conceptual Framework* is that it does not provide guidance for all of the important aspects of and decisions relating to financial reports. In particular, that it provides no definite answers to the question of how to measure the items to be included in financial reports is seen as a barrier to achieving high-quality, consistent and comparable financial reports. Measurement is perhaps one of the most controversial areas in financial reporting. It can be argued that decisions relating to it can be guided by other principles in the *Conceptual Framework* (such as considering the faithful representation and relevance of alternative measures for particular items). However, this does not provide straightforward or clear guidance on what choices should be made for measuring particular financial statement items. The incompleteness of the *Conceptual Framework* in this regard is seen by many as a major weakness.

The *Conceptual Framework* is descriptive, not prescriptive

A further complaint is that the *Conceptual Framework* may be seen as simply reflecting and giving approval to *existing* accounting principles and practices. In other words, the *Conceptual Framework* simply describes accounting principles as currently practised and applied, rather than being prescriptive (normative) and trying to improve practice. This criticism is often based on two arguments. These are:

- The *Conceptual Framework* includes many of the concepts used in accounting practice historically. This argument, however, assumes that these concepts must be incorrect or defective. On the contrary, it could be argued that the *Conceptual Framework* includes 'old' assumptions and principles because these are the appropriate ones to use in preparing financial reports.
- People do not agree with the principles included in the *Conceptual Framework*. For example, some argue that stewardship or accountability is a more appropriate primary objective for financial reports than the objective of providing information useful for decision making.

The concept of faithful representation is inappropriate

A further criticism made of the *Conceptual Framework* relates to the use of faithful representation as this concept is considered to misunderstand the nature of accounting.[28]

Let's consider the meaning of faithful representation. To represent can be seen as meaning to 'portray' or 'describe'. Faithful can be seen as meaning 'true' or 'accurate'. When thinking of the accuracy, one thinks of how close one is to the correct answer. Consequently, many interpret the requirement for financial reports to represent faithfully the transactions and other events to mean that the aim is to provide as accurate a report or description of the financial position and performance of the entity as possible. This implies that there is a single correct financial position and performance measure for an entity. The financial reports that correspond most closely to this correct position or measure will be the most accurate and consequently the most faithful representation.

But is there one 'correct' financial position or performance measure in accounting? Take, for example, the final profit figure for an entity.

The following events and transactions have occurred in the financial year:
- The net profit before depreciation is $250 000.
- The company has the following noncurrent assets:
    - Building A cost $600 000 five years ago. It has a fair value of $1 000 000 and a further useful life of five years.
    - Building B cost $300 000 20 years ago. It has a fair value of $2 000 000 and a further useful life of ten years.

In one set of financial reports, the accountant uses the cost basis; in another, the fair value basis is used. Both are acceptable according to the *Conceptual Framework* and current accounting standards. The financial performance of the entity under each basis is shown in table 2.1.

TABLE 2.1 Reporting profit using cost basis and fair value basis		
	View 1 (at cost)	View 2 (at fair value)
Net profit before depreciation	250 000	250 000
Depreciation building A	60 000	200 000
Depreciation building B	10 000	100 000
Final net profit (loss)	180 000	(50 000)

Which profit figure is correct and represents the 'true' measure of the entity's performance? Both are correct in the sense that they follow generally accepted accounting principles and the alternatives allowed in accounting standards. But how can this be? One view shows the company making a profit; the other a loss.

The problem that many argue here is that the concept of faithful representation treats accounting as similar to a 'hard' science. In science, there is generally one correct objective measure. For example, scientists can measure the distance between the Earth and the moon at a particular point in time. There would only be one correct distance and the most accurate measure (the measure closest to the true distance) would be the one that represents this faithfully. This view of the world as having one single set of objective facts to be discovered is often referred to as the 'realist' perspective. Applying this view to accounting:

> Financial statements . . . are representationally faithful to the extent that they provide an objective picture of an entity's resources and obligations — a reality that exists in the physical world.[29]

An alternative perspective, known as the 'materialist' or 'social constructionist' view, argues that accounting cannot be viewed as a science whose aim is to discover objective facts that simply exist in the world. Although the underlying events and transactions do exist (such as the purchase of a particular asset or the sale of goods to a customer), the accounting measures that are reported (such as income or net assets) are created by accountants and do not exist independently of them. If this approach is accepted, then the concept of faithful representation does not really fit. The question to be decided when preparing the financial reports is not which view represents most faithfully the events and transactions (as this qualitative characteristic asks us to do) but how to *choose* among the possible views that could be used to represent them. This choice does not involve considerations of accuracy (which view is the most 'correct'), but would need to consider the question of which is the *preferred* view to be represented in the financial statements.

This criticism of the *Conceptual Framework* challenges the very nature of accounting. From these arguments, it should be obvious that the principles in any conceptual framework for accounting are not unchangeable or unchallengeable. Principles in accounting are not like the 'laws' in science or mathematics (such as the law of gravity, or $E = mc^2$). Principles, such as the definition of an asset, are decided on by debate and agreement. There will always be alternative views and those who disagree.

Summary

Explain what a conceptual framework is
- A conceptual framework is a set of guiding principles.
- It is a normative theory that sets out the basic principles to be followed in preparing financial statements.
- You should see that it has broad principles, whereas accounting standards relate to a narrow and specific area of financial reporting.

Understand the history, evolution of and current developments in the *Conceptual Framework for Financial Reporting*
- The conceptual framework examined is the *Conceptual Framework for Financial Reporting* issued by the IASB, which derives from conceptual frameworks developed in several countries over the past 30 years, and is currently being revised under a joint project by the IASB and the FASB.

Outline the structure, approach and components of the *Conceptual Framework*
- The *Conceptual Framework* comprises a series of concepts. These relate to the objectives of financial statements, underlying assumptions, qualitative characteristics, definitions and recognition criteria for the elements that make up the financial statements. When complete, it is expected that this will also include principles relating to measurement and presentation of the financial statements.

Explain and evaluate the purpose, objective and underlying assumption of the *Conceptual Framework*
- The *Conceptual Framework* is concerned with general purpose financial reports of a reporting entity.
- There are two views of the objectives of financial reports:
  - stewardship or accountability
  - decision usefulness, which is the objective reflected in the *Conceptual Framework*.
- The going concern assumption underlies financial reports.

Explain the qualitative characteristics of useful financial information in the *Conceptual Framework*
- There are two fundamental qualitative characteristics:
  - relevance
  - faithful representation.
- There are four enhancing qualitative characteristics:
  - comparability
  - verifiability

- timeliness
- understandability.
- The two fundamental qualitative characteristics must be present for financial information to be useful.

Explain the elements of financial statements in the *Conceptual Framework*
- The *Conceptual Framework* identifies and defines the elements of financial statements:
  - assets
  - liabilities
  - equity
  - income
  - expenses.
- The elements must meet the following recognition criteria before they can be recognised in the financial statements:
  - probability
  - reliable measurement.

Explain the benefits of conceptual frameworks
- There are three potential benefits of a conceptual framework in accounting. These are:
  - *technical:* to improve the quality of financial statements by providing guidance to standard setters and for users and preparers
  - *political:* to reduce political interference in the setting of accounting requirements
  - *professional:* to provide a claim of a body of knowledge to ensure the professional status of accountant is maintained.

Explain and evaluate the problems and criticisms of conceptual frameworks, including the *Conceptual Framework*
- Three criticisms of the *Conceptual Framework* are discussed. These are:
  - The *Conceptual Framework* does not work in practice because the principles are too unclear to provide adequate guidance, the guidance in applying the principles is inadequate and the *Conceptual Framework* is incomplete.
  - The *Conceptual Framework* describes current practice, so is mainly descriptive, not normative.
  - The concept of faithful representation as one of the fundamental qualitative characteristics misunderstands the nature of accounting.

Review questions

1. What is a conceptual framework?
2. What is the difference between a conceptual framework and accounting standards?
3. Outline the technical benefits of a conceptual framework. What problems could occur if accounting standards were set without a conceptual framework?
4. How can a conceptual framework help users and preparers understand accounting requirements and financial statements?
5. What is the objective of financial reports according to the *Conceptual Framework*?
6. How is the decision usefulness approach reflected in the *Conceptual Framework*?
7. The *Conceptual Framework* states that 'general purpose financial reports do not and cannot provide all of the information that existing and potential investors, lenders and other creditors need' (paragraph OB6). What information is not provided and why?
8. What is the underlying assumption to be applied in preparing financial reports according to the *Conceptual Framework*? How does this assumption affect the financial report items?

9. Identify the qualitative characteristics of financial information in the *Conceptual Framework*. How are these related to the objectives of general purpose financial reports?
10. Not all relevant and faithfully representative information will be included in financial reports due to the materiality aspect and cost constraint identified in the *Conceptual Framework*. Outline the materiality aspect and the cost constraint on the provision of information. Can you think of any problems in applying these?
11. What is the difference between recognition and disclosure in accounting? According to the *Conceptual Framework*, when should an item be recognised in the financial reports.
12. Why is accounting said to be 'political' in nature? How can a conceptual framework help in the setting of accounting standards in a political environment?
13. It is claimed by some that the reason for conceptual frameworks in accounting is to protect the accounting profession rather than improve accounting practice. Explain the basis for this claim.
14. Some people argue that the conceptual framework is acceptable in theory but in practice it does not work. Explain possible problems with and criticisms of the *Conceptual Framework*. Do you think these problems exist and criticisms are valid?
15. Explain why some people believe that the concept of faithful representation in the *Conceptual Framework* is incorrect.

Application questions

As a group, identify two or three general principles to help guide the making of more specific rules in relation to a particular area, context or task. For example:
- It may be that a group of students is planning on sharing accommodation (such as an apartment).
- You may be required to undertake a group assignment.
  Once you have agreed on the two or three principles, use these to form more specific rules in relation to the context or task. Then consider the following questions:
(a) How easy was it to agree on the basic principles?
(b) Are all the rules consistent with these principles?
(c) Have any members interpreted the principles differently?
(d) How useful were the principles in helping establish more specific rules?
(e) Were there any problems with using principles as a basis for setting the rules? **CT** **SM**

2.2
Look at the accounting standards. Then:
(a) Find examples of how parts of the *Conceptual Framework* (e.g. the definitions, recognition criteria, qualitative characteristics) have been included in them.
(b) Identify any inconsistencies between the requirements in accounting standards and the *Conceptual Framework*. Why do you think these occur? **K** **AS**

2.3
Find the comments letters received on a current exposure draft or proposal. (These can be found from the websites of most standard-setting organisations, such as IASB, AASB or FASB.) Read a sample of comments from a range of respondents (e.g. from accounting bodies, industry, company or corporate bodies) and answer the following questions:
(a) Is there agreement among the various groups?
(b) If there are any concerns or objections, are they based in conceptual issues, practical issues or potential economic consequences? Does this vary among groups?

(c) Have any of the comments letters referred to the *Conceptual Framework* as a basis to support their views?

(d) Do the comments letters suggest that there is support for the *Conceptual Framework*? **K** **AS** **SM**

The following information is provided for two items of property for a company.

Property A was purchased five years ago for $400 000. It was intended to be used to build another factory, but the company has now reorganised its original factory and it is no longer required. The company now intends to sell it. The current property market has dropped but is expected to rise when interest rates fall. If sold now, the property is expected to realise $360 000. Real estate experts have predicted that if the company waits for the property market to recover, it could realise $450 000.

Property B is the current factory. It was purchased ten years ago for $200 000. If sold now, it would be expected to realise $380 000 (and $500 000 if the property market recovers). The company has various estimates about its contribution to the profit of the company. Using current interest rates and various assumptions about future sales and costs, the property is calculated to have a present value (in terms of future cash flows) of $900 000. It is insured for $600 000 because this is the cost required to rebuild it.

The company has always recorded property using the historic cost basis. Other companies in the same industry have traditionally used the same basis, although about 40% now use the fair value basis.

(a) For each of the properties, identify which cost or value would best meet each of the following qualitative characteristics (consider each separately) of:
- faithful representation
- relevance
- verifiability
- comparability
- understandability.

(b) For each of the properties, choose which cost or value should be stated in the financial statements. Explain why you have chosen it and how you balanced the qualitative characteristics.

(c) Do you think everyone would agree with your choices? **J** **K**

Application of definitions and recognition criteria in the *Conceptual Framework*

The following questions (2.5–2.7) require you to apply the definitions and recognition criteria in the *Conceptual Framework* to specific cases. After you have answered these questions, compare your answers with those of other students. Do your answers differ? How did using the *Conceptual Framework* help you to make your decision?

A company has a copper mine in South Africa. It purchased the mining rights ten years ago for $20 million and has been operating the mine for the past ten years. It is estimated that there are about 8 million tonnes of copper in the mine. Because of a fall in world copper prices, the company has closed the mine indefinitely. At current world copper prices, the mine is uneconomic because the costs involved in extracting the copper are greater than the selling price. If copper prices rise by more than 25 per cent, the company has stated that the mine would be reopened.

(a) Applying the principles in the *Conceptual Framework*, explain whether this mine would:
- meet the definition of an asset
- pass the recognition criteria. **J** **K** **AS**

2.6 The company is currently growing and it is expected that in five years an additional factory will need to be built to meet product demand at a cost of $500 000. The directors wish to recognise an expense of $100 000 and a liability (provision for future expansion) for each of the next five years.

(a) Applying the principles in the *Conceptual Framework*, explain whether:
- the definition of a liability or expense is met.
- the recognition criteria for a liability or expense are met. **J K AS**

2.7 The company has recently issued some preference shares. The terms of these shares are:
- A fixed dividend of 3 per cent is payable each year. If no profit is available to pay dividends in one year, these will be back-paid in future years.
- The preference shares will be redeemed (bought back) by the company in three years at their issue price.

(a) Applying the principles in the *Conceptual Framework*, explain whether these preference shares should be considered as equity or a liability. **J K AS**

2.1 CASE STUDY

Code of Ethics — IFAC issues revised code for professional accountants

By Richard George

IFAC's recently released Revised Code of Ethics applies to all professional accountants — whether you work in practice, in industry, in academe, or in government. It is effective from June 30, 2006.

This article is about ethical matters and the activities of the IFAC Ethics Committee. Besides ethics, IFAC Boards and Committees develop international standards on auditing and assurance (ISAs), on education and on public sector accounting. Each of the member bodies of IFAC — there are 163 currently from all parts of the globe — undertakes to use its best endeavours, subject to national laws and regulations, to implement the standards issued by IFAC in each of these fields.

Fundamental principles

The fundamental principles are:
- Integrity
  An accountant should be straightforward and honest in all professional and business relationships. For example, accountants should not be associated with information which they believe contains a false or misleading statement.
- Objectivity
  An accountant should not allow bias, conflict of interest or undue influence of others to override professional or business judgements.
- Professional Competence and Due Care
  An accountant has to maintain professional knowledge and skill at the level required to ensure that a client or employer receives competent professional service. This requires accountants to act diligently and in accordance with current technical, professional and legislative requirements when engaged in professional activities.
- Confidentiality
  An accountant should respect the confidentiality of information acquired as a result of professional and business relationships and should not disclose any such information without proper and specific authority unless there is a legal or professional right or duty to disclose.
- Professional Behaviour
  An accountant should comply with relevant laws and regulations and should avoid any action that discredits the profession.

Where accountants consider that any proposed professional activity might compromise compliance with these fundamental principles they are required to put safeguards in place to mitigate the threat or, where they cannot do so, to desist from the proposed activity.

Threats

The threats identified in the Code are:

- Self Interest Threat

  May occur as a result of a financial or other interest held by the accountant or a family member.
- Self Review Threat

  May occur when a previous judgement needs to be re-evaluated — you cannot audit your own work.
- Advocacy Threat

  May occur when an accountant promotes a position or opinion to the point where subsequent objectivity may be compromised.
- Familiarity Threat

  May occur when, because of a close relationship, the accountant becomes too sympathetic to the interests of others.
- Intimidation Threat

  May occur when an accountant may be deterred from acting objectively by threats — actual or perceived.

The Code contains many examples of situations that may be faced by accountants and of possible safeguards that could mitigate the threats. In some cases, the code makes clear that no safeguard could adequately address the perceived or actual threat to the fundamental principles — for example, the threat to objectivity (or independence) if an auditor held shares in his audit client — and, in such cases, the only option is to walk away, to resign or to refuse the assignment. However, the Code clearly states that the examples are not all inclusive and that the obligation is on the accountant to identify and assess any threats that might arise in the particular circumstances faced — and then to address them appropriately in accordance with the framework approach set out in the Code.

Conceptual framework advantages

The advantages of this conceptual framework approach are that:

- the principles-based standards set out in the Code are robust and can be applied to the diverse and varying circumstances faced by professional accountants;
- it avoids technical evasion of detailed rules;
- it is appropriate for global application; and
- it continues to be applicable in a rapidly changing environment.

Source: Extracted from Richard George, 'Code of ethics: IFAC issues revised code for professional accountants', *Accountancy Ireland.*[30]

Questions

1. Can you identify any potential problems or criticisms of the principles outlined in the conceptual framework in the case? **J** **K**
2. Do you think using these principles would be interpreted and applied consistently between individual accountants in determining whether an action is ethical? **J**
3. How effective do you think such a framework is in (a) ensuring accountants act ethically and (b) enforcing or penalising unethical behaviour? **J** **K**
4. Would a set of specific rules about what constitutes ethical and unethical behaviours in specific circumstances be more or less useful than the principles in the code of conduct outlined? **J**

What's new in water and carbon accounting

By Keryn Chalmers, Jayne Godfrey FCA and Brad Potter

'Water, energy and climate change are inextricably linked. If we truly want to find sustainable solutions, we must ensure that we address all three in a holistic way. They are pieces of the same puzzle and therefore it is not practical to look at them in isolation.'

This was the key message in the World Business Council for Sustainable Development's report *Water, Energy and Climate Change*. Carbon and water information reporting and assurance are gathering momentum in efforts to achieve a common objective — to provide information relevant for decision-making. While the carbon and water reporting and assurance characteristics share similarities, their institutional arrangements differ. Carbon reporting and assurance are being addressed internationally by the International Accounting Standards Board (IASB) and the International Auditing and Assurance Standards Board (IAASB), while responsibility for developing water reporting and assurance standards resides with the national Water Accounting Standards Board (WASB), an advisory board to the Australian Bureau of Meteorology (BOM). Water accounting and assurance is being developed in several countries, with no single body taking responsibility for international standards, although the United Nations is coordinating the reporting of statistics regarding water. These statistical reports differ from the water accounting reports envisaged by the WASB, which are analogous to the three main financial reporting statements and include:

- a statement of physical water flows
- a statement showing holdings of water and water rights and obligations to deliver water
- a statement of changes in water balances and water rights and obligations. This article reviews the respective institutional arrangements, focusing particularly on water accounting.

Progress on carbon

Various bodies internationally are becoming involved in advocating approaches for carbon reporting. For example, the Carbon Standards Disclosure Board, a consortium of business and environmental organisations, released an exposure draft on a proposed reporting framework in May 2009 (refer to cdsb-global.org/). Carbon reporting is also a joint project of the IASB and the Financial Accounting Standards Board (FASB). The IASB/FASB project scope is restricted to emissions trading schemes. Issues to be addressed include:

- whether emissions allowances should be recognised as assets and whether this depends on their genealogy
- if they are assets how they should be measured initially, particularly if they are granted free of charge
- how allowances recognised as assets should be measured subsequent to acquisition
- when and how obligations related to emissions trading schemes should be measured (refer the IASB project page on emissions at iasb.org).

Like any international accounting standard, the global consultative process associated with the issue of an international carbon accounting standard comprises multiple stages. At present, the project is in the planning phase. The IASB agreed to commence the project at its December 2007 meeting and decided its scope in May 2008. Prior to publishing a carbon reporting standard, the IASB may prepare a discussion paper and will need to publish an exposure draft inviting public comments. While the IASB reached some tentative decisions in March 2009 relating to emissions allowances received as government grants, the estimated project completion date has not been determined.

Parallel to the project on an international carbon reporting standard, the IAASB is developing an international assurance standard covering carbon emissions disclosure. Approved as a project proposal in December 2007, a taskforce has been established, roundtable discussions have occurred around the globe and an issues paper was discussed at the IAASB December 2008 meeting. At the time of writing, a draft International Standard on

Assurance Engagements (ISAE) is expected to be tabled for approval at the September 2009 meeting (refer to the project history on ifac.org/IAASB). This will be exposed for public comment prior to ISAE finalisation.

Progress on water

The vision for water accounting in Australia is embodied in the National Water Accounting Development Project, a federally funded project with in-kind support of the state governments and territories. The aim of the project is to improve public knowledge and understanding of Australia's water resources. Standardised water accounting is critical to these aims as it will provide consistent and comparable information to assist water-related policy development, water resource planning and monitoring and water management. The three pillars of water accounting, central to national capacity building are:

- water accounting standards that establish the principles and rules for reporting about water and claims and other rights to water
- reporting obligations and compliance enforcement governing who needs to prepare water accounting reports and when
- independent assurance of the reported information.

While existing international institutional structures are being used to develop carbon reporting and assurance standards, national institutional arrangements have been established for advancing water accounting and achieving the project's outcomes... The key players in this structure are the Australian Parliament, the BOM and the WASB, formerly the Water Accounting Development Committee (WADC). The Government has delegated responsibility for the National Water Accounting Development Project to the BOM. The BOM's responsibilities include reporting on water data and issuing Australian Water Accounting Standards (AWAS). The WASB is an independent advisory board to BOM. Its membership comprises five independent members with accounting standard-setting or water management expertise. Supported by the Water Accounting Development Committee Office (WADCO) and with input on an as-required basis from constituted technical committees and panels, the WASB is responsible for overseeing and coordinating the development of AWAS and recommends their adoption to BOM. While interested in developments in water accounting, the preference of the Australian Accounting Standards Board (AASB) and the Auditing and Assurance Standards Board (AuASB) has been to maintain a watching brief rather than an active role in water accounting standard-setting, unless and until water accounting standards require the preparation of financially denominated water accounts. The WASB currently focuses on volumetric reports and has advised the AASB and the AuASB that it would wish to work with them in order to produce high quality assured water accounts, where appropriate, and will aim to avoid duplication of effort and conflicts of roles. For example, for the all-important auditing and assurance of water accounts, the WASB will refer to relevant existing AuASB standards where appropriate, rather than develop its own standards.

BOM and WASB engage in a consultative standard-setting due process (see bom.gov.au/water/wasb/water-accounting-standard.php), involving state departments and agencies and stakeholder organisations, groups and individuals. Consistent with arrangements for financial accounting standards, the WASB intends that ultimate approval of Australian water accounting standards will reside with the Australian Parliament.

The WASB has endorsed a conceptual framework for water accounting and AWAS development will be guided by these concepts. AWAS will prescribe the basis for the preparation and presentation of general purpose water accounting reports. Their present scope includes the reporting of water volumes and quality. It is intended that the reports will be audited and assured with any specific water-related audit and assurance standards developed in conjunction with the AuASB. Will they be mandatory for water reporting entities? Water accounting is currently voluntary for organisations except those required under the *Water Act 2007* to provide water accounting information to the BOM. The WASB has expressed a preference for the *Water Act 2007* to mandate water reporting obligations and describe the principles governing which entities have legally enforceable reporting obligations. The BOM would be the repository for water accounting reports publicly available through BOM's Australian Water Resources Information System (AWRIS).

Similar trajectories

Carbon and water reporting and assurance are on similar trajectories. The IASB and IAASB are close to issuing exposure drafts. Similarly, the WASB has completed the first Preliminary Australian Water Accounting Standard (refer to bom.gov.au/water/wasb/pawas-download.php). It will be used to prepare the Pilot National Water Account issued by the BOM at the end of 2009 with the intent that the National Water Account post-2009 will be prepared using AWAS. Given public interest in water management, voluntary preparation of general purpose water accounting reports will probably increase rapidly over the next decade. In turn, the global and national water and carbon reporting and assurance developments should deliver important parts of the information puzzle that will assist in delivering sustainable solutions to address climate change.

Source: Article by Keryn Chalmers, Jayne Godfrey & Brad Potter, 'What's new in water and carbon accounting', *Charter*.[31]

Questions
1. In the preface to the water accounting conceptual framework a wide range of users are identified including groups and associations with water related interests, water industry consultants, academics and interested citizens. This is much broader than the primary users that are the focus on the accounting conceptual framework. In the context of water reporting, is such a wide user group appropriate and what possible problems could this result in? **J** **K**
2. Do you think the same qualitative characteristics would be equally important and appropriate to water accounting and reporting? **J**
3. What are the possible advantages and disadvantages of using the *Conceptual Framework for Financial Reporting* as a basis or starting point for conceptual frameworks for reporting in other contexts? **J** **K**

2.3 CASE STUDY

Companies brace for powerful impact of lease accounting changes

By Beth Mattson-Teig

Proposed new accounting standards have been drafted in order to push lease liabilities back onto corporate balance sheets. Such a change would represent a major shift for companies that have typically favoured the off-balance-sheet treatment of operating leases, and it could have a significant impact on corporate decisions to lease or purchase real estate in the future.

The proposed guidelines are a joint initiative by the Financial Accounting Standards Board (FASB) and the International Accounting Standards Board to create a uniform global standard and greater corporate transparency in lease accounting procedures. The most recent draft issued Aug. 17 would establish one method of accounting that requires firms to recognize all lease liabilities and assets on their corporate financial statements.

Another key component is that companies would be required to record the lease value or rent commitment over the entire lease term, including renewal options. Although the intent is to stop off-balance-sheet activity, the changes would add significant weight to corporate balance sheets.

For example, a firm that pays $1 million per year in rent for its corporate headquarters would quickly see its liability multiply depending on whether it has a five-year or 15-year lease. Companies would appear more highly leveraged, which could affect factors such as corporate credit and existing debt covenants.

What makes commercial real estate industry professionals nervous is that it is not clear to what extent the new accounting guidelines would influence tenants' decision-making process. Based on the universe of leased space, the potential impact is enormous.

Although FASB cites data that values leasing activity at $640 billion in 2008, other industry sources estimate that current volume as high as $1.3 trillion in operating leases for U.S. firms alone. Once the guidelines go into effect, which many in the industry believe will occur in 2013, both new and existing leases would be immediately affected.

One fear is that the new accounting practices could deter companies from signing long-term leases, or encourage firms to own rather than lease facilities. Both of those factors could be a detriment to the sale-leaseback and net-lease finance niche where leases typically extend 15 years and beyond.

Source: Extracts from Beth Mattson-Tieg, 'Companies brace for powerful impact of lease accounting changes', *Retail Traffic*. Copyrighted 2011. Penton Media, Inc. 82657:1111SH.[32]

The Joint Accounting Bodies welcome the efforts of the Boards to develop simplified requirements to short-term leases and we believe it appropriate that the lessor can elect not to recognise assets or liabilities arising from a short-term lease. Our response to Question 1 noted our concern with the cost to lessees of complying with the proposals and we do not thing the relief from discounting a real solution, as typically, discounting is not applied to periods of 12 months or less. Further, in practice a short-term lease agreement as defined has more in common with a contract for the provision of a service, as typically the asset is handed back in good condition and rented out again (for example short term car hire and accommodation). We believe that the cost of accounting for a short-term lease even with the proposed concessions is still significant as lessees will be required to implement and maintain information systems that in addition to their application to new leases, capture all open leases on transition and that have an appropriate level of sophistication to enable the estimations and reassessments as proposed.

Accordingly, for reasons of cost/benefit, a better approach would be for the [proposed] Standard to allow the lessee to elect to expense the lease payments and not recognise a right-of-use asset and a corresponding liability to make lease payments (a relief that is similar to that available to lessors). We believe it would be sufficient if the [proposed] Standards were to require the disclosure of information about short-term leases that describes the nature of the underlying asset, the value of lease payments and the length of the lease. We believe it most unlikely that short-term leases would give rise to material assets and liabilities. Nevertheless, if this were so then we suggest that the lessee would conclude that it was inappropriate to make use of the election.

This concession should only be available on leases for less than 12 months with no option to renew; otherwise structuring opportunities may arise.

Source: Extracts from The Joint Accounting Bodies letter, 'Comments on ED/2010/9 Leases'.[33]

Questions

1. The first extract above identifies a number of possible economic consequences if the proposed new lease standard is introduced. Outline the economic consequences identified and discuss whether you believe that the cost constraint in the *Conceptual Framework* would or should require consideration of these. **J** **K** **AS**

2. The second extract discusses the costs to preparers.
   (a) Discuss whether you believe the costs to preparers are valid and whether these should override the benefits?
   (b) The extract proposes that a simpler method be applied to leases for less than 12 months. Discuss any disadvantages of this approach and whether it could be justified using principles in the *Conceptual Framework*? **J** **K**

3. The proposed new leasing standard requires that contingent rental payments (e.g. where a lessee pays additional rent payments if revenue exceeds a certain

amount) be included in the lessee's liabilities using the expected outcome approach that is described in the ED as 'the present value of the probability-weighted average of the cash flows for reasonable number of outcomes' (paragraph 14). The current leasing standard does not have such a requirement and contingent rentals are simply expensed as paid.

(a) Which of these approaches do you believe is more consistent with the definition and recognition criteria for liabilities in the *Conceptual Framework*?

(b) In undertaking the above analysis, identify any problems or alternative interpretations that you had in applying the principles in the *Conceptual Framework*. **J** **K** **AS**

Additional readings and websites

André, P, Cazavan-Jeny, A, Dick, W, Richard, C and Walton, P 2009, 'Fair Value Accounting and the Banking Crisis in 2008: Shooting the Messenger', *Accounting in Europe*, vol. 6, no. 1, pp. 3–24.

Benston, G J, Carmichael, DR, Demski, JS, Dharan, BG, Jamal, K, Laux, R, Rajgopal, S & Vrana, G 2007, 'The FASB's Conceptual Framework for Financial Reporting: A Critical Analysis', *Accounting Horizons*, vol. 21, no. 2, pp. 229–38.

Christensen, J 2010, 'Conceptual frameworks of accounting from an information perspective', *Accounting and Business Research*, vol. 40, no. 3, pp. 287–99.

Hines, RD 1989a, 'The sociopolitical paradigm in financial accounting research', *Accounting, Auditing and Accountability Journal*, vol. 2, no. 1, pp. 52–62.

Hines, RD 1989b, 'Financial accounting knowledge, conceptual framework projects and the social construction of the accounting profession', *Accounting, Auditing and Accountability Journal*, vol. 2, no. 2, pp. 72–92.

Joint Project of the IASB and FASB: www.fasb.org or www.iasb.org.

Lennard, A 2007, 'Stewardship and the Objectives of Financial Statements: A Comment on IASB's Preliminary Views on an Improved Conceptual Framework for Financial Reporting: The Objective of Financial Reporting and Qualitative Characteristics of Decision-Useful Financial Reporting Information', *Accounting in Europe*, vol. 4, no. 1, pp. 51–66.

Leo, KJ & Hoggett, JR 1998, 'Standard-setting reform: neutrality, economic consequences and politics', *Accounting Forum*, vol. 22, no. 3, pp. 330–51.

McCartney, S 2004, 'The use of usefulness: An examination of the user needs approach to the financial reporting conceptual framework', *Journal of Applied Accounting Research*, vol. 7, iss. 2, pp. 52–79.

Peasnell, K, Dean, G & Gebhardt, G 2009, 'Reflections on the revision of the IASB Framework', *Abacus*, vol. 45, iss. 4, pp. 518–27.

Updates and progress on the Conceptual Framework for the Public Sector can be found at: www.ifac.org.

Whittington, G 2008, 'Fair Value and the IASB/FASB Conceptual Framework', *Abacus*, vol. 44, iss. 2, pp. 139–68.

End notes

1. International Accounting Standards Board (IASB) 2010, *Conceptual Framework for Financial Reporting*, p. 4.
2. Ministry of Finance (MOF) 2006, *Accounting standard for business enterprises: basic standard*, 15 February, MOF, China.
3. Rutherford, BA 2003, 'The social construction of financial statement elements under Private Finance Initiative schemes', *Accounting, Auditing & Accountability Journal*, vol. 16, no. 3, pp. 372–96.
4. Sutton, T 2003, *Corporate financial accounting and reporting*, 2nd edn, Prentice Hall, London.
5. International Accounting Standards Board (IASB) 2010, *ED/2010/2 Conceptual Framework for Financial Reporting; The Reporting Entity*, March, p. 8.
6. Lennard, A 2007, 'Stewardship and the Objectives of Financial Statements: A Comment on IASB's Preliminary Views on an Improved Conceptual Framework for Financial Reporting: The Objective of Financial Reporting and Qualitative Characteristics of Decision-Useful Financial Reporting Information', *Accounting in Europe*, vol. 4, no. 1, pp. 51–66.
7. International Accounting Standards Board (IASB) 2010, *Conceptual Framework for Financial Reporting*, pp. 9–10.
8. ibid.
9. Laughlin, R 2008, 'A Conceptual Framework for Accounting for Public-Benefit Entities', *Public Money & Management*, vol 28, no. 4, pp. 247–54.
10. Lennard, A 2007, 'Stewardship and the Objectives of Financial Statements: A Comment on IASB's Preliminary Views on an Improved Conceptual Framework for Financial Reporting: The Objective of Financial Reporting and Qualitative Characteristics of Decision-Useful Financial Reporting Information', *Accounting in Europe*, vol. 4, no. 1, pp. 51–66.
11. International Federation of Accountants (IFAC) 2010, *Exposure Draft (CF–ED1), Conceptual Framework for General Purpose Financial Reporting by Public Sector Entities:* • *Role, Authority and Scope;* • *Objectives and Users;* • *Qualitative Characteristics; and* • *Reporting Entity*.
12. Street, DL & Shaughnessy, KA 1998, 'The quest for international accounting harmonization: a review of the standard setting agendas of the IASC, US, UK, Canada and Australia, 1973–1997', *The International Journal of Accounting*, vol. 33, no. 2, pp. 179–209.
13. Kranacher, M 2006, 'The GAAP between Public and Private Companies', *The CPA Journal*, 1 June, Copyright with permission from the New York State Society of Certified Public Accountants.
14. Poole, V 2010, 'No pain, no gain', *Accountancy Age*, 9 September, p. 10.
15. Rutherford, BA 2003, 'The social construction of financial statement elements under Private Finance Initiative schemes', *Accounting, Auditing & Accountability Journal*, vol. 16, no. 3, pp. 372–96.
16. International Accounting Standards Board (IASB) 2010, *Conceptual Framework for Financial Reporting*, p. 6.
17. Xiao, Z & Pan, A 1997, 'Developing accounting standards on the basis of a conceptual framework by the Chinese government', *The International Journal of Accounting*, vol. 32, no. 3, pp. 279–99.
18. Foster, JM & Johnson, LT 2001, *Understanding the issues: why does the FASB have a conceptual framework?*, FASB.
19. Baker, CR & Hayes, RS 1995, 'The negative effect of an accounting standard on employee welfare: the case of McDonnell Douglas Corporation and FASB 106', *Accounting, Auditing & Accountability Journal*, vol. 8, no. 3, pp. 12–33.
20. Georgiou, G 2004, 'Corporate lobbying on accounting standards: methods, timing and perceived effectiveness', *Abacus*, vol. 40, no. 2, pp. 219–37.
21. Damant, D 2003, 'Accounting standards — a new era', *Balance Sheet*, vol. 11, no. 1, pp. 9–20.
22. Zeff, SA 2002, '"Political" lobbying on proposed standards: a challenge to the IASB', *Accounting Horizons*, vol. 16, no. 1, pp. 43–54.
23. Leo, KJ & Hoggett, JR 1998, 'Standard-setting reform: neutrality, economic consequences and politics', *Accounting Forum*, vol. 22, no. 3, pp. 330–51.
24. Hines, RD 1989b, 'Financial accounting knowledge, conceptual framework projects and the social construction of the accounting profession', *Accounting, Auditing and Accountability Journal*, vol. 2, no. 2, pp. 72–92.
25. Staubus, GJ 2004, 'On Brian P. West's professionalism and accounting rules', *Abacus*, vol. 40, no. 2, pp. 139–56.
26. Xiao, Z & Pan, A 1997, 'Developing accounting standards on the basis of a conceptual framework by the Chinese government', *The International Journal of Accounting*, vol. 32, no. 3, p. 285.
27. IASCF 2002, Accounting for Share-Based Payments, Project Update, IASCF.
28. Hines, RD 1989a, 'The sociopolitical paradigm in financial accounting research', *Accounting, Auditing and Accountability Journal*, vol. 2, no. 1, pp. 52–62.
29. Monson, DW 2001, 'The conceptual framework and accounting for leases', *Accounting Horizons*, vol. 15. no. 3, pp. 275–87.
30. George, R 2005, 'Code of ethics: IFAC issues revised code for professional accountants', *Accountancy Ireland*, www.accountancyireland.ie.
31. Chalmers, K, Godfrey, J & Potter, B 2009, 'What's new in water and carbon accounting', *Charter*, vol. 80, iss. 8, pp. 20–2.
32. Mattson-Tieg, B 2010, 'Companies Brace for Powerful Impact of Lease Accounting Changes', *Retail Traffic*, Altanta, 9 September. Copyrighted 2011. Penton Media, Inc. 82657:1111SH.
33. The Joint Accounting Bodies 2010, 'Comments on ED/2010/9 Leases', letter, 19 November, www.charteredaccountants.com.au.

3 Standard setting

LEARNING OBJECTIVES

After studying this chapter, you should be able to:

1. understand the institutional framework of Australian accounting standard setting

2. explain and define an accounting standard

3. evaluate the distinction between rules-based and principles-based standards

4. apply the concept of regulation to the production of accounting information

5. analyse standard setting as a political process

6. understand the benefits of harmonisation of accounting standards.

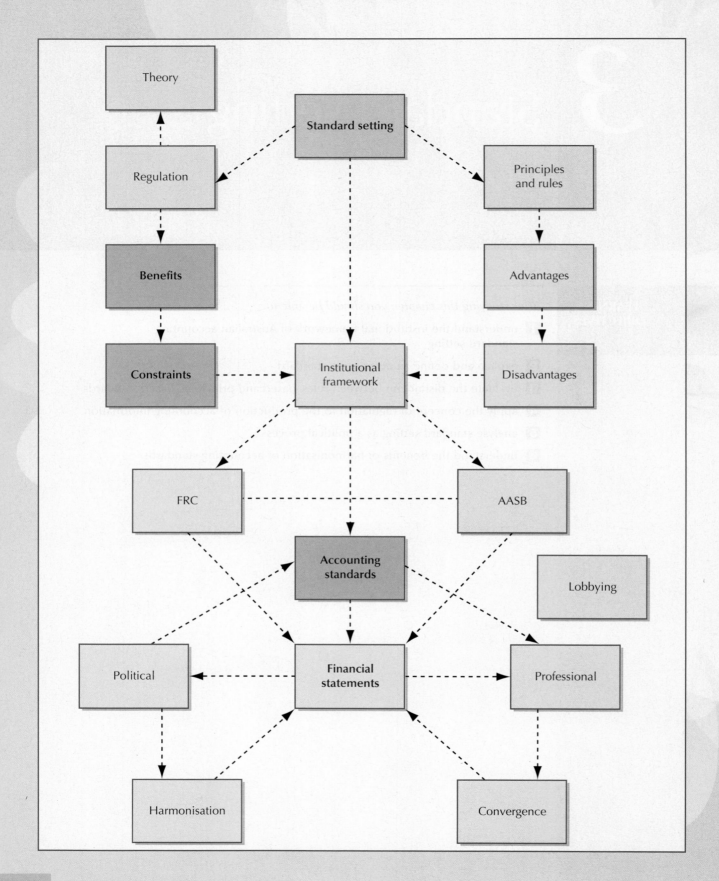

C hapter 2 shows that conceptual frameworks are broad principles used to guide accounting standard setters by providing a base for considering the merits of alternative accounting methods. In contrast, accounting standards provide specific requirements that must be complied with. The international standard setter has no authority to impose accounting standards, as that is left to the authorities in the jurisdictions endorsing the standards.

However, some aspects of conceptual frameworks are also pertinent to standards, particularly the question of whether they should be rules or principles based, as well as the potential influence of political pressures on the standard-setting process. This chapter considers these points and examines the most significant standard-setting development in Australia in recent times: the harmonisation of Australian accounting standards with those issued by the International Accounting Standards Board (IASB).

Before examining the issues, however, the chapter considers the context in which the Australian accounting standards are set and the institutional framework that underlies the Australian regulator.

LO 1 INSTITUTIONAL FRAMEWORK

The Australian Accounting Standards Board (AASB) was established under the *Australian Securities and Investments Commission Act 1991* (ASIC Act), and was designed to improve the quality and independence of the accounting standard-setting process in Australia. Previously, accounting standards were developed and administered by the accounting profession through various professional bodies, particularly the Institute of Chartered Accountants in Australia and CPA Australia.

The AASB is designed as a neutral, independent body, with full legislative backing to enforce the standards it publishes. It is overseen by the Financial Reporting Council (FRC) and is aided in its work by several advisory groups, including interpretations advisory panels and user groups. The structure of this institutional framework is shown in figure 3.1.

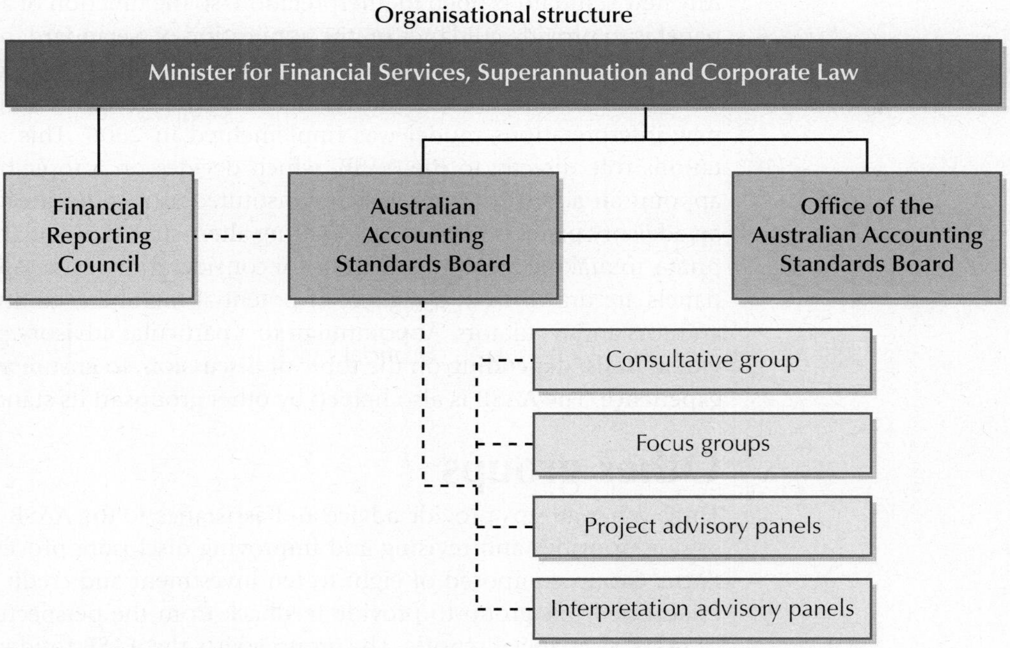

Organisational structure

FIGURE 3.1 Australian accounting standard setting: Organisational structure

Source: Australian Accounting Standards Board, www.aasb.com.au.

Each component of this structure is discussed in further detail in the following sections.

The FRC

The FRC is a statutory body operating within a framework set out in the ASIC Act. It is responsible for broad oversight of the standard-setting process, providing strategic direction and advice to the AASB. The FRC appoints the board members of the AASB.

The AASB

The functions of the AASB are to make accounting standards under the *Corporations Act 2001*, to formulate accounting standards for other purposes, including not-for-profit entities, and to participate in and contribute to the development of a single set of worldwide accounting standards. The AASB accomplishes this by promoting international standards; commenting during the due process period of a proposed standard; providing research input into the early stages of IASB projects; and meeting with individual IASB board members and senior staff as a member of the 'world standard setters' group[1], and regional groupings such as the Asian-Oceanian Standard-Setters Group (AOSSG).

Since 2002, the AASB has been pivotal in mediating the transition from Australian accounting standards to the adoption of IASB accounting standards (known as International Financial Reporting Standards, or IFRSs). This involved the alignment of Australian standards with IFRSs as they were produced by the IASB, as well as adjusting for any unique Australian regulatory conditions. The entire suite of IASB standards came into effect in Australia on 1 January 2005.

Interpretation advisory panel

Any new standard is open to interpretation, so the function of an Interpretation advisory panel is to provide guidance on the application of a standard, particularly as IFRSs apply in Australia to the private sector, the public sector and not-for-profit entities, although IASB standards are focused on business entities. After the implementation of IFRSs, a new interpretations model was implemented in 2006. This model gave the interpretations role directly to the AASB, which decides on a topic-by-topic basis whether to appoint an advisory panel. When constituted as a committee of the AASB, the role of an advisory panel is limited to preparing alternative views of an issue and, where appropriate, to making recommendations for consideration by the AASB. Members of advisory panels are drawn from a register of potential members, composed of preparers, users, auditors and regulators. Appointment to a particular advisory panel is made on an individual basis, depending on the topic of discussion, to ensure a balance of expertise and experience. The AASB is also helped by other groups in its standard-setting role.

Other groups

Three other groups provide advice and assistance to the AASB in formulating standard-setting priorities and revising and improving disclosure processes. The first is the User Focus Group composed of eight to ten investment and credit professionals. The AASB established this group to provide feedback from the perspective of a significant group of users of financial reports. The group assists the AASB to identify issues and priorities of interest to the investment community and to provide input, from a user perspective, during the development phase of projects.

The second group, the Not-for-Profit (Private Sector) Focus Group is also composed of eight to ten professionals drawn from charitable and related organisations. Its purpose is to assist the AASB in reporting issues affecting preparers, donors, credit grantors and community agencies by providing input during the development phase of a project.

Where appropriate, project advisory panels are formed when relevant experts are invited to join an advisory panel to provide advice that will assist the AASB in specific standard-setting projects.

LO 2 ACCOUNTING STANDARDS

The process of standard setting is designed to produce *quality financial reporting*. To ensure that financial statements are of a high quality, accounting standard-setting boards produce 'standards'. The most appropriate definition of a standard from the Macquarie dictionary is: 'anything taken by general consent as a basis of comparison'. It was in this sense that guides to selecting accounting treatments were referred to as Generally Accepted Accounting Principles, or GAAP. When those principles receive authoritative backing from a body such as the Australian federal government, they are referred to as accounting standards. Their purpose is to provide guidance to preparers of financial statements so that the information contained in those statements assists users to make useful decisions about the allocation of their resources.

The standard-setting process

Australia's first accounting standards were issued in 1946. They were not mandatory. Since then, accounting standard-setting boards such as the AASB and the IASB have been established to issue standards guiding the preparation of financial statements. A simplified view of the standard-setting process is provided in figure 3.2 (overleaf).

A standard's origin lies in the identification of a technical issue by the IASB, the IFRS Interpretations Committee or the International Public Sector Accounting Standards Board (IPSASB). The issue is added to the AASB's agenda by developing a project proposal which assesses the potential benefits of undertaking the project, the costs of not undertaking it, the resources available and likely timing. Research into the issue including relevant materials from other standard setters is the next phase. Once this phase is completed, a document such as an exposure draft (ED), an invitation to comment (ITC) or a discussion paper (DP) is made available for public comment. The outcome may be a pronouncement such as a standard, an interpretation, or a conceptual framework document.

Australia's approach has been to adopt the content and wording of IASB standards (IFRSs). Words are changed only when there is a need to take account of the Australian legislative environment; for example, there is a need to include references to Australia's *Corporations Act 2001*. Additionally, in its quest to provide high-quality financial reporting, the AASB may require additional disclosures in adopted IFRSs or may limit the number of optional treatments and disclosure requirements. These changes do not affect the ability of an Australian reporting entity to comply with international standards.

International accounting standards focus on for-profit entities. The AASB has responsibility for setting standards for all reporting entities, including the government and not-for-profit sectors. The AASB must therefore include additional text in international standards to deal with situations applicable to not-for-profit entities and governmental entities. The AASB also writes separate standards for these entities if there are important issues peculiar to that sector that are best dealt with in separate standards.

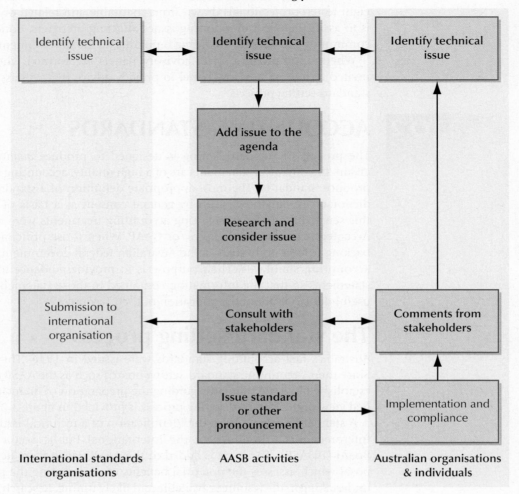

FIGURE 3.2 The AASB standard-setting process

Source: Australian Accounting Standards Board, www.aasb.com.au.

Recently, the surprise collapse of many prominent corporations has prompted questions about the quality and enforceability of standards. Developments in the United States, Australia and Europe, after the high-profile collapses of Enron, WorldCom, Parmalat, HIH and others, have resulted in a questioning of the very basis on which standards are developed: rules-based or principles-based platforms.

LO 3 RULES-BASED VERSUS PRINCIPLES-BASED STANDARDS

Rules-based standards are filled with specific details to meet as many potential contingencies as possible. Supposedly, rules-based standards are a result of preparers demanding them.[2]

Principles-based standards are based on a conceptual framework that provides a broad basis for accountants to follow instead of a list of rules.[3] Principles-based standards focus on the economic substance of a transaction, engaging the professional judgement and expertise of those preparing financial statements.

Rules are sometimes unavoidable. The intent of principles-based standards is not to provide specific guidance for every possible situation but is directed to the principles of the conceptual framework.

The IASB follows a principles-based approach to standard setting. In the United States, the Financial Accounting Standards Board (FASB) and the Securities and Exchange Commission (SEC) are agonising over the benefits and disadvantages of both rules-based and principles-based standards.

The differences between rules-based and principles-based standards can be illustrated as follows. A rules-based standard for depreciation might say:

> Annual depreciation expense for all depreciable assets is to be 10 per cent of the original cost of the asset, until the asset is fully depreciated.

In contrast, the principles-based standard might say:

> Depreciation expense for the reporting period should reflect the decline in the economic value of the asset being depreciated over the period.

You should see that the rules-based standard is very prescriptive in its directions, whereas the principles-based standard is much broader. Contemporary Issue 3.1 demonstrates the flexibility of a principles-based approach.

3.1 CONTEMPORARY ISSUE

Rules-based versus principles-based standards

Four students from an accounting theory class were given the assignment of explaining the difference between principles-based standards and rules-based standards to their student peers. They had a 50-minute class in which to do so. Other than being provided with some readings on the topic, they were given little direction but encouragement to be creative.

Their presentation commenced with the four presenters dividing the class into two groups: the principles group and the rules group. Both groups were supplied with large sheets of white, blank butcher's paper and drawing implements. An ice-age-type scene, an environment of a deep wide valley filled with snow with its sides covered in tall tress to the tree line and a lot of snow above the tree line, was projected onto the wall of the classroom. This provided the context of their exercise.

The students were then asked to develop a design for a village in that environment: one that would provide its inhabitants with the basic needs of shelter and protection. The principles group was unrestricted in the ideas that it could use. The rules group was limited in its choices by many rules that kept changing marginally. The only possible outcome was to build igloo housing and a protective wall of ice bricks!

When each group had completed its task, the environment changed. Global warming set in, increasing temperatures so that the snow melted. Of course, the igloo village was doomed. The principles group had used what was available in the environment to achieve the objective of shelter and safety: timber, a moat outside the timber protective wall and timber and brush houses. Its village, with a few modifications, still satisfied the principle despite the increase in temperatures.

Questions

1. The two principles for the design of the village were shelter and safety. In what ways do accounting standards also provide 'shelter and safety'? **K**
2. Using the example in the above scenario, what are the advantages of principles over rules? **J**

The move away from rules-based standards is related to the problems generated by their misuse in many of the high-profile accounting scandals associated with the collapse of Enron and others. The rules within a rules-based standard limit an auditor's ability to deter aggressive accounting practices. However, Jamal and Tan[4] questioned whether principles-based standards would reduce opportunistic managing of balance sheets as seen in high-profile accounting scandals. Using an experimental situation, the researchers found that the benefits of a principles-based standard may only be realised if the auditor is principles focused. Principles-based auditor training becomes important as standards move to a principles base. The disadvantages of rules-based standards are outlined in the following section.

Advantages of rules-based standards

According to Nobes,[5] the advantages of rules-based standards are:
- improved guidance when there is a lack of a clear and appropriate principle
- improved guidance where standards are inconsistent with the conceptual frameworks of the standard setters
- increased comparability between financial statements
- improved accuracy with which standard setters communicate both their intentions and requirements
- reduced imprecision that leads to aggressive reporting choices by management
- reduced opportunities for earnings management through judgements
- increased verifiability for auditors and regulators
- reduced exposure to litigation for an entity and its auditors when the rules are applied properly.

These advantages, however, seem unable to overcome the perceived disadvantages of rules-based standards and the perceived advantages of principles-based standards as highlighted in the current accounting literature and the following sections.

Disadvantages of rules-based standards

Rules-based standards have some significant disadvantages, mostly related to the attempt to cover all contingencies. The diversity of entities and the many unique situations covered by the reporting system gives rise to some particular problems.
- Rules-based standards can be very complex, and complexity can allow confusion and even manipulation.
- Spelling out rules for every potential situation results in organisations being able to structure transactions to circumvent unfavourable reporting. Enron is a good example, in that special-purpose entities were used to mask the unfavourable financial position it faced.
- Detailed standards are likely to be incomplete or even obsolete by the time they are issued.
- Manipulated compliance with rules makes auditing more difficult because managers can justify their manipulations as compliance. Compliance with the letter of the law may nonetheless be contrary to the spirit of that law.

In contrast, the literature currently finds little to disagree with in relation to *principles-based standards* and much to recommend them. However, Maines et al.[6] stress that the tension between companies and their auditors, investors and regulators is not specific to the nature of standards as principles-based or rules-based. Standards cannot solve the conflicts between reporting entities and their auditors and other stakeholders.

Advantages of principles-based standards

Principles-based standards reflect a more consistent application of the underlying conceptual framework than do rules-based standards. After investing heavily in a conceptual framework, the accounting profession would not like to see it undermined. This conceptual framework provides the basis for the consistency and flexibility inherent in a principles-based system.

- Principles-based standards should be simpler than rules-based standards. The examples given illustrate how simple a standard can be when based on a principle rather than many rules.
- Principles-based standards supply broad guidelines that can be applied to many situations.
- Broad guidelines may improve the representational faithfulness of financial statements.
- Principles-based standards allow accountants to use their professional judgement in assessing the substance of a transaction. Using their judgement is the service that accountants offer to their clients, so principles-based standards highlight their professionalism.
- Evidence suggests that managers are less likely to attempt earnings management when faced with principles-based standards.[7] With rules-based standards, structuring transactions a particular way is 'black or white'. The use of principles makes the structuring more difficult to justify. Auditors are less likely to permit earnings management when standards are principles-based.

Disadvantages of principles-based standards

Despite these positives, all standard systems have inherent disadvantages. The inherent latitude of principles-based standards is a 'double-edged sword', in that managers are able to select treatments that reflect the underlying economic substance of a transaction and those that do not.[8] Managers, audit committee members and auditors must have the desire for unbiased reporting and the expertise to achieve treatments that reflect the underlying economic substance. Even when unbiased statements are produced, the judgement and choice involved in many of the decisions mean that comparability among financial statements may be reduced.

In Australia, an independent government-controlled process with legislative backing governs the standard-setting process. Corporate failures such as those of HIH and One.Tel have focused unwelcome negative attention on this process and, in response to societal demand, the government has moved to increase its regulatory role in the procedures. Government intervention now extends to legal enforcement of financial reporting and audit independence. The purpose of regulation in the standard-setting arena is discussed in the next section.

 **THEORIES OF REGULATION**

'Information is the oil that lubricates markets'.[9] Without accurate and useful information, the market cannot function. Because accounting information is argued to be a public good and is likely to be underproduced without some form of regulation, the production of accounting information and financial statements should be regulated. Others argue that regulation is needed because without it, information would not be produced at all. Ross disagrees: '[D]isclosure regulations are generally neither required nor desirable, since left on their own, firms will have incentives to report accurately.'[10] In contrast, theories of regulation combat the view that financial information is purely technical, being produced in a political and/or social vacuum. The theories behind the justification for regulation fall roughly under several theoretical umbrellas: signalling theory, public interest theory, capture theory and 'bushfire' theory. Before discussing each theory in turn, it is useful to provide the analysis with some definitions and scope.

Defining regulation

The Macquarie dictionary's pertinent definition of the act of **regulation** is to control or direct by rule, principle or method. Regulation is a rule or order, as for conduct, prescribed by authority. Mitnick defines regulation neutrally, extending the concept to self and governmental regulation:

> [R]egulation is the policing, according to a rule, of a subject's choice of activity, by an entity not directly party to or involved in the activity.[11]

According to these definitions, the elements of regulation are:
- *an intention to intervene.* Throughout the history of standard setting, some body, initially the accounting profession, sought to intervene in the production of financial information by reporting entities.
- *a restriction on choice to achieve certain goals.* Accounting standards restrict choices of accounting methods by directing which are to be used.
- *an exercise of control by a party at least nominally independent of those directly involved in the activity.* The control through an accounting standards board is at least nominally independent of those being regulated, although capture theory (outlined later) suggests otherwise.

Signalling theory

Signalling theory, also known as the theory of disclosure regulation,[12] holds that a reporting entity can increase its value through financial reporting. Companies issuing shares face a competitive capital market populated by sophisticated investors. In order to maximise their value, these entities have incentives to disclose all available information. If an entity fails to disclose, it will be identified by interested parties as merely an average entity among all 'tightlipped'[13] or non-disclosing entities.

This gives above-average entities the motivation to show, through financial statements, that they are better than non-reporting entities. The remaining entities are perceived to be of even poorer quality than before, causing them to wish to better their reputation by implementing financial reporting themselves. Consequently, signalling theory is virtually a self-regulating system, in which almost every entity has a reason to issue financial statements to lower its cost of capital.

Public interest theory

Although signalling theory is acclaimed as a self-perpetuating process, it relies on the function of a perfect, free-market economy. Economic markets are, however, rarely perfect or free and are instead subject to various imperfections and inefficiencies. Public interest theory holds that regulation is supplied in response to the demands of the public for the correction of these inefficient or inequitable market practices.[14]

The theory is based on two assumptions:
- Economic markets are fragile so that they are likely to operate inefficiently or inequitably if left unregulated.
- Regulation is virtually costless.

In this theory, accounting standard setting is a response to an inefficient market for financial (or accounting) information. The quantity and quality of an item such as financial information in an unregulated market differ from the social optimum because financial information has the characteristics of a public good. A public good is one for which those who bear the costs of production do not capture its benefits. The inefficient market for financial information is reflected in either its underproduction or overproduction.

Capture theory

Capture theory attempts to build on the evidence that interest groups are intimately involved in regulation. Capture theory holds that regulation is supplied in response to the demands of self-interested groups trying to maximise the incomes or interests of their members. It is based on the assumption that people seek to advance their self-interest and do so rationally. You should note the similarity of this assumption and that underlying positive accounting theory.

The theory is also based on two insights:

- The first is that the coercive power of government can be used to give valuable benefits to particular groups, such as the accounting industry. By making adherence to accounting standards mandatory, government is bestowing benefits on the accounting profession, particularly auditors. One of the early problems for standard-setting bodies was the lack of adherence to standards. Government backing for standards largely eliminates this problem.
- The second important insight is that regulation can be viewed as a product that is governed by the laws of supply and demand. This insight means that attention is focused on the value and cost of regulation to particular groups. Economics tells us that a product will be supplied to those who value it the most, a value that will be weighed against the cost of obtaining the regulation.

Staubus pointed out that management is the interest group which lobbies most on proposed standards. As a producer of financial information, management can afford to invest more than users in lobbying for their point of view. As a result, standards are more likely to reflect benefits for the reporters of financial information than for users of that information.[15]

'Bushfire' theory

Bushfire theory highlights the political and public nature of regulatory influences by attempting to take into account the reactions of users, and society in general, to 'failures' of regulatory processes. Regulations tend to arise from crises such as the collapse of Enron, WorldCom and HIH. These crises tend to occur regularly, although always unexpectedly, and are often spectacular in their explosion. They highlight the shortcomings in accounting, so that the media cries out, 'Where were the auditors?' Media attention results in solutions that are not necessarily of any use to solve the perceived crisis but are understandable to the layperson. The resulting rules do not necessarily deal with the issues that caused the crisis.

According to Watts and Zimmerman, the resulting rules and regulations are designed to gain media exposure so that politicians and their bureaucrats are more likely to gain re-election.[16]

Ideology theory of regulation

Much like the public interest theory of regulation, the ideology theory of regulation relies on market failure but introduces the role of lobbying in influencing the actions of regulators.[17] Lobbying is viewed as a mechanism through which regulators are informed about policy issues. Like capture theory, interest groups lobby regulators to convey their specific knowledge about the issues being regulated. Because non-paying participants in the market for accounting standards cannot be excluded from the benefits of accounting standards, a private market for accounting standards will fail and so the rationale for regulation of standard setting is justified. This theory only predicts that the effectiveness of regulation will depend on the political ideologies of the regulators and the impact of special interest lobby groups.

Unexpected collapses of high-profile organisations have instigated many legislative initiatives worldwide, including the Corporate Law Economic Reform Program (CLERP) 9 in Australia and the Sarbanes–Oxley Act in the United States. Another proposed answer to the crises caused by these collapses is to base standards on principles rather than rules.

Advantages and disadvantages of regulation

There has been much debate about the benefits and costs of regulation. Those in favour promote its benefits; those against tend to emphasise its costs. The commonly offered benefits are listed here, followed by the commonly offered costs.

Advantages of regulation

Proponents of regulation in the standard-setting environment believe in the need for correction of imperfect and inefficient market systems. The nature of accounting information as a free public good means that normal market-pricing mechanisms are unable to operate. Similarly, the organisation is solely responsible for the release of internal information and self-interest suggests significant incentives to under-produce. Regulation intervention is therefore needed to protect the public interest and to increase the production of useful information. The benefits of regulation can be summarised as follows:

* *Increased efficiency in allocating capital.* Information is needed to ensure efficient allocation of capital. Perfect competition requires perfect information. In the absence of a compulsory disclosure system, some issuers of financial statements may conceal or misrepresent information relevant to decision making. Mandatory disclosure should increase the quantity of information communicated and that information should be accurate because the costs of verification are borne publicly by oversight bodies such as the Australian Securities and Investments Commission.
* *Cheaper production.* Mandatory disclosure reduces the redundant production of information because without it, users must produce their own information. If several users produce the same information, too much has been produced. Mandatory disclosure also reduces the search costs of users because they know where to find the information and should understand the form in which it is supplied.
* *Check on perquisites.* In the absence of mandatory disclosure, underwriting costs and management salaries (including perquisites) may be excessive. Recent publicity given to executive compensation casts some doubt on this particular benefit.
* *Public confidence.* Mandatory disclosure increases public confidence because it substantially limits an organisation's ability to remain silent and controls the time, place and manner of disclosure.
* *Standardisation.* Regulation will result in the standardisation of accounting, which will reduce ambiguity in accounting reports. With it, users will be able to make comparisons among reporting entities. Without regulation, incentives do not exist for preparers to conform to any particular model of accounting. Remember that comparability and understandability are two of the qualitative characteristics of the *Conceptual Framework* that are enabled by standardisation.
* *Public good.* As a public good, information has to be regulated to correct market imperfections.

Disadvantages of regulation

Most opponents of regulation argue that free-market mechanisms would generate enough information to reach a socially acceptable level at which the costs of providing that information are equalled by the benefits. Furthermore, it is often argued that users, who mostly bear very little of the cost of providing information, are the most vocal in demanding increased regulation. If this demand is acceded to, it is argued, overregulation could have significant consequences. Some of the arguments against regulation are summarised as follows.

- *Various problems arise when using regulation to achieve efficiency and equity.*
  - Because regulation can benefit some stakeholders to the detriment of others, those with an interest in financial reporting are likely to lobby standard setters, an exercise that can be costly.
  - Problems emerge for regulators from lack of disclosure by regulated entities. The corporate collapses of 2008 illustrate this. Despite many accounting and auditing standards, these entities collapsed without much warning. Regulators are seen to be failures in these situations, losing prestige and legitimacy.
  - What will be disclosed? What will not be disclosed? The IASB declaring in the pertinent international accounting standard that expenditures on intangibles must not be capitalised created difficulties for entities with many intangibles.
  - What or who governs the regulators? The move towards principles-based standards partly answers the question of what governs the regulations — the *Conceptual Framework* should govern standard setters' decisions. Who governs the regulator when that regulator is the IASB is an interesting and problematic question.
- *Determining the optimal quantity of information is problematic.* The public-good argument is unable to determine the optimum amount of information. At what point do users of financial information face information overload?
- *Regulation is difficult to reverse.* Once an accounting standard is in place, considerable time elapses before it is revised or withdrawn. Can you imagine a situation in which all accounting standards would be withdrawn?
- *Communication is restricted.* By reducing ambiguity, regulation also reduces the means of communicating information as well as stifling innovation in ways of presenting financial information.
- *Reporting entities are different.* Regulation of financial reporting on a standardised basis forces different cases into the same mould: regulation does not allow for differences among entities. The arguments against the extension of accounting standards to the public and not-for-profit sectors illustrate the difficulties some reporting entities have with some standards.
- *There is lobbying.* Certain interest groups seek and gain economic rents by investing resources in the pursuit of favourable regulations.
- *Contracts.* Because users can write contracts with management stipulating the provision of information to them, regulation is not needed.
- *Monopolisation of accounting standards.* The monopolisation of accounting standards can lead to the loss of market discipline for the standard setters who may get standards wrong, especially under political pressure.[18]

Despite these arguments, it is unlikely that regulatory bodies will relinquish their control over the current standard-setting process. However, it is almost impossible to remove the regulatory bodies and their functions from the social and political environment in which they operate.

Users are the focus of standards designed to produce general purpose financial reports with all the information required for decision making. As pointed out, there is always inherent tension between reporting entities and their auditors, investors, regulators and other interested parties. Standards cannot resolve these conflicts; nor can the development of a conceptual framework. Because of this tension, standard setters are constantly subject to political pressures.

Theory and accounting regulation research

Although there are regulatory theories, there are few accounting studies which apply these theories to standards setting. A notable study is that by Walker in which he argued that the Accounting Standards Review Board (ASRB, a predecessor of the AASB) was captured by the interest groups that the board was established to regulate. Walker provided a personal account as he had been a member of the ASRB. He argued that the accounting profession had 'managed to influence the procedures, priorities, and output of the Board'. He also argued that in doing so, the profession had ensured that all members appointed to the Board were aligned with the interests of the profession.[19]

Also using capture theory, Cortese, Irvine and Kaidonis examined the setting of an IFRS standard for the extractive industries accounting for pre-production costs. Focusing on the evidence obtained from the processes leading to the standard, they concluded that 'the IASB was captured by the very constituents it was supposed to regulate'.[20]

Perry and Nolke used a political economy perspective for the first post-harmonisation assessment of international accounting regulation. Their focus, via the push for fair value, was on the implications of harmonisation for capitalism, particularly the shift from industrial to finance capitalism, and international accounting regulation by a private authority. They state that 'the shift of accounting regulation to the private IASB has been caused by the sheer dominance of a highly organized financial sector ... [whose] actors are the best connected and most represented in the standard-setting network'.[21] Laughlin notes that 'accounting standard setting may not fulfil the litmus test of being "regulative and amenable to substantive justification" due to its active rejection of a wider stakeholder commitment and the preferential treatment of finance capitalists'.[22]

LO 5 THE POLITICAL NATURE OF SETTING ACCOUNTING STANDARDS

In most democratic countries, there is some mix of public and private participation in the standard-setting process. For example, standard setting in Australia was initially in the hands of the profession but many factors, especially the difficulty of enforcing private standards, led to a public–private partnership. Acceptance of the process by which standards are set does not mean that those on whom they are imposed will necessarily accept them. As can be seen from the several studies of standard setting outlined earlier, standards are controversial.

Why are standards controversial? Various corporate collapses in many countries have caused a legitimacy crisis in the accounting profession for both financial reporting and auditing.[23] Whenever a crisis occurs, someone or something has to take the blame. Most crises in the corporate world resulted in accounting being blamed. To restore confidence in accounting, the *Conceptual Framework* was developed.

In the aftermath of recent corporate collapses, including those of the global financial crisis (GFC), many phenomena have been blamed, including finance models, auditor–client relationships, corporate governance structures, corporate legislation and accounting standards. While accounting escaped the blame for the GFC, the number and size of previous corporate collapses and their impact on stakeholders show that accounting does count. The losses that society suffered from those collapses have undermined confidence in accounting and auditing.[24]

The various parties that have an interest in reporting entities and in accounting standards often have conflicting interests. As outlined in previous chapters and in the composition of the AASB's User Focus Group, users in the form of investors and creditors are the group whose needs will be taken into account by standard setters. However, this is not the only group with an interest. Company accountants and management also have an interest because their performance is often tied to the financial performance of the organisation. Auditors have an interest because they must enforce the rules generated by accounting standards. Governments and governmental agencies are interested particularly in seeing that standards are enforced. There are differences between the IASB and the FASB: the IASB favours a principles-based approach to standards; the FASB favours a more rules-based approach. Other differences exist — for example, the standards-setting boards of Australia, Canada, New Zealand and the United Kingdom have criticised the IASB for focusing too closely on private sector businesses, ignoring the not-for-profit sector and the public sector. Two points are relevant here:

- *The interests of these groups often conflict.* Management is likely to want accounting choices that allow it to produce as favourable a picture of its performance as possible. Shareholders are likely to want to know the 'real' performance of management and the entity under its control.
- *Auditors like auditability, which often translates into objectivity.* However, management never likes having its choices limited.[25]

Remember that standard setting aims at increasing the amount of information available about a reporting entity. Information is said to be the oil that lubricates markets. A perfect market would require perfect information. Given this, what should the goals of those setting standards be when they have to make a choice among different methods and among ways of reporting information? The *Conceptual Framework* is designed to provide guidance and hopefully to reduce the tension among parties interested in the outcomes delivered by standards.

Lobbying

Accounting standard setting is a political process because accounting standards can transfer wealth from investors to creditors, from investors to employees, from present investors to future investors and so on. As a result, those affected by regulation in the form of accounting standards have an incentive to lobby standard setters to achieve a favourable outcome. The standard-setting process offers several opportunities and means by which those affected by the resulting standards can influence the outcomes of the standard-setting process.[26] Contemporary Issue 3.2 demonstrates the lobbying power of stakeholders, in this case government bureaucrats.

**3.2
CONTEMPORARY
ISSUE**

Treasury chiefs revolt over budget rules

Federal and state treasuries are demanding that Australia's main accounting standards body rewrite a sweeping overhaul of the rules that governments must follow when they present their annual budgets and financial reports.

Federal Treasury secretary Ken Henry and the head of the Department of Finance and Administration, Ian Watt, have written to the Australian Accounting Standards Board to say that its proposed new standard for government financial reporting would make budgets unwieldy, confusing and complex.

The AASB is due to meet this week to consider the backlash from governments over its exposure draft of a new standard for financial reporting, which was issued last year in an attempt to harmonise the two existing sets of accounting rules for government budgets.

Sources believe the AASB may give ground on some of the issues raised by the treasury chiefs, in particular a plan for budgets to include a complex, multi-column format for their operating statements, balance sheets and cash-flow statements.

However, fresh divisions have emerged on a separate but critical issue: whether to force governments to produce consolidated financial reports, including information about public corporations in their bottom lines, rather than confining their financial reports to the general government sector.

The former chairman of the AASB, Professor David Boymal, told *The Australian Financial Review* that if the debate about consolidation could not be resolved, then the whole project to produce a harmonised accounting standard for government reporting could collapse.

The disputes have been triggered by a direction from the Financial Standards Council asking the AASB to produce a single accounting standard to replace two existing sets of accounting rules for governments in Australia.

The two sets of rules are the government finance statistics framework produced by the Australian Bureau of Statistics based on International Monetary Fund requirements and existing Australian accounting standards based on generally accepted accounting principles.

The attempt to harmonise these rules into a single standard is the biggest shake-up for government financial reporting since the move from cash-based reporting to accrual accounting in 1999–2000.

It had been anticipated that the AASB would resolve these differences by adopting one treatment for areas where the standards diverge.

However the draft leaves several issues unresolved and suggests instead that financial statements include four columns showing GFS and GAAP results as well as the size of the resulting 'convergence differences'.

In their letter to the AASB, Dr Henry and Dr Watt said they had strong reservations about whether harmonisation had been achieved under this approach.

Source: Excerpts from Mark Davis, 'Treasury chiefs revolt over budget rules', *Australian Financial Review.*[27]

Questions

1. What reasons can you offer for the International Monetary Fund issuing requirements for government financial reporting? **K**
2. What do you think is the fundamental difference between company financial reporting and government reporting? **AS**
3. What do the letters GFS and GAAP stand for? **K**

Those affected by the decisions in the accounting standard-setting process have several decisions of their own to make[28]:

- *Whether they should lobby.* Sutton suggests that self-interest and choice govern lobbying behaviour. In deciding whether to lobby, a potential lobbyist will weigh the costs against the benefits.[29]
- *Which method of lobbying they should use.* Lobbying methods are classified as either direct or indirect. Direct methods involve lobbying the standard setter by communicating with members of the standard-setting board. Indirect methods involve communicating with a member of the board through a third party regarded as influential over him or her. Indirect methods often leave little or no evidence. Which method is chosen will depend on its relative cost effectiveness.[30]
- *When they should lobby.* Sutton suggests that the most effective time to lobby accounting standard setters is at an early stage in the development of the standard. Standard setters' thoughts at this stage are likely to be just crystallising. Because of this, the probability of influencing the outcome is high.[31]
- *What arguments they should use to support their position.* Arguments can be based on technical or non-technical matters. Technical matters are more easily rebuffed while the likely economic consequences of the standard are not so easily countered by standard setters.[32]

Lobby groups

Lobbying is a force in almost all standard-setting environments. Any individual, business, professional association or regulator with an interest in the direction of the standard-setting process can become a lobbyist but some of these are more involved, and more successful, than others.

Reflecting on standard setting by America's FASB, Staubus offered valuable insights into the competition among interest groups for the control of an activity in which more than one group has an interest.[33] (Remember that multiple interest groups have been identified as having an interest in standard setting.)

The *Conceptual Framework*'s mission of decision usefulness makes end-users the fundamental group when listing those with an interest in the products of the financial reporting process. However, users are not a homogeneous group. Staubus divides users into two groups:

- casual non-professional users
- full-time professional users.

Casual non-professional users have difficulty defining what information they require, making them a weak constituency, rarely motivated to lobby on proposals of standard setters. For example, the harmonisation of accounting standards was a major step for Australian accounting standard setting. The move was promoted by CLERP. User groups failed to provide input into the debate about the international harmonisation of Australia's accounting standards. Not one user group lodged a written submission to CLERP.[34]

In contrast, full-time professional analysts spend much of their time seeking pertinent information to give them a comparative advantage over their competitors. Large institutional investors have specialist staff that focus on particular industries. They jealously guard the information they obtain through their efforts and skills, so they do not respond to exposure drafts in case the resulting standard may undermine their efforts. Under the User Focus Group, this particular group now has direct access to the Australian standard setting process.

Similarly, auditors respond but their views are sometimes criticised for not being independent in the standard-setting process.

Academics also come under criticism for their lack of comment on exposure drafts. This is attributed to the research process by which academics are rewarded by other academic scholars rather than by involvement in professional activities, including responding to exposure drafts.

Because financial statements are to managers what marks are to students, managers are more willing to lobby accounting standard setters. They are regarded as more motivated than are members of any other group.

Staubus views the standard-setting process as dominated by management. This phenomenon is known as 'regulatory capture', which was discussed previously in the section on theories about regulation.

The Australian situation

In Australia, the history of standard setting includes many instances demonstrating the influence of political lobbying by various groups to achieve change. The demise of the Accounting Standards Review Board (ASRB) is an obvious example. The ASRB was a standard-setting board established by the federal government in 1984 to be independent of the accounting profession (the precursor to the AASB). The ASRB lasted only one term, forced out by pressure emanating from the various professional bodies, which lamented their loss of control over the standard-setting process.[35]

Individual standards themselves have been vulnerable to the lobbying process as well, most noticeably, the mandatory status of Statement of Accounting Concepts (SAC) 4, part of Australia's original conceptual framework, which was withdrawn after influential lobbying by the G100, a group that represents corporate Australia.

More recently, reforms of Australia's corporate legislation led to the decision to adopt IFRSs rather than harmonise AASB standards with international ones. Although the original reform paper (CLERP paper no. 1) stated that international accounting standards (IASs) were not of a quality that Australia could adopt, it was nevertheless directed to work towards replacing its own standards with international ones. This was despite opposition from the G100, the big accounting firms, the professional accounting bodies, the major banks and academics.

The impetus to adopt rather than harmonise seems to have come from the Australian Securities Exchange (ASX). It was the only organisation (other than the International Accounting Standards Committee, IASC) to make a written submission supporting the adoption of IASs. At the time, the ASX was planning its float as a public company. Collett et al. state that 'through standard-setting reforms that reduce reporting requirements, it is likely that the ASX sought to facilitate offshore listings. Increased listings and easier access to offshore capital would boost the value of the Exchange and the success of the initial public offering.'[36]

Greater insight into the political machinations associated with Australian accounting standard setting can be obtained by reading Walker and Robinson's analysis of the introduction of cash flow reporting in Australia.[37]

LO 6 HARMONISATION

One of the functions of the AASB is to participate in and contribute to the development of a single set of worldwide accounting standards. The concept of international harmonisation is much older than the AASB. The idea can be traced to the 1972 World Accounting Congress, held in Sydney. It was at this conference that the concept of an IASC was developed.

Australia embarked on its international harmonisation program because benefits were expected from reducing diversity in international accounting practice.[38]

Three main benefits were identified:

- International comparability of financial statements would increase, which should encourage the flow of international investment and increase the international markets' operational efficiency.
- The cost of capital should decrease because the risk associated with not fully understanding the financial statements of entities produced under a different accounting regime is reduced.
- By removing the need for entities to produce two or more financial reports to comply with differing standards, listing rules or regulations, reporting costs should be lowered.

Without a single set of global accounting standards, cross-border investment may be distorted, cross-border monitoring of investment may be obstructed, and cross-border contracting inhibited.[39]

Australia and the European Union (EU) 'adopted' IFRSs on 1 January 2005. Although over 100 countries have been said to have adopted IFRSs or have based their national standards on them, the use of the term 'adopted' is problematic. The simplest way to 'adopt' IFRSs is for the regulator to adopt a process of standard setting and thereby the standards produced under that process. No country uses this method to adopt IFRSs.[40] Other methods will possibly result in differences from IFRSs as issued by the IASB. Those methods include rubber stamping in the private sector (Canada); standard by standard endorsement by public authorities (European Union); fully or closely converging (Australia); or partially converging (China). Although China, Japan, Thailand, Hong Kong and Singapore have subscribed to the international standards, only listed companies in Hong Kong and Singapore use IFRSs for reporting purposes. By 2010, Malaysia, Indonesia, India and Korea had also subscribed to IFRSs. A more detailed discussion of harmonisation and convergence is provided in chapter 12 of this book.

An Asian-Oceanian Standard-Setters Group (AOSSG) has been formed. Its aim is to represent Asia's view on financial reporting, although commentators suggest that its membership needs to be widened if its views are to influence the IASB.[41] At the G20 summit in 2010, the G20 leaders called on international accounting bodies to redouble their efforts to achieve a single set of global standards by June 2011. Such an outcome has not eventuated. According to Zeff and Nobes,[42] the alternative implementation strategies used by countries subscribing to IFRSs mean that there will be questions as to whether a particular organisation complies with IFRSs as issued by the IASB.[43] For example, Australia changes the designations of the IAS standards to AASB standards; adds references; inserts departures for not-for-profit entities; and tables the standards in Parliament. The resulting standards are different from their equivalents issued by the IASB.

In a European setting, Hoogendoorn assessed the harmonisation process and found, among other things, that:

- listed entities underestimated the complexities, effects and cost of IFRSs
- there is tension between principles-based interpretations of IFRSs and a rules-based interpretation, and trying to avoid diversity results in a rules-based approach
- under a principles-based approach, the test is not whether accounting treatments are identical but whether they are appropriate in the particular circumstances
- as a result of IFRSs, financial statements have increased by 20 to 30 pages.[44]

Summary

Understand the institutional framework of Australian accounting standard setting
- The FRC is the oversight body. It appoints the standards setters other than the chair of the AASB. The AASB is responsible for:
  - making accounting standards
  - contributing to a set of worldwide standards.

Explain and define an accounting standard
- Accounting standards are authoritative statements that guide the preparation of financial statements.

Evaluate the distinction between rules-based and principles-based standards
- Principles-based standards are based on a statement of accounting principle that is consistent with the objective for accounting as outlined in the *Conceptual Framework*. The standard derives from, and is consistent with, the *Conceptual Framework*.
- Principles-based standards should not allow exceptions.
- Principles-based standards require professional judgement.
- Rules-based standards are characterised by quantitative tests, exceptions, a high level of detail and, often, internal inconsistencies.
- Rules-based standards minimise the use of professional judgement.

Apply the concept of regulation to the production of accounting information
- Regulation is the intervention in an activity by a party nominally independent of those engaged in the activity.
- Signalling theory disputes whether accounting information needs to be regulated because reporting entities have incentives to distinguish themselves from other reporting entities. The cost of capital for a reporting entity provides the incentive to provide accounting information.
- Public interest theory says that accounting is regulated to correct inefficient or inequitable market practices. Accounting information is a public good so, without regulation, it is either under- or overproduced.
- The 'bushfire' approach says that accounting is regulated to overcome the stigma for accounting created by crises such as unexpected corporate collapses.
- Capture theory says that interested bodies 'capture' the regulatory process. The incentive to capture the regulatory process is to claim the perceived valuable benefits created through regulation.

LO 5

Analyse standard setting as a political process

- Various parties have conflicting interests in reporting entities. Standards result in wealth transfers among these parties. Incentives differ between these parties to participate in the standard-setting process. Society must bear the losses that unexpected corporate collapses impose on it. Society, through the media, usually blames accounting for these collapses.

LO 6

Understand the benefits of harmonisation of accounting standards

- Australia embarked on its international harmonisation program because of the perceived benefits in doing so:
  - international comparability of financial statements
  - reduced cost of capital
  - eliminating redundant reporting.
- Australia adopts the content and wording of international standards, although some changes may be made. It also provides technical input and regional insight into the international standard-setting process.

Review questions

1. In what sense are accounting standards 'standards' in the general meaning of the word?
2. How do principles-based standards differ from rules-based standards?
3. What are the functions of accounting standards?
4. What do you think the standard-setting process should achieve?
5. Justify Australia's approach of imposing its set of accounting standards on all reporting entities, irrespective of whether they are profit seeking.
6. Define regulation.
7. In what ways does accounting standard setting conform to your definition of regulation?
8. If the standard-setting process should achieve better information, what criteria would identify better information?
9. Is the setting of accounting standards desirable for society? If so, who should set standards?
10. How does good financial reporting add value to organisations?
11. Are interested parties behaving ethically when they try to influence the standard-setting process?
12. Explain the statement that 'information is the oil that lubricates markets'. How can this statement be used to justify the regulation of accounting information?
13. In your opinion, do the benefits from regulating accounting information outweigh the costs? Justify your answer.
14. How do you reconcile the 'adoption' of international accounting standards with the process of 'harmonisation'?
15. With particular reference to the following opinion expressed by Watts and Zimmerman, discuss whether accounting standards setting is a 'two-edged sword':

   > Regulation affects the nature of the audit. It expands the audit . . . [R]egulation provides the auditor with the opportunity to perform additional services and lobby on accounting standards on clients' behalf. Regulation also provides the auditor with the opportunity to lobby for increasing accounting complexity because of its audit fee effect.[45]

16. Drawing on your knowledge of the *Conceptual Framework* and of principles-based standards, discuss the following statement:

    Ultimately, it is the underlying economic substance that must drive the development of the scope of standards, if … standards are to remain stable and meaningful.[46]

17. What is 'lobbying'? Who would be expected to lobby an accounting standard, and why?
18. Sutton states that accounting standard setting is a political lobbying process, and as such offers several opportunities and means for interested parties to influence its outcomes.[47] What are the opportunities that Sutton mentions? What methods do lobbyists employ to influence the outcomes? How has Australia's adoption of international standards affected lobbying activity by interested parties?
19. Hoogendoorn suggests that there is tension between a principles-based interpretation of IFRSs and a rules-based interpretation.[48] If IFRSs are principles-based standards, why should there be such tension? When the US adopts IFRSs, is this tension likely to increase? Why?
20. In relation to the governance of the IASB, who governs the governor?

Application questions

Laughlin stated the following:

Accounting standard setting may not fulfil the litmus test of being 'regulative and amenable to substantive justification' due to its active rejection of a wider stakeholder commitment and the preferential treatment of finance capitalists'.[49]

(a) What is a 'litmus test'?
(b) Why should accounting standards be 'amenable to substantive justification'?
(c) Does the AASB's User Focus Group provide evidence of 'the preferential treatment of finance capitalists' in the standard-setting process? **J** **K** **AS**

The Australian reported that one of Australia's top accountancy firms said that company annual reports have become too long and it wants IFRSs trimmed. Representatives of the firm said that IFRSs had complicated accounting — for reporting financial instruments alone, there was now more than 300 pages of rules, and guidance that did not exist under 'the old rules'.

(a) Are IFRSs rules-based or principles-based?
(b) If IFRSs are principles-based, why do you think the standard focusing on financial instruments is accompanied by 300 pages of rules and guidance?
(c) Do you think that the existence of such lengthy guidance notes is what Hoogendoorn was referring to when he commented on the tension between a principles-based interpretation of IFRSs and a rules-based interpretation?[50] **J** **K**

Coca-Cola Amatil conducted a campaign against Australia's adoption of IFRSs in 2004. The company lobbied against requirements that meant Coca-Cola Amatil's balance sheet values would have to be written down by as much as $1.9 billion.

(a) What is meant by the term 'lobbying'?
(b) Who would be likely targets of Coca-Cola Amatil's lobbying activities?
(c) Why would adoption of IFRSs so heavily affect Coca-Cola Amatil?
(d) Did harmonisation affect Coca-Cola Amatil's balance sheet? **J** **K** **AS**

A New Zealand newspaper reported that the integrated nature of capital markets, the mobility of capital and the global nature of the financial crisis highlighted the need for a single set of high-quality globally accepted accounting standards. The report went on to state that banks particularly wanted to eliminate differing accounting treatments between jurisdictions. American banks were reported to have spent US$27.6 million on lobbying for such changes.

(a) Why, in particular, would banks be advocating for a single set of global accounting standards?

(b) Why might American banks be so willing to spend so much on lobbying?

(c) If you were an American bank, who would you be lobbying? And why?

Much publicity has been given to the move by James Hardie Industries, a company that mined, manufactured and distributed asbestos and its related products in Australia, to transfer its domicile to The Netherlands and later Ireland, and to move its asbestos-related liabilities to a foundation separate from the company. One of the reasons touted for these moves was the impending introduction of an accounting standard that would have required the company to include the present value of all likely future asbestos-related liabilities in its accounts.

(a) What is the definition of a liability?

(b) What are the recognition tests for the inclusion of liabilities in the financial statements?

(c) How does the long gestation period of diseases resulting from exposure to asbestos complicate the calculation of future liabilities for James Hardie?

(d) Would you have expected the executives of James Hardie to have lobbied against the proposed standard? On what would they have based their argument against its introduction?

(e) Debate the role that the public backlash against James Hardie's moves played in subsequent changes to the foundation holding asbestos-related liabilities.

(f) Debate whether the executives who made the decisions could have behaved more ethically.

3.1 CASE STUDY

Greek bonds raise issue of enforcement of IASs

The Greek economy went into recession in 2009, with the largest budget deficit and government debt to GDP ratios in the European Union. Since then, markets have worried that Greece will not be able to avoid defaulting on its debt. As a result, the value of Greek bonds has fallen well below their par value.

Many European banks hold Greek bonds. The reporting of their holdings on their balance sheets raises concern about the enforcement of International Accounting Standards. Reporting of financial instruments such as Greek bonds is covered by IAS 39 *Financial Instruments: Recognition and Measurement*. Commentators report that some companies, especially French banks, are not following IAS 39. The French securities regulator is faced with a situation where banks within its ambit have acted as if the value of Greek bonds did not fall below par. If the securities regulator forces the banks to change their accounting, then the securities regulator risks incurring the ire of the French government and French banking regulators. If the French securities regulator ignores the lack of compliance with IAS 39, then the inherent weakness of international standards (a lack of consistent enforcement) will be clear.

There is no common legal enforcement mechanism for international accounting standards. The hope was that audit firms would ensure consistency but this has not happened, especially in relation to IAS 39.

Although auditing firms use similar names in various countries, the firms are organised as national partnerships. While the firms make efforts to assure consistency across borders, they are obviously aware of the political aspects of their decisions in various constituencies. Greek bonds should be accounted for as investments in equity instruments — marked to market values. Write-downs do not have to be shown in the income statement unless their values are impaired. France's largest bank argues that the market for Greek bonds is inactive (although there is trading in them happening daily), so market prices are no longer representative of fair value. Greece's largest lending bank categorised most of its holdings of Greek bonds as either 'held to maturity' or 'loans and receivables' which allowed it to avoid using fair value for the bonds so classified.

The IASB reacted to the accounting of Greek bonds by sending a letter to the European Securities and Markets Authority, a letter which was kept secret until it was leaked to a leading British financial paper. This secrecy, as well as the differential treatment of Greek bonds within Europe, raises issues about whether international accounting standards will deliver on the comparability and consistency that was promised as advantages of their adoption.

Source: Based on information from Vincent Papa, 'EU debt crisis highlights shortcomings of financial instrument accounting', *CFA Institute*; Michael Rapoport and David Enrich, 'Officials warn lenders on Greek-debt values', *Wall Street Journal*; and Reuters, 'Accounting board criticizes European banks on Greek debt', *The New York Times*.[51]

Questions

1. What is 'GDP'? **K**
2. What is meant by 'par value'? **K**
3. Do you consider the lack of a common legal enforcement mechanism for IASs a weakness of the concept of common international accounting standards? Give reasons for your answer. **J** **K**
4. (a) Why would commentators regard the letter by the Chairman of the IASB to the European Securities and Markets Authority as a form of lobbying?
   (b) Does the need for the Chairman of the IASB to lobby an authority highlight the weaknesses of the enforcement system for IASs?
   (c) Give reasons why you think the Chairman of the IASB kept the letter secret. **J** **K**
5. The broad principle set out for accounting for financial instruments was that they should be measured at fair value with gains and losses being recognised in the period in which they occur. Why do you think the IASB changed the principle to the rules in the current standard which allows companies to avoid measuring financial instruments at fair value and so violate the principle? **J** **K** **AS**
6. What theory would explain the actions of the IASB? Give reasons for your answer. **J** **K**

3.2 CASE STUDY

International harmonisation of accounting standards

International harmonisation of accounting standards was sold on the idea that such standards would make it easier for investors to compare companies operating in different geographic areas. The argument also proposed that capital would be allocated more efficiently, global companies would find it more difficult to pick regulators to suit them, and accounting scandals would occur less often. However the recent GFC raised several important questions about the International Accounting Standards Board (IASB) and its promotion of so-called high-quality accounting standards based on principles rather than rules. The GFC drew attention to the fundamental question of how to measure what an asset is worth. The IASB had been advocating fair value accounting.

In October 2008, the IASB bowed to pressure from the European Union's regulators by relaxing its stance on fair value accounting by allowing companies to reclassify assets. Companies could transfer non-derivative financial assets out of classifications that required fair value accounting into classifications that allowed amortised cost. This change meant that Chairman of the IASB Sir David Tweedie's desire for accounting precision conflicted with the European view of accounting as a social construct, a tool among other tools to be used to ensure economic stability. According to commentators, Sir David considered resigning over the issue and the IASB only agreed to the change to avoid the European Union's threat to remove sections of the IFRSs relating to fair value practices. Commentators consider that the rule change saved some European banks from collapse as it allowed them to value more favourably loans and bonds that backed securities.

The IASB's bowing to pressure from the European Union compromises its independence, which is also threatened by its ongoing reliance on corporate contributions for its funding. The backdown may result in accounting blocs for Europe, the US (which has still to harmonise with IFRSs) and Asia (which is increasingly harmonising with IFRSs).

Source: Based on information from Phillip Inman, 'UK accounting watchdog threatens to quit over EU rule change', *The Guardian*; Paul Krugman, 'How did economists get it so wrong', *The New York Times*; and Rachel Sanderson, 'Accounting convergence threatened by EU drive', *The Financial Times*.[52]

Questions
1. The conflict between the EU and the IASB suggests that accounting is a social construct. Do you consider accounting to be a social construct or a quasi-science based on precise facts? Justify your answer. **J**
2. What is meant by 'fair value accounting'? **K**
3. Why would accounting scandals occur less often with global accounting standards? **J** **K**
4. Why would trying to establish a standard based on what an asset is worth result in controversy? **J** **K**
5. What lobbying activity, and by whom, would you expect in relation to a measurement standard? You might like to visit the literature about Australia's attempt to resolve measurement issues. **J** **K**
6. Sir David Tweedie has been described as 'combative'. Is this a characteristic that would be desirable in someone who is trying to negotiate global standards and their acceptance globally? **J**
7. Discuss whether individual countries' interpretations of principles-based accounting standards are likely to undermine the uniformity of global standards. **J** **K**
8. Given the dangers identified by Meeks and Swann of a single monopoly standard setter such as the IASB,[53] would it be better to have a duopoly of, say, the IASB and FASB? Would regional accounting blocs be desirable from a competitive point of view? **J** **K**

Additional readings

Bushman, R & Landsman, WR 2010, 'The pros and cons of regulating corporate reporting: a critical review of the arguments', *Accounting and Business Research*, vol. 40, no .3, pp. 259–73.

Meeks, G & Swann, GMP 2009, 'Accounting standards and the economics of standards', *Accounting and Business Research*, vol. 39, no. 3, pp. 191–210.

Stevenson, KM 2010, 'Commentary: IFRS and the Domestic Standard Setter — Is the Mourning Period Over?', *Australian Accounting Review*, vol. 20, no. 3, pp. 308–12.

Walker, RG 1987, 'Australia's ASRB: a case study of political activity and regulatory "capture"', *Accounting and Business Research*, vol. 17, no. 67, pp. 269–86.

Walker & Robinson, SP 1994, 'Competing regulatory agencies with conflicting agendas: setting standards for cash flow reporting in Australia', *Abacus*, vol. 30, no. 2, pp. 119–37.

Watts, RL & Zimmerman, JL 1978, 'Towards a positive theory of the determination of accounting standards', *The Accounting Review*, vol. 53, no. 1, pp. 112–34.

_____ 1979, 'The demand for and the supply of accounting theories: the market for excuses', *The Accounting Review*, vol. 54, no.2, pp. 273–305.

Zeff, S & Nober, CW 2010, 'Commentary: Has Australia (or any other jurisdiction) "adopted" IFRS?', *Australian Accounting Review*, vol. 20, no. 2, pp. 178–84.

End notes

1. Stevenson, KM 2010, 'Commentary: IFRS and the Domestic Standard Setter — Is the Mourning Period Over?', *Australian Accounting Review*, vol. 54, no. 3, pp. 308–12.
2. Maines, LA, Bartov, E, Fairfield, P, Hirst, DE, Iannaconi, TE, Mallett, R, Schrand, C & Vincent, L 2003, 'Evaluating concepts-based vs rules-based approaches to standard setting', *Accounting Horizons*, vol. 17, no. 1, pp. 73–90.
3. Shortridge, RT & Myring, M 2004, 'Defining principles-based accounting standards', *The CPA Journal*, vol. 74, no. 8, pp. 34–8.
4. Jamal, K & Tan, H 2010, 'Joint Effects of Principles-Based versus Rules-Based Standards and Auditor Type in Constraining Financial Managers' Aggressive Reporting', *The Accounting Review*, vol. 85, no. 4, pp. 1325–46.
5. Nobes, CW 2005, 'Rules-based standards and the lack of principles in accounting', *Accounting Horizons*, vol. 19, no.1, pp. 25–34.
6. Maines, LA, Bartov, E, Fairfield, P, Hirst, DE, Iannaconi, TE, Mallett, R, Schrand, C & Vincent, L 2003, 'Evaluating concepts-based vs rules-based approaches to standard setting', *Accounting Horizons*, vol. 17, no. 1, pp. 73–90.
7. Nelson, M, Elliot J, & Tarpley R 2002, 'Evidence from auditors about managers' and auditors' earnings management decisions, *The Accounting Review*, vol. 77, supplement, pp. 175–202.
8. Maines, LA, Bartov, E, Fairfield, P, Hirst, DE, Iannaconi, TE, Mallett, R, Schrand, C & Vincent, L 2003, 'Evaluating concepts-based vs rules-based approaches to standard setting', *Accounting Horizons*, vol. 17, no. 1, pp. 73–90.
9. Staubus, GJ 1995, 'Issues in the accounting standards-setting process', *Accounting theory, a contemporary review*, ed. by Jones, S Romano, C & Ratnatunga, J, Harcourt Brace, Sydney, pp. 189–215.
10. Ross, SA 1977, 'The determination of financial structure: The incentive signalling approach', *Bell Journal of Economics*, vol. 8, pp. 23–40.
11. Mitnick, BM 1980, *The political economy of regulation*, Columbia University Press, New York.
12. Bushman, R & Landsman, WR 2010, 'The pros and cons of regulating corporate reporting: a critical review of the arguments', *Accounting and Business Research*, vol. 40, no. 3, pp. 259–73.
13. Hakansson, NH 1983, 'Comments on Weick and Ross', *The Accounting Review*, vol. 58, no. 2, pp. 381–4.
14. Posner, RA 1974, 'Theories of economic regulation', *Bell Journal of Economics*, pp. 335–58.
15. Staubus, GJ 1995, 'Issues in the accounting standards-setting process', *Accounting theory, a contemporary review*, ed. by Jones, S Romano, C & Ratnatunga, J, Harcourt Brace, Sydney, p. 207.
16. Watts, RL & Zimmerman, JL 1986, *Positive accounting theory*, Prentice Hall, Englewood Cliffs, New Jersey.
17. Bushman, R & Landsman, WR 2010, 'The pros and cons of regulating corporate reporting: a critical review of the arguments', *Accounting and Business Research*, vol. 40, no. 3, pp. 259–73.
18. Meeks, G & Swann, GMP 2009, 'Accounting standards and the economics of standards', *Accounting and Business Research*, vol. 39, no. 3, pp. 191–210.
19. Walker, RG 1987, 'Australia's ASRB: A case study of political activity and regulatory capture', *Accounting and Business Research*, vol. 17, pp. 269–86.
20. Cortese, CL, Irvine, HJ & Kaidonis, MA 2010, 'Powerful players: How constituents captured the setting of IFRS 6, an accounting standard for the extractive industries', *Accounting Forum*, vol. 34, pp. 76–88.
21. Perry, J & Nolke, A 2006, 'The political economy of International Accounting Standards', *Review of International Political Economy*, vol. 13, no. 4, pp. 559–86.
22. Laughlin, R 2007, 'Critical reflections on research approaches, accounting regulation and the regulation of accounting', *The British Accounting Review*, vol. 39, pp. 271–89.
23. Guthrie, J & Parker, L 2003, 'Editorial introduction: AAAJ and accounting legitimacy in a post-Enron world', Accounting, *Auditing & Accountability Journal*, vol. 16, no. 1, pp. 13–18.
24. ibid.
25. Staubus, GJ 1995, 'Issues in the accounting standards-setting process', *Accounting theory, a contemporary review*, ed. by Jones, S Romano, C & Ratnatunga, J, Harcourt Brace, Sydney, p. 192.
26. Sutton, TG 1984, 'Lobbying of accounting standard-setting bodies in the UK and the USA: a Downsian analysis', *Accounting, Organizations & Society*, vol. 9, no. 1, pp. 81–95; Georgiou, George, 2004, 'Corporate lobbying on accounting standards: methods, timing and perceived effectiveness', *Abacus*, vol. 40, no. 2, pp. 219–37; Bushman, R & Landsman, WR 2010, 'The pros and cons of regulating corporate reporting: a critical review of the arguments', *Accounting and Business Research*, vol. 40, no. 3, pp. 259–73.
27. Mark Davis 2006, 'Treasury chiefs revolt over budget rules', *Australian Financial Review*, 3 April.
28. Walker, RG & Robinson, SP 1994, 'Competing regulatory agencies with conflicting agendas: setting standards for cash flow reporting in Australia', *Abacus*, vol. 30, no. 2, pp. 119–37.
29. Sutton, TG 1984, 'Lobbying of accounting standard-setting bodies in the UK and the USA: a Downsian analysis', *Accounting, Organizations & Society*, vol. 9, no. 1, pp. 81–95.
30. Georgiou, George, 2004, 'Corporate lobbying on accounting standards: methods, timing and perceived effectiveness', *Abacus*, vol. 40, no. 2, pp. 219–37.
31. Sutton, TG 1984, 'Lobbying of accounting standard-setting bodies in the UK and the USA: a Downsian analysis', *Accounting, Organizations & Society*, vol. 9, no. 1, pp. 81–95.
32. ibid.
33. Staubus, GJ 1995, 'Issues in the accounting standards-setting process', *Accounting theory, a contemporary review*, ed. by Jones, S Romano, C & Ratnatunga, J, Harcourt Brace, Sydney, p. 192.
34. Collett, PH, Godfrey, JM & Hrasky, SL 2001, 'International harmonisation: cautions from the Australian experience', *Accounting Horizons*, vol. 15, no. 2, pp. 171–83.
35. ibid.
36. ibid.

37. Walker, RG & Robinson, SP 1994, 'Competing regulatory agencies with conflicting agendas: setting standards for cash flow reporting in Australia', *Abacus*, vol. 30, no. 2, pp. 119–37.

38. Collett, PH, Godfrey, JM & Hrasky, SL 2001, 'International harmonisation: cautions from the Australian experience', *Accounting Horizons*, vol. 15, no. 2, pp. 171–83.

39. Meeks, G & Swann, GMP 2009, 'Accounting standards and the economics of standards', *Accounting and Business Research*, vol. 39, no. 3, pp. 191–210.

40. Zeff, SA & Nobes, CW 2010, 'Commentary: Has Australia (or any other jurisdiction) "adopted" IFRS?', *Australian Accounting Review*, vol. 20, no. 2, pp. 178–84.

41. Jauffret, P 2010, 'Asia needs better voice on IFRS', *International Financial Law Review*, 1 March, www.iflr.com.

42. Zeff, SA & Nobes, CW 2010, 'Commentary: Has Australia (or any other jurisdiction) "adopted" IFRS?', *Australian Accounting Review*, vol. 20, no. 2, pp. 178–84.

43. Wild, K 2010, 'Discussion of "Different approaches to corporate reporting regulation: how jurisdictions differ and why"', *Accounting and Business Research*, vol. 40, no. 3, pp. 257–8.

44. Hoogendoorn, M 2006, 'International accounting regulation and IFRS implementation in Europe and beyond — experiences with first-time adoption in Europe', *Accounting in Europe*, vol. 3, pp. 23–6.

45. Watts, RL & Zimmerman, JL 1986, *Positive accounting theory*, Prentice Hall, Englewood Cliffs, New Jersey.

46. U.S. Securities and Exchange Commission, www.sec.gov.

47. Sutton, TG 1984, 'Lobbying of accounting standard-setting bodies in the UK and the USA: a Downsian analysis', *Accounting, Organizations & Society*, vol. 9, no. 1, pp. 81–95.

48. Hoogendoorn, M 2006, 'International accounting regulation and IFRS implementation in Europe and beyond — experiences with first-time adoption in Europe', *Accounting in Europe*, vol. 3, pp. 23–6.

49. Laughlin, R 2007, 'Critical reflections on research approaches, accounting regulation and the regulation of accounting', *The British Accounting Review*, vol. 39, pp. 271–89.

50. Hoogendoorn, M 2006, 'International accounting regulation and IFRS implementation in Europe and beyond — experiences with first-time adoption in Europe', *Accounting in Europe*, vol. 3, pp. 23–6.

51. Papa, V 2011, 'EU debt crisis highlights shortcomings of financial instrument accounting,' *CFA Institute*, 8 August, http://blogs.cfainstitute.org; Rapoport, M & Enrich, D 2011, 'Officials warn lenders on Greek-debt values', *Wall Street Journal*, 31 August, http://online.wsj.com; Reuters 2011, 'Accounting board criticizes European banks on Greek debt', *The New York Times*, 30 August, www.nytimes.com.

52. Inman, P 2008, 'UK accounting watchdog threatens to quit over EU rule change', *The Guardian*, November 12; Krugman, P 2009, 'How did economists get it so wrong', *The New York Times*, 2 September; Sanderson, R 2010, 'Accounting convergence threatened by EU drive', *The Financial Times*, 4 April.

53. Meeks, G & Swann, GMP 2009, 'Accounting standards and the economics of standards', *Accounting and Business Research*, vol. 39, no. 3, pp. 191–210.

4 Measurement

After studying this chapter, you should be able to:

1 analyse the concept of measurement in the context of financial reporting and demonstrate an understanding of its many benefits and limitations

2 describe the standard setters' approach to measurement and evaluate different measurement approaches

3 evaluate the impact of measurement choice on the quality of accounting information

4 explain the controversial nature of fair value as a measurement approach and consider the arguments for and against a shift toward fair value under the accounting standards

5 explain the political nature of accounting measurement by developing an understanding of the different stakeholders in the financial reporting process

6 describe the issues which contribute to the controversial nature of accounting measurement

7 analyse current measurement challenges faced by the accounting profession with particular reference to environmental sustainability, green assets, intangible assets and water assets.

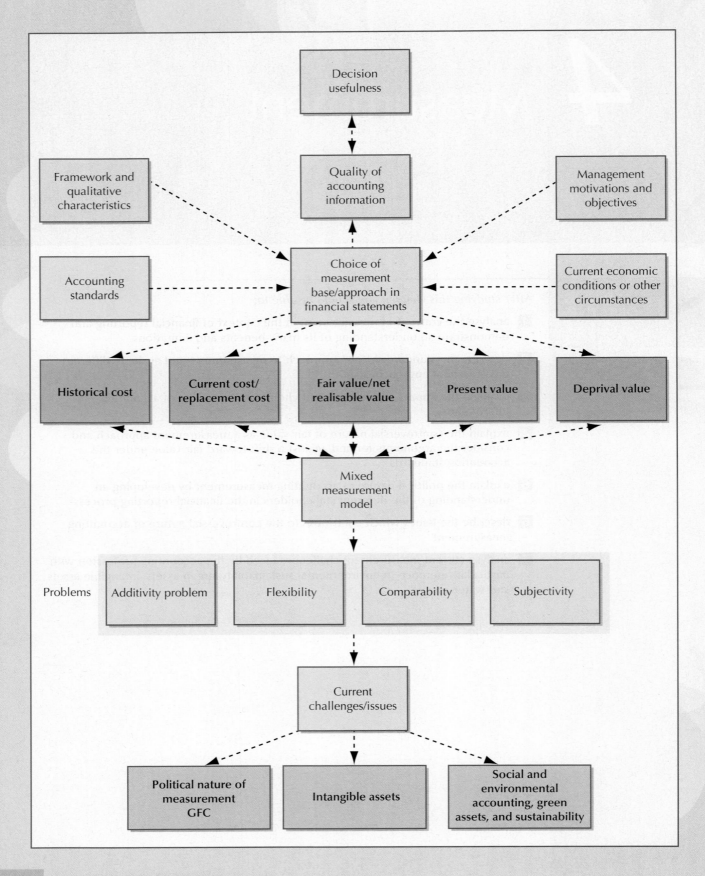

From your previous studies in accounting you would have noted that different items are measured in different ways and we are often faced with a choice as to how we will measure a particular financial statement item. The accounting standard setters have adopted what we call a mixed measurement model when it comes to measurement in accounting. With a recent trend toward measurement of items at fair value, measurement has become very controversial. The political nature of accounting measurement has been highlighted in recent events such as the global financial crisis (GFC). This chapter considers the process of measurement, the benefits, issues and problems associated with the different measurement bases or approaches used in the financial statements, with a particular emphasis on the impact of measurement choice on the quality of accounting information produced. Specific measurement issues and current challenges in accounting measurement are also considered.

LO 1   MEASUREMENT IN ACCOUNTING

The Blackwell Encyclopedic Dictionary of Accounting defines **measurement** as the act or system of measuring, where measuring can have a number of meanings. Measuring can be described as:

- ascertaining the dimensions, quantity or capacity of something
- estimating by evaluation or comparison
- bringing into comparison
- marking off or apportioning, with reference to a given unit of measurement
- allotting or distributing.

Paragraph 4.54 of the *Conceptual Framework for Financial Reporting* (*Conceptual Framework*) issued by the International Accounting Standards Board (IASB) in 2010 defines measurement as:

> the process of determining the monetary amounts at which the elements of the financial statements are to be recognised and carried in the balance sheet and income statement.

Measurement in an accounting context therefore refers to the way the figures on the financial statements are determined. It is interesting to note that the definitions refer to measurement as an act or process. This act or process may involve calculations to determine the quantity of a particular asset held by the entity — for example, inventory. The act or process of accounting measurement can also involve making estimates and comparisons — for example, determination of fair value of an item by reference to market prices or by calculating the net present value of the future cash inflows expected to be derived from an item.

Accounting measurement also involves apportioning or distributing amounts between items or years — for example, depreciation or amortisation of an item to determine the amount or portion of the value that should be included in the financial statements each year to reflect the expense associated with use of the item. It is interesting to see how fundamental concepts put forward in the definition of measurement are reflected in common accounting processes today.

The importance of accounting measurement lies in the purpose for which financial statements are prepared. The *Conceptual Framework* states that the primary objective of general purpose financial reporting is to provide financial information about the reporting entity that is *useful* to existing and potential investors, lenders, and other creditors in making decisions about providing resources to the entity. Financial statements also provide a *stewardship* or *accountability* function by showing the results of how management has performed in managing the resources entrusted to it. The way items are measured in accounting impacts on the quality of accounting information produced. In order to fulfil the **decision usefulness** objective, the financial statements produced must contain good-quality accounting information. The better the quality of the information produced, the more it will assist decision makers in making the right (appropriate) decisions. Poor quality accounting information resulting from the use of inappropriate measurement methods could mislead users and they could potentially make wrong (inappropriate) decisions. If accounting information leads to wrong or inappropriate decisions, then it is not very useful. It would also give the wrong impression as to how well management has performed its role and managed the resources of the entity. Measurement is therefore crucial to be able to provide decision-useful accounting information and accurately appraise the performance of management.

Benefits of measurement

Measurement is fundamental to accounting. It gives meaning to the items included on the balance sheet and income statement. Imagine if we just listed items on the financial statements and put no figures or values against the items. What would the statements tell us? Would users be able to derive any meaning from them that would assist in their decision making?

There are four key benefits of measurement in accounting:

1. It assists in making financial statements *decision useful* by giving meaning to the items included in them. The values placed on items as a consequence of their being measured represent accounting information. The usefulness of the accounting information depends upon the extent to which it possesses the qualitative characteristics outlined in the *Conceptual Framework* issued by the IASB. The impact of choice of measurement approach on the usefulness of accounting information will be discussed later in the chapter.
2. It allows investors, management and other users of accounting information to assess the *financial performance* and *financial position* of the entity.
3. It allows investors, management and other users of accounting information to *compare the entity's performance and position over time*.
4. It allows investors, management and other users of accounting information to *compare entities*.

Limitations of measurement

Measurement in accounting also has a number of limitations or problems. Some flexibility in relation to measurement is necessary. The question lies in how much flexibility is appropriate. With flexibility comes a number of issues.

There are five key limitations of measurement in accounting:

1. There is often *little or no agreement* on what accounting measures should be used. The consequence of this being that management often has *choice* in terms of the approach it adopts to measure an item. This choice is often allowed even within individual standards, where there are a range of possible measurement methods for the same item. This means the same or similar items may be measured using different measurement methods and as a consequence be recorded at different amounts or values.
2. The inherent flexibility and the nature of a mixed measurement approach *reduces comparability* of accounting information. Can any meaning be derived from comparing two entities that have similar items on their financial statements, but have different approaches and make different choices in terms of the specific methods used to measure them?

3. Measurement can be quite *subjective*. Most measurement approaches require exercise of professional judgement or some form of estimation in certain circumstances. This discretion is evident in some approaches more than others. This issue will be explored throughout the chapter.

4. The inherent flexibility is necessary to allow entities to choose the method that will result in the most true and accurate reflection of the fundamental value of the item. Sometimes different approaches might be necessary in different circumstances. For example, in poor economic conditions, measurement at fair value by comparison to market prices may not result in a monetary amount that accurately reflects the true value of an item. This is due to unstable markets causing price volatility. With this flexibility, however, comes opportunity for management to make *opportunistic accounting choices*. The consequence of this being production of accounting information which is potentially misleading and which may even lead to corporate collapse.

5. The current approach to measurement results in what is called the *additivity problem*. Many argue that the items on the financial statements should not be summed and that the totals, such as total assets and net assets, are meaningless. If we think about it, we are potentially adding an item measured at historical cost, to an item measured at present value, to an item measured at fair value. This is the equivalent of adding apples and oranges. Why would you? So what does the total assets figure tell us? Is it logical to try to derive meaning from this total? Similarly, even if the same measurement approach were used for a number of items throughout, it is likely that items were measured at different points in time. This also contributes to the additivity problem.

LO 2 MEASUREMENT APPROACHES AND THE ACCOUNTING STANDARDS

Measurement approaches

The measurement bases discussed below are employed to differing degrees and in varying combinations in the financial statements. The current version of the *Conceptual Framework* does not provide guidance as to which measurement bases should be used when. It recognises that there are a number of different measurement bases which may be appropriate depending upon the nature of the item and the circumstances which exist at the point in time when the item is measured.

Historical cost is the most dominant measurement base used by entities in preparing financial statements. However, it is usually combined with other measurement bases. For example, an item may be predominantly measured at historical cost but where historical cost is unable to deal with the effects of changing prices of non-monetary assets, current cost may be used instead. Fair value has also become more popular in recent times, particularly for measurement of financial instruments and other items which change in substance over time or are traded in an active market. In such circumstances use of fair value represented by the market value of the item makes much more sense than historical cost.

Historical cost

Until recently, historical cost has been the most dominant measurement basis in the preparation of financial statements. Traditional historical cost essentially requires items to be recorded at the amount at which they were purchased or the amount at which they were received. In other words, the amount paid or expected to be paid for a particular item or in relation to a particular expense. In the event of a sale or other income received it is the amount received or expected to be received. All amounts recorded on a historical cost basis are based on transactions which actually occurred in the past.

Paragraph 4.55(a) of the *Conceptual Framework* defines historical cost as a measurement basis according to which:

> Assets are recorded at the amount of cash or cash equivalents paid or the fair value of consideration given to acquire them at the time of their acquisition. Liabilities are recorded at the amount of proceeds received in exchange for the obligation, or in some circumstances (for example, income taxes), at the amounts of cash or cash equivalents expected to be paid to satisfy the liability in the normal course of business.

The key ideas that come out of the definition issued by the IASB in the *Conceptual Framework* are:
- Assets are recorded at the amount paid to purchase them or at the fair value of what has been given up in order to obtain the asset.
- Liabilities are recorded at the amount received in exchange for incurring the obligation or at the amount expected to be paid to settle the liability.
- The amount paid/received or value is the amount as at the time of the transaction. In other words, the amount reflects value at that point in time when the acquisition occurred (in the past) as opposed to its current value.

Current cost — replacement cost

Current and replacement costs are essentially the costs incurred to replace items now. The terms current cost and replacement cost are often used interchangeably. However, they represent two different methods of measuring the cost of replacing items. Current cost requires an item to be valued and recorded at the amount that would be paid at the current time to provide or replace the future economic benefits expected to be derived from the current item. Replacement cost requires an item to be valued and recorded at the amount that would be paid at the current time to purchase an identical item. Current cost is a broader concept in that it represents the costs incurred in order to obtain the same expected future economic benefits that would be received from the current item. These benefits may be achieved or obtained in different ways, not necessarily through the purchase of an identical item. Replacement cost is much more specific in that it refers to the cost associated with purchasing another item identical to the current one.

The *Conceptual Framework* in paragraph 4.55(b) defines current cost as a measurement basis according to which:

> Assets are carried at the amount of cash or cash equivalents that would have to be paid if the same or an equivalent asset was acquired currently. Liabilities are carried at the undiscounted amount of cash or cash equivalents that would be required to settle the obligation currently.

The focus here is on the current acquisition cost of an item as opposed to the amount that was paid to purchase the asset previously, and on the amount needed to be paid here and now to settle a liability. This measurement approach is in a sense a cost based approach designed to try and deal with some of the limitations associated with the historical cost approach to measurement. For example, because an item's cost is reflected by the amount paid now, on the current date, the issue of the cost of items being determined on different dates, at different points in time, is overcome.

Fair value — realisable or settlement value

Fair value is becoming more and more popular as a measurement basis. There has been a significant shift toward the use of fair value with the release of AASB 13/IFRS 13 *Fair Value Measurement*. For a number of reasons, fair value is considered to be more relevant from a decision usefulness perspective. This measurement approach is providing some competition for historical cost.

Fair value is defined in paragraph 9 of AASB 13/IFRS 13 as:

the price that would be received to sell an asset or paid to transfer a liability in an orderly transaction between market participants at the measurement date.

Therefore, fair value is an exit value. It is the value or amount an entity would derive by selling an item. In other words, it represents the market value of an item. **Realisable value** is also an exit value, representing the amount expected to be received upon disposal of an asset. The concepts are similar in nature. Fair value, however, is a more complex concept. It is essentially a theoretical estimation of the market value of an item. There are a number of different ways in which such an estimation may be made. Fair value should be measured by taking into account the characteristics of an asset or liability — for example, the condition and location of the asset, any restrictions on the sale or use of the asset, whether it is a stand-alone asset or liability or whether it is a group of assets, a group of liabilities or a group of assets and liabilities, the most advantageous market for the asset, and the market participants with whom the entity would enter into a transaction in that market. A more detailed discussion of valuation techniques used to determine fair value is provided later in the chapter and fair value is discussed in detail in chapter 10 of this book. Realisable value is the amount an entity expects to realise from the sale of an asset.

Paragraph 4.55(c) of the *Conceptual Framework* defines realisable (settlement) value as a measurement basis according to which:

Assets are carried at the amount of cash or cash equivalents that could currently be obtained by selling the asset in an orderly disposal. Liabilities are carried at their settlement values; that is, the undiscounted amounts of cash or cash equivalents expected to be paid to satisfy the liabilities in the normal course of business.

While realisable value and fair value are similar concepts, realisable value is an entity-specific measurement and fair value is a market-based measurement.

Present value

Present value is a more subjective measurement approach which involves considerable uncertainty. Present value takes the cash flows expected to be received in the future and reduces them so that they reflect their value today. This involves identifying and estimating the future cash flows associated with an item and choosing an appropriate discount rate. The discount rate is applied to adjust the cash flows to reflect the fact that the amount of money expected to be derived from an item in the future does not have the same value as the same amount of money received today.

The *Conceptual Framework* defines **present value** in paragraph 4.55(d) as a measurement basis according to which:

Assets are carried at the present discounted value of the future net cash inflows that the item is expected to generate in the normal course of business. Liabilities are carried at the present discounted value of the future net cash outflows that are expected to be required to settle liabilities in the normal course of business.

In accordance with the definition in the *Conceptual Framework*, this approach involves application of a discount rate to expected future cash flows generated or incurred in the normal course of business. The cash flows are attributable to the particular item being measured. This allows a value to be placed on the item which reflects what the item is worth now in terms of the potential benefits or value that are expected to be associated with the item in the future.

Deprival value

Deprival value is unique in that it is neither a specific cost nor value which is placed on an item, but rather a comparison of already determined costs and values in a 'what if' type scenario to determine the value of an item. Deprival value is essentially the loss that would be suffered if an entity was deprived of the asset. Determination of the deprival value of an asset may incorporate:

- present value if the item was held for use
- net realisable value if the item was held for sale
- replacement cost associated with replacing the item or the services that were received from the item.

Table 4.1 provides a comparison of the different measurement approaches discussed above.

TABLE 4.1 Comparison of measurement approaches

	Historical cost	Current cost	Fair value	Present value	Deprival value
Value is determined using	• the actual amount paid for an item • the actual amount received for an item • actual transactions	• the amount that would be paid at the current time to *purchase an identical item* • the lowest amount that would be paid at the current time to *provide the future economic benefits expected from the current item* • the cost to obtain the same benefits from a different item	• the price that would be received to sell an asset or paid to transfer a liability in an orderly transaction between market participants at the measurement date • market prices	• the present discounted value of the future net cash flows associated with the item • the future cash inflows and outflows associated with the item which need to be identified and then estimated • an appropriate discount rate, which recognises that an amount of money received in one year has a different value to the same amount of money received today	• the loss that a rational person would suffer if they were deprived of the asset • consideration of the action to be taken if the item currently held by the entity was lost (i.e. do nothing or replace the item) • information as to whether the item will actually be replaced and the individual circumstances of the entity
Relevance/ usefulness	• not relevant to current decision making if time span since transaction occurred is long • not necessarily indicative of value	• relevant to current decision making if inflation is high or relative prices are changing • more relevant and useful if asset has no resale value and is used by the entity to provide future economic benefits	• most relevant measure of value for current decision making • the amount that will be received or will need to be paid for an item is decision-useful information	• very relevant to current decision making • directly measures future economic benefits • takes into account the time value of money	• not so relevant, given that the entity still holds the asset and has not been deprived of it • value based on a scenario that may never happen

	Historical cost	Current cost	Fair value	Present value	Deprival value
Subjectivity	• most objective measurement approach • clear audit trail — can usually be proven by documentation	• objective where market prices are used to determine current cost	• objective if fair value is determined by reference to the market price for an item, set by forces outside the entity — not biased by judgement and cannot be manipulated or influenced by management • subjective where items are not regularly traded in an active market and an estimate of fair value is made	• much subjectivity involved in estimating cash flows expected in the future • subjective in the sense that there is a range of discount rates to choose from and there is often much variation between entities in the discount rates chosen • the need for management assertions and assumptions make reliability questionable	• fairly subjective in that there are a range of measures to choose from depending upon the assumptions and decisions made by management
Issues and criticisms	• does not take into account changes in the value of money over time, ignoring price inflation • judgement involved in determining depreciation creates opportunity for inconsistencies or manipulation • unable to determine the cost of some items — items donated with no cost to the entity, items that are internally generated rather than purchased	• current or replacement cost is not necessarily indicative of the value the asset is expected to generate for the entity	• focus on exit values means we are measuring as if we are going to sell off the assets — not logical and goes against the going concern assumption • short-term fluctuations in fair value may be irrelevant and in fact confusing from a user perspective • market prices can be volatile and therefore sometimes not indicative of the market value of an item	• can be difficult or impossible to identify the cash flows attributable to a particular item because the item is used in conjunction with other items to produce cash flows for the entity • lacks objectivity — based on what management think will happen • in effect, management's own opinions and biases are incorporated into the measure of its performance	• depends upon the measure used and how value is determined

Measurement and international accounting standards

The approach to measurement under the international accounting standards is quite complex in that a number of different measurement bases are employed in the preparation of the financial statements. According to the *Conceptual Framework*, these include historical cost, current cost, realisable value and present value. These different measurement bases are employed to different degrees and in varying combinations during the preparation of the financial statements. This approach is called a **mixed measurement model**.

Such a model can lead to variations in accounting practice and, as a consequence, different financial results being reported. The accounting standards prescribe what measurement bases we should be using to a certain extent, but there is still a large amount of flexibility and choice within particular standards. This is demonstrated in figures 4.1, 4.2 and 4.3. There is, however, a need for this flexibility and a need for a mixed measurement model which allows for use of a number of different measurement bases. This is due to the differing circumstances in which entities find themselves and to differences in the substance or nature of transactions.

The major pitfall in the application of such a model is that the discretion allowed provides an opportunity for management to make opportunistic accounting choices, creating a biased picture of reality, perhaps even misleading users and in extreme cases leading to corporate failure.

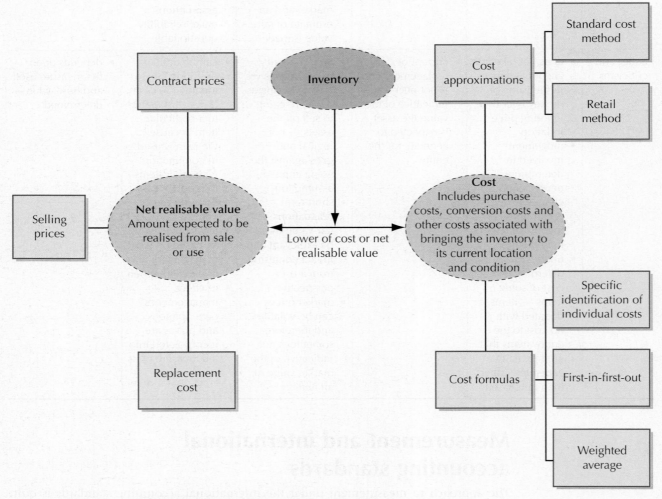

FIGURE 4.1 Measurement approaches: inventory

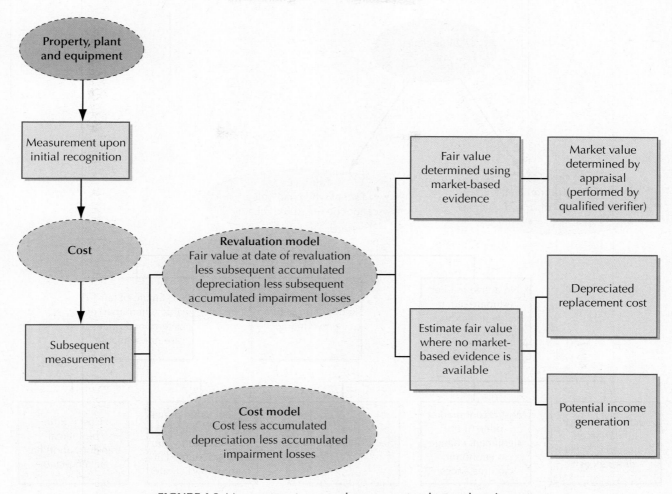

FIGURE 4.2 Measurement approaches: property, plant and equipment

So, one can argue that a mixed measurement model such as the one we have adopted under the international accounting standards is necessary but subjective in nature. A large amount of professional judgement therefore needs to be applied. Applying professional judgement is part of a professional accountant's role. Perhaps the emphasis on professional judgements means there is a role here for ethics as well.

Figures 4.1, 4.2 and 4.3 illustrate what is meant by a mixed measurement model. These diagrams show how a number of important standards incorporate a number of different measurement bases or approaches. They also demonstrate the complexity and variation which exist in terms of how an amount may be determined under a particular measurement approach.

The issue of accounting measurement ranks highly on the IASB agenda. It is being addressed as part of the conceptual framework project being carried out jointly by the IASB and Financial Accounting Standards Board (FASB). The project has been divided into eight phases and measurement constitutes one phase, Phase C. Information regarding the measurement phase of the conceptual framework project can be accessed on the IASB website, www.ifrs.org. A summary of the IASB agenda, discussion, decisions to date, and objectives in relation to accounting measurement has been provided over the following pages.[1]

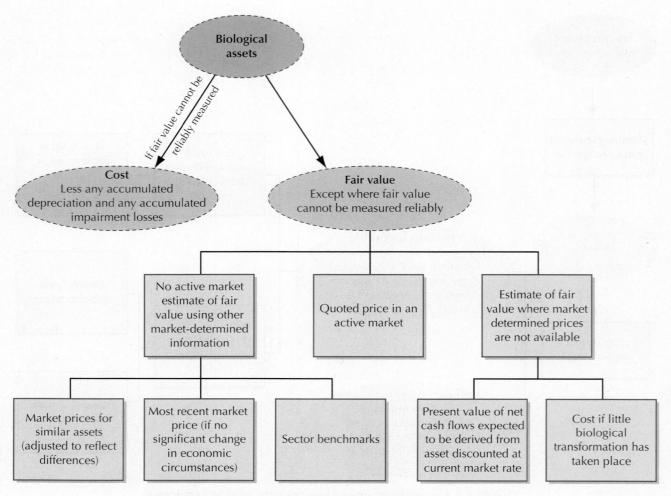

FIGURE 4.3 Measurement approaches: biological assets

The overall objective of the measurement phase of the project is to provide guidance for selecting measurement bases that satisfy the objectives and qualitative characteristics of financial reporting. This guidance has been lacking and has been identified as a weakness in previous versions of the *Conceptual Framework*. In the past, the *Conceptual Framework* has merely stated the main measurement bases that may be used and acknowledged that a mixture of these is adopted as appropriate under the accounting standards.

The decisions to date indicate the beginning of a new approach. The new approach to measurement that has been discussed by the boards is not intended to lead to automatic decisions about what is an appropriate measurement base in particular instances, but rather the approach would describe the circumstances and factors that should be considered when making decisions about accounting measurement. In November 2008, the boards discussed five factors that they thought might be considered when choosing between a number of alternative measurement bases. These factors are:

1. *Method of value realisation.* The relative importance from a user perspective of information about the current value of an asset or liability as opposed to information about the cash flows generated by the item. The ease and precision with which cash flows can be separated from value changes also provides an indication of relevance.

2. *Confidence level.* The confidence that can be placed on different measurements as a representation of the asset or liability provides an indication of faithful representation.

3. *Measurement of similar items.* Use of consistent measurement approaches for items of a similar nature and items used together provides an indication of comparability.
4. *Separability of changes in measurement approach.* Measurement of items that generate cash flows together as a unit should be measured the same way, providing an indication of understandability.
5. *Cost/benefit.* Assessment of the ratio of the benefits that would be derived from alternative measurement approaches to the costs of preparing and using those measurements. This constitutes a major limitation when it comes to financial reporting.

The boards supported these general ideas and over time the approach was developed further. In June 2009, the board decided that these factors were a good starting point for developing a discussion paper. By December 2009, the boards had discussed in depth the circumstances and factors that should be considered as well as other measurement concepts that they thought should have been included in a discussion paper but decided not to go ahead with drafting a discussion paper at that time.

In January 2009, the board also discussed which of the possible measurement approaches should be included in the *Conceptual Framework*. A tentative decision was made to include the following approaches:

- actual or estimated current prices
- actual past entry prices adjusted for interest accruals, depreciation, amortisation, impairments, and other similar items (essentially historical cost adjusted to make the figures more relevant and decision useful)
- prescribed computations or calculations based on discounted or undiscounted estimates of future cash flows (essentially value in use and fair value based measurements).

At the meeting in July 2010, it was decided that the terms historical cost and fair value should not be used in the measurement chapter of the *Conceptual Framework*. The reasoning behind this decision was that in reality neither term clearly and accurately describes the set of possible measurement methods that are to be considered. In order to maximise the information content of financial statement items and represent items faithfully, it is useful to consider possible measurement approaches in a broader sense. At this latest meeting, the boards also agreed on what the measurement chapter should accomplish. It was agreed that it should list and describe possible measurement approaches with a focus on the advantages and disadvantages of each in relation to maximising the decision usefulness of the accounting information produced. How this should be considered in conjunction with the issue of cost constraint to determine the appropriate measurement method or approach was also discussed. It was also agreed that although the chapter would not prescribe specific measurement approaches for particular assets and liabilities, it should include examples or cases that demonstrate how the concepts discussed in the *Conceptual Framework* could be applied. Although there is much work to be done, the discussions that have taken place and the decisions reached by the board so far show progress in the right direction. The foundations that have been laid so far in this phase of the project address many of the critical and fundamental issues that are prevalent in the current version of the *Conceptual Framework*. There has been little progress with regard to this project to date. Contemporary Issue 4.1 discusses the standard setters' approach to determining an appropriate measurement method.

4.1 CONTEMPORARY ISSUE

The standard setters search for the 'best' measurement basis

The current thinking of accounting standard setters about measurement seems to be based on an idealised view of markets as being *complete* and in *perfectly competitive equilibrium*. In such conditions, there is a unique market price based on full information for every asset and liability, and there is an obvious attraction in using this price as the measure for accounting. This explains the apparent enthusiasm for single ideal measurement methods based on market price, such as fair value. In reality, markets are imperfect and incomplete, so that ideal unique market prices are not available for all assets and liabilities. This is why the accounting standards have to resort to a fair value hierarchy. The lower levels of this hierarchy require estimation of what a market price might be if one existed. The liquidity problems evident in the GFC have demonstrated the limitations of markets and the difficulty associated with estimating market prices.

An important source of market imperfection is the existence of information asymmetry, which means that not all market participants are equally well informed. This is the principal reason why accounts are needed. The measurement methods used in preparation of the accounts should be selected with the market context in mind. The idea of having a single preselected measurement method may not best reflect market conditions or meet users' needs.

The IASB and FASB are currently involved in a project to develop a joint conceptual framework. As part of this project they have attempted to identify the *single* measurement basis that best conforms with criteria such as relevance and representational faithfulness that are prescribed by the conceptual framework. These measurement bases are 'pure' bases of measurement such as historical cost, replacement cost, value-in-use or fair value. The objective under this approach being to always estimate the selected measurement basis, other bases allowed only as proxies, where direct measurement is impossible. An example of this concept and the use of proxies is the fair value hierarchy. Fair value (selling price) is the measurement basis, but estimates using other information are allowed when selling prices cannot be directly observed.

This approach does not favour *mixed measurement* approaches, such as the traditional 'lower of historical cost or market value' approach. The view is that there is a problem with mixing different 'pure' measurement bases, even if they are combined in a logical or systematic way. The mixing of different measurement methods is believed to create mismatch problems. The mismatch problem refers to the fact that different items in the same set of accounts are measured on a different basis, making aggregation (totals) misleading. The two boards, after much recent deliberation, have now considered a new approach which might allow mixed measurements. A discussion of the cases for and against a single ideal measurement basis follows.

A single method approach would promote consistency within accounts, avoiding mismatches and allowing more meaningful aggregation. Aggregation problems may still exist within each 'pure' approach. This approach would also improve comparability of accounts across entities.

Fair value has tended to be favoured as a pure measurement base. In the standard setters' deliberations, it has been claimed that this method has the property of relevance because it measures the market's expectation of future cash flows to be derived by the entity. It is also claimed that it has the property of objectivity, reflecting the market's view, rather than the views of the managers associated with the entity.

The adoption of a single measurement method is predicated on the belief that a particular measure will always be the most relevant and will always be able to be reliably measured. This will only be the case if markets are complete and are in perfectly competitive equilibrium. In this situation, a unique market value can be attributed to every asset and liability, so a single measurement method, consistent with fair value is appropriate. Therefore, properties of consistency and comparability can be achieved in a very precise sense.

In reality, markets are not perfect and complete. This ideal information is therefore not available. Beaver and Demski (1979)[2] have pointed out that in a world of perfect and complete markets, accounting would not be required. This is because everybody would be fully informed. They state that the very existence of accounting implies some degree of market imperfection. Beaver and Demski's response to this dilemma is to suggest that, in a realistic setting where market imperfections will always exist, we should regard accounts as providing useful information for decision making rather than definitive measurements. In practical terms, for the standard setters, this means abandoning the search for the single ideal measure and instead, adopting the objective of identifying the information that is most likely to meet the needs of users' decision models. The informational approach is not concerned with measuring the present value of the future cash flows to value the business, but rather to provide information that will help users such as financial analysts to predict future cash flows and perform their own valuations. The nature of such information is likely to be more dependent on specific circumstances than that implied by the 'single ideal' approach. However, it does not preclude the universal use of a single measure if that is justified by users' information needs.

The recent GFC has provided a vivid illustration of the practical importance of market imperfection and incompleteness. Standard setters believed that financial markets were commonly deep and liquid, and therefore financial instruments were selected, in IAS 39, as being suitable for fair value measurement. However, during the global financial crisis, the markets for many financial instruments have become very illiquid and in some cases non-existent. This led the IASB and FASB to relax their fair value reporting requirements.

Source: Adapted from an article by Geoffrey Whittington, 'Measurement in financial reporting', *Abacus*.[3]

Questions

1. What is meant by the term market context? Why is context so important in accounting measurement? **K**
2. Is adoption of a single measurement base approach likely to work in practice? Justify your response. **J** **K**
3. Why do you think standard setters have considered a single measurement base approach? In your response, consider the fundamental problems that such an approach could help resolve and how such an approach would fit with the qualitative characteristics of accounting information prescribed under the *Conceptual Framework*. **K** **CT**

Decision criteria and influences on choice of measurement approach

There are many things which may influence the decision as to which measurement base is most appropriate. Some of the most prominent influences include:

- potential users of the financial statements
- practical considerations
- management's motivations and objectives.

One of the major influences of accounting policy choice lies in the purpose for which the financial statements are being prepared. Before determining the appropriateness of a particular measurement base, the potential users of the information and their needs in relation to accounting information must be understood. In other words, the measurement base or approach which will provide the most decision useful information for users must be chosen.

Similarly, determination of a cost or value using a particular approach must be considered from a practical viewpoint. A particular cost or value may be too difficult or in fact impossible to determine — for example, if the data is not readily available and is too costly or too complex to obtain.

Another practical consideration is the cost of obtaining or calculating the cost or value. The benefits of using a particular measurement approach must outweigh the cost of determining the cost or value. In other words the choice of measurement approach must be cost effective.

Another important influence is the motivations and objectives that underpin management behaviour. For example, if management has a short-term focus because it is on a shorter term employment contract or because its bonus is tied to profits in the current year, it is most likely to choose the measurement approach which produces the best results in terms of higher profits. On the other hand, if management has a long-term focus because it is on a longer employment contract or because its incentive payments are tied to other long-term consequences which reflect its performance, it will most likely be more neutral and objective in its approach to measurement choice. The other factors will have more influence in that they will be more inclined to look for the measurement base which most accurately reflects the cost or value of the item and the one which is most cost effective to determine.

MEASUREMENT AND THE QUALITY OF ACCOUNTING INFORMATION

Measurement is an important aspect in the production of accounting information. The measurement base or approach selected has a great impact on the extent to which accounting information possesses the qualitative characteristics outlined in the *Conceptual Framework*. How an item is measured has a direct impact on the relevance, faithful representation, understandability, comparability and verifiability of the information produced. If the information produced possesses these characteristics, it is considered to be decision useful. This means that measurement plays a key role and choices made in relation to measurement determine whether the financial statements fulfil the decision usefulness objective, which is the purpose for which they are prepared.

Historical cost

Information produced using historical cost as the measurement base is considered to be *less relevant* because the amount an entity paid for a particular item in the past is not necessarily reflective of the value of benefits to be derived from the item now and in the future. For example, what was paid for a machine two years ago is not relevant to a user's decision making if it does not reflect or approximate the value of future benefits to be derived from the machine by the user. However, it can be argued that measurement at historical cost produces accounting information which is *more faithfully represented*. This is because the amounts recorded are based on objective transactions which actually occurred and there is no estimation involved. Values determined for particular assets can be traced back to transaction documentation such as an invoice for verification. Existence of the potential for objective verification and a clear audit trail under the historical cost measurement approach makes the information produced more faithfully represented. The fact that values are determined according to amounts incurred as a consequence of transactions which actually occurred and the fact that there is very little or no estimation involved in the determination of the amount to be recorded, makes the information produced *more neutral*.

Information produced using historical cost is *generally understandable*. The concept is well known and understood. There are no complex formulas or calculations and average users are likely to derive appropriate meaning from the numbers in the financial statements through their understanding of how the items are measured. The danger, however, is that although the information produced is quite simple and understandable, there are some limitations of historical cost measurement which are not well understood and arguably the ability to understand the information produced using this method may be somewhat reduced.

It may be argued that information produced using historical cost is *less comparable*. Items are recorded at the amount for which they are acquired on a particular date. Different items are purchased on different dates and in different years. As the purchasing power of money changes over time, the amounts paid for items at different points in time really cannot be compared from one year to the next. Similarly, one entity may have more old assets and another entity may have mostly newer assets. Therefore, is it really appropriate to compare the total or net asset figures of the two entities?

Fair value

Information produced using fair value as the measurement base is argued to be *more relevant* because it reflects what items are worth now rather than what they were worth when they were purchased. Fair value is also indicative of the value of future potential benefits expected to be derived from an item or the value of future liabilities expected to be associated with an item. The accounting numbers determined using fair value are very relevant from a decision usefulness perspective as they provide useful input into the decision-making process surrounding users' assessment of the current and future value of the entity.

Fair value is generally perceived to be a more subjective measurement approach which is therefore less faithfully represented. However, this is not necessarily the case. If an active market exists for the item, its fair value would be determined by reference to its current market price. The quoted market price for an item is an objective method for determining the fair value of an item and therefore makes the accounting information produced *more faithfully represented*. If there is no active market for the asset, forming a theoretical estimate of what the current market value of the item would be can potentially involve many assumptions and much professional judgement on the part of management. Accordingly, where no active market exists for the asset the faithful representation of accounting information is potentially reduced. Similarly, when there is no objective market price available and estimation and judgement become involved, the determination of fair value becomes *less neutral*.

Information produced using fair value is viewed as being *more understandable* and *comparable*. The concept is simple and straightforward, fair value being the equivalent of the current market value of an item. In other words, what the item would be sold or bought for in the market on the date fair value is to be determined. From a user perspective, this is an easy concept to understand even for those users who are less accounting oriented or financially literate. The fact that the value of all items measured at fair value is current and determined on the same date, for example market values of the items on a particular reporting date, makes the accounting information produced using fair value as the measurement base *more comparable*.

It may also be argued that due to the variation which can exist in the valuation techniques adopted in determining fair value, fair value as a measurement approach actually makes the information produced *less comparable*. These differing valuation techniques should in theory achieve the same outcome in that the amount determined provides a theoretical estimate of the market value of the item. However, in reality differences in values determined under different techniques are likely to occur. We could therefore argue that fair value can also result in accounting information which is less comparable, depending upon the extent to which there is potential for adoption of different techniques and the extent of the differences in the resulting fair values.

Current cost

Current cost produces information which is *more relevant* than that produced using historical cost. Although both approaches are cost based, items recorded at their current cost reflect what would be paid for the same items today or what would be paid to reap the same future benefits that are expected to be received from those items. In other words, their current values — that is, what items which reap similar future benefits are worth now — make information produced using this approach more relevant from a user perspective.

The information produced is generally *faithfully represented* because, in a similar way to historical cost, values are determined by reference to the actual current cost of particular items. The only difference being that this approach is not based on a transaction which occurred previously, but rather it is forward looking based on the current costs that need to be incurred to achieve a similar outcome. It is argued, therefore, that this measurement approach results in information which is *faithfully represented*.

Current cost is essentially more complex than other measurement approaches. There are potentially many different ways in which the same benefits may be derived that would have been received from an item. In its most simplistic form, the cost incurred in replacing the item with another item which is the same would determine the current cost or value of the item. Information produced using this approach is relatively understandable from a user perspective. In reality, an equivalent item would rarely be purchased as the item may no longer be available and technology is constantly changing. More often than not the same outcome will be achieved by some other means as processes are streamlined and completed more efficiently. This makes implementation and valuation using this approach quite difficult in reality, and therefore makes the information produced rather ambiguous as it is often unclear what the amount actually represents. As a result, the information is more difficult to interpret from a decision usefulness perspective and therefore *less understandable*.

Values determined using current cost may be considered *more comparable* in the sense that the cost should always reflect the amount to be paid now to receive the same future economic benefits expected. Amounts are current and determined on the same date, at the same point in time. It may be argued that due to the potential variability which exists in terms of how an entity may choose to achieve the same future economic benefits, the information may be *less comparable*, especially between different companies. This is because different entities have access to different resources and are different in terms of their technological capabilities. It doesn't seem fair to compare an entity which may incur higher costs to achieve the same outcome or future benefits as a consequence of these factors.

Present value

Values determined using present value are *more relevant*. Users are interested in the value or net worth of the entity and present value provides an estimate of the present value of future cash flows expected to be derived from the item. Present value is therefore fairly indicative of the future viability of the firm and its potential as a good investment opportunity.

Present value as a measurement approach *lacks faithful representation* and *neutral depiction*. This is due to the estimation involved, and assumptions and judgement inherent in such an approach. Accounting information produced using present value is *less understandable* than that prepared using some of the other measurement approaches. Such an approach involves complex estimations and formulas. The majority of users of the financial statements would not necessarily understand what an amount determined using present value reflects or means. Knowledge of the assumptions and discount rates used by management in the calculation of present value is required in order to fully understand the amounts or values presented. Generally, users are not necessarily aware of these internal assumptions and discount rates which make it difficult for them to appropriately interpret the values. Although the concept of present value makes logical sense and is relatively simple, the complex calculations and assumptions involved make it *less understandable* from a decision usefulness perspective.

Present value is *comparable* in the sense that all amounts are discounted to the present day and the amounts reflected at the same point in time and in current dollars. On the other hand, due to the fact that there are a number of estimations involved and many different assumptions built in to the calculation of present value, one can argue that information produced using present value is *less comparable*. This is because estimations and assumptions are at management's discretion and have the potential to differ greatly between entities. The consequence is different values which may or may not be comparable depending upon the validity of the assumptions made and the accuracy of estimations formed.

Deprival value

Deprival value is *less relevant* than the other measurement approaches. If an item is held and requires a value to be placed on it, how is the amount of the loss that would be suffered from being deprived of the item relevant? Wouldn't it make more sense to focus on the item itself rather than involving additional calculations and making valuation unnecessarily complicated by looking at loss of production and revenue? Information concerning the amount of loss that would be incurred by the entity if it was deprived of the item is not really relevant from a decision usefulness perspective. This is mainly due to the fact that the value of an item is based on a situation which has not occurred and may not even be likely to occur in the future. In a sense deprival value is a different spin on present value or fair value which are based on the current value determined by estimating what benefits the item is likely to bring in the future. The difference is the concept of deprival value just doesn't make sense, especially from a user perspective.

Following on from the discussion above it is easy to see how deprival value also lacks *faithful representation, neutral depiction* and *understandability*. The estimation involved as well as the management assumptions and decisions inherent in this approach also make accounting information produced using this approach *less comparable*.

Contemporary Issue 4.2 examines the issue of applying qualitative characteristics to different measurement bases in light of the global financial crisis.

**4.2
CONTEMPORARY
ISSUE**

The subprime lending crisis and reliable reporting

A question currently faced by the accounting profession, particularly in light of the recent mortgage meltdown, is whether to use fair value or historical cost for the reporting of assets and liabilities. It is argued that for accounting information to be useful for decision making, it should embody the two primary qualities of relevance and reliability. Fair value or historical cost, on their own, are not likely to achieve both characteristics. In practice, there seems to be an inherent trade-off between these two characteristics. The information which is most relevant is quite often less reliable, depending upon the nature of the item being measured. The information which is the most reliable usually tends to be that which is less relevant. Perhaps, an integration of the two measurement bases may be necessary. Both the IASB and FASB support the use of fair value and are moving away from historical cost and more towards fair value in the financial reporting standards. This means we are unlikely to go back to strict use of traditional historical cost-based accounting despite the issues we face with fair value accounting.

It is argued that reporting assets and liabilities at their fair value provides more relevant information for investment decisions than historical cost. Under fair value accounting, when there is an active and liquid market for the asset or liability, mark-to-market reporting can be used. This provides extremely relevant information because it requires a downward adjustment when the market value of investments decline, thereby revealing problems more quickly. As an example, the savings and loan crisis may have been avoided had fair value accounting been used. The crisis developed when variable interest rates paid on deposits exceeded the fixed interest rates charged on mortgages. Accounting under historical cost allowed resulting losses to be reported gradually over time, where fair value rules would have required earlier recognition (see Ian Michael, 'Accounting and Financial Stability', Financial Stability Review, June 2004, pp. 118–28). Lastly, use of the lower of cost or market rule does not provide relevant accounting reports when fair value significantly exceeds historical cost.

Fair value certainly provides relevant information for decision making, when the information is also reliable. Reliability may be difficult to achieve when we are dealing with hypothetical transactions that are not objectively measurable. This is the situation we face once we move away from the mark-to-market approach when determining fair value. Determining fair value for securities with no active markets using level 3 inputs is extremely difficult, and may therefore adversely affect the reliability and relevance of financial reports.

It is argued that the lower of cost or market rule could be effectively adapted, making reports both relevant and reliable. When fair values exceed costs by a material amount, information related to increases in the value of assets could be provided in footnotes or pro forma statements. In other words, the reliability and relevance of historical cost financial reports could be enhanced by providing fair value information through footnote disclosures or pro forma statements, while the assets are measured using traditional historical cost. Perhaps, a nice balance, to achieve both greater relevance and greater reliability.

Some financial models indicate that using fair value to report financial instruments at market value leads financial institutions to react to market changes in ways they would not normally act. For example, falling prices in an unstable market may worsen market stability. This is because companies tend to react to falling prices by rushing out to sell their assets before their competitors. In comparison, the use of historical cost information by financial institutions tends to dampen the financial business cycle and as a consequence adds stability to the financial markets. Market stability and the nature of the financial business cycle play a large role in the determination of market prices and therefore impact upon the relevance and reliability of accounting information produced.

Obtaining fair values that are reliable can be elusive, particularly for market based instruments that lack objective substance, such as subprime debt obligations. The move to fair value accounting requires inclusion of more hypothetical transactions in the financial statements, which allowed subprime lenders to recognise income well before it was actually earned or received. (see Kenneth F. Fiek, 'Securitized Profits', Journal of Accountancy, May 2008, pp. 54–60). This increases the risk of overstatement of accrual based income not realised in actual transactions. Zoe-Vonna Palmrose, former deputy chief accountant for professional practice at SEC, sees parallels between the subprime lending debacle in 2007 and the stock market crash of 1929. She noted that fair value accounting was popular in the 1920s but was banned by SEC for a number of decades after the stock market crash in 1929.

In a market bubble, values may be overstated and bubble values will not be realisable if many participants in the market decide to sell those assets at the same time. Consequently, financial statements incorporating fair values of assets and liabilities in unstable or illiquid markets are not likely to be relevant or reliable for the purpose of decision usefulness. This problem can be illustrated in subprime lending. When markets for subprime-backed securities were active, applying the market value at which securities were traded might have appeared reasonable and fair. However, the market for subprime securities was not stable and active for long. In the absence of an active and liquid market, how does one establish assumptions for developing estimates for fair values for delinquent loans in a declining market. It is particularly difficult to determine fair values in a speculative and high risk environment like the subprime lending market. Much of the risk due to deceptive practices used in lending to those who did not have the means to repay, encouraging borrowers to take loans with variable interest rates and securitising mortgage loans to relieve lenders of credit risk. Fair value rules require much judgement when adjusting or modifying initially recorded costs for reporting financial assets, including mortgage-backed instruments. The rules may be viewed as weak or ambiguous. We therefore end up suffering in terms of the compromise to relevance and reliability.

Source: Adapted from Benjamin P Foster & Trimbak Shastri, 'The Subprime lending crisis and reliable reporting', *The CPA Journal*. Reprinted from *The CPA Journal*, April 2010, with permission from the New York State Society of Certified Public Accountant.[4]

Questions

1. In practice, which measurement base, historical cost or fair value, would provide the most relevant and reliable accounting information? Draw on the facts presented in the situation above, as well as your knowledge of the global financial crisis, to justify your response. **J** **K**
2. Discuss the role of market stability and the financial business cycle in determining the relevance and reliability of the accounting information produced. **J** **K**

FAIR VALUE

In recent years there has been a significant paradigm shift in relation to measurement. A paradigm is essentially a school of thought or a way of thinking. When it comes to measurement, there appears to have been a distinct move from historical cost to fair value accounting. Dominant thinking in terms of how items should be measured, in particular assets, has changed significantly in recent years with international harmonisation.

Valuation methods

Fair value is reflected by the current market value of an item. The international accounting standards allow for a number of different valuation techniques depending upon the circumstances and the nature of the item. The three valuation techniques which are commonly used to derive the fair value of an item are outlined below.

- *Market approach.* This approach uses prices and other relevant information generated by market transactions involving identical or comparable items — for example, the quoted market price observed in an active market for the items may be the best indicator of current market value.
- *Cost approach.* In some circumstances an item's cost may be the best indicator of current market value. Cost approach reflects the amount that would be required currently to replace the service capacity of an asset (often referred to as current replacement cost).
- *Income approach.* An approximation of current market value is made by estimating the future cash flows or income and expenses expected to be derived from the item and converting them to determine the current amount of those cash flows or income and expenses.

Arguments for fair value

It can be argued that fair value is more relevant than other measurement approaches. Fair value is a form of current value which reflects what the item is worth in the market today. In other words, it reflects the current market price, the amount that would be received if the item was sold in an active and liquid market or the amount that would be paid/owed if the item was purchased on an active and liquid market. It is easy to see how figures determined using a fair value approach are highly relevant from a decision usefulness perspective.

Fair value can also faithfully represent reality where other measurement approaches cannot. For example, consider a security traded in the financial market. The reality of the capital market is that security values fluctuate on a day to day basis and therefore what the security can be sold for at a particular point in time is a true reflection of the real value of the security. The amount the security was purchased for previously is irrelevant from the perspective of those who hold the security and therefore does not faithfully represent the real value of the asset. Another good example is a biological asset such as a tree. Such an asset changes in nature and transforms over time. The tree can potentially change from a small seedling worth a few dollars into a larger tree which produces fruit and has more aesthetic appeal. The fair value, being the net present value of the future revenue that could be derived from selling the fruit produced by the tree, is therefore a true reflection of the real value of the tree. The amount for which the tree or seeds were purchased many years before in their original state is irrelevant and does not faithfully represent reality.

Another key argument in favour of fair value is the neutral depiction of the accounting information produced, given that fair values are primarily determined using objective market prices. It is however important to note that a market price is not always available. Not all assets and liabilities are traded on an active and liquid market, which means sometimes fair value must be determined by some other means, other than the market price.

Fair value also produces more comparable accounting information. This is because items measured at fair value represent the current value of items at the same point in time — that is, as at the current date or as at a particular reporting date. It may be argued that accounting information produced using fair value is more comparable. Historical cost is quite different in that the value recorded is what was paid for the item on a particular date in the past. Potentially, the value placed on the item may be different if the item is purchased at an earlier or later point in time. This is because the effects of price inflation and other economic factors come in to play. In reality, many entities purchase different assets on different dates, making the accounting information produced under historical cost less comparable.

Many also argue that fair value is more understandable than other measurement bases. It is simple and straightforward in that the fair value of an item is reflected by its current market value; in other words, what the item could be sold for in the market today. However, it could argued that when dealing with an item for which there is no active and liquid market, the concept becomes much more complex. When there is no objective market price available and an estimation of the market value of the item needs to be formed, a more complex world is entered into — involving many assumptions, adjustments, formulas and calculations.

Arguments against fair value

One of the main arguments against fair value is the amount of subjectivity and judgement involved in forming estimations of market value in the absence of an objective market price in an active and liquid market. There are also many practical difficulties associated with forming an estimate of market value when the item is not something which is traded or bought and sold regularly in the market. Calculations for adjustments and internal models used are often complex, costly and time consuming. It may be necessary to bring in experts to carry out valuation of an item. The entity itself may not have the expertise or capacity in terms of time and money to determine what the market value of the item would be.

When reporting items at fair value in the financial statements, it is important to note the value recorded is hypothetical in nature and therefore includes gains and losses which have not necessarily been realised. Recognition of unrealised gains and losses leads to volatility in earnings and the potential for reported information to be misleading to the user. For example, recognition of a large amount of unrealised gains, resulting in a higher reported profit will be viewed as good news by investors and they will be expecting a higher dividend payout. In reality, the actual profit available for distribution may not have changed or it could even be less than what was originally expected and be masked by higher values placed on items valued at fair value. Volatile earnings also have the potential to confuse users of the financial statements.

Many argue that accounting information produced using fair value is less faithfully represented. This is largely due to the subjective nature of the valuation process. If an objective market price is not available for the asset, then management's own judgement and assumptions play a key role in forming an estimate of what the market value of an item would be. As calculations and models become more complex, there is also more room for error. By nature, an estimate is just that, an estimate, so the value placed on an item can never be as accurate as using an actual price obtained in an active and liquid market.

Fair value is by far the most controversial measurement approach. It has been the subject of much debate in recent years. The main reason behind such debate and controversy is the subjective nature of the estimates involved in determining fair value when no active market exists for an item. Management assumptions and judgement play a key role and many argue accounting information produced using this measurement approach is more prone to manipulation. Other issues of controversy include the variability in valuation techniques used between entities and the volatility in earnings which occurs as a consequence of changes in fair value from period to period. There was also a lot of debate around the potentially misleading nature of the earnings figure produced under fair value. Chapter 10 explores fair value measurement in depth.

 ## LO 5 STAKEHOLDERS AND THE POLITICAL NATURE OF ACCOUNTING MEASUREMENT

The *Conceptual Framework* recognises that financial statements are used to satisfy different needs for information. The *Conceptual Framework* identifies the primary users of financial information as existing and potential investors, lenders and other creditors. What is important to note is that users have different and sometimes conflicting needs when it comes to accounting information. We do not live in a perfect world where every need of every user can be satisfied by the preparation of one set of financial statements. The question arises as to how these differing needs of many users are balanced out.

Paragraph OB8 of the *Conceptual Framework* deals with this issue by stating that when developing financial reporting standards, the board will seek to provide the information set that will meet the needs of the maximum number of primary users. While all the information needs of each and every user cannot be met, there are needs common to a number of primary users. One would then assume that the best way to achieve the objective is to target the financial statements toward these common needs of the primary users.

The impact and relevance of measurement to investors and other users of the financial statements is obvious in that measurement is essentially how the amounts which appear in the financial statements are determined. The measurement choices made therefore impact on the quality of accounting information produced via the financial statements. It is crucial that two questions are considered when making choices in relation to measurement approaches in accounting.

1. *What do users really need to know?* Measurement will impact greatly on the delivery of information. The choices made in relation to measurement will determine whether the right (useful) information is delivered and also whether the message to the user is delivered as intended. In other words, whether the meaning derived on the part of the user is appropriate.

2. *How do users influence the measurement approach?* It is important to recognise the potential impact of particular users or stakeholders on measurement and measurement choice. Dominant stakeholders will always have greater influence on the choices made and the approaches taken. How does this impact on the quality and usefulness of accounting information produced from the perspective of less dominant stakeholders?

The main user groups are discussed below to demonstrate the connection between measurement and their information needs.

Existing and potential investors

Existing and potential investors are concerned with the risk inherent in, and the return provided by, their investments. Their main interest is in accounting information which assists them in deciding whether to buy, hold or sell their shares. They are also interested in information that enables them to assess the entity's ability to pay dividends. In order to provide information about the potential value and future viability of the entity, the entity will need to adopt a measurement approach which is forward looking with a focus on current values. It would seem that information about items prepared predominantly using a fair value approach would be most useful from the perspective of investors. This is of course assuming that the many issues associated with fair value have also been considered. In order to provide information about its ability to pay dividends, the entity will need to provide an indication of its distributable profits. Profit is based on a historical cost based approach to measurement which is also important as evidence of the entity's current ability to generate profits.

Lenders and other creditors

Lenders and other creditors are interested in information that enables them to determine whether amounts owing to them will be paid when due. Of particular interest to creditors is the entity's net position — the amount of liabilities it has compared to its assets. Again, measurement becomes very important from a valuation perspective in that creditors are interested in accounting information which reflects the current value of assets and liabilities of the entity, giving an indication of the future viability of the entity. Fair value would seem to be the most useful approach, assuming that items can be reliably measured. Creditors would also be interested in profits made in the shorter term as an indicator of funds available to pay the debts. Profit is essentially calculated based upon an historical cost approach to measurement.

It is interesting to note the need for accounting information prepared under the different measurement approaches in order to satisfy the needs of key stakeholders. In most cases, even a particular stakeholder demonstrates a need for information based on more than one measurement approach. This provides evidence to support the argument that measurement really is complex by nature and needs to be considered in context. There is no one size fits all approach. What is appropriate very much depends upon the entity, its objectives and current circumstances. This reinforces the need for a mixed measurement model. It is also important to acknowledge that measurement choice can be a potential issue where there is a need or desire to manage stakeholders and influence their decisions. The last part of this section will focus on the political aspects of accounting measurement.

The political nature of accounting measurement

Accounting measurement is political in the sense that there are a number of different interest groups involved in accounting regulation through the standard-setting process. Each of these interest groups lobby for and favour a particular accounting treatment or measurement method over other alternatives, often biased or influenced by self-serving objectives. Similarly, when it comes to application of the accounting standards, management are sometimes faced with certain choices. Accounting treatment or choice of measurement method is often left to the discretion of management. What makes accounting measurement so political is the fact that management, as well as regulators and other lobby groups involved in the standard-setting process, are largely motivated by their own self-interests and often act to fulfil self-serving objectives. For example, it can be assumed that most parties and interest groups within the economy would act to maximise their own wealth. Wealth transfers are, to a certain extent, a consequence of choices in accounting measurement and how assets are valued. It could therefore be argued that wealth transfers provide the basis or incentive for decisions made in relation to accounting measurement.

Measurement in accounting has come under the spotlight as a consequence of recent events such as numerous corporate collapses and the global financial crisis. Measurement, particularly fair value, has become the subject of much debate. In many ways, measurement is now viewed through a much more sceptical lens as awareness of the role accounting measurement plays as a tool in the political arena increases. Each interest group or entity wants rules and regulations that allow them to satisfy and influence stakeholders through the information they provide in their financial statements. It is important to recognise that different types of entities are acting to satisfy different needs and are attempting to influence stakeholders in different ways. At the same time, regulators attempt to balance the conflicting interests of all stakeholders in the financial reporting process.

Measurement issues that are political in nature and have been highlighted through events in recent times include:

- the validity and acceptance of use of fair value as a measurement approach in times of economic downturn where an attempt at providing accounting information which was more relevant to users only served to highlight losses. As a result of the operation of the capital market, this led to further economic decline as the issue was exacerbated by unfavourable accounting information being released to the market. The resulting impact on prices was a spiral downwards and market prices which did not really reflect the true market values. The initial objective of relevance was no longer being achieved. This becomes political in the sense that the impacts on wealth within the economy need to be considered. It may be argued that certain types of entities are disadvantaged by the decision to adopt fair value as a measurement method for certain assets. This is because the nature of their asset base and the transactions they undertake means they are more vulnerable to economic downturn and the operation of the capital market.

The fact that use of fair value has revealed the truth, highlighting losses that were masked by different accounting treatment, makes financial reporting a public concern.

- the reliability of accounting information prepared using fair value as the measurement base. Where no active market exists for an item and a market price is unavailable, the amount determined becomes very subjective, as an estimate of market value of an item must be formed and this involves application of discretion and substantial judgement on the part of management. This situation has been blamed in several circumstances for allowing manipulation of the financial statements to occur. Although discretion and judgement are necessary in the absence of an active market for an item, with it comes ample opportunity for the potential manipulation of figures determined under the fair value approach. This issue has been highlighted in the recent corporate collapses and has also surfaced in discussions around the feasibility of tightening or loosening the fair value rules as a consequence of the GFC. It is the complex interactions of individuals within society and the consideration of what motivates them to make particular accounting choices and decisions that make accounting measurement political in nature.

- the political nature of measurement is also highlighted by the fact that much of the commentary on recent events blames accounting measurement in some way. Historical cost is blamed for not indicating potential problems, so fair value is used as an alternative, which is then blamed for highlighting the losses. There is much evidence to suggest that accounting has been the scapegoat for many situations and circumstances which have far reaching impacts on the public and are in the public interest. Players have changed their view and opinion of the appropriateness of the various measurement approaches depending upon current political objectives and what needs to be achieved. The literature is fairly inconsistent in that the views put forward are largely dependent on who is writing the piece and on what issues are currently prevalent in the political arena.

- stakeholders' conflicting interests and the difficult nature of managing such political relationships. The most recent example is the conflict arising between regulators and banks and the extent of lobbying that occurred by banks in the context of the GFC.

- inadequate operation of financial markets, resulting in prices which are not necessarily indicative of market value. In relation to the GFC, agency ratings were a key information source and therefore played a role in the market's determination of price. The fact that ratings agencies were paid by the entity means the ratings given were potentially not reflective of true risk. The whole market mechanism and the validity and accuracy of market prices then fell apart. This created a big issue where fair value was determined by reference to market prices. This highlights the complex interaction of many entities acting in their own self-interest and with different objectives. Contemporary Issue 4.3 examines these objectives.

4.3
CONTEMPORARY ISSUE

Current debates on accounting for financial instruments: perspectives in the aftermath of a crisis

We shouldn't neglect the influence of factors that operate in the field of accounting with the purpose of developing accounting standards according to different interests, starting with political factors and self interests of greed, which as seen in history, are dangerous to ignore. There has been evidence of a defensive historical attitude that the accounting standard setting bodies have had, waiting for manifestation of practices of creative accounting that expose the weaknesses of existing accounting standards, and only afterwards reacting in order to manage the identified gaps within the regulations. The consequence of these reactions was that some of the weaknesses were resolved, but not without corresponding side effects.

Results within the trade literature concerning reactions coming from practitioners indicate existence of a complex and confusing environment where the most 'at home' seem to be financial institutions and corporations that are able to exploit the system through choosing accounting practices that favour them in offering the lowest level of informational transparency, but also making significant pressures on regulatory bodies when they issue 'uncomfortable' regulations. There seems to be a need for structural changes within the accounting standards, but the possibility of guiding these changes in the right direction is significantly diminished through mechanisms of political and corporate lobby. What is now obvious is the fact that the current financial crisis has opened for discussion certain areas within the capital market that are less regulated and controlled, such as mortgage markets. A clear effect of the financial crisis is the rethinking and reforming of financial systems through the introduction of new measurement systems and valuation of financial risks, but also through higher control on behalf of regulatory institutions. We therefore find it appropriate that under normal circumstances, assets should be valued at what they are worth from the market's point of view, the market being the only valid standard of value. On the other hand, we do not know what to do when the market does not function normally.

The banking industry argues that fair value would be irrelevant within inactive markets. This means that fair value accounting would not offer any type of useful information to investors, regarding the true economic value of the concerned derivatives. Nevertheless, the decrease in fair values of those derivatives issued last year is fully correlated with the significance of the default degree in comparison with what was expected at the initial moment of the issuance. Since these fair values have the capacity to estimate the impact of a higher degree of defaults on the future and present earnings generated by these derivatives, we assume that we cannot consider them lacking of significance. Based on these assumptions we consider that a present or future limitation of fair value accounting would just 'hide' current realities, only making the mechanism's effect that has triggered the financial crisis longer.

In a valuator's opinion, one of the positive effects of the current financial crisis is bringing light upon the debates concerning the concept of fair value. From a conceptual point of view, creating a balance sheet that has the ability or that needs to offer a true and fair view of the market value of the entity is a great ideal, while the market is far too complex to be captured by an accounting system. The valuation process involves a high degree of subjectivity, and framing this process by a series of accounting rules could be dangerous. Placing value in the center of accounting standard setting bodies' reasoning may induce some assumptions regarding information being efficiently transmitted within the market, generating securities prices that represent a true and fair reflection of the entities' performance. The financial crisis brings significant doubts concerning the above mentioned association. We can therefore state that we are dealing with a valuation crisis; however at the root of the crisis we actually find the growing complexity of the value creating mechanism, the recurrent dynamic between market value and fundamental value. Last, but not least, amplification of the gap between our own intellectual models concerning value and the new paradigm of value. Fundamental value of an entity mainly depends on how its assets are put into good use; however we cannot ignore the opportunities the entity might hope to have in the future based on position or strategy.

Source: Article by Carmen G Bonaci, Jiri Strouhal, and Dumitru Matis, 'Current debates on accounting for financial instruments: perspectives in the aftermath of a crisis', *Review of Business Research*.[5]

Questions

1. 'The market is far too complex to be captured by an accounting system.' Discuss this statement, providing evidence from the global financial crisis. **J** **K** **SM**

2. Analyse the players involved in the recent debate surrounding fair value and its contribution to the global financial crisis. Discuss how this demonstrates the political nature of accounting measurement. **J** **K** **SM**

WHY MEASUREMENT IS A CONTROVERSIAL ACCOUNTING ISSUE

Measurement is by far the most controversial issue in accounting at present. The purpose of this section is to explore why measurement has become such a controversial accounting issue in recent times. One of the key points of controversy is the potential for inappropriate choices in measurement method or approach. Other points of controversy include the variability in measurement approaches used for similar assets, the political influences on measurement decisions, the subjectivity and discretion involved in determination of some values, and the impact of measurement on achievement of other organisational objectives.

The flexibility embedded within the mixed measurement model allows for choices in terms of the measurement method or approach to be adopted. The logic behind choices offered within the standard is to ensure that an entity is able to apply the best approach which suits its current circumstances to provide the most relevant and useful accounting information. A one-size-fits-all measurement approach would most likely compromise the quality and usefulness of accounting information produced. The problem lies in the fact that management may not always make appropriate choices. There is scope for management to make inappropriate choices when determining its approach to accounting measurement for purposes other than providing the most useful and relevant information to users. This may lead to a reduction in the quality of accounting information produced and could also be detrimental to the users' decision-making process.

Some of the most controversial standards, such as those governing accounting for intangibles and biological assets, have resulted in variability in the measurement approaches adopted for similar assets. Controversy has risen over instances where the same or similar assets have been measured differently by different entities. This has sparked huge debate over the accuracy and reliability of the values determined, and such variability also impacts on the comparability of accounting information.

There are a number of political influences on measurement in accounting. Guidance in the form of accounting standards is the product of a number of parties acting in their own self-interest — those with greater power having more influence on the standard-setting process. Accounting measurement has come under the spotlight in recent times, mainly due to the issues and concerns raised by major players in society.

Measurement can also be quite subjective. Most measurement approaches are subjective to a certain extent. Measurement approaches and the values derived are subjective where amounts are not determined by reference to actual transactions or market prices. Subjectivity increases where the amounts determined involve estimation or judgement. There is some element of subjectivity associated with all measurement approaches; however, fair value and net present value may be considered to be the most subjective. They both involve a considerable amount of estimation, with a number of choices and assumptions left at the discretion of management.

How items are measured may also influence the extent to which an entity achieves its objectives. Adoption of different measurement approaches will result in different impacts on profit. Profit is likely to be the main objective or incentive for any business entity. However, most entities also have a number of social and environmental objectives which they attempt to fulfil. The question then is whether measurement choices that result in higher profits will also encourage development and fulfilment of social and environmental aspects of the entity. There have been cases in the past where measurement choices made to achieve higher reported profits have actually worked against the entity as they have been to the detriment of the natural environment. The challenge is to achieve high profits and social and environmental objectives congruently.

LO 7 CURRENT MEASUREMENT CHALLENGES
Green assets and other sustainability issues

There are numerous measurement challenges associated with accounting for social and environmental aspects of an entity. In particular, there are many measurement challenges associated with accounting for green assets. Three key issues which need to be considered from a social and environmental perspective are:

- What needs to be measured and accounted for?
- How can the discretion and subjectivity associated with the estimation of values be managed?
- What are the consequences associated with accounting for social and environmental aspects of the entity?

One of the big questions is in determining what should be accounted for from a social and environmental perspective. This issue in part arises as a result of the *entity concept*. The fact that environmental cost and impacts often extend beyond the boundary of the entity causes a real problem for accountants. How can accountants measure something for which no cost has been incurred or for which knowledge of or control over the potential impact is unknown. There has been much debate over how or in fact whether an entity should measure and account for social and environmental issues. In the absence of actual transactions, an inability to access appropriate data to form an accurate estimate, and a lack of knowledge and control over the possible impacts, measurement in this area has certainly provided a challenge for accountants.

However, sustainability issues are important from a stakeholder perspective. Many stakeholders in the financial reporting process have a keen interest in the extent of sustainability issues and also in the financial impact of these issues. Some stakeholders are more interested in the financial impact (shareholders/potential investors), while other stakeholders are more interested in the nature of the sustainability issues and the potential impact on the environment (environmental groups). What can be reasonably concluded here is that the provision of sustainability information and the inclusion of monetary values representing costs and estimated impacts should be included in an entity's financial report as they are relevant to stakeholders and user decision making.

Burritt and Schaltegger argue the importance of the development of sustainability accounting and reporting and state that the emphasis should be on improving management decision making.[6] This argument has an internal focus in that the priority of preparation of accounting information is on its usefulness to managers to assist them in improving the internal processes and performance of the entity. A need arises for sustainability measurement and reporting whether it stems from inside the organisation, a need to fulfil external accountability, or from a decision usefulness perspective. How items are measured will in a sense depend upon the entity's reporting objective.

The question then is how to determine costs associated with sustainability activities and estimate the likely impacts arising as a consequence of environmental and sustainability issues. For accounting purposes, relevant items need to be measured in dollar terms. This process can be quite subjective and involves extensive professional judgement and discretion on the part of management. For example, upon implementation of a sustainability strategy, should the impact in terms of the future benefits to be derived from the strategy be recognised as an asset or should only the cost be incurred? If an asset is to be recognised, how should its value be measured? The value could be measured using the cost of implementing the sustainability strategy. What exactly would be included as part of this cost? It may also be measured using net present value or fair value. How exactly would fair value or net present value be measured? Does it really make sense? Is it feasible to account for sustainability in this way?

The impact of measurement choice on both the environment and the financial statements needs to be considered. Depending upon how much market conditions change over time, potential exists for fluctuations in profits as a consequence of measuring sustainability activities and incorporating them into the financial statements. Information may become misleading and not convey the appropriate message to users if measurement bases are inappropriate or if the activities cannot be measured. Care also is required to ensure that a focus on measurement from a profit perspective is not to the detriment of the environment. Environmental or sustainability objectives may not be fulfilled if focus is on measurement for the purpose of reporting for profits and growth. Environmental objectives must be considered in making decisions about measurement. The goal is to develop a measurement strategy which achieves both environmental objectives and profit or growth objectives congruently.

It is important that approaches to sustainability measurement and accounting are developed further in order to make sustainability more than an awareness building exercise. According to Burritt and Schaltegger our approach needs to develop sustainability accounting as a provider of solutions and focus on tools which support decision making by different actors, managers and stakeholders in diverse circumstances. There are many deficiencies in our current conventional accounting systems. They are unable to cope with such issues and the matter of accounting for sustainability is something which needs to be carefully considered moving forward.[7]

The environment and natural resource issues have become paramount from a *political perspective*. Rout describes how concerns about energy consumption and the extent to which national forests should be used for timber production or protected wilderness areas are examples of continuing issues.[8] Environmental problems such as pollution and global warming are also highlighted by Rout as receiving much attention and ranking high on the political agenda. There are many challenges associated with accurate measurement of natural assets as a result of the inadequacy of current accounting practice. Limitations include inconsistent treatment of depreciation on artificial and natural assets, and inadequate recognition of degradation of the environment. According to Rout, these limitations or issues result in misleading information, giving the false impression of an increase in income while natural wealth is actually reducing. Rout provides evidence as to some of the key issues associated with green assets. These are:

- effects of environmental protection on economic growth. There has been much debate over the impact of environmental protection on the economy and employment. Studies have shown that placing statutory limits on pollution reduces economic growth.
- distributional effects of natural resource policies. The impact of such policies falls more heavily on some industries or income groups than others. For example, improved water favours higher income groups since most improvement is in urban areas.
- links between trade and natural resource policies. It is important to consider what is going on in other countries.

Measurement of green assets is quite complex and, due to consideration of the issues discussed above, is quite political in nature. Limitations in available data and the controversy associated with varying measurement approaches make this area even more challenging.

Intangible assets

Intangible assets are initially measured at cost. What constitutes cost however is different depending upon whether the intangible was acquired separately, acquired as part of a business combination, or was internally generated. The complexity and variation which exists in terms of how intangible assets are measured on recognition is demonstrated in table 4.2.

TABLE 4.2 Recognising and measuring the cost of intangible assets		
Separate acquisition	Acquisition as part of a business combination	Internally generated
Purchase price *plus* costs directly attributable to preparing the asset for its intended use	Fair value at acquisition date Reflects market participants' expectations at the acquisition date about future economic benefits embodied in the asset that will flow to the entity	Sum of expenditure incurred from date when intangible asset first meets criteria for recognition Includes all directly attributable costs necessary to create, produce and prepare the asset for operating in the manner intended by management

After initial recognition, the entity may choose to subsequently measure the intangible asset using the cost model or the revaluation model. Under the cost model, the asset is carried at cost less any accumulated amortisation and any accumulated impairment losses. Under the revaluation model, the asset is carried at fair value at the date of revaluation less any subsequent accumulated amortisation and any subsequent accumulated impairment losses. Fair value is determined by reference to an active market. If there is no active market for the asset, the asset cannot be revalued and will be carried at cost less any accumulated amortisation and impairment losses.

Measurement of intangible assets is a challenge for both preparers and auditors of financial statements. While such intangibles are acquired separately or internally generated, measurement is cost based and relatively straightforward. However, valuation of intangible assets acquired in a business combination at fair value can be quite messy. Issues arising are outlined below. These issues were highlighted by Crane and Dyson.[9]

- It is difficult to measure the fair value of assets lacking physical substance. This is because the item is not usually something that can be bought and sold in an active market. Such assets are unique in nature and represent something that we cannot see or touch.
- Estimates of fair values are very subjective and are based on the methodology and assumptions applied during the valuation process.
- Most intangibles are difficult to measure because they do not have an active market with readily observable prices for the specific or similar assets which means we cannot use the market approach. A cost approach may also be inappropriate because many intangible assets are unique and there may be little reliable information available on the costs of developing an acceptable substitute. As a consequence, measurement is often based on an income approach, which reflects the entity's own assumptions, making it less reliable. There is much difficulty associated with obtaining supportable fair value measurements.
- There is a risk of earnings management as a result of the use of unsupportable fair value measures.

The issues noted above stem from the attempt to use fair value to measure a type of asset, the nature of which does not really fit or work with the concept of fair value. Use of fair value has its merits in terms of relevance, but when it comes to intangible assets, determining an accurate and reliable measurement of fair value presents a real challenge.

Water assets

Responsibility for developing reporting and assurance standards for water resides with the National Water Accounting Standards Board (WASB). This board operates as an advisory board to the Australian Bureau of Meteorology (BOM). Chalmers, Godfrey and Potter describe the current state of water reporting and accounting in Australia. They note that the WASB currently focuses on volumetric reports and wants to become more involved with the Australian Accounting Standards Board (AASB) and the Auditing and Assurance Standards Board (AUASB).[10] (This article is reproduced in chapter 2 of this book as part of case study 2.2.) The idea is to work together, where appropriate, in an effort to produce the highest quality standards and reports while aiming to avoid duplication of effort and conflicts of roles. This may include referring to relevant existing standards, rather than producing stand-alone standards.

It should be noted that the process employed by the WASB is similar to that undertaken by the main standard-setting bodies when developing financial accounting standards. BOM and WASB engage in a consultative due process and ultimate approval of Australian water accounting standards will reside with the Australian Parliament. This process is underway with the WASB issuing its first preliminary accounting standard entitled *Exposure Draft of Australian Water Accounting Standard 1: Preparation and Presentation of General Purpose Water Accounting Reports*. Further information on water accounting standards can be found at www.bom.gov.au/water/wasb.

It has been highlighted by Chalmers, Godfrey and Potter that water accounting standards are being developed in several countries, with no single body taking responsibility for international standards.[11] There are some questions that need to be explored here. Given recent efforts in regard to harmonisation of financial reporting standards, should the same path be followed in regard to water accounting standards? Would this even be possible given the nature of the asset being dealt with and the differences that exist between countries? Is it more appropriate to set the standards at a national level? Will the standards become mandatory for water reporting entities? Water accounting is currently voluntary, except for those required to provide information to the BOM under the *Water Act 2007*. Given the rising level of public interest in water management, voluntary preparation of general purpose water accounting reports is likely to increase rapidly over the next decade. This view is supported by Chalmers, Godfrey and Potter who recognise that these developments are an important step towards the sustainable solutions we are looking for to address climate change.[12]

Waterlines in Plummer and Tower summarises key issues which demonstrate a need to measure and account for water.[13] Some of these are a need for a better understanding of the relationship between water and the environment, a need for better knowledge to jointly manage surface water and groundwater, to address the over-allocation and/or overuse of water resources, different interpretations of what is meant by a sustainable level, and significant improvement in monitoring and compliance of water resources, just to name a few. There is certainly a need to manage this limited natural resource. In order to manage this resource or asset better, more knowledge and moving forward the implementation of water accounting and production of general purpose water accounting reports should assist in providing adequate information to make appropriate resourcing decisions.

Measurement and valuation

There are a number of issues associated with the measurement or valuation of water as an asset. Some of the key issues are outlined on the next page.

Wide range of stakeholders

Chalmers and Godfrey in Plummer and Tower identify the key stakeholder groups for water as:

- water resource and infrastructure providers — for example, water authorities and the natural environment
- recipients of water and water services — for example, agriculture, industry and households
- regulatory overseeing functions — for example, government authorities and policy makers.[14]

There is a wide range of stakeholders in water, all with diverse interests and differing information needs. This impacts not only on what items should be reported but also on how these items should be measured. When measuring and accounting for water assets, economic factors as well as environmental and social factors need to be considered. This is emphasised by Godfrey, in Plummer and Tower, who argues that for appropriate policy making to occur, water must be accounted for broadly, encompassing economic, environmental and social elements.[15]

How should value be determined?

A number of issues surrounding determination of value have been raised in the literature. Should scientific or volume style measures be used? How should monetary values be determined? Is it appropriate to develop some sort of water trading scheme and, if so, how would appropriate pricing be determined? The issue of pricing water has become quite controversial. Plummer and Tower discuss how, if water is priced too low, water is wasted and if it is priced too high, major welfare inequalities are created.[16] This could potentially lead to serious social turmoil. Are other techniques which focus more on specific inflows and outflows better for determining monetary value? It is difficult to establish what would give a reliable measurement of the value of water. At the moment, methods and procedures used are inconsistent and fairly ad hoc, with a number of different approaches being used across countries.

Water quality and recognition

Upon examining the recognition criteria for a water asset, the question arises whether for *future benefit to be derived* from the asset, should the water be of a particular level of quality? Does the quality of the water then determine what sort of future benefit will be derived and by whom? How will the water quality be determined? Will this impact on the decision as to what the most appropriate measurement approach would be? This is definitely an area where science and accounting start to collide and become interwoven. Scientific issues such as water quality inevitably influence the decisions made from an accounting perspective because there is a connection to value. This is an area which needs to be explored further.

Water is a limited natural resource which needs to be managed. It is therefore appropriate that it is given value and accounted for in the same way as any other asset. Resources are managed better when they have a value placed on them and that value means something. At this stage, there is no question over whether water should be measured and reported. The questions lie in the complexities of *what* exactly should be reported and *how* the items reported should be measured.

Summary

Analyse the concept of measurement in the context of financial reporting and demonstrate an understanding of its many benefits and limitations
- Measurement in an accounting context refers to the way in which the dollar amounts to be included in the financial statements are determined.
- Measurement is important from a decision usefulness perspective and the measurement choices made have an impact on the quality of accounting information produced.
- Evidence suggests that there is a need for accounting measurement but there are a number of issues and problems which also need to be acknowledged.

Describe the standard setters' approach to measurement and evaluate different measurement approaches
- A mixed measurement model approach to standard setting is followed. A number of accounting standards incorporate a number of different measurement approaches, while a particular measurement approach may also offer a number of choices in how a value may be determined. This is necessary to cater for the unique circumstances of each entity and also to cater for changes in economic circumstances over time.
- Key measurement approaches include historical cost, current and replacement cost, fair value, net present value and deprival value.

Evaluate the impact of measurement choice on the quality of accounting information
- There are a number of factors to consider in determining which measurement approach is most appropriate. Management choice in terms of their approach to measurement in certain circumstances can also be explained by these factors and influences.
- Choice of measurement approach impacts on the quality of accounting information produced. For example, depending on the nature of the item being measured, fair value may provide more relevant information than the other measurement approaches.

Explain the controversial nature of fair value as a measurement approach and consider the arguments for and against a shift toward fair value under the accounting standards
- Fair value is reflected by the market value of an item. There are a number of ways in which the market value of an item can be measured.
- As a consequence a number of arguments for and against the use of fair value have been highlighted in recent debate.
- The controversial nature of fair value measurement has become evident in recent events such as the global financial crisis.

 **Explain the political nature of accounting measurement by developing an understanding of the different stakeholders in the financial reporting process**

- There are many different stakeholders who have an interest in how items are measured. The competing interests of different stakeholders makes accounting measurement both political and controversial.

 **Describe the issues which contribute to the controversial nature of accounting measurement**

- Measurement is by far the most controversial issue in accounting at present. One of the key points of controversy is the opportunity for inappropriate choices in measurement method or approach.
- Other points of controversy include variability in measurement approaches used for similar assets, political influences on measurement decisions, the subjectivity and discretion involved in determination of some values, and the impact of measurement on achievement of other organisational objectives.

 Analyse current measurement challenges faced by the accounting profession with particular reference to environmental sustainability, green assets, intangible assets and water assets

- Accountants face a number of current measurement challenges. The most significant challenge is how to cope with measurement in the context of accounting for green assets and other environmental and sustainability issues.
- Another significant challenge lies in the measurement issues and controversy surrounding how intangible assets are accounted for.
- One of the biggest challenges being faced at present is how to measure and account for water as a limited natural resource with a view to sustainability.

Review questions

1. Define measurement in the context of accounting and financial reporting.
2. Why is measurement so important in accounting?
3. Discuss the current approach to measurement adopted by standard setters. Why have they adopted such an approach? What are the issues and problems associated with this approach?
4. Explain the arguments for and against using historical cost as a measurement base.
5. Explain the difference between current and replacement costs.
6. Explain the arguments for and against using fair value as a measurement base.
7. What role does estimation and judgement play in accounting measurement? Discuss with particular reference to present value and deprival value.
8. Identify factors that may influence the choice of measurement approach. Discuss how the measurement approach adopted impacts on the quality of accounting information produced.
9. Why has measurement become such a controversial accounting issue in recent times?
10. Discuss the political aspects of accounting measurement.
11. In your own words, explain what different stakeholders want from financial statements. Assess the impact of measurement on the extent to which accountants are able to fulfil stakeholder needs.

Application questions

4.1 Obtain the annual reports of three companies in the same industry (usually available from company websites) and consider the items included in property, plant and equipment. Answer the following questions.

(a) What range of measures is used to determine amounts for these items in the reports of the individual companies? Do you think it is valid to add the items, given the measures used? How would you interpret the total amount for property, plant and equipment in the financial statements?

(b) Compare the measures used by the different companies for similar items. Are there any inconsistencies in how similar items are measured by the different companies? **J** **K** **SM**

4.2 Examine the requirements for measuring financial instruments in AASB 139/IAS 39 *Financial Instruments: Recognition and Measurement*. What measures are used to determine amounts for these items? Do you think it is necessary to use different measurement bases for different types of financial instruments? Justify your response. **J** **K**

4.3 Examine the requirements for measuring assets at fair value in AASB 138/IAS 38 *Intangible Assets*.

(a) How can fair value be determined under this standard?

(b) What impact would the differences in the methods allowed to determine fair values have on the financial reports? In particular, consider the potential impact on reported profits. **J** **K** **AS**

4.4 Examine the requirements for measuring assets at fair value in AASB 141/IAS 41 *Agriculture*.

(a) How can fair value be determined under this standard?

(b) What impact would the differences in the methods allowed to determine fair values have on the financial reports? In particular, consider the potential impact on reported profits. **J** **K** **AS**

4.5 Do you think the requirement for an active market should be mandatory when measuring at fair value? What problems can occur when determining fair value of an item in the absence of an active and liquid market? Provide examples to justify your response. **J** **K**

4.6 The following information is provided about a particular machine used by a company in its operations. The machine is technological in nature and new models are coming out all the time. The machine originally cost $80 000 and it would cost $140 000 now to replace this machine. The company expects to receive $112 000 (discounted to present value) in cash inflows from using this machine over the next five years. If we were to sell it now, the machine would bring in $60 000. Consider the decision usefulness of accounting information produced when using each of the above figures as a measure of the value of the machine. In particular, consider usefulness from the perspective of the following stakeholders:

(a) Shareholders

(b) Creditors

(c) Employees. **J** **K**

4.7 Obtain the annual reports of two companies in different industries. Assess the decision usefulness of the accounting information contained within these reports from the perspective of the following stakeholders. In your response include an explanation of how the measurement approaches adopted have impacted on the usefulness of the information.

(a) Shareholders
(b) Managers
(c) Government. **J** **K** **SM**

4.8 Obtain the annual reports of two companies in the forestry industry (usually available from company websites) and consider the items included in biological assets. Answer the following questions.

(a) What range of measures is used to determine amounts for these items in the reports of the individual companies? Do you think it is valid to add the items, given the measures used? How would you interpret the total amount for biological assets in the financial statements?

(b) Compare the measures used by the different companies for similar items. Are there any inconsistencies in how similar items are measured by the different companies? **J** **K** **SM**

4.9 Find a current discussion paper or proposal on the IASB website. Discuss the measurement issues raised in the paper and examine the importance of resolving these issues from a standard-setting perspective. **J** **K** **SM**

4.10 Find the comment letters received on a current proposal or discussion paper on the IASB website and answer the following questions.

(a) Have any of the comment letters referred to measurement issues?

(b) Identify the key stakeholder groups. Establish whether there is agreement or disagreement within these groups and between the different groups, as to the appropriate measurement to be used.

(c) Are there any major concerns in relation to measurement? Do you agree or disagree with the comments made? **J** **K** **SM**

4.1 CASE STUDY

Taking account of water

By Matthew Egan and Geoff Frost

We have been hearing for some time that the Murray-Darling Basin (MDB) is sick. For too long agriculture and industry have squeezed more water out of the creeks, rivers, billabongs and lakes within this network than it can sustainably supply. The challenges are interesting ones for accountants to consider. Put simply, we need to develop a balance sheet and a movements statement for this system and ensure that an ecologically sensible net surplus can be maintained from one period to the next.

The Murray-Darling Basin is one of Australia's largest draining divisions, covering one-seventh of the country. Around 3 million people in Australia are directly dependent on its water, and 85 per cent of all irrigation takes place in the basin, supporting an industry worth more than A$9 billion a year.

Through the National Water Initiative, the Australian government is currently working on initiatives that seek an ecologically sensible net surplus. We explore the objective and potential for one particular initiative. In January 2009, the Australian Competition and Consumer Commission (ACCC) released a position paper, 'Water change rules for water planning and management charges'. These water planning and management (WPM) charges are one of three groups of water charges that the Australian government proposes should be levied against water users in the basin. The purpose of these three new proposed water charges as stated on the ACCC's website is:

> Water charge rules applied consistently across the basin will facilitate the efficient functioning of water markets by removing distortions to trade and by sending signals to water users about efficient investment in water infrastructure assets.

Currently authorities apply a variety of inconsistent charges to water users. The definition of WPM provided is very broad and requires the water authorities to determine their administrative, planning and management costs in providing water. The position paper argues that a user pays approach should then be adopted to fully recover these WPM costs. Furthermore, the paper argues that detailed disclosures of these authority's WPM costs and methodology used to determine WPM user charges should also be provided. Together, it is argued, these two initiatives will promote sustainability.

User pays? We've heard this one many times before. However, institutionalised low water user charges in Australia reflect a traditional emphasis on the 'public good' nature of water. As early as 1970, the Senate select committee on water pollution concluded that water pollution was directly attributable to 'the lack of an effective pricing system'. In the 1990s, under the badge of new public management and increased competition, the former Industry Commission and the Council of Australian Governments in their water reform agreement also explicitly supported a user-pays approach. Now the argument has apparently become one of sustainability. Yet none of these efforts have succeeded because of ingrained concern for the public-good nature of water. So what is it about this sustainability dilemma that drives us to reinvestigate a user pays model here? How exactly can that market driven solution contribute to sustainability? If water authorities are seeking to fully recover costs, user charges may become unreasonable, especially given that the key industry impacted is agriculture, one that we otherwise expect to maintain low prices. What about inefficiencies from one authority to another?

From an accounting perspective, the proposed disclosure is also interesting. How exactly does the Australian government expect that disclosing the detail of the water authority's WPM costs and the methodologies for calculating them, will impact the decision making of water users? The ACCC document argues that it will increase transparency, which is undoubtedly true. However, they also argue that water users will use those disclosures to 'assess the way cost recovery arrangements meet other basin water charging objectives such as giving effect to user pays, and promoting greater efficiency and sustainability of water use'.

Why do users need to understand the charges they are required to pay and how the charges relate to the costs of activities particularly given the seasonal uncertainty of environmental assets? Is there a consistent standard relationship between cost and use across the various seasons, and how in particular is it expected that the disclosure of such information will facilitate sustainable decisions up and down the MDB? Aiming for sustainability is important but is any of this going to be an effective tool in that process?

These proposals are not radical in terms of a policy shift. This position paper re-badges the old user-pays argument, this time as a solution to sustainability. It has never been implemented in the water sector in the past so will it work now? Certainly any inconsistency of water charges is not efficient and should be redressed. However, pursuing a full user-pays approach for all water planning and management charges introduces an unprecedented public sector pricing policy that may have adverse impacts on agricultural produce prices and local communities. With the global financial crisis these proposals are undoubtedly becoming increasingly unpalatable.

The key ecological problem in the MDB is the water available is insufficient to meet the demands of all agricultural and urban uses as well as the needs of the environment. The primary solution must therefore include better seasonal measurement of the available volume of water disaggregated by the individual river systems contributing to the basin. This could be coupled with a logical mechanism to determine how much water, in that season, should then be made available for industrial and urban uses. The current development of a national water accounting framework through the water accounting development committee can go a long way towards providing this information. The provision of timely data on the quantum of water flowing through each river contributing to the MDB is vital. But will governments respond to that data appropriately and make the tougher decisions about reducing allocations appropriately?

In the meantime, the ACCC's 'Water change rules for water planning and management charges' position paper is poorly conceived and tacks on a requirement for disclosures that are unlikely to be of any critical use in sustainability decision making.

Source: Article by Matthew Egan and Geoff Frost, 'Taking account of water', *InTheBlack*.[17]

Questions
1. Is it appropriate to place a dollar value on water? Justify your response. **J**
2. In the case above, what is actually measured and how is it measured? **K**
3. What are the potential issues associated with measurement of water? **J** **K**
4. Discuss whether such information is decision useful from the perspective of various stakeholders. **J**
5. What can we expect to achieve through accounting for water? Explain the connection to sustainability decision making. **J** **K**

**4.2
CASE
STUDY**

CMG Worldwide: intangible assets

For four decades, this licensing agency has managed, protected, and marketed the valuable intellectual property rights of celebrity personalities.

James Dean once said, 'If a man can bridge the gap between life and death, if he can live on after he's dead, then maybe he was a great man.' Fifty-five years after his death, the celebrity of James Dean lives on with the same strength he had in life.

Part of that ability comes from actions taken behind the scenes to ensure the James Dean name carried the same merit it has from the start. In the business of managing, protecting, and marketing the valuable intellectual property fight of celebrities, CMG Worldwide has spent the last 40 years ensuring that as generations discover the power behind Dean and other famous celebrities, both living and deceased, the cult of personality is not compromised.

'The most valuable *asset* to celebrities is the goodwill associated with their name and with them,' said Mark Roesler, chairman, founder, and CEO of CMG Worldwide. 'That goodwill is an *intangible asset*, and it's important to protect and manage it, not only right now, but also in the future.'

CMG Worldwide's sports portfolio of clients includes legends such as Babe Ruth, Jackie Robinson, and Lou Gehrig; retired greats like Jim Palmer, Carl Erskin, and White Ford; and current professional athletes. Its entertainment portfolio includes the families of Marilyn Monroe, James Dean, Ingrid Bergman, Bette Davis, and Bettie Page and current celebrities such as Pamela Anderson. In addition, the company represents musicians such as Chuck Berry, Ella Fitzgerald, and Billie Holiday.

But don't let its portfolio confuse you. Although CMG Worldwide works with celebrities, Roesler said the concept behind the company's services is similar to protecting any other brand. 'If you're Gucci or Louis Vuitton, the way your brand is perceived, the way you protect your brand, the way you market it, and the way you position it in the marketplace is very important,' he said. 'It's the same idea for our clients.'

Lawful practices

Now in its fourth decade, CMG Worldwide continues to differentiate itself in the licensing and marketing industry by working exclusively with celebrity personalities. To protect the rights of its clientele, the company developed a legal division to serve as a foundation for its other departments.

'We're often involved in litigation to protect these valuable rights, and that ability distinguishes us from other people,' said Roesler. 'Over the decades, we've been involved in significant cases that resulted in landmark decisions for different famous personalities. That's always been a very important component of what we do.'

CMG Worldwide was a part of litigation involving Major League Baseball, which eventually granted the right for retired players to be shown in their team uniforms while endorsing a product or service. The company also went to bat for the family of James Dean when Warner Bros. attempted to claim ownership of the star's name because he was under contract at the time of his passing.

'Whether it's Dale Earnheardt, Michael Jackson, or any other celebrity that passes away prematurely, all of a sudden you're faced with a whole new frontier: immortality,' Roesler said. 'How do you address those issues? We have to look at future generations and address issues such as what we need to do to get the appropriate amount of protection for our clients, and we have to do these things quickly.'

CMG Worldwide also deals with legal issues pertaining to estate taxes, which Roesler said require the type of long-term experience his employees have. 'There isn't room for someone to learn as they go,' he said. 'We encounter a number of issues every day, and we're ready to handle them.'

Web of power

CMG Worldwide looks after the intellectual property rights of a variety of celebrities such as Pamela Anderson, Ivana Trump, Elvira, and Bette Davis. And although Ms. Davis isn't here to see it, her personality has evolved along with the times.

'The online presence of our various personalities is very important,' said Roesler. 'The fact that they're famous automatically fuels people with a need to have as much information as possible. We look at their official website as the vehicle through which we communicate to the public.'

Social outlets such as MySpace and Facebook provide alternative venues for fans to post information about their favourite personalities. It also gives CMG Worldwide a chance to share any new information that may have surfaced.

The company also uses the web to offer a 24/7 service to licensees interested in working with a particular brand. On each of its client's websites, CMG Worldwide has step-by-step instructions for licensees to learn the requirements and guidelines before proceeding. With more than 4000 licensees working with it at any time, it appears CMG Worldwide has the right idea.

'When you consider the business we're in with most of our clients, we need to ensure people can access these websites at any time,' Roesler said. 'It's as important to be as user friendly as we can.'

Down the road

When looking ahead, Roesler expects CMG Worldwide's client list to continue to grow. He also expects the company's work with copyrights to become a larger part of its business. 'There are a number of collections we're working with on the copyright front,' he said.

But overall, CMG Worldwide will keep its sites on managing valuable intellectual property rights, such as with famous landmarks like the state of New York's program, 'I Love New York.' 'It isn't like a grocery store where we're selling something you can pick up and feel,' he said.

'Whether it's recordings, speeches, artwork, photographs, or rights of publicity, we're here to make sure celebrities maintain the value of their *intangible assets* and the ability to generate revenue.'

Source: CMG Worldwide: intangible assets, *Retail Merchandiser*.[18]

Questions

1. What is an intangible asset? Describe the nature of intangible assets that might be associated with celebrity personalities. **K**
2. Explain how we might measure such assets under AASB 138/IAS 38 *Intangible Assets*. **K** **AS**
3. What are the practical difficulties in measuring an asset of this kind? **J** **K**

Additional readings

AASB 116 *Property, Plant and Equipment*

AASB 138 *Intangible Assets*

AASB 139 *Financial Instruments: Recognition and Measurement*

AASB 141 *Agriculture*

International Accounting Standards Board (IASB) 2010, *Conceptual Framework for Financial Reporting*.

Laux, C & Leuz, C 2009, 'The crisis of fair-value accounting: Making sense of the recent debate', *Accounting, Organizations & Society*, vol. 34, no. 6–7, pp. 826–34.

Water Accounting Standards Board 2010, *Exposure Draft of Australian Water Accounting Standard 1: Preparation and Presentation of General Purpose Water Accounting Reports*.

End notes

1. International Accounting Standards Board & Financial Accounting Standards Board 2010, *Conceptual Framework — Joint Project of the IASB and FASB*, project information page, Norwalk, 23 November, www.fasb.org.
2. Beaver, WH & Demski JS 1979, 'The Nature of income measurement', *The Accounting Review*, vol. 54, no. 1, pp. 38–46.
3. Whittington, G 2010, 'Measurement in financial reporting', *Abacus*, vol. 46, no. 1, pp. 104–10.
4. Foster, BP & Shastri, T 2010, 'The subprime lending crisis and reliable reporting', *The CPA Journal*, vol. 80, iss. 4, pp. 20–5.
5. Bonaci, CG, Strouhal, J & Matis D 2010, 'Current debates on accounting for financial instruments: perspectives in the aftermath of a crisis', *Review of Business Research*, vol. 10, no. 2.
6. Burritt, RL & Schaltegger, S 2010, 'Sustainability accounting and reporting: fad or trend?', *Accounting, Auditing and Accountability Journal*, vol. 23, no. 7, pp. 829–46.
7. ibid.
8. Rout, H 2010, 'Green Accounting: Issues and Challenges', *The IUP Journal of Managerial Economics*, vol. 8, no. 3, pp. 46–60.
9. Crane, M & Dyson, R 2009, 'Risks in applying the new business combination guidance to intangible assets', *The CPA Journal*, vol. 79, no. 1.
10. Chalmers, K, Godfrey, J & Potter, B 2009, 'What's new in water and carbon accounting', *Charter*, vol. 80, iss. 8, pp. 20–2.
11. ibid.
12. ibid.
13. Plummer, J & Tower, G 2010, 'No accounting for water: conflicting business and science viewpoints', *International Business and Economics Research Journal*, vol. 9, no. 9, pp. 65–76.
14. ibid.
15. ibid.
16. ibid.
17. Egan, M & Frost, G 2009, 'Taking account of water', *InTheBlack*, vol. 79, iss. 6, pp. 51–2.
18. Anonymous 2010, 'CMG Worldwide: intangible assets', *Retail Merchandiser*, vol. 50, iss. 3, pp. 74–7.

5 Theories in accounting

LEARNING
OBJECTIVES

After studying this chapter, you should be able to:

1 evaluate how theories can enhance our understanding of accounting practice

2 identify the types of theories used in accounting

3 explain the general tenets of positive accounting theory and examine how it explains accounting practice and disclosures

4 explain institutional theory and examine how it explains organisational structures

5 explain legitimacy theory and examine how it explains accounting disclosure practice

6 explain stakeholder theory and examine how it prescribes and explains accounting disclosure practice

7 explain contingency theory and examine how it prescribes and explains accounting disclosure practice

8 outline the different decisions made by accounting practitioners.

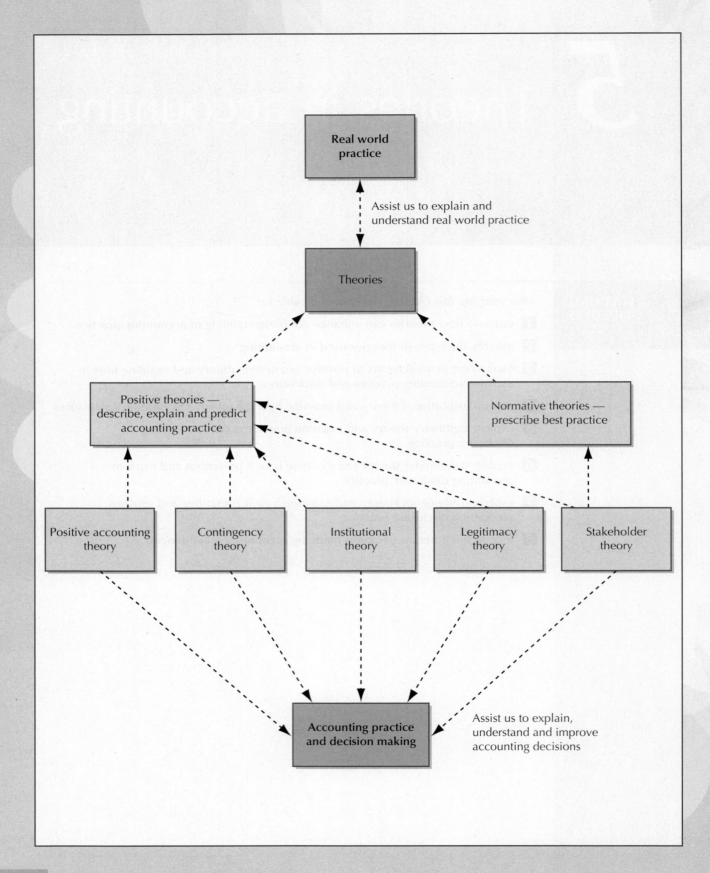

In order to understand the range of decisions that an accountant is required to make, how accounting systems are integrated into an organisation, and demands for accounting information, it is useful to investigate theories which can assist us in these endeavours. What value a theory can offer in attempting to understand accounting practice is initially discussed. We then look at the different types of theories you will encounter, and introduce some theories that are currently used to explain or understand accounting decision making and practice. Finally, how these theories can help to understand accounting decisions from the perspective of preparers of accounting information is examined.

LO 1 WHAT VALUE DOES THEORY OFFER?

Theories are constantly used in the world around us. Builders, engineers and architects rely on structural engineering and mathematical theories in building design and development. Structural theories are based on physical laws and research which explain the structural performance of materials. We observe the outcomes of these theories in the construction of buildings, roads, tunnels and bridges. Governments use monetary and economic theories to formulate and cost policies or when setting taxes. These theories relate to the effect of expenditure or taxes on inflation and the national debt, as well as social justice considerations such as unemployment.

The Reserve Bank of Australia also relies on economic theories to construct monetary policy for the financial system. We see the result of economic theories when the Reserve Bank changes interest rates and we then observe the impact this has on spending and inflation.

Similarly, theories in accounting can help us to understand the decisions of financial information preparers, as well as users of the output of the accounting system, including shareholders, lenders, investors and employees. Despite popular opinion, accounting involves much more than recording financial transactions according to a set of rules or standards. Accounting is an activity that requires accountants to make decisions on what information to provide, how accounting methods are going to be applied, and the extent of information to disclose to users. Accounting is a human activity, and while we can never fully know what motivates people to make the decisions they do, theories can be useful in helping us to understand and explain what might have influenced the decision-making process.

Theories that examine the operation of capital markets explain how share prices change when accounting information is provided to the market. This knowledge allows us to understand how investors make decisions based on accounting information. Other theories explain and predict managerial choice of accounting methods and how they relate to remuneration contracts and lending agreements. Further, theories can explain voluntary disclosure of information to satisfy stakeholder needs or societal expectations. These theories are particularly relevant in understanding why managers present information voluntarily about environmental or social performance, or about financial activities beyond that required by accounting standards.

Theories can also assist us to understand how organisational systems and controls are contingent on both external or environmental and internal or entity-specific factors that affect the organisation. Rather than explaining actions, other accounting theories can assist in determining what appropriate methods should be used or how accounting information should be measured and reported. These theories are designed to provide solutions or improvements.

LO 2 TYPES OF THEORIES

In chapter 1, the following two main types of theories used in accounting were identified:
- normative theories
- positive theories.

This chapter discusses each of these types of theories in more detail.

Normative theories

Normative theories provide recommendations about what *should* happen. They *prescribe* what ought to be the case based on a specific goal or objective. The outcome of a normative theory is derived through logical development and based upon a stated objective. The *Conceptual Framework for Financial Reporting* (*Conceptual Framework*) is one example of a normative theory. With the objective of financial reporting stated in the *Conceptual Framework* as its foundation, a range of prescriptions are made about who should report; what qualities financial information should have; how the financial statement elements, such as assets and liabilities, should be defined; when the information should be recognised within the accounting reports; and how information should be presented to be meaningful.

A normative theory is not necessarily based upon what *is* happening in the world, but on what *should* be the case given the objective upon which it is based. That does not mean that the development of normative theories is completely divorced from reality. Often normative theories evolve from observations and research into practice, undertaken using positive theories.

Positive theories

A positive theory describes, explains or predicts activities. For example, a positive theory could *explain* why managers choose particular accounting methods in situations where accounting standards allow such choice, and *predict* what other organisations might do when faced with similar circumstances. Positive theories can help us to understand what is happening in the world, and why organisations act the way they do. As such they rely on real world observations. Positive theories can help us to understand the decisions users make with regards to accounting information, and this can then lead organisations to make more informed decisions about how and why they present information the way they do.

We will now examine a range of theories commonly used in the accounting and disclosure fields to understand accounting activities. These theories include positive accounting theory, institutional theory, legitimacy theory, stakeholder theory and contingency theory. While most of these theories are positive theories, some also have normative underpinnings.

LO 3 POSITIVE ACCOUNTING THEORY

As the name suggests, positive accounting theory is a *positive* theory used to explain and predict accounting practice. It is 'designed to explain and predict which firms will and which firms will not use a particular method'.[1] The theory, in an attempt to understand accounting policy decisions, examines a range of relationships, or contracts, in place between the entity and suppliers of equity capital (owners), managerial labour (management) and debt capital (lenders or debt holders). Positive accounting theory is based on an underlying economic assumption called the 'rational economic person' assumption, which assumes that all individuals act in their own self-interest and are rational wealth maximisers. It is derived from a number of economic theories including contracting theory and agency theory. We will consider each of these in turn.

Contracting theory

Contracting theory suggests that the organisation is characterised as a legal 'nexus of contracts' or as the centre of contractual relationships, with these contracting parties having rights and responsibilities under these contracts.[2] It is argued that an organisation is an efficient way of organising economic activity.[3] The parties to these contracts include shareholders, lenders, managers, employees, suppliers and customers.[4] While an entity can facilitate this wide array of contractual relationships, positive accounting theory focuses on two, managerial contracts and debt contracts, both of which are agency contracts used to manage relationships where there is a separation between management and capital providers.

Agency theory

Agency theory is used to understand relationships whereby a person or group of persons (the principal) employs the services of another (the agent) to perform some activity on their behalf. In doing so the principal delegates the decision-making authority to the agent. This is generally known as an agency relationship.

While the agent has a legal and fiduciary duty to act in the best interests of the principal, the assumption that both parties are utility maximisers means that the agent will not always act in the interests of the principal.[5] The risk that managers might undertake actions that are detrimental to owners or other principals is often termed moral hazard. If the interests of the agent and principal are not aligned there may be incentives for the manager to act in a way that might not be in the best interests of the principal. As a result of this, Jensen and Meckling identified three agency costs: monitoring costs, bonding costs and residual loss.[6]

Monitoring costs

Monitoring costs are incurred by the principal to measure, observe and control the agent's behaviour. These might include costs to audit the financial reports, putting in place operating rules or costs to set up a management compensation plan. While these costs are initially incurred by the principal, the principal will pass these costs on to the agent. For example, in the relationship between owners and managers, owners as principals who are worried about a manager's performance will have more stringent monitoring systems in place and will pass these costs on to the manager through reduced remuneration. Where a debt contract is concerned, lenders are concerned about the financial performance of companies they lend to and how this might affect the risk involved in lending. Lenders, as principals will also use auditing to monitor managers (who are considered agents acting on behalf of shareholders). Lenders are likely to increase interest rates charged on loans, or lend for a shorter period if they are required to undertake more monitoring of the entity. This means as the costs of monitoring an agent's behaviour increase, the remuneration paid to those agents will decrease or the cost of borrowings will increase. This is known as price protection.

Bonding costs

This price protection means agents will actually bear the costs of monitoring through lower remuneration or higher interest rates. Because of this, managers (the agents in both of these contracts) are likely to provide some assurance that they are making decisions in the best interest of the principals. One example might be incurring the time and effort involved in producing and providing quarterly accounting reports to lenders or by agreeing to link part of the remuneration payment to entity performance. If this is done managers have an incentive to enhance entity performance, which is also in the best interests of owners. These activities are known as bonding costs.

Residual loss

Despite these controls, it is too costly to guarantee an agent will make decisions optimal to the principal at all times and in all circumstances. At times it might cost more to monitor agents than the expected benefits from that monitoring. For instance, it might be too costly to monitor the use of a manager's travel expenses to ensure they are only for business purposes, or his or her use of business stationery for personal use. This additional divergence is referred to as residual loss.

The majority of monitoring and bonding costs are going to be borne by agents through reduced remuneration (in a managerial contract) or higher interest rates (in a debt contract). As this is the case, managers have incentives to minimise these costs. However, principals are never going to perfectly estimate the full impact of the agent's behaviour. Agents know this and perceive that they will not be fully penalised for all their behaviour which is not in the interests of principals. Because of this, residual loss is borne by both the principal and the agent.[7]

Accounting plays a large role in monitoring and bonding mechanisms. Accounting information is used to design the contracts to bond agents' behaviour as well as to monitor performance against those contracts. As such, agency theory relies heavily on the accounting function. We will now discuss how accounting plays a role in both owner–manager relationships and manager–lender relationships.

Owner–manager agency relationships

As previously mentioned, separation of ownership and control means that managers, as agents, are likely to act in their own interest and these actions might not necessarily align with the principal's or owners' interests. One example could be the manager using entity resources, including stationery, office facilities and time during business hours running their own business 'on the side'. Owners bear the costs of this behaviour. The agency theory literature identifies a number of problems that can exist between managers and owners in an agency relationship. It also suggests how contracts and accounting information can be used to 'monitor' managers and 'bond' the interests of owners and managers to reduce these problems. These problems include: the horizon problem, risk aversion and dividend retention.[8]

Horizon problem

Managers and shareholders tend to have differing time horizons in relation to the entity. This is known as the horizon problem. Shareholders have an interest in the long-term growth and value of the entity as the share value of the entity today reflects the present value of the expected future cash flows. Consequently, shareholders want managers to make decisions that enhance the future cash flows of the entity over the long term. Managers, on the other hand, are interested in the cash flow potential only as long as they expect to be employed by the entity. This is particularly a problem for managers who are approaching retirement. Managers who are seeking to move to another entity within the short term are more likely to wish to demonstrate the short-term profitability of the entity as evidence of effective management. Doing so is likely to enhance the remuneration they can command in the new position.

Managers can demonstrate short-term profitability in a number of different ways. They could, for example, delay undertaking maintenance or upgrades to equipment or plant or reduce research and development expenditure. While increasing short-term profitability, these activities can have adverse consequences for longer-term costs relating to future productivity of the entity.

This problem can be reduced by linking management rewards to longer-term performance of the entity. This occurs through the managerial remuneration contract. Linking managerial bonuses to share price, or paying a proportion of managerial remuneration as shares or share options encourages managers to focus on long-term performance because it is likely to affect their own wealth. Tying a greater proportion of managerial pay to share price movements as the manager approaches retirement is also likely to encourage managers to maximise long-term performance.

Risk aversion

Managers generally prefer less risk than shareholders. Shareholders are not likely to hold all their resources as shares in only one entity. They are able to diversify their risk though investing across multiple entities, cash or property investments. Shareholders may also receive regular income from other sources, for example a personal salary. This means they have 'hedged' or minimised the risk of one of these investments losing value. In addition, shareholders' liability is limited to the amount they are required to pay for their shares. Managers, on the other hand, have more capital invested in the entity than shareholders through their 'human capital' or managerial expertise. It is likely that their remuneration is their primary source of income. As such, losing their job or being paid less can substantially impact on their personal wealth.

Economic theory proposes that higher risk has the potential to lead to higher returns. Shareholders, therefore, prefer that managers invest in higher-risk projects, which are likely to increase the value of the business. Managers meanwhile wish to take less risk when deciding on projects for the entity because they have more to lose.

Managerial remuneration contracts can include incentives to encourage managers to invest in more risky projects. For instance linking a bonus partly to profits can encourage managers to consider more risky projects that have the potential to increase profits. Limiting the share-based compensation as a manager's ownership in the company increases is also likely to encourage managers to invest in more risky opportunities. Increasing managerial share ownership increases a manager's risk aversion as it further decreases a manager's ability to diversify risk. A manager is tied to the entity through not only a human capital investment but also a share investment.

Dividend retention

Managers, when compared to shareholders, prefer to maintain a greater level of funds within the entity, and pay less of the entity's earnings to shareholders as dividends. This is known as the **dividend retention problem**. Managers wish to retain money within the business to expand the size of the business they control (empire building) and to pay their own salaries and benefits. Shareholders, on the other hand wish to maximise the return on their own investment through increased dividends.

Paying a bonus which is linked to a dividend payout ratio will likely encourage managers to enhance dividend payouts to shareholders. Similarly, linking bonuses to profits will also encourage managers to seek additional profits, which in turn are likely to be available for dividends.

Profits, and increasingly shares and options, are commonly used as a basis for executive remuneration contracts worldwide. The performance criteria used in executive contracts use a range of accounting measures. Contemporary Issue 5.1 discusses how News Corp used a range of incentive mechanisms to align managers' interests with shareholders.

News Corp reduces agency problems through executive remuneration plans

News Corp's four most senior executives could collect up to US$89.5 million ($98 million) in cash and share bonuses under a new incentive scheme, including US$29 million for chairman, chief executive and largest shareholder Rupert Murdoch.

The scheme, announced on the eve of the media giant's 2009–10 results report this morning, ties the executives' remuneration more closely to News Corp's share price performance. The change follows years of a sluggish stock performance by News Corp in the United States, where its shares have dropped 16 per cent since 2005, compared with a 9.5 per cent decline in the Standard & Poor's 500 Index.

The scheme will take effect on June 30, 2011, and gives Mr Murdoch the chance to earn an annual cash bonus of US$25 million. In recent years, his biggest bonus was US$17.5 million in 2007–08. Mr Murdoch owns 39.7 per cent of News Corp's voting stock.

Chase Carey, who returned to News Corp as deputy chairman and chief operating officer in July 2009 after a seven-year absence, could collect a bonus of between US$10 million and US$20 million a year if the company hits a range of performance targets.

News Corp's previous bonus scheme was based on earning per share (EPS) growth.

Now two-thirds of the four executives' annual bonuses is based on three measures: EPS growth, which accounts for 40 per cent of the performance target, free cash flow growth (40 per cent) and total shareholder return (20 per cent).

The company said the other third was based on 'qualitative factors, including, but not limited to, individual and group contributions to . . . financial and non-financial objectives'.

Mr Murdoch could collect an annual cash bonus of between US$12.5 million and US$25 million. James Murdoch's potential bonus range is US$6 million to $12 million . . . The share-based incentive scheme is on top of these bonuses.

'Tying the bonuses to performance is a step in the right direction and brings News Corp more in line with other companies,' said one fund manager, who did not want to be named.

'But the potential bonuses are still huge. News Corp might be doing well at the moment as media ad markets recover and its cable TV business grows, but is Murdoch worth a potential bonus of US$25 million plus?'

Source: Extracts from Neil Shoebridge, 'News resets top executive pay', *The Australian Financial Review.*[9]

Questions

1. Both the horizon problem and risk aversion are agency problems that relate specifically to the relationship between owners and managers and which contracting can assist in overcoming. Explain these two problems. **K**
2. News Corp Ltd has recently introduced a new pay scheme to link executive pay to a range of performance measures, including share performance through 'total shareholder return'. How does linking bonuses to share performance reduce the horizon problem and risk aversion? **J**
3. Why is it important to link executive bonuses to a range of entity performance measures rather than one, as was previously the case with News Corp? **J**

Compensation policy is argued to be one of the most important factors in organisational success.[10] Not only does the theory suggest it influences how top executives behave, but it also impacts on what kind of executives an organisation attracts.[11]

The most recent research has focused upon the extent to which executive entitlements are linked to entity performance and ultimately shareholder value.[12] Results are mixed, with a number of studies finding either no or an extremely weak relationship between pay and performance. Weak relationships between entity performance and compensation tend to be more evident where the compensation measure used is cash only.[13]

Matolcsy and Wright proposed that it may not be efficient for all types of entities to award equity-based compensation to CEOs. They asserted that if compensation structures are set efficiently, based on the underlying economic characteristics of the entity, then entity performance will be maximised.[14] For some entities this may entail the use of cash-only compensation. The authors divided their sample into two groups based on contract type — entities which provide only cash compensation to the CEO and those which have equity-based compensation schemes in place. A recent study by Rankin examines the level and structure of executive pay in Australian listed entities between 2006 and 2009.[15] Results indicate a variation in both the level and structure of compensation across the executive team. CEO pay varies across industries, with finance entities paying higher levels of salary, although salary as a proportion of total pay is lower than other sectors. Cash payments to CEOs — salary and bonus — are higher in 2009 (following the global financial crisis (GFC)) than for other years, which is likely to indicate a shift towards less risky cash rewards from risky equity payments in periods of economic downturn. The finance sector is more likely to rely on bonuses than other sectors, with mining entity bonuses constituting a significantly smaller proportion of total pay than other industries.

Manager–lender agency relationships

When a lender agrees to provide funds to an entity there is the risk that the lending party may not repay those funds. Agency theory has also been used to understand the relationship between lenders and management. In this situation the lender is the principal and the manager is agent, who is acting on behalf of the owners. In this instance the manager's interests are completely aligned with owners. The agency problems that could arise include: excessive dividend payments to owners; underinvestment; asset substitution and claim dilution.[16]

To avoid higher interest costs (price protection) being imposed by lenders, managers have incentives to contract to show they are acting in a way that is not detrimental to lenders. Debt contracts contain restrictions, known as covenants, which are designed to protect the interest of lenders. As a result of agreeing to the terms of these covenants, managers are able to borrow funds at lower rates of interest, to borrow higher levels of funds or to borrow for longer periods. Accounting data usually form the basis of these covenants.

Excessive dividend payments

When lending funds, lenders price the debt to take into account an assumed level of dividend payout. If managers issue a higher level of dividends, or excessive dividend payments, then this could lead to a reduction of the asset base securing the debt or leave insufficient funds within the entity to service the debt. To reduce this problem managers and lenders agree to covenants that restrain dividend policy and restrict dividend payouts as a function of profits. Dividend payout ratios are a common covenant in Australian debt contracts. Maintaining working capital ratios also alleviates excessive dividend payments.

Underinvestment

Underinvestment as an agency problem arises when managers, on behalf of owners, have incentives not to undertake positive net present value (NPV) projects if the projects would lead to increased funds being available to lenders. This might particularly be the case when the entity is in financial difficulty. Creditors rank above owners in order of payments in the event an entity liquidates and any funds from these projects would go towards debt rather than equity. Covenants that restrict the investment opportunities of the organisation are likely to alleviate this problem. Working capital ratios will also assist by requiring managers to retain a certain level of funds within the entity, which managers are likely to invest in positive NPV assets.

Asset substitution

As we saw previously, shareholders have diversified portfolios and limited liability, and are happy for an entity to invest in risky projects. Shareholders benefit from any excessive gains from such projects. Lenders, on the other hand, determine the interest rate and term of the loan in accordance with the risk level of the asset or project the entity is borrowing funds to invest in. They lend these funds on the assumption that managers will not invest in assets or projects of a higher risk level than agreed. Because managers are working on behalf of owners and are often owners themselves, they have incentives to use the debt finance to invest in alternative, higher-risk assets in the likelihood that it will lead to higher returns to shareholders. Lenders bear the risk of this strategy as they are subject to the 'downside' risk, but do not share in any 'upside' of the investment decision.

To limit asset substitution debt contracts will often restrict the investment opportunities of the entity, including merger activity. The lender might also secure the debt against specific assets. Debt to tangible assets ratios can restrict asset substitution.

Claim dilution

When entities take on debt of a higher priority than that on issue it is referred to as claim dilution. While taking on additional debt increases funds available to the entity, it decreases the security to lenders, making the lending more risky. The most common method of avoiding claim dilution is to restrict the borrowing of higher priority debt, or debt with an earlier maturity date.

In a study of Australian bank private debt contracts, Cotter found that lending agreements most commonly contain leverage covenants, with leverage measured as the ratio of total liabilities to total tangible assets.[17] Contracts also include interest coverage and current ratio constraints. Mather and Peirson conducted a more recent review of both public and private debt covenants.[18] In public debt agreements, while leverage covenants are used (nearly half had restrictions on liabilities), so too are interest cover and dividend coverage ratios. The authors found that interest coverage covenants are commonly used in private debt contracts (78% of their sample). As with public covenants, most contracts have some restriction on liabilities with maximum total liabilities/total tangible assets and secured liabilities/total tangible assets being the most common. Private debt contracts also commonly include covenants requiring minimum current ratios as well as a minimum net worth.

Role of accounting information in reducing agency problems

As previously discussed, accounting information forms one of the major components of both manager remuneration and lending contracts. Terms are written into managerial remuneration contracts to link managers' performance to shareholder interests. Bonuses can be tied to measures of entity financial performance or share performance. Accounting information plays two roles in the contracting process: (1) to write the terms of managerial contracts and (2) to determine performance against the terms of the contracts and consequently the amount of bonus and other pay components managers will receive.

Debt contracts include covenants which reflect different measures of entity performance, such as leverage, dividend payout or interest coverage ratios. Lenders also look to regular financial updates to ensure companies are maintaining the terms of their covenants.

Information asymmetry

In addition to accounting information being used as part of the contracting process, it is also commonly provided in order to reduce information asymmetry. Information asymmetry results from managers having an advantage over investors and other interested parties as they have more information about the current and future prospects of the entity, and can choose when and how to disseminate this information.

Managers can use accounting disclosure, as well as other forms of disclosure and announcements to the market, to signal expectations about the future. These signals could portray either good or bad news. Verrecchia takes the view that unless the information would give competitors an advantage if they knew it, managers have incentives to disclose both good and bad news.[19] If entities did not provide information when other entities in the market did so, it would be assumed they had bad news to report and their share price would suffer as a result. This is often referred to as **adverse selection**. In this instance it is in the entity's best interest to provide news — good or bad — to the market so as to avoid being seen as a poor investment.

LO 4 INSTITUTIONAL THEORY

Institutional theory has been used extensively in the management literature, and is increasingly used in accounting research to understand the influences on organisational structures. It considers how rules, norms and routines become established as authoritative guidelines, and considers how these elements are created, adopted and adapted over time.[20] 'Compliance occurs in many circumstances because other types of behavior are inconceivable; routines are followed because they are taken for granted as "the way we do these things"'.[21] In order to survive, organisations need to conform to the rules and belief systems that prevail in the environment and this will earn the organisation legitimacy.[22]

Much organisational action reflects a pattern of doing things that evolves over time and becomes legitimated within an organisation and an environment.[23] Consequently practices within organisations can be predicted from perceptions of legitimate behaviour derived from cultural values, industry tradition, entity value etc.[24] Multinational corporations are likely to face differing institutional environments in which they operate, and consequently need to adjust their operations accordingly.

Eisenhardt examined compensation in the retail sector, and developed hypotheses relating to the factors likely to influence retail sales compensation under both agency and institutional theories. In doing so, she articulated the difference between the theories.[25] This has been adapted in table 5.1.

TABLE 5.1 Comparison of agency and institutional theories

	Agency theory	Institutional theory
Key idea	Organisational practices arise from efficient organisation of information and risk-bearing costs	Organisational practices arise from imitative forces and firm traditions
Basis of organisation	Efficiency	Legitimacy
View of people	Self-interested rationalists	Legitimacy-seeking satisfiers
Role of environment	Organisational practices should fit environment	A source of practices to which organisation conforms
Assumptions	People are self-interested People are rational People are risk-averse	People are satisfied People conform to external norms

Source: Adapted from Eisenhardt.[26]

Eisenhardt proposed, from an institutional perspective, that the age of the retail store was likely to affect the type of salaries awarded. Older, more traditional stores were likely to use commissions — a practice that had been developed in the 1950s — while newer stores, operating under a changing institutional environment, were more likely to provide salaries to staff. The nature of merchandise sold was also likely to impact on whether staff received a salary or commission. High-priced merchandise, which had its roots in early department stores, was likely to attract a commission.

Campbell proposed that corporate social performance is likely to relate to the institutional environment the entity faces, including legislative forces.[27] The author proposed that corporations were more likely to act in socially responsible ways if strong and well-enforced state regulations or a system of well-organised and effective industrial self-regulation were in place; or if their performance and behaviour was monitored by independent organisations such as non-governmental organisations, institutional investors or the press. Similarly if trade or employer associations were well organised and entities had ongoing dialogue with these associations, it was expected that their social performance would be stronger.

Institutional factors have also been proposed to affect corporate stance on climate change. Kolk, Levy and Pinkse note a shift in entities in energy and transport-related sectors investing substantial amounts in low-carbon technologies and engaging in voluntary schemes to measure, reduce and trade carbon emissions.[28] The authors point to a number of factors likely to influence this change: senior managers have interacted with others on a range of industry associations and climate negotiations, which has led to a convergence in their perceptions and actions about climate change. The authors argue that the global agenda on climate change has become a more important influence on corporate strategy than institutional influences from the entities' home countries.

LO 5 LEGITIMACY THEORY

Legitimacy theory has been used to understand corporate action and activities, particularly relating to social and environmental issues. As such, it is a 'positive theory'. It is based on what has been termed a 'social contract'.

Social contract

The idea of a social contract is drawn from political economy theory. Political economy theory examines the relationships or interplay between government, law, property rights and the economy. It relates to how society, politics and economics all interact,[29] and means that we cannot talk about economic or business issues without considering the social and institutional framework within which it takes place.[30]

A social contract has often been used to describe how business interacts with society. It relates to the explicit and implicit expectations society has about how businesses should act to ensure they survive into the future. A social contract is not necessarily a written agreement, but is what we understand society expects. Some expectations could be explicit (legislation relating to pollution or employee health and safety are examples of explicit expectations), while others are implicit. Evidence of implicit terms of the social contract can be gained from the writing and other communications of a society at a point in time.[31] Membership of environmental groups, or media attention devoted to high executive bonus payments when share prices are declining could be examples of the degree of public importance placed on these issues.

Donaldson says that businesses receive their permission to operate from society and are ultimately accountable to society for how they operate and what they do.[32] That is, an organisation needs to show it is operating in accordance with the expectations in the social contract. The process of maintaining that an organisation is meeting the expectations of society is known as organisational legitimacy.[33]

Organisational legitimacy

Organisational legitimacy, or legitimacy theory, also comes from the political economy perspective.[34] Where the relationship between business and society is explained by a social contract, legitimacy theory can be used to explain the process by which the social contract is maintained. The theory argues that organisations can only continue to exist if the society in which they operate recognises they are operating within a value system that is consistent with society's own.[35] This means that an organisation must appear to consider the rights of the public at large, not just its shareholders.

The values and norm evident in the social contract have changed over time. In the past, legitimacy was considered only in terms of economic performance, with the only expectation of business being to make a profit for its owners.[36] In 1962, Milton Friedman, in discussing the responsibility of corporate managers, stated that:

> there is one and only one social responsibility of business — to use its resources and engage in activities designed to increase its profits so long as it stays within the rules of the game . . .[37]

This has changed and businesses are now expected to consider a range of issues, including the environmental and social consequences of their activities. For example, employees have expectations relating to the range of benefits their employer provides, and the community might be concerned about air or water pollution affecting the immediate environment and what an entity is doing to minimise these. Customers may also be interested in the potential decline in service through business rationalisation and staff cuts or branch closures. Westpac acknowledged that when it closed bank branches in rural areas between 1990 and 1998, it broke its 'social contract' with the community.[38] During a period of high competition, following deregulation of the banking sector, many banks closed branches and agencies across the country, many in rural areas.[39]

Contemporary Issue 5.2 demonstrates how the big four banks have breached an implied social contract by failing to pass on interest rate cuts.

5.2 CONTEMPORARY ISSUE

Banks breaching an implied social contract

Refusing to pass on the rate cut shreds the social contract . . . Treasurer Wayne Swan yesterday declared that the banks needed a kick up the bum because of their reluctance to pass on to their customers the Reserve Bank's latest interest rate cut. The Big Four, unfortunately, are about as likely to be discomforted by a metaphorical slipper from the Treasurer as they would be by a real tickle with a feather.

The problem is that it is not Mr Swan's fault that he can only exhort the banks to do what the Reserve clearly intends them to do. There is an implied social contract that binds the trading banks, the Reserve Bank and the Government, and, as with all such contracts, its effectiveness depends on the willingness of each party to observe its prescriptions. Thus, if the banks persistently refuse to pass on interest rate cuts, then monetary policy ultimately becomes futile, because the customers the banks would normally expect to be enticed by the prospect of cheaper borrowing will not come knocking at the door.

Similarly, the willingness of the Government to protect the banks' business in time of recession by measures such as guaranteeing their deposits, or guaranteeing their own borrowing from overseas banks, also imposes an ethical responsibility. Recognising that banking is not like other kinds of business, since it is the business that makes other business possible, the Government has offered the banks a level of protection other businesses could not expect. And for this, too, there is an implied quid pro quo: when the taxpayer is making extraordinary concessions in extraordinary times, the taxpayer deserves consideration in return . . .

Source: Excerpts from 'The banks take much, but give less and less back, *The Age*.[40]

Questions

1. What is a 'social contract'? **K**
2. What do you think might be the implied terms of the social contract between banks and customers with respect to interest rates and charges? **J**

Legitimacy theory indicates that if an organisation cannot justify it is maintaining its operations in accordance with the social contract, then the community may revoke that contract.[41] Customers might seek alternative sources of products or services, workers may choose other organisations to provide their labour services to, or organisations might find it more difficult to attract sources of either debt or equity capital. Contemporary Issue 5.2 illustrates this point, with the suggestion that customers might look elsewhere for finance.

The media is often one of the main factors that sets or reflects the agenda. O'Donovan considered how Australian corporate executives responded to potentially damaging media attention.[42] He found that corporations pay close attention to issues highlighted by the media, and they in turn present disclosures to either support or counteract any misconceptions that may have come through the media. They saw the media as an important factor in influencing societal views.

Accounting disclosures and legitimation

Organisational legitimation is the process which an organisation uses to address societal expectations. It is in the best interests of organisations to take action to ensure their operations are seen to be legitimate in terms of the implied social contract that exists. Lindblom identifies four ways an organisation can obtain or maintain legitimacy:

1. seek to educate and inform society about actual changes in the organisation's performance and activities
2. seek to change the perceptions of society, but not actually change behaviour
3. seek to manipulate perception by deflecting attention from the issue of concern to other related issues
4. seek to change expectations of its performance.[43]

Legitimation can occur through performance, or through disclosure.[44] Entities can change their organisational processes or systems, but this can be very costly. If an entity is going to do this, it is also likely to publicly disclose information about its activities. For instance an entity might disclose its sustainability policy on its website, together with information about the environmental management system it has implemented, and how it is measuring and documenting carbon emissions — an issue that is of increasing importance to society.

Disclosure of information about an organisation's effect on, or relationship with, society can also be used in each of the strategies.[45] A entity might provide information to offset negative news which may be publicly available. In addition, organisations may draw attention to strengths, for instance awards won for environmental performance or reduction in accident rates, while playing down information about negative activities such as pollution.[46]

Public reporting through the annual report or the entity website can be a powerful tool in showing an organisation is meeting the expectations of society. One of the major functions of corporate reporting is to legitimate corporate operations.[47] Reflective of its striving for organisational legitimacy, the CEO of BHP Billiton, in the 2010 annual report, made reference to meeting its implied 'social contract':

> However we only earn the right to grow this business if we can do it safely, in an environmentally sound manner and in a way that demonstrates our unqualified commitment to working with integrity.[48]

Legitimacy theory has commonly been used to explain disclosure of sustainability or corporate social and environmental information. These issues are considered in detail in chapter 11.

 LO 6

STAKEHOLDER THEORY

Stakeholder theory is also derived from political economy theory, and as such has some links to legitimacy theory, which is discussed above. In fact, they have both been seen as overlapping perspectives which can be used to understand reporting behaviour, 'set within a framework of assumptions about "political economy"'.[49] The essential difference is that stakeholder theory considers the relationships that exist between the organisation and its various **stakeholders** and these stakeholders can be identified. Legitimacy theory, on the other hand, relates to organisational consideration of society in general. Stakeholders have been defined by Freeman as 'any group or individual who can affect or is affected by the achievements of an organisation's objectives'.[50]

There are two versions of stakeholder theory — a normative theory, known as the 'ethical branch', and an empirical theory of management, which is a positive theory.[51]

Normative branch of stakeholder theory

The **normative branch of stakeholder theory** relates to the ethical or moral treatment of organisational stakeholders. It is argued that organisations should treat all their stakeholders fairly, and an organisation should be managed for the benefit of all its stakeholders.[52] Under the ethical branch, stakeholder importance is not determined by the supply of resources to the organisation. This means that one shareholder is not perceived to be any more important than other stakeholders and organisations have a fiduciary duty to all stakeholders.[53] Donaldson and Preston note that stakeholders are important when identifying the 'moral or philosophical guidelines for the operation and management of the corporation'.[54] Stakeholders are identified, and should be considered in organisational decisions because of *their* interest in the activities of the organisation, and not only because they are able to 'further the interests of some other group, such as shareowners'.[55] The ethical or normative branch of stakeholder theory proposes that organisations have a moral obligation to consider how their operations affect stakeholders and should not merely concentrate on maximising profit for the benefit of owners.

Managerial branch of stakeholder theory

The **managerial branch of stakeholder theory** is a positive theory which seeks to explain how stakeholders might influence organisational actions. Drawing from a political economy perspective, it is similar to legitimacy theory in that the organisation is seen as part of a wider social system; however, the theory examines the relationship with different stakeholder groups within society rather than society as a whole. The extent to which an organisation will consider its stakeholders is related to the power or influence of those stakeholders. Managers need to determine which stakeholders they need to consider in their actions and manage these competing interests.

A stakeholder's power is related to the degree of control they have over resources required by the organisation.[56] The more necessary to the success of the organisation the resources the stakeholder controls, the more likely it is that managers will address the stakeholder's concerns. Figure 5.1 reflects the range of stakeholders as organisation needs to consider in its decision-making process.

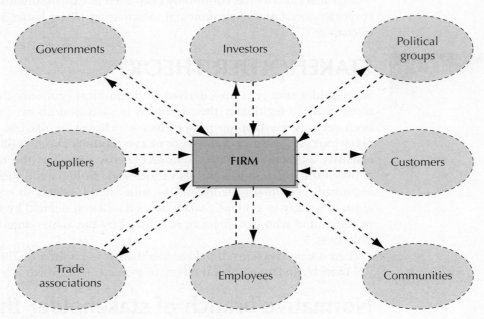

FIGURE 5.1 Organisational stakeholders
Source: Donaldson and Preston.[57]

In addition to power, Mitchell, Angle and Wood also consider legitimacy (socially accepted and expected behaviours) and urgency (time sensitivity or criticality of the stakeholder's claims) as important considerations in determining which stakeholders' wishes or needs to address.[58] One of the major roles of managers is to consider the relative importance of each of their organisational stakeholders in meeting their strategic objectives and manage these relationships accordingly. The level of respective stakeholders' power or influence is likely to change over time and in different circumstances.[59]

Role of accounting information in stakeholder theory

One important way of meeting stakeholders' needs and expectations is providing information about organisational activities and performance. This might be demonstrating how the strategic direction, mission or objectives align with the stakeholders' expectations, or how the organisation's financial or environmental performance meets stakeholders' requirements. Consistent with Lindblom's legitimating strategies discussed previously, providing information to stakeholders is one very important way to gain the support or approval of stakeholders, or to deflect their attention from less desirable activities.[60]

As with legitimacy theory, stakeholder theory has been used to examine disclosure of voluntary information to stakeholders, most commonly relating to social and environmental performance.

CONTINGENCY THEORY

Contingency theory was developed in management literature in the 1960s and 1970s.[61] In essence, the theory proposes that organisations are all affected by a range of factors that differ across organisations. Organisations need to adapt their structure to take into account a range of factors such as external environment, organisational size and business strategy if the organisation is to perform well.[62] Galbraith formulated the theory to propose that there is no one best way to organise, as organisational effectiveness is contingent on context.[63] The central proposition of contingency theory is that organisational performance depends on the fit between organisational context and structure.[64] In turn, organisational effectiveness is achieved by matching organisational characteristics to contingencies.[65] A 'contingency' is defined as 'any variable that moderates the effect of an organizational characteristic on organizational performance'.[66] A number of contingencies have been identified in the literature examining organisational structure and performance, including technology, innovation, environmental change, size and diversification.[67]

Contingency frameworks have been used to evaluate management accounting information and internal control systems (see for example Otley[68] and Chenhall[69]).The contingency approach in management accounting is based on the proposition that there is no universally appropriate accounting system that can be applied to all organisations. Instead, features of appropriate accounting systems are contingent upon the specific circumstances the organisation faces.[70] Contingency theory has been used by Jokipii to examine the effectiveness of internal control systems.[71] The author takes a contingency approach to examining the design of the internal control systems and the important contingency characteristics that should be taken into account when focusing on internal control, and that impact on its effectiveness. Jokipii observes that entities adapt their internal control structure to deal with environmental uncertainty. Entity strategy is also found to impact on internal control structure.[72]

In their study of strategic management accounting, Cadez and Guilding find support for a contingency theory proposition that there is no universally appropriate strategic management accounting system, with factors such as entity size and strategy found to impact on the successful application of strategic management accounting systems.[73]

The next section considers how the theories discussed in this chapter can be used to understand accounting decisions. Many of these accounting issues are discussed in more detail elsewhere in this book.

USING THEORIES TO UNDERSTAND ACCOUNTING DECISIONS

Accountants need to make a range of accounting decisions on a daily basis. In your accounting studies to date you would probably have been given precise information as to the expected useful life of non-current assets, the depreciation method that is to be used, the percentage of accounts receivable anticipated to eventuate as bad debts and the amount of impairment. In reality, this is not the case. Accountants are required to use judgement to make a range of decisions including:
- whether to expense or capitalise costs
- what accounting estimates to use

- whether to recognise an item in the body of the financial statements, or disclose it in the notes only
- whether to disclose additional information, where it is not governed by legislation.

The theories discussed in this chapter can offer some assistance in explaining managers' and accountants' decisions in these areas.

Expensing and capitalising costs

Accountants and managers need to make decisions about the timing and nature of a range of activities including maintenance, machinery overhaul, capital improvements and repairs. Accountants often have discretion over the timing of the recording of these events and many are likely to have considerable impacts on the financial position and performance of the entity. Expensing a transaction rather than capitalising it is likely to reduce short-term profits. Agency theory would hold that managers on compensation contracts which have bonuses tied to a current measure of entity performance, such as profits, would prefer to capitalise these costs, if possible, in order to maximise profits. Similarly, where the entity has a lending agreement with a leverage covenant, managers will want to ensure the value of assets is maximised, which will lead to capitalising costs where possible.

If managers' compensation contracts include measures of medium- or long-term entity performance in order to extend the managers' time horizon, capitalising costs becomes less important and managers are likely to want to smooth income over the medium to long term.[74] Institutional theory would also explain the influence of external norms and expectations on managerial compensation policy. Entities would be expected to follow what are perceived to be 'normal' practices in the industry in setting pay and using a mix of cash and incentive pay.

Accounting estimates

Accountants and managers constantly estimate economic magnitudes to bring to account. Bad debts, provisions for warranties, the expected useful life and salvage value of plant and equipment, and the fair value of financial instruments are just some of these. These estimates require a great deal of judgement and can lead to substantial variations in reported profits and asset balances. Again, agency contracts can explain managerial decisions in this regard. Managers and accountants, acting in self interest, are likely to ensure their own bonuses are maximised and the entity is not at risk of breaching debt contracts.

Disclosure policy

Beyond the specific legal and accounting standard requirements, managers and accountants decide the extent and location of additional disclosures within the annual report.[75] Disclosure policy relates to additional disclosure within the financial statements or notes to the financial statements, in the directors' report or review of operations, additional sections of the annual report or media releases.

Disclosures could relate to financial forecasts, information about social or environmental performance, capital investment plans or research and development opportunities, amongst others. Stakeholder theory would explain these disclosures in terms of providing relevant information to maintain relationships with powerful stakeholders. Legitimacy theory sees voluntary disclosure as a way of maintaining or regaining legitimacy by demonstrating how the entity is meeting societal expectations. The theory has been used to explain disclosure of voluntary environmental information where entities are facing a legitimacy risk due to environmental disasters or poor environmental performance (see for example Deegan & Rankin[76] and Patten[77]). Similarly, institutional theory and contingency theory would explain disclosure policy in relation to the expectations of the norms and external environment.

Information asymmetry between owners and managers is likely to influence the extent and type of information entities disclose. Managers need to be mindful of presenting both good and bad news about the entity, or risk the reputation of the entity and potentially influence entity value.

Summary

Evaluate how theories can enhance our understanding of accounting practice
- Theories can be used to explain and understand accounting practice. They can also be used to prescribe methods to improve accounting practice.

Identify the types of theories used in accounting
- Theories are classified as either positive theories or normative theories.
- Positive theories describe, explain and predict accounting practice. They allow us to understand current practice and identify what accounting methods we can expect similar entities to choose in given circumstances.
- Normative theories prescribe how accounting *should* be done.

Explain the general tenets of positive accounting theory and examine how it explains accounting practice and disclosures
- Positive accounting theory is based on contracting and agency theories and provides guidance on what accounting methods managers are likely to choose given the contracts in place.
- Agency theory concentrates on two agency relationships: the relationships between owners as principals and managers as their agents; and the contractual relationship between lenders as principals and managers, acting on behalf of owners, as agents.
- Contracting is designed to reduce monitoring and bonding costs, and to reduce the resulting residual loss.
- The agency problems leading from the owner–manager contractual relationship are:
  – risk aversion, where managers have incentives to undertake less risky decisions than owners would like, which leads to limiting the potential for long-term value
  – dividend retention, where managers retain funds within the organisation which can be used to expand the business, and increase their 'empire' rather than pay these profits out to shareholders as dividends
  – the horizon problem where managers have an incentive to focus on short-term entity performance, while shareholders are interested in the long-term growth of entity value.
- The agency problems relating to the contractual relationship between lenders and managers are:
  – Excessive dividend payments is a problem where payment of higher dividends could lead to a reduced asset base securing the debt, or leaving insufficient funds within the entity to service the debt.

- Underinvestment arises when managers, on behalf of owners, have incentives not to undertake positive NPV projects if the projects would lead to increased funds being available to lenders.
- Asset substitution arises when lenders lend funds on the assumption that managers will not invest in assets or projects of a higher risk level than agreed. Because managers are working on behalf of owners, and are often owners themselves, they have incentives to use the debt finance to invest in alternative, higher risk assets in the likelihood that it will lead to higher returns to shareholders.
- Claim dilution is when entities take on debt of a higher priority than that on issue. While taking on additional debt increases funds available to the entity, it decreases the security to lenders, making the lending more risky.

• Contracts can be written to reduce agency problems, with many of these contractual terms relying on accounting information. Accounting information plays two important roles in the contracting process including:
  - forming part of the contracts
  - monitoring performance against the contractual terms.
• Information asymmetry is likely to influence corporate disclosure policy as entities are likely to be concerned about their reputation and the impact on entity value if they fail to disclose pertinent information.

Explain institutional theory and examine how it explains organisational structures

• Institutional theory has been used extensively in the management literature and is increasingly used in accounting research to understand the influences on organisational structures. It considers how rules, norms and routines become established as authoritative guidelines and considers how these elements are created, adopted and adapted over time.

Explain legitimacy theory and examine how it explains accounting disclosure practice

• Legitimacy theory has been used to understand corporate action and activities, particularly relating to social and environmental issues. It is based on what has been termed a 'social contract'.
• A social contract is used to describe how business interacts with society. It relates to the explicit and implicit expectations society has about how businesses should act to ensure they survive into the future.
• Businesses receive their permission to operate from society and are ultimately accountable to society for how they operate and what they do.
• Where the relationship between business and society is explained by a social contract, legitimacy theory can be used to explain the process by which the social contract is maintained.
• Disclosure of information about an organisation's effect on or relationship with society can also be used as a legitimating strategy. An entity might provide information to offset negative news which may be publicly available. Organisations may also draw attention to strengths. One of the major functions of corporate reporting is to legitimate corporate operations.

Explain stakeholder theory and examine how it prescribes and explains accounting disclosure practice

• There are two versions of stakeholder theory – a normative theory, known as the 'ethical branch', and an empirical theory of management, which is a positive theory.
• Under the ethical branch, stakeholder importance is not determined by the supply of resources to the organisation. Shareholders are not perceived to be any more important than other stakeholders and organisations have a fiduciary duty to all stakeholders. Organisations have a moral obligation to consider how their operations

affect all stakeholders, and should not merely concentrate on maximising profit for the benefit of owners.

- The managerial branch of stakeholder theory is a positive theory which seeks to explain how stakeholders might influence organisational actions. The extent to which an organisation will consider its stakeholders is related to the power or influence of those stakeholders. Stakeholders' power is related to the degree of control they have over resources required by the organisation.
- Providing information to stakeholders is one way to gain the support or approval of stakeholders, or to deflect their attention from less desirable activities.

Explain contingency theory and examine how it prescribes and explains accounting disclosure practice

- The theory proposes that organisations are all affected by a range of factors that differ across organisations. Organisations need to adapt their structure to take into account a range of factors such as external environment, organisational size and business strategy if the organisation is going to perform well.

Outline the different decisions made by accounting practitioners

- Accounting practitioners and managers make numerous decisions on a daily basis. These include: expensing–capitalising decisions; accounting estimates; whether to recognise an item in the body of the financial reports, or disclose it in the notes only; and whether to disclose additional information, where it is not governed by legislation.

Review questions

1. Differentiate a normative theory from a positive theory. Provide an example of each.
2. Explain what an agency relationship is, and explain the following costs: monitoring costs, bonding costs, residual loss.
3. Why would managers' interests differ from those of shareholders?
4. Outline the three agency problems that exist in the relationship between owners and managers.
5. Outline the four agency problems that exist in the relationship between lenders and managers.
6. What is a debt covenant and why is it used in lending agreements?
7. Why would managers agree to enter into lending agreements that incorporate covenants?
8. What role does accounting information play in reducing agency problems?
9. How might institutional theory explain accounting disclosures?
10. What is a social contract and how does it relate to organisational legitimacy?
11. How can corporate disclosure policy be used to maintain or regain organisational legitimacy?
12. Why would managers decide to voluntarily disclose environmental performance information in an annual report?
13. There are two branches of stakeholder theory. How do they differ?
14. The managerial branch of stakeholder theory proposes that stakeholder power will affect the extent to which an entity meets the stakeholders' needs and expectations. Identify two stakeholder groups and outline how they might have 'power' relating to an organisation's activities.
15. What are the factors a manager might consider in making various expensing–capitalising choices?
16. How can positive accounting theory explain corporate social and environmental reporting?

Application questions

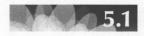

5.1 Making managerial pay contingent on measures of managerial and/or entity performance motivates managers to deliver good performance for shareholders. However, it also burdens them with greater risks than they may like. How do organisations balance these two considerations when choosing managerial pay and performance measures? **J**

5.2 Obtain the remuneration report for a publicly listed company. Examine the compensation contract for the chief executive officer (CEO). Prepare a report which summarises your findings relating to the following issues:
(a) What amount is short term in nature (salary and cash bonus) and what is based on long-term entity or managerial performance?
(b) What proportion of the CEO's pay is performance based and what proportion is not?
(c) What measures of accounting performance are used to determine the CEO's bonus?
(d) Given the accounting entity performance measures in the contract, what accounting decisions could the CEO make in order to maximise his or her bonus?
(e) Can agency theory provide an explanation for the various remuneration components? Justify your answer. **K** **CT** **SM**

5.3 Bonus plans are used to reduce agency problems that exist between managers and shareholders. Discuss two of these problems specific to the relationship between shareholders and managers and identify how bonus plans can be used to reduce the agency problems you have identified. In your answer you should provide examples of specific components that should be added to a bonus contract to address the issues identified. **J** **K**

5.4 You have recently been appointed as a lending officer in the commercial division of a major bank. The bank is concerned about lending in the current economic environment, in which there has been an economic downturn. You have been asked by your supervisor to provide a report indicating how you can safeguard the bank against the risks of lending. In your report you should outline how covenants in debt agreements can be used to reduce the risks, what agency problems the bank should be concerned with, and how accounting information can be used to assist in this process. **K** **CT** **SM**

5.5 A clothing manufacturer has decided to close its factory in a regional Australian town and move its operations offshore to another country where they are going to be able to employ workers at a substantially reduced cost. Closing the factory will result in the loss of 400 jobs in the town. Outline the issues the clothing manufacturer might face with regards to its implied social contract. You should identify what groups or people are likely to be concerned or affected by the decision and whether the decision is likely to be seen as advantageous or disadvantageous to these groups. You should also discuss actions the clothing manufacturer could take to reduce any potential negative reaction to the decision. **J** **K**

5.6 You work for a mining entity which is about to commence exploration in a remote area of the Northern Territory. You have been asked to assist the mining entity to manage its stakeholders to ensure the exploration permit is approved and there is no negative publicity associated with the operation. You are to identify the various stakeholders the mining entity needs to consider and identify the issues each might be concerned with. In your answer you should identify whether these issues are potentially costs or benefits to the entity. **J** **K**

Boral hoses down concerns over debt covenants

By Scott Rochfort

The building materials group Boral has brushed off concerns raised in a broker note that it is at risk of breaching the covenants on a US$700 million 000 bank debt.

A JP Morgan note warns it is 'increasingly likely' Boral could be forced to write down the value of its US assets by as much as $300 million, or a third, a move the broker said could result in a breach of the covenants covering Boral's corporate debt facility.

Boral faces a hefty operating loss from its US operations this year, and a JP Morgan analyst, Andrew Scott, said its asset values would come under closer scrutiny.

'We believe any write-down of the assets may open the door to covenant concerns and reignite speculation regarding an equity raising.'

JP Morgan has forecast Boral's North American business will report a $84 million loss this financial year, compared with a pre-tax and interest profit of $186 million the previous year. The company is the biggest maker of bricks in the US ...

Source: Extracts from Scott Rochfort, 'Boral hoses down concerns over debt covenants', *The Sydney Morning Herald.*[78]

Questions

1. Debt covenants or restrictions are commonly used in Australian lending agreements. Discuss how they are used to reduce agency problems that exist in the relationship between entities and lenders. **J** **K**
2. Why would a company choose to enter into a lending agreement which contains a covenant that puts a restriction on the maximum debt to assets (leverage) that a company can take on? **J** **K**
3. If a company is close to breaching its leverage covenant what actions can it take? **J** **K**

Pay backlash prompts shift to bonuses

By Patrick Durkin

Boards of top-100 companies are paying their chief executives larger annual cash bonuses to avoid an embarrassing investor backlash over pay, experts say.

The fixed pay of CEOs at the top 100 listed companies has doubled over the past five years to an average of $1.8 million — increasing four times faster than pay for ordinary workers, according to a survey of executive pay by the Australian Council of Super Investors [ACSI], which advises 40 superannuation funds that manage more than $250 billion.

The increase compares to a rise of 26.8 per cent in average weekly earnings and a gain of 76.8 per cent in the benchmark S&P/ASX 100 Index over the same period.

ACSI said the more alarming trend was that CEOs were now much more likely to receive an annual bonus. Only four missed out in 2006, compared with one-quarter in 2002.

ACSI said annual bonuses had grown from an average of $769 000 in 2001 to $1.66 million, and more CEOs were receiving them.

'More and more boards seem to be placating executives unhappy at having to meet demanding performance hurdles to get their options by paying them more cash', said ACSI executive officer Phil Spathis.

'Where is the downside for these executives, when so much of their supposed 'at risk' pay is delivered much sooner than later?'

Telstra, AGL, MFS, Suncorp, Babcock & Brown Infrastructure, Leighton Holdings, Toll Holdings and Becton Property Group all faced shareholder protest votes against their remuneration reports this year.

Two of these top-100 companies, Telstra and AGL, faced majority votes against their remuneration reports, and two-thirds of Telstra shareholders, including the Future Fund, voted against Telstra's pay plan and the $11 million pay packet for CEO Sol Trujillo.

Shareholders were concerned his short-term performance pay nearly doubled and the hurdles for his long-term performance pay were less demanding than for other senior executives.

But Geof Stapledon of Risk-Metrics, which conducted the survey, said shareholders typically voted only on long-term grants such as shares, options or equity schemes, rather than short-term annual cash bonuses.

That was one factor driving an increase in the payment of short-term incentives, he said.

'Directors are paid to make tough decisions and it seems many cannot say no to their CEOs when it comes to pay increases,' he said.

The top 10 highest paid CEOs all received a total pay packet of $8.41 million or more, up from $6.49 million the year before.

Source: Extracts from Patrick Durkin, 'Pay backlash prompts shift to bonuses', *The Australian Financial Review*.[79]

Questions

1. One of the problems in the shareholder/manager agency relationship that pay contracts are designed to overcome is the risk aversion problem. Outline what the problem is, and how the contract between managers and shareholders can be designed to reduce risk aversion. **J** **K**

2. How does equity as a pay component work to reduce the horizon problem? What role, if any, does accounting information play in specifying the contractual terms of bonus plans designed to reduce the horizon problem? **J** **K**

3. The article discusses a range of non-salary components that are contained within the management compensation packages of top-100 companies. What is the purpose of including non-salary components in executive pay arrangements? **J** **K**

4. Why would managers prefer short-term cash over long-term equity bonuses? Why does this not align with shareholder interests? Explain your answer. **J** **K**

5. Shareholders of Australian entities have the ability to vote to show either their support or dissatisfaction with companies' remuneration reports. While this is non-binding on the Board, they are obliged to take note of shareholders' views. Explain why shareholders might choose to vote against reports with too high a proportion of pay as short-term cash bonuses rather than long-term incentives. **J** **K**

Additional readings

Deegan, C 2002, 'The legitimising effect of social and environmental disclosures — a theoretical foundation', *Accounting, Auditing and Accountability Journal*, vol. 15, no. 3, pp. 282–311.

Donaldson, T & Preston, LE 1995, 'The stakeholder theory of the corporation: Concepts, evidence and implications', *Academy of Management Review*, vol. 20, no. 1, pp. 65–91.

Gray, R, Kouhy, R & Lavers, S 1995, 'Corporate social and environmental reporting: a review of the literature and a longitudinal study of UK disclosure', *Accounting, Auditing and Accountability Journal*, vol. 8, no. 2, pp. 47–77.

Jensen, M & Meckling, W 1976, 'Theory of the firm: Managerial behaviour, agency costs and ownership structure', *Journal of Financial Economics*, vol. 3, October, pp. 305–60.

Watts, RL & Zimmerman, JL 1986, *Positive Accounting Theory*, Englewood Cliffs, NJ: Prentice Hall.

End notes

1. Watts, RL & Zimmerman, JL 1986, *Positive Accounting Theory*, Englewood Cliffs, NJ: Prentice Hall, p. 7.

2. Smith, CW & Watts, RL 1983, 'The structure of executive contracts and the control of management', unpublished manuscript, University of Rochester.

3. Coase, R 1937, 'The nature of the firm', *Econometrica*, vol. 4, pp. 386–405.

4. Smith, CW & Watts, RL 1983, 'The structure of executive contracts and the control of management', unpublished manuscript, University of Rochester.

5. Jensen, M & Meckling, W 1976, 'Theory of the firm: managerial behaviour, agency costs and ownership structure, *Journal of Financial Economics*, vol. 3, October, pp. 305–60.

6. ibid.

7. ibid.

8. Smith, CW & Watts, RL 1982, 'Incentive and tax effects of executive compensation plans', *Australian Journal of Management*, vol. 7, pp. 139–57.

9. Shoebridge N 2010, 'News resets top executive pay', *The Australian Financial Review*, 5 August, www.afr.com.

10. Jensen, M & Murphy, K 1990, 'CEO incentives — it's not how much you pay, but how', *Harvard Business Review*, May/June, pp. 138–53.

11. ibid.

12. O'Neil, GL & Iob, M 1999, 'Determinants of Executive Remuneration in Australian Organizations: An Exploratory Study', *Asia Pacific Journal of Human Resources*, vol. 37, no. 1, pp. 65–75.

13. Attaway, MC 2000, 'A Study of the Relationship between Company Performance and CEO Compensation', *American Business Review*, vol. 18, no. 1, pp. 77–85; Gregg, P, Machin, S & Szymanski, S 1993, 'The Disappearing Relationship Between Directors' Pay and Corporate Performance', *British Journal of Industrial Relations*, vol. 31, no. 1, pp. 1–9.

14. Matolcsy, Z & Wright, A 2007, 'Australian CEO Compensation: The Descriptive Evidence', *Australian Accounting Review*, November, vol. 17, no. 3, pp. 47–59; Core, JE, Holthausen, RW & Larcker, DF 1999, 'Corporate Governance, Chief Executive Officer Compensation, and Firm Performance', *Journal of Financial Economics*, vol. 51, iss. 3, pp. 371–406; Bushman, RM & Smith, AJ 2001, 'Financial Accounting Information and Corporate Governance', *Journal of Accounting and Economics*, vol. 32, iss. 1–3, pp. 237–333.

15. Rankin, M 2010, 'Structure and level of remuneration across the top executive team', *Australian Accounting Review*, vol. 20, no. 3, pp. 241–55.

16. Smith, CW & Warner, JB 1979, 'On financial contracting: an analysis of bond covenants', *Journal of Financial Economics*, vol. 7, iss. 2, pp. 117–61.

17. Cotter, J 1998, 'Utilisation and restrictiveness of covenants in Australian private debt contracts', *Accounting and Finance*, vol. 38, no. 2, pp. 181–96.

18. Mather, P & Peirson, G 2006, 'Financial Covenants in the Markets for Public and Private Debt', *Accounting and Finance*, vol. 46, no. 2, pp. 285–307.

19. Verrecchia, RE 1983, 'Discretionary disclosure', *Journal of Accounting and Economics*, vol. 5, pp. 179–94.

20. Scott, WR 2001, 'Institutional theory', in George Ritzer (ed.) *Encyclopedia of Social Theory*, Thousand Oaks, CA: Sage Publications.

21. Scott, WR 2001, *Institutions and Organizations*, 2nd ed. Thousand Oaks, CA: Sage Publications, p. 57.

22. ibid; DiMaggio, P & Powell, W 1983, 'The iron cage revisited: Institutional isomorphism and collective rationality in organizational fields', *American Sociological Review*, vol. 48, no. 2, pp. 147–60; Meyer, JW & Rowan, B 1977, 'Institutionalized organizations: Formal structure as myth and ceremony', *American Journal of Sociology*, vol. 83, no. 2, pp. 340–63.

23. Pfeffer, J 1982, *Organizations and organization theory*, Boston: Pitman Publishing; Eisenhardt, KM 1988, 'Agency- and institutional-theory explanations: The case of retail sales compensation', *The Academy of Management Journal*, vol. 31, no. 3, pp. 488–511.

24. Eisenhardt, KM 1988, 'Agency- and institutional-theory explanations: The case of retail sales compensation', *The Academy of Management Journal*, vol. 31, no. 3, pp. 488–511.

25. ibid.

26. ibid.

27. Campbell, JL 2007, 'Why would corporations behave in socially responsible ways? An institutional theory of corporate social responsibility', *Academy of Management Review*, vol. 32, no. 3, pp. 946–67.

28. Kolk, A, Levy, D & Pinkse, J 2008, 'Corporate responses in an emerging climate regime: The institutionalisation and commensuration of carbon disclosure', *European Accounting Review*, vol. 17, no. 4, pp. 719–45.

29. Gray, R, Owen, D & Adams, C 1996, *Accounting and Accountability*, Hertfordshire, UK: Prentice Hall.

30. Gray, R, Kouhy, R & Lavers, S 1995, 'Corporate social and environmental reporting: a review of the literature and a longitudinal study of UK disclosure', *Accounting, Auditing and Accountability Journal*, vol. 8, no. 2, pp. 47–77.

31. Dowling, J and Pfeffer, J 1975, 'Organizational legitimacy: social values and organizational behavior', *Pacific Sociological Review*, vol. 18, no. 1, pp. 122–36.

32. Donaldson, T 1982, *Corporations and Morality*, Englewood Cliffs, NJ: Prentice Hall.

33. Dowling, J and Pfeffer, J 1975, 'Organizational legitimacy: social values and organizational behavior', *Pacific Sociological Review*, vol. 18, no. 1, pp. 122–36.

34. Gray, R, Kouhy, R & Lavers, S 1995, 'Corporate social and environmental reporting: a review of the literature and a longitudinal study of UK disclosure', *Accounting, Auditing and Accountability Journal*, vol. 8, no. 2, pp. 47–77.

35. Gray, R, Owen, D & Adams, C 1996, *Accounting and Accountability*, Hertfordshire, UK: Prentice Hall.

36. Patten, D 1992, 'Intra-industry environmental disclosures in response to the Alaskan oil spill: A note on legitimacy theory', *Accounting, Organizations and Society*, vol. 17, no. 5, pp. 471–75.

37. Friedman, M 1962, *Capitalism and Freedom*, Chicago: University of Chicago Press.

38. Harris, S 1999, 'Westpac chief admits banks failed in the bush', *The Australian*, 20 May, p. 1.

39. ibid.

40. Anonymous 2009, 'The banks take much, but give less and less back', *The Age*, 9 April, www.theage.com.au.

41. Deegan, CM and Rankin, M 1996, 'Do Australian companies report environmental news objectively? An analysis of environmental disclosures by firms prosecuted successfully by the Environmental Protection Authority', *Accounting, Auditing and Accountability Journal*, vol. 9, no. 2, pp. 52–69.

42. O'Donovan, G 1999, 'Managing legitimacy through increased corporate environmental reporting: an exploratory study', *Interdisciplinary Environmental Review*, vol. 1, no. 1, pp. 63–99.

43. Lindblom, CK 1994, 'The implications of organisation legitimacy for corporate social performance and disclosure', *Critical Perspectives in Accounting Conference* (New York), p. 2.

44. Buhr, N 1998, 'A structuration view on the initiation of environmental reports', *Critical Perspectives on Accounting*, vol. 13, no. 1, pp. 17–38; Ashforth, B & Gibbs, B 1990, 'The double edge of legitimization', *Organization Science*, vol. 1, no. 2, pp. 177–94.

45. Gray, R, Kouhy, R & Lavers, S 1995, 'Corporate social and environmental reporting: a review of the literature and a longitudinal study of UK disclosure', *Accounting, Auditing and Accountability Journal*, vol. 8, no. 2, pp. 47–77.

46. Deegan, CM and Rankin, M 1996, 'Do Australian companies report environmental news objectively? An analysis of environmental disclosures by firms prosecuted successfully by the Environmental Protection Authority', *Accounting, Auditing and Accountability Journal*, vol. 9, no. 2, pp. 52–69.

47. Hurst, JW 1970, *The legitimacy of the Business Corporation in the Law of the United States 1780–1970*, Charlottesville, VA: University Press of Virginia.

48. BHP Billiton, *BHP Billiton annual report 2010*, p. 7, www.bhpbilliton.com.

49. Gray, R, Kouhy, R & Lavers, S 1995, 'Corporate social and environmental reporting: a review of the literature and a longitudinal study of UK disclosure', *Accounting, Auditing and Accountability Journal*, vol. 8, no. 2, pp. 47–77.

50. Freeman, R 1984, *Strategic Management: A Stakeholder Approach*, Marshall, MA: Pitman.

51. Hasnas, J 1998, 'The normative theories of business ethics: a guide for the perplexed', *Business Ethics Quarterly*, vol. 8, no. 1, pp. 19–42.

52. ibid.

53. ibid.

54. Donaldson, T & Preston, LE 1995, 'The stakeholder theory of the corporation: concepts, evidence and implications', *Academy of Management Review*, vol. 20, no. 1, pp. 65–91.

55. ibid.

56. Ullman, A 1985, 'Data in search of a theory: a critical examination of the relationships among social performance, social disclosure and economic performance of US firms', *Academy of Management Review*, vol. 10, no. 3, pp. 540–57.

57. Donaldson, T & Preston, LE 1995, 'The stakeholder theory of the corporation: concepts, evidence and implications', *Academy of Management Review*, vol. 20, no. 1, pp. 65–91.

58. Mitchell, RK, Angle, BR & Wood, DJ 1997, 'Toward a theory of stakeholder identification and salience: defining the principle of who and what really counts', *Academy of Management Review*, vol. 22, no. 4, pp. 853–86.

59. Roberts, R. 1992 'Determinants of corporate social responsibility disclosure: an application of stakeholder theory', *Accounting, Organizations and Society*, vol. 17, no. 1, pp. 595–612.

60. Lindblom, CK 1994, 'The implications of organisation legitimacy for corporate social performance and disclosure', *Critical Perspectives in Accounting Conference* (New York), p. 2; Gray, R, Kouhy, R & Lavers, S 1995, 'Corporate social and environmental reporting: a review of the literature and a longitudinal study of UK disclosure', *Accounting, Auditing and Accountability Journal*, vol. 8, no. 2, pp. 47–77.

61. Galbraith, J 2008, 'Organizational design' in T Cummings (ed.) *Handbook of Organisation Development*, Thousands Oaks, CA: Sage Publications.

62. Burns, T, & Stalker, G M 1961, *Management of innovation*. London: Tavistock; Donaldson, L 2001, *The contingency theory of organizations*, Thousands Oaks, CA: Sage Publications; Galbraith, J 1973, *Designing complex organizations*. Reading, MA: Addison Wesley; Gerdin, J & Greve, J 2008, 'The appropriateness of statistical methods for testing contingency hypotheses in management accounting research', *Accounting, Organizations and Society*, vol. 33, iss. 7–8, pp. 995–1009.

63. Galbraith, J 1973, *Designing complex organizations*. Reading, MA: Addison Wesley; Gerdin, J & Greve, J 2008, 'The appropriateness of statistical methods for testing contingency hypotheses in management accounting research', *Accounting, Organizations and Society*, vol. 33, iss. 7–8, pp. 995–1009.

64. Donaldson, L 2001, *The contingency theory of organizations*, Thousands Oaks, CA: Sage Publications; Cadez, S & Guilding, C 2008, 'An exploratory investigation of an integrated contingency model of strategic management accounting', *Accounting, Organizations and Society*, vol. 33, iss. 7–8, pp. 836–63.

65. Morton, NA & Hu, Q 2008, 'Implications of the fit between organizational structure and ERP: a structural contingency theory perspective', *International Journal of Information Management*, vol. 28, iss. 5, pp. 391–402.

66. Donaldson, L 2001, *The contingency theory of organizations*, Thousands Oaks, CA: Sage Publications, p. 7.

67. Morton, NA & Hu, Q 2008, 'Implications of the fit between organizational structure and ERP: a structural contingency theory perspective', *International Journal of Information Management*, vol. 28, iss. 5, pp. 391–402.

68. Otley, DT 1980, 'The contingency theory of management accounting: achievement and prognosis', *Accounting, Organizations and Society*, vol. 5, no. 4, pp. 413–28.

69. Chenhall, R 2003, 'Management control systems design within an organizational context: findings from contingency-based research and directions for the future, *Accounting, Organizations and Society*, vol. 28, no. 2–3, pp. 127–68.

70. Otley, DT 1980, 'The contingency theory of management accounting: achievement and prognosis', *Accounting, Organizations and Society*, vol. 5, no. 4, pp. 413–28.

71. Jokipii, A 2010, 'Determinants and consequences of internal control in firms: a contingency theory based analysis', *Journal of Management and Governance*, vol. 14, iss. 2, pp. 115–44.

72. ibid.

73. Cadez, S & Guilding, C 2008, 'An exploratory investigation of an

integrated contingency model of strategic management accounting', *Accounting, Organizations and Society*, vol. 33, iss. 7–8, pp. 836–63.

74. Sunder, S 1997, *Theory of Accounting and Control*, Cincinnati, O.H.: South-Western College Pub.

75. ibid.

76. Deegan, CM and Rankin, M 1996, 'Do Australian companies report environmental news objectively? An analysis of environmental disclosures by firms prosecuted successfully by the Environmental Protection Authority', *Accounting, Auditing and Accountability Journal*, vol. 9, no. 2, pp. 52–69.

77. Patten, D 1992, 'Intra-industry environmental disclosures in response to the Alaskan oil spill: A note on legitimacy theory', *Accounting, Organizations and Society*, vol. 17, no. 5, pp. 471–75.

78. Rochfort, S 2009, 'Boral hoses down concerns over debt covenants', *The Sydney Morning Herald*, 21 January, p. 1.

79. Durkin, P 2007, 'Pay backlash prompts shift to bonuses', *The Australian Financial Review*, 21 November, p. 3.

6

Products of the financial reporting process

After studying this chapter, you should be able to:

1 evaluate the importance of the identification of the reporting entity

2 outline the debate surrounding the length and frequency of reporting periods

3 discuss the practice of manipulating reported earnings in the production of financial information

4 outline the debate surrounding the exclusion of intangibles and intellectual capital from the financial reporting process

5 explain the options available to companies reporting voluntary disclosures

6 identify three theories that explain the motivation for voluntary disclosures in annual reports.

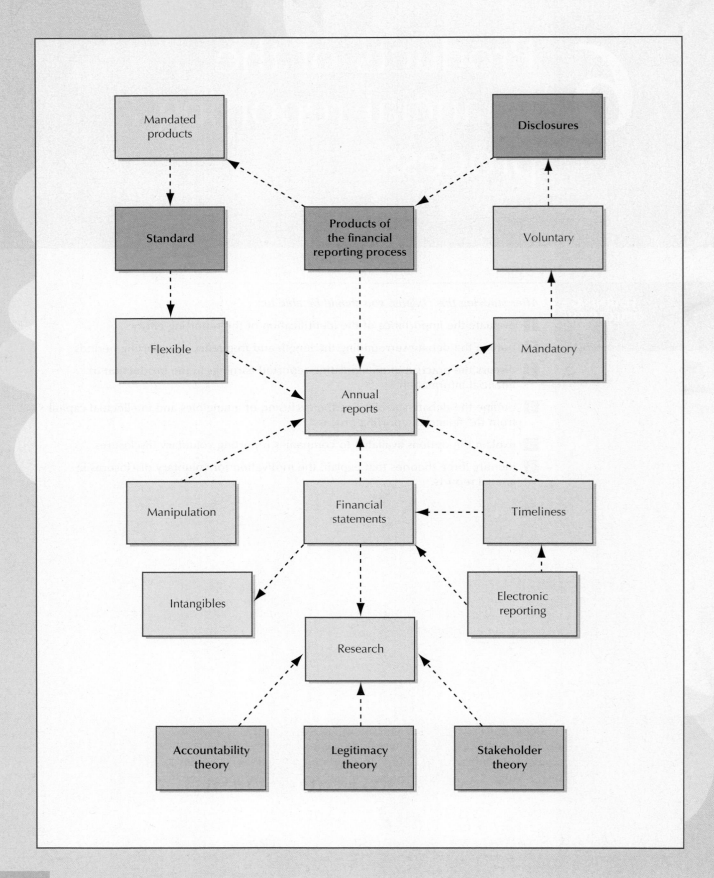

The delivery of financial accounts in the form of financial statements, attested to by a public accounting firm, is the last step in the annual accounting cycle as well as the first step in the publication of accounting information relating to that annual accounting cycle. The publication of the financial statements is highly valued by society because the financial statements impart a sense of reliability and credibility. It is through these statements that claims about economic responsibility, agency and accountability are made. They are the means by which others judge those claims.

Economic responsibility is commonly judged by performance and wealth. The income statement (statement of profit or loss and other comprehensive income) represents the claims by the reporting entity about its economic performance. The balance sheet (statement of financial position) is the dated statement about its wealth.

Accounting regulations are like a straitjacket: what is reported is only one dimension of the reporting entity. In generating its wealth and performance, an entity will engage in activities that are not captured by the accounting process. Many enterprises will give an account of these activities within their annual reports and elsewhere. Back in the 1970s, proposed conceptual frameworks for accounting were in favour of reporting all activities. The corporate report was notable for exploring these issues. More recently, calls for innovation in financial reporting have advocated the inclusion of information apparently relevant to the decisions of users as well as the adoption of new technologies which will change the reporting process from one of publication to one of broadcasting.

Increasingly, accounting's 500-year-old system is being questioned because its methods are seen to be out of touch with the needs of twenty-first century investors and shareholders,[1] especially in light of the global financial crisis. The issues discussed in this chapter relate to some of these criticisms. They are:
- identification of the reporting entity
- the lack of timeliness in the publication of financial reports
- what is included in the financial statements which raises the issue of the conceptual primacy of assets
- the alleged manipulation of reported numbers
- what is omitted from financial statements and how these are reported
- how financial statements are reported, including the adoption of new technologies.

LO 1 IDENTIFICATION OF THE REPORTING ENTITY

For any set of financial statements to be meaningful, the entity whose economic activities are being reported must be clearly identified. In 2010, the IASB promoted a definition of a reporting entity as 'a circumscribed area of economic activities whose financial information has the potential to be useful to existing and potential equity investors, lenders, and other creditors who cannot directly obtain the information they need in making decisions about providing resources to the entity and in assessing whether management and the governing board of that entity have made efficient and effective use of the resources provided'.[2] Under this definition, the reporting entity is not necessarily the same as a legal entity as the entity could include multiple legal entities all bound by the concept of 'control'. If a legal entity controls one or more other legal entities, it should prepare financial statements on a consolidated basis thus reflecting the economic resources and claims of the group of entities as a whole.

Control exists when an investor is exposed, or has rights, to variable returns from its involvement with an investee and has the ability to affect those returns through its power over the investee. Note that the essence of control is the ability to obtain returns. The aim is to restrict opportunities for off-balance-sheet financial schemes such as special-purpose

Definition of "entity"

entities. As such, using the concept of control to determine the composition of a group (reporting entity) has the potential to instigate a range of economic consequences that a controlling entity might want to avoid, such as contracting relationships with implications for debt covenants.

WHEN INFORMATION IS REPORTED

Although by the time annual accounts are published, audited and released there is little news in them, the practice of producing annual financial statements including balance sheets and income statements is well established. International accounting standards require financial reports to be presented at least annually. Annual balancing and closing of accounts has been common in Europe for about 500 years. It was useful in providing arithmetic accuracy.[3] Also, the balance sheet was useful in providing a summary of the financial position to owners who did not manage their businesses. Despite these advantages, many entities did not embrace regular 12-month accounting periods. The introduction of income tax, the separation of ownership from control and the monitoring concerns of shareholders are thought to be responsible for the universal adoption of the annual accounting cycle.[4]

This practice — of producing annual accounts — is so well established that little thought has been given to the possibility of other time periods, other than that of shorter ones. In many countries, listed companies are required to produce interim financial accounts. Real-time reporting, such as with XBRL (discussed later in this chapter), opens up the possibility of non-standardised reporting periods, so that uniformity is surrendered for flexibility.

The practice of producing annual accounts was a response to the continuing nature of reporting entities. The closing of accounts at the completion of a venture was not applicable for continuing enterprises. The idea of an accounting period was to mimic a completed venture. Profit determination for the period represents the liquidation proceeds at the end of a venture. The balance sheet imitates the distributions at the end of the venture.

After a series of high-profile corporate collapses, Australia's *Corporate Law Economic Reform Program (Audit Reform and Corporate Disclosure) Act 2004* aimed to restore public confidence in corporate Australia by requiring better disclosure in both the annual and half-yearly financial reports and in the continuous disclosure regime for Australian-listed companies. Australian-listed companies also comply with Australian Securities Exchange (ASX) listing rules, which require disclosure of share-price-sensitive information as soon as the company becomes aware of it. Share-price-sensitive information is any information that a reasonable person would expect to have a material effect on the price of the company's shares. Generally, this information would relate to earnings, changes in management and bankruptcy.

Arguments for standardisation of reporting periods

The four main arguments for standardisation of the accounting cycle into a 12-month reporting period are briefly outlined in the following.

1. The standardisation of reporting periods allows investors to compare and evaluate the relative effectiveness of managements of different companies or reporting entities.
2. The shareholder requirement for dividends makes it necessary to close the books, calculate profits and declare a dividend based on those profits. In some countries law requires companies to pay dividends only out of profits, so their calculation is integral to paying them.

3. Various company acts require entities under their jurisdiction to supply shareholders with annual balance sheets and profit or loss accounts.
4. Before the twentieth century, stewardship was more important than measuring a rate of return on capital.[5] Accounts were seen as control mechanisms rather than measuring rate of return. Control required standardisation of the reporting period.

Arguments for a more flexible approach to reporting periods

There are several arguments given to support a more flexible approach to reporting periods. For example, any standardised period cuts across many incomplete transactions. Standardisation may result in accountants apportioning unfinished operations and allocating assets to an arbitrary accounting period of 12 months.

Chambers (cited by Luther) argued that the appropriate accounting period is determined by the nature of the entity, so that it should reflect the earnings cycle of the reporting entity.[6] This view was supported by the American Institute of Certified Public Accountants in 1973 but has not been adopted.

Johnson & Kaplan (cited by Luther) argue that standardisation puts pressure on managers to produce profits over short-term periods.[7] Luther quotes several authors who argue that to overcome the problems created by standardisation, annual accounts should have a cumulative component because they are tentative and conjectural statements, the truth of which cannot be verified until the reporting entity has run its entire course.[8]

Interim reporting

Reports issued between annual reports are called interim financial reports to distinguish them from annual reports. There is an accounting standard (AASB 134/IAS 34 *Interim Financial Reporting*) for interim financial reports but it does not mandate their preparation. Nor does the standard mandate their frequency or how soon after the end of an interim period they should be completed. However, if interim reports are prepared, they must, at a minimum, have the following components:

- condensed balance sheet
- condensed income statement
- condensed statement of changes in equity
- condensed statement of cash flows
- selected explanatory notes determined by what is needed to give the user an understanding of the report.

Additionally, comparative information should be supplied.

Remember a key role of financial statements is to summarise relevant information parsimoniously.[9] The statements are intended to be complete within the constraints and definitions of generally accepted accounting principles. In this broad view of financial statements, timeliness is only one dimension.

LO 3 MANIPULATION OF REPORTED EARNINGS

Even though published financial statements have little news, they do have value. Part of the value that comes from the reporting of financial information is in reducing the information asymmetry between company insiders and those outside the firm. Concern about manipulation of reported financial information is not new and researchers and the media have highlighted it since the 1970s. Although both the income statement and the balance sheet are manipulated, the focus of manipulation discovery is mainly on income.

Why does management manipulate the accounts? The main reason suggested relates to the desire to influence wealth transfers among the various stakeholders, including management, controlling shareholders, other shareholders and potential shareholders. Christensen suggests the crux of the problem is the decision-making role given to financial accounting information.[10] Once accounting information is used for performance evaluation, incentives for earnings management arise. Management has an information advantage over outsiders including auditors. This is a moral hazard. Management knows things that owners and other outsiders do not, unless managers reveal what they know. Managers, therefore, have the ability to act opportunistically in their own interests. While auditing reduces the moral hazard problem, it does not eliminate it.

Why are accounts open to manipulation? Managers and controlling shareholders take advantage of the information asymmetry between themselves and existing and potential shareholders.[11] Communication between management and outsiders within the accounting system is limited to financial information. Transactions are combined with managers' inside information within the accrual system.

Manipulation is defined as the:

> use of management's discretion to make accounting choices or to design transactions to affect the possibilities of wealth transfer between the company and society (political costs), funds providers (cost of capital) or managers (compensation plans).[12]

Manipulation that is within the law is called earnings management, which includes income smoothing, big bath accounting and creative accounting. Manipulation that is outside the law is fraud. Often the difference between the two is narrow.

Earnings management

Calculated income (or profit), commonly referred to as 'the bottom line', has become the most widely used indicator of an enterprise's performance. Financial analysts spend a lot of time analysing corporate performances and issue predictions about upcoming performances. These predictions have become so important in some capital markets that it is thought that management 'cook the books' to present as favourable a performance as possible. 'Cooking the books' is a term used in the media; in the accounting literature, the term used is **earnings management**. The investigation of whether earnings management takes place was a hot topic, especially in the period after the world-famous corporate collapses of Enron, WorldCom and others.

Earnings management depends on the timing differences that arise between accrual accounting and cash accounting. Although there are customary ways to treat these differences, earnings management generally brings revenues into the year of 'need' and postpones expenses into the next or subsequent years. Creative compliance is a form of earnings management. It uses schemes to circumvent the law. Lawyers are used to ensure that those schemes are defensible. As a consequence, creative compliance is costly.

Because the measure of corporate success has become whether a corporation has reached its earnings predictions, the temptation for management is to 'manage' earnings to match analysts' forecasts. In this process, as outlined by Macintosh et al., accounting earnings do not reflect the outcomes of an enterprise's strategic decisions.[13] Instead, analysts' predicted earnings determine the strategy of an enterprise to satisfy the prediction. This means management may take predictions about earnings as targets and select investments that are likely to produce reported income equal to or exceeding the analysts' forecasts. Meanwhile, the market incorporates analysts' earnings forecasts into share prices. In this way, share prices, analysts' forecasts and reported income all relate to each other but not to 'true' or underlying income.

Parfet, a representative of preparers of financial reports, defends earnings management by differentiating 'bad' from 'good' earnings management.[14] The bad involves intervening to hide true operating performance by creating artificial accounting entries or by stretching the estimates required in preparing financial statements beyond reasonableness. This, he points out, is the realm of hidden reserves, improper revenue (income) recognition and overly aggressive or conservative accounting judgements.

Good earnings management, on the other hand, involves management taking actions to try to create stable financial performance by acceptable, voluntary business decisions in the context of competition and market developments. The market tends to reward corporations that achieve stable trends of growing income. Good earnings management involves spotting the most beneficial use for the corporation's resources and quickly reacting to unforeseen circumstances. Parfet declares earnings management not to be a bad thing but a reflection of expectations and demands, both inside and outside a business, on the part of all stakeholders in the capital market. Earnings management is addressed in more detail in chapter 9.

Income smoothing

The good earnings management discussed in the previous section is more commonly known as income smoothing. Management artificially manipulates earnings to produce a steadily growing profit stream: above-normal profits in good times are artificially reduced by certain provisions and these provisions are called upon in not-so-good times to inflate the reported profit figure. Management can only smooth income when the entity is making sufficient profits to allow it. Commentators believe management indulges in income smoothing to increase its remuneration, while for controlling shareholders, the benefits lie in transferring wealth to themselves from new shareholders.[15]

The situation in which current income is reduced by a new management team by using as many income-decreasing accruals as possible is known as 'taking a bath' or 'big bath accounting'. The aim is to reduce current income so that reported low income levels may be blamed on the previous management team, as well as providing a reduced basis for future comparisons. Because the future income stream is free of these charges, improved earnings are more likely, and targets within management compensation schemes can more easily be achieved. These issues are covered in more detail in chapter 9.

Pro forma reports: massaging earnings

Pacific Brands, an Australian enterprise which listed on the ASX in 2004, in its first annual report reported pro forma results for the year to balance date as well as a pro forma review of financial performance. **Pro forma results** are primarily used to show 'as though' results — for example, in the case of Pacific Brands, the enterprise had not been operating for a full 12 months so the results and review of operations were 'as though' the company had been operating for 12 months. Pro forma figures have also been used to show the effect of an accounting change for the previous year's results so that the previous year provides a proper comparison with the current year's figures.

However, the use of pro forma financial statements to exclude one-time or unusual items from earnings has generated intense debate between supporters and critics of the practice — particularly in the United States.[16] Pro forma earnings are also known as cash earnings, core earnings, adjusted earnings or earnings before certain items. Policy makers, regulators and the financial press label pro forma statements incomplete, inaccurate and misleading. Supporters argue that pro forma earnings clarify complex accounting disclosures, so providing a clearer picture of core earnings expected to continue in future periods. Critics claim that pro forma reporting is being used to turn a loss under the generally accepted accounting principles (GAAP) into a profit under pro forma reporting, and that pro forma earnings are not comparable across reporting entities or across reporting periods.

It is this aspect of pro forma reporting that worries critics such as Brody and McDonald and Bhattacharya et al., because most of the pro forma results released in the United States reflect higher income levels than if the financial statements were prepared according to accounting standards or GAAP, and pro forma reporting is used by less profitable firms with higher debt levels than other firms in their industry.[17] Entities are more likely to release the pro forma reports when their share price and earnings decline in order to meet analysts' expectations and to downplay bad earnings news. A study revealed that less sophisticated investors with a limited ability to access information trade on pro forma information, while sophisticated, well-informed investors do not.[18]

LO 4   EXCLUSION OF ACTIVITIES FROM THE FINANCIAL REPORTING PROCESS

Although management discretion over accounting numbers can impair or improve the quality of financial statements, accounting regulations themselves may result in inaccurate company assessments because they do not allow certain items to be reported. Remember that the *Conceptual Framework* is based on the definition of an asset. What is recognised as an asset and how it is measured changes as standards change.[19] Currently, this issue centres on the tighter rules relating to the reporting of intangibles, especially the reporting of intellectual capital. Lev stated, 'As much as two-thirds or three-fourths of the real value of the company is based on intangibles, and investors are not getting the information they need to make decisions'.[20] Another issue has been the reporting of social and environmental activities of corporations.

To overcome accounting regulations, firms make voluntary disclosures. These are increasing, particularly among larger companies undertaking to fill the void between what can be reported within accounting rules and the drivers of value generation within firms.[21] Disclosures also seem to be included as corporate management responds to media attention. Disclosures may relate to human resources, the environment, or community, although environment disclosures are the most researched (see chapter 11).

Intangibles

Although accounting authorities have no difficulties in including physical assets in balance sheets, irrespective of whether they have been purchased or internally generated, the rules for intangibles are different. Traditional accounting systems are not able to provide information about corporate intangible assets. Intangibles are identified as the value and growth creators in almost all industries.[22] More and more resources are being put into research and development, brand building, customer relationships, employee training and education, supply chain networks and information technology structure. As such, intangibles are at the centre of an information gap that arises from the forward-looking and uncertain nature of economic activity.[23]

Intangibles are seen to be the reason the book value of corporations has been shrinking in relation to market value.[24] The difference is regarded by capital markets as the value of a corporation's intangible assets. CEOs are concerned that their book values are, on average, a quarter or less than market values.[25] Currently, financial statements do not give an overview of all value-creating activities, so that investors and other stakeholders are unable to properly assess the potential of a reporting entity as well as its ability to achieve sustainable results.

The treatment of intangibles is outlined in the following to show why information about them is limited in financial reporting. This treatment has sparked debate about the focus of the *Conceptual Framework* as well as whether intangibles should be treated differently from other assets. Because the accounting authorities have extended the definition of an asset to include other features and have elaborated the recognition criteria for intangibles, questions have been raised about the balance sheet focus of the *Conceptual Framework*.

Intangible assets are defined as identifiable non-monetary assets without physical substance.[26] AASB 138/IAS 38 *Intangible Assets* declares that identifiable intangible assets should only be recognised when it is probable that the future economic benefits generated by them will flow to the reporting entity and when these benefits can be reliably measured. However, the insertion of 'identifiable' into the definition means that to be recognised, an intangible asset must be able to be separated from the reporting entity or have arisen from contractual or other legal rights. AASB 138/IAS 38 specifically prohibits the recognition of brands, mastheads, publishing titles, customer lists and the like that are internally generated because the IASB believed that they would rarely meet the recognition criteria. Expenditure on research, training, advertising and start-up activities are not to be recognised as intangible assets.

Any recognised intangibles are subject to the impairment test. Revaluations are restricted to those intangibles for which there is an active market. An **active market** is defined in AASB 13/IFRS 13 *Fair Value Measurement* as:

> A market in which transactions for the asset or liability take place with sufficient frequency and volume to provide pricing information on an ongoing basis.

There are not many assets, physical or intangible, that would comply with this test. Yet the test is applied only to intangibles.

Arguably, contractual provisions, particularly those governing the payment of dividends or the issue of additional debt, have generated strong corporate resistance to any changes in the definitions of assets and liabilities, despite the importance of intangibles to the modern organisation.[27] Contemporary Issue 6.1 discusses the state of corporate accounting systems.

**6.1
CONTEMPORARY
ISSUE**

Corporate accounting systems are out of date

By Thorsten Wiesel, Bernd Skiera & Julian Villanueva

The objective of financial reporting is to provide information to help current and potential investors, creditors, and other users (hereinafter, investors) assess the amounts, timing, and uncertainty of prospective cash receipts (Financial Accounting Standards Board [FASB] 1978;[28] International Accounting Standards Board [IASB] 2004).[29] However, the IASB's (2004) Framework for the Preparation and Presentation of Financial Statements acknowledges that financial statements (e.g., balance sheets, profit and loss statements, notes) are not, on their own, sufficient to meet the objective of financial reporting. To bridge the gap between what financial statements are able to achieve and the objective of financial reporting, firms must report additional information that explains the main trends and factors that underlie their development, performance, and position (IASB 2005).[30] In response, the 'Management Discussion and Analysis' ('MD&A') required in the United States (Securities and Exchange Commission [SEC] 2003)[31] and the recently discussed 'Management Commentary' (IASB 2005)[32] require information that supplements and complements information in a firm's financial statements. A recent report on the future of financial reporting published by the Big Six (sec) auditing firms confirms the importance of this discussion (Deloitte 2006).[33]

Specifically, the information requested in the 'Management Commentary' should be future oriented, understandable, relevant, reliable, and comparable and should provide an 'analysis through the eyes of management' (IASB 2005, p. 20).[34] Examples of such information include details about the nature of the business, key resources, risks and relationships, and performance measures and indicators. Moreover, the IASB (2005) discussion paper explicitly mentions customer measures as crucial for assessing operating performance and, therefore, key information that should be reported to investors.[35]

Source: Extracts from Thorsten Wiesel, Bernd Skiera & Julian Villanueva, 'Customer equity: an integral part of financial reporting', *Journal of Marketing*.[36]

Questions

1. Why do financial statements prepared under the IASB's *Conceputal Framework* and standards fail to meet the objective of financial reporting as outlined in the *Conceptual Framework*? **K**
2. Why do you think the author of the extract would expect readers of a marketing journal to be interested in financial reporting? **J** **AS**
3. What difficulties do you see in requiring the disclosed information to be 'reliable and comparable' and 'future oriented'? **J** **AS**

Intellectual capital

Within the debate about intangibles, there is another debate about the reporting and measurement of **intellectual capital**. The term was first used in one of Skandia's annual reports about a decade ago. It is an umbrella term that refers to:

- capital created by employees or purchased, such as patents, computer and administrative systems, concepts, models, and research and development
- relationships with customers and suppliers that consist of brand names, trade marks and the like
- capital embedded in employees, such as through education, training, values and experience.

Under accounting's conservative rules for intangibles, only intellectual capital that has been purchased will be recognised in the financial statements. Knowledge organisations' assets are their employees because of the increasing tendency for technology to be embodied in intellectual property and labour where previously it resided in fixed assets.[37]

Many commentators point out that it is fundamental to an understanding of value creation within firms that users be informed of the categories of expenditures that generate value-creation processes.[38] The rate of return to intellectual capital investment can be determined only through an analysis involving original expenditure data. The general problem of incomplete information suggests that more information is better even if it is uncertain, but regulators have gone the other way, increasingly moving to prevent firms from measuring and reporting internally generated intangible assets.[39] Lev argues strongly for the accounting system to be overhauled in relation to intangibles when he remarks that accounting information failed to give inklings about the late 1990s bubble in technology stocks, failed to alert investors to the major scandals of the early 2000s (such as Enron and WorldCom), and failed to reflect appropriately the values of subprime mortgages. He argues that an overhaul with respect to intangibles should allow accounting information to fulfil its declared purpose of providing information to help investors in assessing future cash receipts.[40]

Because the basic financial statements of balance sheet, income statement and statement of cash flows are not up to the task of providing users with the contextual information necessary for understanding the complex financial affairs of a reporting entity, voluntary disclosure appears to be the answer to the lack of comprehensiveness of financial statements.

VOLUNTARY DISCLOSURES

The traditional, statutory formal communication vehicle between a reporting entity and its interested constituencies is the annual report. Although the annual report is the traditional home of the published financial statements, the purpose of this communication vehicle has been speculated to be: marketing; to project a corporate image; to 'impression manage' to ensure top management is portrayed favourably; to 'sell' an organisation; and to influence the perceptions of stakeholders. Its dominance as a communication device is shown by the many variations in its structure, content and presentation. Reports communicate through words and visual images comprising quantitative information, narratives, photographs, tables and graphs. They are commonly divided into two sections, with the required financial statements usually assigned either to a rear section or to a separate volume. Voluntary disclosures are made in the larger 'up-front' section of an annual report. The glossy overlay of this front half is seen as being capable of overriding the numerical and other statutory messages relegated to the rear.[41]

Annual reports provide management with a unique opportunity to achieve certain purposes. As well as a means to communicate with customers, shareholders, employees, suppliers, media and government, annual reports provide reporting entities with opportunities to provide information to users about corporate activities that are not covered in the financial statements. Annual reports cover governance, employee issues such as health and safety, ethical, environmental and social issues, and information relating to intangibles, particularly intellectual capital. However, the report's role as a communication tool generates controversy because not only can it be used as an information source for investors, it can be used as a marketing tool and conveyor of a particular organisational image to its readers. These uses of annual reports are controversial because the annual report's credibility lies in the inclusion of audited financial statements. Contemporary Issue 6.2 considers this issue further.

6.2 CONTEMPORARY ISSUE

Be kind to shareholders: keep it short, sweet and informative

By Stuart Wilson

The annual report is the single most important document a company sends to its shareholders.

It is also an ever-evolving form of communication, with a phenomenal amount of change in the past few years and some of the biggest improvements expected over the next few years.

Recent years have seen the expansion of the annual report with the introduction of the Corporate Governance and Remuneration Reports as well as the introduction of the International Financial Reporting Standards.

A strongly supported initiative is the 'shareholder friendly report', a concept produced by the Australian Institute of Company Directors and PricewaterhouseCoopers. While it isn't a perfect replacement for a concise annual report (for instance it omits far too many director disclosures), it is a serious attempt to condense a company's annual activities and results into a brief document, and is an initiative to be encouraged.

Some of the key features of the Shareholder Friendly Report include key performance indicator reporting, achievements versus targets and disclosure of new targets for the next year, as well as an overall outlook in the CEO's review of operations, where sensitivities and critical success factors are outlined. Financial statements include an explanation of terms and an elaboration of the data.

The reporting includes the figures for the past five years and the data tie back to the full report to encourage reference to the full document. Shareholder-friendly reporting encourages the company to provide greater interpretation of data. These don't always appear in annual reports, but are considered to be of great value to owners.

A recent survey from Chartered Secretaries Australia suggests that fewer shareholders are reading annual reports. It may be that many are becoming too long, providing information with too much corporate spin or too diverse, or simply incomprehensible to the average person. It may also be that many shareholders own shares in both their own name and their superannuation fund, and have requested only one annual report.

The Shareholder Friendly Report concept also seeks to address the problem that far too many annual reports, including the concise variety, have become overly lengthy. Of course, there are a lot of disclosure requirements these days, however there remains a great deal of wastage, with superfluous photographs and over-the-top graphic design.

Given that the annual report is the most important communication provided by companies to shareholders, it is irksome to see it laden with expensive bells and whistles, while at the same time its creators bang on about how cost-conscious the firm has been over the prior year.

It is essential, therefore, that the board of directors and senior executives maintain control of its content and production, rather than the all too frequent occurrence of letting it get hijacked by the public relations team and graphic artists.

All too often, when a company's performance has been disastrous, it is often described as merely disappointing, or if a good spin doctor has edited the report, mixed. There is, on the other hand a plethora of superlatives for a successful year. If only the chairman actually wrote the chairman's report rather than some lower-level flak.

There are many annual reports that are readable, easily understood and to the point. Let's hope that number continues to grow, and that in the event the economy's dream run starts to fade companies will be as forthcoming about their failings as they have been about their successes.

Source: Extracts from Stuart Wilson, 'Be kind to shareholders', *The Australian*.[42]

Questions

1. Despite reiterating that the annual report is the single most important document a company sends to its shareholders, the writer is critical of annual reports. Outline those criticisms. **K**

2. If annual reports are so important to shareholders, why are fewer people reading them? **K**

3. Why do you think the shareholder-friendly report initiative will not be a 'perfect replacement' for a concise report? **J** **K**

Narrative voluntary disclosures in annual reports provide the means by which management can report corporate achievements, particularly those excluded by accounting standards from the financial statements. An added advantage is that these disclosures can influence and mould readers' expectations about the reporting corporation. Whether the information provided is credible is contestable. Increasingly, this reporting is viewed as an exercise in obfuscation.

Annual reports generally seek images that have positive expected values, while negative images are avoided. Different 'impression management' strategies are adopted for different stakeholders but how powerful a stakeholder group is will influence how much attention they receive.[43]

Impression management is said to be 'proactive' when it is designed to improve a corporation's image. The strategic purpose is to build an image of the corporation that ingratiates it with its stakeholders, to gain their approval (self-promotion). Alternatively, impression management is said to be 'control protective' when it is used to protect an established image under threat as a result of a predicament. The purpose is self-serving. The strategy may be either to admit fault or to deny responsibility by way of excuses, justifications and apologies, disclaimers, self-handicapping and denouncement. Within the annual report, language is used to blur distinctions about the causes of poor performance, presenting the company in a positive light. Interestingly, the annual reports of good performers are easier to read than those of poor performers because they use 'stronger' writing.

Language can be used to blur or bias culpability. This is where responsibility and accountability is said to take on a 'hedonic bias' — that is, a general tendency to attribute anything negative to external, environmental causes ('it's not my fault') and to attribute favourable outcomes to internal dispositional factors ('it's all thanks to my abilities'). Additionally, negative results are explained in technical accounting terms or in convoluted language, while positive performances are explained in strict, simple cause-and-effect terminology so that management's responsibility for them is clear.[44]

Imagery in annual reports displays similar patterns. Symbols are used to guide interpretation to particular outcomes. Because graphs fall outside accounting regulations, financial graphs allow management to present information in a flexible way — a way that is eye-catching, while summarising, distilling and communicating financial information so that it appeals to both unsophisticated and sophisticated users.[45] Financial graphs, however, are frequently distorted to improve perceptions of management performance, so that graphs are more likely to heighten good news, while minimising bad news.[46]

Examining images other than financial graphs in annual reports is still in its infancy. Photography within an annual report serves a number of purposes, particularly a personalisation of an organisation by depicting, for example, what the managers, employees and products look like. These photographs provide a story more impressive than graphs and text because they shape attitudes about the persons portrayed, can convey a sense of credibility and evoke feelings — for example, photographs of executives present investors with an image of competency, stability and success. Images of directors, employees, products, clients, offices, factories and work sites can be designed to give the 'right' message. However, these photographs have been shown to point out the lack of gender and race diversity on boards of directors and other photographs denigrate the role of women in the workforce.[47]

Electronic reporting

Electronic publishing is often confusing, unpredictable and difficult to monitor. Engaging in electronic communications places a corporation at risk of losing control of its public image. Corporations have therefore been slow to develop policies that allow them to take advantage of these new media which include websites, message boards and blogs.[48] Of the corporations that have taken advantage of electronic media, investors are underrepresented in such communications. For example, Lockwood and Dennis found several blogs targeting investors, but these blogs made up less than 5% of the corporate blogs they found on the web, a result surprising to them given the importance of investors to corporations.[49]

Both financial and non-financial information is disclosed on reporting entities' websites. Some annual reports place the reader in an interactive role with access to audio or video downloads, email alerts and links to related sites. Users are able to interpret and analyse the information provided by using spreadsheets and graphical tools. Electronic reporting gives users a wide range of options in relation to the types of information presented as well as the delivery method.

Lack of standardisation in Internet financial reporting arising from such options worries some accounting commentators.[50] Particularly worrying is the possibility that users believe all financial information accessed through a reporting entity's website is audited. The annual report in Internet reporting does not provide the boundary that the physical copy gives to disclosed information. Internet users can unknowingly leave the audited sections. Also, forward-looking statements are provided without adequate disclaimers.

The International Accounting Standards Board has developed a code of conduct for Internet reporting. The guidelines advise that the:
- boundaries of financial reports should be clear
- content of financial reports should be the same as the reporting entity's paper-based reports
- financial reports should be complete, clearly dated and timely
- information provided should be user friendly and downloadable
- information should be appropriately secured to ensure reliability.

Some of these problems are being overcome by new technology, particularly the rise of extensible business reporting language, or XBRL (see Contemporary Issue 6.3). Because XBRL is a language for electronic communication of financial data, it makes possible continuous disclosure by reporting entities. In doing so, it provides major benefits in the preparation, analysis and communication of business information by offering cost savings, greater efficiency, and improved accuracy and reliability to all those involved in supplying or using financial data. The Securities and Exchange Commission has mandated that all US publicly traded companies file their financial statements using XBRL by the year 2011. In 2007, the Canadian Securities Administrators initiated a voluntary XBRL filing program. China requires interactive data filing for the full financial statements of more than 800 listed companies. Japan has mandated XBRL reporting for all listed companies, and Australia implemented Standard Business Reporting (XBRL) in July 2010 (see www.sbr.gov.au).

6.3 CONTEMPORARY ISSUE

Standardised business language cuts operating jargon confusion

By Greg LaRose

One of the big issues in financial data reporting is the use of different terms to identify the financial information provided by companies in their reports. This makes for a confusing lack of consistency and transparency for users — from laypeople to business data analysts. To rectify the problem, a consortium of international government agencies, business organisations and major corporations has developed a computer-based language that converts business and financial data to a standardised form.

Extensible business reporting language, or XBRL, uses XML tags, similar to those used in spreadsheet software such as Microsoft Excel, to identify data. This allows the data to be easily shared and analysed without the need to rekey it. The XBRL consortium has developed a dictionary of commonly used financial reporting terms, and uses it to assign common tags to relevant data. For example, cash and cash equivalents are assigned the same tag, regardless how they are calculated or reported. This means that the need for longhand identification by a skilled specialist is eliminated. The data can then be analysed automatically through software systems.

XBRL is expected to be particularly useful to large, publicly listed companies, with an eventual flow-on effect to medium-sized businesses. However, some commentators believe small businesses could benefit most from XBRL, since capital markets will have increased access to their information.

In the United States, XBRL is also expected to ease the burden of financial reporting analysis by the SEC, as required under the Sarbanes–Oxley Act of 2002. Currently, the law mandates the SEC undertake analysis of a certain percentage of the reports it receives, a tedious and labour-intensive process under current practices. XBRL-tagged reports would make this analysis simpler and far more cost-effective.

Companies such as Edgar Online Inc., based in Norwalk, Conn., which provides normalised data to analysts, are also expected to use XBRL to their advantage. Despite the ability of XBRL to make financial data easily accessible and interchangeable without the need for specialised data processing, Liv Watson, Edgar Online's vice president of XBRL, believes the company will be able to provide intelligent analytical tools, which will further simplify the process. Currently, Edgar Online devotes 80 per cent of its time to mechanically converting data into a searchable and analysable form. Watson expects XBRL will enable the company to focus instead on ways to make this information more marketable.

Source: Excerpts from Greg LaRose, 'Standardized business language cuts operating jargon confusion', *New Orleans CityBusiness.*[51]

Questions

1. What is XBRL? **K**
2. What are the advantages of XBRL as outlined in the extract? **K**
3. Why will companies such as Edgar Online Inc. have to change their focus if they are to survive widespread adoption of XBRL? **J** **AS**

As shown in figure 6.1, interactive data is created by 'tagging' financial information using XBRL. The XBRL tagging process converts the financial information contained within a document such as an excel spreadsheet into a 'document' or computer file with XBRL codes. The subsequent filing of the resulting computer-readable electronic document into a financial information database means that investors, analysts and others can download not only the traditional financial report, but consistent representations of the data that were combined and aggregated to create that report. As a result, investors, analysts and others will not only be able to more quickly and easily do their work, but will also be able to extend their efforts based on the stored data.[52] The growth of this technology will see the advent of real-time financial reporting from corporations, allowing virtually instantaneous analysis and comparisons.

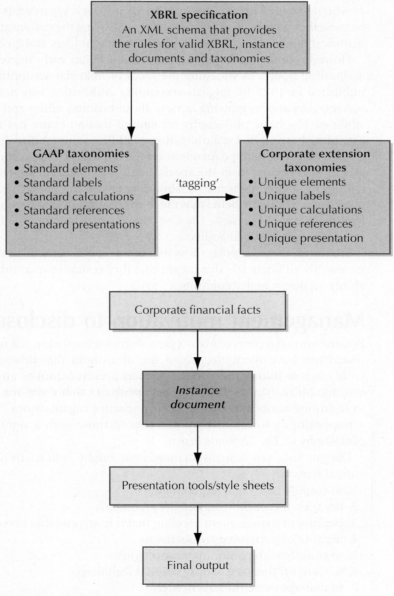

FIGURE 6.1 Creating an XBRL document

LO 6 WHY ENTITIES VOLUNTARILY DISCLOSE

Accounting authorities talk of the need to supply information useful for financial decision making, particularly to investors, yet current accounting standards prevent the recognition of many assets that contribute to the market value of the reporting enterprise. Linked with this lack of recognition is the view, shared by many accounting commentators, that information should be available to groups other than investors because the interactions of a company are not limited to just shareholders but to other stakeholder groups who also have a right to be provided with information about how the activities of the company impact them. Thus, the dissatisfaction with mandatory disclosures and the demand for increased stakeholder reporting have led to initiatives in practically every part of the world, and have encouraged companies to improve their reporting.[53] According to Deegan, those who advocated such socially related disclosures, or who researched non-traditional disclosures, were regarded as both radical and critical, because they were explicitly or implicitly criticising the current structure of the discipline: historical financial accounting reports for shareholders and creditors.[54]

However, much research was engendered by an early interest of some professional accounting bodies in widening the focus of financial accounting. *The Corporate Report*, published in 1975 by English accounting authorities, was notable for its concern for stakeholders and its growing anxiety about business ethics and corporate social responsibilities. The basic philosophy recognised that an entity has multiple responsibilities extending beyond its legal obligations. Public accountability derives from the reporting entity's existence being dependent on the approval of the community in which it operates. It also derives from the special legal and operational privileges afforded to these entities by society, their use of labour, materials and energy resources and community-owned assets, and the belief that the maximisation of shareholders' profits is not the only legitimate aim of business. *The Corporate Report* advocated the need for new accounting methods, such as social audits.

Studies of annual reports show that these reports contain a variety of information, not necessarily all financial. This means that they contain two antithetical forms of accountability: dialogue and accounting.

Management motivation to disclose

Because annual reports contain a great deal of information not required by any authority, researchers have speculated about the motivation that drives management to voluntarily disclose information. Many, such as Beckett & Jonker, attribute the motivation to accountability.[55] In contrast, Deegan speculates that there is a desire by managements to legitimise various aspects of their respective organisations.[56] Accountability implies a responsibility to disclose information to those with a right to know, reflecting the philosophy of *The Corporate Report*.

Deegan lists ten reasons management might voluntarily disclose information in annual reports:
1. to comply with legal requirements
2. because of economic rationality arguments
3. because of management's feeling that it is accountable to stakeholders
4. because of borrowing requirements
5. to comply with community expectations
6. to ward off threats to organisational legitimacy
7. to manage powerful stakeholders
8. to forestall regulations

9. to comply with industry requirements
10. to win reporting awards.[57]

O'Donovan's research suggests that management discloses environmental information in annual reports to:

- align management's values with social values
- pre-empt attacks from pressure groups
- improve corporate reputations
- provide opportunities to lead debates
- secure endorsements
- demonstrate strong management principles
- demonstrate social responsibilities.[58]

Research into annual reports

If you compare the two lists given, you will find factors common to each. Researchers have taken some of these common threads to build theories about why management chooses to disclose certain information in the front half of annual reports. The collective name given to this theorising and its associated research is **corporate social responsibility (CSR)**. In the accounting literature, it is often called corporate social reporting.

Big business is always a target for criticism: the food industry is accused of contributing to obesity, supermarkets are criticised for impoverishing farmers, banks are criticised for closing branches and retrenching staff, chemical manufacturers are criticised for air pollution and so on. The recent high-profile collapses of corporations and the global financial crisis have added corporate governance to the list of grievances associated with the world's corporations. CSR refers to these and other impacts of corporations on society and the need to deal with these impacts in relation to stakeholders. These are generally identified as shareholders, creditors, suppliers, employees and the community.

The main idea underlying CSR is that companies will build shareholder value by engaging non-shareholder stakeholders and by taking account of the companies' impacts on society. This view is in contrast to that which states that businesses should concentrate on what is good for their owners. CSR does not advocate that companies should forgo profitable opportunities, unless they will threaten future profitability by increasing risks or costs, or by threatening revenues and access to capital or labour.[59]

The most common theories about why management would want to disclose its actions in annual reports are accountability theory, legitimacy theory and stakeholder theory.

Accountability theory

Accountability theory views corporations, through their management, as reacting to the concerns of external parties. Accountability involves the monitoring, evaluation and control of organisational agents to ensure that they behave in the interests of shareholders and other stakeholders.[60]

There are two interpretations of this concept. The narrow one deals with the relationship between the company and its shareholders so that the primary focus is on financial information within the annual report. The second interpretation deals with the relationship between a corporation and its stakeholders so that its focus may be any disclosures within an annual report. Because accountability focuses upon the relationship between the corporation and users of its annual reports, information transmission between them depends upon the terms of that relationship.[61] Management is monitored, evaluated and controlled to ensure that it behaves in the interests of shareholders and other stakeholders.[62]

Legitimacy theory

Both Deegan and O'Donovan identified the need to align management's values with social values as a motivation for disclosure. The annual report is a tool with which management signals its reactions to the concerns of society. The underlying assumption is a social contract between society and the organisation. Since corporations only exist because society has provided them with the means to do so, they have obligations to society.

An organisation's survival will be threatened if society perceives that it has breached its social contract. Consequently, reporting entities are controlled by community concerns and values.[63] Values change over time, and reporting entities need to respond to that.[64] Successful legitimation depends on reporting entities convincing society that a congruence of actions and values exists. Management will react to public concern over corporate actions by increasing the level of corporate disclosures in annual reports if it perceives that its legitimacy is threatened by that public concern.[65]

Legitimacy theory is the most widely embraced theoretical perspective in the social and environmental accounting literature to explain corporate motivations for reporting. Researchers using this perspective have been concerned largely with environmental issues. There is mounting evidence that managers should adopt legitimising strategies.[66] Legitimacy theory is discussed in more detail in chapter 5.

Stakeholder theory

Stakeholder theory is actually two theories: an ethics-based theory and a managerial- or positive-based theory. The ethics-based theory largely prescribes how organisations should treat their stakeholders, emphasising the organisations' responsibilities. The managerial-based theory emphasises the need to manage particular stakeholder groups, especially powerful ones. Some stakeholders are powerful because they control resources needed by the organisation's operations and for its survival. For example, lenders, suppliers, regulators and consumers are powerful for this reason.

Information is an important part of the strategy of managing valuable stakeholders. Management informs them of the reporting enterprise's activities through means such as the annual report. In many ways, stakeholder theory is not unlike legitimacy theory. However, while legitimacy theory is concerned with the community as a whole, stakeholder theory is concerned with only those stakeholders powerful enough to endanger the organisation in which they have a stake.

Summary

Evaluate the importance of the identification of the reporting entity
- Accounting regulations define a reporting entity differently from a legal entity.
- The concept of 'control' determines the reporting entity.
- Control is the ability of an investor to obtain returns from an investee.

Outline the debate surrounding the length and frequency of reporting periods
- Arguments for the standardisation of reporting periods to 12 months claim that it allows better comparability between companies, more accurate calculation of dividends, continued compliance with company law and better stewardship.
- Arguments supporting a more flexible approach to reporting periods claim that standardisation creates an artificial and arbitrary halt that may cut across incomplete transactions, be contrary to an entity's internal earnings cycle and put pressure on managers to take a short-term view.
- Some of these issues are overcome by the provision for voluntary interim financial reporting, while the advent of XBRL will allow for real-time reporting and analysis.

Discuss the practice of manipulating reported earnings in the production of financial information
- Managers take advantage of the information asymmetry between themselves and external stakeholders to manipulate the image and financial performance figures of the company.
- Legal manipulation, or 'earnings management', involves the management of revenues and expenses to match analysts' earnings forecasts for the company.
- Income smoothing involves the management of earnings and expenses to provide a stable financial performance. Pro forma reporting, generally used to estimate a recently listed entity's performance before listing, can also be used to exclude one-off or unusual items from earnings as atypical.

Outline the debate surrounding the exclusion of intangibles and intellectual capital from the financial reporting process
- Accounting regulations exclude the reporting of intangibles in annual reports, resulting in a disparity between the reported and market value of entities. To overcome this, entities make voluntary disclosures, which may relate to human resources, the environment or community activities of the firm.
- The treatment of intangibles by accounting standards requires them to be identifiable. This means they must have been generated separately from the entity, excluding

internally generated intangibles such as brands, mastheads, customer lists and research, which are expensed, despite any market value they may generate.

- Intellectual capital refers to the capital created by employees, invested in employees and invested in relationships with customers and suppliers. Only intellectual capital that is purchased is recognised in financial statements. This can create significant issues for knowledge-based organisations.

Explain the options available to companies reporting voluntary disclosures

- Traditionally, voluntary disclosures are made in the first half of the annual report. This section of the annual report can create controversy because it can be used as a marketing tool to manipulate the image of the organisation.
- New technological innovations have resulted in an increase in reporting disclosures made on company websites. The Internet provides increased flexibility and interactivity for the reader but it is not subject to the same auditing requirements as the physical annual report and information cannot be monitored to the same extent. The development of XBRL is designed to resolve this.

Identify three theories that explain the motivation for voluntary disclosures in annual reports

- The theoretical basis for voluntary disclosure is based on corporate social responsibility research, which aims to identify the motivations for companies to make voluntary disclosures about non-financial aspects of the business.
- Accountability theory involves the control and regulation of the relationship between a corporation and its stakeholders, whether shareholders or a wider community, mediated through the disclosures made by the company.
- Legitimacy theory assumes a social contract between society and the organisation, using the annual report as a tool in which management can demonstrate its fulfilment of its obligations to meet community concerns and values.
- Stakeholder theory emphasises the ethical responsibilities of organisations to their stakeholders and, in particular, the need for management of relationships with smaller, more powerful stakeholder groups.

Review questions

1. Why does accounting have regular reporting periods?
2. Consider the arguments for and against standardised reporting periods. Do you agree that accounting periods should be more flexible? Give reasons for your answer.
3. What are the perceived purposes of an annual report?
4. Why are financial statements 'highly valued'?
5. What do you understand by the term 'fair presentation'? Give an example to support your answer.
6. Financial reports have been criticised for their lack of completeness. In what ways do financial reports fail the completeness test?
7. Defend the stand taken by accounting authorities in AASB 138/IAS 38 *Intangible Assets* in relation to the treatment of intangible assets.
8. Define 'earnings management'. Do you consider it to be good or bad? Why?
9. Why are annual reports so well regarded?
10. Researchers speculate that management is motivated to disclose information voluntarily either because it feels accountable or because it wishes to legitimise its activities. Which do you think is the more likely reason and why?
11. Debate whether management should solely pursue profits.

12. What factors appear to instigate voluntary disclosure by management in annual reports?
13. Why should management explain poor performance in technical accounting terms?
14. Why do you think environmental disclosures are more researched than other social disclosures?
15. Why is XBRL a 'language'?
16. Debate whether XBRL is the likely future of financial reporting.

Application questions

6.1

Obtain a copy of an annual report and answer the following questions.

(a) What do you think is the message being conveyed in the annual report? For example, is management optimistic about profitability in the forthcoming financial year? **AS**

(b) How long is the report in pages? **K**

(c) Where are the financial statements located in the report? **K**

(d) Is the company doing well financially? How do this year's results compare with previous results? **J** **K** **AS**

(e) How many pages do the financial statements occupy? **K**

(f) How much of the report is devoted to nonverbal forms of communication? **K** **AS**

(g) Are there photographs in the report? If so, what do they depict? Do they reflect the message being conveyed in the report? **J** **K** **AS**

(h) Are there graphs in the report? If so, what has been graphed? **K** **AS**

(i) What voluntary social disclosures are made in the report? **AS**

(j) What is your overall impression of the annual report? Does it make you want to buy shares in the company? If you already own shares in the company, does it confirm that you have made a good decision in buying them? **J** **AS** **CT**

6.1 CASE STUDY

Reading the annual report: ten issues to consider

The ASIC website publishes a range of information designed to allow amateur investors to avoid the pitfalls of making ill-informed decisions when investing. These tips include advice on the best way to use a company's annual report to make an assessment of its financial performance. They include the ten issues detailed in the following.

There are lots of matters you can check in the annual report. Here are 10 issues you should consider, grouped into three areas:
- Operational and strategic activities of the company: The year's highlights
- Financial results
- Future strategic directions and performance: Looking ahead to next year

The year's highlights...

1. Are the activities reported by the chairman and managing director the same as the activities the company said it was going to do either in its prospectus or last annual report?

Any prospectus the company issued may have included information about markets the directors were aiming to penetrate and the products the company planned to produce. The company may also have made statements in the annual report or announcements to the market about new or different activities it is going to pursue.

Ask:
- Is the company doing the same things shareholders expected it to be doing, for example, was it going to build websites whereas now it is selling computer hardware?
- If it was going to sell products — is it selling the same products?

- If there has been a change in the activities, this may mean the company's prospects are significantly different. There may be different cost structures associated with the different activities and they may require different amounts of development or capital expenditure. There may be differences in the amount and timing of revenue for the company.

2. **Is the current business strategy the same as that described in the prospectus or last annual report? If it has changed, how will it affect the performance of your investment?**

   Business strategy can be described in various ways — future directions, strategic objectives, business plans, corporate goals and vision statements. What are the ultimate goals of the company? Are the company's activities moving towards these goals? For example, did the company say it would develop e-commerce software applications for the banking industry, and now it is considering biotechnology products for the medical industry?

3. **If strategic acquisitions were made during the year, how did they add value to the company?**

   Many companies make strategic acquisitions in other companies. For example, they purchase a substantial shareholding in another company. This company may be complementary because it sells key products to your company or it may provide access to additional markets, new technologies or new products.

   Such investments may or may not generate a direct dividend/revenue stream for the company. Where investments like these have been made, how will these acquisitions help the long-term future of the company? Will the investment assist the company in achieving its short and long-term objectives? For example — if the company's strategy is to establish a significant market presence in Australia, how does acquiring a business in Brazil help achieve this objective?

4. **Has a tangible result been achieved from any money spent on research and development activities, such as developing high technology products or software applications?**

   Companies may spend significant resources on areas described as research and development, product development and intellectual property development. These activities generally aim, among other things, to develop new products, improve existing products and help a company stand out in the market. Such expenditure will not always produce immediate results, but it is important for you to understand the size and purpose of that expenditure and any results that have been achieved.

   A tangible result is something like the first sale of a software application or starting production of a high technology product or entering into a technology licence agreement for another business to use the technology developed by the company.

Financial results...

5. **Did the company receive any revenue from its business activities? If it didn't, did the directors explain why not?**

   In last year's annual report or a recent prospectus, the company may have expected to generate a certain amount of revenue in the coming year. These expectations may have depended on the types of revenue, some of which may be more sustainable over the longer term, and the amount of that revenue.

   When reviewing the financial results, look at the actual revenue of the company and where it came from against these expectations. For example, did it come from selling software products or licensing technology rights to another business?

6. **Did the company make a profit or a loss? If it was a loss, did the directors explain why?**

   Many companies during their 'start-up' phase do not make a profit. If this is the case, the directors may indicate in the annual report when they expect the company will make a profit. If this is not discussed in the report, ask the directors at the AGM. You should also consider the factors that will or may affect whether this profit forecast is achieved.

7. **How did the company fund its activities during the year? Did the company generate its own cashflow from its business activities or did it merely rely on funds from other sources such as funds raised from shareholders, debt financing and asset sales?**

In reviewing the statement of cash flows in the financial report, consider the source of the company's cash for the year.

For example, has the company only used the money raised from the issue of shares or has it borrowed additional funds through loans or by issuing convertible notes (these are debt securities than can be converted to shares at a later stage)? If the company has issued more shares during the year, have these diluted existing investors' shareholdings?

Be aware that the statement of cash flows normally has three sections: operating activities, investment activities and financial activities.

Looking ahead to next year...

8. **Is the company going to change its activities or business strategy for next year?**

Companies operating in a competitive environment have opportunities for the future, and risks or hurdles that must be overcome to achieve success. Think about the key factors that will affect future performance and how the company plans to address these — making the most of the opportunities and minimising the risks.

9. **How long can the company last at its current 'cash-burn' rate? If it looks like it might run out of cash during next year, what is the company proposing to do about this?**

'Cash-burn rate' usually refers to the rate at which the company is using its cash reserves. Where the company is not yet generating cash from its operations, see where cash is being spent and the rate at which it is being spent. Many high technology companies lodge cash flow statements with the ASX at the end of each quarter. You may want to ask for a copy of the company's last couple of cash flow statements.

Where a company is not yet producing revenue but is still using cash to fund its operations, you should assess whether the company will have enough cash on hand until revenue begins to be generated. If it won't, how will the company meet its requirements — will it try to raise more funds? Or will it borrow the money?

10. **Is the company going to make a profit next year? How?**

You should get an idea of what the directors expect for the coming year. If a product is still in the development phase, the directors may think that the company will continue to run at a loss. However, if the company is beginning to develop markets for its product, expectations may be more positive.

You should also distinguish between possible developments, customers and contracts, and those prospects that are more certain.

Source: Australian Securities and Investments Commission, 'ASIC's ten issues to consider when reading annual reports', www.asic.gov.au.[67]

Questions

1. Obtain a copy of an annual report issued by a listed company. **K**
2. Follow the suggestions of the corporate regulator, and analyse the annual report:
   (a) Examine the figures in the financial statements to get an overall impression of the financial performance of the company.
   (b) Note which figures you think are important to an understanding of the financial performance of the company you have chosen.
   (c) Read what management has to say about these figures in the front half of the report.
   (d) Return to the financial report and examine the figures again, taking into account what management has said in the front half. Has your assessment changed in any way? How? **J** **K** **AS** **CT**
3. Write a short assessment of the company as a potential investment. **J** **K** **AS** **CT**

6.2
CASE
STUDY

The impact of the global financial crisis on IAS 39 *Financial Instruments: Recognition and Measurement*

The financial crisis of the late 2000s resulted in the collapse of many large financial institutions, the bailout of banks by national governments and downturns in world stock markets. Among the scapegoats blamed for the crisis was fair value accounting rules. The argument was that companies were forced by fair value accounting to write down their assets to what they hoped was temporarily irrational prices. These write-downs supposedly exacerbated market downturns.

Possibly in response to these arguments and to threats by the European Union to override international accounting standards, the International Accounting Standards Board changed its rules in IAS 39 on balance sheet classifications so that companies could shift many of their financial assets out of categories where fair value accounting was required. This meant a company holding 'dodgy' bonds could delay recognition of future losses on those bonds by simply changing their category on the balance sheet. Such an action is possible because the changes to IAS 39 meant that financial assets could be classified four ways: as fair value through profit or loss; as available for sale; as held to maturity; and as loans and receivables. The first two classifications require financial assets to be marked to market, with those classified as the first category requiring changes in value to go through the income statement, while changes in value for those classified as available for sale would not impact on the income statement. The other classifications allow companies to avoid using fair values on the balance sheet.

In 2009, the Financial Accounting Standards Board also changed its comparable standard to allow companies to keep losses on impaired financial instruments out of net income.

Questions

1. Suppose you are a company holding large quantities of financial instruments the market value of which had declined markedly since purchase. How would you classify those instruments and why? **J** **AS**
2. Compared to the pre-change IAS 39, what are the likely impacts of the changes to IAS 39 on balance sheet values of companies holding large amounts of financial instruments? **K** **AS**
3. Will companies with large holdings of dodgy financial instruments be motivated to disclose information about those instruments? Give reasons for your answer. **J**
4. What types of companies are likely to be affected greatly by the changes to IAS 39? **K**
5. How would the changes impact the truthfulness of financial reporting? **J** **K**
6. How do the changes impact on the comparability of financial statements? **J** **K**
7. Would you expect the 'market' to look through the changes? How can you empirically verify your answer? **J** **K**
8. Argue whether the changes to IAS 39 represent a form of sanctioned earnings management. **J** **K**

Additional readings

Beattie, V & Jones, MJ 1999, 'Australian financial graphs: an empirical study', *Abacus*, vol. 35, no. 1, pp. 46–76.

Stanton, PA & Stanton, PJ 2002, 'Corporate annual reports: research perspectives used', *Accounting, Auditing & Accountability Journal*, vol. 15, no. 4, pp. 478–500.

Walker, RG & Robinson, SP 1994, 'Competing regulatory agencies with conflicting agendas: setting standards for cash flow reporting in Australia', *Abacus*, vol. 30, no. 2, pp. 119–37.

Wright, S 2004, 'Accounting for intangible assets in Australia: exposure draft 109', *Accounting Research Journal*, vol. 17, no. 1, pp. 32–42.

End notes

1. Boerner, H 2005, 'Are corporate accounting systems out-of-date?', *Corporate Finance Review*, vol. 10, no. 2, pp. 35–41.
2. International Accounting Standards Board 2010, *Exposure draft ED/2010/2 — Conceptual Framework for Financial Reporting — The Reporting Entity*, IASC Foundation Publications Department, London, p. 8.
3. Luther, R 2003, 'Uniform accounting periods: an historical review and critique', *Accounting History*, vol. 8, no. 2, pp. 79–100.
4. ibid.
5. ibid.
6. ibid.
7. ibid.
8. ibid.
9. Beaver, WH 2002, 'Perspectives on Recent Market Research', *The Accounting Review*, vol. 77, no. 2, pp. 453–74.
10. Christensen, J 2010, 'Conceptual frameworks of accounting from an information perspective', *Accounting and Business Research*, vol. 40, no. 3, pp. 287–99.
11. ibid.
12. Stolowy, H & Breton, G 2004, 'Accounts manipulation: a literature review and proposed conceptual framework', *Review of Accounting and Finance*, vol. 3, no. 1, pp. 5–69.
13. Macintosh, NB, Shearer, T, Thornton, DB & Welker, M 2000, 'Accounting a simulacrum and hyperreality: perspectives on income and capital', *Accounting, Organizations and Society*, vol. 25, no. 1, pp. 13–50.
14. Parfet, WU 2000, 'Accounting subjectivity and earnings management: a preparer perspective', *Accounting Horizons*, vol. 14, no. 4, pp. 481–9.
15. Stolowy, H & Breton, G 2004, 'Accounts manipulation: a literature review and proposed conceptual framework', *Review of Accounting and Finance*, vol. 3, no. 1, pp. 5–69.
16. Bhattacharya, N, Black, EL, Christensen, TE & Mergenthaler, RD 2004, 'Empirical evidence on recent trends in pro forma reporting', *Accounting Horizons*, vol. 18, no. 1, pp. 27–44.
17. Brody, RG & McDonald, R 2004, 'The next scandal: the undisciplined use of pro forma financial statements', *American Business Review*, vol. 22, no. 1, pp. 34–8; Bhattacharya, N, Black, EL, Christensen, TE & Mergenthaler, RD 2004, 'Empirical evidence on recent trends in pro forma reporting', *Accounting Horizons*, vol. 18, no. 1, pp. 27–44.
18. Bhattacharya, N, Black, EL, Christensen, TE & Mergenthaler, RD 2007, 'Who Trades on Pro Forma Earnings Information', *The Accounting Review*, vol. 82, no. 3, pp. 581–619.
19. Macve, R 2010, 'Conceptual frameworks of accounting: some brief reflections on theory and practice', *Accounting and Business Research*, vol. 40, no. 3, pp. 303–8.
20. Lev, B cited in Boerner, H 2005, 'Are corporate accounting systems out-of-date?', *Corporate Finance Review*, vol. 10, no. 2, pp. 35–41.
21. Hunter, L, Webster, E & Wyatt, A 2005, 'Measuring intangible capital: a review of current practice', *Australian Accounting Review*, vol. 15, no. 2, pp. 4–21.
22. Lev, B & Daum, JH 2004, 'The dominance of intangible assets: consequences for enterprise management and corporate reporting', *Measuring Business Excellence*, vol. 8, no. 1, pp. 6–17.
23. Wyatt, A 2008, 'What financial and non-financial information on intangibles is value-relevant? A review of the evidence', *Accounting and Business Research*, vol. 38, no. 3, pp. 217–56.
24. Lev, B & Daum, JH 2004, 'The dominance of intangible assets: consequences for enterprise management and corporate reporting', *Measuring Business Excellence*, vol. 8, no. 1, pp. 6–17.
25. Lev, B 2008, 'A rejoinder to Douglas Skinner's 'Accounting for intangibles — a critical review of policy recommendations', *Accounting and Business Research*, vol. 38, no. 3, pp. 209–13.
26. Australian Accounting Standards Board (AASB) 2004, AASB 138 *Intangible assets*, Australian Accounting Standards Board, Melbourne.
27. Dyckman, TR & Zeff, SA 2000, 'The future of financial reporting: removing it from the shadows', *Pacific Accounting Review*, vol. 11, no. 2, pp. 89–96.
28. Financial Accounting Standards Board 1978, *Statement of Financial Accounting Concepts No. 1: Objectives of Financial Reporting by Business Enterprises*, FASB, Stamford.
29. International Accounting Standards Board 2004, *Framework for the Preparation and Presentation of Financial Statements*, IASB, London.
30. International Accounting Standards Board 2005, *Management commentary*, IASB, London.
31. Securities and Exchange Commission 2003, *Commission Guidance Regarding Management's Discussion and Analysis of Financial Condition and Results of Operations (Release Nos. 33–8350; 33–48960, FR–72)*, SEC, New York.
32. International Accounting Standards Board 2005, *Management commentary*, IASB, London.
33. Deloitte 2006, *Global capital markets and the global economy: a vision from the CEOs of the International Audit Networks*, Deloitte, London.
34. International Accounting Standards Board 2005, *Management commentary*, IASB, London.
35. ibid.
36. Wiesel, T, Skiera B & Villanueva j 2008, 'Customer Equity: An Integral Part of Financial Reporting', *Journal of Marketing*, vol. 72, no. 3, p. 1.
37. Wyatt, A 2008, 'What financial and non-financial information on intangibles is value-relevant? A review of the evidence', *Accounting and Business Research*, vol. 38, no. 3, pp. 217–56.
38. Skinner, DJ 2008, 'Accounting for intangibles — a critical review of policy recommendations', *Accounting and Business Research*, vol. 38, no. 3, pp. 191–204; Basu, S and Waymire, G 2008, 'Has the importance of intangibles really grown? And if so, why', *Accounting and Business Research*, vol. 38, no. 3, pp. 171–90; Hunter, L, Webster, E & Wyatt, A 2005, 'Measuring intangible capital: a review of current practice', *Australian Accounting Review*, vol. 15, no. 2, pp. 4–21.

39. Wyatt, A 2008, 'What financial and non-financial information on intangibles is value-relevant? A review of the evidence', *Accounting and Business Research*, vol. 38, no. 3, pp. 217–56.

40. Lev, B 2008, 'A rejoinder to Douglas Skinner's "Accounting for intangibles — a critical review of policy recommendations"', *Accounting and Business Research*, vol. 38, no. 3, pp. 209–13.

41. Stanton, PA & Stanton, PJ 2002, 'Corporate annual reports: research perspectives used', *Accounting, Auditing & Accountability Journal*, vol. 15, no. 4, pp. 478–500.

42. Wilson, S 2006, 'Be kind to shareholders', *The Australian*, 9 June, p. 32.

43. Lee, T 1994, 'The changing form of the corporate annual report', *The Accounting Historians Journal*, vol. 21, no. 1, pp. 215–32.

44. Aerts, W 1994, 'On the use of accounting logic as an explanatory category in narrative accounting disclosures', *Accounting, Organizations and Society*, vol. 19, no. 4–5, pp. 337–53; Jones, MJ 1996, 'Readability of annual reports', *Accounting, Auditing & Accountability Journal*, vol. 9, no. 2, pp. 86–91.

45. Beattie, V & Jones, M 2008, 'Corporate reporting using graphs: a review and synthesis', *Journal of Accounting Literature*, vol. 27, pp. 71–110.

46. Beattie, V & Jones, MJ 1992, 'The use and abuse of graphs in annual reports: theoretical framework and empirical study', *Accounting and Business Research*, vol. 22, no. 88, pp. 291–303; Beattie, V & Jones, MJ 1999, 'Australian financial graphs: an empirical study', *Abacus*, vol. 35, no. 1, pp. 46–76; Beattie, V & Jones, MJ 1997, 'A comparative study of the use of financial graphs in the corporate annual reports of major US and UK companies', *Journal of International Financial Management and Accounting*, vol. 8, no. 1, pp. 33–68; Mather, P, Ramsay, A & Serry, A 1996, 'The use and representational faithfulness of graphs in annual reports: Australian evidence', *Australian Accounting Review*, vol. 6, no. 2, pp. 56–63.

47. Bernardi, RA, Bean, DF & Weippert, KM 2005, 'Minority membership on boards of directors: the case for requiring pictures of boards in annual reports', *Critical Perspectives on Accounting*, vol. 16, pp. 1019–33.

48. Cox, JL, Martinez, ER & Quinlan, KB 2008, 'Blogs and the corporation: managing the risk, reaping the benefits', *Journal of Business Strategy*, vol. 29, no. 3, pp. 4–12.

49. Lockwood, NS & Dennis, AR 2008, 'Exploring the Corporate Blogosphere', Proceedings of the 41st Hawaii International Conference on System Sciences.

50. Seetharaman, A, Subramanian, R & Shyong, SY 2005, 'Internet financial reporting', *Corporate Financial Review*, vol. 10, no. 1, pp. 23–34.

51. LaRose, G 2005, 'Standardized business language cuts operating jargon confusion', *New Orleans CityBusiness*, 17 January.

52. Plumlee, RD & Plumlee, MA 2008, 'Assurance on XBRL for Financial Reporting', *Accounting Horizons*, vol. 22, no. 3, pp. 353–68.

53. Boesso, G & Kumar, K 2007, 'Drivers of corporate voluntary disclosure', *Accounting, Auditing & Accountability Journal*, vol. 20, no. 2, pp. 269–96.

54. Deegan, C 2002, 'The legitimising effect of social and environmental disclosures: a theoretical foundation', *Accounting, Auditing & Accountability Journal*, vol. 15, no. 3, pp. 282–312.

55. Beckett, R & Jonker J 2002, 'AccountAbility 1000: a new social standard for building sustainability', *Managerial Auditing Journal*, vol. 17, nos. 1/2, pp. 36–42.

56. Deegan, C 2002, 'The legitimising effect of social and environmental disclosures: a theoretical foundation', *Accounting, Auditing & Accountability Journal*, vol. 15, no. 3, pp. 282–312.

57. ibid.

58. O'Donovan, G 2002, 'Environmental disclosures in the annual report: extending the applicability and predictive power of legitimacy theory', *Accounting, Auditing & Accountability Journal*, vol. 15, no. 3, pp. 344–71.

59. Hopkins, M & Cowe, R 2004, 'Corporate social responsibility: is there a business case?', ACCA, London.

60. Keasey, K & Wright, M 1993, 'Issues in corporate accountability and governance: an editorial', *Accounting and Business Research*, vol. 23, no. 91A, pp. 291–303.

61. Owen, D, Gray, R & Maunders, K 1987, 'Researching the information content of social responsibility disclosures: a comment', *British Accounting Review*, vol. 19, no. 2, pp. 169–75.

62. Keasey, K & Wright, M 1993, 'Issues in corporate accountability and governance: an editorial', *Accounting and Business Research*, vol. 23, no. 91A, pp. 291–303.

63. Islam, MA & Deegan, C 2010, 'Media pressures and corporate disclosure of social responsibility performance information: a study of two global clothing and sports retail companies', *Accounting and Business Research*, vol. 40, no. 2, pp. 131–148.

64. Dowling, J & Pfeffer, J 1975, 'Organizational legitimacy: social values and organizational behaviour', *Pacific Sociological Review*, vol. 18, no. 1, pp. 122–36.

65. Brown, N & Deegan, C 1998, 'The public disclosure of environmental performance information — a dual test of media agenda setting theory and legitimacy theory', *Accounting and Business Research*, vol. 29, no. 1, pp. 21–41.

66. Islam, MA & Deegan, C 2010, 'Media pressures and corporate disclosure of social responsibility performance information: a study of two global clothing and sports retail companies', *Accounting and Business Research*, vol. 40, no. 2, pp. 131–148.

67. Australian Securities and Investments Commission (ASIC) , 'ASIC's ten issues to consider when reading annual reports', www.asic.gov.au.

7 Corporate governance

LEARNING OBJECTIVES

After studying this chapter, you should be able to:

1. explain the interest in corporate governance

2. explain what corporate governance is and why good corporate governance systems are needed

3. discuss the relationship between positive accounting theory and corporate governance

4. discuss the key areas involved in corporate governance

5. explain and evaluate the alternative approaches to corporate governance

6. discuss recent developments and issues in corporate governance

7. explain the role and impact of accounting in and on corporate governance

8. discuss and analyse the role of ethics in corporate governance

9. discuss international perspectives and developments in corporate governance.

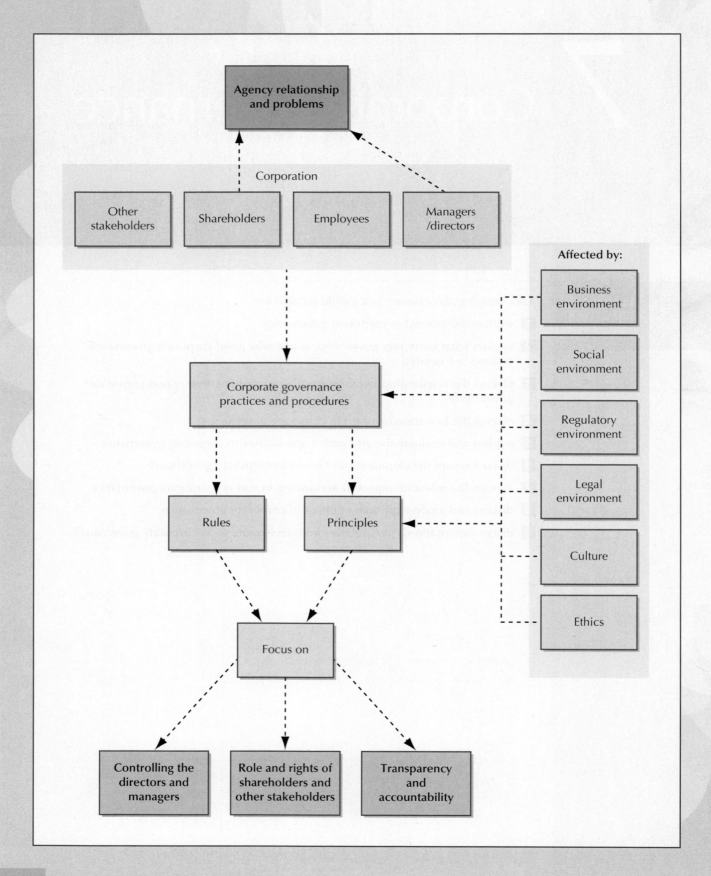

How corporations are managed affects all our lives. They control a large part of the resources of this planet and are increasingly the dominant form of economic organisation. Clearly, decisions made by the people who run corporations affect the prosperity of individuals directly involved with the particular corporations (such as their shareholders and employees) but their decisions also have a much wider impact. In some instances those running companies have abused their positions, or been accused of mismanagement and corporations have been found wanting: the global financial crisis, the collapses of Enron and WorldCom in the United States, the collapse of ABC Learning in Australia and companies polluting the environment, including the BP Gulf of Mexico oil spill, are examples. Ideally, we want those in positions of responsibility in companies to run them properly and to make the 'right' decisions. How can we try to make sure that companies do act appropriately?

'Corporate governance' is the term used to cover the series of principles, mechanisms or procedures developed for this end, and this chapter focuses on some of the underlying causes of corporate governance problems and the role of accounting in effective corporate governance. It must be remembered, however, that decisions are made by people, and so there is a need to consider the behaviour of individuals in companies; this involves us looking at the role of ethics in corporate decision making.

LO 1   THE INTEREST IN CORPORATE GOVERNANCE

Over the past decades, interest in corporate governance practices has increased as a direct result of highly publicised cases of corporate misconduct and concerns over the management of corporations. There is also a growing realisation that good corporate governance can not only help in avoiding problems, but can provide other advantages. Although the corporate structure has many advantages (such as facilitating capital investment and limiting some risk, through the limited liability afforded to shareholders), the separation of the management of the corporation from those who contribute resources (such as shareholders) can lead to problems.

Problems with the management of corporations

Various examples show what type of problems may occur:
- Those managing a company may use the resources to benefit themselves (rather than shareholders). Often this can involve fraud — for example, in the case of Bernard Madoff where a Ponzi scheme was used to defraud investors,[1] and in the case of Parmalat, where documents were forged to hide debt and flows of cash to family members.[2] However, it is often more subtle and in many corporate scandals it has been argued 'false' reporting has sometimes been motivated by the desire to maintain the value of benefits provided to corporate managers (such as the value of share options).
- Corporations may take actions that shareholders (or society) may not consider desirable. For example, Mitsubishi in Japan failed to inform customers of potential safety problems with vehicles or recall the vehicles for repair, which allegedly led to accidents, including one resulting in the death of the driver.[3]
- Corporations may 'hide' or provide 'false' information to shareholders to avoid consequences. For example, Enron failed to inform shareholders of the true level of debt and WorldCom incorrectly recorded expenses as assets to increase reported profits. In the global financial crisis Lehman Brothers was accused of using creative accounting to hide debts.[4]

- In recent times a disparity ('mismatch') has been perceived between the payments received by the managers of corporations and their performance, with directors and executives of corporations receiving massive payments and benefits even when corporate performance is poor or declining.

Although these examples may be the focus of media attention, high-profile corporate scandals and misconduct are not recent occurrences. Of course, it could be argued that the problems mentioned are inevitably part of the risks of 'doing business' and the history of corporations for more than the past 100 years is associated with regulations to protect the public, usually in response to corporate scandals or failures. These have included the need for financial statements and audits. However, good corporate governance practices go beyond reporting and regulations. Furthermore, the risks in not having good corporate governance practices are high — not only to individuals who may be directly involved with specific corporations, but to business and the economy in general. Failures in corporate governance practices have been linked to the recent global financial crisis. For an individual company, the failure to assure others that it has good governance practices can reduce its value; for the economy, a lack of public confidence in corporations can result in reduced economic growth. Given the key role that financial reporting and auditing play in corporate governance, failures or poor corporate governance also risks a loss of confidence in the accounting profession itself.

Advantages of good corporate governance

Companies that can demonstrate good corporate governance practices have advantages. With the increasing globalisation of business and competition for capital, companies that can provide assurances that the company is being appropriately managed can gain a competitive edge. Reducing perceived risks to investors can reduce the cost of capital. Furthermore, the expansion of company shareholdings to a broader base (in many countries, small shareholders are becoming increasingly common, either by direct investment or indirectly through their superannuation/pension plans), combined with more organised and active shareholders lobby groups, is placing more scrutiny on company management.

A key reason for the interest in corporate governance and many of the current prescriptions for best practice is that they are needed for an efficient market and to facilitate economic growth:

> The presence of an effective corporate governance system, within an individual company and across the economy as a whole, helps to provide a degree of confidence that is necessary for the proper functioning of a market economy. As a result, the cost of capital is lower and firms are encouraged to use resources more efficiently, thereby underpinning growth.[5]

 **LO 2**

WHAT IS CORPORATE GOVERNANCE?

Corporate governance in very simple terms is 'the system by which business corporations are directed and controlled'.[6] The definition of corporate governance used by the Organisation for Economic Co-operation and Development (OECD) explains this as:

> The procedures and processes according to which an organisation is directed and controlled. The corporate governance structure specifies the distribution of rights and responsibilities among the different participants in the organisation — such as the board, managers, shareholders and other stakeholders — and lays down the rules and procedures for decision-making. By doing this, it also provides the structure through which the company objectives are set, and the means of attaining those objectives and monitoring performance.[7]

A 'good' corporate governance system ensures that the corporation sets appropriate objectives and then puts systems and structures in place to ensure that these objectives are met, and also provides the means for others, both within and outside of the corporation, to control and monitor the activities of the corporation and its managers.

Corporate governance stakeholders

The determination of whose interests are to be protected and what are 'appropriate' objectives of the corporation are central questions and will influence the related corporate governance systems. The traditional view of the role of the corporation is best stated by Milton Friedman, who argued that:

> Corporate governance is to conduct the business in accordance with the owner or shareholders' desires, which generally will be to make as much money as possible while conforming to the basic rules of the society embodied in law and local customs.[8]

This view that corporate governance relates to ensuring that the interests of the key providers of capital to the corporation (the shareholders) are met underlies many of the current requirements and practices in corporate governance. This view is referred to as the 'Anglo-Saxon' model and is the basis for many corporate governance models currently including, increasingly, in Asia, where there is convergence to this model.[9] This approach views a key role for corporate governance as enabling the efficient use of resources by helping financial markets to work properly and gives priority to shareholder value.[10] The Anglo-Saxon model tends to focus on the problems caused by the relationship between managers and owners (because of the agency relationship discussed in the next section) and often takes a control-oriented approach, concentrating on mechanisms to curb self-serving managerial decisions and actions.

A wider view and more pluralist model that is increasingly being supported is that the responsibility of corporations goes beyond the narrow interests of shareholders and should be extended to a wider group of stakeholders. For example, German models of corporate governance emphasise multiple stakeholders, while other European countries have more focus on employees. Corporate governance systems are more and more considering stakeholders beyond the traditional shareholder groups, and a range of models exists with varying emphases on stakeholders and views of corporate responsibility. This extension of corporate responsibility is also discussed in chapter 11 in relation to sustainability and environmental accounting. Before considering what is involved in practising good corporate governance and briefly examining current guidelines, the next sections consider why there may be a problem with corporate governance and one dominant positive theory in accounting linked to this.

LO 3 THE NEED FOR CORPORATE GOVERNANCE SYSTEMS

Corporate governance rules and prescriptions are needed because of the nature of the company structure. This, at least for all but small family companies, means that the people who have provided the resources to the company (the shareholders and lenders) do not actually run the company directly. These capital contributors need to rely on managers. This separation between capital contributors and management is the source of many issues and problems relating to corporate governance. It could be argued that if managers behaved properly (i.e. acted as though they had contributed the capital), there would be no difficulties. Alternatively, people could opt not to contribute capital to companies; rather, they could only invest in businesses that they themselves manage. A dominant positive theory, positive accounting theory, provides an explanation why these things do not happen and why managers may 'bias' or distort the financial statements. This stream of accounting theory and associated research is referred to as accounting policy choice research and is based on agency theory. It is often referred to simply as 'positive accounting research' because it has been the prevalent positive paradigm in accounting research for more than 30 years.

Positive accounting theory and its relationship with corporate governance

Chapter 5 examines positive accounting theory in detail. As noted previously, many problems with corporate governance are caused by the separation of management and the owners of capital. So why have this separation? With contracting theory as its starting point, positive accounting theory explains that for efficiency reasons companies or firms are formed and can be viewed as a network of contracts or agreements that determine the relationships with and among the various parties involved in the firm: suppliers, employees, distributors, shareholders, lenders and so on. One important **agency relationship** that arises from this nexus is that between the managers and the capital contributors (such as shareholders), as shareholders authorise the managers to make the key business decisions. An agent is considered ethically and often legally to have a fiduciary duty. This means that the agent (i.e. the manager) is placed in a position of trust and assumes a duty to act in good faith and should act in the best interests of the principal (i.e. the shareholder). As chapter 5 outlines, there is a common assumption in economic theory which is, if individuals are rational, they will act in their own best interests. Therefore, although managers should supposedly make decisions that are best for the principals, in some instances they will make decisions that maximise their own wealth, rather than the principals'. Principals are also rational and will expect that the managers will not always act in the shareholders' interests. This leads to three costs associated with this agency relationship:

- *monitoring costs.* These are costs incurred by principals to measure, observe and control the agent's behaviour.
- *bonding costs.* These are restrictions placed on an agent's actions deriving from linking the agent's interest to that of the principal.
- *residual loss.* This is the reduction in wealth of principals caused by their agent's non-optimal behaviour.

This theory also identifies ways in which managers can act against shareholders' interests known as 'agency problems'. These problems involve managers making business decisions that result in less than optimal results from the perspective of the principal. The three 'agency problems' (risk aversion, dividend retention and horizon problem) are outlined in chapter 5. Agency theory explains that these problems can be reduced by linking management's rewards to certain conditions. This in effect 'bonds' the interests of the managers to those of the shareholders. The mechanism to do this is by contracting with the managers, through a bonus plan that specifically deals with each of these problems by linking managers' remuneration to certain performance outcomes (including accounting measures such as profit or share price). Further, given the assumption that individuals act in their own interest, the theory argues that managers will be expected to attempt to maximise any bonuses. A key implication of agency theory is that it provides a reason and explanation for the need for accounting reports: to help monitor and control the activities of managers. In the context of corporate governance the tenets of agency theory are evident in specific prescriptions. For example the OECD principles of corporate governance specify that:

- managers' remuneration should be linked to shareholder interest and that a key responsibility of the board is '[a]ligning key executive and board remuneration with the longer term interests of the company and its shareholders'.
- the remuneration policy for executives and board members needs to be disclosed to shareholders.[11]

Figure 7.1 summarises the key principles of the shareholder–manager relationship in agency theory.

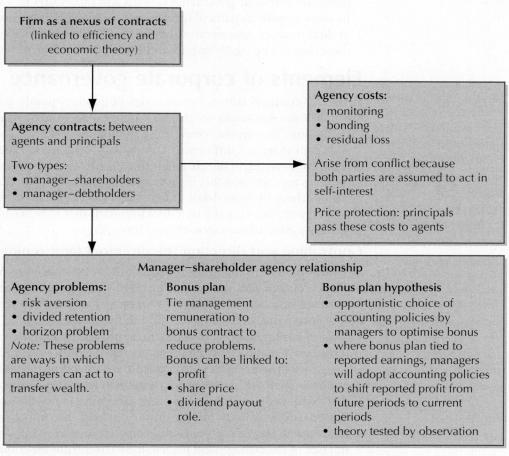

FIGURE 7.1 Overview of the shareholder–manager relationship in agency theory

LO 4 CORPORATE GOVERNANCE GUIDELINES AND PRACTICES

As noted previously, corporate governance involves ensuring that the decisions made by those managing the corporation are appropriate and provides a means to monitor corporate activities and decision making itself. It is primarily concerned with managing the relationship between the shareholders, the key managers of the corporation (usually the board of directors), other senior managers within the corporation and other stakeholders. Many countries have developed suggested (and sometimes required) lists of rules or descriptions of the types of practices that should be included in corporate governance systems. However, it is generally acknowledged that there is no 'one' system of corporate governance. The practices and procedures required or desired will be affected by:

- the nature of the particular corporation and its activities. For example, some companies have dominant shareholders, whereas in others shareholding is more widely spread.
- the environment in which the corporation operates. This will include the legal, regulatory and social environment. For example, in some countries, employees have particular legal rights to information and board representation; in others, directors are individually responsible for decisions; whereas in others, the members of the board of directors may have joint responsibility under law. The legal status and enforcement of particular corporate governance systems and procedures will also affect actual practice. In some countries, particular practices (such as requirements for an audit committee or disclosures of remuneration of directors) will be required by law. In other countries, these may not be legally required, although they may be recommended practice.

Elements of corporate governance

Figure 7.2 contains summaries of codes of good corporate governance as outlined by the OECD, the Australian Securities Exchange (ASX) and the China Securities Regulatory Commission. You should review these summaries now.

Although there are differences among these summaries, many of the principles are similar. As these illustrate, although there is no single model of corporate governance, three areas are common foci in corporate governance. These are interrelated. As this text examines them in more detail, it becomes evident that all of these areas are concerned primarily with reducing the potential problems that may occur in corporations because of the separation of management and ownership.

Controlling and directing the directors (and senior management)

This area focuses on trying to ensure that the key managers make appropriate decisions; that they cannot and do not act in their own interests to benefit themselves against the interest of other stakeholders (in particular shareholders). Examples of possible corporate governance practices in relation to this area include:

- *Codes of conduct for directors.* These aim to promote ethical decision making and will often include statements clarifying the standards of ethical behaviour required of directors, as well as systems or practices put in place to ensure compliance with any legal obligations.
- *Minimum standards or levels of experience for directors.* This will often include a requirement that excludes directors who have certain criminal convictions and may also require professional expertise or training to ensure directors are competent to do their work.
- *Requirements that most of the board of directors be independent.* An independent director is not part of the management team that effectively runs the company. The premise behind this is that there may be a conflict of interest if members of management are part of the board of directors whose duties include evaluating the performance of management.[12]
- *Formation of a nominating committee to identify potential new directors.* This tries to ensure that potential directors are considered on merit.
- *Formation of a remuneration committee.* This aims to ensure that directors and senior management employment contracts are fair, and encourages directors to act in the interests of shareholders, avoiding the situation in which the directors or senior managers are determining and approving their own remuneration.
- *Setting out the responsibilities and duties of directors and specifying the liability of directors who breach their obligations.* This aims to ensure that the respective roles of directors and senior executives within the entity are clearly delineated and defined. This helps to ensure that there is an appropriate allocation of responsibilities (e.g. strategic oversight and guidance are a board responsibility) and associated accountability.

FIGURE 7.2 Various codes of good corporate governance

Summary of OECD's 6 Principles of Corporate Governance

I. Ensuring the basis for an effective corporate governance framework

The corporate governance framework should promote transparent and efficient markets, be consistent with the rule of law and clearly articulate the division of responsibilities among different supervisory, regulatory and enforcement authorities.

II. The rights of shareholders and key ownership functions

The corporate governance framework should protect and facilitate the exercise of shareholders' rights.

III. The equitable treatment of shareholders

The corporate governance framework should ensure the equitable treatment of all shareholders, including minority and foreign shareholders. All shareholders should have the opportunity to obtain effective redress for violation of their rights.

IV. The role of stakeholders in corporate governance

The corporate governance framework should recognise the rights of stakeholders established by law or through mutual agreements and encourage active cooperation between corporations and stakeholders in creating wealth, jobs, and the sustainability of financially sound enterprises.

V. Disclosure and transparency

The corporate governance framework should ensure that timely and accurate disclosure is made on all material matters regarding the corporation, including the financial situation, performance, ownership, and governance of the company.

VI. The responsibilities of the board

The corporate governance framework should ensure the strategic guidance of the company, the effective monitoring of management by the board, and the board's accountability to the company and the shareholders.

Summary of ASX 8 Principles of Corporate Governance

1. Lay solid foundations for management and oversight

Establish and disclose the respective roles and responsibilities of board and management.

2. Structure the board to add value

Have a board of an effective composition, size and commitment to adequately discharge its responsibilities and duties. For example, a majority of the board should be independent.

3. Promote ethical and responsible decision making

Actively promote ethical and responsible decision making. For example establish a code of conduct to ensure someone is responsible and accountable for reporting and investigating reports of unethical behaviour.

4. Safeguard integrity in financial reporting

Have a structure to independently verify and safeguard the integrity of the company's financial reporting. For example, the board should establish an audit committee.

5. Make timely and balanced disclosure

Promote timely and balanced disclosure of all material matters concerning the company.

6. Respect the rights of shareholders

Respect the rights of shareholders and facilitate the effective exercise of those rights. For example, design and disclose a communications strategy to promote effective communication with shareholders and encourage effective participation at general meetings.

7. Recognise and manage risk

Establish a sound system of risk oversight and management and internal control.

8. Remunerate fairly and responsibly

Ensure the level and composition of remuneration is sufficient and reasonable and that its relationship to performance is clear. For example, establish a remuneration committee.

FIGURE 7.2 *(continued)*

Overview of Code of Corporate Governance for Listed Companies in China

Chapter 1: Shareholders and shareholders' meetings

This covers issues and practices to ensure the equal treatment and the protection of legitimate rights and interests of all shareholders, and includes sections on
(1) Protection of the rights of the shareholders
(2) Rules and procedures for meetings
(3) Related party transactions.

Chapter 2: Listed company and its controlling shareholders

This covers issues and practices to regulate the relationship between listed company and its controlling shareholders, and includes sections on
(1) Behaviour rules for controlling shareholders
(2) Independence of listed company.

Chapter 3: Directors and board of directors

This covers issues and practices to strengthen the directors' duties of good faith and due diligence and includes sections on
(1) Election procedures for directors
(2) The duties and responsibilities of directors
(3) Duties and composition of the board of directors
(4) Rules and procedures of the board of directors
(5) Independent director
(6) To establish special committees under of the board of directors.

Chapter 4: The supervisors and the supervisory board

This includes sections on
(1) Duties and responsibilities of the supervisory board
(2) The composition and steering of the supervisory board.

Chapter 5: Performance assessments and incentive and disciplinary systems

This covers issues and practices to establish and strengthen the performance appraisal system assessments and incentive and disciplinary systems for the boards and the management and includes sections on
(1) Performance assessment for the directors, and supervisors and management personnel
(2) Selection of management personnel
(3) Incentive and disciplinary systems for management.

Chapter 6: Stakeholders

This covers issues and practices to ensure the legal rights of interested parties and protection of stakeholders' rights.

Chapter 7: Information disclosure and transparency

This covers issues and practices to strengthen information disclosure and enhance transparency of corporate governance and includes sections on
(1) Listed companies' ongoing information disclosure
(2) Disclosure of information regarding corporate governance
(3) Disclosure of controlling shareholders' interests.

Source: Adapted from OECD principles of corporate governance;[13] Corporate governance principles and recommendations with 2010 amendments;[14] Code of corporate governance for listed companies in China.[15]

These practices are aimed at, first, encouraging directors to make appropriate decisions and, second, preventing abuse of the position of directors by putting in place controls and restraints (e.g. committees or penalties for breaching duties).

Role of shareholders (and other stakeholders)

This area focuses on trying to ensure that shareholders have the ability to protect their interests in the corporation by participating in directing the company and effectively exercising some control at the oversight level. This area also considers, in some cases, a broader category of stakeholders (e.g. employees). Examples of possible corporate governance practices in relation to this area include:

- *the requirement to provide information to shareholders (e.g. the annual report).* This is to ensure that all shareholders have access to adequate and timely information so as to make informed decisions and exercise their rights (e.g. voting rights) effectively.
- *requirements to treat all shareholders equally and take into account the interests of minority shareholders.* These are particularly important if there are controlling shareholders who have the ability to dominate because of the size of their voting rights.
- *rules relating to shareholders' meetings, including notice to be given (to ensure shareholders are informed), and the right to place items on the agenda.*
- *rules relating to shareholders' voting rights.* These include rights to nominate, vote for, and approve the appointment, removal and remuneration of directors, how votes are counted and whether proxy votes are allowed, and whether shareholders vote on the appointment and removal of auditors.
- *rules and rights for shareholders to call extraordinary meetings in particular circumstances, and to take action if their rights are violated.* Corporations law may specify the conditions under which shareholders can require a company to hold such meetings.
- *codes of conduct in relation to other stakeholders.* Such codes often require the company to meet the legal rights of other parties (e.g. creditors and employees).

Many of the rights of shareholders (e.g. those relating to voting rights) will be enforceable by law under specific legislation relating to corporations.

Transparency and accountability

This area focuses on trying to ensure that the stakeholders (including shareholders) are sufficiently informed about the activities of the company and its management, and to allow managers to meet their accountability obligations.

Examples of possible corporate governance practices in relation to this area include:

- *the requirement to prepare quarterly and annual reports, and provide them to shareholders.* In many cases, a time limit is specified in which these reports must be provided.
- *the requirement to have the annual reports audited.* Annual reports contain a large amount of both voluntary and mandatory information and requiring this information to be audited provides some assurance that it gives a fair representation of the entity's operations and performance.
- *rules relating to the appointment of auditors, including the requirement for them to be independent, the establishment of an audit committee, and the rotation of auditors.* For the audit process to provide the intended level of assurance on the information provided, auditors must be (and be perceived as) independent and competent. In many jurisdictions there are legal requirements that specify the professional qualifications and experience required of auditors, and the procedures to be followed to enhance auditor independence.
- *details of specific information to be disclosed.* This may include the disclosure of:
  - related party relationships and transactions (e.g. loans to family members of directors)
  - amounts received by directors (including salary, shares and pension)
  - corporate governance practices.
- *requirements that directors make a declaration that accounts are correct.* In some countries (e.g. the United States), chief financial officers also need to make this statement.

These practices are aimed at ensuring that the company provides adequate, timely and accurate information. Many of these disclosure requirements will be enforceable by law because of specific legislation on corporations, often with penalties if they are not met.

These three areas are interrelated. For example, shareholders may have rights to vote on the remuneration of directors but unless they understand how the remuneration was decided and also have adequate and accurate disclosures on it, they may not be able to assess or identify whether there are problems or concerns. Transparency and accountability are useless without the ability to participate and take action.[16] As stated by Witherell, 'At the end of the day good corporate governance comes down to effective *and* informed owners' (emphasis added).[17]

LO 5 APPROACHES TO CORPORATE GOVERNANCE

Two broad approaches to corporate governance can be identified, although for most countries and corporations the position taken on corporate governance will lie somewhere in between the two. These approaches can be compared with the two divergent methods of accounting standard setting: the rules-based and the principles-based approach.

The rules-based approach to corporate governance

This approach identifies precise practices that are required or recommended to ensure good corporate governance. For example, there may be a rule that an audit or remuneration committee be established. This approach is often associated with enforcement by legislation or listing rules, with imposition of penalties if the rules are not followed. The clearest example of this approach is seen in elements of the Sarbanes–Oxley Act in the United States. It was introduced after a string of accounting abuses (including Enron and WorldCom) and gives legal backing, with associated penalties, to requirements in the corporate governance area. For example, the Sarbanes–Oxley Act:

- requires the chief financial officer to certify the correctness of the financial statements (s. 302) and imposes potential penalties of up to US$5 million and 20 years' imprisonment (s. 906)
- requires audit partner rotation at least every five years
- bans loans to directors (s. 402)
- requires disclosure whether there is a code of ethics for senior financial officers or reasons no code of ethics is in place (s. 406).

The advantages of this approach are that it provides at least a set of minimum corporate governance practices that must be followed by all corporations and there is no uncertainty as to which practices are required. This aids enforcement and helps clarify potential liability in terms of litigation.

The disadvantages of this approach are:

- Although it provides a minimum set of practices, it is likely that good corporate governance requires more.
- It can encourage a 'checklist' (form over substance) approach to corporate governance. This has been seen with 'rules-based' accounting standards, where although corporations may follow the letter of the standard and 'meet' the rules, financial statements may not provide an adequate understanding of the company's performance.
- The legislative backing of rules can result in the view that corporate governance is about dealing with legal liability rather than about promoting the interests of shareholders and stakeholders.[18]

As noted, it is generally accepted that there is no 'one' model of corporate governance and this will vary depending on the specific circumstances of the entity (e.g. the size and influence of particular shareholders). Yet a rules-based approach is essentially a 'one-size-fits-all' approach.

The principles-based approach to corporate governance

Rather than identifying specific practices or rules, this approach identifies general principles or objectives for the corporate governance system to achieve. For example, the general principle may be that the corporation should ensure that there is accurate and adequate disclosure of information. Rather than identifying the exact practices that may help meet this aim (such as directing specific times for rotation of auditors and certification of financial statements), responsibility is placed on the managers to consider which practices are appropriate, given their circumstances.

There are advantages to a principles-based approach, including:

- It arguably places a higher level of duty on directors to determine which corporate governance practices are required, rather than simply accepting a minimum set of practices as being adequate.
- Its flexibility means that the corporate governance practices can be adapted for the particular circumstances and environment of the entity.

The key disadvantage of this approach is that it essentially leaves it to the directors to interpret these principles and decide which corporate governance practices are needed, so it relies on their honesty, integrity and commitment to good governance. If directors are competent and act in good faith, then this would not be a problem, but many of the corporate abuses that have renewed the interest in corporate governance practices have stemmed from people not acting appropriately.

Practical considerations

In practice, in most countries, corporate governance involves various combinations of both the rules and principles-based approaches with:

- *Specific legislation that requires certain corporate governance practices to be followed by law.* The specific practices, plus penalties and degree of enforcement varies from country to country. Common examples of legislated practices are:
  - requirements for audit committees and that accounts be audited
  - shareholders' rights to vote to remove directors
  - requirements to appoint independent directors to the board
  - legal penalties for directors' breaches of duty.
- *Codes of corporate governance practice (based on principles) issued by government or industry groups and also by securities exchanges.* These may suggest specific examples as best practice, although corporations are not required by law to follow them. Common examples are:
  - Best practice recommends separation of the chair of the board of directors and the CEO, although in most countries (e.g. Singapore) this is not legally required.
  - A remuneration committee is recommended best practice in the code of corporate governance but may not be required by law (as in Malaysia).

As Cowan notes, the success of 'voluntary codes depends on the willingness to implement them'.[19] So the actual standard of corporate governance practices will be influenced by the nature of the requirements, the environment in which the corporation operates, and the commitment of management. An illustration of the impact of environmental factors on corporate governance practices is illustrated in Hong Kong. An early study by Allen and Roy found that despite having the highest corporate governance standards in China, Hong Kong had few companies whose practices would be considered world class. They argued this was partly caused by the concentration of ownership and limited shareholder activism in Hong Kong, the voluntary nature of some practices, and the lack of effectiveness of enforcement.[20] In 2005, the Hong Kong Stock Exchange (HKEX) introduced principles of corporate governance with two levels of recommendations: code provisions, which were expected to be complied with and a requirement for an explicit statement of compliance or an explanation of why they were not followed; and best practice recommendations. This approach, combined with close monitoring by the HKEX, has been credited for Hong Kong's corporate governance practices being ranked first (best) by the Asian Corporate Governance Association in 2010. In 2011, the HKEX proposed further changes including upgrading some code provisions to listing rules, with which compliance is mandatory, and upgrading some previous recommendations to code provisions.[21]

LO 6 DEVELOPMENTS AND ISSUES IN CORPORATE GOVERNANCE

As noted previously, there is no 'one' system of corporate governance and it is influenced by the changing environment in which corporations operate. This is reflected, for example, in:
- legal support for specific corporate governance practices via the Sarbanes–Oxley Act in the United States following a number of accounting scandals (including Enron and WorldCom)
- calls for corporations to consider sustainability in the context of concerns about climate change.

More recently the global financial crisis has provided an impetus for regulators, corporations themselves and other organisations to reconsider aspects of corporate governance. Various reviews and investigations have been undertaken into the causes of the global financial crisis (see, for example, reports by the Organisation for Economic Co-operation and Development, United Kingdom House of Commons and the United States Financial Crisis Inquiry Commission) and have attributed the crisis, at least in part, to deficiencies in corporate governance practices such as failures in relation to risk management, remuneration, board practices and the exercise of shareholder rights.[22] The OECD's review concluded that while the espoused principles of corporate governance were sound, there was a 'gap' between the principles and their implementation. The next sections consider two areas of corporate governance that have been or are being influenced as a result of the global financial crisis.[23]

Increased focus on risk management

A repeated theme arising from reviews of the causes of the financial crisis is the failure of many corporations to manage and control risk. It would seem self-evident that to protect and enhance shareholder value a corporation needs to effectively manage risk. However, as noted by the OECD:

> Perhaps one of the greatest shocks from the financial crisis has been the widespread failure of risk management. In many cases risk was not managed on an enterprise basis and not adjusted to corporate strategy. Risk managers were often separated from management and not regarded as an essential part of implementing the company's strategy. Most important of all, boards were in a number of cases ignorant of the risk facing the company . . .
>
> With few exceptions, risk management is typically not covered, or is insufficiently covered, by existing corporate governance standards or codes. Corporate governance standard setters should be encouraged to include or improve references to risk management in order to raise awareness and improve implementation.[24]

The causes of the global financial crisis are not intended to be outlined here in detail. However, the risk management deficiencies noted include:
- a disjointed approach to risk management where risk was not managed or monitored at the entity level, but rather at individual activity level. As a result no effective understanding or oversight of risk for the corporation existed overall.

- information about risks was not reaching the board or board members were unable to understand or appreciate the risks involved
- the organisational culture (pursuing growth in profits) encouraged risk taking
- a 'disconnect' or 'mismatch' existed between the corporation's overall risk strategy and related procedures. For example, many remuneration packages provided incentives for high-risk activities and short-term outlooks.

Risk management in many codes of corporate governance is not given prominence and is subsumed as part of the oversight role of boards. For example, the OECD principles include as part of the responsibilities of the board 'reviewing and guiding corporate strategy including . . . risk policy'.[25] A few codes or models give prominence to risk. For example, the ASX code introduced in 2007 a separate principle (Principle 7: Recognise and manage risk) that provides recommendation on risk management and explicitly recognises that risk management goes beyond 'financial reporting risk' — that is, the risk of material errors in financial statements — and extends to business risks.[26]

The Ernst & Young governance model identifies risk as a key element of good corporate governance as represented in figure 7.3.

Elements of the Effective Governance Model

The foundation of the EGM is the corporate structure that includes the owners of the business in the form of the shareholders, who appoint a number of trustees, in the form of a Board of Directors, to oversee their interests in the business and who in turn hire a chief executive to develop business strategies, employ resources, build and operate processes, generate profits, and increase the value for the shareholders.

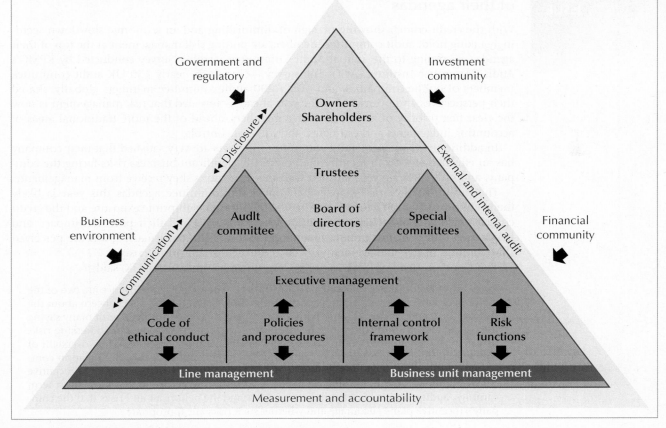

FIGURE 7.3 Elements of the Effective Governance Model

Source: Ernst & Young, *Effective governance model: an operating framework.*[27]

The management of the 'business' aspect of risk is often referred to as 'enterprise risk'. In the wake of the crisis it is apparent that many corporations are endeavouring to introduce more formal and comprehensive risk management policies and procedures and integrate these into their existing corporate governance frameworks. Many companies have now established separate risk management committees to better manage risk. For example, PETRONAS Group in its 2010 annual report states:

> Having regard to the fact that managing risk is an inherent part of the Group's activities, risk management and the ongoing improvement in corresponding control structures in all significant risk areas including among others, financial, health, safety and environment, operations, geopolitics, trading and logistics, remain a key focus of the Board in building a successful and sustainable business. For this endeavour, the Group has established a Risk Management Committee which assists Management in defining, developing and recommending risk management strategies and policies for the PETRONAS Group. In addition, the Risk Management Committee also coordinates Group-wide risk management in terms of building risk management awareness and capabilities, monitoring the risk exposures and planning responses to potential major risk events.[28]

In many committees the task of 'business' risk management had been delegated to the audit committee, expanding its traditional role, which often concentrated on internal controls and financial reporting risks. Contemporary Issue 7.1 discusses the increasing role of audit committees in risk management.

7.1 CONTEMPORARY ISSUE

Audit committees put risk management at the top of their agendas

With the credit crunch showing no sign of diminishing and an economic slowdown seemingly taking hold, audit committee members are putting risk management at the top of their agendas, according to the annual Audit Committee Member Survey conducted by KPMG's Audit Committee Institute (ACI). The survey — in which nearly 150 UK audit committee members of public companies, and over 1,000 audit committee members globally, shared their perspectives and priorities for the year ahead — revealed that risk management is now the clear first priority of audit committee members, ahead of the more traditional areas of accounting judgements and estimates, and internal controls.

In addition, only 46% of audit committee members are very satisfied that their company has an effective process to identify the potentially significant business risks facing the company; and only 38% are very satisfied with the risk reports they receive from management.

The prominence of risk management on audit committee agendas this year is likely fuelled by a number of factors, including the fallout from sub-prime exposure and the credit crunch, increasing awareness of significant business risks and their potential impact, and heightened scrutiny of risk management and its oversight, particularly given the perceived shortcomings of risk management processes during the sub-prime crisis.

Tim Copnell, Head of KPMG's Audit Committee Institute in the UK, said:

> Recession-related risks as well as the quality of the company's risk intelligence are two of the major oversight concerns for audit committee members. But there is also concern about the culture, tone, and incentives underlying the company's risk environment, with many saying the Board and/or audit committee needs to improve their effectiveness in addressing risks that may be driven by the company's incentive compensation structure. While oversight of compensation plans may generally fall within the responsibility of the remuneration committee, audit committees are focusing on the risks associated with the company's incentive compensation structure. In addition to risks associated with an emphasis on short-term earnings, audit committees want to better understand the behaviour and risks that the company's incentive plans encourage and whether such risks are appropriate.

Notwithstanding the oversight of risk management being top of the audit committee's agenda, over half of the Annual Survey respondents expressed some concern that the audit committee has been assigned, or has assumed, too much responsibility for risk oversight (beyond financial reporting risk), and many said the communication and coordination of risk oversight activities among the audit committee, Board, and other committees could be improved.

For most companies, the current business environment poses a major challenge for management — and the pressures to meet expectations will likely increase. Increased complexity and pressures on companies — financial, regulatory, and strategic — make it imperative that the CFO, internal audit, and financial management team have what they need to succeed.

Source: KPMG, Audit committees put risk management at the top of their agendas.[29]

Questions

1. Traditionally, audit committees have primarily focused on managing financial reporting risk (i.e. risk of misstatements in financial statements) and reviewing aspects such as internal control systems. Do you believe the expansion of this committee's role to consider business risk appropriate? **J** **K**
2. The extract notes a link between compensation structures within companies and risk management. Explain how these are related. **K** **AS**

Executive remuneration

The issue of remuneration for corporate directors and executives has long been contentious. This is not surprising given the media regularly reports the million-dollar packages often paid to many corporate executives. However, the global financial crisis has highlighted concerns. First, it was seen as incongruous that directors and executives still received massive bonuses, seemingly unrelated to the actual performance of the company, when company performance was deficient. This was seen as particularly problematic in countries like the United States where public money was used to 'bail' out some companies that otherwise would have failed. Second, investigations into the causes of the global financial crisis argued that remuneration packages that focused on and rewarded short term goals contributed to the crisis itself by encouraging excessive risk taking. As MacFarlane stated:

> The biggest misdirected incentive was the performance-based pay structures which awarded massive bonuses to the management of financial institutions on the basis of short-term profit results...Annual bonuses in the millions or tens of millions of dollars were available to the most successful profit earners, and, of course, were not returnable when the short-term profits were lost in subsequent years. Policymakers around the world, who had previously lacked any 'curiosity and scepticism . . . about what was going on around them' should pay more heed to the risks involved in this type of reward structure.[30]

Linked to these concerns was the perception that shareholders have few effective means to control or question remuneration due to a lack of disclosure that would allow shareholders to assess whether there is any conflict of interest and barriers to shareholders vetoing remuneration to directors. Effective corporate governance requires diligent and effective oversight by owners (shareholders) and all codes of corporate governance include specific principles about the rights of (and responsibilities to) shareholders. Shareholders have voting rights, but often shareholders of large companies are diverse and passive and fragmented in their approach. A number of inquiries into the financial crisis (for example that of the OECD and the House of Commons) found that there were impediments for shareholders to exercise their rights and that institutional investors (often holders of larger equity portions) failed to adequately scrutinise boards' performance. As the House of Commons report states:

> We are particularly concerned that fragmented and dispersed ownership combined with the costs of detailed engagement with firms by shareholders has resulted in the phenomenon of 'ownerless corporations' described to us by Lord Myners.[31]

As Yong states, '[e]xcessive executive pay is actually the most visible form of poor governance'.[32] This visibility, the problems identified in the financial crisis and public concerns have resulted in increased legislation to control executive compensation and to support shareholders rights. For example:

In the United States, the Dodd–Frank Wall Street Reform and Consumer Protection Act includes provisions that require:

- executive compensation to be submitted for shareholder approval via a non-binding vote
- increased disclosure about the nature of compensation packages and payments related to financial performance
- 'claw back' provisions where, if found that compensation paid was based on inaccurate financial statements, the compensation is rescinded
- that non-independent directors cannot sit on remuneration or compensation committees so that these committees are independent of the executives they are rewarding.

In Australia, the federal government commissioned the Productivity Commission to report on executive compensation. The recommendations from the Productivity Commission report resulted in legislation that, as well as requiring increased disclosure and ensuring independence of any remuneration committee (similar to the US requirements), strengthens stakeholders' power via a 'two strikes' rule. The rule proposes that if more than 25% of shareholders vote against the remuneration report for two consecutive years, the board itself can be put up for re-election.

These 'reactions' to the global financial crisis indicate a shift from voluntary regimes to embedding corporate governance practices in law. This is a common regulatory response following crises (as illustrated by the introduction of the Sarbanes–Oxley Act in the United States following the Enron and WorldCom scandals). However, even in the absence of regulation (or perhaps as a response to threats of legislation) companies have responded to increased public and government scrutiny by changing their remuneration policies and practices. Recent studies have indicated that large companies around the world are changing the nature of their bonus plans by linking greater proportions to long-term incentives and deferring part of the compensation. For example:

- A study by Mercer has found that European companies have reduced the bonus components of salary packages, and increased the use of long-term incentives and deferred compensation finding that '[a]round two-thirds of companies have introduced or are considering a so called 'malus' — or opposite of bonus — whereby a major portion of bonuses are deferred and could be reduced if the company posts losses'.[33]
- In Australia, a number of influential listed companies have adjusted their compensation packages to longer-term horizons.[34]

LO 7 ROLE OF ACCOUNTING AND FINANCIAL REPORTING IN CORPORATE GOVERNANCE

Accounting clearly has a central role in directing and controlling a corporation. Internal accounting information (management accounting) provides a significant part of the information on which company operations will be decided. For example, estimates of costs of production, savings in costs of outsourcing or costs involved in reducing the environmental impacts of production processes will often be influential in determining how a company operates (what products it makes and how it makes them). At the other end, accounting also provides the means for outsiders to monitor the corporation and to assess how well those responsible for managing the corporation have performed. You will recall from chapter 2 that, historically, the main purpose of financial statements and accounting was stewardship or accountability. This role of accounting is an integral part of any corporate governance system. Furthermore, a key feature of all corporate governance systems and requirements is the need for corporations to be transparent about what they do. It is not enough for corporations to 'do the right thing', they need to be seen to do it and people outside (such as shareholders) need to be able to check on what is being done. In other words, a critical part of good corporate governance is for corporations to be open and honest and to provide sufficient accurate information for corporate activities to be monitored.

The requirements for corporations to provide financial statements and for these to be audited can be identified as perhaps some of the earliest corporate governance practices, even before the term 'corporate governance' was used.

The origins of corporate governance can be found in the desire to improve the transparency and accountability of financial reporting by listed companies to their shareholders, and although it has since developed far beyond this, transparency and accountability remain the fundamental elements.[35]

Two key roles can be identified for accounting and financial reporting in encouraging good corporate governance.

Deterring, preventing and encouraging certain actions and decisions

There are two ways in which accounting is used to direct and control the managers of a corporation. One is to use accounting information to promote appropriate decisions. As noted in discussing positive accounting theory, linking managers' performance to a bonus that depends on accounting profit, for example, links the interests of managers and shareholders and so encourages managers to make decisions (such as making higher-return investments) that improve profitability. This is a direct way to use accounting information. Indirectly, basing managers' performance (at least in part) on the figures in the financial statements encourages managers to make decisions that will impact positively on financial performance of the corporation, presumably in the best interest of shareholders.

The second way accounting can help corporate governance is through disclosures. Accounting standards require specific disclosures about areas or issues related to corporate governance. For example:

- AASB 124/IAS 24 *Related Party Disclosures* requires extensive disclosures, including the names and compensation of directors and key management personnel, and any transactions between entity and directors (e.g. loans and purchases).
- AASB 2/IFRS 2 *Share-based Payment* includes requirements that share-based payments to directors or other employees be disclosed and also treated as an expense in the profit or loss.

It is natural that a requirement to disclose actions will in some ways control and constrain behaviour. Disclosing the activities (e.g. loans or remuneration) of managers provides a disincentive for inappropriate actions by managers.

Informing shareholders and stakeholders

The key role for financial reporting in corporate governance is to provide the information needed to assess the performance of the corporation and its managers. Historically, accountability was the main purpose of financial statements and accounting, which required the managers to provide a report to the providers of resources to explain how well they have managed the resources. It is still widely considered that an 'absolute core value for corporate governance is to deliver improved accountability' and that accountability is essential for effective corporate governance.[36] Consider a small sporting or social club at which members pay fees and leave the running of the club to a few, often dedicated, individuals. Regardless how much you trust the people who are in charge, would you allow them to say 'trust us' and provide no explanation of how the money is or was to be spent? You would still want an account of where the money went! 'A strong disclosure regime that promotes real transparency is a pivotal feature of market-based monitoring of companies and is central to shareholders' ability to exercise their ownership rights on an informed basis'.[37] However, to be useful, the financial statements provided must be transparent, unbiased and complete. Financial statements are a crucial link enabling shareholders to monitor directors' actions and to assist in identifying any deficiencies in the effectiveness of corporate governance.

There are various mechanisms in force to increase the relevance and faithful representation of financial statements. These include requirements that reports be consistent with accounting standards. AASB 101/IAS 1 *Presentation of Financial Statements* requires that the financial statements present fairly the financial position and performance of the entity and that the entity disclose whether International Financial Reporting Standards (IFRSs) have been complied with.

One impetus behind the spread of adoption of IFRSs is to improve corporate governance. For example, a key recommendation of the Asian Roundtable on Corporate Governance was the priority to converge with international accounting and auditing standards on the basis that:

> Full adoption of international accounting, audit and financial disclosure standards and practices will facilitate transparency, as well as comparability, of information across different jurisdictions. Such features, in turn, strengthen market discipline as a means for improving corporate governance practices.[38]

Following the financial crisis various reports (for example that of the G20) have reiterated the need for a set of high-quality, global and principles-based accounting standards. As noted, requirements for audits, auditors, audit committees and certification of financial statements by managers can also improve the accuracy and reliability of financial statements. This audit element is crucial:

> A good corporate governance structure must be based on a system of checks and balances. Whilst management strives to achieve the right balance between growth and protection of value, auditors provide an objective check that the rules are being followed.[39]

Therefore, accounting is an essential component of any corporate governance system. Furthermore, many of the corporate governance systems and practices (such as audit committees) are in place to ensure that the accounting information to be used for corporate governance (and others) is not compromised. So why are there potential problems with accounting information?

Financial reporting 'problems'

Ideally, financial statements are transparent, complete and unbiased. If they are not, how can corporate governance work? However, historically and in more recent times, there have been financial reporting failures: cases such as Enron, WorldCom and ABC Learning are just some of the most publicised. The nature of accounting itself and the pivotal role accounting and financial reporting play can not only improve corporate governance but can also result in pressures for accounting to be used (or abused) to its detriment.

How accounting can cause financial reporting problems

Financial statements should be transparent and accurate but agency theory explains that managers will be concerned with ensuring that they maximise their own bonuses. Often choices are allowed in accounting methods, so a manager's choice of accounting method may be influenced by the potential impact on his or her bonus. In other words, the choice of accounting policy will not be neutral or unbiased.

Furthermore, increasingly, the share price of corporations is viewed as the ultimate measure of a corporation's (and its management's) success. Indeed, a large part of managers' remuneration is often paid in the form of shares or share options. To maintain the share price, it is necessary to meet the expectations of the market. Again, this can encourage accounting choices or even distortion of accounting information to provide a favourable report to the market. It is paradoxical that the very mechanism for aligning managers' interest with that of shareholders (i.e. bonuses based on accounting profit or issuing shares or share options) has provided incentives for this manipulation. But this has been identified as a contributor to accounting 'abuses' or failures, including Enron. As the Institute of European Affairs states:

> Whereas accounting was traditionally understood as a tool for the board to assess the performance of managers, and a tool for investors to assess the value of a company compared with its peers, it has recently, according to Commissioner Bolkestein, 'become a means for managers to deliver a steady flow of information to the markets in ways that push up or prop up the share price'.[40]

Even if managers do not directly receive shares, having their performance, at least in part, judged on the company's share price provides a powerful incentive to 'show' the market the performance it wants or expects to see. This can also affect the actions taken by companies.

Research in accounting confirms the two key incentives for profit manipulation: first, the contract or agency incentives from bonus contracts identified under agency theory and second, manipulating (or manufacturing) earnings to meet market expectations.[41]

Many accounting standards, particularly principles-based standards, allow choices (this may be a choice to capitalise or expense, or a choice of depreciation methods, for example) and require professional judgement to be exercised in determining them. The flexibility provided by accounting standards is provided to allow the methods that best reflect the economic circumstances of the entity to be selected. However, in reality, in many cases, there have been attempts by management to influence the accountants within the organisation, and the auditors, in the choices made. Pierpont provides the following example:

> Anthony Wight, a former accountant with the Adelaide retailer [Harris Scarfe], told a South Australian court the company had been falsifying its accounts from 1994 until it went into voluntary administration in 2001.
>
> Anthony said Harris Scarfe's chief financial officer, Alan Hodgson, had directed him to falsify accounts in 1994. Hodgson has since pleaded guilty to 32 dishonesty offences and is now completing a six-year term of home detention.
>
> Most of the falsification concerned inflation of inventory records, with the gap between the accounts and reality growing larger every year. By the time Harris Scarfe hit the wall, about one dollar in every six of inventory value wasn't there. And over that period, two successive audit firms missed the falsifications.[42]

Of course, it is in the self-interest of the employees of a corporation (such as their accountants) and the auditors to, wherever possible, meet the needs of management, given that their livelihood can be affected. The ability and willingness to remain independent in the light of pressure from management depends in part on the integrity of the individuals involved, the consequences and what systems are in place to reduce such influence. Some key corporate governance practices (such as the requirement for auditor independence, audit committees and certification of accounts by financial officers) are specifically aimed at reducing the influence of managers and ensuring that the financial statements present an unbiased view.

If the flexibility is removed from accounting standards, for example, with rules-based standards, undue influence in the judgement of accounting policy choice can be avoided, but this may increase the risk that financial statements will not be transparent, complete and unbiased. The problem with a specific rule (such as a requirement to apply consolidation accounting if more than 50% of a company is owned or to recognise a finance-leased asset and liability only if the lease term is for more than 75% of its useful life) is that this allows an entity to avoid the reporting requirements by interpreting or engineering transactions so that the transactions do not meet the specific rule and hence the accounting requirements do not need to be applied. These actions also are often associated with attempts at hiding debt and off-balance-sheet financing and have been associated with corporate reporting 'failures'. As Berkwitz and Rampell state, in relation to rules-based standards:

> The big firms have concocted all kinds of slippery methods that enable companies to comply with the exact letter of the rules while still managing to mislead investors. Case in point: Enron and its multiple 'special purpose entities,' which allowed it to omit substantial liabilities from its balance sheets while staying within the rules of the accounting game.[43]

The problem is that, whether using rules or principles-based standards, financial statements can meet the specific accounting requirements, but still result in misleading or incomplete disclosures. Because unbiased, complete and transparent reporting is considered a critical and necessary condition for effective corporate governance, this is a problem. In the context of the global financial crisis, while there is overall consensus that accounting itself did not cause the financial crisis, problems were identified — for example:

- differences between valuations of assets and incomplete disclosures, allowed by the accounting standards, have been argued to 'contribute to market opacity and reduce the integrity' of financial statements and reduce transparency
- auditors have been accused of 'following accounting standards in an overly mechanistic way without applying sufficient professional judgment'.[44]

These types of financial reporting problems, resulting from flexibility in accounting rules themselves or from engineering transactions to avoid the rules, are often referred to as 'creative accounting'. Essentially, the 'letter of the law' of the accounting requirements is followed, although the interpretations and actions would not be in the 'spirit of the rules'. Some of these may involve deliberate attempts to distort the financial statements; others may be caused by differences in judgements, influenced to varying degrees by self-interest. Of course, some problems in financial reporting (and corporations) are the result of dishonesty, deliberate misstatements and lies in financial statements; in other words, of fraud. Although many corporate governance practices can minimise the opportunity for fraud, wherever people are involved it will inevitably occur. This leads to considering the role of ethics in both accounting and corporate governance.

LO 8 THE ROLE OF ETHICS

Corporations are artificial, legal constructions. People make the decisions in corporations (whether they are directors, executives, auditors, accountants or other employees) and ultimately good corporate governance is about people making the 'right' decisions.

Peter Achterstraat, auditor-general in New South Wales, stated:

> At the core of good governance is 'doing the right thing' by acting with honesty, impartiality, integrity, trustworthiness, respect for the law and due process. A commitment to ethical values is fundamental'.[45]

Ethics is a discipline in its own right, the alternative theories of which will not be considered in detail here. However, in simple terms, to behave ethically can be equated with the common concept of 'do unto others as you would have done unto you'.[46] In the context of corporate governance — the directing and controlling of a company — what makes certain behaviour or decisions 'right'? How does the context change whether a decision is ethical or whether ethical decisions are made? Are there different standards of ethics for a person making a decision as a 'corporate' employee rather than as an individual?

Let's take an example. Mitsubishi in Japan failed to inform customers of potential safety problems with vehicles or recall them for repair. Allegedly, part of the reason for not wanting to make the recall was the impact on the balance sheet that it would have. The failure to make the recall allegedly led to accidents, including one resulting in the death of the driver.[47] Given that a key objective of the corporation is to maintain shareholder value and that recalling vehicles would undoubtedly reduce this, was the decision to not recall the vehicles ethical? You would expect that if family members of corporate employees who knew about these defects owned these vehicles, the family members would have been told about the defects! If the principle 'do unto others as you would have done unto you' is applied, the decision not to recall the vehicles was not ethical. This is perhaps a relatively clear case. If this happens in clear cases, what happens in more ambiguous circumstances? Would it perhaps have been ethical if the defects in the vehicles had been minor and would reduce the life of the vehicles, but were not likely to cause accidents?

As discussed in the context of accounting rules, specific rules, principles or practices do not guarantee acceptable application or outcomes. Interpretation and implementation of these rules and principles, and consideration of the intention and spirit, rather than compliance in form only, matters. The same considerations apply with corporate governance principles and practices. Particular principles, or the existence of particular practices or procedures (such as the auditing of accounts or existence of a remuneration committee), will not guarantee good corporate governance. Indeed, some commentators argue that Enron appeared to practise, and indeed exemplify in some ways, good governance before its downfall. People are often influenced by several factors in making the right decisions and behaving ethically. These include personal integrity, conflicts of interest, pressures and expectations of and from peers and colleagues, and the culture of the corporation itself. The difficulty with corporations is how it can be known whether the managers are ethical. As Flanagan, Little and Watts note:

> When monitoring a company from the outside, it is impossible to observe the character of the directors and their integrity in making decisions. Directors have many ways of erecting smokescreens to hide what they are doing and how they are doing it.[48]

The culture of the corporation — the values it develops and promotes — is considered a key factor in good corporate governance and is widely acknowledged as an essential component. For example:
- The Sarbanes–Oxley Act in the United States requires disclosure of whether or not there is a code of ethics for senior financial officers.
- Guidance by CPA Australia argues that implementation of a corporate governance structure is not sufficient and will only work if the culture of the corporation supports good governance.[49]

- The Hong Kong Institute of Certified Public Accountants guidelines for public bodies places emphasis on the personal qualities of individuals as the foundation for good corporate governance and identifies the qualities of selflessness, integrity, objectivity, accountability, openness, honesty and leadership.[50]

Good corporate governance cannot exist without ethics. Corporate governance relies on people. It is about how people behave and the decisions they make. As Wallenberg states:

> More importantly, corporate governance codes, voluntary or otherwise, are worthless if they are divorced from strong, ethical business leadership. The Enron scandal has demonstrated that in the most regulated market of all, even the best-written governance documents are of little use in the absence of a management culture which embodies real, committed and responsible business ethics. A slavish focus on a rigid set of codes can have the converse effect of encouraging complacency rather than dynamic and proactive management of pressing governance issues.[51]

To be effective, the culture needs to be embedded throughout the corporation and supported. Contemporary Issue 7.2 discusses the role of ethics in corporate governance.

7.2 CONTEMPORARY ISSUE

The individual must take responsibility for doing the right thing

By Alex Malley

The sudden departure of David Jones' chief executive Mark McInnes after inappropriate behaviour towards a 25-year-old woman employee illuminates the need for companies to have good corporate governance to set the checks and balances and boundaries of organisational behaviour.

A robust code of conduct forms an important component of governance practices. If it is applied appropriately, it may reduce the risk of behaviour which, if unchecked, could ultimately cause significant damage — both financially and in terms of reputation.

Promotion of ethical and responsible decision-making and conduct will not only assist in the development of practices which take into account a company's legal obligations, but also maintain confidence in the company's integrity. Reputations can take years to build but be lost overnight, with a loss of customers, the collapse of deals and a plunge in share price all possible consequences, not to mention a decline in staff morale or people who want to work for the company.

A best-practice code of conduct will articulate a company's expectations, procedures and responsibilities towards the individual. It must be more than a statement of aspirational intent. It is important that such a code of conduct operates under well-defined core values to which the board and senior executives are committed.

Companies and their shareholders cannot be protected with absolute certainty from the vagaries of human behaviour. Companies exist within and are part of society, and as such, reflect the ethics and social mores of society. But companies touch the lives of their employees and those who deal with the company, presenting an opportunity to both reflect and promote appropriate conduct.

The role of boards is critical, because the ultimate responsibility for an organisation's activities resides with them. Issues of corporate governance, for example in the assessment of risk, executive remuneration and corporate culture are common, but issues such as the one with which the board of David Jones is dealing are less so, hence the media interest, especially when it involves one of the country's largest retailers.

How well they are handled may depend on how well directors understand their roles. Regulators have a role but it is incumbent on a board to impose a culture of risk assessment, compliance and ethical behaviour on an organisation. Having a whistleblower protection policy in place to protect employees' rights if they report suspected wrongdoing sends a strong message of support and encouragement.

It is impossible to regulate for ethics or common sense. They come about through implementing proper processes and instilling a culture of compliance. Governance and ethics are key components of an accounting education, not least because the accounting profession has a code of conduct that has transparency, ethics, accountability and reporting rigour at its heart.

In its simplest form, an effective corporate governance strategy involves two broad steps. The first is the 'out-of-company experience'. Put yourself in the position of different stakeholders and ask yourself 'what do I want to know about this company? What would make me trust the information I receive?'

The second is the 'inner voice' — What will happen if we don't meet these needs? What are the costs to the business, and corporate reputation? And ultimately can we afford not to meet these needs?

Corporate governance sets the tone, the policy and practices for companies in their efforts to balance business and stakeholder needs. But we must not forget how important it is that we take individual responsibility for doing the right thing — both in the sense of the individual organisation and on the personal level as individuals.

Source: Extracts from Alex Malley, 'The individual must take responsibility for doing the right thing', *The Age.*[52]

Questions

1. This article discusses the issue of a code of conduct in corporate governance. Discuss whether a code of conduct is important for corporate governance. **J** **AS**
2. The article states that it is impossible to legislate for ethics. Do you agree with this? If this is the case, does this mean regulation is ineffective? **J** **K** **AS**

LO 9 INTERNATIONAL PERSPECTIVES AND DEVELOPMENTS

As noted, the Anglo-Saxon model placing emphasis on shareholders' interest dominates in the United States, Australia, Canada and the United Kingdom. Asia is increasingly adopting the Anglo-Saxon shareholder model.[53] However, in many areas, corporate governance codes have now extended — at least in principle — the model to include consideration of the needs of broader stakeholders. This is based on the opinion that the traditional view of corporate responsibility as being to increase profits (as espoused by Friedman) is no longer appropriate. As Hinkley states:

> [T]oday corporations are our most powerful citizens and it is no longer tenable that they be entitled to all the benefits of citizenship, but have none of the responsibilities.[54]

Most European countries, rather than having legislated practices, have voluntary codes of corporate governance practices and compliance varies.[55] In Europe, there is more direct recognition of alternative stakeholders (such as employees in France and creditors in Germany). The key differences between European corporate governance practices and those in other areas results from the emphasis given to employees. Some countries give employees the right to representation on the board of directors.

In Asia, although the Anglo-Saxon model is now increasingly being adopted, particular characteristics and environmental features provide problems in ensuring good corporate governance. In particular, many corporations in the area have dominant shareholders (such as families or the state) and enforcement mechanisms vary considerably throughout the region. It is argued that this has resulted in 'many companies following more the form rather than the substance of corporate governance'.[56]

The primary focus of corporate governance prescriptions has been on larger corporations, particularly those listed on stock exchanges in developed economies. However the inherent advantages that are associated with good corporate governance combined with the increasingly global nature of business (even for smaller entities) has led to a 'push' to extend corporate governance principles to smaller enterprises, including those in developing economies. This has been driven by two key factors. The first is to attract investment. Investors are increasingly looking at the growing Asian economies, but 'investors will not simply put their money into companies that have no transparency or appropriate system of internal control'.[57] A second factor is the 'family' dominance and widespread publicity about a number of scandals in such corporations — for example, Satyam Computer Services, one of India's largest IT companies, failed due to 'family' dealing, abuse and fraud. While the dominance of family 'control' in many Asian corporations has been seen to deter efforts to expand corporate governance, developments indicate that this is now being addressed. For example:

- The OECD has recently published a paper that provides guidelines to both corporations and policy makers to fight abusive related party transactions in Asia.
- In 2008, Pakistan issued the first formal code of corporate governance for family-owned companies which sets out four principles of good governance.

In the future, it is also likely that corporate governance will increasingly consider broader stakeholders. Although a principles-based approach appears to be prevailing at the moment, backed by legislation for particular practices, it is inevitable that future collapses and financial reporting failures will influence future directions and approaches.

Summary

Explain the interest in corporate governance
- Interest in corporate governance has increased as a result of highly publicised corporate scandals.
- Responses to corporate scandals include requirements to produce financial statements and have them audited.
- Advantages of good corporate governance include reduction in the cost of capital and facilitation of economic growth.

Explain what corporate governance is and why good corporate governance systems are needed
- Corporate governance is the system of directing and controlling the corporation.
- Corporate governance is aimed at ensuring that despite the separation of ownership and management, managers act in the best interests of the corporation and its stakeholders.
- A key aim of good corporate governance is to enable markets to operate efficiently.

Discuss the relationship between positive accounting theory and corporate governance
- Positive accounting theory, via agency theory, identifies three costs associated with the agency relationship between managers and shareholders: monitoring costs, bonding costs and residual loss.
- An agency contract is undertaken when the principal delegates decision-making responsibility to an agent. This involves costs due to problems in the manager–shareholder relationship.
- Bonus plans attempt to deal with these issues by linking managers' rewards to shareholders' interests. However, this creates incentives for managers to manipulate accounting figures to increase their bonuses.

Discuss the key areas involved in corporate governance
- Corporate governance principles and practices concentrate on directing and controlling directors and management, shareholders' interests and rights, and transparency and accountability.

Explain and evaluate the alternative approaches to corporate governance
- There are two approaches to corporate governance: rules-based and principles-based, and each has its advantages and disadvantages. In practice, corporate governance is usually a mix of both.

Discuss recent developments and issues in corporate governance

- Corporate governance is influenced by the environment in which it operates. The recent global financial crisis has highlighted problems and this has led to increased scrutiny, reforms and increased regulation of certain aspects of corporate governance. We have considered here risk management and remuneration.

Explain the role and impact of accounting in and on corporate governance

- Accounting information is an essential component of any corporate governance system and has two key roles: to control and direct actions and decisions, and to inform shareholders and other stakeholders.
- The accounting information and reports need to be correct, complete and unbiased.
- However, accounting information can be compromised or manipulated for several reasons.

Discuss and analyse the role of ethics in corporate governance

- Good corporate governance is about people 'doing the right thing'. Despite pre-scribed practices, it essentially can only be achieved through the ethical behaviour of managers.

Discuss international perspectives and developments in corporate governance

- The Anglo-Saxon model placing emphasis on shareholders' interest dominates in the United States, Australia, Canada and the United Kingdom.
- Asia is increasingly adopting the Anglo-Saxon shareholder model.
- Most European countries, rather than having legislated practices, have voluntary codes of corporate governance practices and compliance varies.
- Corporate governance codes have now extended — at least in principle — the model to include consideration of the needs of broader stakeholders.

Review questions

1. Explain what is meant by corporate governance and why it is needed.
2. 'Corporate governance is primarily focused on protecting the interests of shareholders.' Discuss.
3. What are risks of poor corporate governance and the advantages of good corporate governance?
4. Explain what is meant by positive accounting theory and its relationship to corporate governance.
5. Identify the key areas addressed in corporate governance and provide examples of practices related to each of these areas. Explain how any individual practices identified help ensure good corporate governance.
6. What is the rules-based approach to corporate governance and what are the advantages and disadvantages of this approach?
7. What is the principles-based approach to corporate governance and what are the advantages and disadvantages of this approach?
8. Explain the problems identified from the global financial crisis in relation to risk management and how these relate to corporate governance.
9. Explain the problems identified from the global financial crisis in relation to remuneration and how these relate to corporate governance.
10. 'Any corporate governance system is only as good as the people involved in it.' Discuss.

Application questions

7.1 Obtain the annual reports of a range of companies in the same industry and country. Search for any disclosures in relation to corporate governance principles and practices. In relation to these disclosures:
(a) Identify the key areas considered by these companies.
(b) Are there any differences or similarities in corporate governance practices?
(c) Do you believe you could judge or rank the relative standard of corporate governance of these companies based on the information provided? If not, what other information would you need to do so?
(d) Which company would you rank as having the best (or worst) corporate governance from these disclosures? Explain how you have arrived at this decision.
(e) Compare your rankings with those of other students. Identify and discuss the reason for any discrepancies between rankings **J** **CT**

7.2 Obtain the annual reports of a range of companies in the same industry in different countries and search for any disclosures in relation to corporate governance principles and practices. In relation to these disclosures:
(a) Identify any differences or similarities in corporate governance practices.
(b) Can you provide any reasons from the business and regulatory environments in the countries that would explain these differences? **J** **AS**

7.3 Many small companies argue that corporate governance requirements are too costly and onerous and should be restricted to the large 'top' companies.
(a) Do you think that corporate governance principles should apply to smaller companies?
(b) Are there any particular corporate governance practices or principles that you do not think should apply to smaller companies?
(c) What would be the advantages of smaller companies complying with corporate governance principles?
(d) What might be the consequences for smaller companies of not complying with corporate governance principles? **J** **K**

7.4 A friend cannot understand why executives and directors of companies are often paid bonuses and not simply paid a set salary.
(a) Using principles from positive accounting theory, explain the reasons for, and nature of, bonus plans offered to directors and executives.
(b) Because share-based payments to employees (including directors) are now required to be recognised as expenses, would this reduce the desire by companies to use shares or share options as part of a manager's remuneration package? **K**

7.5 Obtain the annual report for a listed company and examine the remuneration packages provided for executives.
(a) Identify the key components of the remuneration packages for directors and executives. Do the principles of agency theory provide a rationale for each of these components?
(b) Would these packages provide incentives for these executives to manipulate accounting figures?
(c) How much information is provided about any bonuses paid? Is this information sufficient to allow shareholders to determine if these packages are reasonable? **J** **AS**

 **7.6** In many countries in Asia it is claimed that concentration of corporate ownership/control by families causes particular difficulties with corporate governance. For example, Hong Kong billionaire Richard Li owns 75% of Singapore-listed Pacific Century Regional Developments.[58]

(a) Examine corporate governance guidelines and identify specific recommendations for practice aimed at protecting minority investors.

(b) Would these suggested practices be effective where there is a higher concentration of family control in a company? **J** **K**

 **7.7** Each year various bodies give corporate governance awards. For example, in Malaysia, an annual award is given by Malaysian Business, sponsored by the Chartered Institute of Management Accountants (CIMA), and The Australasian Reporting Awards (Inc.), an independent not-for-profit organisation, gives annual awards.

(a) Locate the criteria on which these awards are based and compare these for different awards.

(b) Are there any significant differences between the criteria?

(c) In what areas of corporate governance reporting did winning companies outperform other companies?

(d) Does the winning of an award for reporting necessarily mean that these companies have the best corporate governance practices? **K** **SM**

 **7.8** Australian companies listed on the ASX must report on their corporate governance practices on the basis of 'comply or explain'. That is, they are not required to comply with all of the specific corporate governance practices detailed by the ASX, but if they choose not to comply, they must identify which guidelines have not been followed and provide a reason for their lack of compliance.

(a) Examine the corporate governance disclosures of some Australian-listed companies and identify any instances where best practice recommendations of the ASX have not been met.

(b) Do you believe that the noncompliance in these instances is justified?

(c) What are the advantages of having a 'comply or explain' requirement rather than requiring all companies to comply with all best practice recommendations? **K** **SM**

 **7.9** In the 2009 annual report of Boral Ltd (an Australian-listed company), the corporate governance disclosures include the following note:

> The Board has considered establishing a nomination committee and decided in view of the relatively small number of Directors that such a Committee would not be a more efficient mechanism than the full Board for detailed selection and appointment practices. The full Board performs the functions that would otherwise be carried out by a Nomination Committee.

(a) Examine the ASX corporate governance principles and identify the best practice recommendations in relation to nomination committees.

(b) What potential governance problems are these recommendations designed to meet?

(c) Is Boral's deviation from these best practice recommendations justified?

(d) In March 2010 (see 2010 annual report), Boral did introduce a Nomination Committee (as part of the Remuneration Committee) although it is noted that the number of directors remained the same. What reason can you think of for this change, given Boral's previously stated reason for not complying with this best practice recommendation? **J** **K**

7.10 In the 2010 annual report of Biota Ltd (an Australian-listed company), the corporate governance note disclosed an audit and risk committee composed of two directors (chaired by an independent non-executive director and supported by one other non-executive director).

(a) Examine the ASX corporate governance principles and identify the best practice recommendations in relation to audit committees.

(b) What potential governance problems are these recommendations designed to meet?

(c) Does Biota's audit committee meet these guidelines and, if not, is any deviation from these best practice recommendations justified?

 **7.11** At times there are problems (and subsequent investigations) with corporate governance, which include deficiencies in financial reporting.

(a) Search the website of regulatory authorities (such as the Australian Securities and Investments Commission or the Securities and Exchange Commission in the United States) and identify a case that has been investigated that involves issues of corporate governance.

(b) Briefly discuss the corporate governance issues and what part financial reporting played in these.

(c) Suggest what procedures or practices would prevent these abuses occurring.

| 7.1 CASE STUDY | |

Critical questions of governance

By Sanjay Anandaram

The recent case of Satyam Computers trying to use its cash reserves to acquire the two infrastructure companies held by the promoter's sons is certainly newsworthy. Not because it was unusual — far from it, especially in India — but because it was withdrawn thanks to angry protests by shareholders. Corporate governance, ethics and reputation were the casualties in this case.

A friend of mine was till recently a senior executive in a family-owned financial services company. He worked long hours, was extremely diligent, hard working, cost-conscious and highly conscientious. One day, he decided to leave the company in pursuit of better prospects. The chairman of the company then tried to talk my friend out of the decision. He was told how well he was doing, how highly he was thought of by all and was offered additional responsibilities. My friend took some time to think through the decision. After two weeks, with his decision remaining unchanged, he informed the chairman of his desire to leave. Then, things erupted. The chairman started yelling at his senior executive and even threatened to run him off the financial services industry. 'I'll see that you don't find a job in the industry,' he said, while throwing in a few colourful epithets.

A senior professional executive was recently brought into a young family owned and managed company. The CEO's wife routinely assigned 'work' to an employee who reported into this executive without the executive being aware of the entire situation. The executive was naturally very upset.

A few employees recently quit a start-up to start off on their own. They promptly joined a competitor and quite brazenly used their logins to access the information in their previous company, for the benefit of their new employer.

I'm sure all of us have many more similar stories to share. The above examples throw up critical questions of culture, ethics and governance. They reflect how we behave, how we react to situations and are a mirror to the larger issue of flexible ethics in our country.

In the first instance, the chairman took the departure of the executive rather personally, as if his departure were an affront to him. His feudal hierarchical mindset could not stomach the idea of someone lower down the pecking order rejecting his overtures. His outburst against the executive is understandable but inexcusable. There was no effort made to understand the reasons for the executive's departure, his sense of being neglected and ignored. Throwing money at a problem isn't a substitute for treating people with respect and regard.

In the second case, the lack of governance systems in the company is shockingly glaring. What business does the CEO's wife have ordering employees around? Her rights as a shareholder do not give her the rights to interfere with management of a company. Again, a combination of ignorance and a feudal attitude (for instance, I'm the CEO's wife) cause enormous grief to competent professional executives. The role and responsibilities of shareholders and management need to be clearly understood.

In the third case, dishonest and unethical employees tried to take advantage of their previous employer — not an unheard of situation. The company did not, obviously, have adequate safeguards to protect its interests. The employment contracts had to be reworked to include a non-compete clause, protection of confidential information and a non-disclosure agreement. The internal systems had to be re-jigged to have passwords of departing employees immediately disabled and so on.

But there's a larger issue at stake here. One that involves company culture and ethics. Do the CEO and the rest of the leadership team walk the talk? How often does the CEO communicate the company's vision and culture to all employees? Is there a written document that captures this? Do all employees understand what this means? Is the culture and code of conduct applicable to all employees or to just some employees? What parts of a company culture are negotiable and what aren't? What happens to a senior executive guilty of violating the code of conduct vis-à-vis a junior employee? Do customers and vendors also fall under the purview of the code of conduct? If not, how is the code of conduct communicated to them? Is the company, especially a start-up, willing to live with the consequences of acting against some of its star employees, major suppliers or major customers on grounds of their having questionable integrity? If there's a grey area, how will the company react? Will it give the benefit of doubt to the accused? Do family members understand that the company is not a personal zamindari or fiefdom to be lorded over and plundered?

At the end of the day, is each one of us willing to stand up for ethics, governance and integrity?

What do you think?

Source: Excerpts from Sanjay Anandaram, 'Critical questions of governance', *Financial Express*.[59]

Questions

1. This article discusses the issue of corporate governance in family-dominated businesses. Go to the Center for International Private Enterprise website, www.cipe.org, and locate the Pakistan Institute of Corporate Governance document 'The Corporate Governance Guide: Family Owned Companies'. This guide includes four principles. Do you think these principles would address the types of problems identified in the extract? **J** **AS**
2. Do you think regulation would be effective in dealing with the types of problems identified? **J** **K**
3. The article argues that the larger issue relates to culture and ethics. Do you agree? How critical is the CEO in this? **K** **AS**

7.2 CASE STUDY

Reining in executive pay

By Sarah Anderson & Sam Pizzigati

JOEL GEMUNDER, the CEO of Omnicare, retired on July 31, almost exactly one year after his company announced a wide array of wage cuts and layoffs. The former head of the nation's top provider of pharmaceuticals for seniors won't have to worry much about his economic security. He's walking into his golden years with a getaway package worth at least $130 million.

Gemunder's sweet deal only hints at the excess still pulsing through America's executive suites. Since 2008, the year the nation collapsed into the Great Recession, 50 major U.S. corporations have each axed more than 3000 jobs. Yet their CEOs, as our just-released report for the Institute for Policy Studies documents, last year took home 42 percent more pay on average than the S&P 500 CEO average.

At America's top 50 companies, CEO pay — after adjusting for inflation — is running at quadruple the 1980s average and eight times the average in the mid-20th century. Is executive pay going to forever trend upward? Or can somebody, anybody, do something?

Actually, Congress has just done something. The landmark financial reform legislation passed in July includes reforms advocated for years by those who believe that empowering shareholders will clean up the executive pay mess. The most notable proposal — shareholder 'say on pay' — now stands as the law of the land, not just for financial companies but for all publicly traded U.S. corporations.

All shareholders now will have the right to express their disapproval of executive pay packages. And if directors ignore that disapproval, shareholders will soon have the tools, through new SEC regulations, to get their own director candidates on corporate board ballots.

Point by point, Congress has codified almost the entire shareholder-driven agenda for pay reform. Among other things, corporate board compensation committees must be independent, and corporations must disclose how their executive pay relates to actual financial performance.

These are all positive steps. But will they end the outrageous incentives for reckless executive misbehavior that excessive rewards create? Unfortunately, no.

All these reforms rest on the shaky assumption that shareholders, once suitably empowered, will rise up and end executive pay excess. We don't make this assumption for other corporate problems. We don't, for instance, expect shareholders to prevent corporations from poisoning our water or employing child labor. We endeavor, instead, to enact laws and regulations to prevent such practices. So why should we rely on shareholders to fix executive pay?

We're all stakeholders, after all, in executive pay decisions, either as consumers or workers or residents of communities where corporations operate. In recent years, executives chasing after paycheck jackpots have engaged in actions that have put us all at risk, such as toxic securities and job-killing mergers. Why should we leave the responsibility for executive pay decisions to shareholders and shareholders alone?

Instead, we can start with a different assumption: that our tax dollars must in no way subsidize executive excess. Currently, corporations can deduct from their income taxes all those millions they lavish on their execs. One bill before Congress would deny tax deductions on any executive pay that runs over $500 000 or 25 times the pay of a company's lowest-paid workers.

Another promising proposal would give a leg up in federal contract bidding to companies that pay their executives less than 100 times what their workers make.

We already deny government contracts to companies that discriminate, by race or gender, in their employment practices because we don't want our tax dollars subsidizing such inequality. We need to apply this same reasoning to extreme economic inequality.

Lawmakers in the current Congress, to their credit, have quietly taken some baby steps down this alternate executive pay reform road. The health care reform legislation enacted this year lowers the tax deduction that health insurers can take on executive pay to $500 000.

Even better, the new financial reform law includes a provision that requires all U.S. corporations to annually report the ratio between their CEO compensation and the median pay that goes to their workers.

Corporate lobbyists are now working furiously, behind the scenes, to defang this mandate. They have good reason to feel panicked. The first step to limiting the vast pay gap that divides CEOs and workers is disclosing that gap. We've now taken that step. Let's keep going.

Source: Excepts from Sarah Anderson & Sam Pizzigati, 'Reining in executive pay', *Virginia Pilot*.[60]

7.3 CASE STUDY

Limits to governance; corporate reforms often have unintended consequences

By Ed Waitzer and Marshall Cohen

One cumulative impact of governance failures (in both the private and public sectors) has been a massive loss of trust in leadership. Demand for more government (and consequential regulation) is re-emerging, although what this is to do is less clear. The continuing focus on the use of regulatory instruments to curb executive compensation may be instructive and illustrative of a broader problem: unrealistic expectations, both about corporate governance and, as importantly, efforts to effectively regulate it.

In recently announcing a new review into how to foster a long-term focus for corporate Britain, the U.K. Business Secretary noted that the remuneration of the FTSE 100 CEOs had risen on average 15% a year between 1999 and 2008, while the FTSE 100 index had fallen 3% and average earnings growth had been 4%.

A universal regulatory response, including a recently announced initiative of the Canadian Securities Administrators, is to require more disclosure on executive pay. Regulated disclosure of executive compensation has consistently served to ratchet up pay levels. Few boards think their CEO shouldn't be in the top quartile of compensation rankings. The problems are almost always elsewhere. In a recent PWC survey of U.S. corporate directors, 83% thought their board's compensation committee was effectively managing CEO compensation, while 58% thought boards, generally, were having trouble controlling CEO compensation (and another 8% were unsure).

Likewise, the shift in compensation from salary to stock options was dramatically accelerated by changes to U.S. tax laws designed to curb excessive employee remuneration. In hindsight, the flaws in this result — encouraging excessive risk-taking and short-term focus — have become painfully obvious.

While it may be counterintuitive, the rise of boards composed primarily of 'independent' directors — encouraged or mandated by regulation — may have also contributed to the explosion in executive compensation. Typically, such directors have less intimate knowledge of a corporation's affairs and tend to be more focused on their monitoring role. The resultant power vacuum in widely held corporations (i.e., where there is no controlling shareholder) has tended to shift authority to the CEO (who generally controls information flow). Directors often feel that they are hostage to their CEOs — replacing one is disruptive and the costs are high.

A recent study by three University of Southern California professors goes one step further, finding that strongly independent directors (and powerful institutional shareholders) had a negative impact on the performance of a sample of 296 of the world's largest banks, brokerages and insurance companies (125 of them U.S.-based and all with assets of more than US$10-billion) during the 2007–08 financial crises. Other efforts to strengthen boards — directors with financial expertise, risk committees or the separation of CEO and chair functions — didn't appear to help.

Less surprisingly, another recent study confirmed that as the proportion of 'independent' directors who joined a board after the CEO assumed office increases, board monitoring decreases and CEO pay level increases, as does firm risk.

Board independence and otherwise trying to regulate executive compensation are just two of many examples where regulatory instruments dictating governance structures have often failed to achieve intended results and have led to unintended consequences. Consider, for example, the demand for audit and credit-rating services, largely driven by regulatory requirements. Aside from being a huge revenue generator for the service providers, one obvious problem is the resultant lack of market discipline on quality (and on conflicts of interest). Similar demand is now emerging for the regulation of proxy advisory services as a regulatory-driven shift from director to more shareholder-centric governance models increases the complexity of shareholder voting decisions.

This is not to suggest that regulation and resulting governance structures are unimportant. It is striking, however, how public distrust in corporate governance continues to escalate in the face of enormous investments made to better regulate through mandated structures and processes. Not surprisingly, many directors feel frustrated and increasingly less certain as to their role and how they might make a difference.

One difficulty with trying to regulate conduct based on the assumption that actors are purely self-interested is that precisely such behaviour will be reinforced. Building layers of governance mechanisms in the hope of channelling behaviour often serves to frustrate meaningful stewardship on the part of corporate directors and management. Regulation of compensation, independence or other structural requirements will never be the answer, in isolation.

It has become almost a matter of conventional wisdom to observe that the lesson to be learned from the collapse of our 'efficient' financial markets paradigm is the need to focus on long-term, sustainable value creation. Simplistic notions of short-term market performance and regulatory imposed 'better' behaviour will not work. What remains elusive is the prescription to accomplish this end.

Perhaps we must look deeper into the DNA of the corporate model to understand and affirm its role in creating long-term value for individuals, firms, shareholders and communities. For example, we need to understand better the role of culture, character and reputation — on management, on the board, on the institutional owner community — in defining and implementing a meaningful sense of 'ownership' and responsibility. Perhaps we have to challenge the structural paradigm itself, if we are to achieve meaningful and permanent change.

Asking deeper questions must come first. Doing so is essential if we are to find effective answers and thereby restore public trust.

Source: Excerpts from Ed Waitzer & Marshall Cohen, 'Limits to governance; Corporate reforms often have unintended consequences', *Financial Post*.[61]

Questions

1. This article discusses the increased use of regulation in corporate governance issues arguing that this may produce 'unintended consequences'. Can you identify any unintended consequences that could occur? **K** **AS**
2. The focus of reforms on the need for sufficient independent directors is discussed in this article. What is the underlying rationale for inclusion of independent directors? Should independence override concerns of competence and expertise? **J** **K**

Additional readings

Christensen, J, Kent, P & Stewart, J 2010, '2010 Corporate Governance and Company Performance in Australia', *Australian Accounting Review*, vol. 20, iss. 4, pp. 372–86.

Corporate Governance: An International Review, published by Wiley-Blackwell, accessed via www.wiley.com.

Corporate Governance, published by Emerald, accessed via www.emeraldinsight.com.

Fitzpatrick, G 2009, 'The corporate governance lessons from the financial crisis', *Financial Market Trends*, vol. 2009/1, OECD.

International Journal of Corporate Governance, published by Inderscience Publishers, accessed via www.inderscience.com.

OECD Steering Group on Corporate Governance 2010, *Corporate governance and the financial crisis: conclusions and emerging good practices to enhance implementation of the Principles*, 24 February, www.oecd.org.

Singh, JP, Kumar, N & Uzma, S 2010, Satyam fiasco: corporate governance failure and lessons therefrom, *Journal of Corporate Governance*, vol. 9, iss. 4, pp. 30–9.

Solomon, J 2010, *Corporate Governance and Accountability*, third edition, John Wiley & Sons Ltd, UK.

The Reports on the Observance of Standards and Codes (ROSC) by the World Bank, This provides reports and assessment of corporate governance frameworks and practices assessed against a template in various developing countries and can be accessed at www.worldbank.org.

Yong, L 2009, *Lessons in Corporate Governance from the Global Financial Crisis*, CCH Australia Ltd, Sydney, p. 23.

End notes

1. Fuerman, RD 2009, 'Bernard Madoff and the solo auditor red flag', *Journal of Forensic & Investigative Accounting*, vol. 1, no. 1, pp. 1–38.

2. Anonymous 2004, 'Parma splat: what are the lessons from the scandal at Europe's largest dairy-products group?, *The Economist*, 15 January.

3. Anonymous 2004, 'Another denial in Mitsubishi trials', *The Asahi Shimbun*, 7 October.

4. Jones, M 2011, *Creative accounting, fraud and international accounting scandals*, John Wiley & Sons Ltd, Chichester.

5. Organisation for Economic Co-operation and Development 2004, *OECD principles of corporate governance*, OECD Publications Service, Paris.

6. Cowan, N 2004, *Corporate governance that works!*, Prentice Hall Pearson Education, Singapore, p. 15.

7. Organisation for Economic Co-operation and Development 1999, *OECD principles of corporate governance*, OECD Publications Service, Paris.

8. India Infoline 2005, 'What is corporate governance?', www.indiainfoline.com.

9. Allen, J 2000, *Code convergence in Asia: smoke or fire?*, Asian Corporate Governance Association, 1 CGI, www.acga-asia.org.

10. Cornford, A 2004, *Enron and internationally agreed principles for corporate governance and the financial sector*, G-24 discussion paper series, no. 30, June, United Nations, p. 10.

11. Organisation for Economic Co-operation and Development 2004, *OECD principles of corporate governance*, OECD Publications Service, Paris.

12. Colley, JL Jr, Doyle, JL, Logan, GW, Stettinuis, W 2005, *What is corporate governance?*, McGraw-Hill, New York, p. 80.

13. Organisation for Economic Co-operation and Development 2004, *OECD principles of corporate governance*, OECD Publications Service, Paris.

14. ASX Corporate Governance Council 2010, *Corporate governance principles and recommendations with 2010 amendments*, 2nd edn, Australian Securities Exchange, Sydney.

15. China Securities Regulatory Commission State Economic and Trade Commission 2002, *Code of corporate governance for listed companies in China*, China Securities Regulatory Commission, Beijing.

16. Shailer, GEP 2004, *An introduction to corporate governance in Australia*, Pearson Sprint Print, ANU, p. 13.

17. Witherell, B 2004, 'Corporate governance, stronger principles for better market integrity', *OECD Observer*, no. 243, May.

18. Bruce, R 2004, 'Courtrooms concentrate the minds — corporate governance', *Financial Times*, 9 September, p. 2.

19. Cowan, N 2004, *Corporate governance that works!*, Prentice Hall Pearson Education, Singapore, p. 165.

20. Allen, J & Roy, F 2001, *Corporate governance in greater China: a comparison between China, Hong Kong and Taiwan, from structuring for success: the first 10 years of capital markets in China*, Asian Corporate Governance Association, www.acga-asia.org.

21. Quah, M 2010, 'Have governance levels slipped? Singapore ceded top spot to Hong Kong in a recent study of corporate governance in Asia', *The Business Times*, 31 March.

22. OECD Steering Group on Corporate Governance 2010, *Corporate governance and the financial crisis: conclusions and emerging good practices to enhance implementation of the Principles*, 24 February, www.oecd.org; Financial Crisis Inquiry Commission (FCIC) 2011, *The financial crisis inquiry report, final*

report of the National Commission on the causes of the financial and economic crisis in the United States, U.S. Government Printing Office, Washington; House of Commons Treasury Committee 2009, *Banking crisis: reforming corporate governance and pay in the city: Ninth Report of Session 2008–09,* The Stationery Office Limited, London.

23. OECD Steering Group on Corporate Governance 2010, *Corporate governance and the financial crisis: conclusions and emerging good practices to enhance implementation of the Principles,* 24 February, www.oecd.org.

24. ibid.

25. ibid.

26. ASX Corporate Governance Council 2010, *Corporate governance principles and recommendations with 2010 amendments,* 2nd edn, Australian Securities Exchange, Sydney.

27. Ernst & Young 2009, *Effective governance model: an operating framework,* Ernst & Young, South Africa, p. 9.

28. PETRONAS 2010, Annual report 2010, Petroliam Nasional Berhad (Petronas), Kuala Lumpur.

29. KPMG 2008, *Audit committees put risk management at the top of their agendas,* news release, KPMG Corporate Communications, London, 16 June.

30. Saulwick, J & Irvine, J 2008, 'Huge executive bonuses broke economy', *Business Day,* 4 December, www.businessday.com.au.

31. House of Commons Treasury Committee 2009, *Banking crisis: reforming corporate governance and pay in the city: ninth report of session 2008–09,* The Stationery Office Limited, London.

32. Yong, L 2009, *Lessons in corporate governance from the global financial crisis,* CCH Australia Ltd, Sydney, p. 23.

33. Valente, C 2011, 'Banks, insurers cut bonuses, mull clawbacks — study', Reuters, 8 February, http://in.reuters.com.

34. Wilson, S 2010, 'Companies see value of long-term thinking: long-term

incentives', *The Australian,* 20 October, www.theaustralian.com.au.

35. Hong Kong Institute of Certified Public Accountants 2004, 'Corporate governance for public bodies: a basic framework', www.hkicpa.org.hk.

36. Cowan, N 2004, *Corporate governance that works!,* Prentice Hall Pearson Education, Singapore, p. 167.

37. Organisation for Economic Co-operation and Development 2004, *OECD principles of corporate governance,* OECD Publications Service, Paris, p. 49.

38. Organisation for Economic Co-operation and Development 2003, 'Corporate governance in Asia', white paper, OECD Publications Service, Paris, p. 6.

39. Ernst & Young 2009, *Effective governance model: an operating framework,* Ernst & Young, South Africa, p. 8.

40. Institute of International and European Affairs 2003, 'EU–US Project Group EU–US relations: corporate governance', www.iiea.com.

41. Lambert, C & Sponem, S 2004, 'Corporate governance and profit manipulation: a French field study', *Critical Perspectives on Accounting,* vol. 16, no. 6, pp. 717–48.

42. Sykes, T 2004, 'Perspective: Pierpont's dubious distinction awards for 2004', *Australian Financial Review,* 29 December, p. 22.

43. Berkwitz, A & Rampell, R 2002, 'The accounting debate: principles vs. rules', *Wall Street Journal Online,* 2 December.

44. House of Commons Treasury Committee 2009, *Banking crisis: reforming corporate governance and pay in the city: ninth report of session 2008–09,* The Stationery Office Limited, London, p. 76.

45. Anonymous 2009, 'A matter of public importance', *InTheBlack,* vol. 79, no. 8, pp. 44–5.

46. Cowan, N 2004, *Corporate governance that works!,* Prentice Hall Pearson Education, Singapore, p. 9.

47. Anonymous 2004, 'Another denial in Mitsubishi trials', *The Asahi Shimbun,* 7 October.

48. Flanagan, J, Little, J & Watts, T 2005, 'Beyond law and regulation — a corporate governance model of ethical decision-making', *Advances in Public Interest Accounting,* Ed. C Lehman, vol. 11, pp. 271–302.

49. CPA Australia 2004, *A guide to understanding corporate governance.*

50. Hong Kong Institute of Certified Public Accountants 2004, 'Corporate governance for public bodies: a basic framework', www.hkicpa.org.hk.

51. Wallenberg, J 2004, 'Viewpoint: Achieving 3Cs is no mean feat — conformance, competition and culture are the key to good corporate governance', *The Banker,* 1 July.

52. Malley, A 2010, 'The individual must take responsibility for doing the right thing', *The Age,* June 23.

53. Allen, J 2000, *Code convergence in Asia: smoke or fire?,* Asian Corporate Governance Association, 1 CGI, www.acga-asia.org.

54. Hinkley cited in Burmeister, K 2000, 'Corporate responsibility: a matter of ethics or strategy?', *The Issues,* no. 1, Blake Dawson Waldron, Sydney, pp. 23–5.

55. Anonymous 2004, 'Parma splat: what are the lessons from the scandal at Europe's largest dairy-products group?, *The Economist,* 15 January, p. 4.

56. Allen, J 2000, *Code convergence in Asia: smoke or fire?,* Asian Corporate Governance Association, 1 CGI, www.acga-asia.org.

57. Dixon cited in Hodge, N 2010, 'Code Comfort', *Financial Management,* October, pp. 18–22.

58. Wai-yin Kwok, V 2006, 'Richard Li's Tangled Web', 28 September, www.forbes.com.

59. Anandaram S 2008, 'Critical questions of governance', *Financial Express,* 26 December, www.financialexpress.com.

60. Anderson, S & Pizzigati, S 2010, 'Reining in executive pay', *Virginia Pilot,* Norfolk, 19 September, p. B9.

61. Waitzer, E & Cohen, M 2010, 'Limits to governance; Corporate reforms often have unintended consequences', *Financial Post,* 8 December, p. 15.

8 Capital market research and accounting

After studying this chapter, you should be able to:

1 explain the role of capital market research for accounting

2 differentiate between an event study and an association study

3 outline the relationship between accounting measures of financial performance and share prices

4 identify findings of capital market research relevant to accounting

5 explain the role of information and information intermediaries in capital markets

6 distinguish between behavioural finance findings and mainstream finance findings

7 discuss how behavioural research contributes to an understanding of decision making.

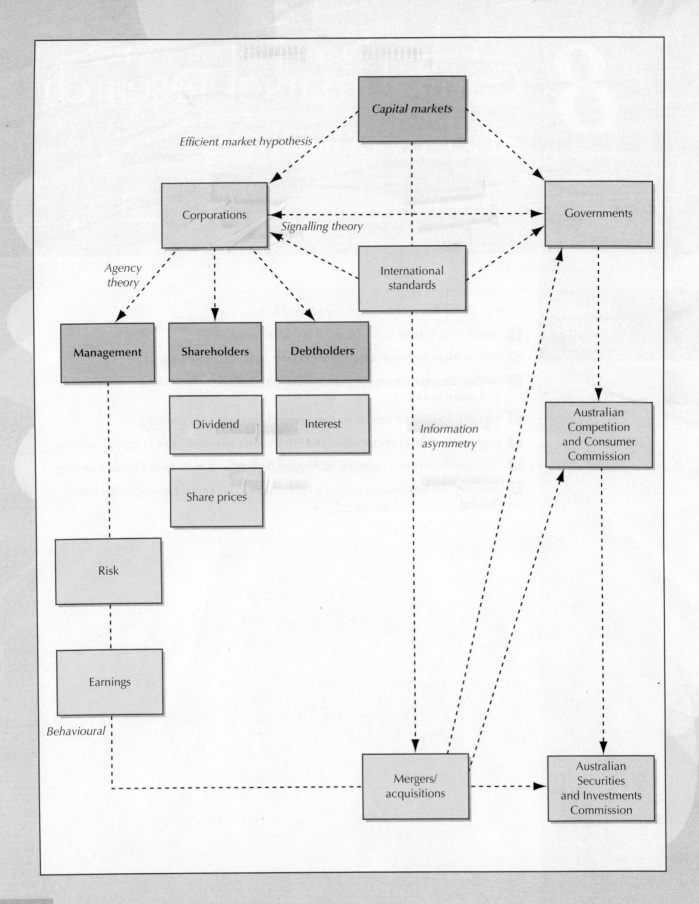

S hare markets have been popularised over the past two decades. This is reflected in regular media reports on the state of the daily markets. Share markets have particular importance to accounting because of the generally held assumption that accounting informs capital or share market participants. In Australia, this assumption is embedded in the *Conceptual Framework*. According to that framework, accounting aims at providing investors with relevant information for investment decision making, enabling investors to predict future cash flows and assess future risk and returns associated with particular shares.

The assumption that accounting provides information useful to participants in share or capital markets raises the issue of whether those participants actually use accounting information in their decisions. This is an important issue for accounting because if capital market participants do not use accounting information when making decisions relating to share transactions, what then is the purpose of accounting? Since the development of a conceptual framework for accounting, its policy makers have concentrated on improving this kind of information, so finding that it does not inform capital markets would be devastating for accounting and its policy makers.

LO 1 CAPITAL MARKET RESEARCH AND ACCOUNTING

Capital markets have been extensively researched, more so in the context of the United States than any other country. Since the seminal study by Ball & Brown,[1] more than 1000 papers have been published covering various aspects of the capital markets. Because the important issues for accounting are whether accounting information informs capital markets and whether capital market based research can inform the standard-setting process, the focus in this chapter is on research investigating the relationship between the two. However, there are limitations to the value of capital markets based research to accounting. First, accounting standards require the specification of social preferences — that is, how to measure and weigh the net benefits to some capital market participants and the net costs to others. No capital market based study does this.[2] Second, because the research concentrates on the United States, the results of capital market research should be viewed with caution as the findings may not be relatable to countries such as Australia.

Capital market research adopts either an information perspective or a measurement perspective. The information perspective focuses on accounting providing information to users of financial statements about a firm's financial position and performance. In short, how well do accountants summarise information related to economic events? This is consistent with the *Conceptual Framework*'s objective to provide useful information to users of financial statements to help them make economic decisions relating to the reporting entity. The measurement perspective focuses on accounting amounts as measures of the firm's resources (assets), claims to those resources (liabilities) and components of performance (revenues and expenses) — in short, how well accounting income numbers measure economic income, and how well an accounting asset number or liability number measures the associated economic asset or liability.[3] This perspective is consistent with the *Conceptual Framework*'s criteria for recognition and measurement — that is, an item after meeting the asset definition is suitable for financial statement recognition if it is probable that future economic benefits will flow to the entity and these benefits can be measured reliably.

How do accounting earnings numbers relate to share returns? The theoretical framework to answer this information perspective question has been developed by Beaver and reworked by Nichols and Wahlen, and this section relies heavily on that framework.[4] Beaver identified three links between earnings and share prices:

1. earnings of the current period provide information to predict future periods' earnings, which
2. provide information to those interested (shareholders and analysts) to develop expectations about dividends in future periods, which
3. provide information to determine share value (the present value of expected future earnings).[5]

This theoretical framework is outlined in figure 8.1.

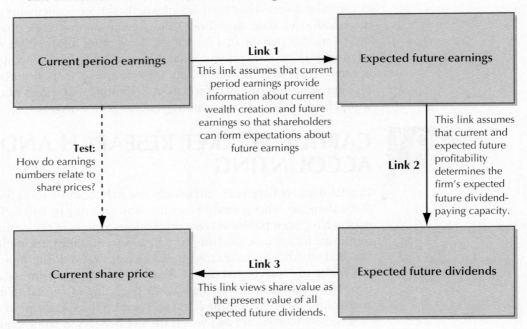

FIGURE 8.1 Links relating earnings to share returns

Source: Adapted from Nichols and Wahlen.[6]

To understand this framework, some clarification is necessary. There are two measures of firm performance. There is the measure termed 'earnings' which refers to accounting profit — the 'bottom-line' accounting measure of an firm's performance — which is measured by accrual accounting over an accounting period. The second measure is the firm's share return — the change in the firm's market value over a period of time plus any dividends paid — which represents the capital market's measure of the firm's performance. These two measures of the firm's performance are rarely, if ever, equivalent. Much research focuses on how the two measures relate. Three important assumptions underlie this research. They are:

- that the accounting measure provided by financial reporting can be used by shareholders to form expectations about current and expected future profitability;
- which, in turn provides shareholders with information about dividends, both current and expected; and
- these expectations will influence shareholders' decisions to retain or to sell their shares, so determining the market price of the shares.

A share price represents the present value of future dividends to shareholders.

While the linkage model, shown in figure 8.1, provides an intuitive framework for understanding the relation between earnings and share prices, it also demonstrates the importance of whether the earnings are expected to continue. Earnings that are expected to continue into future periods, will contribute more to share value than earnings which are expected to be short-lived. This model implies that if earnings exceed expectations, share prices increase; if earnings fall short of expectations, share prices fall. However, this is too simple an explanation because the capital market's use of information is a 'complex and dynamic process'.[7] The four factors that are commonly considered by capital market researchers are accounting information in the form of earnings/profitability, expectations about earnings, asset pricing and market efficiency. But these factors cannot be isolated individually so capital market researchers use statistical and econometric tests to examine the association (not the cause) between share prices and unexpected earnings numbers.

The first factor, *accounting information in the form of earnings*, may not provide useful information to capital markets because earnings announcements may have been pre-empted by other sources such as the financial press, or accounting standards do not allow a firm to recognise certain information (for example, research and development expenditures), or capital market participants may suspect earnings management. Researchers using expectations about earnings rely heavily on analysts' forecasts, and if they are not available, on prior period earnings. The difference between the reported accounting numbers and the forecasts about those earnings is assumed to be new information.

The second factor is *unexpected earnings* — that is, new information conveyed by the earnings number. How do researchers know what information is new? They take the earnings that were predicted by a consensus of analysts' forecasts and the difference between the earnings announcement and the consensus number is assumed to be 'unexpected' or new information.

Asset pricing, the third factor, uses models that assume that shares should provide a rate of return sufficient to compensate their holders for forgoing consumption and bearing the risk associated with the shares. Share purchases come with opportunity costs: purchasing shares means that the purchaser has less money to spend on other purchases. To entice the purchase of particular shares, the shares need to offer an expected rate of return that will supposedly place the purchaser in a better position than if they had purchased other items, or saved their money.

The fourth factor is the *market efficiency* which refers to the efficiency with which markets handle information. Definitions of market efficiency are linked with assumptions about what information is available to investors and thus reflected in the price. The efficiency with which the market uses information gives rise to three forms of market efficiency. Under weak form efficiency, the current share price reflects all the information contained in past prices, suggesting that technical analyses that use past prices alone would not be useful in finding undervalued stocks. Under semi-strong form efficiency, the current price reflects the information contained not only in past prices but all public information (including financial statements) and no approach that was based on using and manipulating this information would be useful in finding undervalued stocks. Under strong form efficiency, the current share price reflects all information, public as well as private or hidden, and no investors will be able to consistently find undervalued stocks. An efficient market is one in which share prices reflect fully all available information, including accounting information. Under this hypothesis, corporate disclosure is critical to the functioning of capital markets. But not all corporate disclosure is accounting based. Firms disclose using, annual reports, including the financial statements and notes, management discussion and analysis, regulatory filings, and voluntary disclosures such as management forecasts, press releases, websites and so on. Information arising from firms is supplemented by financial analysts, industry experts and the financial press.

Accounting's policy makers, particularly standard setters, rely on the assumption of market efficiency because decisions relating to matters such as changes in accounting policies should not affect share price. An alternative view is that capital market efficiency provides justification for using the behaviour of share prices as an operational test of the usefulness of information provided by financial statements.[8] Market efficiency, however, is being challenged. Some findings of capital market research and the causes of the global financial crisis (GFC) suggest that markets are not efficient. Behavioural finance research also contradicts the assumption that capital markets are efficient. Contemporary Issue 8.1 outlines some of these issues.

8.1 CONTEMPORARY ISSUE

Economists and the global financial crisis

By JE King

John Maynard Keynes famously remarked on the importance of ideas:

> The ideas of economists and political philosophers, both when they are right and when they are wrong, are more powerful than is commonly understood. Indeed the world is ruled by little else. Practical men, who believe themselves to be quite exempt from any intellectual influences, are usually the slaves of some defunct economist. Madmen in authority, who hear voices in the air, are distilling their frenzy from some academic scribbler of a few years back. I am sure that the power of vested interests is vastly exaggerated compared with the gradual encroachment of ideas.

The global financial crisis of 2008–09 has proved him right, albeit in a manner that he would have hated: the financial crisis and the ensuing recession in the real economy were both made by the political influence of erroneous economic ideas.

The age of neoliberalism is most often interpreted in microeconomic terms, as an epoch of privatisation, public–private partnerships and market-mimicking arrangements of many different types, all based on the assertion that 'state failure' was invariably a more serious problem than market failure... beginning in the early 1970s, neoliberalism conquered academic economics... The discipline was becoming more mathematical, and therefore — supposedly — more scientific, at precisely the same moment as its practitioners were becoming neoliberal.

There was also, and crucially, a macroeconomic dimension to this process. Or, rather, there were two macroeconomic dimensions. The first was a belief in the underlying stability of the (private) capitalist economy, if it was not disturbed ('shocked') by mistaken government intervention. The second was a belief in the efficiency of financial markets, which therefore required only the lightest of government regulation, if any at all...

First, the 'efficient market hypothesis': according to the classic definition by Eugene Fama, 'A market in which prices always "fully reflect" available information is called "efficient"'... Now 'efficiency' is obviously a good thing, and having 'the right price' is evidently socially beneficial. Hence theorists already favourably disposed towards free markets on ideological grounds could not resist the fatal elision from the true statement that financial markets are subject to random disturbances and therefore impossible to predict, to the false statement that they should be left to regulate themselves... The consequent far-reaching deregulation of national and international financial transactions was fundamental to the subsequent global financial crisis... the efficient market hypothesis did a great deal of harm, both in encouraging foolhardy behaviour on a massive scale by large corporate players in financial markets and in discouraging any serious attempt at governmental regulation...

So what should non-economists do, in order to make sense of the global financial crisis? First, they should take a deep breath and learn some mainstream economics, if only... to avoid being deceived by economists. Second, they should also learn some heterodox macroeconomics... since this will throw at least some light on existing economic reality. Third, they should encourage interdisciplinary contacts, including links between the disciplines of international political economy and (heterodox) economics.

Source: Excerpts from JE King, 'Economists and the global financial crisis', *Global Change, Peace & Security*.[9]

Questions

1. Who was John Maynard Keynes?
2. To what does the author attribute the causes of the global financial crisis?
3. How did the efficient market hypothesis contribute to the crisis?

RESEARCH METHODS: EVENT STUDIES AND VALUE RELEVANCE

Because of the complexity of the relationship between accounting information and share prices, researchers can never be certain that accounting information causes share price reactions. The common aim is to test whether accounting information in the form of earnings numbers reflects information that capital markets believe is relevant and faithfully represented, two of the qualitative characteristics for accounting information promoted by the *Conceptual Framework*. To do so, researchers rely on statistical and econometric tests to examine the association between unexpected earnings and share returns, assuming capital market efficiency. If capital markets are efficient, share prices must reflect fully and quickly any new information, including accounting information. New information causes market participants to revise their expectations of future cash flows. Their revisions cause them to act so that share prices change.

There are two main methods that are used to examine whether share prices react to accounting information: an event study and an association study.

An **event study** examines the changes in the level or variability of share prices or trading volume over a short time around the release of accounting or other information. Information is assumed to be 'new' if the release revises the market's expectation, as evidenced by changes in level of prices or in the variability of prices around the disclosure date.

An **association study** does not assume a causal connection between an accounting performance measure and share price movements. Rather, this type of study aims to see how quickly accounting measures capture changes in the information that is reflected in share prices over a given period. Accordingly, an association study looks for correlation between an accounting performance measure (such as earnings or income) and share returns where both are measured over relatively long, contemporaneous time periods. Association studies are used to assess the value relevance of accounting information.

WHAT THE INFORMATION PERSPECTIVE STUDIES TELL US

Most event studies focus on earnings announcements. The general intuitive assumption underlying the research is that an earnings announcement with good news should cause a share price to increase; one with bad news should cause a share price to decrease. Observing the volatility of returns on announcement days can indicate whether earnings convey information to investors. Releases of earnings numbers should also result in significant increases in trades if they are a source of information for investors.

Ball and Brown, and Beaver were the first to show that earnings announcements lead to significant share price changes, or increases in trading volumes.[10] Subsequent research, such as that by Hew et al. in the United Kingdom, shows that disclosures of earnings have information content since positive (negative) unexpected annual earnings announcements caused significant positive (negative) returns.[11] These results have been confirmed in countries as varied as the United States, Finland, Spain, Malaysia and

China. The assumption of some studies that the greater the surprise in disclosures, the larger will be the investor reaction has also been confirmed, with trading volumes, volatility of returns or mean abnormal returns all positively related to the size of unexpected earnings.[12]

Association studies also show that accounting earnings capture part of the information set that is reflected in share prices. Although this is good news for accounting, there is some bad news. The evidence suggests that much of the information is captured from non-accounting sources that compete with the earnings number. This means that annual financial statements are not a timely source of information for the capital market.

Interim disclosures of accounting information may help investors predict the annual earnings number. Share price reactions to half-year releases are statistically significant, but their information content appears to be less than that of the annual report.[13]

Certain factors such as firm size and the ability of investors to use accounting information seem to modify results. The larger the market value of the firm, the smaller its abnormal returns at announcement dates. For large firms, information disclosed at typical announcement dates is usually pre-empted by the attention given to large firms by investment analysts and fund managers. Sophistication of investors also accounts for the positive association between price changes and unexpected earnings. Unsophisticated investors are defined as those who react mechanically to reported earnings. A positive investor sophistication effect has been observed. Less sophisticated investors react to good news but underreact to negative unexpected earnings in comparison with their sophisticated counterparts.[14]

Prices lead earnings

As mentioned above, not all of the information captured in share prices is accounting information. Beaver, Lambert and Morse put forward the idea that the information reflected in prices is richer than the information in accounting earnings.[15] This idea is called **prices lead earnings**, which means that the information set reflected in prices contains information about future earnings.

So why do earnings numbers lag prices? The fundamental principles in the calculation of earnings relate to revenue realisation and expense matching. These principles are conservative. According to Kothari, accounting 'garbles' an otherwise 'true' earnings signal about firm value.[16]

The divide between accounting measures of earnings and share prices is referred to as the *deficient-GAAP* argument. This argument suggests that financial statements are slow to incorporate all of the information that investors use to value shares, including information about human capital and other intangibles. There is information asymmetry between managers and outsider investors. This information asymmetry, together with the threat of litigation against managers by outsiders, produces a demand for and supply of conservative accounting numbers. The generally accepted accounting principles (GAAP) have responded by having different timings for good and bad news: bad news is disclosed more timely than good news. In other words, accounting recognition criteria are less stringent for losses than for gains.

Because of the differences in accounting's recognition criteria, accruals and cash flows are the two most commonly examined components of earnings.[17] Accruals are the means by which accountants attempt to transform operating cash flows into an earnings figure that is more informative about firm performance. From positive accounting theory, it is known that managers might use accounting information opportunistically and so manipulate accruals for their own ends, distorting the earnings figure as a measure of firm performance.

Post-earnings announcement drift

Much evidence indicates that the stock market under-reacts to earnings information. This means that the market does not recognise accounting earnings information as soon as the figure is released. Instead, the market recognises its full impact gradually. This evidence is inconsistent with the assumption of capital market efficiency. An efficient market should react instantaneously and completely to value-relevant information.

This gradual adjustment in prices makes it seem that investors underreact to the information. This phenomenon is termed **post-earnings announcement drift**. According to Nichols and Wahlen, post-earnings drift is one of the most puzzling anomalies in accounting (and finance and economics) based tests of capital market efficiency in relation to earnings information.[18] It was one of the first areas to suggest that markets may not be efficient with respect to accounting data.[19] The drift seems to be related to the extent of good news in an announcement. Unexpected good news causes the market to react as predicted by the **efficient market hypothesis**, but drift follows bad news announcements. Contrary evidence has been found — for example, in Finland, post-announcement drift is higher following positive earnings surprises.[20] Johnson and Schwartz show that the drift persists in the United States among small firms and among firms with little analyst coverage.[21] In Australia, Chan et al. find that both growth and value firms have significant negative post-earnings announcement drift following non-routine bad news forecasts.[22] Truong shows that a post-earnings announcement drift exists in the New Zealand equity market.[23]

Not all studies concentrate on the association between share prices and earnings. Some studies have used inflation-adjusted earnings, residual earnings and operating cash flows as measures. Recently, performance measures such as comprehensive income compared with earnings per share, economic value added against earnings, or measures specific to particular industries have been used. Evidence from these studies is important to accounting because it suggests that performance measures that have evolved in an unregulated environment are more informative than those mandated by regulation.[24]

Cosmetic accounting choices

Because accounting allows management to make some choices about accruals and methods, management is likely to have incentives to convey self-serving information when preparing financial statements. When accounting choices are used to achieve a particular goal, the choice is described as earnings management. According to Beaver, although earnings management appears to be widespread, it may not be management discretion but a proxy for some other factor.[25]

Earnings management occurs when managers use judgement in financial reporting and in structuring transactions to alter financial reports to either mislead some stakeholders about the underlying economic performance of the company or to influence contractual outcomes that depend on reported numbers.[26] In an earlier definition, Schipper emphasised the purposefulness of the process order to obtain some private gain to managers and perhaps shareholders.[27] The discretion they use may not be necessarily opportunistic. Healy & Palepu, for instance, view earnings management as the means by which management conveys either its private information about the firm's prospects or a more accurate picture of the firm's performance.[28] For example, informed management imparts information to less informed users about the timing, magnitude and risk of future cash flows. For earnings management to be successful, users of the financial statements must be either unable or unwilling to unravel the effects of earnings management.[29]

Recent research has focused on whether management compensation contracts provide incentives for managers to achieve desired financial reporting objectives. Managers are hypothesised to select accounting methods to increase their compensation or to reduce the likelihood of violating debt covenants. The debt covenant hypothesis predicts that when a firm is close to violating an accounting-based debt covenant restriction, its managers are expected to make income-increasing accounting choices to relax the debt covenant restriction and lower the expected costs of technical default, such as renegotiation costs or bankruptcy costs.

Managers seem to take advantage of discretion in methods to manage reported earnings to increase their compensation.[30] Some contradictory evidence suggests that an income-smoothing hypothesis better explains the evidence. Other evidence suggests that management may engage in 'big bath' accounting. When earnings for a period are below expectations, managers may write off as many costs as possible in that period to allow improved performances in subsequent periods. Similar actions have been observed with changes in executives or CEOs. The evidence suggests that investors react positively to such actions.[31] Additionally, managers seem to manipulate discretionary accruals in the period before announcing a management buyout, presumably to reduce the share price.

Capital markets and their participants' reaction to accounting disclosures

In an efficient market, firm value is defined as the present value of expected discounted future net cash flows.[32] An important input into the market's assessment of value is a firm's current performance, reflecting the *Conceptual Framework*'s focus on financial statements providing information useful in assessing the amounts, timing and certainty of future cash flows.

Disclosures of accounting earnings numbers lead to share price changes or increases in the volume of trading, providing evidence that capital market participants do use accounting information, reacting more quickly to bad news than good. However, the conservative principles that govern the calculation of accounting earnings 'garble' the signal sent to the capital market.

The good news for accounting is that participants use accounting information; the bad news is that accounting earnings numbers are poor measures of the relevant events that are incorporated into share prices. Forecasts of future revenues, expenses, earnings and cash flows are the core of valuation. Financial statements, with their backward focus, are poor indicators of value. Accounting's reliability and recognition principles are blamed for financial statements not providing forward-looking information.

Managers' behaviour suggests that they believe accounting information is used by capital market participants. The reaction of investors to voluntary disclosures by management and to some earnings management strategies confirms that accounting information is used by them.

LO 4 DO AUDITORS OR INTERMEDIARIES ADD VALUE TO ACCOUNTING INFORMATION?

Capital providers require firms to employ an independent auditor as a condition of financing, even when it is not required by regulations. Although little or no research has examined the reasons capital providers require independent audits, the fact that they do implies that capital providers consider that auditors increase credibility. Audited financial statements are generally accepted as giving credibility to the annual report in which they are found. Intuitively, qualified audit reports should be more valued by market participants. However, they do not provide timely signals to capital markets, basically because the qualification has been expected.[33]

In contrast, the work of financial **intermediaries** adds value in the capital market because they use and interpret accounting data so that share prices reflect the result of their research.[34] Analysts' earnings forecasts are more accurate than time-series models of earnings. Their accuracy is affected by innate ability, company assignments, brokerage affiliation and industry specialisation. Their earnings forecasts and recommendations affect share prices. However, analysts' forecasts have been found to be biased in an overly optimistic direction, especially when their brokerage house has been hired to underwrite particular security issues.[35] Interestingly, research shows that firms with more intangible assets attract more analysts who expend more effort to follow them.[36]

Voluntary disclosure theory

According to Core, the voluntary disclosure literature offers the best opportunity for increasing understanding of the role of accounting information in firm valuation and corporate finance.[37] The most important questions relate to which firms voluntarily disclose, how stakeholders use this information in allocating capital to firms and how the various people who produce or use this information verify, regulate and interpret it. Although the literature has theorised about voluntary disclosure, empirical evidence from reputable studies is scant.

Voluntary disclosure theory predicts that shareholders optimise disclosure policy, corporate governance and management incentives to maximise firm value.[38] Increased disclosure lowers information asymmetry, thus lowering the cost of capital. However, this has to be weighed against the costs associated with incentives, litigation and proprietorship. Increased disclosure does not mean credible or unbiased disclosure because it is too costly to eliminate all the ways that managers can use to add some bias. The theory predicts that even though disclosure is somewhat biased, on average it will be credible. Although manipulation of disclosures is possible, corporate governance is designed to constrain managers to follow the optimal policy. Firms will differ in their disclosures according to their disclosure policy and the ability of the individual firm's governance to enforce the policy.

Managers with shares or share options may take actions to manipulate the prices of their share or option holdings.[39] They delay disclosing good news and speed up the release of bad news before their stock option award periods to maximise their stock-based compensation. Managers may find it more profitable to buy shares before their stock options are awarded.[40] Management forecasts are associated with trading by insiders in the firm's shares, and with share option compensation that is at risk because of firm performance. Firms with greater information asymmetry use more share and option incentives. Greater information asymmetry is associated with more voluntary disclosure, because managers do not want to bear any risk associated with any misvaluation of shares. Firms that warn investors that bad news is imminent have significantly more negative returns per unit of unexpected earnings than firms that do not warn, suggesting that firms are penalised for disclosing bad news early.[41]

LO 5 VALUE RELEVANCE

Recall that association studies regress accounting numbers on capital market data to test for significant relationships to assess the **value relevance** of information. Value relevance research has two major features.[42] First, this research requires in-depth knowledge of accounting institutions, accounting standards and reported accounting numbers.

Second, timeliness is not an important issue as it is in an event study. An item of accounting information is considered relevant if it has the ability to make a difference to the decisions of financial statement users. An accounting number is value relevant if it conveys information that results in the modification of investors' expectations about future payoffs or associated risk.[43] Value relevance research attempts to assess the relevance and reliability of accounting amounts because accounting's *Conceptual Framework* stresses the importance of accounting information being both relevant and faithfully represented. An accounting amount is faithfully represented if it represents what it purports to represent. Value relevance research tests relevance and faithful representation jointly as it is difficult to test these characteristics separately. Figure 8.2 depicts graphically the two concepts. Relevance relates to two aspects of the underlying economics of the investment: a value construct of some kind (such as expenditure on acquisition of goodwill), and the process by which value is expected to be created. Faithful representation refers to two links: the relevance link and a measure that is capable of reflecting the economic substance of the value construct and process. Faithful representation is affected by accounting rules (GAAP), economic uncertainty–especially if it causes the link from the value construct to value creation to be ill-defined — and management discretion to communicate credibly with investors.[44]

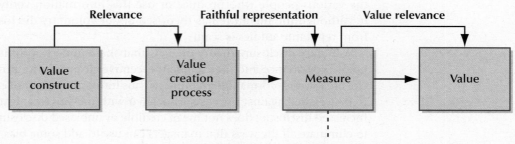

1. Impacted by uncertainty about link from value construct to value creation (e.g. purchased goodwill)
2. Impacted by GAAP (e.g. full expensing of research and development)
3. Impacted by management discretion.

FIGURE 8.2 The relationship between relevance and reliability, and value relevance

Source: Adapted from Wyatt, A 2008, 'What financial and non-financial information on intangibles is value-relevant? A review of the evidence', *Accounting and Business Research*, vol. 38, no. 3, pp. 217–56. © Taylor & Francis Group, www.informaworld.com.[45]

Value relevance research does not attempt to assess the usefulness of accounting numbers. Nor can it be inferred from the statistical test alone that the information of interest causes the level of market value, changes in share prices, or financial performance. Value relevance tests provide a statistical association only, an association that is not backed up by theory of the underlying links between accounting, standard setting and value.[46]

Studies have focused on accounting information by examining four different associations:
- earnings and security returns
- the value relevance of non-earnings data
- the value relevance of different accounting practices
- the value relevance of different GAAP.

Studies examining these associations use three different research methods as follows.
- Relative association studies compare the association between stock market values or changes in those values and alternative bottom-line accounting measures. The accounting number with the greater R^2 is described as being more value relevant.

R^2, known as the coefficient of determination, is a measure used in statistical model analysis to assess how accurately a model explains and predicts future outcomes.

- Incremental association studies investigate whether the accounting number of interest is helpful in explaining value or returns over a long period. The accounting number is said to be value relevant if its estimated regression coefficient is significantly different from zero.
- Marginal information content studies investigate whether a particular accounting number adds to the information set available to investors. Typically, these are event studies examining whether the release of an accounting number is associated with value changes. Price changes are considered evidence of value relevance. These studies represent less than 10% of the value relevance studies.[47]

Note that these studies explore an association. An association signifies that when two or more sets of numbers are regressed and give an R^2 that suggests a relationship between the numbers, they may be related. However, the use of the term association signifies the lack of theory to explain why the sets of numbers are related.

Holthausen and Watts find two implicit but different theories in this literature.[48] The first assumes that accounting earnings tend to be highly associated with equity market value changes. In the second theory, accounting's role is to provide information on inputs to valuation models that investors use in valuing firms' equity. Most researchers assume that the main role of financial reporting is to provide measures associated with value or measures of value or information relevant for equity valuation, an assumption criticised by Holthausen and Watts. As noted in previous chapters, accounting information is an important input into other contexts, not just capital markets and is used by many non-investor user groups.

Holthausen and Watts identify three assumptions underlying the value relevance literature:

- Equity investors are assumed to be the main or dominant users of financial reports. They are assumed to use those reports mainly for the valuation of equity.
- Share prices adequately represent investors' use of information in valuing equity securities.
- Share-price-based tests of relevance and reliability measure relevance and reliability as defined by FASB statements (reflecting the heavy dominance of American researchers in stock market research).[49]

LO 6 WHAT VALUE RELEVANCE STUDIES TELL US

Studies of the relationship between accounting earnings and share returns have analysed data from most of the world's major stock exchanges. Results show that any relationship evident is at best weak.

Reported earnings are not good measures of the value-relevant events that are built into share prices in the periods studied. The relatively low association between reported earnings and share prices suggests that earnings do not capture all the information incorporated into share prices.

One reason for this may be that investors focus on all events that affect future cash flows, while earnings only capture those events that meet the criteria for accounting recognition. Nichols and Wahlen disagree.[50] They report that annual earnings changes contain more value relevant information than changes in cash flows. Other reasons suggested for the low association between reported earnings and share prices refer to managers' risk preferences and negative earnings. Risk-averse managers are likely to report more conservative earnings figures than less risk-averse ones and are likely to report bad news earlier. Both of these actions have been confirmed. Another explanation may be that negative earnings are not value relevant because investors do not expect losses to persist, but firms with losses are included in test samples, lowering the association. Additionally, losses do not provide information about a firm's ability to generate future cash flows.

Relevance and faithful representation

Value relevance research examines the association between accounting amounts and equity market values.[51] An accounting amount is considered value relevant if it has an association with share prices although the literature uses the term *equity market values*. As mentioned, value relevance research focuses on the relevance and faithful representation criteria that are used in the *Conceptual Framework* to choose among accounting methods. The assumption is that an accounting amount will be value relevant only if the amount reflects information relevant to investors in valuing the firm and if the amount is measured reliably enough to be reflected in share prices.

Some studies have tried to decompose earnings and test the association of decomposed items with share prices. The evidence conflicts. Some studies show that partitioning earnings into pre-exceptional, exceptional and extraordinary improves the association, while others contradict these findings, especially in relation to extraordinary earnings. Earnings are more correlated with share returns than cash flows for short periods, but with increased time intervals both tend to have the same level of correlation with returns. Inclusion of non-earnings variables increases the correlation between returns and accounting data.[52]

Consolidated earnings were found to have an incremental information content beyond that of the parent company, so that consolidation improves the value relevance of earnings. However, no value relevance was found for the minority interest portion of earnings and equity.

For Finnish investors at least, restating local GAAP earnings to conform to international accounting standards has helped meet foreign investor needs but appears to have been of limited use for domestic investors. Asset revaluations under Australian GAAP, on the other hand, are relevant and estimated with some reliability but are not considered timely.[53] The degree of association for value relevance of earnings differs internationally. The degree of association is lower in countries with bank-oriented rather than market-oriented economies, in countries in which private-sector bodies are not involved in the standard-setting process and in continental Europe. Differences, especially between the United Kingdom and the United States, seem to be sensitive to the earnings measure analysed.[54]

Measurement perspective research

Fair value accounting is a focus of value relevance research. Much of the US-based research has focused on banks because most of their assets and liabilities are financial. That research suggests that for investment securities, loans and derivatives, fair values are incrementally informative relative to their book values in explaining bank share prices.[55] Other research has focused on pension and other post-retirement assets and liabilities. These are perceived by investors as assets and liabilities of the firm, although they are less reliably measured than other recognised assets and liabilities.[56] The fair value of pension assets measures the pension asset implicit in share prices more reliably than the book value of those pension assets. Other findings are that disaggregated costs are potentially more informative to investors than aggregated costs. Investors perceive the fair value estimates of debt and equity securities and bank loans as more value relevant than historical cost amounts. As well, investors perceive fair values of derivatives as reflecting more precision than their notional amounts in relation to the underlying economic value.

The costs of intangible assets are relevant to investors and are reflected in share prices with some reliability. Investors perceive expenditures on research and development and advertising as capital acquisitions. As well, capitalised software, patents and goodwill are found to be relevant to investors. In contrast, fair value estimates of tangible long-lived assets are not value relevant, although this may be because these values are not always reliably estimated. Because Australian and British accounting standards permitted revaluation, some of the research focused on the revaluation of tangible long-lived assets. Revaluations were found to have incremental explanatory power relative to earnings and changes in earnings and that the market finds revaluation estimates made by external appraisers more informative and reliable than those made by internal appraisers such as directors. Evidence of whether fair value measurements are likely to be used by firms facing financial distress is contradictory. Relations between revaluations and share prices are weaker for firms with high debt-to-equity ratios, suggesting that managers of these firms manipulate the earnings numbers via asset revaluation. However, Danish bank regulators have used mark-to-market accounting for Danish banks for a long time and there is no reliable evidence that Danish banks manage mark-to-market to avoid regulatory constraints.[57] Landsman also reports that US-based evidence on share options suggests that managers facing incentives to manage earnings are likely to do so when fair values of share options must be estimated using entity-supplied estimates for the options.

Landsman concludes from the evidence relating to fair values and value relevance that fair values are informative to investors but the level of informativeness is affected by measurement error and the source of the estimates of fair value (external appraisers or management).[58] The evidence also suggests that investors are provided with information that is somewhat faithfully represented and relevant.

LO 7 THE EFFICIENCY OF CAPITAL MARKETS

Capital markets are assumed to be efficient. The hypothesis suggests that if accounting choices and changes do not affect cash flows, investors will not alter their assessment of share prices. Therefore, market efficiency is important to accounting because the assumption means that investors would see through alternative or opportunistic accounting choices. If markets are not efficient, then discretionary accruals (or earnings management) can fool investors.

Researchers have had little success in resolving the question of whether markets are efficient in relation to discretionary or cosmetic accounting choices. Tests for earnings management generate results with little explanatory power for earnings management.[59] Dechow and Skinner argued that it is sufficient in well-functioning markets for information to be disclosed, because rational investors will process the information appropriately.[60] Not all empirical evidence is consistent with this opinion.[61]

Testing whether capital markets are efficient

Market efficiency is important to accounting because this assumption means that investors would see through alternative or opportunistic accounting choices. If markets are not efficient, then discretionary accruals can fool investors. Tests of market efficiency in the late 1970s and 1980s began to undermine the efficient market hypothesis, although the research methods employed were unable to determine whether investors could see through cosmetic changes or mandated accounting changes.[62]

Most short-window event studies are generally consistent with market efficiency although sometimes the market does not react quickly to information, so that there is a 'drift', which contradicts market efficiency. Longer-period tests assume that the market can over or under react to new information because of human judgement and behavioural biases. Recent evidence such as large abnormal returns spread over several years after well-publicised events such as initial public offerings also contradict market efficiency. According to Kothari, collectively this research poses a formidable challenge to the efficient market hypothesis.[63]

Evidence in studies examining manipulation of discretionary accruals immediately before initial public offerings and other equity offerings also challenges market efficiency. These studies suggest that the market fails to recognise the optimistic bias in earnings forecasts, even though owners, managers and analysts have incentives to issue overly optimistic forecasts.[64]

Statistical anomalies continue to appear in studies using the capital asset pricing model (CAPM). Investors were shown not to react 'logically' to new information.[65] In 1992, Eugene Fama, a key figure in the development of the CAPM model, withdrew his support from it. Defenders of the efficient market hypothesis began to argue that noisy data, measurement errors and selection bias could explain anomalies. Fields, Lys and Vincent note that the evidence about market efficiency is not conclusive on whether markets are inefficient or not.[66] Both before and after the GFC, researchers, finding evidence of market inefficiency, are beginning to draw on the behavioural literature for support, arguing that investors are not necessarily rational.

Prices in an efficient market theoretically reflect all that there is to know about capital assets. This ideology endorsed markets as a perfect allocative device. However, as discussed, anomalies (information that conflicts with the efficient market hypothesis) appeared. The main anomalies are:

- *The small firm effect.* CAPM understates cross-sectional returns of listed firms with low market values of equity and overstates those of firms with high market values of equity.
- *The neglect effect.* Returns of firms not followed by analysts are inferior to those of firms followed by many analysts.
- *The exchange effect.* Investor interest and publicly available information vary according to the market in which a firm's shares are traded.
- *The exotic effect.* There are end-of-month, end-of-year, weekend, Yom Kippur and January effects. For example, many of the abnormal returns for smaller firms occur during the first half of January and stock returns are predictably negative over weekends. These results cannot be explained by the efficient market hypothesis and CAPM combination.

Contemporary Issue 8.2 discusses the failure of the efficient market hypothesis and other mathematical models in predicting the GFC.

8.2 CONTEMPORARY ISSUE

Mathematical models

In relation to the GFC, the popular belief is that conventional economics and finance have failed because their models failed to predict the GFC, to prevent the GFC, and even caused the GFC. What particularly seemed to fail were the efficient market hypothesis (EMH) and the widespread use of mathematical financial models.

Did the mathematical models fail? Is mathematics the curse of economics and finance? Investment banks and hedge funds hired well-qualified mathematicians ('quants') to help them understand and model the markets using complex mathematics. Around 2000, new mathematical models were invented that made it easier to price collateralised ▾

debt obligations (CDOs). One of these models was the Gaussian Copula Function, devised by a quant (David X Li) working at JPMorgan. The formula allowed determination of the correlation between the default rates of different securities. As one commentator put it, if this model was correct, it would tell you the likelihood that related CDOs would explode, as well as the likelihood that a given set of corporations would default on their bond debt in quick succession. Various commentators have said that the formula will go down in history as the instrument that brought the world financial system to its knees. Li is unlikely to get a Nobel Prize as was believed when his formula was adopted.

As profit margins on CDOs narrowed, subprime housing loans and other lesser-quality loans were brought into the CDOs. Then the market started doing things that the model had not expected — a model that had not been extensively tested by those putting it into use. Events underlying the CDOs were not independent or random, but complex and difficult to analyse. Li's formula had oversimplified things, not recognising that there could be correlations between random events because of factors such as employer linkages, geographic regions, or acts of God. Despite not understanding it, many adopted the model, assuming its accuracy.

In relation to other models also blamed for the GFC, Paul Krugman, the Nobel Prize winning economist, said that economists mistook beauty, clad in impressive looking mathematics, for truth. Warren Buffet warned his shareholders to 'beware of geeks bearing formulas'. Others have said that the desire for elegant mathematical models plays down the role of bad behaviours. The quants are not entirely to blame — some blame must rest with those who bought the instruments that they created.

Source: Based on information from JE King, 'Economists and the global financial crisis', *Global Change, Peace & Security*; Steve Keen, 'Was the GFC a mathematical error?', *Business Spectator*; and Damien Wintour, 'The equation that sank Wall Street?', *Necessary and Sufficient*.[67]

Questions

1. If mathematical models were abandoned, what could replace them? **J**
2. Discuss whether mathematical models are better to be partly right rather than totally wrong. **J**
3. Should decision makers be more mathematically literate so that they understand the limitations of the models they use or should the models be extensively tested before use? **J**

LO 8 BEHAVIOURAL FINANCE

The global financial crisis of 2008 increased uncertainty over whether capital markets are efficient. As a consequence, behavioural finance has become a topic of considerable interest. Although the origins of behavioural finance date to 1951, about the same time as modern finance was being born, interest in it did not gain momentum until the late 1980s. This renewed interest seems to have been engendered by two developments:

- mounting empirical evidence suggesting that existing finance theories appear to be deficient in fundamental ways. In particular, theories as to why individual investors trade, how they perform, how they choose their portfolios and why returns vary across shares for reasons other than risk.[68]
- the development of **prospect theory** by Kahneman and Tversky. This theory is based on the simple idea that the pain associated with a given amount of loss (say $100) is greater than the pleasure derived from an equivalent gain, so that investors attach more importance to avoiding the loss.[69] The underlying assumptions of this alternative model of decision making are more realistic than those of existing finance theories.[70] Contemporary Issue 8.3 reviews this model of investor behaviour.

Road to wealth may lie in marching out of step

By Ross Gittins

If the price of a share you owned fell below what you'd paid for it, would that make you more likely or less likely to want to sell it?

One company's profits have been buoyant in recent times, whereas another company hasn't been doing at all well. Which company's shares would you be more inclined to buy?

If in answer to the first question you said you'd be less likely to want to sell a share that had fallen below what you paid for it, congratulations — you're normal.

Unfortunately, you're also sadly misguided. That fact should have no bearing on your decisions about whether to sell the share.

Why not? Because what you paid for a share is in the past. There's nothing you can do to change it, so you should ignore it. It's what economists call a 'sunk cost' and what accountants call 'irrelevant information'.

The point is that the only thing you can hope to influence is the future, so that's what you should focus on. And the question you should ask yourself is this: do I know of any other share (or other investment) that offers a better prospect of gain than the share I've got my money in now?

If so, sell the old one and buy the new one. If not, stick with the old one. If there isn't a lot in it, sit tight — because you pay brokerage fees every time you change horses.

But why do so many investors find it so hard to live by that simple rule? Why do we find it so hard to ignore what we paid for our T2 Telstra shares, for instance?

Well, as we're reminded in an interesting little booklet from JP Morgan Asset Management, *A Primer in Behavioural Finance Theory*, these are the sort of questions that specialists in 'behavioural finance' seek to answer.

The two American psychologists who pioneered this school of thought, Daniel Kahneman and Amos Tversky, discovered almost 30 years ago that losses create much more distress among investors (and ordinary consumers) than the happiness created by equivalent gains.

Whereas conventional economists believe people are 'risk averse', it's more accurate to say most people are 'loss averse'. They're highly reluctant to crystallise a paper loss by selling up and, in fact, often are willing to take more risks to avoid losses than to realise gains.

The behavioural finance specialist Professor Terrance Odean examined data on the whole of the Taiwanese share market and found that, similar to previous studies, people were four times more likely to sell a winner than a loser.

He also looked at investors who repurchased shares they'd previously owned and found they were much more likely to repurchase a stock they sold for a gain than for a loss.

Our obsession with the price we paid for shares is a specific instance of a wider behavioural bias psychologists call 'anchoring' — we make decisions based on a single fact or figure that should have little bearing on the decision.

Salespeople often exploit our tendency to focus on figures of limited relevance. Car salespeople, for example, may anchor their prospective buyers to a vehicle's sticker price.

Bargaining with the buyer and slowly lowering that price makes the buyer think they're getting a good deal. But the sticker price may have been deliberately set too high.

The JP Morgan booklet says even experienced investment analysts can be guilty of anchoring. When faced with new information that contradicts their forecast, they tend to dismiss it as a short-term phenomenon.

This is in direct contradiction to conventional finance theory — the 'efficient market hypothesis' — which holds that all new information is almost instantly incorporated into the market and reflected in share prices.

OK, let's turn to the second question: more inclined to buy the share of a buoyantly profitable company or one that hasn't been doing so well?

Of course you'd buy the one that had been doing well. And, simply because so many other people act that way, it's a pretty good bet you'd be rewarded by seeing the price of the share keep rising after you'd bought it.

The efficient market hypothesis holds that, because all new information is immediately incorporated into a share's price, and because we don't know whether the next bit of information to come along will be good or bad, it's impossible to predict whether the next move in a share's price will be up or down.

But the behavioural finance people had disproved that contention, demonstrating that if a share price has been rising, it's more likely to rise further than to fall back. Similarly, if it's been falling, it's more likely to keep falling.

In other words, share prices tend to develop momentum. And the market contains a lot of 'momentum traders' who follow a policy of buying shares whose price is rising and selling shares whose price is falling.

But going along for the ride will benefit you only in the short term. Longer term, it's quite likely that a share whose price has risen a long way because everyone's been piling into it may by now be overvalued.

Similarly, a share whose price has fallen a long way may by now be undervalued — and so represents good buying.

Studies show that shares with a low P/E (ratio of price to earnings) tend to outperform those with a high P/E. (They get a low P/E by being undervalued and a high P/E by being overvalued.)

And then you have that familiar statutory warning — 'past performance is no guarantee of future performance' — we all keep forgetting to heed.

Just because a company's had a good run of profits lately doesn't mean the good run's likely to continue.

And just because another company's had a bad run lately doesn't mean the bad run's likely to continue.

Indeed, there's a statistical phenomenon called 'reversion to the mean' which says an exceptionally good run is more likely to be followed by a weak performance, while an exceptionally bad run is more likely to be followed by a strong performance.

Why? Because, in the end, most things tend to average out.

JP Morgan's point about behavioural finance is that, because so many investors act irrationally, but in systematic and hence predictable ways, there ought to be ways for the better-informed investor to make a quid out of second-guessing them.

Source: Article by Ross Gittins, 'Road to wealth may lie in marching out of step', *The Sydney Morning Herald.*[71]

Questions

1. Why should the price you paid for a share be irrelevant to your decision to hold it, or to sell that share? **J**
2. What is meant by the phrase that 'people are loss averse'? **J** **K**
3. Explain 'anchoring.' How does anchoring contradict the efficient market hypothesis? **K** **AS**

In their work, Kahneman and Tversky integrated psychology and economics, so providing the intellectual foundations of behavioural finance. Their focus was decision making under uncertainty, a characteristic of capital markets. They demonstrated that decision making involves the use of **heuristics** and systematically departs from the laws of probability. Modern finance involves little or no examination of individual decision making. Deduction is prominent, so that decision making is a 'black box'. Because finance is concerned with prediction rather than description or explanation, finance theorists constructed abstractions of the decision process.[72]

Investment decisions are characterised by high exogenous uncertainty because future performance must be estimated from a set of noisy and vague variables. Investors who make decisions have an intuitive, less quantitative, emotionally driven perception of risk than that implied by finance models. Decision makers' preferences tend to be multifaceted, easily changed and often only formed during the decision-making process. They seek satisfactory rather than optimal solutions. The typical investor can be termed *homo heuristics*, not *homo economics*, a completely rational decision maker focused on utility or wealth maximisation.[73]

Cornerstones of behavioural finance

An important cornerstone of behavioural finance is cognitive psychology. Because cognitive psychology is the study of how people perceive, speak, think, remember, or solve problems, it suggests the following:

- People make systematic errors in the way they think. They use heuristics or rules of thumb to make decision making easier, which can lead to biases and sub-optimal investment decisions.
- People are overconfident about their abilities. Men are more overconfident than women. Entrepreneurs are especially likely to be overconfident.
- People put too much weight on recent experience so that they underweigh long-term averages.
- Mental accounting separates decisions that should be combined.
- *Framing* says that how a concept is presented to people matters. This refers to the old adage about whether a glass is half full or half empty and how each gives us a different perception about the quantity in the glass.
- People avoid realising paper losses but seek to realise paper gains. This behaviour is called the *disposition effect*.
- *Anchoring* says that people tend to rely on a numerical anchor value that is explicitly or implicitly presented to them and use it as an initial starting point. When things change, people tend to be slow to pick up on the changes as well as to underreact because of their conservatism. Any evaluation of returns is distorted by the size of the anchor.
- *Representativeness* says that people tend to rely on stereotypes — for example, past performances are extrapolated without considering the exogenous uncertainty and randomness of financial markets. Good brand image and high brand awareness result in a lower perception of investment risk.
- *Affect heuristic* indicates that emotions affect risk–return perceptions and investment behaviour. Positive emotional associations result in lower perceived investment risk.

Whether expertise moderates these outcomes is uncertain. Some findings show that investor expertise has no influence on the use of heuristics.[74] Other evidence suggests that individual knowledge has a moderating effect.

These observations contradict the core theories of modern finance, which assume that:

- Investors are perfectly rational (or markets act as if they were).
- Markets are efficient.
- Transaction costs are so small that informed traders quickly notice and take advantage of mispricing, driving prices back to 'proper' levels.[75]

Behavioural finance argues that investors, based on these observations, are not rational, so that there are observable biases. The list of biases is growing and includes:

- *overconfidence*. The tendency of investors to overestimate their skills.
- *endowment effect*. The tendency of individuals to insist on a higher price for something they wish to sell than to buy the same item if they do not already own it.
- *loss aversion*. The tendency for people to be risk averse in relation to profit opportunities but to be willing to gamble to avoid a loss.
- *anchoring*. The tendency for people to make decisions based on an initial estimate that is later adjusted, but not sufficiently adjusted to eliminate the influence of the initial estimate.

- *framing*. The tendency to make different choices based on how the decision is framed, especially if it is framed in terms of a likelihood of a good outcome or the reciprocal bad outcome.
- *hindsight*. The tendency to read the present into assessments of the past.

Those who study capital markets are becoming increasingly disillusioned with the assumptions that underlie the notion that markets are efficient. So what are the implications for accounting of markets not being efficient and of behavioural finance? Accounting policy makers have relied on market efficiency to make choices between accounting methods. How will the tenets of behavioural finance affect accounting policy choice? This is one issue that relies on a 'wait and see' answer.

Summary

Explain the role of capital market research for accounting
- Capital market research suggests that the main role of financial reporting is to provide information relevant for equity valuation.
- Capital market research indicates which disclosures have information content for investors.

Differentiate between an event study and an association study
- The main difference is time: an event study is conducted over a short period; an association study over relatively long periods.
- Event studies examine changes in the level or variability of share prices or trading volumes.
- Association studies examine the correlation between accounting performance measures and share returns.

Outline the relationship between accounting measures of financial performance and share prices
- Accounting information provides investors with information relevant for investment decision making.
- Disclosures of earnings lead to significant share price changes or increases in trading volumes.
- Financial performance numbers are slow to incorporate all of the information investors use to value shares.

Identify findings of capital market research relevant to accounting
- Annual financial statements are not a timely source of information for capital markets.
- Interim disclosures of accounting information have less information content than annual reports.
- The relation between security returns and contemporaneous earnings is low.
- Capital market research validates the relevance of accrual accounting.
- Consolidated accounting data is more value relevant than unconsolidated data.
- No relation has been observed between inflation accounting and share prices and returns.
- The information content of accounting varies with firm and country characteristics.

Explain the role of information and information intermediaries in capital markets
- Information informs capital markets.
- Share prices reflect available information.

- Capital markets react to new information.
- Auditors appear to add credibility to financial information.
- Financial analysts' forecasts affect share prices.
- Managers, as intermediaries, voluntarily disclose information.

Distinguish between behavioural finance findings and mainstream finance findings

- Mainstream finance assumes that investors are rational; behavioural finance shows that investors are not rational.
- Mainstream finance assumes decision making is a 'black box'; behavioural finance studies decision making.

Discuss how behavioural research contributes to an understanding of decision making

- Behavioural finance argues that investors are not rational.
- There are observable biases such as overconfidence, endowment effects, loss aversion, anchoring, framing and hindsight.
- Investors tend to use heuristics in their decision making.

Review questions

1. Explain what is meant by an 'efficient market'.
2. Distinguish an event study from an association study.
3. Explain why accounting earnings do not capture all the information contained in share prices.
4. Explain how accounting's recognition and realisation principles affect the relationship between earnings and share prices.
5. What is meant by the term 'post-earnings announcement drift'? What implications does this phenomenon have for the efficient market hypothesis?
6. In what ways are the finance definition of 'relevance' and the *Conceptual Framework* definition provided in chapter 2 similar?
7. When is an accounting number said to be 'value relevant'?
8. Explain why earnings are not good measures of value relevance.
9. International accounting standards are conservative in their treatment of intangibles. Will this conservative treatment conflict with investors' perceptions of the value of intangibles to a firm?
10. Summarise the main findings of the value relevance literature in relation to accounting.
11. What principles are blamed for financial statements being poor indicators of value? How do these principles inhibit valuation?
12. Read the section on earnings management in chapter 6. How does that view of earnings management differ from the view held in the finance literature? Why would investors react positively to earnings management?
13. What is prospect theory? What are the implications of prospect theory for finance?
14. In the literature on which this chapter is based, the notions of the efficient market hypothesis and the CAPM are referred to as a 'paradigm'. Findings that conflict with these hypotheses are called 'anomalies'. Find definitions of these terms. How do they explain the progress of knowledge in the finance discipline?
15. Behavioural finance, in contrast to mainstream finance, focuses on what aspects of capital markets?
16. What does cognitive psychology tell us about investors?

17. Does cognitive psychology supply explanations of why investors have flocked to subscribe in high-profile companies such as Woolworths or Telstra?
18. Evaluate whether behavioural finance is able to explain the main anomalies of efficient markets.
19. What are heuristics? How can they lead to poor decision making?
20. How would you evaluate large amounts of research findings that are based on associations, without much theoretical underpinning?

Application questions

8.1

Marcus Padley, a stockbroker, made the following statements in an article in *The Sydney Morning Herald*.

> I love 'The Warren Buffet Way'. In fact, one of my first clients introduced himself by saying, 'I am Fred and I'd like to invest the Warren Buffet Way'. Well whoopee do! What shall we do? Get the annual reports of the top 200 companies. Analyse the accounts of each, assess 'value' and then go to the stock market and find out that 'wow, I'm right and the whole market is wrong' and the share price is trading below the true 'value'. Then purchase the shares and wait for that value to inevitably emerge.
>
> In fact most Warren Buffett-based approaches are terrible at timing, which in reality is about the only thing that really matters. In an increasingly impatient market it is not just about 'what', it is becoming all about 'when'. Investors who sat through the 54.5 per cent fall in the market in the financial crises need to earn 113% to get their money back. That's 13 years of compounding average annual returns. Not caring about 'when' just cost us 13 years.[76]

(a) Critically evaluate the two statements made by Marcus Padley in the context of capital market research. **J** **K** **AS** **CT**

8.2

In December 2008, OZ Minerals wrote down its assets by $201 million. In its 2010 accounts it reversed this impairment charge, recording an increase of $141.1 million to net profit. The impairment reversal was a non-cash adjustment — it did form part of OZ Minerals' operating earnings. As a result, the market was reported to have found the reversal of historical interest only. However, after the announcement of its 2010 earnings, OZ Minerals' share price outperformed the broader mining market, rising by over 3%.

(a) If the reversal was of 'historical interest only', how can the share price reaction be explained? **J** **AS**

8.3

In September 2008, the Seven Network revealed it had incurred losses on its strategy to 'park' hundreds of millions of dollars in listed securities which were the result of the sale of half of its television and magazine interests to a private equity firm, a strategy which the company had not revealed to the market. Seven's share price closed at its lowest level since January 2005.

(a) What is a 'private equity firm'?
(b) Why do you think the share price fell?
(c) Was it a response to the lack of disclosure?
(d) Was it a response to the losses incurred by the strategy? **J** **K**

8.4

Talking to the financial press about the David Jones 2010 earnings from its department store business, the company's CEO acknowledged that it had been a tough time for the company due to the departure of its former CEO after sexual harassment claims against

the former CEO. The current CEO said the company should be judged on two indicators: sales and share price. He distinguished between the man (the former CEO) and David Jones' 170-year-old brand. David Jones' shares rose 2%.

(a) Do you agree that a company such as David Jones should be judged on sales and share price? **J**

(b) Why is the distinction between the 'man' and the 'brand' important? **AS**

(c) If brands are so important to a company's share price, why are internally generated brands not recognised under accounting rules? **AS**

 **8.5** The alleged behaviour of the former CEO of David Jones apparently did not impact on the company's share price. However, according to a study by two American economists, the transgressions of golfer Tiger Woods were responsible for wiping up to US$12 million off the value of his sponsors (Gatorade, Nike, Gillette, Electronic Arts). Gatorade and Nike were the worst hit of his sponsors.

(a) How can this apparent contradiction between the impact of the allegations against David Jones' CEO and Tiger Woods be explained? **J**

(b) What does the impact on sponsors' shares say about the adage that 'any publicity is good publicity'? **J**

 **8.6** Read accounting standard AASB 133/IAS 33 *Earnings per Share* and answer the following questions.

(a) How is earnings per share calculated? **K**

(b) What are some of the allocations, predictions and wild guesses that go into the calculation of net income? **K**

(c) In light of the allocations, predictions and guesses, how reliable do you think the earnings per share are as a summary of a firm's activities for a period? **J** **AS**

 **8.7** For the 2010 financial year, Phoslock Water Solutions reported:

- revenues from ordinary activities up by 79%
- earnings before depreciation, amortisation, tax and interest improved by 40%
- net loss for the period improved by 33% over the previous year's loss.

(a) What would you intuitively expect to be the market reaction? **J**

(b) Over the following two weeks, the company's share price fell by one-third. The directors could not offer a business reason for the fall. Can you suggest a reason(s) for the fall? Explain your reasoning. **J** **AS**

 **8.8** Geoffrey Hill, a private share consultant, made the following statements.[77] Comment on each statement, noting that some might require some research on your part.

(a) First statement:

> The trouble with all of this overseas money flowing into our market and pushing it to new levels is that overseas investors have different views on what 'value' means. The sheer weight of money obviously increases share prices but the institutions investing for overseas investors have scant regard to the level of risk that they are adding to everyone's portfolios.

(i) What do you understand by 'value' in the context of this statement? **SM**

(ii) What is a portfolio? What role does risk play in the composition of a portfolio? **K**

(b) Second statement:

> We have become accustomed to low oil prices, over the past 20 years. This has created a disincentive to developing alternative energy supplies due to

economics. But it is a different story now with the oil price near US$50 a barrel. Pacific Hydro operates hydro and wind farms in Australia, Chile, Fiji and the Philippines. As new projects come on line, the economics and profit become stronger. It is trading on a P/E of 16 and dividend yield of 1.4%. There is no value here for the Chartist's Portfolio so we will not be investing.

(i) What is a 'Chartist'? **K** **SM**

(ii) What makes his or her share purchasing decisions distinctive? **K**

The listed investor, Djerriwarrh, had a solid year in 2009, but not according to IAS rules. Its net operating profit rose by 21.1% despite holding nearly 29% of its portfolio in bank shares. Because of AASB 139/IAS 39 *Financial Instruments: Recognition and Measurement*, it had to report a pre-tax 'impairment' charge of $70.9 million and a net charge of $49.7 million, pushing its results to a loss of $14.1 million. Shares in the Djerriwarrh portfolio qualified for the charge, shares that were not even remotely close to going broke but were affected by the global financial crisis. The problem is that as share prices recover, impairment charges already taken against earnings cannot be reversed.

(a) Does the accounting impairment rule, as it stood in 2009, make sense? **J**

(b) What changes were made to AASB 139/IAS 39 *Financial Instruments: Recognition and Measurement* as a result of the unforeseen consequences such as that suffered by Djerriwarrh? **K**

(c) As a result of the changes, will investment companies that book impairment losses to the balance sheet be able to report dividend income as income? **K**

8.1
CASE
STUDY

Who needs credit ratings? They should be optional

By Adam Creighton

Imagine if we all needed our very own personality rating. People would demand to see it even before doing coffee. You would routinely pay a company with emotional expertise to rate you from AAA... right down to CCC... A higher rating would snare you a bigger pool of potential friends. This ridiculous arrangement would only last if governments could enforce it. Character analysis is best performed bilaterally; individuals have the most incentive to get it right. Finance should work like this too. Banks and investors should thrive or die by the quality of their own assessments of credit risk. They have the most incentive to get it right. But for decades government regulators, through the Basel II bank regulations to take one example, have in effect required all companies and countries to have credit ratings that indicate how likely a particular entity is to default. For regulators, ratings are a simple and cheap way to monitor and compare the riskiness of financial institutions. The world's largest rating agencies, which enjoy regulatory clout, Standard & Poor's, Moody's and Fitch, have grown fat and powerful on the back of these mandates. They now underpin the world's financial system; their ratings critically influence the composition of every bank's balance sheet.

If only the ratings were any good: Bear Stearns and Lehman Brothers were 'investment grade' only days before they collapsed. Greece was recently rated A. Amazingly, before 2008 US sub-prime mortgages were packaged up and sold in AAA-rated securities, facilitating the spread and popularity of sub-prime mortgages throughout the world's financial system. And poor ratings are not only a North Atlantic or recent problem—Enron, WorldCom and Australia's very own HIH Insurance were all 'investment grade' before they collapsed in the early 2000s.

Perhaps it is no surprise these credit ratings have been crap. The agencies rarely disagree with each other, they are paid exclusively by borrowers who hanker for higher ratings, their regulatory sinecure protects them from any competition, and as mere opinions, they cannot be held legally accountable for stuffing up. The proliferation of ratings has absolved banks and investors from having to think carefully about credit risk. Yet credit assessment is meant to be the primary skill of banks. One wonders what the massive army of highly trained and paid financial 'risk management professionals' were doing in the lead-up to the global financial crisis. Surely not helping, to the bank's advantage, the arcane rules of Basel II? Moreover, being able to contract out expensive and time-consuming analysis of credit risk has helped banks become huge and hold assets they don't fully understand.

Following such embarrassing stuff-ups, regulators in Europe and America are now considering regulation of rating agencies themselves. But this will only undermine the quality of ratings even further—agencies will come to capture regulators as much as large financial institutions have. And the incentives for banks and investors to think for themselves will dwindle even further.

The insidious nexus between bureaucrats and rating agencies needs to be broken. Credit ratings and agencies should be excised from every government regulation everywhere. Credit rating agencies may still thrive independent of regulatory fiat. Individual investors, less skilled in credit analysis and without adequate information, might want to pay for a second opinion, for example. But governments should set an example and agree to stop paying agencies for a credit rating. Australia could issue a few bonds without one and see what happens. Governments' accounts, their economic circumstances and history are already widely published. You didn't need Moody's to tell you Greece is a bad credit risk and has borrowed too much, or Standard & Poor's that the US's credit position has deteriorated. To be sure, without shorthand credit ratings it will be harder to regulate and constrain banks. But that only matters if governments are implicitly standing ready to absorb banks' losses. And regulators could still talk to individual banks about how they monitor their own assets. The No.1 priority for regulators and politicians everywhere should be to destroy entirely the implicit guarantee the finance sector has enjoyed for many years. That will mean tough decisions: perhaps breaking up banks, or bestowing limited liability on businesses only when it is clearly in the public interest, for instance.

The finance sector is and has been, overwhelmingly, the most regulated sector of the economy, the most replete with moral hazard and chock full of malign incentives. And it is the sector that has wrought such damage on the economy. Making credit ratings optional would be a sensible way to help cure these perversions.

Source: Article by Adam Creighton, 'Who needs credit ratings? They should be optional', *Crikey.*[78]

Questions

1. What is the function of a credit rating agency? **K**
2. Why have these agencies prospered? **J**
3. Why do credit ratings 'underpin the world's financial system'? **K**
4. Can you offer reasons why credit rating agencies would have valued US subprime mortgages as AAA? **J** **K**
5. Why does the author have a low opinion of credit ratings? **J** **K**
6. What is meant by 'moral hazard'? **K**
7. Explain the statement that the finance sector is 'replete with moral hazard and chock full of malign incentives'. **J** **K**
8. Can you suggest why making credit ratings optional would 'cure these perversions'? **J** **K**
9. Research the following:
   (a) The author is a research fellow of the Centre for Independent Studies. Is this Centre 'independent'? **J** **K**
   (b) How have ratings been used to regulate the investment decisions of local government? **J** **K**
   (c) How have the ratings resulted in large investment losses for many NSW local governments? **J** **K**

8.2 CASE STUDY

Women take more risks when investing: survey

By Anna Fenech

Women are greater risk takers than men when investing, new research revealed this week. Women are also more exposed to growth assets than men, especially as they head towards retirement.

The research appears to debunk previous findings showing women are more conservative investors than men because they tend to have fewer overall assets.

Conducted by BT Financial Group and the University of Western Australia (UWA), the research, which spans more than three decades and draws on BT funds data for 850 000 investors, also confirmed that men trade more frequently than women.

The study, presented at a University of NSW superannuation conference this week, collected demographic details, including age, gender, postcode; whether the investor is a direct investor or is advised; 6.8 million daily transactions data; and more than 1.8 billion investor-fund-days (that is, the number of days investors were invested).

Supporting the so-called life-cycle theory of investing, the research shows those in their 20s are exposed to growth assets 60 per cent of the time. But by the time they hit their 60s, this had fallen to 46 per cent.

Being wealthy does affect the riskiness of assets invested in, with 'growth assets' (stocks and listed property style investments) accounting for 61 per cent of investor fund days of the wealthiest investors, but only 50 per cent of those in the lowest tax quartile.

'The research also found that conservative, wealthy, older and male investors were more likely to sell their winning investments and hold their losers than other types of investors,' says Tracey McNaughton, an economist at BT and a co-author of the survey. 'As expected, the research did confirm that men trade more frequently than women, wealthier investors have a greater proportion of their portfolio in riskier assets and, supporting the "life-cycle theory of investing", older investors are more likely to move from risky to safe assets as they age.'

This research also appears to demonstrate that managed fund investors act more rationally than their direct equity (those investing in shares) counterparts when choosing to sell investments, she says.

'Previous research on the same subject shows that direct share investors found gains are realised 50 per cent more often than losses. That is, investors tend to sell winners and hold on to their losers.'

And yes, this does affect investment performance. The same research found unsold losers returned 5 per cent in the next year while sold winners returned a further 11.6 per cent.

McNaughton says a well-documented finding in behavioural finance is the tendency for investors to hold on to losing investments while selling winners. The BT/UWA research found this bias was not displayed by Australian managed fund investors.

'And, in stark contrast to one of the most robust findings in behavioural finance, the research found that overall female investors have a greater appetite for risk than men,' McNaughton says.

A need to catch up later in life might be one reason, she says.

Source: Article by Anna Fenech, 'Women take more risks when investing: survey', *Weekend Australian*.[79]

Questions

1. What do you understand by a 'life cycle theory of investing'? Does the research by BT and UWA support this theory? **J** **K** **AS**
2. How does being wealthy affect investment choices? **J**
3. What other factors seem to affect investment activity? **K**
4. How do the findings by BT and UWA differ from the findings and predictions of behavioural finance? **J** **AS**
5. In what ways do the BT and UWA findings confirm or deny the predictions and findings of behavioural finance? **J** **AS**

Additional readings

Dechow, P & Skinner, D 2000, 'Earnings management: reconciling the views of accounting academics, practitioners and regulators', *Accounting Horizons*, vol. 14, no. 2, pp. 235–50.

Healy, PM & Wahlen, JM 1999, 'A review of the earnings management literature and its implications for standard setting', *Accounting Horizons*, vol. 13, pp. 365–84.

Schipper, K 1989, 'Commentary on earnings management', *Accounting Horizons*, vol. 3, pp. 91–102.

End notes

1. Ball, R & Brown, P 1968, 'An empirical evaluation of accounting income numbers', *Journal of Accounting Research*, vol. 16, no. 2, pp. 159–78.
2. Barth, ME 2006, 'Research, Standard Setting, and Global Financial Reporting', *Foundations and Trends in Accounting*, vol.1, no. 2, pp. 71–165.
3. Barth, ME 2000, 'Valuation-based accounting research: Implications for financial reporting and opportunities for future research', *Accounting and Finance*, vol. 40, iss. 1, pp. 7–31.
4. Beaver, W 1968, 'The information content of annual earnings announcements', *Journal of Accounting Research*, vol. 6, pp. 67–92; Nichols, DC & Wahlen, JM 2004, 'How do earnings numbers relate to stock returns? A review of classic accounting research with updated evidence', *Accounting Horizons*, vol. 18, no. 4, pp. 263–86.
5. Beaver, W 1968, 'The information content of annual earnings announcements', *Journal of Accounting Research*, vol. 6, pp. 67–92.
6. Nichols, DC & Wahlen, JM 2004, 'How do earnings numbers relate to stock returns? A review of classic accounting research with updated evidence', *Accounting Horizons*, vol. 18, no. 4, pp. 263–86.
7. ibid.
8. Ball, R & Brown, P 1968, 'An empirical evaluation of accounting income numbers', *Journal of Accounting Research*, vol. 16, no. 2, pp. 159–78.
9. King, J E (2009) COMMUNICATION Economists and the global financial crisis, *Global Change, Peace & Security*, vol. 21, no. 3, pp. 389–96.
10. Ball, R & Brown, P 1968, 'An empirical evaluation of accounting income numbers', *Journal of Accounting Research*, vol. 16, no. 2, pp. 159–78; Beaver, W 1968, 'The information content of annual earnings announcements', *Journal of Accounting Research*, vol. 6, pp. 67–92.
11. Hew, D, Skerratt, L, Strong, N & Walker, M 1996, 'Post-earnings announcement drift: some preliminary evidence for the United Kingdom', *Accounting and Business Research*, vol. 26, no. 4, pp. 283–93.
12. Dumontier, P & Raffournier, B 2002, 'Accounting and capital markets: a survey of the European evidence', *The European Accounting Review*, vol. 11, no. 1, pp. 119–51.
13. Foster, G 1977, 'Quarterly accounting data: time-series properties and predictive ability results', *Accounting Review*, vol. 52, no. 1, pp. 1–21; Firth, M 1981, 'The relative information content of the release of financial results data by firms', *Journal of Accounting Research*, vol. 19, no. 2, pp. 521–9.
14. Dumontier, P & Raffournier, B 2002, 'Accounting and capital markets: a survey of the European evidence', *The European Accounting Review*, vol. 11, no. 1, pp. 119–51.
15. Beaver, W, Lambert, R & Morse, D 1980, 'The information content of security prices', *Journal of Accounting and Economics*, vol. 2, no. 1, pp. 3–28.
16. Kothari, SP 2001, 'Capital markets research in accounting', *Journal of Accounting and Economics*, vol. 31, nos. 1–3, pp. 105–231.
17. ibid.
18. Nichols, DC & Wahlen, JM 2004, 'How do earnings numbers relate to stock returns? A review of classic accounting research with updated evidence', *Accounting Horizons*, vol. 18, no. 4, pp. 263–86.
19. Beaver, WH 2002, 'Perspectives on Recent Capital Market Research', *The Accounting Review*, vol. 77, no. 2, pp. 453–74.
20. Booth, G, Kallunki, J & Martikainen, T 1996, 'Post announcement drift and income smoothing: Finnish evidence', *Journal of Business Finance and Accounting*, vol. 23, no. 8, pp. 1197–211.
21. Johnson and Schwarz cited in Dumontier, P & Raffournier, B 2002, 'Accounting and capital markets: a survey of the European evidence', *The European Accounting Review*, vol. 11, no. 1, pp. 119–51.
22. Chan, H, Faff, R, Ho YK & Ramsay, A 2006, 'Asymmetric Market Readctions of Growth and Value Firms with Management Earnings Forecasts', *International Review of Finance*, vol. 6, no. 1–2, pp. 79–97.
23. Truong, C 2010, 'Post earnings announcement drift and the roles of drift-enhanced factors in New Zealand', *Pacific-Basin Finance Journal*, vol. 18, no. 2, pp. 139–57.
24. Kothari, SP 2001, 'Capital markets research in accounting', *Journal of Accounting and Economics*, vol. 31, nos. 1–3, pp. 105–231.
25. Beaver, WH 2002, 'Perspectives on Recent Capital Market Research', *The Accounting Review*, vol. 77, no. 2, pp. 453–74.
26. Healy, PM & Wahlen, JM 1999, 'A review of the earnings management literature and its implications for standard setting', *Accounting Horizons*, vol. 13, no. 4, pp. 365–84.
27. Schipper, K 1989, 'Commentary on earnings management', *Accounting Horizons*, vol. 3, no. 4, pp. 91–102.
28. Healy, PM & Palepu, KG 2001, 'Information asymmetry, corporate disclosure, and the capital markets: a review of the empirical disclosure

literature', *Journal of Accounting and Economics*, vol. 31, nos. 1–3 , pp. 405–40.

29. Fields, TD, Lys, TZ & Vincent, L 2001, 'Empirical research on accounting choice', *Journal of Accounting and Economics*, vol. 31, nos. 1–3, pp. 255–307.

30. ibid.

31. ibid.

32. Kothari, SP 2001, 'Capital markets research in accounting', *Journal of Accounting and Economics*, vol. 31, nos. 1–3, pp. 105–231.

33. Healy, PM & Palepu, KG 2001, 'Information asymmetry, corporate disclosure, and the capital markets: a review of the empirical disclosure literature', *Journal of Accounting and Economics*, vol. 31, nos. 1–3, pp. 405–40.

34. Beaver, WH 2002, 'Perspectives on Recent Capital Market Research', *The Accounting Review*, vol. 77, no. 2, pp. 453–74.

35. Healy, PM & Palepu, KG 2001, 'Information asymmetry, corporate disclosure, and the capital markets: a review of the empirical disclosure literature', *Journal of Accounting and Economics*, vol. 31, nos. 1–3, pp. 405–40.

36. Barth, ME 2000, 'Valuation-based accounting research: Implications for financial reporting and opportunities for future research', *Accounting and Finance*, vol. 40, iss. 1, pp. 7–31.

37. Core, JE 2001, 'A review of the empirical disclosure literature: discussion', *Journal of Accounting and Economics*, vol. 31, nos. 1–3, pp. 441–56.

38. ibid.

39. Aboody, D & Kasznik, R 2000, 'CEO stock options awards and the timing of corporate voluntary disclosures', *Journal of Accounting and Economics*, vol. 29, iss. 1, pp. 73–100.

40. Healy, PM & Palepu, KG 2001, 'Information asymmetry, corporate disclosure, and the capital markets: a review of the empirical disclosure literature', *Journal of Accounting and Economics*, vol. 31, nos. 1–3, pp. 405–40.

41. Core, JE 2001, 'A review of the empirical disclosure literature: discussion', *Journal of Accounting and Economics*, vol. 31, nos. 1–3, pp. 441–56.

42. Beaver, WH 2002, 'Perspectives on Recent Capital Market Research', *The Accounting Review*, vol. 77, no. 2, pp. 453–74.

43. Barth, ME, Beaver, WH & Landsman, WR 2001, 'The relevance of the value relevance literature for financial accounting standard setting: another view', *Journal of Accounting and Economics*, vol. 31, nos. 1–3, pp. 77–104.

44. Wyatt, A, 2008, 'What financial and non-financial information on intangibles is value-relevant? A review of the evidence', *Accounting and Business Research*, vol. 38, no. 3, pp. 217–56.

45. ibid.

46. ibid.

47. Holthausen, RW & Watts, RL 2001, 'The relevance of the value-relevance literature for financial accounting standard setting', *Journal of Accounting and Economics*, vol. 31, nos. 1–3, pp. 3–75.

48. ibid.

49. ibid.

50. Nichols, DC & Wahlen, JM 2004, 'How do earnings numbers relate to stock returns? A review of classic accounting research with updated evidence', *Accounting Horizons*, vol. 18, no. 4, pp. 263–86.

51. Barth, ME, Beaver, WH & Landsman, WR 2001, 'The relevance of the value relevance literature for financial accounting standard setting: another view', *Journal of Accounting and Economics*, vol. 31, nos. 1–3, pp. 77–104.

52. Dumontier, P & Raffournier, B 2002, 'Accounting and capital markets: a survey of the European evidence', *The European Accounting Review*, vol. 11, no. 1, pp. 119–51.

53. Barth, ME, Beaver, WH & Landsman, WR 2001, 'The relevance of the value relevance literature for financial accounting standard setting: another view', *Journal of Accounting and Economics*, vol. 31, nos. 1–3, pp. 77–104.

54. Dumontier, P & Raffournier, B 2002, 'Accounting and capital markets: a survey of the European evidence', *The European Accounting Review*, vol. 11, no. 1, pp. 119–51.

55. Landsman, WR 2007, 'Is fair value accounting information relevant and reliable? Evidence from capital market research', *Accounting and Business Research*, vol. 37, no. 3, pp. 19–30.

56. Barth, ME, Beaver, WH & Landsman, WR 2001, 'The relevance of the value

relevance literature for financial accounting standard setting: another view', *Journal of Accounting and Economics*, vol. 31, nos. 1–3, pp. 77–104.

57. Landsman, WR 2007, 'Is fair value accounting information relevant and reliable? Evidence from capital market research', *Accounting and Business Research*, vol. 37, no. 3, pp. 19–30.

58. ibid.

59. Kothari, SP 2001, 'Capital markets research in accounting', *Journal of Accounting and Economics*, vol. 31, nos. 1–3, pp. 105–231.

60. Dechow, P & Skinner, D 2000, 'Earnings management: reconciling the views of accounting academics, practitioners and regulators', *Accounting Horizons*, vol. 14, no. 2, pp. 235–50.

61. Fields, TD, Lys, TZ & Vincent, L 2001, 'Empirical research on accounting choice', *Journal of Accounting and Economics*, vol. 31, nos. 1–3, pp. 255–307.

62. ibid.

63. Kothari, SP 2001, 'Capital markets research in accounting', *Journal of Accounting and Economics*, vol. 31, nos. 1–3, pp. 105–231.

64. ibid.; Fields, TD, Lys, TZ & Vincent, L 2001, 'Empirical research on accounting choice', *Journal of Accounting and Economics*, vol. 31, nos. 1–3, pp. 255–307.

65. Olsen, RA 1998, 'Behavioral finance and its implications for stock-price volatility', *Financial Analysts Journal*, vol. 54, no. 2, pp. 10–18.

66. Fields, TD, Lys, TZ & Vincent, L 2001, 'Empirical research on accounting choice', *Journal of Accounting and Economics*, vol. 31, nos. 1–3, pp. 255–307.

67. King, JE 2009, 'Economists and the global financial crisis', *Global Change, Peace & Security*, vol. 21, no. 3, pp. 389–96; Keen, S 2009, 'Was the GFC a mathematical error?', *Business Spectator*, 29 December, www. businessspectator.com.au; Wintour, D 2009, 'The equation that sank Wall Street?', *Necessary and Sufficient*, 2 June, www.necessaryandsufficient.net.

68. Sunbrahmanyam, A 2007, 'Behavioural Finance: A Review and Synthesis', *European Financial Management*, vol. 14, no.1, pp. 12–29.

69. Fuller, RJ 1996, 'Amos Tversky, behavioral finance, and nobel prizes', *Financial Analysts Journal*, vol. 52, no. 4, pp. 7–8.

70. Olsen, RA 1998, 'Behavioral finance and its implications for stock-price volatility', *Financial Analysts Journal*, vol. 54, no. 2, pp. 10–18.

71. Gittins, R 2006, 'Road to wealth may lie in marching out of step', *The Sydney Morning Herald*, 30 September, p. 38.

72. Olsen, RA 1998, 'Behavioral finance and its implications for stock-price volatility', *Financial Analysts Journal*, vol. 54, no. 2, pp. 10–18.

73. ibid.

74. Jordan, J & Kaas, K 2002, 'Advertising in the mutual fund business: The role of judgmental heuristics in private investors' evaluation of risk and return', *Journal of Financial Services Marketing*, vol.7, no. 2, pp. 129–40.

75. Gilson, RJ & Kraakman, R 2003, 'The mechanisms of market efficiency twenty years later: the hindsight bias', *Journal of Corporation Law*, vol. 28, no. 4, pp. 715–42.

76. Padley, M 2010, 'Buffett investment style has the market cornered', *The Sydney Morning Herald*, 20 March, www.smh.com.au.

77. Hill, G 2004, 'Bullish winds of change', *The Courier-Mail*, 27 November, p. 83.

78. Creighton, A 2011, 'Who needs credit ratings? They should be optional', *Crikey*, 23 August, www.crikey.com.au.

79. Fenech, A 2006, 'Women take more risks when investing: survey', *Weekend Australian*, 22 July, p. 40.

9

Earnings management

After studying this chapter, you should be able to:

1 describe the importance of earnings in assessing the success of an organisation

2 explain what earnings management is

3 describe a number of common methods of earnings management, including accounting policy choice, accrual accounting, income smoothing, real activities management and big bath write-offs

4 explain why entities manage earnings

5 identify the consequences of earnings management

6 assess the role corporate governance plays in controlling earnings management.

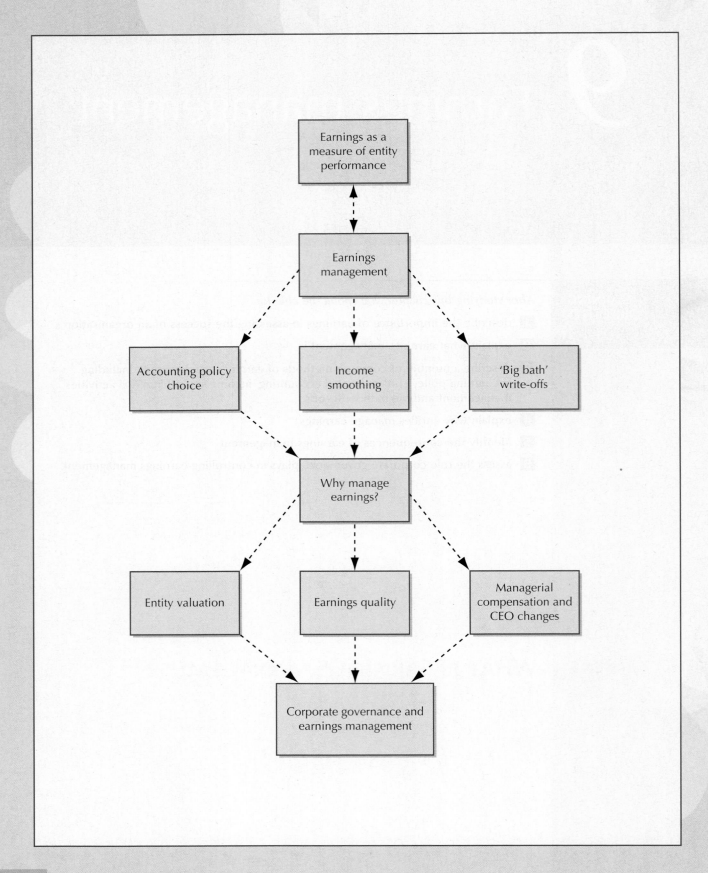

The beginning of the twenty-first century saw a series of accounting scandals worldwide. Following the largest corporate bankruptcy in the United States — Enron in 2001 — evidence surfaced about a number of financial misstatements.[1] Further evidence of substantial irregularities in other companies around the globe followed. Examples include WorldCom and Xerox in the United States, Parmalat in Italy and HIH, One.Tel and Harris Scarfe in Australia. Central to all these failures was aggressive earnings management, in which entities misstated earnings or presented misleading accounting information.[2]

This chapter investigates what is meant by earnings management and how it is conducted. We will start by discussing the importance of earnings as a reporting concept and what we mean by earnings management. Common methods of earnings management are then discussed. We then examine why entities might engage in earnings management and how earnings management relates to the quality of earnings. Finally, the roles of corporate governance and executive and employee issues in earnings management are detailed.

THE IMPORTANCE OF EARNINGS

Before the meaning of earnings management is discussed, the importance of earnings needs to be investigated. **Earnings** are sometimes called the 'bottom line' or 'net income'. As a measure of entity performance, they are of great importance to financial statement users and indicate the extent to which an entity has engaged in activities that add value to it. The financial press provides many instances of earnings or profit announcements and a discussion of why earnings might deviate from that which was forecasted previously. Both financial analysts and managers provide forecasts of earnings. The theoretical value of an entity's stock is the present value of its future earnings.[3] Increased earnings signal an increase in entity value, while decreased earnings represent a decrease in that value.[4]

Earnings are used by shareholders to both assess managers' performance — a stewardship role — and to assist in predicting future cash flows and assessing risk.[5] Francis, Schipper and Vincent found that earnings are more closely associated with stock prices than are cash flows, sales or other financial statement data.[6] Lenders use earnings as a component in debt covenants to reduce the risk associated with lending and to monitor performance against covenants. Customers may use earnings to evaluate whether products and services are likely to be supplied into the future, and employees use earnings to assess the entity's future prospects and evaluate the level of job security they are likely to hold.[7] Correctly assessing entity performance depends on the level of accounting information quality or earnings quality. Earnings quality, a concept that will be discussed later, can be affected by earnings management.

WHAT IS EARNINGS MANAGEMENT?

There are several definitions of **earnings management** that are commonly understood in the academic and professional literature. Schipper defines it as 'a purposeful intervention in the external financial reporting process with the intent of obtaining some private gain (as opposed to, say, merely facilitating the neutral operation of the process)'.[8] Healy and Wahlen argue that 'earnings management occurs when managers use judgement in financial reporting and in structuring transactions to alter financial reports to either mislead some stakeholders about the underlying economic performance of the company, or to influence the contractual outcomes that depend on reported accounting numbers'.[9] McKee meanwhile defines earnings management more conservatively as 'reasonable and legal management decision making and reporting intended to achieve stable and predictable financial results'. He states that earnings management is not to be confused with activities that do not reflect economic reality — which may be evidence of fraud.[10]

The above definitions differ on the basis of whether normal financial decisions are part of the definition, or whether the purpose of earnings management is to mislead. Management can take a relative position on accounting issues based on the perspective of the management team. This can be conservative, with few if any non-recurring or unusual items, or, at the other extreme, a more aggressive or even fraudulent perspective. This range of earnings management definitions has been classified by Ronen and Yaari as white, grey or black.[11] White, or beneficial earnings management, enhances the transparency of financial reports; black involves misrepresentation, reducing transparency or even fraud; while grey defines earnings management as choosing an accounting method that is either opportunistic — that is, it maximises wealth of managers — or could be economically efficient for the entity concerned.

Earnings management can therefore range from being beneficial, in that it signals long-term entity value to stakeholders, can be harmful because it conceals real entity value in either the short or long term, or can be neutral if it documents short-term true performance.[12] Giroux supports this view where he considers that earnings management 'includes the whole spectrum, from conservative accounting through fraud' and provides useful examples of the range of alternatives, which have been adapted in table 9.1.[13]

TABLE 9.1 Earnings management relating to different entity objectives

	Conservative	Moderate	Aggressive	Fraud
Revenue recognition on services	Services are prepaid and performed in full	Services prepaid and partially performed	Services are agreed to but not yet performed	Fraudulent scheme
Inventory	Lower of cost and net realisable value is consistently applied	Slow to write down slow-moving inventory	Obsolete inventory is still recorded as an asset	Overstate inventory where non-existent inventory is recognised
Accounts receivable	Conservative credit terms and bad debts allowances used	Liberal credit terms and bad debts provision estimates	Liberal use of credit policies to expand sales; understate bad debts provisions or reduce bad debts by ignoring likely defaults	Fictitious receivables established to support non-existent sales or services
Depreciation	Conservative useful life and residual value computed	Liberal useful life and residual value computed	Restate useful life and residual value upward	Change useful life and residual value estimates to meet earnings targets
Advertising, marketing	Expensed as incurred	Expensed based on a formula; perhaps sales-based	Marketing costs are capitalised	Costs are capitalised and manipulated to meet earnings targets

Source: Adapted from Giroux.[14]

LO 3 METHODS OF EARNINGS MANAGEMENT

There are a range of techniques that commonly fall within the category of earnings management. The most widely used, which will be discussed in this section, include: accounting policy choice, the use of accruals, income smoothing, real activity management, and an extreme example of loss recognition known as taking a 'big bath'.

Accounting policy choice

Choosing between the available acceptable accounting policies is one of the most commonly used forms of earnings management. Accounting choices are made within the framework of applicable accounting standards. This decision could relate to a choice between straight-line and accelerated depreciation, FIFO or weighted average for inventory valuation, or deciding to be a voluntary early adopter of a new accounting standard. Earnings management can occur when management have flexibility in making accounting choices in line with accounting standard requirements. These choices will lead to different timing and amounts of expense recognition and asset valuation. It is difficult to determine if these choices are made because they reflect the economic nature of the underlying transactions, or if management is seeking to delay expense recognition to a later date.

Entities may even choose to change accounting method in some circumstances. It is generally thought that once an entity chooses an accounting method it needs to maintain this. However, this is not necessarily the case. Provided the entity can put a case forward to the auditors that the new principle or practice is preferable, it is free to change this policy. A change in accounting method could relate to a change in accounting principle (e.g. straight-line or reducing balance depreciation) or a change in accounting estimate (e.g. extending the useful life of a non-current asset or changing the estimated salvage value). The auditors will require the entity, if the result is a material change, to justify this decision.

Accrual accounting

Rather than reporting erratic changes in revenue and earnings year on year, managers prefer to generate consistent revenues and earnings growth. Shareholders prefer to invest in an entity that exhibits consistent growth patterns, not one that has uncertain and changing earnings patterns. For this reason, managers will have incentives to use **accrual accounting** techniques to manage earnings over time. The IASB discusses the importance of using accrual accounting to users:

> Accrual accounting attempts to reflect the effects of transactions and other events and circumstances that have cash (or other) consequences for an entity's resources and the claims to them in the periods in which they occur or arise. The buying, producing, selling, and other operations of an entity during a period, as well as other events that affect its economic resources and the claims to them, often do not coincide with the cash receipts and payments of the period. The accrual accounting information in financial reports about an entity's resources and claims and changes in resources and claims generally provides a better basis for assessing cash flow prospects than information solely about the entity's current cash receipts and payments. Without accrual accounting, important economic resources and claims on resources would be excluded from financial statements.[15]

Accrual accounting techniques generally have no direct cash flow consequences and can include: under-provisioning for bad debts expenses, delaying asset impairments, adjusting inventory valuations, and amending depreciation and amortisation estimates and adjustments.

Research attempts to measure accruals management by identifying 'unexpected' accounting accruals reflected in earnings, where unexpected accruals are used as a proxy for exercising discretion to manage earnings. One of the most commonly used methods to determine earnings management was developed by DeAngelo and involves comparing the accruals component of earnings in one year to accruals the previous year as an estimate of 'normal' accruals. The DeAngelo model is presented below:

$$AC_t = NPAT_t - CFO_t$$

where:

AC_t = the accruals component of earnings in year t;

$NPAT_t$ = net operating profit after interest and tax in year t;

CFO_t = cash flows from operations in year t.[16]

To calculate earnings management through accruals accounting, unexpected or discretionary accruals are calculated as the difference between the change in net operating profit after interest and tax and the change in cash flow from operations from year $t-1$ (the previous year) to year t (the current year).[17] This is reflected in the following model:

$$\Delta AC_t = AC_t - AC_{t-1}$$

Income smoothing

A definition of **income smoothing** has been provided by Copeland.[18] 'Smoothing moderates year-to-year fluctuations in income by shifting earnings from peak years to less successful periods'. The practice can relate to a wide range of accrual accounting practices including: early recognition of sales revenues, variations to bad debts or warranty provisions, or delaying asset impairments. Research has found that some entities will undertake hedging with financial instruments to encourage income smoothing.[19] Anandarajan, Hasan and McCarthy found that Australian banks used loan loss provisions to manage earnings, with their use being more pronounced in listed commercial banks and in the post-Basal period.[20]

Real activities management

Management can also manage earnings by managing operational decisions, not just accounting policies or accruals. This is referred to as **real activities management**.[21] Some examples observed in the research literature include: accelerating sales, offering price discounts, reducing discretionary expenditures, altering shipment schedules, and delaying research and development and maintenance expenditures.[22] Graham et al., in a survey of US managers, finds:

> strong evidence that managers take real economic actions to maintain accounting appearances. In particular, 80% of survey participants report that they would decrease discretionary spending on R&D, advertising, and maintenance to meet an earnings target. More than half (55.3%) state that they would delay starting a new project to meet an earnings target, even if such a delay entailed a small sacrifice in value...[23]

Real activities management can have an effect on cash flows and in some cases accruals. One negative outcome of real activities management could be a reduction in entity value because actions taken in the current accounting period to increase earnings can have a negative effect on cash flows in later periods.[24] As an example, aggressive price discounting to increase volume of sales to maximise short-term earnings can lead customers to expect the same discounts in the future, which will lead to lower margins on future sales.[25] Real activities management is less likely to draw the attention of auditors than accruals management as auditors are not likely to question actual pricing and production decisions.

Big bath write-offs

There will occasionally be situations when management are required to significantly restructure the organisation, which might mean selling off subsidiaries or operational units. This will result in a large loss reported against income — normally referred to as a **big bath write-off**. As McKee notes, charging such a large loss is likely to have a negative impact on share price as it indicates bad news about the company.[26] However, if the loss is accompanied by information indicating a major restructure and operational changes that are going to lead to a positive outcome for the company in the long-term, the share price is likely to only decline in the short term. **Big bath accounting** is often used when there is a change in the management team, with the need to write-off assets or operational units being blamed on the outgoing managers' poor management of resources. This will lead to future reductions in expenses and benefits the new management team by presenting a reduced base upon which future valuations and comparisons of the management team's performance can be assessed. Common circumstances when a big bath is taken can include: restructuring of operations; troubled debt restructuring; asset impairment and write-down; disposal of operations.[27]

LO 4 WHY DO ENTITIES MANAGE EARNINGS?

Instead of being viewed as negative, earnings management can be beneficial to shareholders. Arya, Glover and Sunder state:

> That earnings management reduces transparency is a simplistic idea. A fundamental feature of decentralized organizations is the dispersal of information across people. Different people know different things and nobody knows everything. In such an environment, a managed earnings stream can convey more information than an unmanaged earnings stream. A smooth car ride is not only comfortable, but it also reassures the passenger about the driver's expertise.[28]

There are two main motivations for engaging in earnings management:
1. Earnings are managed for the benefit of the entity for a number of reasons including: to meet analysts' and shareholder expectations and predictions; to maximise share price and company valuation; to accurately convey private information; or to avoid violating restrictive debt covenants.
2. Earnings are managed to meet short-term goals which lead to maximising managerial remuneration and bonuses.

McKee points out that these two viewpoints are not necessarily in conflict and managers can be motivated by both objectives at the same time.[29] If the entity performs well financially, this is also likely to lead to managers maximising their own remuneration.

Managers may manage earnings to present some private information, or personal knowledge to shareholders about the entity's operations. For example, a different depreciation rate for computer technology could be used than what is normally accepted in the industry because the entity is signalling that anticipated technological advances will make equipment obsolete sooner than has been the industry norm.[30] Managers are also likely to use earnings management as a way of conveying their own expectations of future cash flows. It is costly for managers to mislead the market, so they are likely to use accounting methods that are efficient — that is, that reflect the actual transactions of the entity.

Breaching debt covenants can be very costly for an entity. It can lead to the need to refinance debt, normally at a higher interest rate, placing the entity under closer scrutiny of lenders and, at the extreme, to the requirement to repay debt in full immediately. This means that entities which are close to breaching debt constraints are likely to engage in earnings management to ensure they maintain accounting measures below targets. This has been referred to as the debt hypothesis in agency theory and is covered in more detail in chapter 5.[31]

Many examples are reported in the financial press of companies not meeting analysts' forecasts of earnings. Realised earnings that are below forecasts can lead to investors reacting to this negative signal, resulting in significant declines in share prices — even where there is a small gap.[32] Because of this, managers are likely to manage earnings to ensure they do not fall below forecasts. A survey of managers finds that meeting analyst expectations is a fundamental earnings target.[33] Athanasakou et al. find that large entities will change the classification of small core expenses to appear as non-recurring items so that they meet analysts' expectations with core earnings.[34]

Management of earnings to enhance entity value and to meet analysts' expectations is linked to the concepts of entity valuation and earnings quality. These will be addressed in the next two sections. This will then be followed by a discussion of managerial remuneration motives to manage earnings.

Entity valuation

To understand why managers might manage earnings to maximise share price it is important to consider how a company is valued. There are a number of different methods commonly used to determine the value of a company. They generally rely on determining current value by forecasting the future value of one of the following measures:

- book value of the company (reflected in the balance sheet)
- operating cash flow
- net income.[35]

Research by Dechow indicates that share prices are more highly aligned with net income than operating cash flows.[36] As such, net income, or earnings, is commonly used to determine entity value. An entity's value is effectively the present value of future income discounted at a risk–adjusted discount rate, which is usually the cost of capital. In doing so, analysts generally forecast earnings for a five-year period.[37] Because determining entity value relies on some measure of risk, entities with more volatile patterns of earnings are likely to have a higher risk measure and therefore are likely to have a lower entity value. Earnings volatility could be an indication of an increased chance of insolvency.

As a result of this, managers are more likely to engage in income smoothing to reduce volatility and therefore risk of investment. This is anticipated to send a stronger message to shareholders and lead to an increase in entity value.

Earnings quality

Quality of earnings can also affect a company's share price. The last section shows that current earnings are commonly used to forecast future earnings. Earnings quality relates to how closely current earnings are aligned with future earnings. Current earnings which are highly correlated to future earnings are said to have high earnings quality and lead to a more accurate future earnings forecast. On the other hand, if current earnings have a low correlation with future earnings, low earnings quality is said to be present.

Contemporary Issue 9.1 considers earnings quality from a practical investment perspective.

Considering earnings quality in investment decisions

When considering the purchase of a company's stock, it's important to not just look at how much they earn, but also how they earn. We do this by looking at a company's 'quality of earnings'.

The better the quality of earnings, the more consistently the company should be able to deliver solid results.

A company's total profit after tax can often by misleading. This year's record profit could cause you to overlook the past three years of losses.

Alternatively, that record profit could be inflated due to the sale of property or thanks to a quirk of tax accounting.

But even if the profit is growing year to year in line with its normal business, concerns could be raised because the company has only one customer.

All of these factors are just as important to understand as the company's end profit. Quality of earnings is usually analysed through three criteria:

1. Trend in profit results. How consistent is the company's profits? Do profits vary wildly from year to year? Or has the company consistently grown profits over a significant time-frame? A company that has an established track record of growing profits should, all things being equal, present a more attractive opportunity than a company with volatile earnings. This information should be easily sourced from the company's website or in their annual reports.

2. Operating/non-operating mix. What part of the business generated profits? Were profits produced by the company's operating business or did abnormal items prop up earnings? Companies will disclose this information in their statement of financial position (in their annual report) and operating revenue will usually be called 'ordinary activities'.

3. Earnings base. Where does the company source its revenues from? More attractive companies should have a spread of earnings through different geographic regions and markets. For example, a resources company with only one mine should be seen as an investment with inherently greater risk than a miner with operations spread across several mines.

Many companies will detail this mix in their annual report under segment reporting. (Of course, companies can fall into disfavour because they have too much of a spread and are unable to harness scale or synergies, so a balance needs to be struck.)

An analysis of these three factors, and if the company performs well against each benchmark, should mean your purchase has less downside risk.

And, as you know, protecting the downside is just as important as benefiting from the upside.

Source: 'Earnings quality', *Herald Sun*.[38]

Questions

1. Explain the three criteria usually considered important in assessing earnings quality. **K**
2. Outline two advantages to a company from having high quality earnings. **J**
3. Given the information you have already addressed in this chapter, what are some methods companies could use to ensure they present consistent profits? **J**

The above article reflects earnings quality from an accounting perspective. Earnings quality as a concept is difficult to observe and measure. Research has not determined a consensus view on what characterises 'high quality' earnings.[39] This is, in part, due to the fact that different parties are looking for different outcomes from accounting earnings. For example, standard setters might be interested in how objective entities have been in applying accounting regulations, while analysts and shareholders might be more interested in earnings as a good predictor of future earnings or cash flows.

Much of the research in earnings quality has focused on the role of accruals in financial reporting.[40] Current earnings have been found to be a better predictor of future cash flows than current period cash flows.[41] Dechow found that earnings explain a larger proportion of share returns than do cash flows.[42] Given the difference between earnings and cash flows are accounting accruals, the greater explanatory power of earnings can therefore be attributed to accounting accruals. Ultimately, over the life of an asset or a business, cash flows will equal accruals; however, accruals are used in such a way as to smooth earnings over time and to predict future cash flows.

As we discussed previously, accounting accruals can be classified as either discretionary or non-discretionary. Non-discretionary accruals are the 'normal' part of earnings that result from applying accounting rules in a neutral way. Discretionary accruals are those that result from conservative or aggressive accounting policy choices. If entities have large levels of discretionary accruals, when compared to total accruals they are deemed to have low earnings quality.

Dechow and Dichev examine the quality of working capital accruals and earnings, and determine how they relate to operating cash flow realisations.[43] They argue that poor mapping between working capital accruals and operating cash flow realisation signals low quality of earnings. Dechow and Dichev also find that there is an inverse relationship between working capital accruals and various aspects of business such as the length of the operating cycle and the incidence of losses. Larger entities also tend to have higher quality accruals.[44]

Research which examines income smoothing and its relationship to earnings quality tends to have competing views on whether smoothed income indicates high earnings quality. One view is that smoothed income is a way of managers signalling they have used their discretion over the available accounting alternatives and have chosen those methods that minimise fluctuations to give a better reflection of future performance.[45] The other is that smoothed earnings in some way hide the true changes in underlying entity performance.[46] This research argues that managers use discretionary accruals to mask the true performance of the accounting period, which could lead to investors not being able to correctly assess the economic environment the entity is facing.[47] Both views have found support in the research literature.

While there are different measures of earnings management, as discussed previously, each are likely to have some impact on earnings quality — that is, they are likely to affect how useful current reported earnings are in predicting future earnings potential for a company.

Managerial compensation and change in CEO

Senior managers, including the chief executive officer (CEO) and the chief financial officer (CFO), play an integral role in generating and reporting earnings. While key decisions are approved by the board of directors, it is the management team that makes the key decisions about strategy, investments, budgets, operations and acquisitions. While managers are appointed to operate the business for the benefit of shareholders, their objectives do not necessarily always align. Agency theory is often used to understand the separation of ownership and control of corporations, which means that managers, as agents, are likely to act in their own interest, and these actions might not necessarily align with the principals' or owners' interests.

Agency theory literature identifies a number of problems that can exist between managers and owners in an agency relationship. These problems include: the horizon problem, risk aversion and dividend retention.[48] For more details of these problems, refer to the discussion in chapter 5. Rewarding managers for their contribution to the entity is an important part of ensuring strong entity performance. Managerial remuneration contracts are used to reduce the three agency problems mentioned above. Managerial compensation generally has a number of parts: (1) base salary; (2) cash bonus, which is usually based on some measure of earnings performance; (3) shares or share options, which are generally awarded or vested subject to certain performance hurdles; and (4) various perquisites such as travel or motor vehicle.

The remuneration package for senior managers, therefore relates payment of cash, shares and options to various performance measures, where performance could include a combination of share returns and earnings, as well as a number of non-financial performance targets. Some common performance measures that directly relate to earnings include, but are not restricted to:

- acounting returns
- sales revenue
- net interest income
- a balanced scorecard index of multiple indicators
- economic value added (EVA).[49]

Given the extent to which managerial pay relies on meeting entity performance targets, it is not surprising that research has found a link between earnings management and managerial pay. Healy was the first to investigate this relationship in the United States, and found that bonuses were paid when earnings reached a defined minimum level; however, there was a point at which no further bonuses were paid, despite earnings being significantly higher.[50] That is, there was a defined maximum and minimum level of earnings which led to a bonus payment. Healy observed that managers will manage earnings in such a way that they maximise their bonus.[51] If earnings are so low that they are unlikely to meet their targets, they are likely to engage in big bath write-offs to ensure they meet earnings targets the next year. Other authors have observed managers in this circumstance engaging in income smoothing techniques.[52] Richardson and Waegelein find that where entities adopt a long-term bonus plan in addition to a short-term plan, the long-term plan mitigates earnings management and leads to higher annual returns.[53]

Share-based compensation has increasingly been used in recent years and comes in a range of forms, including: share grants; restricted share grants where managers are restricted from selling their shares until a certain time elapses or the entity reaches specific performance goals; and share performance rights, which offer the right to receive shares when specific performance goals are reached.[54] Research examining equity-based compensation generally supports the existence of earnings management that is intended to inflate earnings.[55]

Research has found that earnings management is particularly evident around the time a CEO changes. This research has looked at two distinct issues: (1) whether the departing CEO used earnings management to mask poor performance, which can lead to a higher bonus upon leaving; and (2) whether the incoming CEO used earnings management in the form of a big bath write-off to blame poor performance on his or her predecessor and in turn increase earnings the following year.

US evidence generally finds that earnings management techniques can depend upon whether the CEO is aiming to take a seat on the board upon retirement. If this is the case, earnings are likely to be managed upwards.[56] Forced departure generally follows poor entity performance, which is likely to lead to upwards earnings management to reduce the appearance of this poor performance. In this case, Pourciau finds that entities record downwards earnings management in the year of departure, which she explains as a likely result of increased monitoring by the board where an entity has poor performance.[57]

Research has found that incoming CEOs are more likely to take an earnings bath in the first year and then the following year show large earnings increases.[58] Godfrey, Mather and Ramsay in a study of earnings and impression management surrounding Australian

CEO changes, find evidence that in the year of a CEO change, earnings are managed downwards, with upwards earnings management in the year after a CEO change. The authors note that the results were strongest where the CEO change was prompted by a resignation rather than a retirement.[59]

LO 5 CONSEQUENCES OF EARNINGS MANAGEMENT

The consequences of earnings management decisions will depend upon the nature and extent of earnings management that has taken place. A number of studies examine the entity value consequences of earnings management by examining share price reactions surrounding a significant event such as an initial public offering (IPO) or a management buyout. For example, Teoh, Wong and Rao find that companies will use accruals accounting to manage earnings upwards during an IPO. The authors notice poor share performance after the IPO and attribute this to the market temporarily overvaluing the entity, and then being disappointed by earnings declines, leading to share price reductions in the following year.[60] This has not been found in all cases. Brav, Geczy and Gompers found that investors undo the effects of the upwards earnings management and share price does not react negatively following earnings management associated with an IPO.[61]

Researchers have also examined the share price reaction to evidence of fraudulent reporting. Dechow, Sloan, and Sweeny; Palmrose, Richardson, and Scholz; and Beneish all find that the market reacts negatively to the disclosure that there has been fraudulent manipulation, implying that investors were surprised and interpret the information as negative news.[62]

Chapman, in an examination of real activities management by supermarkets, observed stock discounting in the last fiscal quarter. He also finds evidence that entities engage in persistent, longer-term price reduction to meet analysts' forecast targets. The author also notes that earnings management incentives at one entity are related to competitor price discounting.[63]

LO 6 CORPORATE GOVERNANCE AND EARNINGS MANAGEMENT

While the management team is responsible for the day-to-day operations of the organisation and for developing plans, strategies and investment decisions, the board of directors is responsible for approving these and ensuring they are in the long-term interests of shareholders. How the board functions is essential to the overall operation and future of the company, as well as the earnings management environment of the entity.[64]

The composition of the board, including the number of members, their expertise and independence are important in determining how likely it is that managers are able to manipulate or manage earnings. A board made up of internal rather than independent directors is less likely to question a CEO who may want to use aggressive earnings management strategies. Strong governance means a balance between corporate performance and an appropriate level of monitoring.[65] It is important that the board exhibits an optimal mix of monitoring and expertise, and is not just seen as providing a 'rubber stamp' to decisions of the CEO. If this is the case, it is more likely that inappropriate earnings management can result.

Research has found that there is likely to be greater levels of earnings management when the proportion of independent directors on the board is low.[66] Beasley also found that the presence of independent directors reduces the likelihood of fraudulent earnings management.[67]

Boards often delegate certain responsibilities to separate specialist committees. The audit committee plays an important role in ensuring financial reports are credible and controls the extent of earnings management. It is likely to play the main 'gatekeeper' role in limiting aggressive or fraudulent earnings management. An audit committee is mandated for the top 500 Australian companies, in accordance with the *Corporations Act 2001*. Similarly, the ASX Corporate Governance Council best practice guidelines recommend that all listed companies have an audit committee. Research has found that the effectiveness of an audit committee in constraining earnings management relates to the level of committee independence.[68] Similarly, a stronger audit committee is also associated with higher quality earnings.[69] Corporate governance is examined is detail in chapter 7.

Summary

Describe the importance of earnings in assessing the success of an organisation
- Earnings are sometimes called the 'bottom line' or 'net income'. As a measure of entity performance, they are of great importance to financial statement users and indicate the extent to which an entity has engaged in activities that add value to the entity.
- Earnings are used by shareholders to both assess managers' performance — a stewardship role — and to assist in predicting future cash flows and assessing risk.

Explain what earnings management is
- Earnings management occurs when managers use judgement in financial reporting and in structuring transactions to alter financial statements to either mislead some stakeholders about the underlying economic performance of the entity, or to influence the contractual outcomes that depend on reported accounting numbers.
- Earnings management encompasses the whole spectrum, from conservative accounting through to fraud.

Describe a number of common methods of earnings management, including accounting policy choice, accrual accounting, income smoothing, real activities management and big bath write-offs
- Accounting policy choice
  - Choosing between the available acceptable accounting policies is one of the most commonly used forms of earnings management.
- Accrual accounting
  - Accrual accounting techniques generally have no direct cash flow consequences, and can include: under-provisioning for bad debts expenses, delaying asset impairments, adjusting inventory valuations, amending depreciation and amortisation estimates and adjustments.
- Income smoothing
  - Rather than reporting erratic changes in revenue and earnings year on year, managers prefer to generate consistent revenues and earnings growth. Shareholders prefer to invest in an entity that exhibits consistent growth patterns, not one that has uncertain and changing earnings patterns. For this reason, managers will have incentives to use accrual accounting techniques to promote smooth earnings over time.
- Real activities management
  - Management can also manage earnings by managing operational decisions, not just accounting policies or accruals. This is referred to as real activities

management. Some examples observed in the research literature include: accelerating sales, offering price discounts, reducing discretionary expenditures, altering shipment schedules, and delaying research and development and maintenance expenditures.
- Big bath write-offs
  - Big bath accounting occurs when large losses are reported against income as a result of a significant restructure of operations.
  - Common circumstances when a 'big bath' is taken can include: restructuring of operations; troubled debt restructuring; asset impairment and write-down; and disposal of operations.

Explain why entities manage earnings
- Instead of being viewed as a negative thing, earnings management can be beneficial to shareholders.
- Management of earnings to enhance entity value and to meet analysts' expectations is linked to the concepts of entity valuation and earnings quality, or to maximise managerial compensation.
- Entity valuation
  - Determining entity value relies on some measure of risk. Therefore, companies with more volatile patterns of earnings are likely to have a higher risk measure, and therefore are likely to have a lower entity value. Earnings volatility could be an indication of an increased change of insolvency. As a result of this, managers are more likely to engage in income smoothing to reduce volatility, and therefore risk of investment.
- Earnings quality
  - Earnings quality relates to how closely current earnings are aligned with future earnings. While there are different measures of earnings management, each is likely to have some impact on earnings quality.
- Managerial compensation and change in CEO
  - Senior managers, including the chief executive officer (CEO) and the chief financial officer (CFO), play an integral role in generating and reporting earnings.
  - Given the extent to which managerial pay relies on meeting entity performance targets, research has found a link between earnings management and managerial pay.
  - Earnings management is particularly evident around the time a CEO changes.

Identify the consequences of earnings management
- In initial public offerings (IPOs) or a management buyout, earnings management may result in poor share performance as the market may temporarily overvalue the entity and then be disappointed by earnings declines.
- Evidence suggests the share market reacts negatively to the disclosure that there has been fraudulent manipulation of earnings.
- Real activities may be managed by some entities — for example, supermarkets may discount stock in the last fiscal quarter. Entities may also engage in persistent, longer-term price reduction to meet analysts' forecast targets.

Assess the role corporate governance plays in controlling earnings management
- How the board functions is essential to the overall operation and future of the company as well as the earnings management environment of the entity.
- The composition of the board, including the number of members, their expertise and independence, is important in determining how likely it is that managers are able to manipulate or manage earnings.
- There is likely to be greater earnings management when the proportion of independent directors on the board is low.

Review questions

1. Define what is meant by 'earnings' and outline why it is important to shareholders.
2. Explain what is meant by earnings management.
3. Is earnings management always bad? Explain your answer.
4. How can accounting policy choice be considered earnings management? Explain your answer.
5. What is income smoothing and how is it commonly used to manage earnings?
6. Why and in what circumstances would a management team consider engaging in big bath accounting?
7. Provide two reasons why entities might engage in earnings management.
8. How is earnings management related to entity valuation?
9. What is 'earnings quality' and how is it related to earnings management?
10. Explain why managers who receive a cash bonus as part of their remuneration might wish to manage earnings.
11. Why is corporate governance important for evaluating corporate earnings management?

Application questions

Table 9.1 presents examples of some common accounting decisions, and how companies following a conservative, moderate, aggressive or fraudulent strategy might use these to manage earnings. Prepare a similar table and complete it in relation to the following accounting decisions:
(a) revenue recognition from services
(b) intangible assets
(c) impairment of non-current assets
(d) revaluation of non-current assets. **J K**

Examine the 2010 annual report of Qantas Airways Ltd, available at www.qantas.com.au. Review the corporate governance statement and evaluate how successful you think the board structure is likely to be in limiting earnings management. In particular, consider the board size, independence, and committees in place. Prepare a report of your findings. **J K CT**

Outline the three methods discussed in this chapter that entities can use to manage earnings. Discuss the circumstances in which entities are likely to use each method. **K**

You have recently been appointed as a researcher for a firm of share analysts. As one of your first roles you are required to prepare a report for your manager to outline common techniques used to manage or manipulate earnings. From your prior accounting knowledge you would have gained an understanding of techniques you can use to examine entity performance and profitability, including trend analysis. Document what strategies you might use as an analyst to detect earnings management using accounting information. **J K CT**

Obtain the remuneration report for a publicly listed company. Examine the compensation contract for the CEO. Document the range of remuneration components used in the CEO pay arrangements and what performance targets are used to determine both cash and equity payments. What earnings management techniques would the management team be likely to use in these circumstances to maximise their short-term and long-term remuneration? Explain your answer. **J K**

The ethics of earnings management

By James Gaa and Paul Dunmore

The directors of almost any organisation, whether business, government, or non-profit, must manage the organisation's external disclosures.

A common method of managing disclosures is to manage earnings. Because New Zealand applies substantially the same accounting standards to public and private organisations, public sector bodies can manage earnings in much the same way as businesses do.

The ethical status of earnings management is controversial. Whether acts of earnings management are ethically justifiable depends essentially on management's intention either to be truthful or to mislead readers of the statements. This article looks at the ethics of income smoothing, which is one form of earnings management . . . The financial reports of the New Zealand Symphony Orchestra Ltd (NZSO) during the late 1990s provide a useful example of income smoothing. Based on the publicly available information contained in its financial statements, we can conclude that the income smoothing conducted by the NZSO in the late 1990s is informative and not misleading, and therefore is ethically justifiable. Through this example, we can see that income smoothing, which is a specific type of earnings management, is at least some times ethically justifiable.

The NZSO's smoothed income

Organisations which depend on sponsorship and donations need to pay particular attention to their financial performance. If the organisation makes a loss, doubts about its management and viability may make contributors wary of committing further funds. But a big surplus is equally risky, because it shows that the management has not used all the resources available to it. Contributors may then decide that some of their money is no longer needed, and may direct their funds elsewhere. For most such organisations, then, the ideal result is a surplus which is so small as to be immaterial.

The NZSO shows how this works. It has three major streams of revenue: concert sales, sponsorship and government funding. For the year ended 30 June 1998, these revenues were about $2.7, $1.4 and $8.9 million respectively. Like many other similar organisations, the NZSO's expenses are largely fixed, even before the start of the season. The concert programmes, the required orchestral forces, conductors and soloists and the associated costs are all set in advance. The main uncertainties about the success of a season concern the subscription and door sales revenue from its concerts.

The financial year starts half-way through the concert season. By that time, the result for the first half of the financial year is nearly unalterable, and that for the second half depends largely on the attractiveness of the next season to subscribers and sponsors.

For this reason, the NZSO has little opportunity to manage earnings, either by making discretionary accruals or by structuring real transactions in the short term. However, in the medium term, an unexpected cash surplus in one year (perhaps from a particularly successful concert) can be used up by providing extra services in later years, thus incurring an offsetting deficit. Not-for-profit organisations are expected not to amass large surpluses, except to be used in future operations. By smoothing out reported short-term surpluses and deficits, management may show that it has credible ways of using its resources in full, to break even over the medium term. As we suggested above, allowing a large surplus to be reported without smoothing may put the organisation's future revenue at risk.

Source: Excerpts from James Gaa & Paul Dunmore, 'The ethics of earnings management', Chartered Accountants Journal.[70]

Questions

1. Why would the NZSO wish to smooth income? **J** **K**
2. Were the earnings management techniques the NZSO used ethical? Explain your answer. **J** **K**
3. What factors would you consider when determining whether such a decision was ethical? **J** **K**

Mastering corporate governance: when earnings management becomes cooking the books

By Ira Millstein

The line between legitimate and inappropriate accounting techniques can be a blurry one, but the audit committee must endeavour to make a clear distinction.

The polestar of the audit committee is shifting — rather than focus exclusively on mechanics, structures and controls (which are necessary but not sufficient), it is turning towards the overriding policy issue, namely whether or not financial disclosure presents a 'true and fair' view of the company's state of affairs. Faced with intense pressure to meet earnings estimates from analysts and investors, executives at many companies use a variety of 'earnings management' techniques to help them 'make the numbers'. These techniques will frequently exploit loopholes in generally accepted accounting principles (GAAP) to manipulate deliberately the company's revenues.

'Earnings management' includes both legitimate and less than legitimate efforts to smooth earnings over accounting periods or to achieve a forecasted result. It is the responsibility of the audit committee members to identify, by appropriate questioning and their good faith judgment, whether particular earnings management techniques, accounting estimates and other discretionary judgments are legitimate or operate to obscure the true financial position of the company . . .

Source: Excerpts from Ira Millstein, 'When earnings management becomes cooking the books', *The Financial Times.*[71]

Questions

1. What earnings management techniques are outlined in the above article? **J** **K**
2. What role can the audit committee play in detecting and/or limiting earnings management? **J** **K**
3. What relationship does the audit committee have with the external auditors in ensuring earnings management is within acceptable limits? **J** **K**

Additional readings

Dechow, P 1994, 'Accounting earnings and cash flows as measures of firm performance: the role of accounting accruals', *Journal of Accounting and Economics*, vol. 18, no. 1, pp. 3–42.

Dechow, PR & Dichev, I 2002, 'The quality of accruals and earnings: the role of accruals estimation error', *The Accounting Review*, vol. 77, supplement, pp. 35–59.

Dunmore, P 2008, 'Earnings management: good, bad or downright ugly?', *Chartered Accountants Journal*, vol. 87, no. 3, pp. 32–7.

Godfrey, J, Mather, P & Ramsay, A 2003, 'Earnings and impression management in financial reports: The case of CEO changes', *Abacus*, vol. 39, no. 1, pp. 95–123.

Godfrey, JM & Jones, KL 1999, 'Political cost influences on income smoothing via extraordinary item classification', *Accounting and Finance*, vol. 39, no. 3, pp. 229–54.

Sloan, R 1996, 'Do stock prices fully reflect information in accruals and cash flows about future earnings?' *The Accounting Review*, vol. 71, no. 3, pp. 289–315.

End notes

1. Goncharov, I 2005, *Earnings management and its determinants: closing gaps in empirical accounting research*, Frankfurt, Germany: Peter Lang.

2. Giroux, G 2004, *Detecting earnings management*, Hoboken, N.J.: John Wiley and Sons Inc.

3. McKee, TE 2005, *Earnings management: an executive perspective*, Mason, O.H.: Texere, Thomson Higher Education.

4. Lev, B 1989, 'On the usefulness of earnings and earnings research: lessons and directions from two decades of empirical research', *Journal of Accounting Research*, vol. 27, supplement, pp. 153–201.

5. Ronen, J & Yaari, V 2008, *Earnings management: emerging insights in theory, practice, and research*, New York, N.Y.: Springer.

6. Francis, J, Schipper, K & Vincent, L 2003, 'The relative and incremental explanatory power of earnings and alternative (to earnings) performance measures for returns', *Contemporary Accounting Research*, vol. 20, no. 1, pp. 121–64.

7. Goncharov, I 2005, *Earnings management and its determinants: closing gaps in empirical accounting research*, Frankfurt, Germany: Peter Lang.

8. Schipper, K 1989, 'Commentary on earnings management', *Accounting Horizons*, vol. 3, iss. 5/6, pp. 91–102.

9. Healy, PM & Wahlen, JM 1999, 'A review of the earnings management literature and its implications for standard setting', *Accounting Horizons*, vol. 13, pp. 365–83.

10. McKee, TE 2005, *Earnings management: an executive perspective*, Mason, O.H.: Texere, Thomson Higher Education, p. 1.

11. Ronen, J & Yaari, V 2008, *Earnings management: emerging insights in theory, practice, and research*, New York, N.Y.: Springer.

12. ibid.

13. Giroux, G 2004, *Detecting earnings management*, Hoboken, N.J.: John Wiley and Sons Inc., p. 2.

14. ibid., p. 3.

15. International Accounting Standards Board (IASB) 2006, *Discussion Paper — Preliminary views on an improved conceptual framework for financial reporting: The objective of financial reporting and qualitative characteristics of decision-useful financial reporting information*, London, UK: IASB.

16. DeAngelo, LE 1986, 'Accounting numbers as market valuation substitutes: a study of management buyouts', *The Accounting Review*, vol. 61, no. 3, pp. 400–20.

17. Godfrey, J, Mather, P & Ramsay, A 2003, 'Earnings and impression management in financial reports: the case of CEO changes', *Abacus*, vol. 39, no. 1, pp. 95–123.

18. Copeland, R 1968, 'Income smoothing', *Journal of Accounting Research*, vol. 6 (supplement), pp. 101–16.

19. Pincus, M & Rajgopal, S 2002, 'The interaction between accrual management and hedging: evidence from oil and gas firms', *The Accounting Review*, vol. 77, no. 1, pp. 127–60.

20. Anandarajan, A, Hasan, I & McCarthy, C 2007, 'Use of loan loss provisions for capital, earnings management and signalling by Australian banks', *Accounting and Finance*, vol. 47, iss. 3, pp. 357–79.

21. Roychowdhury, S 2006, 'Earnings management through real activities manipulation', *Journal of Accounting and Economics*, vol. 42, iss. 3, pp. 335–70.

22. Healy, PM & Wahlen, JM 1999, 'A review of the earnings management literature and its implications for standard setting', *Accounting Horizons*, vol. 13, iss. 4, pp. 365–83; Fudenberg, D & Tirole, J 1995, 'A theory of income and dividend smoothing based on incumbency rents', *Journal of Political Economy*, vol. 103, no. 1, pp. 75–93; Dechow, PM & Skinner, DJ 2000, 'Earnings management: reconciling the views of accounting academics, practitioners and regulators', *Accounting Horizons*, vol. 14, no. 2, pp. 235–50; Roychowdhury, S 2006, 'Earnings management through real activities manipulation', *Journal of Accounting and Economics*, vol. 42, iss. 3, pp. 335–70.

23. Graham, JR, Harvey, CR & Rajgopal, S 2005, 'The economic implications of corporate financial reporting', *Journal of Accounting and Economics*, vol. 40, nos. 1–3, pp. 3–73.

24. Roychowdhury, S 2006, 'Earnings management through real activities manipulation', *Journal of Accounting and Economics*, vol. 42, iss. 3, pp. 335–70.

25. ibid.

26. McKee, TE 2005, *Earnings management: an executive perspective*, Mason, O.H.: Texere, Thomson Higher Education.

27. ibid.

28. Arya, A, Glover, JC & Sunder, S 2003, 'Are unmanaged earnings always better for shareholders?' *Accounting Horizons*, vol. 17, supplement, pp. 111–16.

29. McKee, TE 2005, *Earnings management: an executive perspective*, Mason, O.H.: Texere, Thomson Higher Education.

30. ibid.

31. Watts, RL & Zimmerman, JL 1986, *Positive accounting theory*, Englewood Cliffs, NJ: Prentice Hall.

32. Skinner, D & Sloan, R 2002, 'Earnings surprises, growth expectations, and stock returns or don't let an earnings torpedo sink your portfolio', *Review of Accounting Studies*, vol. 7, iss. 2, pp. 289–312; Burgstahler, D & Eames, M 2006, 'Management of earnings and analysts' forecasts to achieve zero and small positive earnings surprises', *Journal of Business Finance and Accounting*, vol. 33, no. 5/6, pp. 633–52.

33. Graham, JR, Harvey, CR & Rajgopal, S 2005, 'The economic implications of corporate financial reporting', *Journal of Accounting and Economics*, vol. 40, nos. 1–3, pp. 3–73.

34. Athanasakou, VE, Strong, NC & Walker, M 2009, 'Earnings management or forecast guidance to meet analyst expectations?', *Accounting and Business Research*, vol. 39, no. 1, pp. 3–35.

35. McKee, TE 2005, *Earnings management: an executive perspective*, Mason, O.H.: Texere, Thomson Higher Education.

36. Dechow, P 1994, 'Accounting earnings and cash flows as measures of firm performance: the role of accounting accruals', *Journal of Accounting and Economics*, vol. 18, no. 1, pp. 3–42.

37. McKee, TE 2005, *Earnings management: an executive perspective*, Mason, O.H.: Texere, Thomson Higher Education.

38. Anonymous 2007, 'Earnings quality', *Herald Sun*, 6 October, p. 90.

39. Goncharov, I 2005, *Earnings management and its determinants: closing gaps in empirical accounting research*, Frankfurt, Germany: Peter Lang.

40. Bowen, RM, Burgstahler, D & Daley, LA 1997, 'The incremental information content of accrual versus cash flows', *The Accounting Review*, vol. 62, no. 4, pp. 723–47; Dechow, P

1994, 'Accounting earnings and cash flows as measures of firm performance: the role of accounting accruals', *Journal of Accounting and Economics*, vol. 18, no. 1, pp. 3–42.

41. Dechow, P, Kothari, SP & Watts, RL 1998, 'The relation between earnings and cash flows', *Journal of Accounting and Economics*, vol. 25, no. 2, pp. 133–68.

42. Dechow, P 1994, 'Accounting earnings and cash flows as measures of firm performance: the role of accounting accruals', *Journal of Accounting and Economics*, vol. 18, no. 1, pp. 3–42.

43. Dechow, PR & Dichev, I 2002, 'The quality of accruals and earnings: The roe of accruals estimation error', *The Accounting Review*, vol. 77, supplement, pp. 35–59.

44. ibid.

45. Givoly, D & Ronen, J 1981, '"Smoothing" manifestations in fourth quarter results of operations: some empirical evidence', *Abacus*, vol. 17, iss. 2, pp. 174–93.

46. Bhattacharya, U, Daouk, H & Welker, M 2003, 'The world price of earnings opacity', *The Accounting Review*, vol. 78, no. 3, pp. 641–78.

47. Schipper, K & Vincent, L 2003, 'Earnings quality', *Accounting Horizons*, vol. 17, supplement, pp. 97–110.

48. Smith, CW & Watts, RL 1982, 'Incentive and tax effects of executive compensation plans', *Australian Journal of Management*, vol. 7, no. 2, pp. 139–57.

49. Ronen, J & Yaari, V 2008, *Earnings management: emerging insights in theory, practice, and research*, New York, N.Y.: Springer.

50. Healy, P 1985, 'The effect of bonus schemes on accounting decisions', *Journal of Accounting and Economics*, vol. 7, no. 1–3, pp. 85–107.

51. ibid.

52. Holthausen, RW, Larcker, DF & Sloan, RG 1995, 'Annual bonus schemes and the manipulation of earnings', *Journal of Accounting and Economics*, vol. 19, no. 1, pp. 29–74.

53. Richardson, VJ & Waegelein, JF 2002, 'The influence of long-term performance plans on earnings management and firm performance',

Review of Quantitative Finance and Accounting, vol. 18, no. 2, pp. 161–83.

54. Bushman, RM & Smith, AJ 2001 'Financial accounting information and corporate governance', *Journal of Accounting and Economics*, vol. 32, no. 1–3, pp. 237–333; Murphy, KJ 1999, 'Executive compensation', *Handbook of Labor Economics*, vol. 3, Ashenfelter, O & Card, D eds, Amsterdam: North Holland, pp. 2485–563; Rankin, M 2010, 'Structure and level of remuneration across the top executive team', *Australian Accounting Review*, vol. 20, no. 3, pp. 241–55.

55. Ronen, J & Yaari, V 2008, *Earnings Management: emerging insights in theory, practice, and research*, New York, N.Y.: Springer.

56. Reitenga, AL & Tearney, MG 2003 'Mandatory CEO retirements, discretionary accruals, and corporate governance mechanisms', *Journal of Accounting, Auditing and Finance*, vol. 18, no. 2, pp. 255–80.

57. Pourciau, S 1993, 'Earnings management and nonroutine executive changes', *Journal of Accounting and Economics*, vol. 16, no. 1–3, pp. 317–36.

58. ibid; Strong, J & Meyer, J 1987, 'Asset writedowns: managerial incentives and security returns', *Journal of Finance*, vol. 42, no. 3, pp. 643–62.

59. Godfrey, J, Mather, P & Ramsay, A 2003, 'Earnings and impression management in financial reports: the case of CEO changes', *Abacus*, vol. 39, no. 1, pp. 95–123.

60. Teoh, SH, Wong, TJ & Rao, G 1998, 'Are Accruals During Initial Public Offerings Opportunistic?', *Review of Accounting Studies*, vol. 3, nos. 1–2, pp. 175–208.

61. Brav, A, Geczy, C & Gompers, P 2000, 'Is the abnormal return following equity issuances anomalous?', *Journal of Financial Economics*, vol. 56, iss. 2, pp. 209–49.

62. Dechow, PM, Sloan, RG & Sweeney, AP 1996, 'Causes and consequences of earnings manipulation: an analysis of firms subject to actions by the SEC', *Contemporary Accounting Research*, vol. 13, iss. 1, pp. 1–36; Palmrose, Z, Richardson, V & Scholz, S 2004, 'Determinants of

Market Reactions to Restatement Announcements', *Journal of Accounting and Economics*, vol. 37, no. 1, pp. 59–89; Beneish, M 1997, 'Detecting GAAP violation: implications for assessing earnings management among firms with extreme financial performance', *Journal of Accounting and Public Policy*, vol. 16, iss. 3, pp. 271–309.

63. Chapman, CJ 2008, 'The effects of real earnings management on the firm, its competitors and subsequent reporting periods' unpublished working paper, Harvard Business School, www.kellogg.northwestern.edu/accounting/papers/chapman.pdf.

64. Giroux, G 2004, *Detecting earnings management*, Hoboken, N.J.: John Wiley and Sons Inc.

65. Cadbury, A 1997, *Board focus: the governance debate*, London, UK: Egon Zehnder International.

66. Peasnell, KV, Pope, PF & Young, S 2005, 'Board monitoring and earnings management: do outside directors influence abnormal accruals?', *Journal of Business Finance and Accounting*, vol. 32, no. 7–8, pp. 1311–46; Davidson, R, Goodwin-Stewart, J & Kent, P 2005, 'Internal governance structures and earnings management', *Accounting and Finance*, vol. 45, no. 2, pp. 241–67.

67. Beasley, MS 1996, 'The relationship between board characteristics and voluntary improvements in audit committee compensation and experience', *Contemporary Accounting Research*, vol. 18, pp. 539–70.

68. Davidson, R, Goodwin-Stewart, J & Kent, P 2005, 'Internal governance structures and earnings management', *Accounting and Finance*, vol. 45, no. 2, pp. 241–67.

69. Ronen, J & Yaari, V 2008, *Earnings management: emerging insights in theory, practice, and research*, New York, N.Y.: Springer.

70. Gaa, J & Dunmore, P 2007, 'The ethics of earnings management', *Chartered Accountants Journal*, vol. 86, no. 8, pp. 60–2.

71. Millstein, I 2005, 'When earnings management becomes cooking the books', *The Financial Times*, 27 May, p. 4.

10 Fair value accounting

After studying this chapter, you should be able to:

1 discuss the role of fair value in accounting

2 evaluate the traditional definition of fair value

3 describe the key aspects of the new definition of fair value

4 explain how fair value should be determined for assets and liabilities

5 describe the three valuation techniques and the importance of the input hierarchy

6 apply the general disclosure requirements for items measured at fair value

7 discuss some specific issues that arise from the fair value standard.

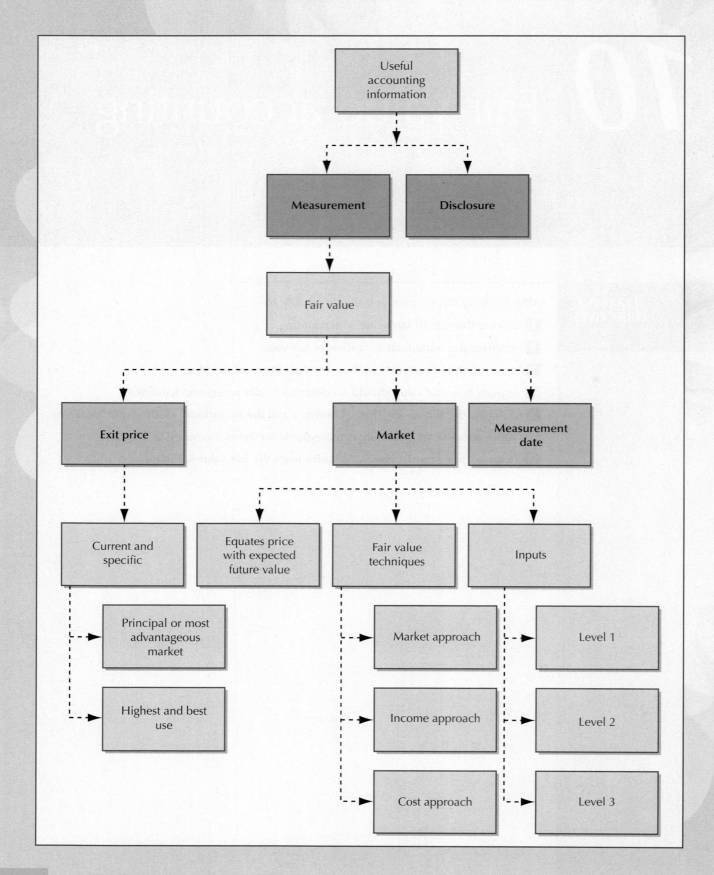

There has been a steady shift in accounting standards over the past few years, moving away from historical cost measures towards fair value. Proponents view this as a way to deal with traditional criticisms of accounting valuation (sometimes referred to as the apples and oranges problem) while making information more relevant to users. Opponents are concerned that the information contained in financial statements will lose its reliability and that the opportunities to overstate the balance sheet and income statement will prove too tempting for today's managers.

This chapter will discuss the fair value standard. The fair value standard may be regarded as a derivative standard as it considers the issue of fair value referenced across a number of other standards instead of considering a new or specific area of accounting. While the International Accounting Standards Board (IASB) described this standard as 'evolutionary not revolutionary' it certainly has the potential to significantly impact on the practice of accounting in a range of areas. It introduces a rigorous and consistent approach to the determination of fair values and requires potentially significant additional disclosure as described later in the chapter.

 ## LO 1 THE ROLE OF FAIR VALUE IN ACCOUNTING

The concept of fair value in accounting is ubiquitous, appearing in many standards as the preferred alternative to modified historical cost. It is seen to provide more useful information that is relevant to decision makers. A search of the accounting standards will easily turn up more than 2000 references to the term 'fair value' in more than 35 standards and interpretations. A similar search for the word 'cost' has only around 1300 matches.

Some of the key standards including fair value are:
- AASB 3/ IFRS 3 *Business Combinations*
- AASB 7/IFRS 7 *Financial Instruments: Disclosures*
- AASB 102/IAS 2 *Inventories*
- AASB 116/IAS 16 *Property, Plant and Equipment*
- AASB 118/IAS 18 *Revenue*
- AASB 119/IAS 19 *Employee Benefits*
- IAS 26 *Accounting and Reporting by Retirement Benefit Plans*
- AASB 133/IAS 33 *Earnings per Share*
- AASB 134/IAS 34 *Interim Financial Reporting*
- AASB 136/IAS 36 *Impairment of Assets*
- AASB 138/IAS 38 *Intangible Assets*
- AASB 139/IAS 39 *Financial Instruments: Recognition and Measurement*
- AASB 140/IAS 40 *Investment Property*
- AASB 141/IAS 41 *Agriculture*

Despite its prevalence in the accounting standards fair value is a nuanced concept in practice, which can be difficult to operationalise and interpret, potentially leaving open the door for organisations to manipulate financial statements with the use of inappropriate valuation to achieve financial or political ends. The matter is also complicated by the fact that in the process of standard creation it is a term that has been, in some cases, given slightly different definitions in different standards or indeed no definition at all. This inconsistency in guidance has made financial reporting unnecessarily mystifying; an already difficult concept has become, at times, even more confusing.

In order to address these concerns, the IASB released IFRS 13 *Fair Value Measurement* to draw together the disparate definitions and explanations of fair value into a single standard which is to be applied across all relevant accounting standards. This standard has an effective date of 1 January 2013, with early adoption permitted. The Australian Accounting Standards Board has released an Australian equivalent of this standard as AASB 13 *Fair Value Measurement*.

The usefulness of fair value as an economic measure and its relationship to the fundamental assumptions

The point of using fair value measures is to allow accounting to provide information that is both useful and relevant. Traditionally accounting has mostly used a valuation concept known as modified historical cost as the key measurement foundation. As will be discussed later, under normal circumstances at transaction date, when an asset is acquired or a liability incurred, cost is seen as an appropriate valuation that is equivalent to the item's fair value. Issues arise, however, as time passes and we attempt to keep accounting information relevant. How is the 'true' value of an asset or liability to be measured? Traditionally accounting has sought to 'adjust' this cost to reflect changes in expectations about the item's use and/or the value of money and/or its condition. Approaches based on depreciation/amortisation have generally been used for non-current assets. Time value of money is often considered for liabilities. For inventory, the lower of cost and market rule is used. These are seen as attempts to adjust the historical cost in such a way that the accounts provide some kind of useful information as time goes by.

Given that under the current *Conceptual Framework* a range of users are interested in the accounting information, it is sometimes difficult to ascertain to what use the information will be put and therefore what measurement base would be most appropriate. The definitions of assets and liabilities themselves, however, offer some tantalising clues. Both have their value defined in terms of future cash flow — assets by the economic benefit or cash inflow, liabilities by the economic sacrifice or cash outflow. If accountants could go some way towards accurately capturing this estimated future (and therefore inherently uncertain) cash flow, they would have information that was both relevant and faithfully represented, and on which users could go forward and make their diverse decisions. The fair value standard is an attempt to capture this quality of 'value' in a way that satisfies the requirements of the *Conceptual Framework*.

 ## THE TRADITIONAL DEFINITION

The traditional definition of fair value, prior to the introduction of the fair value standard, could be exemplified by a number of standards. For example, AASB 3/IFRS 3 *Business Combinations* Appendix A defined fair value as:

> The amount for which an asset could be exchanged, or a liability settled between knowledgeable, willing parties in an arms-length transaction.

As previously mentioned, this definition was not consistent across all standards, but provides a representative example. It was generally considered an adequate definition in most circumstances. It was premised on a hypothetical transaction ('could be') that removed the item from the balance sheet in a defined transaction. However, with the release of the fair value exposure draft the IASB identified a number of concerns it had with this definition.

Shortcomings of the traditional definition

The use of the word 'exchanged' is problematic. In this hypothetical transaction, is the asset being measured from the point of view of the buyer or the seller? This could give a significantly different valuation, particularly where there is a substantial bid–ask spread. For example, a car may be bought for $12 000 today, but the same car may be expected to sell at the same time for only $10 000 because of the differences in the market expectations for buyers and sellers of cars.

Applying the definition to liabilities is a little confusing. First, what do we mean by 'settle a liability'. Is it what it could hypothetically cost to make the liability 'go away'? What if this 'settlement' can be achieved via illegal means such as bribery? Further, a liability isn't settled with knowledgeable and willing parties, but rather a creditor who has a right to receive the money.

The definition does not make it clear on which date this exchange should be valued. While it is generally assumed to be reporting date, this is not explicitly clear. This can also be problematic if it is evident the market is rapidly changing, or is illiquid with infrequent exchanges.

What does it mean to be a 'willing' party? An organisation may be in distress and in urgent need of cash and therefore willing to sell an asset at a deep discount for rapid reimbursement. This situation would presumably not be seen to result in an item being measured at its fair value, although this is not clear.

AASB 13/IFRS 13 *FAIR VALUE MEASUREMENT*

To address concerns about the disparate definitions, disseminate advice, and suggest shortcomings of the old definition of fair value, the IASB stated in paragraph BC6 of the Basis for Conclusions to IFRS 13 that the fair value standard has the following objectives:

(a) to establish a single source of guidance for all fair value measurements required or permitted by IFRSs to reduce complexity and improve consistency in their application;
(b) to clarify the definition of fair value and related guidance in order to communicate the measurement objective more clearly; and
(c) to enhance disclosures about fair value to enable users of financial statements to assess the extent to which fair value is used and to inform them about the inputs used to derive those fair values.

The IASB was explicit in its desire not to substantially change the current interpretation of fair value, but rather gather that information into a single standard. This would then more clearly annunciate the board's intentions with regards to measuring fair value. It would also provide more complete and comprehensive disclosure of fair value information to allow users to adequately understand how value was determined. To this end, AASB13/IFRS 13 paragraph 5 states:

> This Standard [IFRS] applies when another Standard [IFRS] requires or permits fair value measurements or disclosures about fair value measurements (and measurements, such as fair value less costs of disposal, based on fair value or disclosures about those measurements) . . .

However certain transactions are explicitly excluded from the scope of AASB 13/IFRS 13 (paragraph 6), being:

- share-based payments (when they are captured by AASB 2/IFRS 2 *Share-based Payment*)
- leasing transactions (when they are captured by AASB 117/IAS 17 *Leases*)

- measurements that may appear similar to fair value but are not termed as such; examples include 'net realisable value' used in AASB 102/IAS 2 *Inventories* and 'value in use' used in AASB 136/IAS 36 *Impairment of Assets*.

Fair value defined

The definition of **fair value** in paragraph 9 of AASB 13/IFRS 13 *Fair Value Measurement* is:

> The price that would be received to sell an asset or paid to transfer a liability in an orderly transaction between market participants at the measurement date.

There are a number of key parts to this definition that seek to address and clarify the concerns raised regarding the traditional definition. For an asset the value is based on the price that would be *received* if the asset were to be *sold*. For a liability the value is based on the price that would be *paid* to *transfer* the liability. This transaction is assumed to occur as an **orderly transaction** between *market participants* expanding our understanding of the market in which these transactions are occurring. All of this is done at measurement date, confirming what was always assumed to be the case.

Another important part of the definition is the term *would*. This makes it clear that the transaction does not have to occur, and in most cases is a hypothetical transaction that would occur should the entity decide to sell the item. Paragraph 21 of AASB 13/IFRS 13 makes this clear:

> Even when there is no observable market to provide pricing information about the sale of an asset or the transfer of a liability at the measurement date, a fair value measurement shall assume that a transaction takes place at that date, considered from the perspective of a market participant that holds the asset or owes the liability. That assumed transaction establishes a basis for estimating the price to sell the asset or to transfer the liability.

The focus on an exit price — why?

The first thing to note is that the price is based on an **exit price**. That is, the price the entity would receive if the asset were sold. This is certainly not the only value that could have been used.

When the IASB sought initial views via a discussion paper on how to proceed with regard to fair value it identified nine potential valuation bases, which are listed below (it is outside of the scope of this chapter to discuss each in detail):
- past entry price
- past exit price
- modified past amount
- current entry price
- current exit price
- current equilibrium price
- value in use
- future entry price
- future exit price.

As already noted, modified past amount is what in reality the traditional historical cost methods have used. Current exit price is what the standard uses. Value in use is perhaps the most relevant of the definitions for users, assuming that use is given a broad definition, but is considered difficult in reality to accurately estimate. However, value in use plays an important role in the definition of fair value as discussed later.

The use of an exit price offers a number of advantages. First, it is current. It allows users to focus on a value today, not some historical price that may or may not be relevant under today's conditions. Second, it is specific. It focuses on the asset or liability at hand, rather than the price to purchase a generic equivalent item. Third, it has a level of independence by introducing, if only hypothetically, an external party into the transaction. The value is based on its estimate of value, not the price the entity was, or is, prepared to pay for the item.

The importance of the concept of a market

The focus on the price an external party is prepared to pay for an asset grounds its value in some of the most important foundations of economics theory, namely the efficient markets hypothesis and the economic rationalism assumption. According to the efficient markets hypothesis, information available is impounded into the price of an item. In an appropriately efficient market, therefore, there will be sufficient information available for the participants to assess the likely future economic benefit to be derived from an asset (or sacrifice for a liability) and this value will be reflected in the value for which they are prepared to buy/sell the item.

Assume we have an asset — for example, a machine that makes widgets (some hypothetical item that we can sell to the market). We have two choices of what we can do with the machine: we can use it and sell the product or sell the machine. The efficient market hypothesis leads us to assume, accepting some level of uncertainty, we can estimate the potential sales to be made from the asset and can therefore assign a value in use to it. Appropriately adjusted for risk, and the time value of money, this sets a floor on the amount we would expect to receive to be prepared to sell the item. That is, self-interest and utility maximisation mean we will only sell the item if we are offered more money than we can reasonably expect to receive using the asset. However, it is assumed that the potential buyers will have access to the same information and markets that we have and therefore would expect about the same return should they use the asset. This sets an effective ceiling on the amount they are prepared to offer for the item.

The point where a sale will occur is therefore constrained by the minimum the current owner will accept and the maximum the potential buyer will pay, and both are determined with reference to the expected future benefit to be received from the asset. There may be some difference in opinion or potential benefit or risk tolerance based on access to skills or markets, but in a reasonably efficient market these differences will not be significant. Therefore, the sales price of an asset can be taken as a fair estimate of its future value or the expected future economic benefit to be realised, which is a fundamental part of the definition of an asset.

Economic rationalism assumes that the organisation and management are attempting to maximise, directly or indirectly, profit (within reasonable societal bounds). This is certainly an assumption of the Australian *Corporations Act 2001*, which calls on the directors and management to maximise shareholder wealth.

What are the characteristics of the market

One of the key considerations for AASB 13/IFRS 13 is whether a market actually exists in which the exit price can be measured. Paragraph 15 of the standard discusses at some length the characteristics that indicate the existence of such a market.

> A fair value measurement assumes that the asset or liability is exchanged in an orderly transaction between market participants to sell the asset or transfer the liability at the measurement date under current market conditions.

An orderly transaction is defined in Appendix A of AASB 13/ IFRS 13 as:

> A transaction that assumes exposure to the market for a period before the measurement date to allow for marketing activities that are usual and customary for transactions involving such assets or liabilities; it is not a forced transaction (e.g. a forced liquidation or distress sale).

Appendix B to the standard, which contains the application guidance, devotes considerable discussion to how to identify when a market is not to be considered active, and therefore not amenable to an orderly transaction and so not an appropriate basis for assigning a fair value. The factors identified in paragraph B37 include:

(a) There are few recent transactions.
(b) Price quotations are not developed using current information.
(c) Price quotations vary substantially either over time or among market-makers (e.g. some brokered markets).
(d) Indices that previously were highly correlated with the fair values of the asset or liability are demonstrably uncorrelated with recent indications of fair value for that asset or liability.
(e) There is a significant increase in implied liquidity risk premiums, yields or performance indicators (such as delinquency rates or loss severities) for observed transactions or quoted prices when compared with the entity's estimate of expected cash flows, taking into account all available market data about credit and other non-performance risk for the asset or liability.
(f) There is a wide bid-ask spread or significant increase in the bid-ask spread.
(g) There is a significant decline in the activity of, or there is an absence of, a market for new issues (i.e. a primary market) for the asset or liability or similar assets or liabilities.
(h) Little information is publicly available (e.g. for transactions that take place in a principal-to-principal market).

A lot of the concerns associated with inactive markets came as part of the global financial crisis. Collateralised debt obligations (CDOs) had become a popular way to turn specific individual debt, generally mortgages, into a marketable security via pooling and dividing (tranching). When it was realised there was serious, and previously unrecognised, systemic risk associated with these financial instruments the market for them dried up. While it was generally agreed that many CDOs had some value, albeit reduced, the asset itself was considered 'toxic', no-one wanted it in their balance sheet even though rationally there was a future economic benefit. Accordingly, the market activity dropped and there was significant difference between market value and estimated future cash flows. Organisations holding this debt were forced to value it using hugely depressed market prices as no 'inactive market' out clause previously existed.

The standard makes it clear that an entity is not required to undertake 'exhaustive' analysis to determine whether the market is active or not, but cannot ignore relevant information that would indicate one way or the other. It would appear that the first assumption in most cases should be that the market is active and that the accountant would need substantial evidence to be able to justify the assertion that it was not.

Under AASB 13/IFRS 13, if it is determined that the market is not active, then an entity may determine that significant adjustments are needed to quoted prices to accurately reflect estimated fair value, or in fact market prices may not be used at all. Instead, an alternative valuation technique (or techniques) may be used if deemed appropriate. The standard does not describe a method for making these adjustments should they be deemed necessary. However alternative valuation techniques are describe in the standard, as discussed later.

In addition to establishing the existence of a market, AASB 13/ IFRS 13 also considers the possibility that multiple markets might exist. As discussed previously, key assumptions underlying accounting, and in particular the fair value standard, are those of an efficient market hypothesis and economic rationalism. So it is assumed that an organisation has the information and desire to establish the most appropriate market for the item it is attempting to measure.

Paragraph 16 of the standard indicates that a fair value measurement assumes that the transaction to sell the asset or transfer the liability takes place either:

(a) in the *principal market* for the asset or liability; or
(b) in the absence of a principal market, in the *most advantageous market* for the asset or liability.

The **principal market** is defined in Appendix A as:

The market with the greatest volume and level of activity for the asset or liability.

While the **most advantageous market** is defined in Appendix A as:

The market that maximises the amount that would be received to sell the asset or minimises the amount that would be paid to transfer the liability, after taking into account transaction costs and transport costs.

Paragraph 16 has caused some unease for entities and their auditors who are concerned that significant effort may need to be expended to identify and confirm that the principal or most advantageous market has been identified. Paragraph 17 of AASB 13/ IFRS 13 makes it clear that it would be assumed (economic rationalism) that the entity would normally enter a transaction in its principal or most advantageous market and that exhaustive searches are not required to be undertaken by the entity, nor should auditors require or seek out exhaustive evidence that this is the case.

Paragraph 19 places an important limitation on the market by introducing the term 'access', it also creates the potential for significant variation in the value that could be assigned to similar assets by different organisations.

The entity must have access to the principal (or most advantageous) market at the measurement date. Because different entities (and businesses within those entities) with different activities may have access to different markets, the principal (or most advantageous) market for the same asset or liability might be different for different entities (and businesses within those entities).

This limitation is closely tied to the discussion of highest and best use in the next section.

An important part of the market definition is that of participants. As can been seen in paragraph 9, the price is based on a transaction between **market participants**. This term is defined extensively in Appendix A of AASB 13/IFRS 13 as:

Buyers and sellers in the principal (or most advantageous) market for the asset or liability that have all of the following characteristics:
(a) They are independent of each other, i.e. they are not related parties as defined in AASB 124 [IAS 24], although the price in a related party transaction may be used as an input to a fair value measurement if the entity has evidence that the transaction was entered into at market terms.
(b) They are knowledgeable, having a reasonable understanding about the asset or liability and the transaction using all available information, including information that might be obtained through due diligence efforts that are usual and customary.
(c) They are able to enter into a transaction for the asset or liability.
(d) They are willing to enter into a transaction for the asset or liability, i.e. they are motivated but not forced or otherwise compelled to do so.

Importantly, the fair value is calculated using the assumptions that these market participants would consider relevant when pricing the specific asset or liability the entity is considering. This is discussed in more detail in the next section.

LO 4 FAIR VALUES ARE SPECIFIC, WHAT FACTORS SHOULD BE CONSIDERED?

The standard is very clear that the asset or liability being fair valued is that held by the entity — that is, the fair value must be specific to the item under consideration. Paragraph 11 of AASB 13/IFRS 13 states:

> A fair value measurement is for a particular asset or liability. Therefore, when measuring fair value an entity shall take into account the characteristics of the asset or liability if market participants would take those characteristics into account when pricing the asset or liability at the measurement date. Such characteristics include, for example, the following:
> (a) the condition and location of the asset; and
> (b) restrictions, if any, on the sale or use of the asset.

This requirement to focus on the specific item held by the entity can have a significant impact on the ease with which an item can be valued. At one end of the spectrum many financial assets, like shares of the same type in the same company, are generic, one share being identical in all respects to another. Therefore, although the share held by the entity may not have been traded recently, trade in a share of the same class in the same entity can proxy as a fair value for that specific share held. In the middle of the spectrum there would be assets that are mass produced but subject to individual wear and tear, like a motor vehicle. There are generally enough transactions occurring with regards to a specific make and model of vehicle to establish a fairly robust average price for the asset, but adjustments may need to be made to take into account aspects of the specific item being considered, like mileage, or damage. At the far end of the spectrum will be unique items where virtually no relevant market exists at all. This could be the case for a highly specialised piece of machinery or intellectual property like a patent. This obviously makes the valuation more difficult in many cases as it is not for some generic item, but rather what is held by the entity.

Each type of asset and liability is going to have its own set of characteristics that will affect the fair value. It is expected that the entity will be able to identify these characteristics and the adjustments that would be necessary to any valuation to account for these issues.

Any restrictions on the use or disposal of the asset must also be accounted for if market participants would consider the restrictions when pricing the asset at the measurement date.

Discussion of the highest and best use for non-financial assets

The standard introduces an additional step to the measurement process for non-financial assets. While not defined in the standard, financial assets would include cash, shares and items like accounts receivable, and would represent a direct interest in cash. Non-financial assets on the other hand would include property, plant and equipment or intangible assets, like patents, which represent a potential income stream.

Non-financial assets are inherently harder to value and therefore paragraph 27 of AASB 13/IFRS 13 introduces additional guidance as follows:

> A fair value measurement of a non-financial asset takes into account a market participant's ability to generate economic benefits by using the asset in its *highest and best* use or by selling it to another market participant that would use the asset in its highest and best use.

Highest and best use is defined in Appendix A of AASB 13/IFRS 13 as:

> The use of a non-financial asset by market participants that would maximise the value of the asset or the group of assets and liabilities (e.g. a business) within which the asset would be used.

While for any asset there may be a range of potential uses, paragraph 29 of AASB 13/IFRS 13 indicates that the valuation should be based upon the highest and best use from an economic perspective, no matter what use it is actually being put to by the entity. Again this is a concept very much based in economic rationalism and utility maximisation. The idea is that if an entity chooses not to put an item to its best use, the value it is extracting from the asset, directly or indirectly, must be at least as much as that best use. An accountant, however, would be wise to question a fair value based on a best use that is substantially different from the value estimated for the actual use. Also, the standard again does not require extensive searching for alternative potential uses unless the evidence suggests the current use is not the best use.

Paragraph 30 of AASB 13/IFRS 13 identifies an example where an asset may not be used for its best use — for example, a defensive asset:

> To protect its competitive position, or for other reasons, an entity may intend not to use an acquired non-financial asset actively or it may intend not to use the asset according to its highest and best use. For example, that might be the case for an acquired intangible asset that the entity plans to use defensively by preventing others from using it. Nevertheless, the entity shall measure the fair value of a non-financial asset assuming its highest and best use by market participants.

Imagine a situation where a company holds two patents for drugs that treat a specific disease. The patent for one is utilised to produce a compound that is marketed and sold for the disease treatment. The other patent is held simply to stop other entities from being able to use it to compete. The second patent is not being used directly to generate income but can be valued based on the amount that would be received if the patent were to be sold in a hypothetical transaction. The assumption is that the benefit perceived to be gained from holding the patent, in terms of increased sales revenue from the first patent, must be greater than the expected return should the second patent be sold.

When considering the highest and best use, paragraph 28 of AASB 13/IFRS 13 imposes three limitations to keep the estimates realistic and focused on the specific asset to be valued: (1) the use must be physically possible, taking into account, for example, the location or condition of the asset; (2) it must be legally permissible, considering, for example, zoning regulations; and (3) it must be financially feasible, meaning that even if physically and legally possible, it would be fiscally sensible to put the asset to the nominated best use.

The legally permissible limitation on the surface is relatively straightforward. Again we can imagine a company that produces cocaine for the medicinal market. In theory, the highest and best use *from a purely monetary perspective* could be selling the product on the street, which is clearly illegal and totally unethical. The valuation to be used would be based on its existing, legal markets. A less extreme example could be an organisation which owns land zoned for commercial usage. It could be argued that the highest and best use in the current market is to build residential apartments. Due to the zoning restrictions, however, that is currently not legal and therefore should not be used as a valuation base. This however can be complicated as the organisation could conceivably spend money (transaction costs) to have the land rezoned. If it is probable that the land could be rezoned, then the organisation can use the potential use as a basis for valuation after considering the potential costs.

Figure 10.1 provides an example of how the measurement of fair value is affected by restrictions placed on an asset.

IE29 A donor contributes land in an otherwise developed residential area to a not-for-profit neighbourhood association. The land is currently used as a playground. The donor specifies that the land must continue to be used by the association as a playground in perpetuity. Upon review of relevant documentation (e.g. legal and other), the association determines that the fiduciary responsibility to meet the donor's restriction would not be transferred to market participants if the association sold the asset, i.e. the donor restriction on the use of the land is specific to the association. Furthermore, the association is not restricted from selling the land. Without the restriction on the use of the land by the association, the land could be used as a site for residential development. In addition, the land is subject to an easement (i.e. a legal right that enables a utility to run power lines across the land). Following is an analysis of the effect on the fair value measurement of the land arising from the restriction and the easement:

(a) *Donor restriction on use of land.* Because in this situation the donor restriction on the use of the land is specific to the association, the restriction would not be transferred to market participants. Therefore, the fair value of the land would be the higher of its fair value used as a playground (i.e. the fair value of the asset would be maximised through its use by market participants in combination with other assets or with other assets and liabilities) and its fair value as a site for residential development (i.e. the fair value of the asset would be maximised through its use by market participants on a stand-alone basis), regardless of the restriction on the use of the land by the association.

(b) *Easement for utility lines.* Because the easement for utility lines is specific to (i.e. a characteristic of) the land, it would be transferred to market participants with the land. Therefore, the fair value measurement of the land would take into account the effect of the easement, regardless of whether the highest and best use is as a playground or as a site for residential development.

FIGURE 10.1 IFRS 13 Illustrative Examples, Example 9 — Restrictions on the use of an asset
Source: IASB, IFRS 13 Fair Value Measurement Illustrative Examples.[1]

An asset may have a different value if it is considered stand-alone or as part of a group of assets. That is to say there may be synergy derived from the use of an asset in combination with other assets that will not be realised if the asset were to be sold on its own. This gives rise to the concept of a value 'in use' versus a value 'in exchange'. Paragraph 31 of AASB 13/IFRS 13 states:

(a) The highest and best use of a non-financial asset might provide maximum value to market participants through its use in combination with other assets as a group (as installed or otherwise configured for use) or in combination with other assets and liabilities (e.g. a business).

  (i) If the highest and best use of the asset is to use the asset in combination with other assets or with other assets and liabilities, the fair value of the asset is the price that would be received in a current transaction to sell the asset assuming that the asset would be used with other assets or with other assets and liabilities and that those assets and liabilities (i.e. its complementary assets and the associated liabilities) would be available to market participants.

(ii) Liabilities associated with the asset and with the complementary assets include liabilities that fund working capital, but do not include liabilities used to fund assets other than those within the group of assets.

(iii) Assumptions about the highest and best use of a non-financial asset shall be consistent for all the assets (for which highest and best use is relevant) of the group of assets or the group of assets and liabilities within which the asset would be used.

(b) The highest and best use of a non-financial asset might provide maximum value to market participants on a stand-alone basis. If the highest and best use of the asset is to use it on a stand-alone basis, the fair value of the asset is the price that would be received in a current transaction to sell the asset to market participants that would use the asset on a stand-alone basis.

The entity can, in most cases, value the assets using the method that would return the highest value in use. There is an exception for financial assets which must always be measured on an exchange basis.

Application to liabilities and equity: general principles

The main focus of this chapter so far has been on valuing assets. Assets are considered theoretically easier to fair value in many ways as there is more likely to be an active market for the exchange of assets, whereas liabilities and, to a lesser extent, equity tend, in most situations, to remain with the original party to the transaction. While acknowledging this reality, paragraph 34 of AASB 13/IFRS 13 states that:

A fair value measurement assumes that a financial or non-financial liability or an entity's own equity instrument (e.g. equity interests issued as consideration in a business combination) is transferred to a market participant at the measurement date. The transfer of a liability or an entity's own equity instrument assumes the following:

(a) A liability would remain outstanding and the market participant transferee would be required to fulfil the obligation. The liability would not be settled with the counterparty or otherwise extinguished on the measurement date.

(b) An entity's own equity instrument would remain outstanding and the market participant transferee would take on the rights and responsibilities associated with the instrument. The instrument would not be cancelled or otherwise extinguished on the measurement date.

The standard sets out a hierarchy for valuing liabilities and equity. In the first instance, if there is an active market for the debt or equity, then this market will provide a fair value for the debt or equity. This could be the situation for publicly traded debentures and shares, it is not, however, a common arrangement for most liabilities. When public prices aren't available for the debt or equity, according to paragraph 37 of AASB 13/ IFRS 13 the entity should, where possible, 'measure the fair value of the liability or equity instrument from the perspective of a market participant that holds the identical item as an asset at the measurement date'.

This approach supports the early discussion of the efficient markets approach, as stated by the IASB in the Basis for Conclusions paragraph BC88–BC89 to IFRS 13:

the fair value of a liability equals the fair value of a properly defined corresponding asset (i.e. an asset whose features mirror those of the liability), assuming an exit from both positions in the same market. In reaching their decision, the boards considered whether the effects of illiquidity could create a difference between those values . . . The boards concluded that there was no conceptual reason why the liability value would diverge from the corresponding asset value in the same market because the contractual terms are the same...

Furthermore, the boards concluded that in an efficient market, the price of a liability held by another party as an asset must equal the price for the corresponding asset. If those prices differed, the market participant transferee (i.e. the party taking on the obligation) would be able to earn a profit by financing the purchase of the asset with the proceeds received by taking on the liability. In such cases the price for the liability and the price for the asset would adjust until the arbitrage opportunity was eliminated.

The most contentious part of the valuation hierarchy for liabilities and equity is the final level. Should no corresponding asset exist for a liability or equity then the entity needs to use a valuation technique based on the assumptions that would be used by market participants. In most circumstances this is going to affect calculations for liabilities. Paragraph B31 of Appendix B of AASB 13/IFRS 13 states:

> When using a present value technique to measure the fair value of a liability that is not held by another party as an asset (e.g. a decommissioning liability), an entity shall, among other things, estimate the future cash outflows that market participants would expect to incur in fulfilling the obligation. Those future cash outflows shall include market participants' expectations about the costs of fulfilling the obligation and the compensation that a market participant would require for taking on the obligation.

An example of a liability with no corresponding asset might be the requirement to rehabilitate land at the completion of mining operations. As the mine develops the corresponding rehabilitation liability will increase and need to be valued. The valuation is potentially controversial because the entity itself may have the skills and the intention to rehabilitate the land at a cost significantly lower than would have to be paid to a third party to achieve the same outcome. The current standard requires the entity to value the liability based on the higher, external, cost. This is demonstrated very clearly in illustrative example 11 that accompanies the standard.

Included in the calculation of the fair value of the liability is the **non-performance risk**. In effect, the value of a liability is affected by the perceived chance that the entity will not be able to pay it. This can lead to some counter-intuitive outcomes when measuring the fair value of liabilities as is shown in figure 10.2.

IE32 Assume that Entity X and Entity Y each enter into a contractual obligation to pay cash (CU500) to Entity Z in five years. Entity X has a AA credit rating and can borrow at 6 per cent, and Entity Y has a BBB credit rating and can borrow at 12 per cent. Entity X will receive about CU374 in exchange for its promise (the present value of CU500 in five years at 6 per cent). Entity Y will receive about CU284 in exchange for its promise (the present value of CU500 in five years at 12 per cent). The fair value of the liability to each entity (i.e. the proceeds) incorporates that entity's credit standing.

FIGURE 10.2 Measuring liabilities — illustrative examples IE2

Source: IASB, *IFRS 13 Fair Value Measurement Illustrative Examples.*[2]

In this example, though both entities will be required to pay CU500 in five years time, the entity with the higher credit rating recognises a larger liability at inception. The key issue is that this reflects the willingness of a lender to hand over more cash at day one. The entity with the lower credit rating will ultimately end up paying a higher amount of interest as the liability increases as maturity date approaches.

In the United States, failure to follow this approach has led to some unusual outcomes as discussed in Contemporary Issue 10.1.

How to conjure up billions

By Jonathan Weil

Bailed-out American car giant GM has made $32 billion appear out of thin air.

It will be a long time before General Motors can shake the stigma of being called Government Motors. Here's another nickname for the bailed-out car maker: Goodwill Motors.

Sometimes the wackiest accounting results are those driven by accounting rules themselves. Consider this: how could it be that one of GM's most valuable assets, listed at US$30.2 billion (A$32.57 billion), is the intangible asset known as goodwill, when it has been only a little more than a year since the company emerged from Chapter-11 bankruptcy protection?

The company said it would not have registered any goodwill under fresh-start reporting if it had booked all its identifiable assets and liabilities at their fair market values. However, GM recorded some of its liabilities at amounts that exceeded fair value, primarily related to employee benefits. The company said the decision was in accordance with US accounting standards.

The difference between those liabilities' carrying amounts and fair values gave rise to goodwill. The bigger the difference, the more goodwill GM booked. In other instances, GM said it recorded certain tax assets at less than their fair value, which also resulted in goodwill.

On the liabilities side, for example, GM said the fair values were lower than the carrying amounts on its balance sheet because it used higher discount rates to calculate the fair value figures. The higher discount rates took GM's risk of default into account, driving fair values lower.

Here's where it gets really funky. If GM's creditworthiness improves, this would reduce the difference between the liabilities' fair values and carrying amounts. Put another way, GM said, the goodwill balance implied by that spread would decline. That could make GM's goodwill vulnerable to write-downs in future periods, which would reduce earnings.

A similar effect would ensue on the asset side if GM's long-term profit forecasts improved. Under that scenario, GM could recognise higher tax assets and bring their carrying amount closer to fair value, narrowing the spread between them.

So, to sum up, the stronger and more creditworthy GM becomes, the less its goodwill assets may be worth in future. An intuitive outcome this is not.

Source: Excerpts from Jonathan Weil, 'How to conjure up billions', *The Sydney Morning Herald*.[3]

Questions

1. What is the relationship between liabilities and the recording of goodwill? **K**
2. Explain how GM can argue that because it has a higher risk of default the fair value of the liabilities would be lower than their carrying amount. **J** **K**
3. Discuss what would be most relevant to the users of GM's financial statements with regards to the valuation of the liabilities. **J** **K** **AS**

 **LO 5**

FAIR VALUE TECHNIQUES

AASB 13/IFRS 13 acknowledges that it may be difficult to find the price at which an item would be exchanged in the market. Paragraph 38 therefore discusses three valuation techniques that it believes would be appropriate to establish a fair value. Whichever approach is adopted, the intention is to use the most accurate and reliable information available. While the Basis for Conclusions to IFRS 13 explicitly states that this is not a hierarchy of preferred valuation techniques, it seems that a market approach should be used unless it is clear that the income approach will give a more relevant and reliable approximation of fair value, likewise the cost approach should only be used if there are significant shortcomings in using the market or income approach. These three approaches are now discussed.

Acceptable valuation techniques

The core principle to be applied when attempting to measure fair value is contained in paragraph 61 of AASB 13/IFRS 13, which states that:

> An entity shall use valuation techniques that are appropriate in the circumstances and for which sufficient data are available to measure fair value, maximising the use of relevant observable inputs and minimising the use of unobservable inputs.

Paragraph 62 then goes on to state that there are three widely used techniques, discussed below, and that the entity 'shall use valuation techniques consistent with one or more of those approaches to measure fair value'. The techniques are outlined in some detail in Appendix B of AASB 13/IFRS 13.

The **market approach** is based on the ability to identify a market for an identical or comparable asset or liability. This approach is theoretically most directly related to the intention of the standard. Depending on the nature of the market, adjustments may need to be made to take existing transactions and best approximate the price that would be relevant to the specific item under consideration. The share market would be an example of a market for identical assets. In theory, any share of the same type in a given company is identical to the last one sold and therefore a direct valuation can be used (assuming a liquid market). A motor vehicle could be an example of a comparable market. While there is generally a market for various models of vehicle, adjustments would need to be made to market prices to account for quantitative (e.g. distance) and qualitative (e.g. condition) characteristics of the specific vehicle being valued.

The **income approach** is based on converting future cash flows or income and expense into a single present value. Usually this would mean using discounted cash flow models, but could alternatively use much more complex models such as a Black–Scholes–Mertons options pricing approach. As explained earlier, it is expected that there will be a close relationship in any efficient market between the market price and the expected future economic benefit to be extracted from the item under consideration. In the absence of a market price the expected net income/expense should proxy for a market price. However, it is likely in all but the most trivial examples that this will involve a number of assumptions that could significantly affect the derived value.

The **cost approach** is based on an estimate of the cost of replacing the 'service capacity' of the asset under consideration. This is what is known as the current replacement cost in accounting theory. The cost is calculated not based on a new asset, rather an asset that would substitute to derive comparable benefit, taking into account the 'obsolescence' of the current asset. Obsolescence describes those characteristics, like physical condition, technological changes etc., that would reduce the value of the asset in the eyes of the market. Through some circular reasoning, paragraph B9 in Appendix B of AASB 13/IFRS 13 argues that the cost approach is approximate to the income approach because 'a market participant would not pay more for an asset than the amount for which it could replace the service capacity of that asset'.

The technique chosen is clearly a matter for professional judgement and will depend on the circumstances and information available to the accountant attempting to make the valuation. However, paragraph 67 of AASB 13/IFRS 13 requires that the accountant maximise relevant observable inputs and minimise unobservable inputs. These are discussed in detail in the next section. In practice this would mean that the market approach is most likely to be preferred. However, this also means that where a market is inactive, as previously discussed, alternative valuation methods are available to an entity.

AASB 13/IFRS 13 in paragraph 65 states that whatever valuation technique is chosen should be applied consistently — that is, unless there is a change in the circumstance or the information available to the entity the same approach should be used from period to period. If a change in method is expected to provide better, more reliable information this will be treated as a change in policy and must be disclosed in accordance with AASB 108/IAS 8 *Accounting Policies, Changes in Accounting Estimates and Errors*.

Figure 10.3 provides of example of the measurement of the fair value of a machine held and used.

FIGURE 10.3 IFRS 13 Illustrative Examples, Example 4 — Machine held and used

IE11 An entity acquires a machine in a business combination. The machine will be held and used in its operations. The machine was originally purchased by the acquired entity from an outside vendor and, before the business combination, was customised by the acquired entity for use in its operations. However, the customisation of the machine was not extensive. The acquiring entity determines that the asset would provide maximum value to market participants through its use in combination with other assets or with other assets and liabilities (as installed or otherwise configured for use). There is no evidence to suggest that the current use of the machine is not its highest and best use. Therefore, the highest and best use of the machine is its current use in combination with other assets or with other assets and liabilities.

IE12 The entity determines that sufficient data are available to apply the cost approach and, because the customisation of the machine was not extensive, the market approach. The income approach is not used because the machine does not have a separately identifiable income stream from which to develop reliable estimates of future cash flows. Furthermore, information about short-term and intermediate-term lease rates for similar used machinery that otherwise could be used to project an income stream (i.e. lease payments over remaining service lives) is not available. The market and cost approaches are applied as follows:

(a) The market approach is applied using quoted prices for similar machines adjusted for differences between the machine (as customised) and the similar machines. The measurement reflects the price that would be received for the machine in its current condition (used) and location (installed and configured for use). The fair value indicated by that approach ranges from CU40,000 to CU48,000.

(b) The cost approach is applied by estimating the amount that would be required currently to construct a substitute (customised) machine of comparable utility. The estimate takes into account the condition of the machine and the environment in which it operates, including physical wear and tear (i.e. physical deterioration), improvements in technology (i.e. functional obsolescence), conditions external to the condition of the machine such as a decline in the market demand for similar machines (i.e. economic obsolescence) and installation costs. The fair value indicated by that approach ranges from CU40,000 to CU52,000.

IE13 The entity determines that the higher end of the range indicated by the market approach is most representative of fair value and, therefore, ascribes more weight to the results of the market approach. That determination is made on the basis of the relative subjectivity of the inputs, taking into account the degree of comparability between the machine and the similar machines. In particular:

(a) the inputs used in the market approach (quoted prices for similar machines) require fewer and less subjective adjustments than the inputs used in the cost approach.

(b) the range indicated by the market approach overlaps with, but is narrower than, the range indicated by the cost approach.

(c) there are no known unexplained differences (between the machine and the similar machines) within that range.

Accordingly, the entity determines that the fair value of the machine is CU48,000.

FIGURE 10.3 *(continued)*

> IE14 If customisation of the machine was extensive or if there were not sufficient data available to apply the market approach (e.g. because market data reflect transactions for machines used on a stand-alone basis, such as a scrap value for specialised assets, rather than machines used in combination with other assets or with other assets and liabilities), the entity would apply the cost approach. When an asset is used in combination with other assets or with other assets and liabilities, the cost approach assumes the sale of the machine to a market participant buyer with the complementary assets and the associated liabilities. The price received for the sale of the machine (i.e. an exit price) would not be more than either of the following:
> (a) the cost that a market participant buyer would incur to acquire or construct a substitute machine of comparable utility; or
> (b) the economic benefit that a market participant buyer would derive from the use of the machine.

Source: IASB, IFRS 13 Fair Value Measurement Illustrative Examples.[4]

Inputs into valuation

Appendix A of AASB 13/IFRS 13 defines inputs as:

> The assumptions that market participants would use when pricing the asset or liability, including assumptions about risk, such as the following:
> (a) the risk inherent in a particular valuation technique used to measure fair value (such as a pricing model); and
> (b) the risk inherent in the inputs to the valuation technique.
> Inputs may be observable or unobservable.

Observable inputs are those values that can be obtained independently from available market data, possibly with some adjustment for the specific asset, which would be used by market participants when valuing an asset or liability. Unobservable inputs are based on information that is not available to the market but must be inferred or estimated based on the best information available.

The fair value hierarchy

In line with the requirement of using a market based approach to measure fair value, the standard includes a hierarchy of inputs into the valuation model. The entity should maximise the use of observable inputs and minimise the use of unobservable inputs. Observable inputs are split into two levels that mirror the discussion in the section on market valuation. Some observable inputs do not need to be adjusted, they are based on active markets for identical assets or liabilities — these inputs are termed Level 1 inputs. Other observable inputs require adjustment to reflect quantitative or qualitative differences between the item under consideration and the market observed — these inputs are termed Level 2 inputs. Level 3 inputs are based on unobservable inputs that require estimation and inference by the entity.

In establishing the fair value of an item, the entity will most likely have to use a range of inputs. Paragraph 73 of AASB 13/IFRS 13 is clear:

> The fair value measurement is categorised in its entirety in the same level of the fair value hierarchy as the lowest level input that is significant to the entire measurement.

'Significant' requires professional judgement to interpret.

For example, in measuring the fair value of an asset we might start by using a market valuation based on adjusted market prices (Level 2). Alternatively, we could use an income valuation model which at its simplest might start with the risk-free interest rate (Level 1), adjust it for specific asset related risks (making it Level 2) and apply this to estimated future cash flows (Level 3). In this circumstance the market valuation is clearly preferable as it does not include significant Level 3 inputs.

Level 1 inputs

Level 1 inputs are defined in paragraph 76 of AASB 13/IFRS 13 as:

> quoted prices (unadjusted) in active markets for identical assets or liabilities that the entity can access at the measurement date.

The standard introduces the concept of an active market into this definition. An **active market** is defined in Appendix A to AASB 13/IFRS 13 as:

> A market in which transactions for the asset or liability take place with sufficient frequency and volume to provide pricing information on an ongoing basis.

Deciding whether a market transaction involves an identical asset can be difficult. While it is clear that many financial assets can be considered identical (such as specific shares), it is less clear when it comes to physical assets. The assumption is that for physical assets adjustments will have to be made for individual quantitative and qualitative characteristics and therefore even where market prices exist, they are not identical and cannot be treated as Level 1 inputs.

As already discussed, the ability to access the market is key, not necessarily the right to sell the asset or transfer the liability at that date. There could be specific restrictions in place at this point in time (AASB 13/IFRS 13, paragraph 20). However if this restriction is likely to remain in place and it would affect the amount market participants were willing to offer for the item then this becomes an adjustment and changes the measure to a Level 2 input.

Level 2 inputs

Level 2 inputs are defined in paragraph 81 of AASB 13/IFRS 13 as:

> inputs other than quoted prices included within Level 1 that are observable for the asset or liability, either directly or indirectly.

The definition of Level 2 inputs is very similar to that of Level 1 inputs, but they fail to meet the strict requirements to be a Level 1 input, usually requiring some adjustment to the price. It may be that the market is not active and so prices are not current and require some adjustment. The inputs may be observable (for example, interest rates), but not actual market prices. If the adjustments that need to be made to the observed prices or inputs are significant, this may in fact then mean that the measurement becomes a Level 3 measurement. Paragraph B35 of Appendix B to AASB 13/IFRS 13 contains examples of Level 2 inputs. Figure 10.4 outlines these examples.

FIGURE 10.4 Examples of Level 2 inputs for particular assets and liabilities

Examples of Level 2 inputs for particular assets and liabilities include the following: . . .
(c) *Receive-fixed, pay-variable interest rate swap based on a specific bank's prime rate.* A Level 2 input would be the bank's prime rate derived through extrapolation if the extrapolated values are corroborated by observable market data, for example, by correlation with an interest rate that is observable over substantially the full term of the swap.
(e) *Licensing arrangement.* For a licensing arrangement that is acquired in a business combination and was recently negotiated with an unrelated party by the acquired entity (the party to the licensing arrangement), a Level 2 input would be the royalty rate in the contract with the unrelated party at inception of the arrangement.

FIGURE 10.4 *(continued)*

(f) *Finished goods inventory at a retail outlet.* For finished goods inventory that is acquired in a business combination, a Level 2 input would be either a price to customers in a retail market or a price to retailers in a wholesale market, adjusted for differences between the condition and location of the inventory item and the comparable (i.e. similar) inventory items so that the fair value measurement reflects the price that would be received in a transaction to sell the inventory to another retailer that would complete the requisite selling efforts.

(g) *Building held and used.* A Level 2 input would be the price per square metre for the building (a valuation multiple) derived from observable market data, e.g. multiples derived from prices in observed transactions involving comparable (i.e. similar) buildings in similar locations.

Source: IASB, IFRS 13 *Fair Value Measurement*, paragraph B35.[5]

Level 3 inputs

Level 3 inputs are defined in paragraph 86 of AASB 13/IFRS 13 as:

unobservable inputs for the asset or liability.

At the bottom of the hierarchy are unobservable inputs, which should only be used if observable inputs are unavailable. This will generally be because there is no market activity available to use directly or on an adjusted basis. However the entity is still to use one of the three valuation methods to approximate a market price for the item under consideration. In doing so it must attempt to obtain the best data it can, generally based on internal information, which would reflect the concerns of the market when attempting to value the item. This being said, the standard (AASB 13/IFRS 13, paragraph 89) indicates that an entity will not be required to undertake exhaustive searches to establish what a market would require to appropriately value an asset; unless clearly otherwise indicated its assumptions will be assumed correct. Paragraph B36 of Appendix B to AASB 13/IFRS 13, contain examples of Level 3 inputs. Figure 10.5 outlines these examples.

Examples of Level 3 inputs for particular assets and liabilities include the following:
(a) *Long-dated currency swap.* A Level 3 input would be an interest rate in a specified currency that is not observable and cannot be corroborated by observable market data at commonly quoted intervals or otherwise for substantially the full term of the currency swap.

(b) *Three-year option on exchange-traded shares.* A Level 3 input would be historical volatility, i.e. the volatility for the shares derived from the shares' historical prices. Historical volatility typically does not represent current market participants' expectations about future volatility, even if it is the only information available to price an option . . .

(e) *Cash-generating unit.* A Level 3 input would be a financial forecast (e.g. of cash flows or profit or loss) developed using the entity's own data if there is no reasonably available information that indicates that market participants would use different assumptions.

FIGURE 10.5 Examples of Level 3 inputs for particular assets and liabilities
Source: IASB, IFRS 13 *Fair Value Measurement*, paragraph B36.[6]

One significant criticism of the proposed standard has been the use of the term 'fair value' to describe a value derived primarily from Level 3 inputs. It has been suggested that a different term should be used to describe these values to avoid confusion about how they have been derived. This suggestion has not been accepted by the board, as described in paragraph BC173 of the Basis for Conclusions:

(a) The proposed definition of fair value identifies a clear objective for valuation techniques and the inputs to them: consider all factors that market participants would consider and exclude all factors that market participants would exclude. An alternative label for Level 3 measurements would be unlikely to identify such a clear objective.

(b) The distinction between Levels 2 and 3 is inevitably subjective. It is undesirable to adopt different measurement objectives on either side of such a subjective boundary.

Rather than requiring a different label for measurements derived using significant unobservable inputs, the IASB concluded that concerns about the subjectivity of those measurements are best addressed by requiring enhanced disclosure for those measurements . . .

In business there are often going to be assets that are difficult to value. While fair value particularly based on Level 3 valuations may come with the risk of overvaluation, those risks exist even without, and in fact may be mitigated by, fair value measurement. Contemporary Issue 10.2 gives an example of the risk associated with the overvaluation of a patent.

10.2 CONTEMPORARY ISSUE

Serial floats and patent porkies

By Kate McClymont and Michael West

In early 2005, Canadian-born entrepreneur Shawn Richard was emailing a Hong Kong-based trader, Jack Flader, to seek advice about their Australian assets in the wake of the brutal murder of their business partner Matthew Littauer.

For years, Littauer was involved in an array of stockbroking scams, which ended only when he was stabbed to death in his office in Tokyo's red-light district in December 2004. His murder remains unsolved.

In his emails to Flader, Richard discussed their half-ownership of Advanced Medical Institute.

Doyle told BusinessDay that in early 2005 Richard introduced him to Flader, whom he believed to be one of Richard's business associates and funders. The three men came up with a plan — to float AMI on the US stock exchange. When AMI Inc listed in the US in March 2005, its only assets were the Australian sexual dysfunction operations . . .

Halfway through 2005, an ingenious plan was put in motion. AMI's promoter Vaisman had lodged an 'innovation patent' for a nasal spray to treat premature ejaculation with Australian authorities. It only takes a minute to fill out the documentation online and, not long after, you are granted an 'innovation patent' to protect your idea until it can be scientifically verified.

An innovation patent is completely different to a standard patent. Millions of dollars and rigorous medical trials are required for a drug to be patented. According to a former AMI executive: 'The company has never owned any patents . . .'

But American investors weren't to know this. They were told in mid-2005 that the company had been 'awarded' an innovation patent by the Commonwealth Patent Office. Not only that, the company holding the Australian rights to the patent (which had cost Vaisman a mere $150) was now being acquired by AMI Inc for an astronomical $24 million.

The pattern was repeated the following year when a second company — owner of the global rights, as opposed to Australian rights — was acquired by Vaisman's publicly listed US company for 'the aggregate acquisition price of A$24.05 million,' the Securities and Exchange Commission was informed . . .

Vaisman and Doyle received millions of dollars for these two deals. Doyle said there was nothing inappropriate about the transactions as they had been 'independently valued by a major Australian accounting firm'.

After these transactions Doyle said he had no 'major involvement' with Flader and Richard. He said that he had not communicated with Flader for more than two years.

Doyle also said, 'I have not had any business interaction with Richard for an extended period.'

Doyle, whose offshore companies still own shares in AMI, claims AMI owes him $600 000. Fairfax Media, the owner of *The Age* and *The Sydney Morning Herald*, is also a creditor.

Source: Excerpts from Kate McClymont & Michael West, 'Serial floats and patent porkies', *The Sydney Morning Herald*.[7]

Questions

1. Describe the three acceptable valuation techniques and how they could be used to determine the fair value of the patent in this scenario. **K**
2. Provide examples of the inputs you could use to establish the fair value of the patent and to what level those inputs would be assigned. **J** **K** **AS**
3. Given that the valuation of the patent did involve a sales transaction would this indicate that the market approach was the appropriate one to use in this case? What weight can be placed on the 'independent valuation'? **J** **K**

LO 6   DISCLOSURES

Prior to the release of AASB 13/IFRS 13 the requirements as to the disclosures required around fair value were very dependent on exactly which standard was being applied. The IASB has two main goals with regards to disclosures under this standard: they should be both useful to users and consistent. The principles for disclosure are set out in paragraph 91 of AASB 13/IFRS 13:

> An entity shall disclose information that helps users of its financial statements assess both of the following:
> (a) for assets and liabilities that are measured at fair value on a recurring or non-recurring basis in the statement of financial position after initial recognition, the valuation techniques and inputs used to develop those measurements.
> (b) for recurring fair value measurements using significant unobservable inputs (Level 3), the effect of the measurements on profit or loss or other comprehensive income for the period.

Obviously for assets and liabilities measured at fair value the amount shown in the statement of financial position will be the fair value. The standard then requires a note (or notes) that provide additional information on how the valuation was determined. The amount of information is dependent on the level of input to the valuation (remembering that the lowest 'significant' level defines the overall level for that item class), with particularly extensive requirements for items based on Level 3 inputs.

A concept introduced into the disclosure section is that of recurring and non-recurring fair value measurements. Recurring fair value measurements are those that other standards require or permit in the balance sheet at the end of each reporting period. Non-recurring fair value measurements are those that other standards require or permit in the balance sheet only in particular circumstances.

The following disclosures are required according to paragraph 93 of AASB 13/IFRS 13:

> (a) for recurring and non-recurring fair value measurements, the fair value measurement at the end of the reporting period, and for non-recurring fair value measurements, the reasons for the measurement . . .
> (b) for recurring and non-recurring fair value measurements, the level of the fair value hierarchy within which the fair value measurements are categorised in their entirety (Level 1, 2 or 3).

(c) for assets and liabilities held at the end of the reporting period that are measured at fair value on a recurring basis, the amounts of any transfers between Level 1 and Level 2 of the fair value hierarchy, the reasons for those transfers and the entity's policy for determining when transfers between levels are deemed to have occurred (see paragraph 95). Transfers into each level shall be disclosed and discussed separately from transfers out of each level.

(d) for recurring and non-recurring fair value measurements categorised within Level 2 and Level 3 of the fair value hierarchy, a description of the valuation technique(s) and the inputs used in the fair value measurement. If there has been a change in valuation technique (e.g. changing from a market approach to an income approach or the use of an additional valuation technique), the entity shall disclose that change and the reason(s) for making it. For fair value measurements categorised within Level 3 of the fair value hierarchy, an entity shall provide quantitative information about the significant unobservable inputs used in the fair value measurement.

(e) for recurring fair value measurements categorised within Level 3 of the fair value hierarchy, a reconciliation from the opening balances to the closing balances, disclosing separately changes during the period attributable to the following:

  (i) total gains or losses for the period recognised in profit or loss, and the line item(s) in profit or loss in which those gains or losses are recognised.

  (ii) total gains or losses for the period recognised in other comprehensive income, and the line item(s) in other comprehensive income in which those gains or losses are recognised.

  (iii) purchases, sales, issues and settlements (each of those types of changes disclosed separately).

  (iv) the amounts of any transfers into or out of Level 3 of the fair value hierarchy, the reasons for those transfers and the entity's policy for determining when transfers between levels are deemed to have occurred (see paragraph 95). Transfers into Level 3 shall be disclosed and discussed separately from transfers out of Level 3.

(f) for recurring fair value measurements categorised within Level 3 of the fair value hierarchy, the amount of the total gains or losses for the period in (e)(i) included in profit or loss that is attributable to the change in unrealised gains or losses relating to those assets and liabilities held at the end of the reporting period, and the line item(s) in profit or loss in which those unrealised gains or losses are recognised.

(g) for recurring and non-recurring fair value measurements categorised within Level 3 of the fair value hierarchy, a description of the valuation processes used by the entity (including, for example, how an entity decides its valuation policies and procedures and analyses changes in fair value measurements from period to period).

(h) for recurring fair value measurements categorised within Level 3 of the fair value hierarchy:

  (i) for all such measurements, a narrative description of the sensitivity of the fair value measurement to changes in unobservable inputs if a change in those inputs to a different amount might result in a significantly higher or lower fair value measurement. If there are interrelationships between those inputs and other unobservable inputs used in the fair value measurement, an entity shall also provide a description of those interrelationships and of how they might magnify or mitigate the effect of changes in the unobservable inputs on the fair value measurement. To comply with that disclosure requirement, the narrative description of the sensitivity to changes in unobservable inputs shall include, at a minimum, the unobservable inputs disclosed when complying with (d).

(ii) for financial assets and financial liabilities, if changing one or more of the unobservable inputs to reflect reasonably possible alternative assumptions would change fair value significantly, an entity shall state that fact and disclose the effect of those changes. The entity shall disclose how the effect of a change to reflect a reasonably possible alternative assumption was calculated. For that purpose, significance shall be judged with respect to profit or loss, and total assets or total liabilities, or, when changes in fair value are recognised in other comprehensive income, total equity.

(i) for recurring and non-recurring fair value measurements, if the highest and best use of a non-financial asset differs from its current use, an entity shall disclose that fact and why the non-financial asset is being used in a manner that differs from its highest and best use.

Figure 10.6 provides examples of disclosures from the illustrative examples accompanying IFRS 13.

FIGURE 10.6 Fair value disclosures

Illustrative Example 15 — Assets measured at fair value

IE60 For assets and liabilities measured at fair value at the end of the reporting period, the IFRS requires quantitative disclosures about the fair value measurements for each class of assets and liabilities. An entity might disclose the following for assets to comply with paragraph 93(a) and (b) of the IFRS:

(CU in millions)		Fair value measurements at the end of the reporting period using			
Description	**31/12/X9**	**Quoted prices in active markets for identical assets (Level 1)**	**Significant other observable inputs (Level 2)**	**Significant unobservable inputs (Level 3)**	**Total gains (losses)**
Recurring fair value measurements					
Trading equity securities[(a)]:					
Real estate industry	93	70	23		
Oil and gas industry	45	45			
Other	15	15			
Total trading equity securities	153	130	23		
Other equity securities[(a)]:					
Financial services industry	150	150			
Healthcare industry	163	110		53	
Energy industry	32			32	
Private equity fund investments[(b)]	25			25	
Other	15	15			
Total other equity securities	385	275		110	
Debt securities:					
Residential mortgage-backed securities	149		24	125	
Commercial mortgage-backed securities	50			50	
Collateralised debt obligations	35			35	
Risk-free government securities	85	85			
Corporate bonds	93	9	84		
Total debt securities	412	94	108	210	

FIGURE 10.6 *(continued)*

(CU in millions)		Fair value measurements at the end of the reporting period using			
Description	**31/12/X9**	**Quoted prices in active markets for identical assets (Level 1)**	**Significant other observable inputs (Level 2)**	**Significant unobservable inputs (Level 3)**	**Total gains (losses)**
Recurring fair value measurements *(continued)*					
Hedge fund investments:					
Equity long/short	55		55		
Global opportunities	35		35		
High-yield debt securities	90			90	
Total hedge fund investments	180		90	90	
Derivatives:					
Interest rate contracts	57		57		
Foreign exchange contracts	43		43		
Credit contracts	38			38	
Commodity futures contracts	78	78			
Commodity forward contracts	20		20		
Total derivatives	236	78	120	38	
Investment properties:					
Commercial — Asia	31			31	
Commercial — Europe	27			27	
Total investment properties	58			58	
Total recurring fair value measurements	1 424	577	341	506	
Non-recurring fair value measurements					
Assets held for sale[c]	26		26		(15)
Total non-recurring fair value measurements	26		26		(15)

(a) On the basis of its analysis of the nature, characteristics and risks of the securities, the entity has determined that presenting them by industry is appropriate.

(b) On the basis of its analysis of the nature, characteristics and risks of the investments, the entity has determined that presenting them as a single class is appropriate.

(c) In accordance with IFRS 5, assets held for sale with a carrying amount of CU35 million were written down to their fair value of CU26 million, less costs to sell of CU6 million (or CU20 million), resulting in a loss of CU15 million, which was included in profit or loss for the period.

(Note: A similar table would be presented for liabilities unless another format is deemed more appropriate by the entity.)

FIGURE 10.6 (continued)

Illustrative Example 16 — Reconciliation of fair value measurements categorised within Level 3 of the fair value hierarchy

IE61 For recurring fair value measurements categorised within Level 3 of the fair value hierarchy, the IFRS requires a reconciliation from the opening balances to the closing balances for each class of assets and liabilities. An entity might disclose the following for assets to comply with paragraph 93(e) and (f) of the IFRS:

(CU in millions)	Fair value measurements using significant unobservable inputs (Level 3)										
	Other equity securities			Debt securities			Hedge fund investments	Derivatives	Investment properties		Total
	Healthcare industry	Energy industry	Private equity fund	Residential mortgage-backed securities	Commercial mortgage-backed securities	Collateralised debt obligations	High-yield debt securities	Credit contracts	Asia	Europe	
Opening balance	49	28	20	105	39	25	145	30	28	26	495
Transfers into Level 3				60 (a)(b)							60
Transfers out of Level 3				(5) (b)(c)							(5)
Total gains or losses for the period											
Included in profit or loss			5	(23)	(5)	(7)	7	5	3	1	(14)
Included in other comprehensive income	3	1									4
Purchases, issues, sales and settlements											
Purchases	1	3			16	17		18			55
Issues				(12)							
Sales							(62)				(74)
Settlements								(15)			(15)
Closing balance	53	32	25	125	50	35	90	38	31	27	506
Change in unrealised gains or losses for the period included in profit or loss for assets held at the end of the reporting period			5	(3)	(5)	(7)	(5)	2	3	1	(9)

(a) Transferred from Level 2 to Level 3 because of a lack of observable market data, resulting from a decrease in market activity for the securities.

(b) The entity's policy is to recognise transfers into and transfers out of Level 3 as of the date of the event or change in circumstances that caused the transfer.

(c) Transferred from Level 3 to Level 2 because observable market data became available for the securities.

(Note: A similar table would be presented for liabilities unless another format is deemed more appropriate by the entity.)

IE62 Gains and losses included in profit or loss for the period (above) are presented in financial income and in non-financial income as follows:

(CU in millions)	Financial income	Non-financial income
Total gains or losses for the period included in profit or loss	(18)	4
Change in unrealised gains or losses for the period included in profit or loss for assets held at the end of the reporting period	(13)	4

(Note: A similar table would be presented for liabilities unless another format is deemed more appropriate by the entity.)

Example 17 — Valuation techniques and inputs

IE63 For fair value measurements categorised within Level 2 and Level 3 of the fair value hierarchy, the IFRS requires an entity to disclose a description of the valuation technique(s) and the inputs used in the fair value measurement. For fair value measurements categorised within Level 3 of the fair value hierarchy, information about the significant unobservable inputs used must be quantitative. An entity might disclose the following for assets to comply with the requirement to disclose the significant unobservable inputs used in the fair value measurement in accordance with paragraph 93(d) of the IFRS:

(CU in millions)	Quantitative information about fair value measurements using significant unobservable inputs (Level 3)			
Description	Fair value at 31/12/X9	Valuation technique(s)	Unobservable input	Range (weighted average)
Other equity securities:				
Healthcare industry	53	Discounted cash flow	weighted average cost of capital	7%–16% (12.1%)
			long-term revenue growth rate	2%–5% (4.2%)
			long-term pre-tax operating margin	3%–20% (10.3%)
			discount for lack of marketability[a]	5%–20% (17%)
			control premium[a]	10%–30% (20%)
		Market comparable companies	EBITDA multiple[b]	10–13 (11.3)
			revenue multiple[b]	1.5–2.0 (1.7)
			discount for lack of marketability[a]	5%–20% (17%)
			control premium[a]	10%–30% (20%)
Energy industry	32	Discounted cash flow	weighted average cost of capital	8%–12% (11.1%)
			long-term revenue growth rate	3%–5.5% (4.2%)
			long-term pre-tax operating margin	7.5%–13% (9.2%)
			discount for lack of marketability[a]	5%–20% (10%)
			control premium[a]	10%–20% (12%)
		Market comparable companies	EBITDA multiple[b]	6.5–12 (9.5)
			revenue multiple[b]	1.0–3.0 (2.0)
			discount for lack of marketability[a]	5%–20% (10%)
			control premium[a]	10%–20% (12%)
Private equity fund investments	25	Net asset value[c]	n/a	n/a

(continued)

FIGURE 10.6 *(continued)*

FIGURE 10.6 (continued)

| (CU in millions) | Quantitative information about fair value measurements using significant unobservable inputs (Level 3) | | | |
Description	Fair value at 31/12/X9	Valuation technique(s)	Unobservable input	Range (weighted average)
Debt securities:				
Residential mortgage-backed securities	125	Discounted cash flow	constant prepayment rate probability of default loss severity	3.5%–5.5% (4.5%) 5%–50% (10%) 40%–100% (60%)
Commercial mortgage-backed securities	50	Discounted cash flow	constant prepayment rate probability of default loss severity	3%–5% (4.1%) 2%–25% (5%) 10%–50% (20%)
Collateralised debt obligations	35	Consensus pricing	offered quotes comparability adjustments (%)	20–45 –10%–+15% (+5%)
Hedge fund investments:				
High-yield debt securities	90	Net asset value(c)	n/a	n/a
Derivatives:				
Credit contracts	38	Option model	annualised volatility of credit(d) counterparty credit risk(e) own credit risk(e)	10%–20% 0.5%–3.5% 0.3%–2.0%
Investment properties:				
Commercial — Asia	31	Discounted cash flow	long-term net operating income margin cap rate	18%–32% (20%) 0.08–0.12 (0.10)
		Market comparable approach	price per square metre (USD)	$3000–$7000 ($4500)
Commercial — Europe	27	Discounted cash flow	long-term net operating income margin cap rate	15%–25% (18%) 0.06–0.10 (0.80)
		Market comparable approach	price per square metre (EUR)	€4000–€12 000 (€8500)

(a) Represents amounts used when the entity has determined that market participants would take into account these premiums and discounts when pricing the investments.

(b) Represents amounts used when the entity has determined that market participants would use such multiples when pricing the investments.

(c) The entity has determined that the reported net asset value represents fair value at the end of the reporting period.

(d) Represents the range of the volatility curves used in the valuation analysis that the entity has determined market participants would use when the pricing contracts.

(e) Represents the range of the credit default swap spread curves used in the valuation analysis that the entity has determined market participants would use when pricing the contracts.

(Note: A similar table would be presented for liabilities unless another format is deemed more appropriate by the entity.)

Source: IASB, IFRS 13 Fair Value Measurement Illustrative Examples.[8]

LO 7 SPECIFIC ISSUES

How to deal with transaction costs

The concept of transaction costs is referred to in a number of places in AASB 13/IFRS 13 and has the potential to cause confusion. The term is linked to determining the principal or most advantageous market in Appendix A of AASB 13/IFRS 13. Transactions costs are defined in Appendix A as:

> The costs to sell an asset or transfer a liability in the principal (or most advantageous) market for the asset or liability that are directly attributable to the disposal of the asset or the transfer of the liability and meet both of the following criteria:
> (a) They result directly from and are essential to that transaction.
> (b) They would not have been incurred by the entity had the decision to sell the asset or transfer the liability not been made.

The transaction costs are considered in determining which market valuation to use. However, once the market is determined the price used to measure the fair value of the item is not adjusted for those costs (AASB 13/IFRS 13, paragraph 25). The reason for this is that transaction costs are not an inherent quality of the item being valued — they are an artefact of the market. To confuse matters, although in keeping with this logic, transport costs are excluded from the definition of transaction costs as location is a specific characteristic of an item and so it is included both in the determination of the most advantageous market and the fair value that is ascribed to the item based on the price that would be received in this market.

How blocks of assets are dealt with

The factors of supply and demand can heavily influence market valuations. A particular situation that could arise is where an entity holds a high number of relatively rare assets. This could be the situation with shares, but also commodities. If the entity were to 'flood' the market with all its holdings at one time the expected market response would be to drop the per unit price. AASB 13/IFRS 13 indicates in paragraph 69 that a blockage factor is not permitted in a fair value measurement — that is, the fair value is determined for each asset individually as though it was the only single item being sold.

Fair value at initial recognition different to cost

The price that an entity pays for an asset or receives to assume a liability is an entry price. So this may not always be the same as the fair value of the asset or liability which is based on an exit price, although usually it would be assumed that these values are not going to be materially different at day one. This assumption may not hold if the transaction was not a genuine market transaction as defined by AASB 13/IFRS 13. According to paragraph B4 of Appendix B to AASB 13/IFRS 13, indications of this would include:

(a) the transaction is between related parties . . .
(b) the transaction takes place under duress or the seller is forced to accept the price in the transaction. For example, that might be the case if the seller is experiencing financial difficulty.
(c) the unit of account represented by the transaction price is different from the unit of account for the asset or liability measured at fair value. For example, that might be the case if the asset or liability measured at fair value is only one of the elements in the transaction, the transaction includes unstated rights and privileges that are separately measured or the transaction price includes transaction costs.

(d) The market in which the transaction takes place is different from the principal market (or most advantageous market). For example, those markets might be different if the entity is a dealer that enters into transactions with customers in the retail market, but the principal (or most advantageous) market for the exit transaction is with other dealers in the dealer market.

Where there is a difference between the fair value at initial recognition and the cost of the item the entity (unless explicitly prohibited by another standard) can adjust the value in the balance sheet and recognise the resultant change through profit or loss. Figure 10.7 provides an example where fair value at initial recognition and the cost of an item differ.

Illustrative Example 7 — Interest rate swap at initial recognition

IE24 Entity A (a retail counterparty) enters into an interest rate swap in a retail market with Entity B (a dealer) for no initial consideration (i.e. the transaction price is zero). Entity A can access only the retail market. Entity B can access both the retail market (i.e. with retail counterparties) and the dealer market (i.e. with dealer counterparties).

IE25 From the perspective of Entity A, the retail market in which it initially entered into the swap is the principal market for the swap. If Entity A were to transfer its rights and obligations under the swap, it would do so with a dealer counterparty in that retail market. In that case the transaction price (zero) would represent the fair value of the swap to Entity A at initial recognition, i.e. the price that Entity A would receive to sell or pay to transfer the swap in a transaction with a dealer counterparty in the retail market (i.e. an exit price). That price would not be adjusted for any incremental (transaction) costs that would be charged by that dealer counterparty.

IE26 From the perspective of Entity B, the dealer market (not the retail market) is the principal market for the swap. If Entity B were to transfer its rights and obligations under the swap, it would do so with a dealer in that market. Because the market in which Entity B initially entered into the swap is different from the principal market for the swap, the transaction price (zero) would not necessarily represent the fair value of the swap to Entity B at initial recognition. If the fair value differs from the transaction price (zero), Entity B applies IAS 39 *Financial Instruments: Recognition and Measurement* or IFRS 9 *Financial Instruments* to determine whether it recognises that difference as a gain or loss at initial recognition.

FIGURE 10.7 IFRS 13 Illustrative Examples, Example 7 — Interest rate swap at initial recognition

Source: IASB, *IFRS 13 Fair Value Measurement Illustrative Examples.*[9]

The role for third party valuations

An issue that has arisen is the use of third party valuations to establish a fair value for an item. This is likely to become an increasingly common approach to valuation and is certainly not precluded by the standard. However, in paragraphs 16–18 of the Basis for Conclusions that accompanied the original exposure draft for IFRS 13 the IASB stated that the entity is in effect simply outsourcing the provision of a fair valuation under this standard. That is, a third party valuation cannot substitute for a fair valuation and the entity is still required to appraise the valuation given within the framework of the standard.

The implication is that the entity does not avoid the requirements of the standard by obtaining a third party valuation and must still consider what level of inputs were used by the external party in arriving at its valuation. This also has implications for auditors who must review whether the entity has appropriately disclosed the fair value.

Summary

Discuss the role of fair value in accounting
- To ensure accounting information is relevant and useful to decision makers, the role of fair value is to establish a framework for measuring assets and liabilities using fair value, and to require consistent disclosures of items measured at fair value.

Evaluate the traditional definition of fair value
- The traditional definition of fair value was not consistent across all standards.
- While generally viewed as sufficient, there were a number of shortcomings identified with the interpretation of certain concepts within the traditional definition.

Describe the key aspects of the new definition of fair value
- The new definition of fair value is 'The price that would be received to sell an asset or paid to transfer a liability in an orderly transaction between market participants at the measurement date.'
- Fair value is based on exit prices.
- The transaction is based on one that would occur in an orderly transaction.
- The transaction is assumed to be between market participants.
- The transaction can be hypothetical.
- The valuation for a non-financial asset is based on its highest and best use.

Explain how fair value should be determined for assets and liabilities
- Fair value measurement is specific to the asset or liability being valued.
- The characteristics of the item under consideration, along with any restrictions on it, should be considered if they would influence the value placed on the item by market participants.
- A non-financial asset should be valued based on its highest and best use, even if this is different from the use it is being put to by the entity.
- The highest and best use must be physically possible, legally permissible and financially feasible.
- Liabilities and equity are fair valued based on the price to transfer the instrument to a third party.
- In most cases the value of a liability should match the fair value assigned to the corresponding asset by the counterparty.

Describe the three valuation techniques and the importance of the input hierarchy
- The market approach is based on the ability to identify a market for an identical or comparable asset or liability.

- The income approach is based on converting future cash flows or income and expense into a single present value.
- The cost approach is based on an estimate of the cost of replacing the 'service capacity' of the asset under consideration.
- The approach chosen should maximise observable inputs and minimise unobservable inputs.
- Some observable inputs do not need to be adjusted; they are based on active markets for identical assets or liabilities. These are termed Level 1 inputs.
- Other observable inputs require adjustment to reflect quantitative or qualitative differences between the item under consideration and the market observed. These are termed Level 2 inputs.
- Level 3 inputs are based on unobservable inputs that require estimation and inference by the entity.

Apply the general disclosure requirements for items measured at fair value
- There are two main goals with regards to disclosures under AASB 13/IFRS 13: they should be both useful to users and consistent.
- The principles for disclosure are set out in paragraph 91 of AASB 13/IFRS 13 and are quite extensive.

Discuss some specific issues that arise from the fair value standard
- Transaction costs should be considered in identifying the principal or most advantageous market, but do not form part of the valuation.
- When valuing large groups of items the entity should not take into account the impact on the market of transferring a large number of assets or liabilities.
- Where there is a difference between the fair value at initial recognition and the cost of the item, the entity (unless explicitly prohibited by another standard) can adjust the value in the balance sheet and recognise the resultant change through profit or loss.
- Third party valuations can be useful but cannot be relied on to establish the fair value of an item under consideration.

Review questions

1. Why has the IASB decided to release a standard on 'fair value', given that it is a general term, rather than a specific accounting issue?
2. What alternative measures are used in accounting to value items? Provide specific examples.
3. What are the main arguments against the old definition of fair value?
4. Identify and discuss the objectives of the fair value standard.
5. What is the new definition of fair value? Explain the key parts of this definition.
6. Why has the IASB chosen to use exit price as the primary measure of fair value?
7. Assuming an entity does not want to sell an asset, how is exit price useful to the users of that entity's financial statements?
8. The existence of a market is very important in determining fair value. What factors would indicate an appropriate market exists?
9. If it is determined that markets for the item under consideration are inactive, does that mean they cannot be fair valued? Discuss.
10. While fair values are based on market prices, the standard also states that fair values are based on the specific item being valued. What does this mean when considering the valuation of a share in a company? A large piece of mining equipment?

11. What are the limitations on determining the highest and best use for an asset when establishing fair value?
12. Identify and discuss the hierarchy for fair valuing liabilities.
13. Describe the valuation techniques that can be used to fair value an asset. Which method is preferred?
14. Describe the 3 levels of inputs that can be used in valuing an item under AASB 13/IFRS 13. How is the valuation level ultimately determined?
15. What information must be disclosed when an item in the balance sheet is measured at fair value? How are the disclosures different depending on the level of input?

Application questions

10.1 In light of the *Conceptual Framework for Financial Reporting* what are the broad arguments for and against the use of fair value and modified historical cost in accounting? **J** **K**

10.2 The fair valuing of liabilities has proved problematic for the IASB. Discuss the old definition and contrast it with the new definition. Have the problems been satisfactorily dealt with? Are there other issues to consider? **J** **K**

10.3 As noted in the chapter, potential valuation bases were considered when deciding how to measure fair value. Describe each and, where appropriate, give examples of how these are already used in accounting. **K**

10.4 Paragraph 16 of AASB 13/IFRS 13 indicates that fair value should be based on the principal or most advantageous market for an item. What do these terms mean and how does this relate to the value of the item to the entity itself? **K**

10.5 XYZ Ltd owns a land based drilling rig. It is in near perfect condition and unmodified. The company wishes to establish a fair value for the rig and identified two markets where almost identical rigs are being actively traded. In Market A, the price that would be received is $27 000, there will be a commission payable to a selling agent of 10%, and it will cost $3000 to transport the rig to that market. In Market B, the price that would be received is $26 000, there are no commissions to pay, and the costs to transport the asset to that market are $3000. What fair value would be placed on the asset based on this information? Show workings and explain. **K** **AS**

10.6 An entity wants to fair value some of its motor vehicle assets, which consist of approximately 20 motor vehicles of various, but common, commuter type cars. How would the entity go about fair valuing those motor vehicles and what factors would it need to consider? **J** **K** **AS**

10.7 The concept of highest and best use to value an asset was criticised by a number of respondents to the fair value exposure draft. They argued that it may not reflect the actual use of the asset by the entity and therefore provides a misleading valuation for the asset under consideration. Why did the IASB propose this definition and how is it justified in situations where the use is clearly different? **J** **K**

10.8 10 years ago your organisation bought a block of land on the Perth foreshore for $500 000. Over the next two years an apartment block was constructed on the site at a cost of $5 000 000. The apartments are currently owned by your organisation and sublet to tenants on a variety of leases not longer than five years. You want to establish the fair value of the property using AASB 13/IFRS 13. You have ascertained the following information for your assessment:

(i) Two separate expert valuations have been received. One valuer said the property is worth around $9 000 000 ($1 000 000 for the land and $8 000 000 for the building). The other valuer said it is worth $6 000 000 ($750 000 for the land and $5 250 000 for the building). Both valuers acknowledge that valuing the building in the current economic climate is difficult as there have been few sales of comparable buildings recently. They have used their experience of prior markets to estimate the values.

(ii) The current cost of replacing the building has been established as $7 500 000, determined based on the current design with today's construction costs, including labour, materials and overhead.

(iii) Present value of future cash flows:
Average net cash inflows over the next 20 years is estimated to be $650 000 per year, based on projected cash flows from rent, tax savings and expenditures. It is assumed after 20 years the building will need to be replaced, and the land will be worth $1 000 000. The current borrowing rate for the entity is 12%.

(iv) Depreciation is currently being charged on a straight-line basis using the same assumptions presented in (iii).

(a) Discuss each of the above four values as a basis for establishing fair value. In accordance with AASB 13/IFRS 13, which methodology do you believe is most appropriate? What additional information would you like to obtain to make a better estimate? **J** **K** **AS**

10.1
CASE
STUDY

Former FDIC Chief: Fair value caused the crisis

By David M Katz

Things were fine before the accounting standards-setters barged in and 'destroyed hundreds of billions of dollars of capital,' he contends.

In perhaps the most sweeping indictment of fair-value accounting to date, the chairman of the Federal Deposit Insurance Corporation during the 1980s savings-and-loan debacle told the Securities and Exchange Commission today that mark-to-market accounting rules caused the current financial meltdown.

Speaking at an SEC panel on mark-to-market accounting and the recent period of market turmoil, William Isaac, FDIC chairman from 1978 to 1985 and now the chairman of a consulting firm that advises banks, said that before FAS 157, the controversial accounting standard issued in 2006 that spells out how companies should measure assets and liabilities that have been marked to market, took hold, subprime losses were 'a little biddy problem.'

Isaac rhetorically asked the participants how the financial system could have come upon such hard times in under two years. 'I gotta tell you that I can't come up with any other answer than that the accounting system is destroying too much capital, and therefore diminishing bank lending capacity by some $5 trillion,' he asserted. 'It's due to the accounting system, and I can't come up with any other explanation.'

As of late 2006, Isaac, now chairman of The Secura Group, a financial institutions consulting firm, argued, 'inflation was under control, economic growth was good, unemployment was low, and there were no major credit problems in the banking system.' There were $1.2 trillion worth of U.S. subprime mortgages, with about $300 billion provided by FDIC-insured banks and the rest held by investors world-wide.

Since subprime losses were estimated to be about 20 percent in 2006, federally insured U.S. banks had lost about $60 billion in that market, according to Isaac. But those banks had recorded about $150 billion in after-tax earnings and had $1.4 trillion of capital.

The devastation that followed stemmed largely from the tendency of accounting standards-setters and regulators to force banks, by means of their litigation-shy auditors, to mark their illiquid assets down to 'unrealistic fire-sale prices,' the former FDIC chief asserted. The fair-value rules 'have destroyed hundreds of billions of dollars of capital in our financial system, causing lending capacity to be diminished by ten times that amount,' he said in his prepared remarks.

Noting that 157 was issued in 2006, Isaac noted that he wasn't 'asking that we change the whole system of accounting that has been developed for centuries.' Instead, he said, 'I'm asking for a very bad rule to be suspended until we can think about this more and stop destroying so much capital in our financial system. I think that's a basic step that needs to be taken immediately.'

Isaac added that it's his 'fervent hope that the SEC will recommend in its report to Congress that we abandon mark-to-market accounting altogether.' The panel was held as part of the commission's effort to comply with a requirement in the Emergency Economic Stabilization Act signed earlier this month that the SEC complete a study of mark-to-market's role in the current crisis by Jan. 2, 2009.

Isaac's remarks seemed to underline the highly polarized current state of the fair-value debate, with the banking industry pitted in fierce opposition to mark-to-market against the strong defense of investors and auditors. The latter point of view was represented by Ray Ball, a professor of accounting at the University of Chicago's graduate school of business. Noting that fair value has been a subject of accounting debate for five decades, he declared, 'I think it would be a terrible shame if we shoot the messenger and ignore the message' mark-to-market accounting conveys about the current condition of banks.

Similarly, Vincent Colman, a partner at PricewaterhouseCoopers, encouraged the SEC to look at the 'root causes' of the crisis, 'including those that go beyond accounting and financial reporting.' In particular, regulators should refine current capital guidelines and enforce 'an independent standards-setting process' that's free of political influence, he said.

The auditor urged the commission to keep the current fair-value rules intact during the credit crisis. 'Any fundamental change to fair value runs the risk of reducing confidence among investors,' he said, 'which tends to restrict the flow of capital.'

Espousing a middle position in the debate, Damon Silvers, associate general counsel for the AFL-CIO, asserted that there were errors on both sides. Countering fair value's critics on the banking side, he said that the opacity in the reporting of mortgage securitizations is a root cause of the credit freeze.

Further, even if fair-value accounting were eliminated, the trillions of dollars of distressed mortgage-backed assets on bank balance sheets 'are never going to be worth their full value,' he said. 'Assuming that those people who are thrown out of their homes will return with a pile of cash is deeply deluded.'

On the other hand, 157's provision that companies holding assets and liabilities in inactive markets need to use models to value them runs the risk of 'making a complete hash of financial statements,' according to Silvers.

The provision causes companies to move 'further and further away from the stated mark-to-market regime,' he observed. 'If we don't have that market [on which to base valuations], we move to a more baroque series of arrangements.'

Source: Article by David M Katz, 'Former FDIC Chief: Fair value caused the crisis', www.cfo.com.[10]

Questions

1. A number of observers suggest that fair valuing of CDOs under the old definition caused the global financial crisis of 2008. What do you think of this argument? **J** **AS**
2. What indications were there that the market was not working properly? **J** **AS**
3. Under AASB 13/IFRS 13, how would these financial instruments have been valued? **J** **AS**

NewForrest Mining is attempting to value a rehabilitation liability it has because of a mine development in northern Western Australia. The entity is legally required to rehabilitate the site to its former condition once mining is complete (estimated to be in 10 years time).

The entity has decided to use the expected present valuation technique and has established the following information. The mine is about 50% complete. Based on estimates to rehabilitate the mine in its current state it is estimated the labour costs (using in-house expertise) would be approximately $250 000, although a sensitivity analysis of the estimates indicates there is a 25% chance that that it would cost $50 000 less and a 25% chance it could cost $50 000 more. The real value of these wages is not expected to change significantly over the coming years. In addition to wages, there would also be overhead and equipment costs that would add about 80% to the total rehabilitation costs.

If an external party were asked to undertake the project, these costs would be comparable. In addition, an external contractor would include a mark up of around 20% to cover its requirements to make a reasonable profit. Further, given that there is a time factor due to the 10-year time frame, it is estimated that the external contractor would probably require a 5% premium after inflation to compensate it for risks associated with the inherent uncertainty of what could happen over the next 10 years.

Inflation is expected to continue to be around 4% for the foreseeable future. The risk-free interest rate on 10-year government bonds is 5%. The entity estimates its risk of non-performance is approximately 3.5%

Questions

1. Identify the three valuation techniques that could be used for establishing fair value and discuss their appropriateness in this situation. **K**
2. There are two present value approaches outlined in AASB 13/IFRS 13. How are they different and how would it have changed your approach to establishing fair value in this case study? **J** **K**
3. Calculate the expected present value of the liability in accordance with AASB 13/ IFRS 13. **AS**
4. How would your value have differed if you had simply calculated the valuation based on the entities expected discounted cash flow? **J** **AS**
5. How is this difference in valuation, which has caused concern in the mining industry, justified by the IASB? **J** **K**
6. What is non-performance risk and why is it included in the calculation? **K**

Additional readings

Gwilliam, D & Jackson, RHG 2008, 'Fair value in financial reporting: problems and pitfalls in practice: a case study analysis of the use of fair valuation at Enron', *Accounting Forum*, vol. 32, iss. 3, pp. 240–59.

International Accounting Standards Board 2011, IFRS 13 *Fair Value Measurement*,

Rayman, R 2007, 'Fair value accounting and the present value fallacy: the need for an alternative conceptual framework', *The British Accounting Review*, vol. 39, no. 3, pp. 211–25.

Ronen, J 2008, 'To fair value or not to fair value: a broader perspective', *Abacus*, vol. 44, no. 2, 181–208.

Whittington, G 2008, 'Fair value and the IASB/FASB conceptual framework project: an alternative view', *Abacus*, vol. 44, no. 2, pp. 139–68.

End notes

1. International Accounting Standards Board (IASB) 2011, *IFRS 13 Fair value measurement illustrative examples*, IASB, London.
2. ibid.
3. Weil, J 2010, 'How to conjure up billions', *The Sydney Morning Herald*, 13 September, www.smh.com.au.
4. International Accounting Standards Board (IASB) 2011, *IFRS 13 Fair value measurement illustrative examples*, IASB, London.
5. International Accounting Standards Board (IASB) 2011, IFRS13 *Fair value measurement*, IASB, London.
6. idid.
7. McClymont K & West, M 2011, 'Serial floats and patent porkies', *The Sydney Morning Herald*, 4 January, www.smh.com.au.
8. International Accounting Standards Board (IASB) 2011, *IFRS 13 Fair value measurement illustrative examples*, IASB, London.
9. ibid.
10. Katz, DM 2008, 'Former FDIC chief: fair value caused the crisis', 29 October, www.cfo.com.

11

Sustainability and environmental accounting

LEARNING OBJECTIVES

After studying this chapter, you should be able to:

1 explain the meaning of sustainability and why an entity might embrace sustainable development practices

2 explain sustainability reporting and describe a range of methods used to report on sustainability and environmental performance

3 describe the commonly used guidelines for sustainability reporting, and articulate how they can assist corporate reporting of sustainability performance

4 evaluate the range of stakeholders that can influence sustainable business practice, and how entities can engage with these stakeholders

5 explain how entities can use environmental management systems to improve environmental performance and reporting

6 evaluate the implications of climate change for accounting.

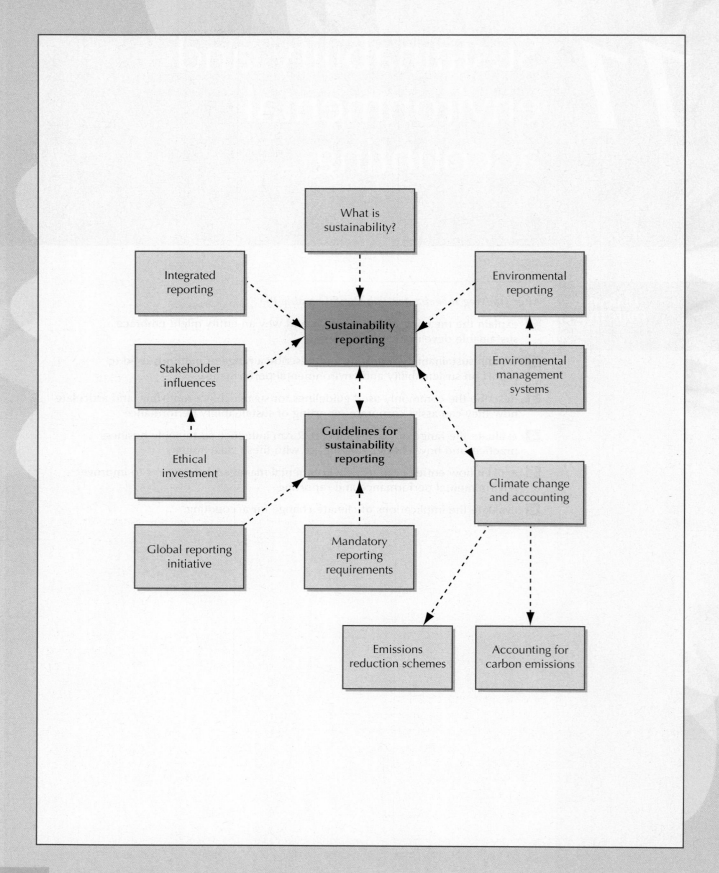

Sustainability issues, and particularly those resulting from climate change, have an increasing influence on the business environment and, in turn, on the role of accountants. A need to measure and report on social and environmental performance and to consider how greenhouse gas emissions are generated by the entity impacts on its information systems and reporting practices.

In this chapter we examine sustainability and how it impacts on the accounting profession. Sustainability reporting and the recently proposed 'integrated reporting' are introduced. We will consider some of the mandatory requirements for sustainability reporting globally and discuss guidelines to assist in preparing sustainability reports. While shareholders are traditionally seen as the most important stakeholders with regard to financial performance, sustainability and **environmental accounting** tends to consider a broader range of stakeholder interests. How environmental management systems can be used to assist in documenting, measuring and reporting environmental performance is also examined. The chapter will conclude with an examination of accounting for carbon emissions — an emerging area impacting the accounting arena.

LO 1 WHAT IS SUSTAINABILITY?

Before considering how **sustainability** affects the contemporary business environment and the accounting profession, the meaning of sustainability needs to be clarified. **Sustainable development** was identified as a significant issue by the General Assembly of the United Nations in 1987, when it commissioned a report — *Our Common Future* — to foster a global solution to ongoing pressures on the environment. The report was presented by the United Nations World Commission on Environment and Development (known as the Brundtland Commission after its Chair, Gro Harlem Brundtland) and subsequently became known as the Brundtland Report. The report defined sustainable development as 'development that meets the needs of the present without compromising the ability of future generations to meet their own needs'.[1] This definition relates to three main areas: economic development, environmental development and social development.

The Brundtland definition highlights the importance of both intergenerational and intragenerational equity. **Intergenerational equity** has a long-term focus and recognises that consumption of resources should not affect the quality of life of future generations. **Intragenerational equity** relates to the ability to meet the needs of all current inhabitants. This means strategies need to consider poverty and access to basic food, water and shelter for all inhabitants Together, intragenerational and intergenerational equity have been termed eco-justice. The above sustainability definition also considers what is known as eco-efficiency — a focus on the efficient use of resources to minimise their impact on the environment. While the definition of sustainability has received widespread debate, there is general agreement that it involves preservation and maintenance of the environment and involves some duty of social justice.[2]

While the definition of sustainability initially considered global development at a government level, it is intended to also relate to organisations and companies. Given corporate entities are in control of the majority of the earth's resources, this means that any moves towards sustainability will not happen unless entities consider how their operations affect the environment and society. While it is essential for an entity to make a profit in order to continue operations, if it is to do this sustainably, it needs to consider how to do so without causing any damage to the environment and society. Embracing sustainability could make good business sense for an entity.

Figure 11.1 demonstrates how BHP Billiton has considered why it embraces sustainable development from not only a business case, but also considers factors beyond the business case.

FIGURE 11.1 Why BHP Billiton embraces sustainable development

The business case for sustainable development

Our bottom-line performance is dependent on ensuring access to resources and securing and maintaining our licence to operate and grow. Maximising the bottom-line is, however, about recognising the value protection and value add that can be achieved through enhanced performance in HSEC aspects. Delivery of this enhanced performance is a core expectation of our management teams. This is termed our sustainability value add and the value it can bring to our business is recognised through the following.

Reduced business risk and enhanced business opportunities

Understanding and managing risk provides greater certainty for shareholders, employees, customers and suppliers, and the communities in which we operate. By managing our business risk we can be better informed, more decisive and can pursue growth opportunities with increased confidence.

The aim is to embed risk management in all critical business systems and processes so that risks can be identified and managed in a consistent and holistic manner.

Gaining and maintaining our licence to operate and grow

Access to resources is crucial to the sustainability of our business. Fundamental to achieving access to resources is effectively addressing heightened political and societal expectations related to the environmental and social aspects of our business.

Improved operational performance and efficiency

Many key operational performance indicators are inextricably linked to sustainability performance. For example, improving energy efficiencies reduces both costs and greenhouse gases; increasing plant life reduces maintenance cycles, which then reduces requirements for consumables and replacement items. Reducing wastes immediately eliminates operational costs. The application of innovation and business improvement processes can not only improve operational efficiency and performance but also deliver sustainability gains.

Improved attraction and retention of our workforce

Our workforce is an essential element of our business, and being able to attract and retain a quality workforce is fundamental to our success.

Maintaining a healthy and safe workplace is a universal value of all employees. Effective employee development and training programs, attractive remuneration packages, addressing work/life balance, and providing a fair and non-discriminatory work environment all contribute to employee attraction and retention.

Maintained security of operations

Asset security is a critical element that can be significantly impacted by the nature of relationships with host communities. Trusting and supportive relationships can lead to reduced security risks, whereas distrustful relationships can lead to heightened security risks. This is particularly critical for our operations in parts of the world with politically unstable environments.

Enhanced brand recognition and reputation

The benefits of enhanced brand recognition and reputation are many but often difficult to quantify. Understanding what our stakeholders perceive as responsible behaviour, meeting these expectations and achieving recognition from financial institutions, investors and customers can deliver value.

For example, enhanced reputation may foster an increased belief that the Company has the credibility and capabilities to deliver on its commitments. This can promote shareholders' faith in proposed investments, communities' faith in community development plans, governments' faith in successful delivery of projects, and business partners' faith that we are reliable and competent in all that we do.

FIGURE 11.1 *(continued)*

Enhanced ability to strategically plan for the longer term

By anticipating and understanding trends in society — new regulations, heightened societal expectations and improved scientific knowledge — and assessing these against our business models, our ability to proactively plan for the longer term is improved. This includes entering emerging markets, revising product mixes or changing operational technologies.

Beyond the business case

Beyond the business case described above, there are also many clear societal benefits that flow from our ability to integrate aspects of sustainability into our business. These benefits include, but are not limited to, contributing to improved standards of living and self-sustaining communities.

The diagram below illustrates the many facets of value creation at BHP Billiton.

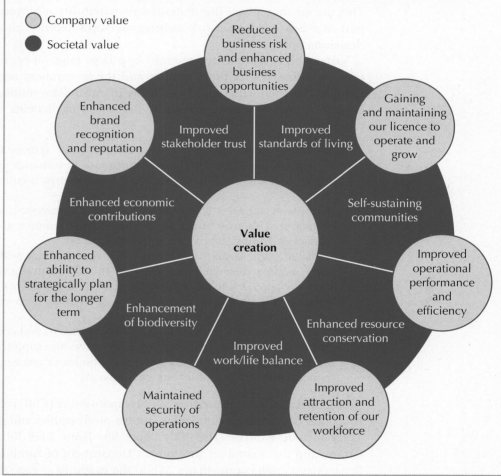

Source: BHP Billiton, *BHP Billiton sustainability report.*[3]

LO 2 SUSTAINABILITY REPORTING

With the increasing importance of sustainable development to business, reporting on sustainable performance has also increased. A number of terms are commonly used for **sustainability reporting**. It has been referred to as corporate social reporting, corporate social responsibility reporting, triple bottom line reporting, sustainability reporting, environmental reporting, social audit, environmental, social and governance (ESG) reports and stakeholder reports. Many of these terms are used interchangeably. While the term **triple bottom line reporting** was commonly used until approximately 2006 and ESG appears to be emerging as a more prominent term, the use of the term 'sustainability reporting' is still the most common and will be used in this chapter.

The term 'triple bottom line' reporting was initially coined by John Elkington in reference to the three main areas that are the focus of sustainable development — economic, environmental and social development.[4] A **triple bottom line report (TBL)** or **sustainability report** refers to a report that not only presents information about the economic value of an entity, but provides information upon which stakeholders can also judge the environmental and social value of an entity. Elkington points out that it not only reflects reporting requirements, but can be used as a model to assist with performance measurement, accounting, auditing and reporting.[5] This means that a well implemented sustainability reporting system can be used as part of a broader framework to integrate sustainability into business management decisions.[6]

Sustainability reports are presented by a large range of organisations from most sectors, including not-for-profit entities and the government sector. The Australian government, in producing guidelines to assist Australian entities determine appropriate environmental indicators, identified the following benefits of sustainability or TBL reporting:

- *Embedding sound corporate governance and ethics systems throughout all levels of an organisation.* Currently many corporate governance initiatives are focused at the Board level. TBL helps ensure a values-driven culture is integrated at all levels.
- *Improved management of risk through enhanced management systems and performance monitoring.* This may also lead to more robust resource allocation decisions and business planning, as risks are better understood.
- *Formalising and enhancing communication with key stakeholders such as the finance sector, suppliers, community and customers.* This allows an organisation to have a more proactive approach to addressing future needs and concerns.
- *Attracting and retaining competent staff by demonstrating an organisation is focused on values and its long-term existence.*
- *Ability to benchmark performance both within industries and across industries.* This may lead to a competitive advantage with customers and suppliers, as well as enhanced access to capital as the finance sector continues to consider non-financial performance within credit and investment decisions.[7]

Sustainability, TBL or corporate social responsibility (CSR) reports have been presented by a range of Australian companies, not-for-profit entities and government departments. These include Westpac, The Body Shop, Rio Tinto, BHP Billiton, CSR, Lion, Foster's Group, and the Australian government Department of Families, Housing, Community Services and Indigenous Affairs. While the extent of organisations presenting sustainability reports has increased, there has been limited guidance on appropriate methods of developing sustainability reports.[8] Reporting in many countries is currently voluntary (more information on reporting guidance in different jurisdictions will be presented later in the chapter) and it is the responsibility of the organisation to develop their own measurement and reporting format. A widely accepted format for the integration of sustainability concepts into business and reporting of sustainability aspects is reflected in the Global Reporting Initiative (GRI). GRI is discussed later in the chapter. Initially, we will consider a new initiative currently being developed — integrated reporting.

Integrated reporting

Integrated reporting is a recent initiative designed to improve sustainability reporting and integrate it more closely with financial and governance reporting. In August 2010, the Prince of Wales' Accounting for Sustainability Project (A4S) and GRI announced the formation of an International Integrated Reporting Committee (IIRC). The IIRC members represent a cross-section of society, including members from the corporate, accounting, securities, regulatory, non-governmental organisation (NGO), intergovernmental organisation (IGO) and standard-setting sectors. The mission statement of the IIRC is:

> To create a globally accepted integrated reporting framework which brings together financial, environmental, social and governance information in a clear, concise, consistent and comparable format. The aim is to help with the development of more comprehensive and comprehensible information about organizations, prospective as well as retrospective, to meet the needs of the emerging, more sustainable, global economy.[9]

The IIRC aims to 'reach a consensus among governments, listing authorities, business, investors, accounting bodies and standard setters for the best way to tackle the challenges of Integrated Reporting'.[10] Amongst a range of other activities, the IIRC is charged with developing an 'overarching Integrated Reporting framework, which sets out the scope and key components of Integrated Reporting' and to consider whether standards in the area should be voluntary or mandatory.[11] Further information about the IIRC can be found on its website, www.theiirc.org.

The development of a proposal for integrated reporting followed the global financial crisis and resulted from a perceived need for a 'new economic model that can protect businesses, investors, employees and society from a cycle of successive and increasingly debilitating crises'.[12] Governments and business leaders recognise there needs to be a change in emphasis of corporate reporting given it currently does not adequately reflect material ESG factors such as resource usage, social impacts, human rights and how businesses may contribute to climate change.[13] It is perceived that integrated reporting which includes all these non-financial but critical risk factors will increase the quality of corporate reporting as it will ensure businesses report on and consider the issues critical to long-term sustainability and success.[14]

At time of writing, the IIRC has developed a number of key milestones moving forward, including the release of an Integrated Reporting discussion paper; and a two-phase pilot program which encompasses initial company and investor testing as the first phase, followed by a full two-year pilot program — launched in September 2011 — which will allow companies to apply the principles of Integrated Reporting to be proposed in the IIRC's discussion paper and inform the future development of the framework.

Environmental reporting

Environmental reporting is a subset of sustainability reporting. Entities, when presenting sustainability reports, generally include information about their environmental performance and impacts. Information about environmental activities could be found as a separate section of the annual report, in a separate environmental report or as part of a comprehensive sustainability, ESG, CSR or TBL report.

A large body of research has examined environmental disclosure.[15] Much of this research has examined disclosure from the perspective of legitimacy theory, which is based on the notion of a social contract, and argues that organisations can only continue to exist if the society in which they operate recognises they are operating within a value system that is consistent with society's own.[16] This means that an organisation must appear to consider the rights of the public at large, not just its shareholders. This theory is discussed in more detail in chapter 5. If you refer to figure 11.1, BHP Billiton refers to its 'licence to operate', which equates to meeting the terms of its social contract.

To date, research has not drawn any clear conclusions as to the relationship between environmental performance and environmental disclosure. Legitimacy theory would propose that entities with poor environmental performance would more likely produce more, or higher-quality environmental information to address potential legitimacy threats. Entities that have been subjected to environmental threats such as prosecutions due to emissions or large spills have been found to provide greater levels of environmental information.[17] Al-Tuwaijri, Christensen and Hughes II took a holistic approach to examine how management's overall strategy jointly affects environmental disclosure, environmental performance and economic performance. They find that good environmental performance is positively associated with both good economic performance and more extensive quantifiable environmental disclosures of specific pollution measures. In doing so, Al-Tuwaijri et al. indicate that managers should change their strategic outlook from fixating on the cost of regulatory compliance considering the opportunity costs of environmental pollution and the consequent positives associated with good environmental performance.[18]

Clarkson, Li, Richardson and Vasvari in an examination of discretionary environmental disclosures by a sample of US firms from the most polluting industries, found a positive association between environmental disclosures and environmental performance.[19] The authors conclude that their results support an economic-based voluntary disclosure theory which predicts that firms that are good performers will more likely present greater levels of disclosure to differentiate themselves from poor performers.[20] The results of Clarkson et al. do not support a legitimacy argument where poor performers are more likely to increase disclosure to detract attention from their poor performance.[21] These theories are discussed in more detail in chapter 5.

Another factor that could affect environmental reporting is firm reputation and strategic risk management.[22] Managers have a desire to manage stakeholder views of environmental performance in an effort to portray the firm as environmentally and socially responsible, with the expectation that environmental or social risk management will lead to maximising earnings potential and investment in the company. Bebbington, Larrinaga and Moneva explore this issue and conclude that reputation risk management, while not a competing explanation to legitimacy motives, can further add to our understanding of the motivations for social and environmental reporting.[23]

In the following sections we examine both voluntary guidelines and current global mandatory reporting requirements that might be used to guide corporate sustainability reporting.

LO 3 GUIDELINES FOR SUSTAINABILITY REPORTING

There are a range of guidelines which have emerged to provide direction on appropriate sustainability reporting. The United Nations (UN) has been responsible for a number of these initiatives. The UN Global Compact is a strategic policy initiative for businesses which are committed to aligning their operations and strategies with principles in the areas of human rights, labour, environment and anti-corruption.[24] Entities joining the Global Compact are required to annually communicate on their progress, with the Global Reporting Initiative's reporting framework being the preferred method of reporting.

The UN has also produced Principles for Responsible Investment, aimed at integrating social and environmental factors into financial practices. Signatory companies, usually institutional investors, are required to communicate their application of the Principles annually to the UN.[25]

The United Nations Conference on Trade and Development (UNCTAD), in 2008, produced guidance on the use of corporate sustainability indicators in annual reports. The objective of the document, which was developed with reference to the Global Reporting Initiative Guidelines and International Financial Reporting Standards, is to provide detailed guidance on the preparation of reports using selected indicators. In doing so the guidance discusses key stakeholders and their information needs, including an overview of users and their uses for corporate responsibility reporting, and selection indicators along with detailed guidance on reporting each of these indicators. The selection indicators chosen are presented in table 11.1.

TABLE 11.1 Overview of selection indicators

Group	Indicator
Trade, investment and linkages	• Total revenues • Value of imports versus exports • Total new investments • Local purchasing
Employment creation and labour practices	• Total workforce with breakdown by employment type, employment contract and gender • Employee wages and benefits with breakdown by employment type and gender • Total number and rate of employee turnover broken down by gender • Percentage of employees covered by collective agreements
Technology and human resources development	• Expenditure on research and development • Average hours of training per year per employee broken down by employee category • Expenditure on employee training per year per employee broken down by employee category
Health and safety	• Cost of employee health and safety • Work days lost to occupational accidents, injuries and illness
Government and community contributions	• Payments to government • Voluntary contributions to civil society
Corruption	• Number of convictions for violations of corruption related laws or regulations and amount of fines paid/payable

Source: Adapted from UNCTAD, *Guidance on corporate responsibility indicators in annual reports.*[26]

The Organisation for Economic Co-operation and Development (OECD) includes as part of its *Guidelines for Multinational Enterprises*, a section on 'Disclosure', which encourages multinational enterprises to provide disclosures on their non-financial performance in addition to financial performance.[27]

The International Organization for Standardization (ISO) has developed standards dealing with a range of issues. Of relevance to sustainability reporting is the ISO 14000 series on environmental management and the ISO 26000 guidance standard on social responsibility. ISO 14001 requires management to develop a policy of communication of environmental performance. The new ISO 26000, which was issued in 2010, requires organisations to demonstrate their accountability by reporting significant impacts related to social responsibility to concerned stakeholders.[28]

The most widely recognised guidelines, however, are provided by the Global Reporting Initiative (GRI). These guidelines will be detailed in the next section.

Global Reporting Initiative

GRI was launched in 1997 as an initiative to develop a globally accepted reporting framework to enhance the quality of sustainability reporting and is a joint initiative of the Coalition of Environmentally Responsible Economies (CERES) and the United Nations Environment Program (UNEP).[29] The aim is to enhance transparency, comparability and clarity, amongst other principles.

Sustainability reports based on the GRI Framework can be used to 'demonstrate organizational commitment to sustainable development, to compare organizational performance over time, and to measure organizational performance with respect to laws, norms, standards and voluntary initiatives'.[30] GRI provides a framework of principles and performance indicators that organisations can use to measure and report their economic, social and environmental performance. The cornerstone of the framework is the *Sustainability Reporting Guidelines* (the Guidelines). While the initial guidelines were produced in 2000, the third-generation (G3) Guidelines were released in 2006, with an update (G3.1) being issued in March 2011. The G3.1 Guidelines include a range of new disclosures, new indicators or adjusted disclosure requirements compared to the previous G3 Guidelines.

The G3.1 Guidelines present a number of principles that should be used to define reporting content and to ensure reporting quality. The guidelines are presented in two parts as follows:

Part 1 — Reporting Principles and Guidance
- Principles to define report *content*: materiality, stakeholder inclusiveness, sustainability context, and completeness.
- Principles to define report *quality*: balance, comparability, accuracy, timeliness, reliability, and clarity.
- Guidance on how to set the report *boundary*.

Part 2 — Standard Disclosures
- Strategy and Profile
- Management Approach
- Performance Indicators.[31]

They include 55 core indicators and 29 additional indicators across environmental, economic and social performance areas. Table 11.2 presents the range of performance indicators reflected in the G3.1.

The updated G3.1 Guidelines now include expanded guidance for reporting on human rights, local community impacts and gender. GRI has also produced Sector Supplements which address the relevant issues to specific sectors and present tailored guidelines to assist companies in these sectors to prepare relevant sustainability reports. Sector Supplements are currently provided for the following sectors: airport operators, construction and real estate, electric utilities, financial services, food processing, mining and metals and non-governmental organisations. Further guidance is currently under development for media, oil and gas, and event organisers.

In 2011, GRI also produced a Technical Protocol which provides process guidance on how to define the content of a sustainability report. This includes deciding on the scope of a sustainability report, the range of topics to be covered, and the priority and level of coverage to be given to each topic.[32]

TABLE 11.2 Range of performance indicators reflected in the G3.1 Guidelines	
Economic	• Revenues, operating costs, employee compensation, donations and other community investments, retained profits, and payments to investors and governments • Financial implications and other risks and opportunities due to climate change • Policy, practices, and spending on locally based suppliers • Procedures for local hiring and proportion of senior management hired from the local community • Coverage of the organisation's defined benefit plan obligations • Development and impact of infrastructure investments and services provided primarily for public benefit • Range of ratios of standard entry level wage by gender compared to local minimum wage
Environmental	• Materials used and recycled • Energy consumption, savings, including initiatives to reduce energy usage • Water use and recycling • Biodiversity, including protection and conservation • Habitats protected and restored • Emissions, effluent and waste measurement and management • Environmental impacts of products • Non-compliance with environmental laws • Impacts of transport
Labor Practices and Decent Work	• Workforce by employment type, region and gender • Rate and number of new employee hires and turnover by age and gender • Return to work and retention rates by gender • Percentage of employees covered by collective bargaining agreements • Rates of injury, occupational diseases and absenteeism • Education, training, counselling and risk control programs in place • Average hours of training per year per employee
Society	• Percentage of operations with local community engagement • Operations with significant potential or actual negative impact on local communities • Anti corruption policies and practices, including staff training • Monetary value of fines and non-monetary sanctions relating to breach of laws and regulations
Human Rights	• Percentage and number of investment agreements and contracts that have undergone human rights screening • Details of human rights screening of suppliers, contractors and business partners • Incidents of discrimination and action taken • Details of screening of suppliers for incidents of child labour and forced or compulsory labour risks
Product Responsibility	• Assessment of life cycle stages for health and safety risks • Details of programs for adherence to laws, standards and voluntary codes relating to marketing, promotion, communications and sponsorship

Source: Adapted from GRI, *Sustainability reporting guidelines 3.1.*[33]

In addition, GRI has an Application Levels system which was introduced with the release of the G3 Guidelines in October 2006. The Application Levels indicate the extent to which The Guidelines have been applied in sustainability reporting and meet the needs of reporting organisations in terms of objectively displaying their use of the GRI Guidelines. They communicate which part of the reporting framework has been addressed and reflect the degree of transparency in reporting.[34]

The Application Levels are not a measure of sustainability performance. There are three different Application Levels: A, B and C. Reporting entities are required to assess their Application Level and have the additional opportunity to have GRI check the Application Level applied.[35] Figure 11.2 shows the Application Level diagram, which lists the requirements for each Application Level.

Report Application Level		C	C+	B	B+	A	A+
Standard disclosures	G3 Profile disclosures — Output	Report on: 1.1 2.1–2.10 3.1–3.8, 3.10–3.12 4.1–4.4, 4.14–4.15	Report externally assured	Report on all criteria listed for Level C plus: 1.2 3.9, 3.13 4.5–4.13, 4.16–4.17	Report externally assured	Same as requirement for Level B	Report externally assured
	G3 Management approach disclosures — Output	Not required		Management approach disclosures for each indicator category		Management approach disclosures for each indicator category	
	G3 Performance indicators & sector supplement performance indicators — Output	Report on a minimum of 10 performance indicators, including at least one from each of: economic, social and environmental.		Report on a minimum of 20 performance indicators, at least one from each of economic, environmental, human rights, labor, society, product responsibility.		Report on each core G3 and sector supplement* indicator with due regard to the materiality principle by either: a) reporting on the indicator or b) explaining the reason for its omission.	

*Sector supplement in final version

FIGURE 11.2 GRI Application Level criteria

Source: GRI, *Application Levels.*[36]

GRI is currently working on the G4 version of its Guidelines and anticipates it will be published in 2013.[37]

Mandatory sustainability reporting requirements

There are increasing instances of mandatory ESG reporting requirements around the globe, some of which are considered in this section.

Australia

The *Corporations Act 2001* requires directors to outline the company's performance in relation to environmental regulations. In November 2005, the parliamentary Joint

Committee on Corporations and Financial Services and the Corporations and Markets Advisory Committee conducted enquiries into the desirability of mandatory reporting of social and environmental impacts. While a report was released this has not resulted in increasing mandatory reporting requirements.[38]

The *National Greenhouse and Energy Reporting Act 2007* (NGER Act) introduced a national framework for reporting and dissemination of information about greenhouse gas (GHG) emissions and energy use by certain corporations.[39]

Canada

The Canadian securities regulators require public companies to produce an Annual Information Form that reports on the current and future financial and operational effects of environmental protection requirements. In addition, some companies are required to report information about pollutant emissions, which are included in a National Pollutant Release Inventory.[40] This is required under the Canadian Environmental Protection Act 1999 (CEPA 1999). From 2004, CEPA 1999 set up the Greenhouse Gas Emissions Reporting Program which requires large emitters to report GHG emissions.[41]

Denmark

The Danish Act of 16 December 2008 requires Denmark's largest companies to include their ESG activities in their annual reports or justify the absence of this information. This requirement relates to state-owned public companies and large listed companies.[42]

Norway

The Norwegian government issued a white paper titled *Corporate social responsibility in a global economy* which announced the government's intention to propose that large companies should report their social and environmental performance to stakeholders. It suggests GRI as an appropriate reporting tool. Legislation is yet to be enacted.[43]

United States

The US Environmental Protection Agency proposed a mandatory GHG reporting rule, which became effective on 29 December 2009. It requires reporting of GHG emissions information by facilities that emit GHGs and for supplies of fuel and industrial gases.[44] In addition, the Securities and Exchange Commission (SEC) requires disclosure of some general information, including disclosure of capital expenditure for environmental control facilities, and about environmental claims.[45]

LO 4 STAKEHOLDER INFLUENCES

An understanding of why entities adopt sustainable reporting practices can be gained from examining the range of organisational stakeholders and how they have changed. Traditionally, shareholders were seen as the primary stakeholder, where entities run a business with the sole objective of maximising profitability and shareholder value. Contemporary entities now consider a range of stakeholders in their decision making. These might include employees, customers, suppliers, the media, government, superannuation funds and other institutional investors, lenders and community groups. Entities following GRI are required to undertake stakeholder assessment as part of their reporting process. Similarly, businesses as a matter of course identify and engage with stakeholders as a means of reducing risk and managing reputation.

Figure 11.3 reflects AGL Energy Ltd's approach to stakeholder engagement and is reflected in its sustainability report.

Stakeholder engagement

Engaging in constructive dialogue with stakeholders keeps us responsive to issues important to our customers, employees, investors, regulators and the wider community.

The diagram below outlines how AGL incorporates the AA1000 principles of inclusivity, materiality and responsiveness into our business and sustainability strategy.

AGL approach to integrating the principles of inclusivity, materiality and responsiveness into business practices

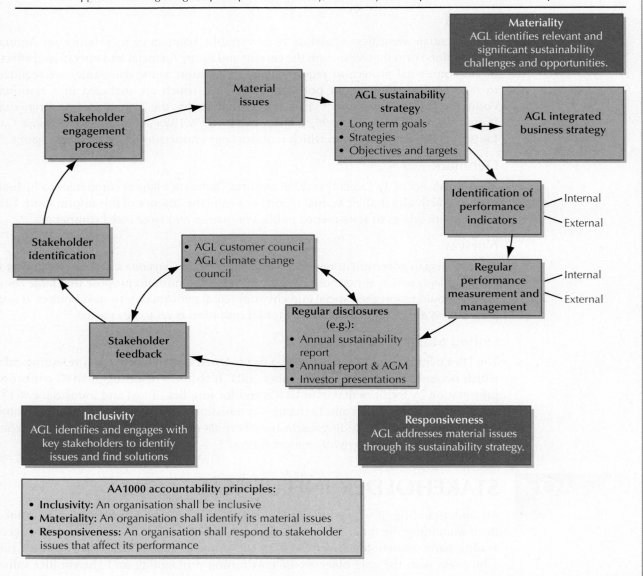

FIGURE 11.3 AGL Energy Ltd's approach to stakeholder engagement

Source: AGL Energy Ltd, *AGL summary sustainability report 2009.*[46]

Stakeholders are increasingly concerned with issues of sustainability. Growing recognition of **climate change** and the impact corporations have on global warming has likely led to this increase. Accounting for the issues resulting from climate change is addressed later in this chapter.

Table 11.3 provides examples of stakeholders and why they might be interested in corporate sustainability.

Stakeholder	Interest in corporate sustainability
Shareholders	Sustainability can improve entity value. Others consider sustainability issues in their investment decisions.
Customers	Some customers are interested in the source of products and actively seek 'green' or 'fairtrade' products.
Fund investors	Some investors invest in funds that make investments on socially responsible grounds.
Community groups	These groups are invested in services and facilities offered in the local community, as well as job creation, health and emissions information.
Media	The media can voice concerns of other stakeholders as well as set the public agenda relating to corporate sustainability issues.
Government and regulators	In some jurisdictions government and regulators are required to monitor mandatory reporting of sustainability or environmental issues.
Creditors or banks	Financial institutions need to consider the environmental impacts of projects they fund.

TABLE 11.3 Stakeholder interests in corporate sustainability

The relationship between organisations and their stakeholders is considered in stakeholder theory. The managerial branch of stakeholder theory seeks to explain how stakeholders might influence organisational actions. The extent to which an organisation will consider its stakeholders is related to the power or influence of those stakeholders. Managers need to determine which stakeholders they should consider in their actions and manage these competing interests.

A stakeholder's power is related to the degree of control they have over resources required by the organisation.[47] The more necessary to the success of the organisation are the resources the stakeholder controls, the more likely it is that managers will address the stakeholder's concerns. One of the major roles of managers is to consider the relative importance of each of their organisational stakeholders in meeting their strategic objectives, and manage these relationships accordingly. Hedberg and Von Malmborg found that Swedish companies produce social and environmental information to satisfy powerful stakeholders in the form of their financiers.[48] Orij also found stakeholders influenced corporate social reporting, particularly in countries where there was a close relationship between organisations and their stakeholders.[49] Stakeholder theory is considered in more detail in chapter 5.

Ethical investment

Ethical investment and ethical investment funds pose a growing influence on corporate sustainability performance and reporting. Entities are challenged by the social, environmental and regulatory pressures as institutional investors increasingly voice their concerns about the economic, financial and regulatory risks of global warming. Many institutional investors have increased their demand for sustainability reporting by becoming signatories to the **Carbon Disclosure Project (CDP)**. The CDP represents several large institutional investors, holding assets of over US$71 trillion, such as the Investor Group on Climate Change, Goldman Sachs, JB Were, Catholic Super, and Booz and Company. These investors are concerned about the risks associated with climate change, and thus are calling for more information about how companies are addressing the challenges of climate change. The CDP questions companies about their policies, particularly in regard to lowering emissions and climate change resilience.[50]

The CDP is a voluntary effort to encourage standardised reporting procedures for companies to provide investors with relevant information about the business risks and opportunities from climate change.[51] Recent research has shown that the CDP has influenced corporate GHG disclosure. For example, Okereke observed that the top UK companies began to disclose their actions to reduce GHG emissions as a result of increased pressure from powerful institutional investors supported by institutions such as the CDP, the Sustainable and Responsible Investment (SRI) Fund and the Institutional Investors Group on Climate Change (IIGCC).[52] Using global governance, institutional and commensuration theories, Kolk et al. analysed company disclosures of GHGs in response to the CDP questionnaire for years 2003–2007. They found responses to the CDP are growing and corporate GHG disclosure has achieved some progress in technical terms, but acknowledge the problems of self reporting, the lack of rigorous GHG disclosure guidelines and associated global regulation.[53]

In addition to direct investment in an ethical investment fund, investors have the opportunity to identify investments from benchmark indices which categorise investments on the basis of sustainability in addition to financial performance. Launched in 1999, the Dow Jones Sustainability Indexes (DJSIs) track the financial performance of the leading sustainability-driven companies worldwide.[54] Based on the cooperation of Dow Jones Indices and Sustainable Asset Management (SAM) — an international investment group — the DJSIs provide asset managers with reliable and objective benchmarks to manage sustainability portfolios. In addition to providing information to investors, the DJSIs provide feedback to participating companies on their sustainability performance, and how they rank when compared to industry averages.

ENVIRONMENTAL MANAGEMENT SYSTEMS

In conjunction with increased interest in sustainable reporting, interest in environmental management systems (EMSs) has also intensified. An EMS is a system that organisations implement to measure, record and manage their environmental performance. Implementation of an EMS suggests an organisation's commitment to better monitor, manage, measure and report environmental matters. An EMS not only provides organisations with an environmental management tool, but also facilitates the organisation's communication to stakeholders.

Malmborg emphasises that the EMS is a tool not only important for an organisation's environmental management tasks, but also to assist with communication and organisational learning. An essential role of the EMS is to provide information that can enhance communication regarding a company's environmental and sustainable development in response to community concerns.[55]

The international standard ISO 14001 *Environmental management*, which governs EMSs, was released in 1996. This standard relates to the development and audit of EMSs and requires certifying companies to establish and maintain communication, both internally and externally. It requires companies to develop policies, objectives and targets, and assess environmental performance against these requirements.[56] Patten and Crampton provide evidence that companies who certify their EMS using ISO 14001 have a higher level of environmental disclosures. Having a certified EMS is also more likely to address risk concerns of stakeholders.[57]

LO 6 CLIMATE CHANGE AND ACCOUNTING

One of the most pressing sustainability issues is climate change. The United Nations Framework Convention on Climate Change (UNFCCC) has developed a framework for international action designed to reduce climate change, known as the Kyoto Protocol.[58] The **Kyoto Protocol** is an agreement that commits signatories to achieve GHG or **carbon emissions** reduction. As part of this endeavour, signatory countries have committed to achieving specific GHG emissions reduction targets.

Under the Kyoto Protocol, countries were allocated allowed emissions in the form of assigned units that corresponded to their agreed emission targets. If countries hold units in excess of their targets, these units can be traded. In this section we will examine emissions schemes that are increasingly being used to reduce the impacts of climate change, and the accounting issues that stem from climate change and emissions trading.

Emissions reduction schemes

One response that is being used around the globe to mitigate or reduce climate change is the development of emissions reduction schemes. These can be in the form of either an emissions trading scheme or a carbon tax. An **emissions trading scheme (ETS)**, often referred to as a cap and trade scheme, is a system that is designed to control emissions by allowing participants to trade excess emissions permits. Emissions trading schemes work differently in different jurisdictions, but essentially governments create tradeable emissions permits which are based on the Kyoto target. Permits are either given to business, sold or auctioned. A cap or limit is set on the level of emissions organisations are permitted. Organisations are required to obtain permits that equal the amount of their emissions. If their emissions levels exceed the amount of permits they hold, they are required to buy additional permits to avoid substantial fines. This has led to the creation of secondary markets where GHG permits can be bought or sold, where the price is determined by demand and supply in the market. Over time governments can lower the cap, thus moving towards achieving the national emissions reduction target.

The alternative is the application of a carbon tax based on the amount of emissions or GHGs. There is no cap set on the level of emissions and it is thought by some that a carbon tax is less likely to lead to a reduction in emissions because of this.[59] However, the alternative view is that a carbon tax sends an immediate price signal to the market which addresses the externality imposed on society by the polluter.[60]

The most established ETS is the European Union Emissions Trading Scheme (EU ETS), which commenced in January 2005. A mandatory ETS commenced in New Zealand on 1 July 2010, with Canada and Japan both proposing compulsory trading schemes. Japan has had a voluntary scheme in operation since 2005. In addition to participating in the EU ETS, the United Kingdom has proposed the introduction of the CRC Energy Efficiency Scheme (formerly known as the Carbon Reduction Commitment) to apply across public sector entities not currently covered by the EU ETS. The United States government also proposed the introduction of an ETS in the 2010 budget.

The New Zealand ETS is being progressively introduced, with all industries expected to be included by 2015. It commenced with the forestry sector, with electricity, industrials and transport also now included. Agriculture will commence on 1 January 2015. The New Zealand government has pledged to cut GHG emissions by between 10 and 20% on 1990 levels by 2020.[61]

The Australian government proposed the Carbon Pollution Reduction Scheme (CPRS) originally developed by respected economist Professor Ross Garnaut.[62] The proposed CPRS is a market-based solution designed to encourage business to invest in GHG reduction.[63] The CPRS had many detractors however, particularly from the powerful mining and energy lobbies which argued that their industries would lose competitive advantage if GHGs were priced.[64] At the time of writing, the Australian government has put its CPRS on hold, and a multi-party climate change committee, in addition to a separate business roundtable, has been set up to develop a GHG reduction policy. On 12 October 2011, the Australian House of Representatives passed a Clean Energy legislative package. This legislation is intended to put a price on carbon in a move to create an incentive to invest in clean energies, thus reducing pollution. This legislation passed the Australian Senate on 8 November 2011 and has since received Royal Assent. A fixed carbon price of $23 a tonne will apply from 1 July 2012, moving to a flexible price after 3 years.[65]

While emissions trading schemes generally target high emitters, it is anticipated that every business is affected in some way, through increased power or transport costs for example. There is an increase in demand by some businesses for products to be carbon neutral, or for suppliers to disclose their carbon footprint. Contemporary Issue 11.1 presents an example of the New Zealand wine industry making moves towards carbon neutrality.

**11.1
CONTEMPORARY
ISSUE**

Perfect timing for world's first carbon neutral winery

By Bruce Gilkison

In September 2006, the New Zealand Wine Company Ltd (NZWC) announced that it had been independently certified as 'carbon-neutral', the first winery in the world to get such certification. Its timing was impeccable. The world was becoming increasingly concerned about carbon emissions. Millions of people had already seen Al Gore's movie 'An Inconvenient Truth'. And a month later, the Stern Review was released in the UK, prompting widespread concern about the economic effects of climate change and issues such as 'food miles'.

NZWC's carboNZero certification brought the winery much media and public attention. But what was this status actually worth?

CarboNZero program

The carboNZero programme is a certification scheme for minimising climate change impacts. It is administered by Landcare Research NZ Ltd, a Crown Research Institute, and is available to an organisation, or for a product, service, event or individual.

For certification, the greenhouse gas emissions associated with that source must be measured, managed and mitigated.

Value of certification

CarboNZero certification seems to be a very valuable asset for NZWC. But because this was the first company in NZ to be certified, Landcare Research wanted to be certain that it was, and engaged me to assess the value of this 'brand' to the winery.

Findings

The economic effects of certification were positive, and probably more than anyone had initially expected.

1. There had been a dramatic increase in demand for NZWC's products, particularly from UK supermarket chains.
2. I expected to see major energy savings as a result of NZWC's involvement in the carboNZero programme. In fact, although there had been big savings these were attributed to initiatives already taken.
3. NZWC's costs of certification and mitigation were quite low, and brought immediate benefits.

4. The impetus for this initiative had come from staff who had a strong commitment to sustainability. While certification had achieved marketing advantages, these were not the driving force behind it.
5. Certification provided some extremely cost-effective promotion. The Prime Minister, Helen Clark, has referred to Grove Mill's example in speeches on a number of occasions, and there have been many references to it in the media.
6. It is possible that sales, instead of increasing that year, might actually have dropped if the company had not been so well informed and prepared for the 'food miles' debate.

Source: Bruce Gilkison, 'Perfect timing for world's first carbon neutral winery', *Chartered Accountants Journal.*[66]

Questions

1. Outline the potential costs and benefits of making moves towards carbon neutrality. **J**
2. The 'food miles' movement is increasing in strength in the United Kingdom, with some major retailers, for example Tesco, asking suppliers to label products with their carbon footprint. Evaluate what impact this move could have on the New Zealand wine industry. **J**

An ETS provides a mechanism by which economic activities of an organisation can be linked to climate change benefits. However, an ETS scheme is not anticipated to be without costs to organisations.[67] These may include significant costs to meet reporting requirements such as compliance and monitoring costs, in addition to the costs of future investments to mitigate and manage emissions. Companies may also be required to re-evaluate their strategies, operational and control systems.[68]

If the ETS operates as a market scheme there is likely to be additional costs or at the very least price fluctuations and uncertainty involved in the event that carbon credits need to be purchased. Lund examined the cost impacts of the EU ETS on energy intensive manufacturing industries. He observed direct costs associated with the carbon reduction requirements stated in the EU directive. Indirect costs resulting from a higher electricity price were also noted.[69]

Multinational corporations are particularly affected by the development of ETSs. They are likely to face a wide variety of schemes that differ in scope and enforcement, thus leading to differing institutional constraints and reporting requirements across the locations in which they operate.[70]

Accounting for carbon emissions

As previously mentioned, ETSs are either currently operating or proposed across a number of jurisdictions. Despite this, there is currently no guidance on how to account for carbon pollution permits or emissions trading activities. In 2004, prior to the commencement of the EU ETS, the IASB issued IFRIC 3 *Emission Rights*. However there was considerable criticism of the proposal, with many arguing it involved inconsistent accounting of assets and liabilities and potential volatility. Following these criticisms it has since been withdrawn. The IASB project on **accounting for carbon emissions** and emissions trading schemes is currently paused, with the IASB considering its agenda in early 2012.

The operation of a carbon trading scheme creates a number of short-term and long-term financial implications for organisations.[71] In the short term, organisations are required to account for both purchased and allocated emissions allowances. One issue facing organisations is how to account for allowances allocated by government on an annual basis. Are they to be recorded at fair value or at cost — effectively zero? Should there be a difference in treatment for allocated versus purchased emissions allowances? The treatment of allowances is likely to be related to their classification as either an intangible asset or a financial instrument.

Organisations also need to consider how to account for their obligation to deliver allowances to the government at the end of the reporting period to 'pay' for their emissions. It has also been suggested that organisations should be permitted to use hedge accounting to reduce the risk associated with their allowance asset and emissions liability.[72] Table 11.4 demonstrates the range of accounting approaches currently in use in Europe to account for emissions credits and trading rights.

TABLE 11.4 Accounting approaches for the EU ETS — PWC view

	Full market value approach (IFRIC 3)	Cost of settlement approach	
		Alternative approach 1	Alternative approach 2
Initial recognition — granted allowances	Recognise when able to exercise control; corresponding entry to government grant, at market value at date of grant.	Recognise when able to exercise control; corresponding entry to government grant, at market value at date of grant.	Recognise when able to exercise control; recognise at cost, which for granted allowances is a nominal amount (e.g. nil).
Initial recognition — purchased allowances	Recognise when able to exercise control, at cost.	Recognise when able to exercise control, at cost.	Recognise when able to exercise control, at cost.
Subsequent treatment of allowances	Allowances are subsequently held at cost or revalued amount, subject to review for impairment.	Allowances are subsequently held at cost or revalued amount, subject to review for impairment.	Allowances are subsequently held at cost, subject to review for impairment.
Treatment of deferred income	Government grant amortised on a systematic and rational basis over compliance period.	Government grant amortised on a systematic and rational basis over compliance period.	Not applicable.
Recognition of liability	Recognise liability when incurred.	Recognise liability when incurred.	Recognise liability when incurred.
Measurement of liability	Liability is remeasured fully based on the market value of allowances at each period end, whether the allowances are on hand or would be purchased from the market.	Remeasure liability at each period end. For allowances held, remeasure to carrying amount of those allowances (i.e. market value at date of recognition if cost model is used; market value at date of revaluation if revaluation model is used) on either a FIFO or weighted average basis. A liability relating to any excess emission would be remeasured at the market value at the period end.	Remeasure liability at each period end. For allowances on hand, at the carrying amount of those allowances (nil or cost) on a FIFO or weighted average basis. A liability relating to any excess emission would be remeasured at the market value at the period end.

Source: PricewaterhouseCoopers, *Trouble-Entry Accounting — Revisited.*[73]

Climate change also has an impact on traditional financial accounting as it affects the value of assets and asset impairment decisions. Climate change can affect the value of physical assets such as land, and assets used to produce products no longer in demand due to falling demand and consumer change in preference to 'green' products and technologies. Climate change also affects the disclosure of risk and risk management strategies required in financial reports.

Summary

Explain the meaning of sustainability and why an entity might embrace sustainable development practices

- Sustainability relates to development that meets the needs of the present without compromising the ability of future generations to meet their own needs.

Explain sustainability reporting and describe a range of methods used to report on sustainability and environmental performance

- With the increasing importance of sustainable development to business, reporting on sustainable performance has also increased. A number of terms are commonly used for sustainability reporting.
- The term 'triple bottom line' (TBL) reporting refers to the three main areas that are the focus of sustainable development: economic, environmental and social development.
- Sustainability, TBL or corporate social responsibility reports have been presented by a range of Australian companies, not-for-profit entities and government departments.
- Integrated reporting is a recent initiative designed to improve sustainability reporting and integrate it more closely with financial and governance reporting.
- Environmental reporting is a subset of sustainability reporting. Currently, no separate guidelines for environmental reporting exist.

Describe the commonly used guidelines for sustainability reporting, and articulate how they can assist corporate reporting of sustainability performance

- The most widely recognised is the Global Reporting Initiative (GRI). GRI was launched in 1997 as an initiative to develop a globally accepted reporting framework to enhance the quality of sustainability reporting.
- GRI includes 55 core indicators and 29 additional indicators across environmental, economic and social performance areas.

Evaluate the range of stakeholders that can influence sustainable business practice, and how entities can engage with these stakeholders

- Traditionally shareholders were seen as the primary stakeholder, where entities run a business with the primary objective to maximise profitability and shareholder value. Contemporary businesses now consider a range of stakeholders in their decision making.
- Stakeholders are now more concerned with issues of sustainability. Increasing recognition of climate change and the impact corporations have on global warming has likely led to this increase.

- Ethical investment and ethical funds pose a growing influence on corporate sustainability behaviour. Institutional investors have increased their demand for sustainability reporting through signing to the Carbon Disclosure Project. In addition to the CDP, investment in ethical funds has increased substantially in recent years. Investors also have the opportunity to identify investments from benchmark indices which identify investments on the basis of sustainability, in addition to financial performance.

LO 5   **Explain how entities can use environmental management systems to improve environmental performance and reporting**

- An environmental management system (EMS) is a system that organisations implement to measure, record and manage their environmental performance. Implementation of an EMS suggests an entity's commitment to better monitor, manage, measure and report environmental matters. An EMS not only provides companies with an environmental management tool, but also facilitates the entity's communication to stakeholders.

LO 6   **Evaluate the implications of climate change for accounting**

- One response that is being used around the globe to mitigate or reduce climate change are emissions trading schemes. An emissions trading scheme (ETS) is a system that is designed to control emissions by allowing participants to trade excess emissions permits.
- While emissions trading schemes generally target high emitters, every organisation is expected to be affected in some way.
- There is currently no guidance on how to account for carbon pollution permits or emissions trading activities.

Review questions

1. Explain the meaning of sustainability and outline why corporations might consider it in their business operations.
2. Explain the difference between eco-justice and eco-efficiency, and explain how both might relate to business activities.
3. What reasons can an entity provide for adopting sustainable development?
4. Identify what information entities are likely to provide if they use triple bottom line reporting.
5. Explain the difference between sustainability reporting and traditional financial reporting.
6. What benefits should entities expect from preparing sustainability reports?
7. What is international integrated reporting and how does it differ from the current financial reporting system we have?
8. What is the Global Reporting Initiative, and what is its purpose?
9. Identify four corporate stakeholders and explain how they affect a business's operations.
10. For the four corporate stakeholders you have identified above, document how an organisation might engage with them about sustainability issues.
11. Identify how ethical investment can affect corporate decision making regarding sustainable business operations.
12. Explain what an environmental management system is and how it can be used to improve environmental performance.
13. Explain how emissions trading schemes are likely to affect financial reporting.

Application questions

11.1 There are currently no formal accounting standards for the reporting of social and environmental activities. Evaluate what issues this has for preparation of financial reports. **J** **K**

11.2 In this chapter a range of stakeholders have been identified that managers should consider when determining their sustainability performance and reporting. Determine how managers should engage with each of these stakeholders and document what sustainability issues they would be likely to discuss during this engagement process. **J** **K**

11.3 Obtain the 2011 sustainability report for Toyota Motor Corporation. Prepare a report that addresses the following issues:
(a) Document Toyota's vision and mission statement, and articulate how these might relate to sustainability, if at all.
(b) Outline Toyota's stakeholders and explain how they have engaged each of these stakeholder groups.
(c) Outline governance mechanisms in place on the Board of Directors to address sustainability.
(d) Articulate how Toyota links sustainability to its risk management systems.
(e) Outline any guidance Toyota used in implementing environmental and social performance and reporting systems. **J** **K** **CT**

11.4 You are the accountant of a company that is considering expanding its operations to a country in the developing world. You are to prepare a report to the CEO outlining what issues the company should consider from a sustainability perspective when making this decision. **J** **CT**

11.1 CASE STUDY

Turning the heat on

By Christine Grimard

After being trained by former US vice-president Al Gore, Mike Sewell FCPA is convinced that the weight of scientific evidence behind climate change and the global effects we're seeing today should be enough to push businesses and individuals to take action.

Sewell is the general manager and company secretary for the Nossal Institute for Global Health, which is actively involved in research, education and inclusive development health practices in developing countries. In July this year, he underwent an intensive climate change course, along with a group of other volunteers under the Australian Conservation Foundation's Climate Project. The training was led by Nobel Prize winner Al Gore, whose Oscar award winning documentary *An Inconvenient Truth* helped bring mass international attention to climate change...

His interest in climate change grew earlier this year when he read an article in the medical journal *The Lancet* drawing the link between the developing world where his work is focused, and the magnified effects of climate change in these areas. He says that it's only in understanding the massive impact of climate change that organisations and individuals will start to take action.

'Climate change affects all of us but it affects developing countries more,' says Sewell. He notes that a lack of resources and already poor infrastructure amplifies the devastation caused by climate change.

In acknowledging these global incidences Sewell puts aside the debate over whether the scientific arguments of global warming are valid. It's a separate argument he says. 'We have to acknowledge that things are happening to the world and that we need to change things if we want to protect the next generation.'

'I'd say the majority of small businesses haven't addressed the issues because they don't acknowledge the problems and they aren't aware of the effects,' Sewell says.

The effects, however, are becoming more tangible for organisations around the globe, as their carbon footprints begin to appear on their balance sheets with the introduction of carbon emissions trading schemes.

'It's important for CPAs to understand what the carbon emissions trading scheme is about, and what drives it. What we as accountants need to do is to understand the fundamentals that are driving the scheme and make sure that the desired result comes through. These are exciting times for us because as accountants we can drive significant global change,' says Sewell, who's president of CPA Australia's Victoria division.

'There's no doubt that it will increase costs,' he notes. 'But we were always going to pay a price for carbon reduction. In the short term we'll pay a price, but in the long term we'll learn to develop a model that's more sustainable...'

Source: Excerpts from Christine Grimard, 'Turning the heat on', *InTheBlack*.[74]

Questions

1. Outline how climate change is likely to affect Sewell's business operations in developing countries. **J** **K**
2. Evaluate the social issues likely to impact on a business operating in a developing country. **J** **K**
3. Evaluate the role accountants can play in addressing climate change in a business environment. **J** **K**

**11.2
CASE
STUDY**

Dutch group seeks to tie executive bonuses to social responsibility

By Richard Milne and Michael Steen

DSM wants focus on 'people, profits, planet'.

Two Dutch companies have proposed linking top managers' pay to broad measures of environmental sustainability and worker and customer satisfaction, giving a novel twist to the debate on how to reward executive performance.

DSM, the Dutch life sciences group, will announce today that half the bonuses for its management board will be tied to targets such as the reduction of greenhouse gas emissions and energy use, the introduction of new environmentally friendly products and improvements in workforce morale. This week, TNT, the Dutch mail operator, unveiled similar plans that also include customer satisfaction.

Source: Excerpts from Richard Milne & Michael Steen, 'Dutch group seeks to tie executive bonuses to social responsibility', *The Financial Times*.[75]

Questions

1. The company that employs you is a manufacturing firm. It is considering following the lead of DSM and developing some performance indicators to tie executive bonuses to environmental performance. Outline what some of these might be. **J** **K**
2. Document measures of performance relating to social issues, such as employee and consumer relations that should also be considered. Explain your answer. **J** **K**

**11.3
CASE
STUDY**

Super funds set to track carbon footprints

By Derek Parker

Superannuation funds are emerging as a crucial driver in the shift towards a carbon constrained economy, according to a key report commissioned by the Australian Institute of Superannuation Trustees.

The report, *Carbon Counts 2008: The Carbon Footprints of Australian Superannuation Investment Managers*, was provided by Trucost, a UK-based consulting firm recognised as a leader in the analysis of the environmental performance of companies. It examines 14 of the largest superannuation funds in Australia, accounting for $31.6 billion in equity holdings, and looks at the greenhouse gas emissions associated with 100 equity portfolios that employ different investment styles.

'This will have a very significant impact on the investment strategies of super funds,' says Andrew Barr, policy and research manager for AIST . . . 'There is also a lot of difference between funds, with a 36 per cent difference between the largest and smallest carbon footprints of the 14 funds, and an eight-fold variation in efficiency between individual portfolios.

Understandably, some investment categories have a smaller carbon footprint than others, with the sustainability and growth groups showing a better performance than the index. The utilities and basic resources groups recorded carbon footprints at the higher end of the scale. But Barr points to the need to properly understand the figures and the nature of superannuation investment.

'A crucial aspect of the *Carbon Counts* report is that it shows that portfolios can be designed to reduce their carbon intensity by the careful selection of companies within each category. This approach rebalances holdings to overweight carbon-efficient companies and underweight carbon-intensive companies relative to a benchmark. There are carbon-efficient companies in all investment categories.

'The bottom line is that a portfolio's overall exposure to carbon liabilities can be reduced without sacrificing financial returns.'

Source: Excerpts from Derek Parker, 'Super funds set to track carbon footprints', *The Australian*.[76]

Questions
1. Identify why you would expect the finance sector, investment funds in particular, to have an interest in climate change. **J** **K**
2. Outline potential sources of information that superannuation funds could use to gather data about a company's sustainability operations. **J** **K**
3. Outline methods superannuation funds could use to encourage companies to take a more active role in managing climate change. **J** **K**

Additional readings

Bebbington, J & Larrinaga-Gonzalez, C 2008, 'Carbon trading: Accounting and reporting issues', *European Accounting Review*, vol. 17, no. 4, pp. 697–717.

Chalmers, K, Godfrey, J & Potter, B 2009, 'What's new in water and carbon accounting', *Charter*, vol. 80, iss. 8, pp. 20–2.

Cook, A 2009, 'Emissions rights: From costless activity to market operations', *Accounting, Organizations and Society*, vol. 34, pp. 456–68.

Dellaportas, G 2008, 'Accounting for carbons', *Charter*, June, pp. 64–5.

Malkovic, T 2010, 'Seeking sustainability', *Charter*, March, pp. 32–6.

Milne, M, Ball, A & Mason, I 2010, 'The Kyoto seesaw: accounting for GHG emissions 2008 to 2012', *Chartered Accountants Journal*, February, pp. 25–7.

O'Connor, J 2009, 'Creating a 3D bottom line', *InTheBlack*, September, pp. 34–7.

Parker, L 2008, 'Wine's carbon footprint', *Charter*, November, pp. 20–2.

Stebbens, P & Spicer, M 2009, 'Carbon and impairment', *Charter*, May, pp. 64–6.

Stringer, A & McWilliams, K 2009, 'Update on carbon emissions', *Charter*, June, pp. 60–1.

End notes

1. United Nations World Commission on Environment and Development 1987, *Our common future — The Brundlandt Report*, University of Oxford Press, Oxford.
2. Gray, R 2010, 'Is accounting for sustainability actually accounting for sustainability... and how would we know? An exploration of narratives of organisations and the planet', *Accounting, Organizations and Society*, vol. 35, iss. 1, pp. 47–62.
3. BHP Billiton 2006, 'BHP Billiton sustainability report', BHP Billiton, Melbourne, p. 6.
4. Elkington, J 1997, *Cannibals with forks — the triple bottom line of 21st century business*, Capstone Publishing, Oxford.
5. ibid.
6. Suggett, D & Goodsir, B 2002, *Triple bottom line measurement and reporting in Australia. Making it tangible*, The Allen Consulting Group, Melbourne; Christen, EW, Shepheard, ML, Meyer, WS, Jayawardane, NS & Fairweather, H 2006, 'Triple bottom line reporting to promote sustainability of irrigation in Australia', *Irrigation and Drainage Systems*, vol. 20, iss. 4, pp. 329–43.
7. Department of the Environment and Heritage, Environment Australia 2003, *Triple Bottom Line Reporting in Australia: a guide to reporting against environmental indicators*, Commonwealth of Australia, Canberra, p. 6.
8. Dillard, JF, Brown, D & Marshall, RS 2005, 'An environmentally enlightened accounting', *Accounting Forum*, vol. 29, no. 1, pp. 77–101.
9. International Integrated Reporting Committee 2011, *Mission statement*, International Integrated Reporting Committee, London, viewed 21 October 2011, www.theiirc.org.
10. ibid.
11. ibid.
12. Stevenson, N 2011, 'New dawn for reporting', *Accountancy Futures: Critical Issues for Tomorrow's Profession*, 3rd edn, ACCA, pp. 10–13.
13. ibid.
14. ibid.
15. See for example: Patten, DM 1992, 'Intra-industry environmental disclosures in response to the Alaskan oil spill: a note on

legitimacy theory', *Accounting, Organizations and Society*, vol. 17, no. 5, pp. 471–5; Roberts, RW 1992, 'Determinants of corporate social responsibility disclosure: An application of stakeholder theory', *Accounting, Organizations and Society*, vol. 17, no. 6, pp. 595–612; Deegan, C & Rankin, M 1996, 'Do Australian companies report environmental news objectively? An analysis of environmental disclosures by firms prosecuted successfully by the Environmental Protection Authority', *Accounting, Auditing & Accountability Journal*, vol. 9, no. 2, pp. 52–67; Brown, N & Deegan, C 1998, 'The public disclosure of environmental performance information — a dual test of agenda setting theory and legitimacy theory', *Accounting and Business Research*, vol. 29, no. 1, pp. 21–41; Deegan, C, Rankin, M & Tobin, J 2000, 'An examination of the corporate social and environmental disclosures of BHP from 1983–1997: a test of legitimacy theory', *Accounting, Auditing & Accountability Journal*, vol. 15, no. 3, pp. 312–43; Alciatore, ML & Dee, CC 2006, 'Environmental disclosures in the oil and gas industry, Environmental Accounting: Commitment or Propaganda', *Advances in Environmental Accounting & Management*, vol. 3, pp. 49–75; Cho, CH & Patten, DM 2007, 'The role of environmental disclosures as tools of legitimacy: A research note', *Accounting, Organizations and Society*, vol. 32, no. 7/8, pp. 639–47; Gibson, K & O'Donovan, G 2007, 'Corporate governance and environmental reporting: an Australian study', *Corporate Governance: An International Review*, vol. 15, no. 5, pp. 944–56.
16. Gray, R, Owen, D & Adams, C 1996, *Accounting and Accountability*, Hertfordshire, UK: Prentice Hall.
17. Deegan, C & Rankin, M 1996, 'Do Australian companies report environmental news objectively? An analysis of environmental disclosures by firms prosecuted successfully by the Environmental Protection Authority', *Accounting, Auditing & Accountability Journal*, vol. 9, no. 2, pp. 52–67.

18. Al-Tuwaijri, SA, Christensen, TE & Hughes II, KE 2004, 'The relations among environmental disclosure, environmental performance and economic performance: a simultaneous equations approach', *Accounting, Organizations and Society*, vol. 29, iss. 5/6, pp. 447–71.
19. Clarkson, P, Li, Y, Richardson, G & Vasvari, FP 2008, 'Revisiting the relation between environmental performance and environmental disclosure: an empirical analysis', *Accounting, Organizations and Society*, vol. 33, nos. 4/5, pp. 303–27.
20. Dye, RA 1985, 'Disclosure of nonproprietary information', *Journal of Accounting Research*, vol. 23, no. 1, pp. 123–45; Verrecchia, RE 1983, 'Discretionary disclosure', *Journal of Accounting and Economics*, vol. 5, no. 1, pp. 179–94.
21. Clarkson, P, Li, Y, Richardson, G & Vasvari, FP 2008, 'Revisiting the relation between environmental performance and environmental disclosure: an empirical analysis', *Accounting, Organizations and Society*, vol. 33, nos. 4/5, pp. 303–27.
22. Unerman, J 2008, 'Strategic reputation risk management and corporate social responsibility reporting', *Accounting, Auditing and Accountability Journal*, vol. 21, no. 3, pp. 362–4.
23. Bebbington, J, Larrinaga, C & Moneva, JM 2008, 'Corporate social reporting and reputation risk management', *Accounting, Auditing and Accountability Journal*, vol. 21, no. 3, pp. 337–61.
24. United Nations Global Compact 2011, *What is the Global Compact?*, UN Global Compact Office, New York, viewed 24 October 2011, www.unglobalcompact.org.
25. UNEP Finance Initiative & UN Global Compact, *Principles for responsible investment*, UN Environment Programme Finance Initiative and UN Global Compact, London, viewed 24 October 2011, www.unpri.org.
26. United Nations Conference on Trade and Development (UNCTAD) 2008, *Guidance on corporate responsibility indicators in annual reports*, United Nations, New York and Geneva, pp. 17–18.

27. OECD 2011, *OECD Guidelines for Multinational Enterprises*, 2011 edn, OECD Publishing, Paris, viewed 24 October 2011, www.oecd.org.
28. International Organization for Standardization 2010, *ISO 26000: 2010 Guidance on social responsibility*, International Organization for Standardization, Geneva, viewed 24 October 2011, www.iso.org.
29. Global Reporting Initiative (GRI) 2006, *Sustainable Reporting Guidelines 3.0*, Global Reporting Initiative, Amsterdam, viewed 24 October 2011, www.globalreporting.org.
30. Global Reporting Initiative (GRI) 2011, *Sustainability reporting guidelines 3.1*, Global Reporting Initiative, Amsterdam, viewed 24 October 2011, www.globalreporting.org.
31. ibid.
32. Global Reporting Initiative (GRI) 2011, *Technical protocol — applying the report content principles*, Global Reporting Initiative, Amsterdam.
33. Global Reporting Initiative (GRI) 2011, *Sustainability reporting guidelines 3.1*, Global Reporting Initiative, Amsterdam, viewed 24 October 2011, www.globalreporting.org.
34. Global Reporting Initiative (GRI) 2011, *Application levels*, Global Reporting Initiative, Amsterdam, viewed 24 October 2011, www.globalreporting.org.
35. ibid.
36. ibid.
37. Global Reporting Initiative (GRI) 2011, *G4 developments*, Global Reporting Initiative, Amsterdam, viewed 24 October 2011, www.globalreporting.org.
38. United Nations Environment Program (UNEP), KPMG, The Global Reporting Initiative (GRI) & Unit for Corporate Governance in Africa 2010, *Carrots and Sticks — Promoting transparency and sustainability*, Global Reporting Initiative, Amsterdam, viewed 24 October 2011, www.globalreporting.org.
39. Department of Climate Change and Energy Efficiency 2011, *National greenhouse and energy reporting*, Commonwealth of Australia , Canberra, viewed 24 October 2011, www.climatechange.gov.au.
40. Environment Canada 2011, *National pollutant release inventory*, Government of Canada, Ottawa, viewed 24 October 2011, www.ec.gc.ca.
41. United Nations Environment Program (UNEP), KPMG, The Global Reporting Initiative (GRI) & Unit for Corporate Governance in Africa 2010, *Carrots and Sticks — Promoting transparency and sustainability*, Global Reporting Initiative, Amsterdam, viewed 24 October 2011, www.globalreporting.org; Environment Canada 2011, *Greenhouse gas emissions reporting program*, Government of Canada, Ottawa, viewed 24 October 2011, www.ec.gc.ca.
42. Observatoire sur la Responsabilité Sociétale des Entreprises (ORSE) 2011, *Danish legal framework*, Observatoire sur la Responsabilité Sociétale des Entreprises (ORSE), Paris, viewed 24 October 2011, www.reportingcsr.org.
43. Observatoire sur la Responsabilité Sociétale des Entreprises (ORSE) 2011, *Norwegian legislative framework*, Observatoire sur la Responsabilité Sociétale des Entreprises (ORSE), Paris, viewed 24 October 2011, www.reportingcsr.org.
44. U.S. Environmental Protection Agency, *Greenhouse gas reporting program*, Federal government of the United States, Washington, viewed 24 October 2011, www.epa.gov.
45. Observatoire sur la Responsabilité Sociétale des Entreprises (ORSE) 2011, *American legal framework*, Observatoire sur la Responsabilité Sociétale des Entreprises (ORSE), Paris, viewed 24 October 2011, www.reportingcsr.org.
46. AGL Energy Ltd 2009, *AGL Summary Sustainability Report 2009*, AGL Energy Ltd, Sydney, viewed 24 October 2011, www.aglsustainability.com.au.
47. Ullmann, AA 1985, 'Data in search of a theory: a critical examination of the relationship among social disclosure and economic performance of US firms', *Academy of Management Review*, vol. 10, no. 3, pp. 540–57.
48. Hedberg, CJ & Von Malmborg, F 2003, 'The Global Reporting Initiative and corporate sustainability reporting in Swedish companies', *Corporate Social Responsibility and Environmental Management*, vol. 10, iss. 3, pp. 153–64.
49. Orij, R 2010, 'Corporate social disclosure in the context of national cultures and stakeholder theory', *Accounting, Auditing and Accountability Journal*, vol. 23, no. 7, pp. 868–89.
50. Carbon Disclosure Project (CDP) 2011, *CDP global 500 report 2011 — Accelerating low carbon growth*, Carbon Disclosure Project (Trading) Ltd, London, viewed 24 October 2011, www.cdproject.net.
51. Kolk, A, Levy, D & Pinkse, J 2008, 'Corporate responses in an emerging climate regime: the institutionalization and commensuration of carbon disclosure', *European Accounting Review*, vol. 17, no. 4, pp. 719–45.
52. Okereke, C 2007, 'An exploration of motivations, drivers and barriers to carbon management: the UK FTSE 100', *European Management Journal*, vol. 25, no. 6, pp. 475–86.
53. Kolk, A, Levy, D & Pinkse, J 2008, 'Corporate responses in an emerging climate regime: the institutionalization and commensuration of carbon disclosure', *European Accounting Review*, vol. 17, no. 4, pp. 719–45.
54. CME Group Index Services LLC and SAM Indexes GmbH 2011, *Dow Jones Sustainability Indexes*, Zurich, viewed 24 October 2011, www.sustainability-index.com.
55. Malmborg, FB 2002 'Environmental management systems, communicative action and organizational learning', *Business, Strategy and the Environment*, vol. 11, no. 5, pp. 312–32.
56. International Organization for Standardization 2004, *ISO 14001:2004 Environmental management systems*, International Organization for Standardization, Geneva, viewed 24 October 2011, www.iso.org.
57. Patten, DM & Crampton, W 2004, 'Legitimacy and the Internet: an examination of corporate web page environmental disclosures', *Advances in Environmental Accounting and Management*, vol. 2, iss. 3, pp. 31–57.
58. United Nations Framework Convention on Climate Change 1998, *Kyoto Protocol to the United Nations Framework Convention on Climate Change*, United Nations, Bonn, viewed 24 October 2011, unfccc.int.
59. Anonymous 2009, 'To cap or tax?', *InTheBlack*, vol. 79, no. 10, pp. 46–8.
60. ibid.

61. Ministry for the Environment 2011, *The New Zealand Emissions Trading Scheme*, New Zealand, Wellington, viewed 24 October 2011, www.climatechange.govt.nz.

62. Garnaut, R 2008, *The Garnaut Climate Change Review Final Report*, Cambridge University Press, Melbourne.

63. ibid.

64. Pearse, G 2009, 'Quarry vision: coal, climate change and the end of the resources boom', *Quarterly Essay*, vol. 33, pp. 1–122.

65. Department of Climate Change and Energy Efficiency 2011, Clean energy bills receive Royal Assent, Commonwealth of Australia, Canberra, viewed 17 January 2012, www.cleanenergyfuture.gov.au.

66. Gilkison, B 2008, 'Perfect timing for world's first carbon neutral winery', *Chartered Accountants Journal*, vol. 87, iss. 4, pp. 56–9.

67. Bui, B, Fowler, C & Hunt, C 2009, 'Costs of an ETS', *Chartered Accountants Journal*, vol. 88, no. 9, pp. 36–8.

68. ibid.

69. Lund, P 2007, 'Impacts of EU carbon emission trade directive on energy-intensive industries — Indicative micro-economic analyses', *Ecological Economics*, vol. 63, no. 4, pp. 799–806.

70. Pinkse, J & Kolk, A 2007, 'Multinational Corporations and Emissions Trading: Strategic responses to new institutional constraints', *European Management Journal*, vol. 25, no. 6, pp. 441–52.

71. Bebbington, J & Larrinaga-Gonzalez, C 2008, 'Carbon trading: Accounting and reporting issues', *European Accounting Review*, vol. 17, no. 4, pp. 697–717.

72. Cook, A 2009, 'Emissions rights: From costless activity to market operations', *Accounting, Organizations and Society*, vol. 34, nos. 3/4, pp. 456–68.

73. PricewaterhouseCoopers 2007, *Trouble-Entry Accounting — Revisited**, PricewaterhouseCoopers, London, p. 27.

74. Grimard, C 2009, 'Turning the heat on', *InTheBlack*, vol. 79, no. 11, p. 19.

75. Milne, R & Steen, M 2010, 'Dutch group seeks to tie executive bonuses to social responsibility', *The Financial Times*, 24 February, p. 1.

76. Parker D 2009, 'Super funds set to track carbon footprints', *The Australian*, 23 January, p. 25.

12 International accounting

LEARNING OBJECTIVES

After studying this chapter, you should be able to:

1 discuss the nature of international accounting

2 outline evidence of the diversity of international accounting practice

3 explain the environmental, cultural and religious factors that lead to diversity of international accounting practice

4 discuss international adoption of IFRSs, explain the difference between harmonisation and convergence and identify the benefits and limitations of IFRSs adoption

5 describe the FASB and IASB convergence project

6 evaluate the impact of international accounting and tax issues on multinational enterprises.

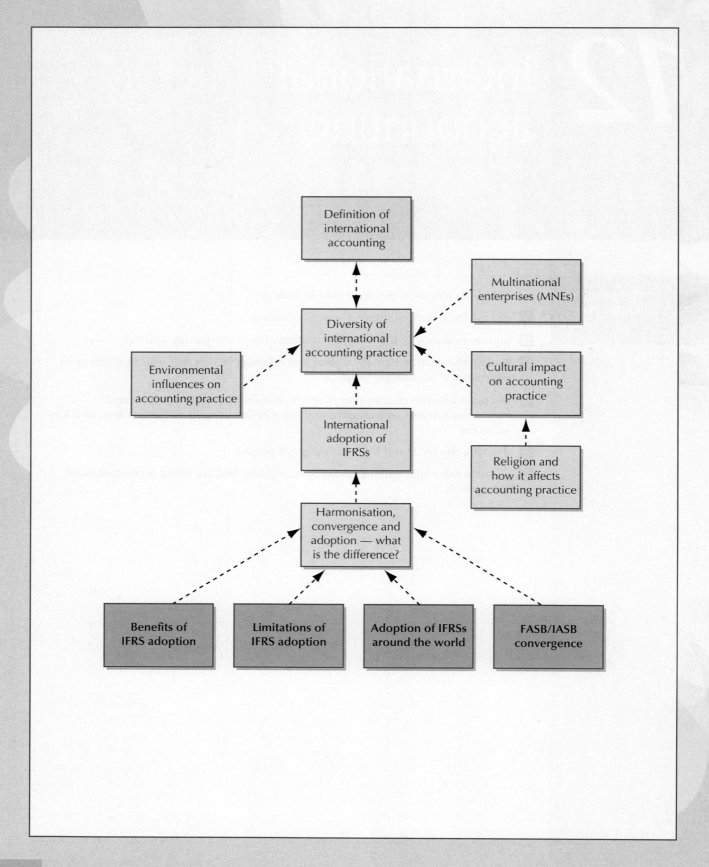

International business in the twenty-first century is increasing rapidly. There is increasing foreign investment and capital markets are opening up in countries that were previously closed, such as China. Accountants and managers need to keep up to date with the changing accounting and financial complexities of doing business on a global stage and the regulations that impact on financial reporting of their business activities globally.

This chapter introduces international accounting and highlights a range of issues that impact on financial reporting around the world. It starts with an explanation of what is meant by international accounting. This is followed by a discussion of the global environment of financial accounting, including examples of internationally diverse accounting practices, and how culture, legal and environmental factors influence accounting at a national level. Adoption of International Financial Reporting Standards (IFRSs) is then explored. Lastly, we examine how the global regulatory and reporting environment affects the operation of multinational enterprises, and the challenges that foreign currency transactions place on business accounting.

LO 1 DEFINITION OF INTERNATIONAL ACCOUNTING

International accounting refers to a description or comparison of accounting in different countries and the accounting dimensions of international transactions. While it encompasses financial accounting, management accounting, auditing, taxation and management accounting systems, this broad range of areas is beyond the scope of this chapter, so we restrict our examination to external financial reporting.

Doupnik and Perera note that international financial reporting can be defined at three levels:

1. supranational, universal or world accounting;
2. the company level standards, guidelines and practices that companies follow relating to their international business activities and accounting for foreign subsidiaries; and
3. comparative or international accounting.[1]

Universal or world accounting is the largest in scope and relates to standards, guidelines and rules issued by supranational organisations such as the Organisation for Economic Co-operation and Development or the International Federation of Accountants. Under this definition accounting is considered a universal system that can be adopted by all countries. Practices and principles would be applicable to all countries.[2] As we will discuss later in this chapter, over the last ten years we have been moving closer to achieving a goal of international standardisation of accounting practices and principles, with over 100 countries adopting IFRSs in addition to the convergence project between the International Accounting Standards Board (IASB) and the United States Financial Accounting Standards Board (FASB).

Company-level accounting is the definition of international accounting with the narrowest focus and relates to the accounting process required to account for a range of international transactions, including parent-foreign subsidiary consolidations, accounting for foreign investments and foreign currency transactions.

Comparative accounting is the study of rules, standards and guidelines that exist in different countries, and a comparison of these items across countries. Comparative accounting considers the diversity of accounting practices across the globe and assesses the impact of these diverse practices on financial reporting.[3]

It is important to understand the differences in accounting practices across a range of countries. Such practices can impact on multinational enterprises when expanding their operations or seeking foreign investment, and can contribute to our understanding of the accounting standard convergence process. In this chapter, we examine some of the factors that can lead to different accounting practices.

DIVERSITY OF INTERNATIONAL ACCOUNTING PRACTICE

Accounting practices can differ substantially across countries. For example, entities in the United States are not permitted to capitalise any research and development expenditure, while entities in Australia are permitted to capitalise development costs if certain conditions are met. Property, plant and equipment in Australia must be recorded at historical cost, while European entities are permitted to use market values.

A variation in accounting requirements can result in significant differences being recorded in company accounts when they are required to report under the rules of different jurisdictions. Westpac Banking Corporation in its 2007 annual report included a note reconciling its report prepared in accordance with Australian accounting requirements (A-IFRS) to United States generally accepted accounting principles (US GAAP). Net profit as reported under A-IFRS was \$3 451 000 000, while according to US GAAP it was \$3 824 000 000 — a difference of nearly \$375 000 000 or 10% of net profit.[4] In December 2007, the US Securities and Exchange Commission (SEC) announced that foreign companies listed on the New York Stock Exchange (NYSE) that accounted under IFRSs no longer had to reconcile to US GAAP. As a result, Westpac Banking Corporation and other multinational corporations which list on the NYSE only have to prepare one set of accounts, thus decreasing costs of preparation.[5]

While there have been some moves to harmonise (or converge) accounting practices globally, there are still a number of environmental and cultural factors which are likely to lead to diversity in accounting practices around the world.

ENVIRONMENTAL INFLUENCES ON ACCOUNTING

Internationally, accounting is influenced by a range of economic, political, legal and social factors. These environmental influences are represented in figure 12.1. At a national level, accounting systems will be influenced by the taxation system, sources of finance, the political system, the stage of economic growth and development, the stage of development of a capital market, the legal system, the existence of an accounting profession and the nature of accounting regulation. All of these influences are equally likely to impact on financial reporting in different countries.

The taxation system can affect accounting practice in countries where financial reports are used to determine an entity's tax liabilities. This is the situation in France, Japan and Germany for example. On the other hand, in Australia, the United Kingdom and the United States financial statements are adjusted for tax purposes, with separate reports being sent to taxation authorities. In Germany, the expense deductible for taxation purposes is the same expense used to calculate financial income. Consequently, German entities are more likely to use accelerated depreciation methods to reduce income and minimise tax. In Australia, which adopts IFRSs, different depreciation rates are permissible. While an entity may use accelerated depreciation for tax purposes, a straight-line method might be used to calculate financial income. These differences will lead to deferred income taxes. Accounting rules are generally aligned with tax laws.[6]

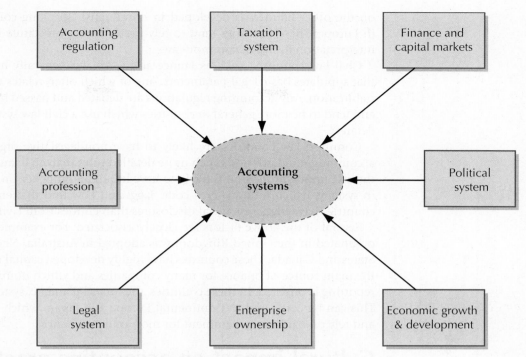

FIGURE 12.1 Environmental influences on accounting

Source: Adapted from Lee Radebaugh, Sidney Gray & Ervin Black, *International accounting and multinational enterprises.*[7]

Sources of finance differ across countries. Major sources of finance include banks, government, families and shareholders.[8] In Germany, for instance, the majority of finance is obtained from banks, while in the United States funds are more likely to be raised through share issues on the stock exchange. In this case, there is going to be greater levels of information disclosure to external shareholders. This also relates to the extent to which the capital market has been developed. A highly developed capital market will mean there are many external users of accounting information, which will affect accounting disclosure practices. A difference in sources of finance will often lead to a difference in financial statement orientation, with shareholders more interested in profits (an income statement focus), and banks placing a greater emphasis on solvency and liquidity (a balance sheet focus).[9]

The political system in place also plays a large role in the nature of the accounting system, which will reflect political philosophies and objectives. Similarly, the extent of economic growth and development and the nature of the economic system will influence the accounting practice. A change from a predominantly agricultural economy to a manufacturing economy — for example, as is the case in China — will pose challenges relating to leasing and depreciation of machinery.

When enterprises are owned by a larger range of external shareholders, in comparison to high levels of family or state ownership, it may be expected that public disclosure will be greater. Where state ownership is prevalent — for example, in China — the state is likely to influence the nature of accounting requirements.

The legal system plays a significant role in corporation law and accounting regulation. There are two major legal systems — common law and codified Roman law (often referred to as civil law). Common law, which originated in England, relies on a limited amount of statute law, which is interpreted by the courts, resulting in case law. Civil law, on the other hand, was developed in non-English speaking countries and originated in Europe. These countries tend to rely more heavily on statute law, without the court interpretation found in common law.

Civil law countries, such as France and Germany, generally have a corporation law that stipulates basic legal parameters, one of which often relates to financial statements publication. Any accounting regulations are debated and passed by a national legislature and tend to be more general in countries which use a civil law system, with little specific detail.[10]

Common law countries are likely to have non-legislative organisations developing accounting standards and much more detailed rules than civil law countries.[11] Similarly, the accounting profession is likely to have less of an influence on accounting regulation in systems which follow a civil code. Jaggi and Low find that entities in common law countries have higher financial disclosures than entities from civil law countries.[12]

Several of the above factors are closely associated. For example, the legal system that originated in the United Kingdom was adopted in Australia, New Zealand, the United States and Canada. These countries have highly developed capital markets which provide the main source of finance for many companies and which dominate the way financial reporting is oriented. In these countries, the financial and tax systems operate separately. This can be compared to Continental Europe and Japan, which have civil law systems and rely on banks or government for most of their finance.

Cultural impact on accounting practice

In addition to economic and political determinants, national culture has increasingly been recognised as a factor that influences diversity of accounting systems. The term 'culture' has traditionally been used in sociology and anthropology to explain different social systems.[13] Harrison and McKinnon incorporated culture into a proposed framework for analysing changes in financial reporting regulation at a national level.[14] Gray further proposed a theoretical framework, again incorporating culture, that could be used to explain international differences in accounting systems.[15] The work is based on earlier research by Hofstede who, in his original work, identified four cultural dimensions that could be used to describe general characteristics of cultures around the world.[16] In subsequent work, Hofstede added a fifth cultural dimension. These dimensions are as follows:

1. *Individualism versus collectivism.* **Individualism** relates to a preference for a loosely knit social framework where individuals take care of themselves and their immediate family. In this system families tend to be nuclear rather than extended. **Collectivism** refers to a preference for a tightly knit social framework where relatives or clans look after each other and there is a large amount of loyalty amongst relatives.
2. *Large versus small power distance.* **Power distance** refers to the extent to which members of society view power in organisations as distributed unequally. People in large power distance societies accept there is a hierarchical order in place and this is not questioned. Conversely, in a small power distance society people look towards equality and seek justification for any power inequalities.
3. *Strong versus weak uncertainty avoidance.* **Uncertainty avoidance** refers to how comfortable members of society are with uncertainty and ambiguity. Strong uncertainty avoidance societies tend to have rigid codes of belief and behaviour. Weak uncertainty avoidance societies are happy to tolerate uncertainty and do not attempt to control the future.
4. *Masculinity versus femininity.* **Masculinity** relates to a preference for assertiveness, achievement and material success, while societies with feminine traits have a preference for nurturing and caring for the weak.

5. *Long-term versus short-term orientation.* Long-term orientation relates to respect for social and status obligations — a thrifty approach to resources, encouragement of large savings levels. Conversely, a short-term orientation encourages respect for social obligations and status, regardless of the cost. It engenders social pressure to overspend and a concern for appearances.[17]

Hofstede went on to summarise studies that had replicated or extended his research, and concluded that most had confirmed his findings, indicating that his framework gave a real insight into cultural values at the national level.[18] Hofstede did, however, note that societal values are likely to change over time.[19] Gray recognised that societal values are likely to influence accounting systems internationally.[20] He noted that 'a methodological framework for incorporating culture may be used to explain and predict international differences in accounting systems and patterns of accounting development internationally'.[21] He adapted Hofstede's categories for accounting, and identified four accounting values:

1. *Professionalism versus statutory control.* A preference may exist for the exercise of individual professional judgement and self-regulation rather than compliance with prescriptive legal requirements and statutory control. The development of professional organisations and their influence on accounting is more evident in Anglo-American countries such as the United Kingdom, the United States and Australia. They are less prevalent in developing countries and continental European countries, where statutory control takes a greater role.

2. *Uniformity versus flexibility.* A preference may exist for the enforcement of uniform accounting practices between companies and for the consistent use of such practices over time, compared to flexibility in accordance with the perceived circumstances of individual companies. Some countries have well established uniform accounting plans and tax rules for measurement purposes. France is an example. In contrast, in the United States there is a greater need for flexibility and inter-company comparability.

3. *Conservatism versus optimism.* A preference may exist for a cautious approach to measurement so as to cope with the uncertainty of future events, as opposed to being optimistic and taking risks. Conservatism or prudence in asset measurement and reporting of profits is a fundamental principle of accounting. However, conservatism varies according to country, ranging from a strongly conservative approach in Europe to a less conservative and to some extent risk-taking approach in the United Kingdom and the United States.

4. *Secrecy versus transparency.* This reflects a preference for confidentiality and disclosure only to those who are most closely involved with management and financing, as opposed to a more transparent, open and publicly accountable approach. While conservatism relates to the measurement function of accounting, secrecy relates to the disclosure function. Disclosure practices vary across countries, with lower levels generally evident in Japan and Europe than in the United Kingdom and Australia.[22]

The accounting values with the greatest association to accounting disclosure and financial reporting are conservatism and secrecy. Countries that require limited disclosures in financial statements (high secrecy) are expected to be more conservative in measuring assets and liabilities. According to Gray, this would include less-developed Latin countries such as Mexico.[23] Conversely, Anglo countries, such as the United States, Australia, the United Kingdom, Canada and New Zealand, sit at the opposite end of the spectrum, with low levels of conservatism (or high optimism) and low levels of secrecy (or high transparency). Doupnik and Tsakumis conduct a comprehensive review of research that has tested Gray's theory of cultural relevance. The authors find much support for Gray's framework in the literature.[24]

In a study of accounting systems in a developing country, Baydoun and Willett note that accounting systems in developing countries have been imported from the West through a number of mechanisms, including colonialism through western multinational companies and the influence of professional associations and loan agencies. The authors examine the relevance of the French Unified Accounting System (UAS) in Lebanon and apply the Hofstede-Gray scheme to analyse the system's usefulness. They conclude that a distinction needs to be made between accounting measurement and accounting disclosure, and it may well be the disclosure aspect of an accounting system that is most likely to fail to satisfy the needs of users in developing countries.[25]

Religion and how it affects accounting practice

Religion is often seen as a subset of culture and can have a significant effect on business practice in some jurisdictions. This is particularly true of Islam. Two aspects shape the relationship between Islam and accounting:

1. Islamic law regulates all aspects of life, and accountants must perform their duties in accordance with the rules and regulations of Islam.
2. In addition to providing a set of business ethics, certain Islamic economic and financial principles have a direct impact on accounting practices. In particular, these include the obligation to pay *zakat* (a religious levy) and prohibition on *riba* (usury) and the institution of an interest-free economic system.[26]

Under Islam, it is incumbent on the Islamic state to guarantee a minimum level of food, clothing, shelter, medical care and education.[27] To guarantee a fair standard of living, *zakat* is the most important instrument for the redistribution of wealth. This is a compulsory levy which is collected by the state or Islamic banks, where a *zakat* fund is established.[28]

The one aspect of Islamic economics that is probably most controversial from a Western accounting and finance perspective is the prohibition of interest (*riba*).[29] The taking of interest as it would normally occur in a Western finance system is prohibited, so investors are compensated by other means.[30]

Muslims cannot compartmentalise their behaviour into religious and secular dimensions — including business and commerce — and their actions are always bound by Islamic law.[31] Values reflected in Islamic law include: *iqtisad* (moderation), *adl* (justice), *amanah* (honesty) and *infaq* (spending to meet social obligations). Conversely, there are a number of negative values that should be avoided: *zulm* (tyranny), *hirs* (greed), *iktinaz* (hoarding of wealth) and *israf* (extravagance).[32]

The Accounting and Auditing Organization for Islamic Financial Institutions (AAOIFI) — a standard-setting body based in Bahrain — has been active in developing Islamic accounting standards which consider the transactions carried out by Islamic financial institutions. These have been considered by the Malaysian Accounting Standards Board (MASB), which has developed a range of accounting standards dealing with Islamic accounting and reporting. With MASB's move to convergence with IFRSs, a decision has been made by the MASB to issue further guidance for Islamic-based transactions as technical releases instead of accounting standards.[33]

LO 4 INTERNATIONAL ADOPTION OF IFRSs

After examining worldwide accounting diversity and some of the factors that have led to that diversity, it becomes apparent that this diversity creates challenges for international business operations and investment. It is costly for multinational enterprises to restate their accounts to meet the requirements of every jurisdiction in which they are listed. Investors also incur costs in comparing results of companies when their financial reports are prepared using different rules. International investment is also likely to be reduced as the risks of investing across borders increase with inconsistencies associated with accounting diversity.

As a result, accounting standard setters and governments have been under pressure to reduce diversity and align accounting requirements worldwide. In this section the efforts of the IASB towards international harmonisation or convergence are discussed. The difference between these terms can sometimes be confusing, so we will start with a definition of harmonisation, convergence and adoption. The benefits and limitations of adoption of IFRSs are also discussed.

Harmonisation, convergence and adoption — what's the difference?

A number of different terms are used when discussing the implementation of a common accounting system worldwide. Harmonisation can sometimes mean different things to different people. To some it refers to adoption or standardisation, where the one set of accounting standards are adopted around the globe, whereas others see harmonisation as a reduction of alternatives while maintaining a degree of flexibility.[34] **Harmonisation** implies reconciling different points of view and reducing diversity, while allowing countries to have different sets of accounting standards. Harmonisation leads to increased communications in a form that can be interpreted and understood internationally.[35] It is a process that takes place over time.

Convergence, while also a process that takes place over time, implies the adoption of one set of standards across the globe. This is often referred to as 'adoption' and 'standardisation'. The predecessor to the IASB — the International Accounting Standards Committee (IASC) — was working towards an objective of harmonisation. However, with the formation of the IASB in 2001, the focus changed to one of global adoption of accounting standards.

Benefits of IFRS adoption

There are a range of advantages to IFRS adoption. Many countries, and developing nations in particular, do not have well codified accounting standards. Adoption of IFRSs is a cost-effective way to institute a comprehensive system of accounting standards.[36] Adoption of IFRSs would also enhance the operation and globalisation of capital markets. Financial statements would be more comparable, making it easier for investors to evaluate a range of investment opportunities. This would lead to a reduction in risk to investors through international diversification.[37]

IFRS adoption would reduce the costs of financial report preparation when companies seek to cross-list on multiple exchanges. This would enhance the ability of multinational firms to access less expensive capital in other countries, as well as reducing the costs associated with investors acquiring a company's shares.[38] Further, it would reduce the cost of preparation and audit of consolidated financial statements.

Limitations of IFRS adoption

Zeff questions the desire for international comparability of accounting practices through IFRS adoption or convergence. He indicates that enhancing comparability may be difficult to achieve for a number of reasons, primarily concerning differences in business, financial and accounting culture from one country to another.[39] The diversity of legal and political systems across the world was discussed earlier in the chapter. One of the greatest obstacles to global adoption of IFRSs is the magnitude of these differences, and the costs involved in overcoming them, if indeed they should be overcome through convergence. Zeff cites as an example the different business customs and corporate structures that exist.[40] For example, in Japan and Korea companies tend to encompass networks of entities with interlocking relationships where it is not clear which is the holding company.[41] As such, it could be questioned whether an accounting standard on consolidated financial statements could be applied to provide comparability with financial reports of companies operating in other countries with clear hierarchical relationships between holding companies, or parent entities and subsidiaries.

Fair value accounting is becoming more common in IFRSs. However, in many countries there may not be asset pricing markets with sufficient depth to generate a reliable fair value measure.[42] In this case, artificial methods are likely to be used in order to meet the accounting standard requirements, which may produce figures that lack comparability.

As discussed previously, religion can also be a factor that affects accounting practices. This presents a challenge to harmonisation or convergence. Any move towards uniformity of accounting standards conflicts with 'the economic, social and cultural contexts of different accounting systems, and even with some manifestations of national sovereignty'.[43] The purpose of financial reporting in Islamic organisations is different to that proposed by the IASB. In its framework, the IASB highlights that the purpose of financial reporting is to provide information to assist resource providers to make decisions about the allocation of scarce resources. They also assume a profit motive. This is contrary to the purpose of accounting and reporting in the Islamic system, where businesses operate with an ethical motive.[44]

As noted above, the primary benefits of IFRS convergence are to enhance the operation and globalisation of capital markets by making financial statements more comparable and therefore making it easier for investors to evaluate a range of investment opportunities. This implies that everyone wants to invest on global markets or seek foreign investment. While convergence might be beneficial for large multinational entities and institutional investors, it is unlikely to benefit entities which operate only in one jurisdiction and do not seek international sources of funds through global markets. For these entities, the increased compliance costs would likely outweigh the benefits of convergence. Therefore, whether it is appropriate in some instances to override local accounting rules with global standards that do not consider country-specific legal and political circumstances is questionable.

Finally, even if worldwide adoption of IFRSs eventuates, the range of reporting or measurement options available under some IFRSs can mean there is limited comparability of reporting practices.

Contemporary Issue 12.1 outlines the perceived benefits of IFRS adoption in Asia.

12.1 CONTEMPORARY ISSUE

Adopting IFRS in Asian countries vital

As Sri Lanka is complying with International Financial Reporting Standards (IFRS) by 2011, it is important to create a better understanding of the challenges and solutions prepared in comparative financial statements by 2010.

IFRS by 2011

- Increased benefits having a commonly understood financial reporting framework supported by strong globally accepted standards
- Mixed picture in cost of equity capital in Europe
- IFRS to drive organizations through the journey of implementing standards successfully.

Get Through Guides (GTG) CEO, Vandana Saxena said that there were numerous misunderstandings about the different IFRS in local Generally Accepted Accounting Principles (GAAP) and many people believe that the conversion will only affect the finance function.

Asia was the first to recover from the global finance meltdown. Therefore, adopting the IFRS in Asian countries is vital, as it will have a conducive effect over the world's economy in the near future, she said.

She said that as the forces of globalization prompt more countries to open their doors to foreign investments and expand business the public and private sectors have increasingly recognized the benefits of having a commonly understood financial reporting framework supported by strong globally accepted standards.

The IFRS adoption in Europe was fairly smooth and it helped the companies to enhance their management reporting in an effective manner.

The benefits viewed by Indian professionals noted that comparability and credibility was high with the enhanced conducive investment environment.

Enhanced business opportunities and easy access to finance are the other benefits in adopting the IFRS to the Indian financial statements, Saxena said.

Source: Excerpts from 'Adopting IFRS in Asian countries vital', *Daily News (Sri Lanka)*.[45]

Questions

1. Outline the benefits of adoption of IFRSs in Sri Lanka. **J** **K**
2. What are the challenges expected to be faced by the country in adopting IFRSs from 2011? **J**

Adoption of IFRSs around the world

Table 12.1 lists a selection of IFRS users around the globe. The information is adapted from a more complete table updated by Deloitte's annually. A number of countries are in the process of adopting IFRSs, including Canada, which adopted from 2011, and Malaysia, which will adopt from 2012.

Jurisdictions will have differing degrees of convergence with IFRSs. In some jurisdictions (e.g. Australia) IFRSs are required for all corporate reporting for listed and unlisted entities. By contrast, in others, IFRSs are required for consolidated reporting of listed entities, while unconsolidated reporting is still *allowed* to use national rules (e.g. Denmark, the Netherlands and the United Kingdom) or is *required* to use national rules (e.g. Belgium, France and Spain).[46]

Nobes develops a theory for the motives and opportunity for the emergence of different national variants of IFRS practice. He suggested that the environmental factors — financial systems, legal systems and taxation systems — that have previously been associated with international differences in accounting still can be used to explain differences in IFRS adoption practices across jurisdictions.[47]

Use of IFRSs

Europe

From 2005 all EU listed companies have been required to adopt IFRSs for reporting purposes. EU member states can extend this to non-listed companies, which has been carried out by most member states.[48] As noted above, some either require or allow national standards for unconsolidated reporting.

From December 2008, for non-EU companies listed on EU stock exchanges, the EU designated the GAAP from a range of countries including the United States, Australia, Japan, Canada and Korea to be equivalent, so any companies reporting under these jurisdictions do not have to prepare separate EU accounts.[49]

TABLE 12.1 A selection of IFRS users around the globe

Location	IFRSs not permitted	IFRSs permitted	Required for some domestic listed companies	Required for all domestic listed companies
Abu Dhabi (UAE)				X
Argentina	X (d)			From 2012
Australia				X (c)
Austria				X (a)
Bangladesh	X			
Bermuda		X		
Brazil				From 2010
Cambodia	No stock exchange. Companies may use IFRSs.			
Canada				From 2011
Chile				X
China		(k)		
Czech Republic				X (a)
Dubai (UAE)				X
Fiji				X
France				X (a)
Germany				X (a)
Haiti		X		
Hong Kong				X (c)
India	X (i)			
Indonesia	X			
Iran	X			
Iraq				X
Israel		All except banks		
Japan		X		
Kenya				X
Malaysia	X (d)			
Maldives		X		
Mexico		X (d)		From 2012
Morocco		Non-banks	Banks	
New Zealand				X (c)
Pakistan	X			
Papua New Guinea				X
Philippines	X (e)			
Russia	X			
Saudi Arabia			X (j)	
Singapore	X (d)(e)			
South Africa				X
Sri Lanka		X		

Location	IFRSs not permitted	IFRSs permitted	Required for some domestic listed companies	Required for all domestic listed companies
Taiwan	X (h)			
Thailand	X			
Turkey		X (f)		
United Kingdom				X (a)
United States	X (g)			
Vietnam	X			
Zimbabwe		X		

Notes:

(a) Audit report and basis of presentation note to the financial statements refer to IFRSs as adopted by the European Union (EU).

(b) By law, all companies must follow IFRSs approved by the local government, and approval is not up to date with the Standards and Interpretations issued by the IASB.

(c) Local standards identical to IFRSs, but some effective dates and transitional provisions differ.

(d) All domestic listed companies must use IFRSs starting 2012.

(e) Most IFRSs adopted, but various significant modifications were made.

(f) Turkish companies may follow English versions of IFRSs, or Turkish translation. If the latter, because of the translation delay, audit report and basis of presentation refer to 'IFRSs as adopted for the use in Turkey'.

(g) SEC permits foreign private issuers to file financial statements prepared under IFRSs as issued by the IASB without having to include a reconciliation of the IFRS figures to US GAAP.

(h) Plan announced for full adoption of IFRS starting 2013, including financial institutions supervised by the Financial Supervisory commission of Taiwan except for credit cooperatives, credit card companies and insurance intermediaries who will be required to adopt Taiwan-IFRS starting 2015.

(i) Phasing in of IFRSs for listed companies 2011 to 2014.

(j) All listed banks and insurance companies must use IFRSs.

(k) The new Chinese Accounting Standards for Business Enterprises (CAS) were published by the Ministry of Finance (MoF) in 2006 and became effective on 1 January 2007. These standards are substantially converged with IFRSs, except for certain modifications (e.g., disallow the reversal of impairment loss on long term assets) which reflect China's unique circumstances and environment. In April 2010, the MoF released the roadmap for continuing convergence of CAS with IFRSs. The CASs are now mandatory for entities including PRC-listed companies, financial institutions (including entities engaging in securities business permitted by China Securities Regulatory Commission), certain state-owned enterprises, private companies in certain provinces. In the roadmap, the MoF has indicated its intention to have all large and medium-sized enterprises (regardless whether they are listed companies or private companies) adopt the new CAS by 2012. In December 2007, the HKICPA recognized CAS equivalence to HKFRS, which are identical to IFRSs, including all recognition and measurement options, but have in some cases different effective dates and transition requirements. From then the CASC and HKICPA together with the IASB created an ongoing mechanism to reinforce continuously such equivalence. In December 2010, the Hong Kong Stock Exchange decided to allow mainland-incorporated companies listed in Hong Kong to have an option to present financial statements using CASs and audited by an approved mainland audit firm. A number of such companies have chosen to present financial statements using CASs for annual reporting. The EU Commission permits Chinese issuers to use CAS when they enter the EU market without adjusting financial statement in accordance with IFRS endorse by EU.

Source: Adapted from Deloitte Touche Tohmatsu, *IFRS in your pocket 2011.*[50]

Canada

Publicly accountable Canadian entities are required to apply IFRSs from 1 January 2011; however, earlier use is permitted upon approval of the securities regulator.

South America

Use of IFRSs has developed across the region. Chile phased in IFRSs use by listed companies in 2009. Brazil required use of IFRSs by listed companies and banks in 2010 and Mexico will start phasing in use from 2012. IFRSs are already required in a number of other Latin American or Caribbean countries such as Bermuda.[51]

Asia–Pacific region

Asian jurisdictions take a range of approaches to IFRS adoption. IFRSs have replaced national GAAP in Mongolia, while in Hong Kong, Australia, Korea and New Zealand national standards are virtually word for word the same as IFRSs. The Philippines and Singapore have adopted nearly all IFRSs but have made significant modifications.[52]

In India, Malaysia, Pakistan and Thailand some IFRSs have been adopted to date; however, significant differences exist for others. India is moving towards full adoption in the future — between 2012 and 2014 — while Malaysia will adopt IFRSs as Malaysian Financial Reporting Standards by 2012.[53]

While there has been extensive adoption of IFRSs around the world, some question whether convergence of accounting standards actually leads to convergence of accounting practices.[54] Research shows that the institutional differences in culture, legal, taxation, political and socioeconomic systems may in fact lead to non-comparable accounting figures despite similar accounting standards.[55] This concern is likely to be more pronounced in emerging economies, such as China, where accountants, auditors and regulators do not have the expertise to support compliance.[56] This issue has been examined in China as a case of an emerging and transitional market economy.[57] Peng et al. point out that standards developed by the IASB are primarily aimed at countries with highly developed capital markets, and it can be questioned whether the resulting standards are optimal for developing and transitional economies that lack the infrastructure to monitor financial reporting decisions.[58]

The Chinese capital market has increased rapidly since it was established in the early 1990s, where it comprised 14 companies. This has risen to 1488 companies by the end of 2006.[59] The market at the end of 2006 was the eighth biggest in the world with a market capitalisation equivalent to US$500 billion.[60] The rapid expansion and the desire to attract foreign investment has provided an incentive for the Chinese government to put in place measures to improve the quality of financial reporting.[61] The Chinese share market is segmented into A-share and B-share markets. A-shares can be owned and traded only by Chinese citizens, while B-shares can be owned and traded only by foreign investors.[62] Companies which issue both A-shares and B-shares are required to supply two sets of annual accounts — one in Chinese GAAP and the other in accordance with IFRSs.

China has made substantial changes to Chinese GAAP since 1992 in an effort to converge domestic standards with IFRSs. Since 1992, China has issued four sets of accounting regulations (in 1992, 1998, 2001 and 2006), with each replacing the previous standards. The standards are considered to increasingly conform to IFRSs.[63] However, research has found little relationship between Chinese GAAP and IFRS-based net income for Chinese listed companies in both 1992 and 1998.[64] Peng et al. and Chen and Zhang find the level of convergence has improved with the advent of the 2001 standards.[65]

FASB AND IASB CONVERGENCE

Any moves towards global adoption of IFRSs are dependent upon whether the United States adopts or converges with IFRSs. One issue that has stood in the way of convergence to date is a differing underlying 'philosophy' of the two standards. While the IASB standards are 'principles-based', the FASB have previously taken a 'rules-based' approach to standard setting. However, while the SEC and FASB in United States were previously reluctant to embrace IFRSs, there have recently been moves towards convergence.

The IASB and FASB formed the *Norwalk Agreement* — a memorandum of understanding — in 2002, aimed at removing any differences between international standards and

US GAAP. In the interim, the SEC requirement for non-US companies that use IFRSs to provide a reconciliation to US GAAP when they list on US securities exchanges was removed from 2007. It is generally thought that US GAAP reconciliations were looked upon as a 'mostly futile and expensive exercise',[66] which acts as a barrier to entry for foreign companies seeking to list on the US securities exchanges. Most investors were not relying on the reconciliation to US GAAP in their investment decisions and instead were using IFRSs.[67]

The convergence commitment was further strengthened in 2006 when the FASB and IASB set milestones to be reached by 2008.[68] While the two boards are still progressing towards convergence, there have been delays and the milestones outlined in 2006 were not reached. In 2008, the two boards issued an update to the memorandum of understanding, which identified a series of priorities and milestones to complete the remaining major joint projects by 2011.[69]

In June 2010, the standard setters jointly announced a modification to their convergence strategy as a result of concerns about the number of draft standards due for publication over a short period of time. While the June 2011 target date was still set to complete those projects for which the need for improvement of IFRSs and US GAAP is the most urgent, a later completion date was given to those projects with a relatively low priority or for which further research and analysis is necessary.

The convergence project is continuing, with priority projects as at 2011 including:
- financial instruments
- leases
- revenue recognition
- consolidations
- fair value measurement
- derecognition
- insurance contracts.

Other projects include:
- post-employment benefits
- joint ventures
- financial statement presentation
- financial instruments with characteristics of equity
- emissions trading schemes.[70]

LO 6 MULTINATIONAL ORGANISATIONS

As indicated previously, multinational enterprises are particularly affected by the range of environmental factors and accounting systems in the different countries in which they operate. As such they face a range of issues not faced by domestic entities.

Multinational enterprises (MNEs) can be differentiated from domestic enterprises because they operate simultaneously in a number of countries. They tend to be larger and have more complex business operations than their domestic counterparts.

MNEs operate across different countries with often different legal, tax and reporting requirements, and different currencies. They are likely to have a large number of intra-corporate transactions between their operating units located in different countries. Internally, decision-making authority is likely to be delegated to subsidiary managers who can respond to local conditions. However, this practice is difficult to manage where subsidiary managers are required to meet operational and reporting requirements in their respective countries which might not align with the organisational culture. Any strategic decisions need to consider the national culture in which the MNE subsidiaries operate.

When looking to globalise business operations an entity needs to decide to what extent decision making should be held in a few key centres, or spread across a large number of units.

As we previously saw, taxation systems can vary significantly across the globe. MNEs face the challenge of understanding how their operations are taxed in the countries in which they operate. Countries can offer tax incentives to either attract foreign investors or to encourage export of goods and services.

MNEs need to consider inter-corporate **transfer pricing** — the pricing of goods and services that are transferred between members of a corporate family. These transfers can relate to raw materials, finished goods, loans, fees and allocation of fixed costs. There may be differing internal and external factors that influence transfer prices. Transfer pricing can be a management control tool designed to maximise performance, obtain financial efficiencies and minimise costs or maximise profits. This may not align with external motivations stemming from tax laws in the various countries in which the MNE operates, however. Contemporary Issue 12.2 outlines some tax challenges facing MNEs relating to taxation of internal transactions.

**12.2
CONTEMPORARY
ISSUE**

Survey finds multinationals facing new tax challenges

Multinationals are facing new tax challenges due to growing transfer pricing (TP) scrutiny by world's tax authorities, according to a survey.

The survey by international accounting firm Ernst & Young found a dramatic increase in the scope of TP documentation required by governments with penalties imposed more frequently and at higher levels when multinationals get it wrong.

Given the need for governments to raise revenues in this challenging economic climate and the changing regulatory environment, the study anticipates heightened litigation in the near future.

The expectation is driven by the almost universal trend towards increased TP investigation resources within tax authorities, it said, adding that this trend is also shared by Malaysia.

'As governments search for tax revenues to offset growing budget deficits, many are sharpening their focus on compliance, enforcement and legislative approaches,' said Ernst & Young Malaysia's partner and head of transfer pricing, Janice Wong.

Source: Excerpts from 'Survey finds multinationals facing new tax challenges', *Organization of Asia-Pacific News Agencies.*[71]

Questions
1. How can multinationals use transfer pricing to minimise their taxation burden? **K**
2. Why do you think taxation authorities would get involved in transfer pricing? **J** **K**

Summary

Discuss the nature of international accounting
- There are a number of views of the meaning of international accounting. International accounting can be defined at three levels:
  1. supranational, universal or world accounting
  2. the company-level standards, guidelines and practices that companies follow relating to their international business activities and accounting for foreign subsidiaries
  3. comparative or international accounting.

Outline evidence of the diversity of international accounting practice
- Accounting practices can differ substantially across countries. A variation in accounting requirements can result in significant differences being recorded in company accounts when they need to report under the rules of different jurisdictions.

Explain the environmental, cultural and religious factors that lead to diversity of international accounting practice
- Accounting systems at a national level will be influenced by:
  - the taxation system
  - sources of finance
  - the political system
  - the stage of economic growth and development
  - the stage of development of a capital market
  - the legal system
  - the existence of an accounting profession
  - the nature of accounting regulation.
- In addition to economic and political determinants, national culture has increasingly been recognised as a factor that influences diversity of accounting systems.
- Religion is often seen as a subset of culture, and can have a significant effect on business practice in some jurisdictions.

Discuss international adoption of IFRSs, explain the difference between harmonisation and convergence and identify the benefits and limitations of IFRSs adoption
- Harmonisation implies reconciling different points of view and reducing diversity, while allowing countries to have different sets of accounting standards. It leads to increased communications in a form that can be interpreted and understood internationally.
- Convergence, a process that takes place over time, implies the adoption of one set of standards across the globe.

- Adoption of IFRSs is a cost-effective way to institute a comprehensive system of accounting standards. Adoption of IFRSs would enhance the operation and globalisation of capital markets. Financial statements would be more comparable, making it easier for investors to evaluate a range of investment opportunities.
- One of the greatest obstacles to global adoption of IFRSs is the magnitude of these differences and the costs involved in overcoming them. Critics question the real benefits that can be achieved from IFRS adoption on a global scale, citing the current existence of a well-developed global capital market.

Describe the FASB and IASB convergence project

- The IASB and FASB formed the *Norwalk Agreement* — a memorandum of understanding — in 2002, aimed at removing any differences between international standards and US GAAP.
- In December 2007, the SEC announced that foreign companies listed on the New York Stock Exchange which accounted under IFRS no longer had to reconcile to US GAAP.

Evaluate the impact of international accounting and tax issues on multinational enterprises

- MNEs operate across different countries with often different legal, tax and reporting requirements, and different currencies.
- MNEs are likely to have a large number of intra-corporate transactions between their operating units located in different countries.
- MNEs need to consider transfer pricing when pricing goods and services that are transferred between members of a corporate family.
- Transfer pricing can be a management control tool designed to maximise performance, obtain financial efficiencies and minimise costs or maximise profits.

Review questions

1. Outline and differentiate the various definitions of international accounting.
2. Explain the environmental factors that lead to national differences in accounting.
3. What are the two main legal systems operating worldwide? How might these affect accounting?
4. Countries that rely on capital markets for finance, as opposed to banks and governments, are likely to expect greater levels of public disclosure in their accounting systems. Evaluate this argument and provide examples.
5. Outline and discuss three cultural aspects that can differ across countries. How do these cultural differences relate to differences in accounting systems?
6. What does accounting harmonisation mean? Differentiate harmonisation from convergence or adoption.
7. Explain the benefits of global adoption of IFRSs.
8. What are advantages of having one set of accounting standards worldwide?
9. What are the limitations of global adoption of IFRSs?
10. Outline the key challenges of US GAAP and IFRS convergence.
11. What is transfer pricing and how does it affect the operation of MNEs?

Application questions

Visit the website of the IASB and FASB and read the documents relating to US GAAP and IFRS convergence. Prepare a summary of the progress to date and the timelines for future convergence. **K**

12.2 The New York Stock Exchange (NYSE) is the largest exchange in the United States. Visit the website of the NYSE, www.nyse.com, and determine the number of foreign companies listed on it. Choose three of these companies and analyse their latest financial reports, available from the companies' websites. Document how the companies have addressed the difference, if any, between their reporting requirements for United States purposes and those for their home jurisdiction. Why would foreign companies have gone to the effort of listing their shares on the NYSE and the expense of preparing separate financial statements in some cases? **J** **SM**

12.3 Find the financial reports available on the websites of one domestic company and one foreign company that operate in the same industry and complete the following:

(a) Document what accounting principles the foreign and domestic companies used to prepare their financial reports.

(b) Document any differences between the formats of the reports or the accounting principles used between your two companies.

(c) Document any differences in the directors' report for each company.

(d) Prepare a table which outlines the similarities and differences you have observed. **J** **K** **AS** **SM**

12.4 Form small teams and have each team select two countries from different cultural areas. Identify and compare each country's environmental, cultural and accounting values. **J** **K** **CT**

12.5 Visit the website of the Australian Securities Exchange, www.asx.com.au. Select a large company that is listed on the securities exchange that also has operations in different countries — an MNE. You may need to refer to the company website or annual report for this information. Access the latest annual report and evaluate the impact of operating across countries on the company's financial reporting requirements. **J** **K** **SM**

12.1 CASE STUDY

US accounting switch to aid multinationals

By Patrick Durkin

An expected switch by the United States from the US Generally Accepted Accounting Principles to the International Financial Reporting Standards will benefit investors and multinationals, observers said yesterday. The move by the US Securities and Exchange Commission comes after the chairman of the International Accounting Standards Board, David Tweedie, provided the SEC with evidence that the international accounting standards were better at uncovering problems during the credit crisis. 'The value of Australia moving to IFRS has always been diminished by the US not participating,' said National Australia Bank chief financial officer Mark Joiner. The switch is expected to benefit US companies with Australian operations including General Electric, Citigroup and ExxonMobil.

Source: Excerpts from Patrick Durkin, 'US accounting switch to aid multinationals', *Australian Financial Review*.[72]

Questions

1. Outline some reasons the US regulators are likely to accept financial reports prepared under IFRSs rather than US GAAP for listing purposes. **J** **K**

2. What would you perceive to be negative aspects of convergence between the FASB and IASB? Explain your answer. **J** **K**

3. How do you think the agreement to accept IFRSs will impact on US companies? **J** **K**

Making the most of IFRS

By V Balakrishnan

International Financial Reporting Standards (IFRS) is fast becoming the de facto accounting standard across the world. The adoption of IFRS would result in one set of high-quality, globally accepted accounting standards that would bring uniformity in reporting and make the world one common market place. Different countries have taken different paths towards adopting IFRS. Some of the countries have gone for full-fledged adoption of IFRS, while some others, including India, have taken the path of convergence rather than adoption.

There are varied views on adoption vs convergence. Some are of the view that adoption is the only way to achieve the goal of getting to a single set of high-quality, globally accepted accounting standards. The world is becoming one single market and adoption would result in reduced reporting costs for multinational companies, better comparability of performance of companies across the world and improved allocation of capital by global investors. The other point of view supports convergence, arguing that adoption of IFRS would result in countries giving up significant control of the standard setting process. The argument further goes that convergence, over a period of time, will help corporates in concerned countries to have a soft landing, while adopting certain standards in IFRS could put their companies in a disadvantageous position.

India has taken the route of convergence to IFRS by 2011. There is a clear road map for companies to converge, with the set of converged standards to be issued by the domestic accounting standard setters. While the government has taken this view and is moving towards it with a plan, it is important to debate whether this is the right thing to do for India.

India should be at the forefront of adopting IFRS and shaping the global debate on the standard setting process; it should forcefully participate in the global accounting standard setting process. Whether we like it or not, global investors will look down on India for having converged with IRFS in contrast to countries that adopt IFRS fully. IFRS is also a global opportunity for India on the accounting services front. It is a great opportunity for Indian accountants to service the external world . . .

Also, the cost of capital for Indian corporates will remain high as global investors would attach a risk premium as Indian corporates would have converged and not adopted IFRS fully. Finally, this would affect Indian corporates in their globalisation process as it would become more onerous for them to list in global equity markets.

Source: Excerpts from V Balakrishnan, 'Making the most of IFRS', *Financial Express (India)*.[73]

Questions

1. Outline the arguments both for and against full adoption rather than harmonisation with IFRSs. **J** **K**
2. What are the benefits to India of convergence? **J** **K**
3. As an investor looking to invest in the Indian market, what do you see as the obstacles to investment? **J** **K**

Additional readings

Delloite IAS Plus Publications: http://www.iasplus.com/dttpubs/pubs.htm

Depoupnik, T. and Perera, H. (2009) *International Accounting*, 2nd edn, McGraw-Hill Irwin, Boston MA.

Radebaugh, L.H., Gray, S.J. and Black, E.L. (2006) *International Accounting and Multinational Enterprises*, 6th edn, John Wiley & Sons Inc. Hoboken NJ.

Geert Hofstede: http://www.geert-hofstede.com/.

End notes

1. Doupnik, T & Perera, H 2009, *International Accounting*, 2nd edn, McGraw-Hill Irwin, Boston MA.
2. Weirich, TR, Avery, CG & Anderson, HR 1971, 'International Accounting: Varying definitions', *Journal of Accounting Education and Research*, Fall, pp. 79–87.
3. Jones, S & Riahi-Belkaoui, A 2010, *Financial Accounting Theory*, 3rd edn, Cengage, Melbourne.
4. Westpac Banking Corporation 2007, *Westpac 2007 annual report*, Westpac Banking Corporation, Sydney, viewed 28 October 2011, www.westpac.com.au.
5. NYSE Euronext 2011, *Going public in the US: tips for foreign private investors*, NYSE Euronext, New York, viewed 28 October 2011, www.nyse.com.
6. Choi, FDS & Meek, GK 2005, *International Accounting*, 5th edn, Pearson Prentice Hall, Upper Saddle River NJ.
7. Radebaugh, LH, Gray, SJ & Black, EL 2006, *International Accounting and Multinational Enterprises*, 6th edn, John Wiley & Sons Inc, Hoboken NJ, p. 16.
8. Doupnik, T & Perera, H 2009, *International Accounting*, 2nd edn, McGraw-Hill Irwin, Boston MA.
9. ibid.
10. ibid.
11. ibid.
12. Jaggi, B & Law, PY 2000, 'Impact of culture, market forces, and legal system on financial disclosures', *International Journal of Accounting*, vol. 35, no. 4, pp. 495–519.
13. Hofstede, G 1980, *Culture's consequences: international differences in work-related values*, Sage Publications, London.
14. Harrison, GL & McKinnon, JL 1986, 'Cultural and accounting change: A new perspective on corporate reporting regulation and accounting policy formulation', *Accounting, Organizations and Society*, vol. 11, no. 3, pp. 233–52.
15. Gray, SJ 1988, 'Towards a theory of cultural influence on the development of accounting systems internationally', *Abacus*, March, pp. 1–15.
16. Hofstede, G 1984, 'Cultural dimensions in management and planning', *Asia Pacific Journal of Management*, vol. 1, no. 2, pp. 81–99.
17. Hofstede, G & Bond, MH 1988, 'The Confucian connection: from cultural roots to economic growth', *Organizational Dynamics*, vol. 16, no. 1, pp. 4–21.
18. Hofstede, G 2001, *Culture's consequences: Comparing values, behaviours, institutions and organizations across nations*, 2nd edn, Sage Publications, Thousand Oaks CA.
19. ibid.
20. Gray, SJ 1988, 'Towards a theory of cultural influence on the development of accounting systems internationally', *Abacus*, March, pp. 1–15.
21. ibid.
22. ibid.
23. ibid.
24. Doupnik, TS & Tsakumis, GT 2004, 'A critical review of tests of Gray's theory of cultural relevance and suggestions for future research', *Journal of Accounting Literature*, vol. 23, pp. 1–48.
25. Baydoun, N & Willett, R 1995, 'Cultural relevance of western accounting systems in developing countries', *Abacus*, vol. 31, no. 1, pp. 67–92.
26. Lewis, MK 2001, 'Islam and accounting', *Accounting Forum*, vol. 25, no. 2, pp. 103–27; Baydoun, N & Willett, R 2000, 'Islamic corporate reports', *Abacus*, vol. 36, no. 1, pp. 71–90.
27. Lewis, MK 2001, 'Islam and accounting', *Accounting Forum*, vol. 25, no. 2, pp. 103–27.
28. ibid.
29. ibid.
30. ibid.
31. ibid.
32. ibid.
33. Malaysian Accounting Standards Board (MASB) 2009, *Policy Statement*, MASB, Kuala Lumpur, viewed 1 November 2011, www.masb.org.my.
34. Doupnik, T & Perera, H 2009, *International Accounting*, 2nd edn, McGraw-Hill Irwin, Boston MA.
35. ibid; Jones, S & Riahi-Belkaoui, A 2010, *Financial Accounting Theory*, 3rd edn, Cengage, Melbourne.
36. Jones, S & Riahi-Belkaoui, A 2010, *Financial Accounting Theory*, 3rd edn, Cengage, Melbourne.
37. Doupnik, T & Perera, H 2009, *International Accounting*, 2nd edn, McGraw-Hill Irwin, Boston MA.
38. ibid.
39. Zeff, SA 2007, 'Some obstacles to global financial reporting comparability and convergence at a high level of quality', *British Accounting Review*, vol. 39, iss. 4, pp. 290–302.
40. ibid.
41. ibid.
42. ibid.
43. Hoarau, C 1995, 'International accounting harmonization: American hegemony or mutual recognition with benchmarks', *European Accounting Review*, vol. 4, no. 2, pp. 217–33.
44. Karim, RAA 2001, 'International accounting harmonization, banking regulation and Islamic banks', *The International Journal of Accounting*, vol. 36, no. 2, pp. 169–93.
45. Anonymous 2009, 'Adopting IFRS in Asian countries vital', *Daily News (Sri Lanka)*, 16 December.
46. Nobes, C 2008, 'Accounting classification in the IFRS era', *Australian Accounting Review*, vol. 18, no. 3, pp. 191–8.
47. Nobes, C 2006, 'The survival of international differences under IFRS: towards a research agenda', *Accounting and Business Research*, vol. 36, no. 3, pp. 233–45.
48. Deloitte Touche Tohmatsu Limited 2011, *IFRS in your pocket 2011*, Deloitte, London.
49. ibid.
50. Deloitte Touche Tohmatsu Limited 2011, *IFRS in your pocket 2011*, Deloitte, London, pp. 19–27.
51. Deloitte Touche Tohmatsu Limited 2011, *IFRS in your pocket 2011*, Deloitte, London.
52. ibid.
53. ibid.
54. Street, DL & Bryant, SM 2000, 'Disclosure level and compliance with IASs: a comparison of companies with and without U.S. listing and filings', *The International Journal of Accounting*, vol. 35, no. 3,

pp. 305–29; Chen, JJ & Zhang, H 2010, 'The impact of regulatory enforcement and audit upon IFRS compliance — evidence from China', *European Accounting Review*, vol. 19, no. 4, pp. 665–92.

55. Schultz, JJ & Lopez, TJ 2001, 'The impact of national influence on accounting estimates: implications for international accounting standard-setters', *The International Journal of Accounting*, vol. 36, no. 3, pp. 271–90; Ball, R, Robin, A & Wu, J 2003, 'Incentives versus standards: properties of accounting income in four East Asian countries', *Journal of Accounting and Economics*, vol. 36, no. 1/3, pp. 235–70.

56. Chen, JJ & Zhang, H 2010, 'The impact of regulatory enforcement and audit upon IFRS compliance — evidence from China', *European Accounting Review*, vol. 19, no. 4, pp. 665–92.

57. See for example Peng, S, Tondkar, RH, van der Laan Smith, J & Harless, DW 2008, 'Does convergence of accounting standards lead to the convergence of accounting practices? A study from China', *The International Journal of Accounting*, vol. 43, no. 4, pp. 448–68; Chen, JJ & Zhang, H 2010, 'The impact of regulatory enforcement and audit upon IFRS compliance — evidence from China', *European Accounting Review*, vol. 19, no. 4, pp. 665–92.

58. Peng, S, Tondkar, RH, van der Laan Smith, J & Harless, DW 2008, 'Does convergence of accounting standards lead to the convergence of accounting practices? A study from China', *The International Journal of Accounting*, vol. 43, no. 4, pp. 448–68.

59. Chen, JJ & Zhang, H 2010, 'The impact of regulatory enforcement and audit upon IFRS compliance — evidence from China', *European Accounting Review*, vol. 19, no. 4, pp. 665–92.

60. ibid.

61. ibid.

62. Peng, S, Tondkar, RH, van der Laan Smith, J & Harless, DW 2008, 'Does convergence of accounting standards lead to the convergence of accounting practices? A study from China', *The International Journal of Accounting*, vol. 43, no. 4, pp. 448–68.

63. Chen, JJ, Sun, Z & Wang, Y 2002, 'Evidence from China on whether harmonized accounting standards harmonize accounting practices', *Accounting Horizons*, vol. 16, no. 3, pp. 183–97; International Accounting Standards Board (IASB) 2011, 'Convergence between IFRSs and US GAAP', IASB, London, viewed 28 October 2011, www.ifrs.org.

64. Chen, JPC, Gul, FA & Su, X 1999, 'A comparison of reported earnings under Chinese GAAP versus IAS: evidence from the Shanghai Stock Exchange', *Accounting Horizons*, vol. 13, no. 2, pp. 91–111; Chen, JJ, Sun, Z & Wang, Y 2002, 'Evidence from China on whether harmonized accounting standards harmonize accounting practices', *Accounting Horizons*, vol. 16, no. 3, pp. 183–97.

65. Peng, S, Tondkar, RH, van der Laan Smith, J & Harless, DW 2008, 'Does convergence of accounting standards lead to the convergence of accounting practices? A study from China', *The International Journal of Accounting*, vol. 43, no. 4, pp. 448–68; Chen, JJ, Sun, Z & Wang, Y 2002, 'Evidence from China on whether harmonized accounting standards harmonize accounting practices', *Accounting Horizons*, vol. 16, no. 3, pp. 183–97.

66. Dzinkowski, R 2007, 'A roadmap to US IFRS convergence', *InTheBlack*, June, pp. 58–9.

67. ibid.

68. International Accounting Standards Board (IASB) 2011, *A Roadmap for Convergence between IFRSs and US GAAP — 2006–2008 Memorandum of Understanding between the FASB and the IASB — 27 February 2006*, IASB, London, viewed 2 November 2011, www.ifrs.org.au.

69. International Accounting Standards Board (IASB) 2011, 'Convergence between IFRSs and US GAAP', IASB, London, viewed 28 October 2011, www.ifrs.org; International Accounting Standards Board (IASB) 2011, *Completing the February 2006 Memorandum of Understanding: a progress report and timetable for completion September 2008*, IASB, London, viewed 2 November 2011, www.ifrs.org.au.

70. International Accounting Standards Board (IASB) 2011, *Progress Report on Commitment to Convergence of Accounting Standards and a Single Set of High Quality Global Accounting Standards — 29 November 2010*, IASB, London, viewed 2 November 2011, www.ifrs.org.au.

71. Anonymous 2009, 'Survey finds multinationals facing new tax challenges', *Organization of Asia-pacific News Agencies*, 1 November.

72. Durkin, P 2008, 'US accounting switch to aid multinationals', *Australian Financial Review*, 12 August, p. 6.

73. Balakrishnan, V 2010, 'Making the most of IFRS', *Financial Express (India)*, FE Special, 9 September.

13 Corporate failure

After studying this chapter, you should be able to:

1 outline what is understood by the term 'corporate failure'

2 examine the causes of corporate failure

3 identify the costs of corporate failure

4 evaluate the factors used to predict corporate failure

5 assess the likely indicators of corporate failure

6 evaluate the relationship between corporate governance and failure

7 evaluate how regulation has been used to alleviate the effects of corporate failure

8 evaluate the anatomy of a corporate failure

9 critically evaluate the causes and consequences of the global financial crisis (GFC) and evaluate how governments have intervened to alleviate the effects of the GFC.

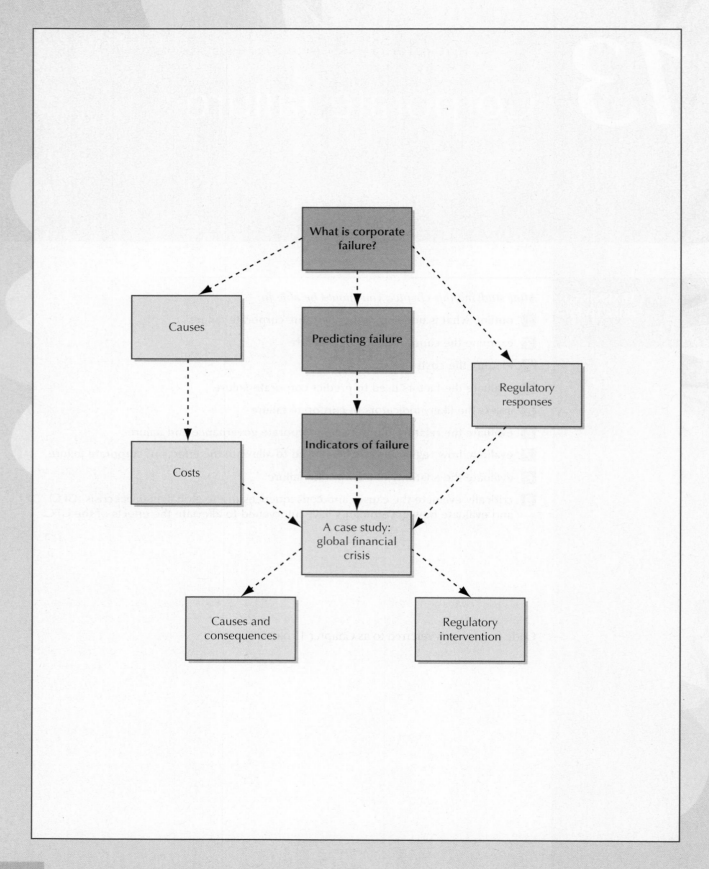

The first decade of the twenty-first century started with corporate failures of a vast scale and ended with a global financial crisis. Enron — perhaps the most prominent failure — highlighted evidence of fraud, corporate greed and earnings manipulation. Many other entities collapsed across the globe — HIH Insurance and One.Tel in Australia, WorldCom in the United States and Parmalat in Europe. In this chapter we will look at corporate failure and see what can be learned from failures of the past. We will discuss what corporate failure means and common causes of failure, using past failures as examples.

The search for an accurate method of predicting corporate distress continues, nevertheless we will look at common prediction models used by financial analysts. Regulatory responses to corporate failure which are generally aimed at corporate governance or strengthening the financial reporting process are also investigated.

The global financial crisis (GFC) has led to, and continues to result in, economic downturn and in some cases recession. We will use the GFC as a case study and in doing so examine both its origins and its consequences. The impact of the GFC on the finance sector will be a particular focus.

LO 1   WHAT IS CORPORATE FAILURE?

There is a lack of agreement as to what 'corporate failure' means and in the terminology used. This can also vary across jurisdictions; for example, in the United States corporate failure is referred to as **bankruptcy**, while in Australia the term **insolvency** is generally used to represent the state of bankruptcy for a corporate entity, with 'bankruptcy' reserved for individuals. A person can also be considered 'insolvent' if they are unable to meet their debts, but there has not been a debtor's petition lodged. In reality, these terms are often used interchangeably, along with other terms such as 'failure' and 'default'.

When conducting research into business failure, a number of definitions are commonly used by researchers. In the United States, Altman and Narayanan note that failure could relate to: a company filing for bankruptcy; delisting for a range of reasons which might include a merger; or liquidation.[1] It could also include appointment of a receiver or administrator to assist the company to trade out of financial difficulties. Altman, when developing the original Z-Score bankruptcy prediction model, defined failure quite narrowly as those companies which file for bankruptcy where the company ceases trading and goes out of business.[2] Taffler and Tisshaw present a broader definition and see failed entities as those that enter receivership, creditors' voluntary liquidation, compulsory winding up by order of the court or government action in the form of a bailout.[3]

A significant indication of corporate failure could be the appointment of voluntary administrators. In the United States, this is governed by Chapter 11 of the Bankruptcy Code (commonly referred to as Chapter 11 bankruptcy). In Australia, a voluntary administrator can be appointed by directors or in some circumstances by secured creditors in an attempt to resolve the company's future direction quickly. This entails the administrator investigating the affairs of the company and trying to find a way to save the business. If this is not possible, the administrator manages the affairs of the company to maximise the return to creditors prior to liquidation.

There is a distinction between companies entering voluntary and involuntary liquidation in Australia.[4] Companies may enter voluntary liquidation only if they are able to pay debts in full upon liquidation (s. 494 of the *Corporations Act 2001*).

Dunn & Bradstreet, a global entity that researches business failures and undertakes credit collection services adopts a wide definition of business failure:

> businesses that cease operation following assignment or bankruptcy; those that cease with loss to creditors after such actions or execution, foreclosure, or attachment;

those that voluntarily withdraw, leaving unpaid obligations, or those that have been involved in court actions such as receivership, bankruptcy reorganization, or arrangement; and those that voluntarily compromise with creditors.[5]

Default on a debt agreement can also be associated with corporate distress. A **technical default** usually is seen when a company has violated a condition of a debt agreement — for example, exceeding a leverage ratio specified in a loan agreement. This can lead to renegotiation of the loan — which can be very costly — but could also signal grounds for legal action against the company.[6]

Therefore, business failure can relate to anything from technical default on a debt agreement, signalling the company is having liquidity issues, through to bankruptcy or insolvency where the company ceases to operate after being determined insolvent.

LO 2 CAUSES OF CORPORATE FAILURE

There are many reasons why companies fail, and indeed most fail for multiple reasons. Corporate decline can stem from multiple sources both inside and outside the organisation, making it difficult for managers to see and respond to problems.[7] Outside factors can include changes in technology, recession, competitors' actions, deregulation or changes in import protection in an industry, or interest rate changes; while factors inside the organisation that can lead to a downturn can include weak strategy, financial mismanagement, and dysfunctional culture amongst others.[8]

Altman and Hotchkiss note that, despite the many factors that can contribute to corporate failure, management inadequacies are often at the core.[9] This can be reflected in management not being able to read the market and not understanding the effect external factors could have on the entity's operations.

Following an in-depth examination of a number of high profile corporate failures, including Enron, Barings Bank, WorldCom, Tyco and Parmalat, Hamilton and Micklethwait believe that the main causes of failure can be grouped into six categories:

1. *Poor strategic decisions.* Companies fail to understand the relevant business drivers when they expand into new products or markets, leading to poor strategic decisions.
2. *Greed and the desire for power.* High achieving executives can be ambitious, eager for more power and may attempt to grow the company in a way that is not sustainable.
3. *Overexpansion and ill-judged acquisitions.* Integration costs often far exceed anticipated benefits. Cultural differences and lack of management capacity can also be problems.
4. *Dominant CEOs.* Boards can sometimes become complacent and not adequately scrutinise the CEO.
5. *Failure of internal controls.* Internal control deficiencies may relate to complex and unclear organisational structures and failure to identify and manage operational risks. This can lead to gaps in information flow, control and risk management systems.
6. *Ineffective boards.* While directors are expected to provide an independent view, occasionally they can become financially obliged to management, which can impede their judgement.[10]

A number of these issues stem from organisational governance, which will be examined shortly.

Lamers points to the importance of cash flow in ensuring the ongoing viability of a business.[11] There needs to be enough cash to pay staff, GST obligations, debtors and other operational expenses. Dunn & Bradstreet CEO Christine Christian notes that businesses are more likely to fail because of poor cash flow than poor sales.[12] She commented, 'The risk is that in relatively good economic times executives ignore the critical role of cash flow to the overall health of their business, focusing instead on revenue and sales numbers'.[13]

Cash flow is often affected in times of economic recession or downturn. Usually, this is as a result of waiting extra time to receive payment from customers or other businesses. National Credit Insurance (Brokers) Pty Ltd, which offers insurance to protect companies in the event of bad debts in their debtors' lists, reported a significant rise in the number of claims against bad debtors following the GFC, indicating businesses were not prepared for the slowdown in the economy, resulting in a strain on cash flows.[14]

COSTS OF FAILURE

Corporate distress and failure can result in a range of direct and indirect costs to a company. Direct costs include expenses to hire lawyers, accountants, restructuring advisers and a range of insolvency practitioners. They also include additional interest on holding debt that cannot be discharged due to lack of cash flow, or refinancing debt if debt covenants have been breached.

Indirect costs are more difficult to identify. They often relate to reputation and opportunity costs. For example, some entities might suffer lost sales and profit as customers will choose not to deal with a company that is in receivership or attempting to trade out of insolvency.[15] Higher debt costs are often common as are more costly credit terms with suppliers. A financially distressed or failing company may lead to loss of key employees or managers. Lost opportunities can also arise because the management team is focused on ensuring the survival of the company, not on identifying potential opportunities.

PREDICTING CORPORATE FAILURE

Investors as well as professionals in the finance sector use a range of methods to assess corporate financial performance and to search for signs of financial distress. For some time, ratios derived from figures reported in financial statements have been used to assess a range of corporate performance characteristics including liquidity and profitability. There are also, however, a range of bankruptcy prediction models available to assist in identifying companies in financial distress. While there are many models in use, they tend to all involve a range of quantifiable financial indicators of corporate performance, with some also including additional variables to attempt to capture some qualitative elements likely to indicate distress.[16]

Probably the best known is Altman's Z-Score.[17] In developing his model, Altman examined the financial records of a sample of 33 failed US manufacturing entities, and compared these to a sample of 33 healthy entities, which he matched on industry and size. He examined subtle differences in financial ratios between the failed and healthy entities. While he started with 22 potentially helpful ratios, Altman included only five ratios in his final Z-Score model.[18] The model he developed was:

$$Z = 1.2X_1 + 1.4X_2 + 3.3X_3 + 0.6X_4 + 1.0X_5$$

where:
- Z = *overall index or score.*
- X_1 = *working capital/total assets.* Measures the net liquid assets of the entity relative to the total capitalisation.
- X_2 = *retained earnings/total assets.* A measure of the cumulative profitability over the life of the entity. It also measures the leverage of the entity, as those entities with high

retained earnings compared to total assets have financed their assets through retention of profits rather than borrowings.

- X_3 = *earnings before interest and tax/total assets*. Measures the productivity of the entity's assets. Given an entity's ultimate existence is based on the earning power of its assets, this ratio is particularly relevant.[19]
- X_4 = *market value of equity/book value of total liabilities*. Shows how much an entity's assets can decline in value before the liabilities exceed the assets and the entity becomes insolvent.[20]
- X_5 = *sales/total assets*. A capital turnover ratio that gives an indication of the sales-generating ability of the entity's assets. This ratio is often left out of the model as there is likely to be great variability across industry sectors.

Altman used multiple discriminant analysis (MDA), which is a statistical technique used to classify observations into groupings depending on their characteristics.[21]

A Z-Score of 3.0 or more defines a healthy entity. A score of 1.8 to 2.9 indicates an entity in the 'danger zone', while a score below 1.8 indicates a high probability of entity failure. Despite many new models being developed, Altman's Z-Score is still popular amongst financial analysts.[22] Uebergang 'bench tested' Altman's Z-Score on a group of 84 Australian ASX-listed entities that had experienced an insolvency event such as the appointment of a receiver or an administrator.[23] He found that one third of the sample was classified as financially distressed three reporting periods before the insolvency occurred and about half by the date of the second-last annual report. One year before the event, two-thirds were under the danger zone threshold of 1.8. While the level of accuracy was below that found by Altman in his original study,[24] Uebergang supported the use of Altman's Z-Score as one means of detecting financial distress in Australian entities.[25]

A variety of other models have been developed since Altman's original work. Many of these are based on the original Z-Score but with some refinement. Others, while still relying on financial ratios from company financial reports, make greater use of cash flow analysis and/or non-financial determinants. One such model is the CAMEL (Capital adequacy, Asset and Management quality, Earnings, Liquidity) model, which as its name suggests, uses a range of financial and non-financial indicators.[26] Sharma and Iselin confirm the relevance of cash flow information to solvency assessments by comparing judgements made by commercial lending managers to models using both cash flow and accrual information.[27] They found that in the case of both behavioural judgements by lenders and the quantitative model, cash flow information produced decisions of higher accuracy than accrual information.

 # INDICATORS OF CORPORATE FAILURE

The Australian Securities and Investments Commission (ASIC) has set up the National Insolvent Trading Program, which aims to:

- make company directors aware of their company's financial position
- make directors of potentially insolvent companies aware of their responsibilities and the implications of continued trading if they know they are insolvent
- encourage directors to seek external advice from accountants and lawyers on restructuring
- encourage directors to seek advice from insolvency professionals where appropriate.[28]

ASIC has identified some key operational and financial practices which, in combination with other practices, indicate a company is at significant risk of insolvency. They include:

- poor cash flow, or no cash flow forecasts
- disorganised internal accounting procedures

- incomplete financial records
- absence of budgets and corporate plans
- continued loss-making activity
- accumulating debt and excess liabilities over assets
- default on loan or interest payments
- increased monitoring and/or involvement of financier
- outstanding creditors of more than 90 days
- instalment arrangements entered into to repay trade creditors
- judgement debts
- significant unpaid tax and superannuation liabilities
- difficulties in obtaining finance
- difficulties in realising current assets (e.g. stock, debtors)
- loss of key management personnel.[29]

As indicated previously, corporate decline can result from factors both inside and outside the entity. Managers and directors need to be aware of the factors or forces that can lead to problems. Managers often rely on 'filtered' information which includes written and verbal reports, memos and summaries. This can lead to information being 'filtered' to such an extent that managers do not get enough information, or the correct information that can trigger warnings about potential problems.[30]

LO 6 CORPORATE GOVERNANCE ISSUES

Corporate governance practices are often at the heart of corporate failure. As noted previously, some of the main contributing factors to failure include ineffective boards and failure of internal controls — both of which are reflective of corporate governance. Corporate governance reform across the globe following the collapse of Enron and other high-profile corporate failures in the early twenty-first century points to potential deficiencies of governance surrounding failed companies. These regulatory responses will be discussed shortly.

Before identifying the corporate governance characteristics that might lead to ensuring entities are sustainable long term, the meaning of 'corporate governance' should be discussed (corporate governance is considered in more detail in chapter 7). Corporate governance relates to the 'duties and responsibilities of a company's board of directors in managing the company and their relationships with the shareholders of the company and the stakeholder groups'.[31] Haspeslagh sees the role of governance as going beyond shareholder protection and notes that corporate governance is the system of rules and regulations by which managers and owners are held accountable for whatever performance society expects. It is commonly viewed that one of the main focuses of governance is accountability.[32]

Despite an increasing reliance on regulation and corporate governance guidelines, governance is ultimately an issue that needs to be addressed at a company level, as each will have a different system, if any, of checks and balances. Companies are less likely to get into financial difficulty if boards of directors are active in their roles. Strong corporate governance, at a company level, will have the following characteristics:
- Boards are active in setting and approving the strategic direction of the company. They are effective at goal setting and understand the importance of risk assessment and management.
- Boards are effective in overseeing risk and setting an appropriate risk level for the entity. They have strong performance management systems in place to ensure managers are working towards the goals and strategies set by the board. Along with this goes appropriate development and rewards for company leadership. This also involves

appropriate selection strategies to ensure the company has a management team that is able to meet organisational goals.[33]

BusinessWeek, a business journal in the United States, annually rates boards on their corporate governance. The principles of good governance they look for include:

1. *Independence.* No more than two directors should be current or former company executives, and none should do business with the company. The audit, compensation and nominating committees should be made up solely of independent directors.
2. *Stock ownership.* Each director should own an equity stake in the company
3. *Director quality.* Boards should include at least one independent director with experience in the company's core business. Directors should be expected to attend at least 75% of board meetings and should be limited in terms of the number of boards they sit on.
4. *Board activism.* Boards should meet regularly without management present and should evaluate their own performance annually.[34]

Boards are sometimes in the difficult situation of having to oversee and question the management team on the one hand and to give support on the other. This can be a difficult role. They also need to ensure they receive adequate information to assess the risk and performance of the organisation and managerial decisions. Having quality processes in place is also essential to ensuring strong governance practices.

LO 7 REGULATION AND POLITICAL RESPONSES TO CORPORATE FAILURE

Historically, every major event where we have seen significant levels of corporate failure has led to a focus on corporate governance and a demand for corporate reform.[35]

In Australia, corporate failures in the 1980s were thought to result from inadequate accounting disclosures. This led to government control over the accounting standard-setting process and stronger governance legislation.

Following a spate of corporate collapses at the start of the twenty-first century, a range of significant legislative and regulatory changes were made in many countries, including Australia, the United States and the United Kingdom. Responding to the perceived limitations in corporate governance legislation that led to the collapse of Enron, with charges of fraud, conspiracy and unethical behaviour, the US government took a primarily legislative route and enacted the Sarbanes–Oxley Act in 2002. This was designed to tighten accounting standards and enhance external auditor independence. Donald Jacobs, a former dean of Northwestern University's Kellogg School of Business was quoted as saying 'Enron is bringing about the most sweeping structural changes in governance that have ever occurred'.[36]

In Australia, following a number of corporate failures in 2001, including HIH Insurance, One.Tel and Harris Scarfe, legislative changes also occurred, but at a slower pace than in the United States. Changes were not restricted to legislation and included:

- the Financial Reporting Council introduced International Accounting Standards from 1 January 2005
- establishment of the ASX Corporate Governance Council and publishing best practice corporate governance guidelines for listed companies in 2003. These have since been revised and re-released
- the *Corporate Law Economic Reform Program (Audit Reform and Corporate Disclosure) Act 2004* (known as CLERP 9) which resulted in changes to the *Corporations Act 2001* effective from 1 July 2004. Following Sarbanes–Oxley in the United States this was designed to strengthen financial disclosure, including executive remuneration

cators and how they were manifested in failed companies.

Cash flow has been seen to be a major contributing factor to corporate failure and this is particularly evident in the retail sector. Some prominent retailers in Australia, such as Gowings and Brashs have disappeared completely, while others like Harris Scarfe and Sportsgirl have been rescued by new owners.[37] In retail, poor control systems and inventory management, expanding too fast, debt management and occupancy rates can all contribute to problems with cash flow. Retailers often suffer from poor planning, inadequate understanding of product costing and margin setting and unrealistic sales forecasting, all of which can lead to problems.[38]

After being placed into voluntary administration in 2001, the administrators of Harris Scarfe documented $93 million owed to unsecured trade creditors, in addition to $67 million owed to secured creditor ANZ Banking Group and $6 million to employees.[39] At the time there were reports of some suppliers entering the flagship store in Rundle Mall in Adelaide and retrieving their stock from the shelves.

Retail is not the only industry affected by cash flow. One of the primary causes of the collapse of HIH Insurance was the consistent failure to set aside enough cash to pay claims.[40] The auditors and regulators contributed to these ongoing issues as it emerged during a Royal Commission that both Arthur Andersen and the Australian Prudential Regulation Authority (APRA) had ignored a document in July 1998 which highlighted that HIH Insurance had been substantially under-reserved for many years.[41] This led to an examination of the role corporate governance strength plays in corporate failure.

Deficiencies in the audit process have been found to play a role in the collapse of both Enron and HIH Insurance. Audit firm personnel were over-represented on the boards of failed entities. In fact, the issue of audit independence was of fundamental importance to the HIH Insurance collapse. Arthur Andersen performed the financial audit of HIH Insurance from 1971 until its collapse in 2001.[42] At the time of its liquidation, HIH Insurance had three former Arthur Andersen partners on its board — one was chief operating officer and another was the chairman. Due to the personal relationship between these directors and the current Arthur Andersen partners and staff, the independence of the audit process was compromised. A further indication of questionable independence was evident when it was revealed that Arthur Andersen paid consulting fees to the HIH Insurance chairman totalling $190 977.60.[43]

Similar conflicts of interest were observed in the audit of Enron, also conducted by Arthur Andersen. In addition to being appointed the external auditors, Enron also subcontracted its internal audit function to Arthur Andersen, which resulted in the effective removal of one layer of the checks and balances necessary in an internal control system.[44]

The independence of the audit committee also appears to be a factor in the HIH Insurance failure. The board members who were audit partners were also members of the audit committee. In the cases of One.Tel, Harris Scarfe and HIH Insurance, there

As we have seen so far there is often not one indicator that a company is likely to become

LO 8 THE ANATOMY OF A CORPORATE FAILURE

of countries, including New Zealand in 2004 and India in 2009.

Corporate governance best practice codes or guidelines have been instituted in a range

increase disclosure requirements relating to these services.

as the US legislation in prohibiting audit firms from providing other services, it did

disclosure and audit independence. While the Australian legislation did not go as far

capitalisation, on average, for the failed companies examined. This can be compared to less than 1% of market capitalisation for the average ASX 100 company.[49]

Contemporary Issue 13.1 outlines factors leading to the appointment of receivers to RedGroup Retail — the owners of the Borders and Angus & Robertson book chains.

13.1 CONTEMPORARY ISSUE

Not open and shut

Reports of the death of books are greatly exaggerated.

The collapse of RedGroup Retail, which went into voluntary administration last week with debts of about $130 million, has fuelled fears of a crisis in the publishing and book selling trade.

RedGroup operates Angus and Robertson, Australia's largest chain of book stores, as well as Borders. A&R, established in Sydney in 1886, has 169 stores around the country, Borders has 26 and another part of the group in New Zealand has 60. Together they employ about 2500 people.

The company blames many of its problems on falling sales caused by the drift of customers to online shopping, as well as high prices caused by import barriers which protect the local publishing industry.

Others, including some rival retailers, publishers and politicians, have been quick to suggest that the management of RedGroup and its private equity owner only have themselves to blame.

There is no dispute that book sales have declined in the past few years, not only in Australia. Like other retail sectors, book shops are suffering from a general loss of confidence and a softening of consumer spending in the wake of the global financial crisis.

The rising value of the Australian dollar has not translated into cheaper books here but has increased the purchasing power for those who buy on the internet from the US and other countries, where books tend to be significantly cheaper.

Some local retailers have called on the Federal Government to impose the 10 per cent goods and services tax on internet purchases but that is unlikely and besides, it would hardly make a dent in the trade because the savings that consumers make on the net are so big.

Eventually, inevitably, the market is going to decide the future of book sales. The internet makes a mockery of national markets and it is becoming more costly and less feasible to maintain trade barriers and insulate business from the power of consumer choice but Australians still do love books and they still love buying works by local authors.

Source: Excerpts from the Editorial, 'Not open and shut', *The Mercury.*[50]

Questions

1. Discuss how trade barriers may have contributed to the failure of the RedGroup. **J** **K** **AS**
2. From the previous discussion, what other issues can the retail sector face which might lead to corporate distress? **J** **K** **AS**
3. Outline some ways the sector could change its operations to sustain and compete in a global market where the internet dominates. **J** **K** **AS**

LO 9 A CASE STUDY: THE GLOBAL FINANCIAL CRISIS

Some economists propose that the global financial crisis (GFC) is the worst financial crisis since the Great Depression,[51] and based on measures of world industrial output, world trade and stock markets may in fact be worse on a global scale.[52] The GFC is widely viewed to have commenced with a downturn in the US housing market and a consequential liquidity shortfall in the banking system. This resulted in the collapse of a number of large financial institutions, a downturn in stock markets and the government bailout of banks in a number of countries. This section examines the proposed causes and consequences of the GFC and discusses the resulting regulatory intervention in a number of jurisdictions.

Causes and consequences of the GFC

The GFC is said to have started in the US housing sector.[53] The health of the housing sector is understood to be a critical indicator of the health of the economy in any country. This results from a number of factors including 'the size of the sector, its linkage to other sectors in the economy, and the social and political implications of the industry that is interwoven into the fabric of the family, the community, and the economy'.[54] Housing and home ownership is seen to be a main focus of the social and economic system in many countries, including the United States, Australia, the United Kingdom and New Zealand. Home ownership, from a sociological point of view, is said to promote community-based values, respect for law and order, and provide stability and prosperity; while from an economic standpoint the steady appreciation of home values, often the main asset a household owns, provides the basis for continuous increase in consumption, leading to a strengthened economy.[55]

Leading up to the financial crisis there was a substantial increase in housing prices, with historically low interest rates. This created an environment which promoted borrowing, with lending standards relaxing and subprime mortgages increasingly being used. **Subprime lending** refers to lending to people who may have difficulty maintaining the payment schedule. This might include people who have a limited credit history, limited assets, no savings history, or have defaulted on payments in the past. In 2006, in the United States, subprime mortgages accounted for somewhere between 20% and 34% of new mortgage originations, compared to only 6% in 2002.[56] This period has been referred to as a 'housing bubble', which peaked in 2006. An **asset bubble** occurs when the price of an asset (in this case housing) goes far beyond its underlying value.

Some attribute the cause of the housing bubble to a broad political agenda to promote home ownership, particularly to the middle and lower middle class.[57] This was done through generous underwriting policies of the government-sponsored enterprises Fannie Mae and Freddie Mac, low risk weights on bank capital adequacy requirements for holding mortgages, and the Community Reinvestment Act that required banks to serve their communities — an obligation often met by making mortgage loans.[58]

Towards the end of 2006 house prices started declining, with significant defaults and foreclosures on mortgages following in early 2007. This also coincided with an increase in interest rates and saw a number of financial companies filing for bankruptcy. Increasing losses in the finance sector continued in 2008, with Bear Stearns being an early victim.[59] In July 2008, the stock prices of Fannie Mae and Freddie Mac fell over 80% in value and Lehman Brothers declared bankruptcy in September of that year.[60] Lehman Brothers was the fourth largest investment bank in the United States behind Goldman Sachs, Morgan Stanley and Merrill Lynch.

While most market participants originally thought the United States was entering a subprime crisis, this quickly turned into a financial crisis which affected credit markets and jeopardised the banking system.[61] By the end of 2008, the financial crisis had developed into an economic crisis that affected not only the United States, but caused the rest of the world to head into recession.[62]

Research has shown that the end of major asset bubbles can have a significant effect on other markets.[63] Case, Quigley and Shiller find that stock market and real estate fluctuations significantly affect household consumption levels, with declines in housing prices having a greater effect than stock price fluctuations.[64]

Internal management and governance in the finance sector played a contributing role to the GFC. Risk taking was perceived to be a significant issue, with credit default swaps, which were originally designed to insure bond investors against default risk, being used for speculation purposes. The market for credit default swaps and derivatives was effectively unregulated in the United States at the time.[65] Two days after Lehman Brothers declared bankruptcy the US government bailed out American International Group Inc. (AIG) — an insurance company. The government was concerned about the consequences of having AIG default on counterparties to credit default swaps at a time when the market reaction to Lehman Brothers was so severe.[66]

The financial and economic effects of the GFC were transferred to other countries through three mechanisms.[67] The first was the exposure of the world's financial system to the US system through direct funding of the US subprime mortgage market. Some international banks that have experienced difficulties as a result of this exposure include BNP Paribas (France), Halifax Bank of Scotland (United Kingdom) and KKB Deutsche Industriebank AG, SachsenLB, BayernLB and WestLB, all from Germany.[68] The second is through declining international demand and supply, which had a flow-on effect to unemployment. Finally, housing bubbles existed in many countries at the same time. The bursting of the US bubble resulted in other countries experiencing the same situation.[69]

The impact of the GFC in Australia was relatively minor in comparison to other countries. The Australian banking sector was protected to a certain extent by prudential capital requirements and with further government intervention avoided a technical recession.[70] New Zealand, however, was affected to a greater extent. The situation in New Zealand was also affected by a fragile manufacturing sector, with global demand slipping.[71]

Government intervention in the GFC

Both the Australian and New Zealand governments responded to the GFC by announcing stimulus packages to 'kick start' the economy and to avoid a full recession. In Australia, the government granted $900 to taxpayers who met certain conditions. They also guaranteed bank deposits and increased first home buyers' grants. A second, larger economic stimulus package followed in early 2009, which provided funding to schools to embark on a building program, funding for road repairs and infrastructure, cash bonuses of $950 for taxpayers and small business tax breaks.[72]

The health of Australian authorised deposit-taking institutions (ADIs) following the GFC, is as a result of regulation by the Australian Prudential Regulation Authority (APRA), seen as a model for corporate governance of financial institutions around the world. The regulation of ADIs goes well beyond capital and liquidity requirements.[73] The London G20 Conference 2009 examined the role played by APRA with the view to reforming corporate and securities law in line with the existing ADI regulation in Australia.[74]

Contemporary Issue 13.2 highlights the changes to US legislation as a consequence of the GFC.

13.2 CONTEMPORARY ISSUE

Penalties, enforcement key to real reforms

When crisis erupts and the public clamour ensues, the usual response from the authorities is new regulation. This is particularly so in the US. Thus, the Great Financial Crisis (GFC) of 2008 has last week led to the passing by the House of Representatives of Bill HR4173, the Wall St Reform and Consumer Protection Act of 2009.

There is no doubt that there is pressing need for something to be done to rein in excessive risk-taking on Wall Street. Salaries, especially, have to be capped in view of the fact that large amounts of taxpayer money were used to bail out the banks that are now paying huge bonuses, even comparable to the halcyon days of 2007.

But US regulators — as well as those in other jurisdictions – should bear in mind that rules are only one side of the regulatory coin and that without strong penalties and strict enforcement, there can be no lasting change. Worse, the public may well be lulled into a false sense of security.

It is worth recalling, for instance, that contrary to popular belief, there were already plenty of rules and protective legislation in place in the US before the GFC. For example, the new Bill proposes a council of regulators to police the financial landscape for systematic risks and to identify firms 'too large to fail' whose collapse could jeopardise the financial system. Yet, this was supposed to have been the job of the US Treasury, whose mission was, and is, to ensure the 'safety, soundness and security of the US and international financial system' and the Federal Reserve, which is supposed to supervise the banks, regulate credit and money supply and keep a check on lending. Insurance companies, in the meantime, were supposed to be under the control of state regulators and protecting the interests of investors was, and is, supposed to be the job of the Securities and Exchange Commission which ensures investment banks and stockbrokers make all proper disclosures and discharge their fiduciary duties properly.

Hopefully, whatever does finally pass will be strictly enforced with heavy penalties, because regulation without enforcement is form without substance. It provides only an illusion of reform, which is not only meaningless but, to the extent that it replaces real reform, is also dangerous.

Source: Extracts from the article 'Penalties, enforcement key to real reforms', *The Business Times*.[75]

Questions

1. The article above highlights regulatory changes in the United States as a result of the GFC. Research the main outcomes from this legislation and document how this is anticipated to improve governance in the finance sector. **K** **SM**
2. Outline the arguments both in favour of and against increasing regulation, given the extent of regulation already in the market. **K** **SM**

Summary

Outline what is understood by the term 'corporate failure'

- Failure could relate to a company filing for bankruptcy; delisting for a range of reasons, which might include a merger; or liquidation. It could also include appointment of a receiver or an administrator to assist the company to put in place a strategy to enable it to trade out of difficulties.
- In Australia, there is a distinction between companies entering voluntary and involuntary liquidation.
- Default on a debt agreement can also be associated with corporate distress.

Examine the causes of corporate failure

- Corporate decline can stem from multiple sources both inside and outside the organisation, making it difficult for managers to see and respond to problems.
- Outside factors can include changes in technology, recession, competitors' actions, deregulation or changes in import protection in an industry, or interest rate changes.
- Inside factors can include weak strategy, financial mismanagement and dysfunctional culture.
- Despite the many factors that can contribute to corporate failure, management inadequacies are often at the core.

Identify the costs of corporate failure

- Corporate distress and failure can result in a range of both direct and indirect costs to a company.
- Direct costs include expenses to hire lawyers, accountants, restructuring advisers and a range of insolvency practitioners.
- Indirect costs are more difficult to identify. They often relate to reputation and opportunity costs. Higher debt costs are often common, as are more costly credit terms with suppliers. A financially distressed or failing company may also lead to loss of key employees or managers.

Evaluate the factors used to predict corporate failure

- There are a range of bankruptcy-prediction models available to assist in identifying companies in financial distress. Probably the best known is Altman's Z-Score. Altman's Z-Score is still popular amongst financial analysts.
- A variety of other models have been developed since Altman's original work. Many of these are based on the original Z-Score, but with some refinement. Others, while still relying on financial ratios from company financial reports, make greater use of cash flow analysis and/or non-financial determinants. Sharma and Iselin confirm the

relevance of cash flow information to solvency assessments by comparing judgements made by commercial lending managers to models using both cash flow and accrual information.

Assess the likely indicators of corporate failure

- ASIC has identified some key operational and financial practices which, in combination with other practices, indicate a company is at significant risk of insolvency, including:
  - poor cash flow, or no cash flow forecasts
  - disorganised internal accounting procedures
  - incomplete financial records
  - absence of budgets and corporate plans
  - continued loss-making activity
  - accumulating debt and excess liabilities over assets
  - default on loan or interest payments
  - increased monitoring and/or involvement of financier
  - outstanding creditors of more than 90 days
  - instalment arrangements entered into to repay trade creditors
  - judgement debts
  - significant unpaid tax and superannuation liabilities
  - difficulties in obtaining finance
  - difficulties in realising current assets (e.g. stock, debtors)
  - loss of key management personnel.

Evaluate the relationship between corporate governance and failure

- Corporate governance practices are often at the heart of corporate failure. Strong corporate governance, at a company level, will have the following characteristics:
  - Boards are active in setting and approving the strategic direction of the company.
  - Boards are effective in overseeing risk and setting an appropriate risk level for the entity.

Evaluate how regulation has been used to alleviate the effects of corporate failure

- Responding to the perceived limitations in corporate governance legislation that led to the collapse of Enron, with charges of fraud, conspiracy and unethical behaviour, the US government took a primarily legislative route and enacted the Sarbanes–Oxley Act in 2002. This was designed to tighten accounting standards and enhance external auditor independence.
- In Australia legislative changes following corporate failures in 2001 included:
  - introduction of International Accounting Standards in 2005
  - establishment of the ASX Corporate Governance Council
  - CLERP 9.
- Corporate governance best practice codes or guidelines have been introduced in a number of countries, including New Zealand in 2004 and India in 2009.

Evaluate the anatomy of a corporate failure

- There is often not one indicator that a company is likely to become distressed or fail.
- Cash flow has been seen to be a major contributing factor to corporate failure. This is particularly evident in the retail sector.
- Deficiencies in the audit process have been found to play a role in the collapse of both Enron and HIH Insurance. The independence of the audit committee also appears to be factor in the HIH Insurance failure.
- IA Research found that the majority of failed companies had an ownership structure dominated by a single shareholder with effective control (60%) when compared with

39% of ASX 100 companies. Boards also tended to contain below average numbers of independent directors and it is common to find the board dominated by founders or relatives of founders. Executive remuneration packages are often also an issue at failed companies.

Critically evaluate the causes and consequences of the global financial crisis (GFC) and evaluate how governments have intervened to alleviate the effects of the GFC

- The GFC is widely viewed to have commenced with a downturn in the US housing market and a consequential liquidity shortfall in the banking system. This resulted in the collapse of a number of large financial institutions, a downturn in stock markets and the government bailout of banks in a number of countries.

- The health of the housing sector is understood to be a critical indicator of the health of the economy in any country. Leading up to the financial crisis there was a substantial increase in housing prices, with historically low interest rates. This created an environment which promoted borrowing, with lending standards relaxing and subprime mortgages increasingly being used. Towards the end of 2006 US house prices started declining, with significant defaults and foreclosures on mortgages following in early 2007.

- Internal management and governance in the finance sector played a contributing role to the GFC.

- The financial and economic effects of the GFC were transferred to other countries through three mechanisms. The first was the exposure of the world's financial system to the US system through direct funding of the US subprime mortgage market. The second is through declining international demand and supply, which had a flow on effect to unemployment. Finally, housing bubbles existed in many countries at the same time.

- Both the Australian and New Zealand governments responded to the GFC by announcing stimulus packages to 'kick start' the economy and to avoid a full recession.

- The health of Australian authorised deposit-taking institutions (ADIs) following the GFC is, as a result of regulation by the Australian Prudential Regulatory Authority (APRA), seen as a model for corporate governance of financial institutions around the world.

Review questions

1. What is corporate failure?
2. Articulate what is meant by bankruptcy and insolvency. In doing so, highlight the similarities and differences.
3. What are four common causes of corporate failure?
4. What external factors can influence corporate failure?
5. What internal factors can influence corporate failure?
6. Researchers and professionals have highlighted the importance of cash flow in avoiding corporate failure. Explain why this factor is important.
7. What direct costs can result from corporate failure?
8. What indirect costs can result from corporate failure?
9. Discuss what financial indicators can be used by analysts to assist in predicting whether companies might be at risk of distress or failure.
10. What factors should investors look for to assess the likelihood of corporate failure? Explain how each might be related to the likelihood of corporate failure.
11. Corporate governance has been highlighted as an important factor in alleviating the risk of corporate failure. Evaluate which aspects of corporate governance are likely to guard against corporate failure.

12. What is the global financial crisis (GFC)?
13. How did the GFC start?
14. Articulate the relationship between the housing sector and the finance sector.
15. How was the housing sector so integral to the development of the GFC?
16. Why have Australian financial institutions been able to avoid the worst of the GFC?

Application questions

13.1 Identify a delisted Australian company from the website www.delisted.com.au. Access the financial reports for the previous five years. Work in teams to determine and calculate a range of financial ratios which may have been used to assess the signs of financial distress that might have been evident to investors in the five years leading up to failure. **J** **CT** **SM**

13.2 You are interested in investing in shares in an Australian company, but are worried the company might be in financial distress. Prepare a list of factors you might look at in deciding whether it might be considered to be a sound investment, or that could indicate potential distress. **J** **K**

13.3 Access the Australian Prudential Regulation Authority (APRA) website www.apra.gov.au. Document what rules and regulations it has in place to oversee governance of ADIs. Identify any proposals it is examining that may affect future governance requirements. **J** **K**

13.1 CASE STUDY

ABC Learning 'reliant' on debt to cover cash shortfalls

By Danny John

The failed childcare operator ABC Learning almost certainly became insolvent in the first half of 2008, about six months before the directors appointed administrators to take control of the company, creditors have been told.

According to financial statements prepared by the administrators Ferrier Hodgson, the company went from a positive cash flow of $207 million from its operating activities in its 2007 full year accounts to a deficit of almost $20 million in the first half of 2008.

The cash flow had grown significantly from 2004 when ABC emerged as a significant player in the childcare industry – it ran 327 centres by June that year. Run by Eddy Groves, the company had listed on the ASX in 2001 with 43 centres.

Ferrier noted in its report to creditors yesterday that its analysis showed a 'significant deterioration' in the net cash flow from its operations in the last few months of its corporate life.

Ferrier moved into ABC Learning on November 6 2008, days after its board concluded the company had insufficient cash to pay its debts. Its banks, owed nearly $1 billion, called in receivers immediately.

Ferrier put down ABC's failure to a combination of factors including:
- 'Inadequate focus' on day-to-day practices and results of operations;
- Lack of strategy to integrate businesses it bought over seven years;
- A dependency on compensation payments, liquidated damages and fee guarantees from developers to provide revenue;
- Too high a reliance on debt to fund acquisitions and to support a shortfall of cash from operations.

The administrator Greg Moloney said the company's business model became 'unsustainable'. ABC's former directors and management are under examination to help determine the detailed causes of the company's failure.

Creditors will be asked next week to decide whether to wind up the company and appoint a liquidator to consider claims of insolvent trading, breaches of directors' and auditors' duties, uncommercial transactions and unreasonable director-related deals.

Source: Danny John, 'ABC Learning "reliant" on debt to cover cash shortfalls', *The Sydney Morning Herald.*[76]

Questions

1. Outline the importance of cash flow to ensuring the ongoing operation of a company. **J** **K**
2. Discuss the corporate governance and board mechanisms that could have served to limit the chances of corporate failure in the case of ABC Learning. **J** **K**

13.2
CASE
STUDY

Company failures soar by 40 pc

By Maria Slade

Failures of New Zealand companies are up over 40 per cent on the same time last year.

Ministry of Economic development figures show that in the seven months since July 2008 a total of 3487 companies have run aground – 3270 have gone into liquidation, a further 217 into receivership.

In the same period the previous year, 2424 companies hit the wall, made up of 2344 liquidations and 80 receiverships.

Liquidator Damien Grant of Waterstone Insolvency said applications to the court where a creditor applies to have a debtor company wound up were way up. His records show there were 236 applications in February.

Grant said the tax department was behind many of the liquidations. 'Applications made by the IRD are really starting to crank.'

He was also noticing companies taking much greater advantage of the 10-day rule, in which they had 10 days after a creditor application was made to put themselves into liquidation.

A year ago many businesses did not seem aware they had that option.

Kerry Downey, partner in insolvency specialists McGrath Nicol, said the pain was being felt across the board.

Businesses were being hit by factors such as declining orders and customers not paying.

Businesses were even trying to renegotiate their leases in an attempt to cut costs, a strategy that smacked of desperation, Downey said.

McGrath Nichol was doing a lot of assessment work, coming up with remedial plans for businesses heading into trouble.

Source: Excerpts from Maria Slade, 'Company failures soar by 40 pc', *The New Zealand Herald.*[77]

Question

1. Discuss how the GFC could have affected business health in New Zealand. **J** **K**

Additional readings

Altman, EI & Hotchkiss, E 2006, *Corporate financial distress and bankruptcy*, John Wiley & Sons Inc., Hoboken, NJ.

Forster, J 2010, *Global financial crisis: implications for Australasian businesses*, John Wiley & Sons Australia Ltd: Milton.

Hamilton, S & Micklethwait, A 2006, *Greed and corporate failure: the lessons from recent disasters*, Palgrave Macmillan: New York, NY.

End notes

1. Altman, E & Narayanan, P 1997, 'An international survey of business failure classification models', *Financial Markets, Institutions and Instruments*, vol. 6, no. 2, pp. 1–57.
2. Altman, E 1968, 'Financial ratios, discriminant analysis and the prediction of corporate bankruptcy', *Journal of Finance*, vol. 23, no. 4, pp. 189–209.
3. Taffler, R & Tisshaw, H 1977, 'Going, going, going — four factors which predict', *Accountancy*, vol. 50, March, pp. 50–4.
4. Sharma, D & Iselin, E 2003, 'The relative relevance of cash flow and accrual information for solvency assessments: a multi-method approach', *Journal of Business Finance & Accounting*, vol. 30, no. 7/8, pp. 1115–40.
5. Altman, EI & Hotchkiss, E 2006, *Corporate financial distress and bankruptcy*, John Wiley & Sons Inc., Hoboken, NJ, p. 6.
6. ibid.
7. Anonymous 2006, 'How to succeed in identifying failure', *Strategic Direction*, vol. 22, no. 1, pp. 9–11.
8. ibid.
   Altman, EI & Hotchkiss, E 2006, *Corporate financial distress and bankruptcy*, John Wiley & Sons Inc., Hoboken, NJ.
9. ibid.
10. Hamilton, S & Micklethwait, A 2006, *Greed and corporate failure: the lessons from recent disasters*, Palgrave Macmillan, New York, NY.
11. Lamers, R 2009, '8 warning signs of financial distress', *Dynamic Business Magazine*, 9 September, viewed 2 November 2011, www.dynamicbusiness.com.au.
12. Heaney, C 2011, 'GFC still taking its grim toll, warns Dunn & Bradstreet', *Herald Sun*, 24 February.
13. ibid.
14. Lamers, R 2009, '8 warning signs of financial distress', *Dynamic Business Magazine*, 9 September, viewed 2 November 2011, www.dynamicbusiness.com.au.
15. Altman, EI & Hotchkiss, E 2006, *Corporate financial distress and bankruptcy*, John Wiley & Sons Inc., Hoboken, NJ.

16. ibid.
17. Altman, E 1968, 'Financial ratios, discriminant analysis and the prediction of corporate bankruptcy', *Journal of Finance*, vol. 23, no. 4, pp. 189–209.
18. ibid.
19. ibid.
20. Altman, EI & Hotchkiss, E 2006, *Corporate financial distress and bankruptcy*, John Wiley & Sons Inc., Hoboken, NJ.
21. Altman, E 1968, 'Financial ratios, discriminant analysis and the prediction of corporate bankruptcy', *Journal of Finance*, vol. 23, no. 4, pp. 189–209.
22. Uebergang, M 2006, 'Predicting corporate failure', *JASSA*, iss. 4, Summer, pp. 10–11.
23. ibid.
24. Altman, E 1968, 'Financial ratios, discriminant analysis and the prediction of corporate bankruptcy', *Journal of Finance*, vol. 23, no. 4, pp. 189–209.
25. Uebergang, M 2006, 'Predicting corporate failure', *JASSA*, iss. 4, Summer, pp. 10–11.
26. Bongini, P, Classens, S & Ferri, G 2001, 'The political economy of distress in East Asian financial institutions', *Journal of Financial Services Research*, vol. 19, no. 1, pp. 5–25.
27. Sharma, D & Iselin, E 2003, 'The relative relevance of cash flow and accrual information for solvency assessments: a multi-method approach', *Journal of Business Finance & Accounting*, vol. 30, no. 7/8, pp. 1115–40.
28. Australian Securities and Investments Commission (ASIC) 2010, *ASIC's National Insolvent Trading Program*, ASIC, Gippsland, viewed 2 November 2011, www.asic.gov.au.
29. ibid.
30. Anonymous 2006, 'How to succeed in identifying failure', *Strategic Direction*, vol. 22, no. 1, pp. 9–11.
31. Pass, C 2004, 'Corporate governance and the role of non-executive directors in large UK companies: an empirical study', *Corporate Governance*, vol. 4, no. 2, pp. 52–63.
32. Haspeslah, P 2010, 'Corporage governance and the current crisis',

Corporate Governance, vol. 10, no. 4, pp. 375–7.
33. ibid.
34. Lavelle, L 2002, 'The best & worst of boards: how the corporate scandals are sparking a revolution in governance', *BusinessWeek*, 7 October, pp. 104–14.
35. Vinten, G 1998, 'Corporate governance: an international state-of-the-art', *Managerial Auditing Journal*, vol. 13, no. 5, pp. 419–31.
36. Lavelle, L 2002, 'The best & worst of boards: how the corporate scandals are sparking a revolution in governance', *BusinessWeek*, 7 October, pp. 104–14.
37. Atkinson, B 2007, 'Cry for help — how to avoid receivership in retailing', *Inside Retailing Magazine, Inside Retailing Online*, 28 June, viewed 2 November 2011, www.insideretailing.com.au.
38. ibid.
39. Peacock, S 2001, 'Probe reveals the extent of Scarfe's debts', *The West Australian*, 11 April, p. 65.
40. Robins, F 2006, 'Corporate governance after Sarbanes–Oxley: an Australian perspective', *Corporate Governance*, vol. 6, no. 1, pp. 34–48.
41. ibid; Main, A 2002, 'APRA lacked insurance depth', *The Australian Financial Review*, 8 November, p. 8.
42. Mirshekary, S, Yaftian, AM & Cross, D 2005, 'Australian corporate collapse: The case of HIH Insurance', *Journal of Financial Services Marketing*, vol. 9, no. 3, pp. 249–58.
43. ibid.
44. Hamilton, S & Micklethwait, A 2006, *Greed and corporate failure: the lessons from recent disasters*, Palgrave Macmillan, New York NY.
45. Watts, T 2002, *A report on corporate governance at five companies that collapsed in 2001*, IA Research, Melbourne.
46. ibid.
47. ibid.
48. ibid.
49. ibid.
50. Editorial 2011, 'Not open and shut', *The Mercury*, 22 February, www.themercury.com.au.
51. Pendery, D 2009, 'Three top economists agree 2009 worst financial

crisis since Great Depression; Risks increase if right steps not taken', IHS press release, *Reuters*, 27 February, www.reuters.com.

52. Adams, R 2009, *Governance and the Financial Crisis, ECGI — Finance Working Paper No. 248/2009*, working papers, *Social Science Research Network*, 4 May, www.ssrn.com.

53. Bardhan, A 2010, 'Of subprimes and sundry symptoms: The political economy of the financial crisis' in *Lessons from the Financial Crisis*, RW Kolb Series in Finance, John Wiley & Sons Inc., Hoboken NJ.

54. ibid.

55. ibid.

56. ibid.

57. Scott, HS 2009, *The Global Financial Crisis*, Foundation Press, New York NY.

58. ibid.

59. Bardhan, A 2010, 'Of subprimes and sundry symptoms: The political economy of the financial crisis' in *Lessons from the Financial Crisis*, RW Kolb Series in Finance, John Wiley & Sons Inc., Hoboken NJ.

60. ibid.

61. Scott, HS 2009, *The Global Financial Crisis*, Foundation Press, New York NY.

62. ibid.

63. Congleton, RD 2010, 'The political economy of the financial crisis of 2008' in *Lessons from the Financial Crisis*, R.W.Kolb Series in Finance, John Wiley & Sons Inc., Hoboken NJ.

64. Case, KE, Quigley, JM & Shiller, RJ 2001, 'Comparing wealth effects: the stockmarket versus the housing market', *Cowles Foundation Discussion Paper 1335*, Yale University, New Haven, CT.

65. Friedman, HH & Friedman, LW 2010, 'The global financial crisis of 2008: what went wrong?' in *Lessons from the Financial Crisis*, RW Kolb Series in Finance, John Wiley & Sons Inc., Hoboken NJ.

66. Scott, HS 2009, *The Global Financial Crisis*, Foundation Press, New York NY.

67. Forster, J 2010, *Global financial crisis: implications for Australasian businesses*, John Wiley & Sons Australia Ltd: Milton.

68. ibid.

69. ibid.

70. ibid.

71. ibid.

72. Canstar 2009, 'Global Financial Crisis — What caused it and how the world responded', Canstar Cannex, Brisbane, viewed 3 November 2001, www.canstar.com.au/global-financial-crisis.

73. Peters, M 2010, 'Corporate governance of Australian Banking: A lesson in law reform or good fortune', UNSW Australian School of Business, research paper, *Social Science Research Network*, www.ssrn.com.

74. ibid.

75. Anonymous 2009, 'Penalties, enforcement key to real reforms', *The Business Times*, Singapore, 18 December.

76. John, D 2010, 'ABC Learning 'reliant' on debt to cover cash shortfalls', *The Sydney Morning Herald*, 19 March, p. 5.

77. Slade, M 2009, 'Company failures soar by 40 pc', *The New Zealand Herald*, 10 March.

14

Special reporting issues

After studying this chapter, you should be able to:

1 analyse the background leading to the issue of whether intangible assets and heritage assets should be recognised in financial statements

2 explain why capitalisation is contentious and apply the asset definition and recognition tests of the *Conceptual Framework*

3 analyse whether intangibles pass the definition and recognition tests

4 explain the implications of non-recognition of intangibles

5 analyse whether heritage assets pass the definition and recognition tests

6 explain the implications of recognition of heritage assets.

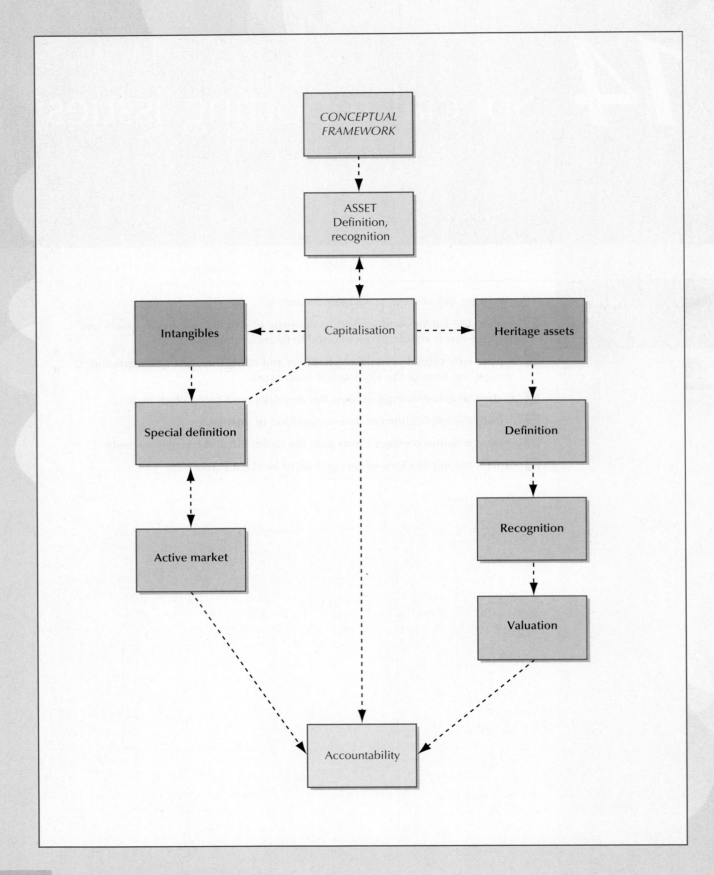

After reading the previous chapters, you know that the *Conceptual Framework for Financial Reporting* (the *Conceptual Framework*) is the driving force behind the decisions made by the International Accounting Standards Board (IASB). The *Conceptual Framework* has a balance sheet focus in that the definition of an asset determines the definition of the other elements: liabilities, revenue, expenses and equity. This chapter looks at two reporting issues: the reporting of (1) intangible assets and (2) heritage assets. These asset types are interesting in that intangibles are a reporting problem for the for-profit sector, while heritage assets are largely located in the public and not-for-profit sectors. This chapter examines whether these two types of assets comply with the definition of an asset in the *Conceptual Framework*, the recognition problems associated with these assets, and the reporting problems that their lack of recognition creates for their relevant sectors.

Both asset types have attracted the attention of the international accounting standard setters. In the case of intangibles, standard setters have been reluctant to recognise intangibles despite pressures to do so, while in relation to heritage assets, standard setters have been keen to recognise them despite pressure not to do so. In 2006, the International Public Sector Accounting Standards Board (IPSASB) issued a consultation paper, in partnership with the UK Accounting Standards Board (ASB), on the topic of heritage assets under accrual accounting.[1] The IASB has contemplated undertaking a project on the accounting for intangible assets (but excluded goodwill and intangible assets acquired in a business combination) because of concerns that the current accounting requirements lead to inconsistent treatments for some types of intangible assets. In December 2007, the IASB decided not to add the project to its active agenda. However, national standard setters are carrying out research for a possible future project. The IASB will consider whether to restart the project when it considers its future agenda.

LO 1 BACKGROUND

Despite the definition of an asset providing the primary conceptual basis for deliberations by accounting standards setters for standards regulating financial reporting, the resulting standards issued by the IASB limit the reporting of many items that may be regarded as assets or liabilities or one of the other elements. Because certain 'assets' and 'liabilities' are missing from published balance sheets, a listed company has two values that are often reported in the financial press: book value and market value. The book value of a company is that reported on the balance sheet as the difference between a company's assets and liabilities. The market value of a company is determined by the number of its issued shares and the price at which those shares are trading on the company's listing stock exchange. The difference between these two values is increasing. As accounting moves towards a more balance sheet centric view of a company, many commentators attribute this difference to those items that the IASB says do not meet the definition of an element and/or do not meet the recognition test.

Unlike most other countries which have adopted or harmonised with international accounting standards issued by the IASB, Australia's and New Zealand's accounting standards apply to all reporting entities. This means that reporting entities, whether listed on a stock exchange or not, whether they are in the for-profit sector, the not-for-profit sector or the government sector, must comply with standards that assume that complying entities pursue a profit-maximisation strategy. This one-size-fits-all approach can create problems for entities whose purpose is not profit maximisation.

Added to these difficulties is the issue that accounting information is being criticised currently. Some of the criticisms relate to the absence of some items, particularly intangibles, from financial statements as well as accounting information's inability to alert investors and other users to financial happenings such as the late 1990s bubble in information technology stocks, the major bankruptcy scandals of the early 2000s (such as Enron, WorldCom, and HIH), and to reflect appropriately the values of subprime mortgages which led to the 2008 global financial crisis.[2] That accounting information failed to give inklings about and thereby warnings of these damaging events suggests that accounting information is due for an overhaul. Wyatt says the general problem of incomplete information suggests that more information is better even if it is uncertain.[3] Accounting regulators, however, have gone the other way — for example, increasingly moving to prevent entities measuring and reporting internally generated intangible assets.

LO 2 WHAT EXPENDITURES SHOULD BE CAPITALISED?

Sterling argued that:

> We accountants do not resolve issues, we abandon them . . . We debate them loud and long . . . until another issue comes along . . . The explanation for our inability to resolve issues is to be found in the way we conceive issues. We conceive of the issues in such a way that they are in principle irresolvable.[4]

Whether certain items are 'assets', is another unresolved issue. Perhaps the longest running issue in this regard is whether goodwill is an asset. However, disagreement about the status of particular items such as goodwill, intangibles or heritage items would be quickly settled if the definition of the term 'asset' was first agreed upon. In other words, definitions are like a language — they help to provide the 'dictionary', so that one understands what another means.[5] An explicit definition of an 'asset' would solve the question of what expenditures should be capitalised, with the remaining 'left-over' expenditures being expensed.

Prior to the development of conceptual frameworks for accounting, expenditures on intangibles, largely research and development (R&D), were expensed. In the 1970s, the decision to expense such costs as incurred was based on the high failure rate of new products, a rate too high to justify capitalisation.[6] As well, early studies failed to find a causal relationship between expenditure on intangibles and increases in future economic benefits.[7] In the 1980s and 1990s, decisions about capitalisation began to change. Expenditure on development was capitalised and recognised if the reporting enterprise could establish technical feasibility, interpreted as the completed intangible being available for sale within a demonstrated market, and, secondly, if a reporting enterprise could measure reliably the expenditure attributable to the intangible.

The non-capitalisation of intangibles was due to the perceived lack of usefulness in assessing future earning capacity of an enterprise. Such a notion raises the question of whether the objective of financial reporting is to value a reporting enterprise, and questions the concerns mentioned earlier about the differences between market values and reported accounting values. The current *Conceptual Framework* rejects the valuation objective, in that the stated objective for financial reporting is to provide information useful in users' decision making. Financial reporting does so by providing information about economic resources (that is, expenditures which should be capitalised), which raises the question about what economic resources should be included.

In relation to heritage assets, the issue is whether the 'asset' in question constitutes an economic resource *per se*, thereby rendering it capable of financial recognition under the *Conceptual Framework*. There is a degree of controversy about this issue since accounting regulators first proposed the inclusion of heritage assets, both cultural and environmental, on the balance sheets of reporting entities as reportable assets. There is no universal consensus on recognition and valuation of these assets. Asset managers, particularly in the not-for-profit museum sector, have shown themselves to be disinclined to capitalise collections, either for financial reporting purposes or to discharge accountability requirements.

The *Conceptual Framework* is intended to settle these kinds of issues by providing guidance as to what resources should be reported in the information provided to users for their decision making. What is an economic resource should be determined by the definition of an asset in the *Conceptual Framework*.

Applying the asset definition and recognition tests

According to paragraph 4.4 of the *Conceptual Framework*, an asset is defined as:

> a resource controlled by the entity as a result of past events and from which future economic benefits are expected to flow to the entity.

This definition generates three characteristics that determine whether an item is an asset:

1. *Future economic benefits.* This is a term which roughly translates to mean that the item being considered is an asset that has a value which someone is willing to pay for,[8] although the IASB's explanation in paragraph 4.8 of the *Conceptual Framework* refers to the asset's potential to contribute directly or indirectly to the flow of cash and cash equivalents to the entity. Paragraph Aus54.2 of the *Framework for the Preparation and Presentation of Financial Statements* (the predecessor to the *Conceptual Framework*) modifies this explanation in relation to not-for-profit entities to explain that for these entities, which typically do not charge or do not fully charge for the goods and services they provide, the future economic benefits that arise from assets enable them to meet their objectives of providing needed services to beneficiaries.

2. *Control by the entity.* This translates into the power of an entity to obtain the future economic benefits flowing from the underlying resource and the power to restrict the access of others to those benefits.

3. *The asset is the consequence of a past transaction or event.* According to paragraph 4.14 of the *Conceptual Framework*, this includes donations but excludes intentions to purchase from giving rise to assets.

Although a resource/item may meet the definition of an asset, it must pass the recognition test contained in paragraph 4.38 of the *Conceptual Framework*. The test consists of two recognition criteria:

1. the future economic benefit associated with the item will probably flow to the controlling entity

2. the asset has a cost or value that can be measured with reliability.

The important thing to note here is that the *Conceptual Framework* does not define any differences between assets. It does not specify that tangibility, separability, ownership and existence of markets for the asset are relevant in the decision about whether to record and report an asset although reliability is a necessary condition for recognition. Paragraph 26 of the US Financial Accounting Standards Board's (FASB) *Statement of Financial Accounting Concepts No. 6* explains that assets commonly have other features that help identify them, such as acquisition at a cost, tangibility, exchangeability, or legal enforceability. The statement goes on to say that these features are not essential characteristics of assets and their absence, by itself, is not sufficient to preclude an item qualifying as an asset. That is, assets may be acquired without cost, they may be intangible, and although not exchangeable, they may be usable by the entity in producing or distributing other goods or services. Interestingly, the Australian Group of 100's policy on accounting for intangible assets agrees — expenditures satisfying the definition of an asset and asset recognition criteria should be recognised as an asset irrespective of whether it is purchased or internally developed.[9] This view was also expressed in the Australian Accounting Standards Board (AASB) discussion paper which, additionally, recommended that if an internally generated intangible did not meet the recognition criteria, a description of the asset and why it fails to meet the relevant criteria should be disclosed.[10] The G100's policy raises yet another issue about what expenditures should be capitalised, as generally accepted accounting principles have always capitalised purchased 'assets' while not capitalising most internal developments of certain 'assets'. This issue will be addressed later in this chapter.

At the time the FASB's conceptual framework was introduced, several notable commentators criticised the definition of an asset included in that framework, a definition that mirrors the one in the IASB *Conceptual Framework*. Echoing Sterling's statement quoted above, Scheutze, a former Securities Exchange Commission chief accountant, suggested that FASB's definition is 'so complex, so abstract, so open-ended, so all-inclusive, and so vague that we cannot use it to solve problems'.[11] He went on to say that: '[t]he definition does not discriminate and help us to decide whether something or anything is an asset.' In his opinion, the definition describes 'a large empty box' that is so open to interpretation that 'almost everything and anything can be fit into it'. Thus, Scheutze suggested that the asset definition is useless for the purpose of resolving accounting issues.[12]

We will now proceed to examine the veracity or otherwise of these criticisms. The remainder of the chapter will be devoted to examining the *Conceptual Framework* definition of an asset, first by applying it to the controversial area of intangibles and second by determining its appropriateness in the management of heritage assets.

 **LO 3**

DO INTANGIBLES PASS THE DEFINITION AND RECOGNITION TESTS?

As stated previously, the function of a definition is to provide a meaning so that everyone understands what is meant when the term being defined is used. If the *Conceptual Framework* definition of an asset is clear, then there would be no need to expand the definition in particular accounting standards applying to assets, such as intangibles. However, AASB 138/IAS 38 *Intangible Assets* defines an **intangible asset** in paragraph 8 as 'an identifiable non-monetary asset without physical substance'. This definition effectively creates barriers to recognition in financial statements for *intangible* assets that otherwise comply with the *Conceptual Framework* definition (and pass the recognition test). These additional barriers relate to the insertion of 'identifiable' in the definition of an intangible asset and its associated test of separability, legal rights, active markets and issues relating to what can be termed 'boundaries'.

What is so different about intangibles?

Before addressing the additional features that an intangible item must possess before it can be acknowledged as an asset, let us look at what is so different about intangibles that they deserve this definition that modifies the *Conceptual Framework* definition of an asset.

Skinner, and Basu and Waymire between them identify five features of intangibles that differentiate them from other assets.[13] They are:

1. Intangibles are largely knowledge assets which are fundamentally different from tangible assets in that their existence cannot be verified merely by visual inspection of the person carrying the knowledge. Rather, the asset's existence is only demonstrable by observing the economic transactions coordinated by the individual carrying the knowledge.

2. As such, many intangibles are not separate, saleable, or discrete items. Examples of these assets are customer satisfaction, employee loyalty and some brand names. Because these resources increase in value as the result of many different and inter-related activities and expenditures, it is hard to uniquely identify the costs associated with these assets.

3. The well-defined property rights associated with most tangible and financial resources currently recognised as assets often do not extend to intangibles. For example, it is often very difficult to exclude others from enjoying the benefits associated with these resources. Basu and Waymire define this feature as non-rival — consumption by one person does not preclude consumption by another because there is no physical feature that is transformed by consumption.

4. Largely because of the above characteristics, there are no liquid secondary markets for many intangibles, making it difficult to measure reliably the value of these resources. This means that it will be difficult to estimate reliably fair values for these types of resources.

5. Because many intangibles are not separable and saleable and because of poorly defined property rights, it is often difficult to write fully specified contracts for intangibles.[14]

AASB 138/IAS 38's definition of an intangible asset

Using the *Conceptual Framework* definition of an asset, none of these features precludes an intangible item from being identified as an asset. Perhaps Scheutze is right when he suggested that the asset definition is useless for the purpose of resolving accounting issues.[15] As noted previously, the IASB in responding to the issue of intangibles has developed a special definition just for them. However, what is an economic resource should be determined by the definition of an asset in the *Conceptual Framework*, not by a special definition outside of the *Conceptual Framework*. Let us closely examine this extended definition.

- 'Intangible' accords with the *Macquarie* dictionary definition of something that is 'incapable of being perceived by the sense of touch'.
- The 'non-monetary' criterion is necessary to distinguish certain intangibles from the traditionally recognised intangibles such as cash and investments.
- The 'identifiable' criterion is justified by separating an intangible asset from goodwill, another traditionally recognised intangible.
- The definition introduces other criteria — that the asset must be *separable* and arise from *contractual or other legal rights*. Paragraphs 11–12 of AASB 138/IAS 38 indicate that separability (the capacity of being separated from the entity and sold, transferred, licensed, rented or exchanged) together with contractual or legal rights, demonstrates identifiability of an intangible in order to distinguish it from goodwill.
- Contractual or other legal rights demonstrate *control* over the asset.

In arguing that a separate definition is essential for intangibles, AASB 138/IAS 38 contends that control is difficult to demonstrate in the absence of legal rights enforceable in a court of law as well as allow for the reliable measurement of the item which forms part of the recognition test. The examples offered, technical knowledge, skilled staff and customer portfolios, imply that without legal rights, an intangible should not be recognised. However, legal rights are not a necessary condition for control since the economic benefits that flow from the resources may be protected in other ways — for example, the recipe for Coca-Cola is protected by secrecy. Contemporary Issue 14.1 discusses the myth of conservative accounting as it relates to intangibles.

14.1 CONTEMPORARY ISSUE

The myth of 'conservative accounting'

By Baruch Lev

Five or six years ago, when I began discussing the problems caused by the accounting system's mismeasurement of investment in intangible assets, the common wisdom was that the immediate expensing of intangibles was good because it was 'conservative'. (Conservative in the accounting sense means that you underestimate earnings and the value of assets.) However, the lives of the assets, their creation costs, and the cash flows generated have a time dimension, which is fixed. Therefore, if you are 'conservative' in some periods, you will end up being 'aggressive' (inflating earnings) in others.

The exhibit that I have included shows the results of a model that two colleagues and I developed that relates the rate of growth in R&D spending to three popular measures of company performance: return on equity, return on assets, and growth in earnings (what analysts call 'momentum'). The solid line in the exhibit shows corporate performance if the R&D spending is capitalized; the dashed line shows the performance resulting from the immediate expensing of R&D or other intangibles.

As the model shows, companies with high growth rates of R&D spending report conservatively when they expense intangibles. However, companies with low growth rates actually report aggressively. For these companies, the reported levels of return on equity, the return on assets, and the growth in earnings *appear to be much better than they really are*. The inflection point occurs when the rate of spending growth is equal to the company's cost of capital.

It is therefore a myth that the mismeasurement of profitability and assets due to the expensing of investment in intangibles results in conservative accounting. Expensing intangibles is conservative for some companies, aggressive for others, and erroneous for all.

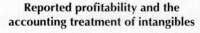

Reported profitability and the accounting treatment of intangibles

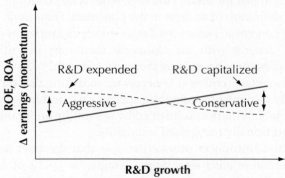

Source: Baruch Lev, 'Remarks on the measurement, valuation, and reporting of intangible assets, *Economic Policy Review*.[16]

Questions

1. Define 'conservative' as the term is used by the author. **J**
2. What is the 'myth' that is exposed by the author? **J** **AS**
3. Who would be harmed by the failure to capitalise intangible assets? **J** **AS**

Recognition issues for intangibles

In addition to a special definition for intangibles, paragraph 63 of AASB 138/IAS 38 names some intangibles that are specifically banned from being recognised — for example, customer lists. Let us consider a customer list. A customer list passes the *Conceptual Framework* definition and recognition tests as well as the AASB 138/IAS 38 definition of an intangible. Customer lists are identifiable; they are non-monetary; they are separable in that customer lists are routinely bought and sold. This evidence of a market for customer lists is a good indication of control and the ability to measure reliably an item's value. With control comes the ability to buy, sell or withhold from a market, characteristics that are argued to indicate the notion of an asset. Internally developed customer lists cannot be recognised; however, those purchased externally may be recognised.

AASB 138/IAS 38 offers the argument that expenditure on internally generated brands, mastheads, publishing titles, customer lists and such cannot be recognised because expenditure on them cannot be distinguished from expenditure that develops the business as a whole. Prior to harmonisation with international accounting standards in 2005, Australia rejected this argument — these kinds of intangibles could be recognised if they met the asset definition and the recognition criteria. Because the standard specifically bans these items, account preparers and their auditors are not allowed to exercise their professional judgement in assessing whether certain expenditures such as those on brand development, mastheads, publishing titles and customer lists should be capitalised and recognised.

In relation to the recognition test, the standard requires that an intangible asset be initially measured at cost, although revaluations to fair value are allowed where fair value is determined by reference to an *active market*. An **active market** is defined in AASB 13/IFRS 13 *Fair Value Measurement* as:

> A market in which transactions for the asset or liability take place with sufficient frequency and volume to provide pricing information on an ongoing basis.

Paragraph 78 of AASB 138/IAS 38 argues that it is 'uncommon' for an active market to exist for intangible assets. It gives the examples where such markets may exist — for example, taxi and fishing licences and production quotas. The paragraph further asserts that such markets cannot exist for intangibles such as brands and customer lists 'because each asset is unique', which creates an inconsistency. The 'unique' argument is not applied to a unique tangible item such as an artwork. Each artwork is unique and its uniqueness gives it value.

The concern that the 'fair value' of particular intangibles, such as brands and mastheads, may be difficult to appraise to the point of deeming that active markets are unlikely to exist establishes a test that many tangibles, as well as reported intangibles, cannot pass. Land, for example, in itself is unique, specified by its location and resources, and, therefore, is not homogeneous. Additionally, due to there being one seller of a particular parcel of land, there is information asymmetry (discussed in the next section). The owner of a parcel of oil-bearing land is more likely to obtain more accurate information of its reserves and value than potential buyers. In the case of used plant and equipment, by the history of prior usage each piece is unique and there is only one potential seller. The outcome of an active market, known prices, cannot be met in any of the prior examples. Both seller and buyer have no certainty about the ultimate productivity of a piece of land.

While the valuation of internally generated brands, mastheads and similar intangibles carries the risk of information asymmetry, they do not represent a separate or unique asset class. Rather, the tradeable rights of licences and quotas are the unique class because of their regulated contrivance rather than their possession of the properties of an active market — only one or two taxi licences may be issued for a particular locality, a practice not unknown in small towns. While prices for tradeable rights may be known, they have no closer correspondence to 'fair value' than any other price sought by a buyer or seller under bounded rationality and imperfect information. Accounting normally recognises assets because there is a possibility of a sale if the owner decides that they no longer need the item. The same applies to intangibles such as customer lists and published titles.

Commentators such as Wrigley, a financial analyst, hoped that AASB 138/IAS 38 would bring some clarity through greater disclosure and commonality of capitalisation for expenditure on intangibles. If the standard was done well, the divergence in accounting practice and company accounts would become more comparable, a huge potential benefit for analysts. Wrigley concludes that the reality is that every analyst now has a significantly more complicated spreadsheet.[17]

 ## LO 4 IMPLICATIONS OF NON-RECOGNITION OF INTANGIBLES

Information asymmetry

Purchased intangibles are recognised; internally developed intangibles are not recognised. For example, expenditures to purchase a brand name are capitalised. Expenditures to build a brand name are immediately expensed. This differential treatment does not make economic sense as it generates **information asymmetry**. The differential treatment is not common sense as it can have serious consequences. One consequence at a time when reliance on intangibles is growing is a lessening in the information content of financial statements. Understatement of assets because intangibles are not recognised allows gains to be diverted from external-to-the-entity shareholders to insiders, who are knowledgeable about the non-recognised intangible items. Another consequence of the policy is that companies with significant investment in intangible items are likely to be undervalued.

Goodwill

The asymmetric treatment of intangibles has traditionally applied to **goodwill**. For over a century, the definition, measurement, and accounting for goodwill have been a controversial issue in financial accounting.[18] As with other intangibles, the usual distinction is made between internally generated goodwill and purchased goodwill, and whether the former, like other internally generated intangibles, should be accounted for is at the centre of the controversy. In the accounting literature, internally generated goodwill is presumed to be developed by processes and non-specific expenditures within the entity itself. Because these matters are generally difficult to identify, isolate and measure, such goodwill is not accounted for. The solution is the asymmetric treatment. Because goodwill cannot be purchased or sold as a separate item, it can only be recognised when an entity has acquired another entity or part of another entity. Recognition of goodwill requires the valuation of all identifiable assets, both tangible and intangible, at fair value. Goodwill then becomes a balancing item, the difference between the purchase consideration given (cost of the business combination) and the fair value of the identifiable net assets acquired.[19] In other words, the amount recognised is the excess of the entity's economic value over its identifiable book value. Skinner says that such treatment is evidence that the current accounting model fails to recognise all the assets of a business.[20]

Capital markets

A strong advocate for greater information about intangibles in financial statements, Lev points out that capital market participants consider intangibles to be assets of the firm.[21] He says that evidence shows that information about investments in intangibles and the outcomes of this investment such as patents is highly relevant to investors. As to questions about the reliability of information relating to intangibles, many investments such as product developments, and employee training, are factual and easily subject to auditor verification.

Wyatt reviewed the literature on the relevance and reliability of expenditures on intangibles and goodwill.[22] While pointing out that it is difficult to know whether variation in the size of the regression coefficient is due to relevance or reliability or both, she found that a wide variety of financial and non-financial information on intangibles is value relevant. Expenditures on R&D are value relevant but appear to be less reliable than tangible items, and appear less reliable than tangible items in signalling future benefits. R&D is generally not reliably measured and may be less relevant in some contexts than others, such as established versus growth entities. While purchased goodwill and some non-financial measures of brands and customer satisfaction are value relevant, they do not appear to be reliable indicators of future benefits, nor do they appear to be measured reliably.

Wyatt also found evidence that accounting regulators would better facilitate value relevant disclosures about intangibles if they gave discretion to management to report their entity's economic reality. In this respect, there is evidence from the pre-2005 Australian setting that management discretion to report intangible assets was associated with the financial reporting of value relevant identifiable intangible assets. Before the adoption of international accounting standards in 2005, purchased and internally generated intangibles (with the exclusion of basic research) could be reported by Australian entities. The evidence suggests that the least regulated intangibles were the most value relevant which suggests that discretion is associated with a balance of relevance and reliability.[23] Wyatt found that R&D assets and purchased goodwill were not value relevant where investors know that managers have discretion to report identifiable intangible assets that are informative about the source of future benefits.[24]

Wyatt concludes that the general problem of incomplete information suggests that more information is better even if it is uncertain.[25] She points out that accounting regulators have gone the other way, moving to prevent entities measuring and reporting internally generated intangible assets. However, she points out that even unreliable numbers can be useful signals that (unobservable) assets exist, pointing investors in the direction of additional relevant information sources.[26]

What should be done about the issue of intangibles?

Lev promotes two proposals:
1. the capitalisation of certain investments in intangibles
2. the facilitation of improved *standardised* disclosures about intangibles.[27]

Why does he promote this? Because, as he says, the current practice of expensing intangibles understates asset values and earnings. In America, CEOs are concerned that their book values are, on average, a quarter or less than market values and capitalising intangibles would be a reasonable solution to this problem. However, because entities are not permitted to capitalise most intangibles, there is very little data available to test whether capitalisation or expensing is the answer.

A return to measuring income rather than trying to value intangible assets and so get the balance sheet right is advocated by Skinner, and Basu and Waymire.[28] This approach would be a return to the primacy of measuring income through an income statement approach rather than a balance sheet approach to the *Conceptual Framework*. However, Skinner suggests the best solution is to disclose information about intangibles, with regulators providing guidance as to the forms that these disclosures should take.[29]

The next section examines heritage assets. Most heritage assets are tangible (although some are intangible and are treated much like other non-heritage intangibles). Like intangibles, heritage assets provide evidence of the problem of accounting standard setters looking somewhere other than the *Conceptual Framework* for answers as to how they should or should not be reported. Note the contrast that the two issues provide: for intangibles, the standard setters are arguing that they do not conform to the definition of an asset and the associated recognition criteria. For heritage assets, the standard setters are arguing that, despite opposition that says otherwise, heritage assets do conform to the definition and the associated recognition criteria.

DO HERITAGE ASSETS PASS THE DEFINITION AND RECOGNITION TESTS?

The official AASB position on the recognition of heritage assets is that they 'are a subset of property, plant and equipment that should be subject to the same definition, . . . recognition, measurement and presentation requirements as for other categories of property, plant and equipment'.[30] The AASB did concede that the nature of heritage assets might require additional disclosures. However, this rather facile response to a joint UK ASB and International Public Sector Accounting Standards Board consultation paper tends to oversimplify the issues surrounding the definition and recognition of heritage assets.[31]

What is so different about heritage assets?

Generally speaking, heritage assets are tangible examples of the cultural or natural environments that a particular community is desirous of preserving. There is no single official definition but the UK ASB's approach in paragraph 2 of *Financial Reporting Standard 30: Heritage Assets* is typical:

> A tangible asset with historical, artistic, scientific, technological, geophysical or environmental qualities that is held and maintained principally for its contribution to knowledge and culture.

The South African ASB is slightly more expansive, defining heritage assets in paragraph .04 of *Standard of Generally Recognised Accounting Practice Heritage Assets (GRAP 103)* as:

> assets that have a cultural, environmental, historical, natural, scientific, technological or artistic significance and are held indefinitely for the benefit of present and future generations.

Examples of heritage assets vary widely in their scope and character and include, but are not limited to, national and marine parks, museum collections, historic buildings and industrial and cultural artefacts. This heterogeneous assemblage of objects and places that society wishes to preserve range from entries on the World Heritage List to items at a local community level. What are not included are intangibles, which largely disenfranchises a substantial component of indigenous heritage which is predominantly based on an oral tradition.

The issues for heritage assets in an Anglo-centric accounting system are:

- Should heritage assets be treated in the same manner as other assets?
- Would heritage assets be considered assets in accordance with the *Conceptual Framework* definition?
- Are *Conceptual Framework* definition and recognition criteria appropriate for entities managing heritage assets?
- Are heritage assets capable of financial measurement?
- Should heritage assets be financially measured? [32]

Applying the *Conceptual Framework* definition

Recall that the *Conceptual Framework* definition of an asset has three parts:

1. future economic benefits
2. control by the entity
3. consequence of a past transaction or event.

After 'passing' these three tests, the asset in question is subject to the recognition criteria.

Do heritage assets embody future economic benefits?

Commentators such as Barton argued that heritage assets do not satisfy the asset definition and should not be recognised in the accounts.[33] He claimed that heritage and other like assets (including infrastructure) are public goods, are not for sale and are for the public benefit — and monetary value does not represent the future benefit of the assets to the managing entities. There is, therefore, no value-in-use or value-in-exchange for heritage assets in a financial sense.

The problem is the *Conceptual Framework*'s concept of 'economic benefit', which is essentially one that is financially quantifiable. Generally speaking, benefits relating to heritage assets are not financial, in that they do not generate cash or cash equivalents. On the contrary, it can be seen that heritage assets are likely to lead to significant cash, or other resource, outflows due to maintenance and upkeep, without the mitigation of a corresponding revenue stream. While the *Conceptual Framework* sees no anomaly in this as the payoff for a not-for-profit entity is the meeting of objectives of providing needed services to beneficiaries, it does seem a bit of a stretch to describe these services as 'future economic benefits' in the meaning of the *Conceptual Framework*. They may entail use of economic resources to provide them but, in general, the services are embodied in the provision of an incidental sense of community wellbeing, not financially quantifiable benefits to the controlling entity.

Are heritage assets a liability?

Mautz suggested that because of the continual financial outgoings associated with heritage assets, they could be viewed as liabilities rather than assets.[34] However, any commitment to expenditure, either past or prospective, is not to be viewed as a liability. No matter how much a particular 'asset' is a drain on resources or is completely unproductive (for example, a monument), it does not constitute a present obligation to an outside entity, the key feature of a liability under any conceptual framework.[35]

Who controls heritage assets?

It is extremely problematic whether public sector and/or not-for-profit entities have the requisite degree of control over the heritage assets they manage, or for which they are custodians. For instance, it is arguable whether access to the benefits of many heritage assets is excludable — for example, national parks. Additionally, many environmental assets are technically owned by the States but 'are subject to varying degrees of control by the [Commonwealth] government'.[36] In some cases, this amounts to joint control, which, in accounting parlance, is not control at all. In other cases, effective control is vested (by deed or grant) in another funded or sponsored instrumentality or local community voluntary organisation.

An example of the uncertainties that can arise under the aforementioned situation was the case of the iconic steam locomotive 3801, formerly of the NSW Government Railways. From 1986 until 2006, this important artefact of railway heritage was leased from the NSW Rail Transport Museum (RTM) by 3801 Limited, both entities being quasi-official not-for-profit voluntary organisations trading in a corporate form (limited by guarantee). The NSW Government had originally transferred the locomotive to the RTM, via an instrument styled a 'deed of gift in perpetuity', while claiming (later) to retain nominal ownership. None of the entities concerned recognised the locomotive as an asset on a balance sheet, because they implicitly deemed there to be a lack of control with respect to their entity.[37] Specifically, control meant the ability of any party to freely dispose of the asset. Thus the government did not recognise items that had been decommissioned (notwithstanding retention of nominal ownership), 3801 Limited did not recognise a capital lease because of the peppercorn rental of $38.01 per annum, and the RTM did not recognise an asset which they regarded as held in trust. This case highlights the difficulty of the attribute of control being a determinant in the recognition of heritage assets when the form of management of the asset is complex or the presence of control is not clear cut.

However, according to paragraph 13 of Appendix 1 of the UK ASB's *Financial Reporting Standard 30: Heritage Assets*, the concept of 'inalienability' (constraint against disposal) is 'not a robust concept . . . even statutory restrictions are not immutable . . . because it is imprecise . . . [it] does not therefore provide a suitable criterion for framing accounting requirements'. This attitude indicates either flexibility or expediency on the part of a regulator (in this case, the UK ASB), depending on one's personal perspective. It does seem to show a propensity to vary the intellectual underpinnings of a concept (control) in order to propagate a desired outcome (financial reporting of heritage assets as tangible fixed assets).

Valuation issues for heritage assets

Recall that, commonly with all assets, the *Conceptual Framework* also requires that recognition criteria be satisfied, even if the definitional attributes are present, before heritage assets are recognised in financial statements. If the regulatory view can be accepted, that 'future economic benefits' is a synonym for, or equivalent to, service potential or utility of purpose, then the first criterion is probably satisfied. That is, the probability of deriving the benefit (giving the service) is more, rather than less, likely. However, the criterion of reliable measurement of the asset would seem to be another story.

By the very nature of heritage assets, in most cases there is not a ready market or, alternatively, management is prevented, in the community interest, from selling them.[38] Nevertheless, Australian government departments, under paragraph 7.4.7 of AAS 29 *Financial Reporting by Government Departments* (now superseded), were encouraged to regularly revalue heritage and community assets to their 'written-down current cost'. According to paragraph 7.4.8, this was to be 'determined by reference to current market buying prices of the remaining future economic benefits embodied in the asset' or, if not available, an estimate. AAS 29 recognised that 'practical difficulties' may preclude recognition (paragraph 7.4.7). With respect to museum collections, many items are only able to be reliably valued when actually sold. A number of methods have been proposed to overcome these obstacles, each of which has its own limitations. Briefly, the main methods are:

- *Valuation at a nominal amount ($1)*. The obvious limitation of this approach is it is meaningless, but has been used in the past.
- *Travel cost method*. This involves a survey of visitors to determine the resources embodied in their visit. The result is extrapolated to the relevant population.

- *Contingent valuation method.* This approach involves a survey of a representative group in society who are asked what they are willing to pay (for example, tax impost or loss of benefits) to retain a particular heritage asset. Once again, the result is extrapolated to society at large. The limitations for each of the last two methods are the usual ones for surveys — is the sample representative, are the respondents rational, are the questions appropriate, is the description of the asset accurate, are the assumptions valid?
- *Valuation based on market values of surrounding private properties.* This approach can sometimes work for buildings in an urban environment, but has serious shortcomings when dealing with properties that have restrictions, such as parklands.

It would seem, therefore, that the reliable measurement criterion cannot be satisfied with any degree of confidence. Contemporary Issue 14.2 discusses some of the challenges relating to the valuation of heritage assets.

**14.2
CONTEMPORARY
ISSUE**

How do you value an asset like the Rosetta Stone?

By Ray Jones

In 2004, the Accounting Standards Board kicked off an ambitious project to find a way to account for heritage assets.

It published a discussion paper in 2006 with an impressive image of the Rosetta Stone on its front cover. The stone, with its priestly decrees from the time of Ptolemy V, was seen as epitomising the difficulty of valuation. How do you value a unique asset that provided the key to the understanding of Egyptian hieroglyphs, acquired as a spoil of the Napoleonic Wars?

Five years' thought from the best accounting brains in the country produced no convincing answer. The new accounting standard on heritage assets, FRS 30, which applies to financial years starting on 1 April 2010 and onwards, takes the same line as the Statement of Recommended Practice. Both say that if you know the cost of a heritage asset or can value it, do so. If you can't, provide further explanation in the accounts so people at least understand the nature of the asset.

However, the new standard requires some sensible extra information. Most interestingly, details are now required on the extent of access permitted to heritage assets. This is relevant to questions of public benefit and might also help to prevent a 'private collection' mentality from developing among curators and trustees.

But there are other areas of accounting where valuation is tricky, such as volunteers. The SORP asks for valuation when the donated service is provided by an individual as part of their trade or profession. Again, when valuation is impractical or simply produces the wrong answer, the solution is to explain the contribution of volunteers. Its approach is simple and avoids difficult questions such as, for example, whether someone laying the flowers at a church altar is a volunteer or a worshipper.

Because convergence with new International Financial Reporting Standards is in the pipeline, the debate on valuation is sure to resurface. The IFRS uses a principle of 'fair value'. Most would agree that an asset such as freehold property donated to a charity should be valued in its accounts.

The SORP talks of including the value to the charity of the gift. In my view, where the property is saleable, logic dictates including the gift at its market value. Some argue that if a charity was gifted a mansion in Mayfair but only needed a basement in Brixton, then the accounts should include the value of the latter. This seems wrong to me, because it does not capture 'fair value'.

So if you get something that you really cannot value, like the Rosetta Stone, make sure you describe it well and if you can value a gift, then please do it fairly.

Source: Article by Ray Jones 2010, 'How do you value an asset like the Rosetta Stone?', *Third Sector.*[39]

Questions

1. How does the author summarise the requirements of the British standard and its associated statement of recommended practice (SORP) in relation to heritage assets?
2. Why is valuing a heritage object such as the Rosetta Stone difficult?
3. How does convergence with IFRSs complicate valuing heritage assets? **J** **K**

Recognition issues for heritage assets

The FASB's conceptual framework and its definition of an asset, mentioned earlier in this chapter, was the impetus for the FASB to propose a requirement for not-for-profit museums to capitalise their collections. This proposal was vigorously resisted by the affected parties, and accounting commentators, in the main, were similarly critical.[40] In Australia, there were contemporaneous proposals to capitalise heritage assets in the public sector in each of the State, Territory and Commonwealth jurisdictions.[41] Some jurisdictions had reference to heritage assets (usually coupled with infrastructure) in their asset management manuals, while others were in the process of policy development.

It would be useful to note at this point that the regulatory regimes (but not the thrust of the conceptual frameworks) are fundamentally different in Australia and the United States. The AASB is (now) an overarching authority which has responsibility for all sectors involved in financial reporting, private and public, for-profit and not-for-profit. In contrast, at a national level in the United States, the FASB looks after the private sector (both profit and not-for-profit) while the federal agencies (public sector) are covered by the Federal Accounting Standards Advisory Board (FASAB). This has implications for the treatment of certain types of heritage assets, most notably national parks, which will be covered later in the chapter.

With respect to the capitalisation proposals of the early 1990s, Australian commentators were no less vigorous in their criticism of regulatory requirements pertaining to public sector heritage assets, especially museum collections, than were their American counterparts a few years earlier.[42] They argued that public collections should not be recognised for financial reporting purposes since 'collections held in the public domain are prized for their cultural, heritage, scientific and educative qualities — and those attributes cannot be quantified in monetary terms'.[43] Furthermore, referencing the stewardship objective of financial reporting, Rentschler and Potter chided the proponents of recognition for trying to constrain assessment of museum managers' accountability into narrow and exclusively financial terms. They concluded that '[t]he traditional notion of accountability commonly applied in non-profit museums and performing arts organisations has been hijacked by accountants and economists'.[44] The accountability template referred to was not based on economic rationalism but rather the 'viability' of the entity (not linked merely to financial solvency) and the 'vitality' of the museum/arts experience, a relatively abstract but palpable concept, presumably not well captured in a balance sheet. A decade later, a similar proposal of capitalisation of museum collections in New Zealand was met with the same out-cries of dismay by the institutions affected and another flurry of activity by accounting commentators.[45]

However, unlike the case in the United States, where the FASB proposal was ultimately shelved, there was a more vocal (albeit less numerous) chorus of commentators who supported financial recognition of heritage assets in the Australian context.[46] They also had powerful allies in the various Australian states' auditors-general.[47] In essence, they supported the approach of Rowles (the official line) and refuted the views of Carnegie and Wolnizer.[48] They contended the (superseded SAC 4) definition of an asset was perfectly capable of being satisfied as were the recognition criteria. Their overall view can be encapsulated thus:

> the valuation of public collections is an essential component of any sound system of management of the resources applied to the running of activities such as public museums and art galleries.[49]

Arguably, however, the assertions by the preceding authors are those of the faithful. The regulatory view does not seem to have been tested by empirical research, rather it is an implementation of a public policy attitude. As mentioned previously, the official view is that heritage assets are a subset of property, plant and equipment, specifically regulated by AASB 116 *Property, Plant and Equipment* (paragraph Aus 6.2). This is supplemented within the standard by the Australian implementation guidance (paragraphs G1–G4) for heritage and cultural assets held by not-for-profit public sector entities and for-profit government departments.

14.3 CONTEMPORARY ISSUE

The sum of us

By Ruth Laugesen

Te Papa dealt with the thorny issue of valuation by valuing much of its collection in bulk. Sections of the collection for which there is a ready market, such as fine arts and ceramics, have been relatively easy to value, with many pieces valued individually. In other collections, the sale of a similar item internationally may provide a benchmark. The feather cloak given to Captain James Cook by a Hawaiian chief was valued at $5.3m after a similar item was sold in the United States. The Maori collection has had a high and growing valuation . . . because of the thriving international market for treasures from indigenous cultures.

Archives [New Zealand] was faced with the task of valuing 77 km of records. It grappled with whether to value each famous signature individually. In the end Archives decided to assess all but a few exceptional documents by the metre. Documents are divided into categories of age, and then simply multiplied by the length of shelving they take up. Boxes of files from 1852 or before are valued at $202 400 per metre of shelving, while the 1945–1970 category comes in at just $2200 per metre.

Source: Ruth Laugesen, 'The sum of us', *Sunday Star-Times*.[50]

Questions

1. Why would Te Papa resort to valuing its collections 'in bulk'?
2. How could the price per metre be derived and defended?
3. Do you regard the use of benchmarks of similar items a defensible method of obtaining a value for infrequently traded items? **J**

LO 6 IMPLICATIONS OF RECOGNITION OF HERITAGE ASSETS

When discussing heritage assets, there is an additional aspect of financial reporting that needs to be considered. This relates to the definition of reporting entity by the AASB in Statement of Accounting Concepts SAC 1 *Definition of the Reporting Entity* and the narrow definition of **accountability** in SAC 2 *Objective of General Purpose Financial Reporting*. Under the Australian conceptual framework there is an implicit assumption that users exist who demand financial information about heritage assets. These users (according to the conceptual framework) require information about heritage assets to make decisions about the allocation of scarce resources. Under SAC 2, accountability of an asset controller is always linked to the production of a general purpose financial report. Accountability is discharged when a financial report is decision-useful to identified users, paradoxically rendering the objective superfluous.

There are two points at issue here (1) are there identifiable users who require financially oriented information about heritage assets and (2) is the accountability of those who have custody of heritage assets best assessed by financial indicators? The answers to these questions are largely a matter of perception and perspective. Certainly a broader scope accountability would mean a mix of qualitative and quantitative performance indicators, for example 'quality of experience', rather than relying merely on the financial report. This would seem to cater more to the subjective social attribute inherent in heritage assets. As for the 'users', this has, seemingly, not been well established by objective means; it is largely a matter of presumption and an express policy attitude. It is reasonable to assume that users exist who are interested in the management of heritage assets but it is arguable that their decisions would be based on the financial statements *per se*.

What should be done with heritage assets?

There needs to be some consensus about accountability for heritage assets and recognition that the *Conceptual Framework* is inadequate in this respect. The objectives of financial reporting should be turned on their head in this area, so that accountability should be the primary objective for custodians and financial valuation a distant second. As an example, the FASAB in paragraph 38 of *Statement of Federal Financial Accounting Standards 29 Heritage Assets and Stewardship Land* has determined that some heritage assets, described as 'stewardship land' (national parks, forest and grazing land) will not be ascribed a value when no cost has been incurred. However, there has to be significant, structured, qualitative disclosure about all classes of heritage assets, including a mission statement, number of physical units, their condition and maintenance, acquisitions and disposals. The standard of reporting of these disclosures is contained in *Statement of Federal Financial Accounting Standards 8 Supplementary Stewardship Reporting*. The AASB could apply the same principles to good effect.

Summary

Analyse the background leading to the issue of whether intangible assets and heritage assets should be recognised in financial statements

- The book value of a company is different from its market value. Commentators attribute this difference to items that the IASB says do not meet the definition and recognition tests for assets.
- Because Australia and New Zealand have adopted a one-size-fits-all policy to accounting standards, heritage assets should be recognised in the financial statements of their controlling entities which are usually in the not-for-profit and government sectors.
- Inconsistencies in the treatment of certain items for financial reporting purposes and the implications of the recent global financial crisis have generated criticism of accounting information.

Explain why capitalisation is contentious and apply the asset definition and recognition tests of the *Conceptual Framework*

- The *Conceptual Framework* definition of an asset and its associated recognition test should solve questions of what expenditures are capitalised, and what are expensed.
- Financial reporting should provide information about economic resources (expenditures that should be capitalised) determined by the *Conceptual Framework* definition and recognition tests. However, some items that appear to pass these tests are not included in financial statements, and some that appear to fail these tests are included.
- The conceptual definition of an asset generates three characteristics that determine whether an item is an asset:
  - future economic benefits
  - controlled by the entity reporting
  - a consequence of a past transaction.
- The definition of an asset does not require that an asset needs to be tangible, separable, to be owned rather than controlled, or to have an active market.
- The *Conceptual Framework* has two recognition criteria for an asset:
  - the future economic benefit associated with the item will probably flow to the controlling entity
  - the asset has a cost or value that can be measured with reliability.

LO 3 **Analyse whether intangibles pass the definition and recognition tests**

- Intangibles appear to meet the *Conceptual Framework* definition of an asset.
- However, the IASB has developed special tests for intangibles which include additional characteristics to the *Conceptual Framework*'s characteristics and requirements for recognition as assets.
- AASB 138/IAS 38 *Intangible Assets* defines intangibles as non-monetary, identifiable and separable.
- Identifiable means the intangible arises from contractual or other legal rights as well as having an active market in which its fair value can be determined.
- The argument for intangibles' exclusion from balance sheets rests on the notion that expenditure on intangibles cannot be distinguished from expenditure that develops the business as a whole.
- Prior to harmonisation with international accounting standards, Australia rejected this argument. The argument means that financial statement preparers and their auditors cannot exercise their professional judgement.
- The active market argument is a test that many tangible assets cannot pass.

LO 4 **Explain the implications of non-recognition of intangibles**

- The differential treatment of intangibles creates implications in the following areas:
  - *Information asymmetry.* At a time when reliance on intangibles is growing it results in a lessening in the information content of financial statements. Understatement of assets, because intangibles are not recognised, allows gains to be diverted from external-to-the-entity shareholders to insiders.
  - *Goodwill.* A distinction is made between internally generated goodwill and purchased goodwill. This asymmetric treatment provides evidence that the current accounting model fails to recognise all the assets of an entity.
  - *Capital markets.* Expenditures on research and development are value relevant (i.e. may influence the value of a market on a securities exchange), but appear to be less reliable than tangible items, and appear less reliable than tangible items in signalling future benefits.
- Methods identified for dealing with these implications include:
  - capitalisation of certain investments
  - improved standardised disclosures.

LO 5 **Analyse whether heritage assets pass the definition and recognition tests**

- The *Conceptual Framework*'s concept of economic benefits is essentially one that is financially quantifiable which implies that assets should generate cash or cash equivalents.
- Heritage assets are examples of the cultural or natural environments that a particular community is desirous of preserving — they are unlikely to generate cash flows.
- Control is also an issue because for heritage assets, it is difficult to deny or regulate access to benefits. Additionally, control is often joint control, which is not control at all. By the very nature of heritage assets, there is not usually a ready market for them, or management is prevented from selling them. Reliable measurement cannot be satisfied.
- To justify the inclusion of heritage assets in financial statements, future economic benefits are defined in terms of providing needed services to beneficiaries, which is stretching the meaning of the term in the *Conceptual Framework*.

LO 6 **Explain the implications of recognition of heritage assets**

- There are two important implications:
  - Are there identifiable users who require financially oriented information about heritage assets?
  - Is the accountability of those who have custody of heritage assets best assessed by financial indicators?

Review questions

1. What are the distinctive features of an intangible asset?
2. Which of the features of an intangible asset are irrelevant to the *Conceptual Framework* definition of an asset?
3. What are the distinctive features of a heritage asset?
4. Which of the features of a heritage asset are irrelevant to the *Conceptual Framework* definition of an asset?
5. What impact has the accounting standard AASB 138/IAS 38 *Intangible Assets* had on the balance sheet?
6. Justify the recognition (and associated valuation) of heritage assets on their controlling entity's balance sheet.
7. What is your understanding of the term 'economic' in the *Conceptual Framework* definition of an asset?
8. Explain whether the definition of an asset would be less problematic if the definition included the term 'financial' instead of 'economic'.
9. Name the generally accepted intangible assets that are recognised on a balance sheet.
10. How does 'recognition' differ from 'disclosure'?
11. What are the implications of disclosing information about an asset rather than recognising it?
12. What do you think accounting standard setters should do in relation to:
    (a) intangible assets?
    (b) heritage assets?
    Justify your position.
13. Why do you think there was widespread opposition to the recognition of heritage assets?
14. Why is the element of 'control' problematic for the recognition of heritage assets?
15. How is the presence or absence of a market vital to the justifications advanced for the treatment of intangible and heritage assets? Evaluate these justifications.
16. How would you conceive the problem of what an asset is so that standard setters do not have to release further information to clarify whether an item is, or is not, an asset?

Application questions

Obtain a copy of your university's annual report.
(a) What intangibles does it report?
(b) Does it capitalise intellectual capital?
(c) Does it disclose information about its most valuable intangible, its intellectual capital?
(d) Does it recognise or disclose any information about any heritage assets it may control?

14.2

Read the following passage:

The immediate expensing of practically all internally generated intangible investments in the United States, a questionable procedure given the substantial future benefits of many such investments, is often justified by the conservatism principle. Conservative accounting procedures, goes the argument, counter managers' prevalent optimism, and are appropriate given the generally high level of uncertainty associated with the outcome of intangible investments. However, no accounting procedure consistently applied can be conservative (or aggressive) forever. Over the lifetime of the enterprise, if reported earnings under a conservative accounting rule are understated (relative to a less conservative rule) during certain periods, they have to be overstated in other periods, given that conservative/aggressive accounting procedures essentially shift earnings from one period to another.[51]

(a) What is the 'conservatism principle'?
(b) How is it applied to intangibles?
(c) Why do the authors believe that expensing of intangibles is 'questionable'?
(d) Why can't accounting procedures generated by the conservatism principle be conservative forever? **J** **K**

 **14.3** The following passage was taken from the article 'R&D reporting biases and their consequences'.

> We find evidence consistent with investor fixation on the reported profitability measures. Thus, the stocks of conservatively reporting firms appear to be undervalued, while the stocks of aggressively reporting firms appear to be overvalued, and these misvaluations appear to be corrected when the reporting bias reverses from conservative to aggressive, or vice versa. In addition, the misvaluations are significant for both ROE and earnings momentum profitability indicators. The misvaluation evidence we detect is consistent with well-established behavioral finance findings and, in particular, with the heuristic of representativeness that makes investors view patterns in reported data as representative about future patterns and thus overreact. The social relevance of systematic mispricing of securities is that it leads to misallocation of resources in both the real and capital markets.[52]

(a) What do the authors mean by 'investor fixation'?
(b) How does investor fixation on profitability lead to misvaluations of stocks?
(c) Explain the heuristic of 'representativeness'? **J** **K**

 **14.4** Jim Peterson made the following comments about PricewaterhouseCoopers' announcement that they officially abandoned their 'perfectly serviceable name in favour of the three-letter vernacular' (i.e. PwC):

> When the accounting profession's very survival rests on the ability to sell a basic core product — assurance on financial information — the essence of that delivery is the maintenance of confidence among issuers and users in consistent, solid and predictable quality service. That has been more than challenge enough, in difficult times for the profession. But its messages can and should be pretty stolid. A slightly boring orthodoxy is not a bad thing . . . We may of course expect defensive messages from the branding types at PwC, justifying what must be massive expenditure for this effort, along the lines of 'we wanted to shake things up' and 'we have an exciting new set of messages'. Trouble is, they don't, and the world of assurance users doesn't want it.[53]

(a) Would PwC be able to recognise the expenditure on its new 'three-letter vernacular' on its balance sheet? Justify your answer.
(b) How could PwC defend the 'massive expenditure' on its new brand?
(c) What message does the spending send in relation to expected future economic benefits?
(d) If you were PwC's auditor, would you allow the expenditure to be capitalised? Why? **J** **K**

14.5 In their article on 'Intangibles and the OFR', Vivien Beattie and Sarah Jane Thomson included the following graph:

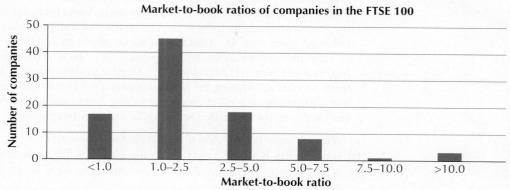

Market-to-book ratios of companies in the FTSE 100

Source: From 'Intangibles and the OFR' by Vivien Beattie and Sarah Jane Thompson, *Financial Management*, June 2005 © CIMA.[54]

(a) What does a market-to-book ratio tell you about how complete a company's financial statements are?
(b) What does a market-to-book ratio of less than 1.0 mean?
(c) The authors report that GlaxoSmithKline, a leading pharmaceutical manufacturing and research company, had the highest ratio. Where would you expect media companies to be positioned on the chart? Why? **J** **K**

14.6 Australian government departments were formally encouraged (under AAS 29 *Financial Reporting by Government Departments*) to value their heritage assets by their 'written-down current cost' determined by reference to current market prices for the future economic benefits embodied in the asset or an estimate of those market prices.

(a) What difficulties do you envisage in applying this requirement to:
  (i) A ruined abbey?
  (ii) A dinosaur skeleton?
  (iii) A steam locomotive? **J** **K**

14.7 The following information was reported in the New Zealand *Sunday Star-Times* newspaper:

> For a decade, Treasury has required institutions like Archives New Zealand, Te Papa and the National Library to tot up the value of their treasures. Archives' holdings are currently estimated to be worth $524m, including the $20m for the 1835 declaration of independence of northern chiefs, and $10m for the women's suffrage petition that led to New Zealand becoming the first country in the world to give women the vote, Te Papa's treasures have been valued at $526m, while the rate books and manuscripts at National Library have been valued at $671m. [Rodney Wilson] has concerns that publishing the value of Auckland Museum's collections would give strength to museum sceptics. 'It raises political issues, the sort of stupid comment you sometimes hear in local body politics, well if they've got all that money let them sell something' he says.[55]

(a) What is the danger envisaged by the valuation of heritage assets?
(b) Does a sale of a Maori feather cloak in the United States indicate a market for such items along the lines of AASB 138/IAS 38 *Intangible Assets*?
(c) Can items from indigenous cultures be considered an 'active market' in terms of the definition of an active market in AASB 13/IFRS 13 *Fair Value Measurement*? **J** **K**

14.8 The article cited above goes on to say:

> Putting a value on the nation's treasures has made no difference to funding the three organisations, but it has made the crown look wealthier. The assets make up more than $1.7b of the crown's $72b of assets in the latest financial year. But you won't find the Americans rushing to have the Declaration of Independence valued. New Zealand, followed soon after by Australia, is so far alone in requiring its public institutions to view its heritage assets with a gimlet eye...New accounting standards from the Institute of Chartered Accountants...require beancounters in local governments and trusts to start accounting for heritage assets just like any other item of property, plant and equipment. The edict covers everything from public monuments erected by local authorities to the butterfly specimens in regional museums.[56]

(a) Who or what is the 'crown' to which the article refers?

(b) Has valuing heritage assets made the crown actually wealthier? Why?

(c) Why do you think New Zealand and Australia were alone in valuing their heritage assets?

(d) How can their stance on heritage assets be justified in terms of the *Conceptual Framework*?

14.9 More from the article in the *Sunday Star-Times* newspaper:

> [T]here is revolt among the country's big regional museums, who say they don't need a dollar sign on a balance sheet to recognise an item of immense value. [Three museums] are all refusing to comply with the new accounting standards...The country's biggest regional museum is the Auckland War Memorial Museum...It is preparing to publish its annual accounts...in a form that makes accountants everywhere blanch — with a caveat attached to the accounts...the caveat will be mildly worded, explaining that the museum refuses to comply with the new rules. 'It's not a good look, but it's a bad look that we're prepared to live with. Somebody has to fly the flag of common sense. It's dogma. They've come up with something which in accounting terms makes a lot of sense to them. But it makes no sense in many places out in the market place'.[57]

(a) Would you expect an audit qualification for the financial statements in response to the caveat attached to the accounts? Justify your answer.

(b) Why do you agree/disagree with the museum manager that 'Somebody has to fly the flag of common sense'?

(c) What alternative measure or measures could be taken to 'recognise' the value of items in the museums?

14.10 Read the following article from *Business Wire* on Interbrand's methodology for valuing brands:

> Brands create value, both for consumers who use their preferred brands and for the companies that own the brands. For more than 25 years, Interbrand...has been evaluating exactly how much brands are worth. Now its brand valuation methods have been certified according to International Standards Organization (ISO) 10668:2010, making Interbrand the first brand consultancy in the world to achieve ISO 10668 certification [which] is the international norm that sets minimum standard requirements for the procedures and methods used to determine the monetary value of brands. It defines a coherent and reliable approach for brand valuation that takes into consideration financial, legal and behavioural science aspects.[58]

(a) Argue whether the 'reliable' approach of brand valuation by Interbrand would satisfy the reliability part of the recognition test for assets.

(b) Debate whether the awarding of the ISO standard will impact the accounting for internally generated intangible assets. **J K AS**

14.1 CASE STUDY

Fund managers, intangibles and private disclosure

By John Holland

[M]ajor problems of ignorance and uncertainty in stock selection and in asset allocation decisions...arose due to the limitations of public domain information sources, but they were exacerbated by an increasing intellectual capital and intangibles component to share prices. As a result, the case FMs [fund managers] used private meetings with company management to understand how value arose through intangibles as well as through tangible assets. The case data revealed the nature of this private information agenda concerning intellectual capital or intangibles and the dynamic connections between these variables in the value creation process. This private information was combined with public sources to create a knowledge advantage within case fund management teams. The learning and knowledge advantages played a central role in framing FM perceptions of corporate gains and losses and risks. The knowledge advantage and prior framing were used by FMs to estimate future corporate performance variables and hence to value the company... The private information sources were used to remove black holes or very poor performers from the portfolio. In addition, they were used to understand which companies and sectors were likely to be winners and losers under forecast macro conditions... This fund management behaviour has important implications for regulatory policy issues on insider information, on corporate disclosure, the corporate governance role of financial institutions, and for the governance of financial institutions.

Source: Excerpts from John Holland, 'Fund management, intellectual capital, intangibles and private disclosure', *Managerial Finance.*[59]

Questions

1. What is meant by 'intellectual capital'? **K**
2. Why do you think intellectual capital has been the only named intangible by the author? **J** **K**
3. The fund managers are being informed in a private way. Argue whether this advantage should be treated as insider information. **J** **K**
4. Who benefits from this inside information? **K**
5. Argue the case whether the market benefits that fund managers gain in this way should be regulated. **J** **K**
6. Identify any ways this private disclosure process could be used to improve the public disclosure process via financial reporting. **K** **AS**
7. Undertake research to ascertain the governance of fund managers; who or what governs fund managers. **J** **K** **AS**
8. Who governs those who govern the fund managers? **K**

14.2 CASE STUDY

Kakadu: mining versus intangible values

Kakadu National Park contains many natural and cultural values. Its river systems, major landforms, wildlife and Aboriginal cultural sites led to its recognition on the UNESCO World Heritage List. Kakadu is one of only 22 World Heritage sites listed for both its natural and cultural heritage. It is also on the National Heritage List and on the Register of the National Estate because of its national significance to the Australian people. Its wetlands are recognised for their international significance under the (Ramsar) Convention on Wetlands of International Importance.

Kakadu is an ecologically and biologically diverse area with many different landforms and habitats. These include the sandstone plateau and escarpment, areas of savanna woodlands and open forest, rivers, billabongs, floodplains, mangroves and mudflats. There are over 60 species of mammals and a great many reptiles including goannas, frill-necked lizards, saltwater crocodiles, water pythons and a number of highly venomous snakes. Kakadu also supports more than 280 species of birds, or about one-third of Australia's bird species. Aboriginal people have lived in Kakadu continuously for at least 50 000 years. There is a rich heritage of Aboriginal art (rock carvings and cave paintings) and archaeological sites throughout the region.

But Kakadu is also rich in minerals, notably uranium, deposits of which have been identified at the Koongarra, Nabarlek, Ranger and Jabiluka sites. Announcements to mine at these sites have received fervent public opposition and generated debate over the uses of Kakadu. In 1990, an inquiry was held to determine:

1. whether the potential gain from mining in what was then the Kakadu Conservation Zone outweighed the permanent harm that would be done to the immediate area around the mine
2. the risk posed to the conservation zone
3. any loss from not being able to use the conservation zone as part of Kakadu while mining took place.

Contingent valuation was used to determine that a conservative estimate of the benefits of preserving the conservation zone by adding it to Kakadu as $435 million. The estimated present value of the proposed mine was $102 million. The government decided to preserve the conservation zone, stating its chief reason was Aboriginal concerns.

More recently, controversy over whether a mine would be developed at Jabiluka, an area surrounded by Kakadu but not legally part of it, arose over the juxtaposition of issues concerning uranium mining, conservation of heritage values, and Aboriginal land rights. The concern is that mining would jeopardise the integrity of the key values for which Kakadu had been listed on the World Heritage List. Despite traditional owners opposing the development of the Jabiluka uranium deposit, Energy Resources of Australia announced in April 2011 that it intended to develop the deposit because the uranium was worldclass and development would benefit all stakeholders. In response, a traditional owner when calling for the inclusion of Jabiluka in Kakadu, expressed sadness that Ranger uranium had been exported to Japan for use in the Fukushima plant. In Mirrar dreaming, a sacred dangerous power, Djang, was unleashed when disturbed on their land. An elder had warned the Australian government in the 1990s that the Djang might kill if disturbed at Ranger. The Ranger mine was developed despite opposition from traditional owners.

Sources: ABC News 2010, 'Green group wants end to Kakadu uranium mining', *ABC News*, 30 May; Aplin, G 2004, 'Kakadu National Park World Heritage Site: deconstructing the debate, 1997–2003', *Australian Geographical Studies*, vol. 42, no. 2, pp. 153–74; Carson, RT, Wilks, L & Imber, D 1994, 'Valuing the preservation of Australia's Kakadu conservation zone', *Oxford Economic Papers*, vol. 46, supplement, pp. 727–49; Fitzgerald, B 2011, 'Jabiluka still on, says ERA', *The Sydney Morning Herald*, 14 April; Statham, L 2011, 'Kakadu owners want stop to uranium mining', *The Sydney Morning Herald*, 7 April.[60]

Questions

1. In one sentence summarise the debate that is the focus of this article. **K**
2. Prepare a list of:
    (a) the tangible assets of Kakadu
    (b) the intangible assets of Kakadu
    (c) the heritage assets of Kakadu. **J**
3. Which of the assets identified would pass the *Conceptual Framework* definition of an asset? Justify your answer. **J K**
4. Of those assets identified in (3), which would pass the *Conceptual Framework* recognition test? Give reasons for your answer. **J K**
5. On what grounds did you identify some of Kakadu's assets as heritage assets? **J K AS**

6. When decisions have to be made, for example as in the use of Kakadu, how has the inability to value intangible and heritage assets reliably disadvantaged the case for their preservation? **J** **K** **CT**

7. Which of the unique geological formations, plants, animals and minerals of Kakadu would
(a) pass the active market test of AASB 13/IFRS 13 *Fair Value Measurement?*
(b) satisfy the capitalisation provisions of FRS 30 *Heritage Assets?* **J** **K** **AS**

8. How do you weigh up the benefits of mining against more intangible values? **J** **K** **CT**

Additional readings

Barton, AD 2005, 'The conceptual arguments concerning accounting for public heritage assets: a note', *Accounting, Auditing & Accountability Journal*, vol. 18, no. 3, pp. 434–40.

Basu, S & Waymire, G 2008, 'Has the importance of intangibles really grown? And if so, why', *Accounting and Business Research*, vol. 38, no. 3, pp. 171–90.

Carnegie, GD & Wolnizer, PW 1999, 'Unravelling the rhetoric about the financial reporting of public collections as assets: a response to Micallef and Peirson', *Australian Accounting Review*, vol. 9, no. 1, pp.16–21.

Hooper, K, Kearins, K & Green, R 2005, 'Knowing "the price of everything and the value of nothing": accounting for heritage assets', *Accounting, Auditing & Accountability Journal*, vol. 18, no. 3, pp. 410–33.

Micallef, F & Peirson, G 1997, 'Financial reporting of cultural, heritage, scientific and community collections', *Australian Accounting Review*, vol. 7, no. 1, pp. 31–7.

Rentschler, R & Potter, B 1996, 'Accountability versus artistic development: the case for non-profit museums and performing arts organizations', *Accounting, Auditing & Accountability Journal*, vol. 9, no. 5, pp.100–13.

Scheutze, WP 1993, 'What is an asset?', *Accounting Horizons*, vol. 7, no. 3, pp. 66–70.

Skinner, DJ 2008, 'Accounting for intangibles — a critical review of policy recommendations', *Accounting and Business Research*, vol. 38, no. 3, pp. 191–204.

Wyatt, A 2008, 'What financial and non-financial information on intangibles is value-relevant? A review of the evidence', *Accounting and Business Research*, vol. 38, no. 3, pp. 217–56.

End notes

1. Accounting Standards Board (ASB) 2006, *Heritage assets: can accounting do better?*, Accounting Standards Board, London.
2. Lev, B 2008, 'A rejoinder to Douglas Skinner's 'Accounting for intangibles — a critical review of policy recommendations', *Accounting and Business Research*, vol. 38, no. 3, pp. 209–13.
3. Wyatt, A 2008, 'What financial and non-financial information on intangibles is value-relevant? A review of the evidence', *Accounting and Business Research*, vol. 38, no. 3, pp. 217–56.
4. Sterling, RR 1975, 'Toward a science of accounting', *Financial Analysts Journal*, vol. 31, no. 5, pp. 28–36.
5. Bal, M 1997, *Narratology: Introduction to the theory of narratives*, University of Toronto Press.
6. Upton, WS 2001, 'Business and financial reporting, challenges from the new economy', *Financial Accounting Series*, FASB, Norwalk, Connecticut.
7. Financial Accounting Standards Board, 1974, 'Accounting for Research and Development Costs', Statement of Financial Accounting Standards No. 2, FASB, Norwalk, Conneticut.
8. Storey & Storey cited in Upton, WS 2001, 'Business and financial reporting, challenges from the new economy', *Financial Accounting Series*, FASB, Norwalk, Connecticut, p. 63.
9. Group of 100 2005, *Accounting for intangible assets*, Group of 100 Inc., Southbank, viewed 10 November 2011, www.group100.com.au.
10. Australian Accounting Standards Board (AASB) 2008, *Initial accounting for internally generated intangible assets*, discussion paper, Australian Accounting Standards Board, Melbourne.

11. Scheutze, WP 1993, 'What is an asset?', *Accounting Horizons*, vol. 7, no. 3, pp. 66–70.

12. ibid.

13. Skinner, DJ 2008, 'Accounting for intangibles — a critical review of policy recommendations', *Accounting and Business Research*, vol. 38, no. 3, pp. 191–204; Basu, S & Waymire, G 2008, 'Has the importance of intangibles really grown? And if so, why', *Accounting and Business Research*, vol. 38, no. 3, pp. 171–90.

14. ibid.

15. Scheutze, WP 1993, 'What is an asset?', *Accounting Horizons*, vol. 7, no. 3, pp. 66–70.

16. Lev, B 2003, 'Remarks on the measurement, valuation, and reporting of intangible assets, *Economic Policy Review*, vol. 9, no. 3, pp. 17–22.

17. Wrigley, J 2008, 'Discussion of What financial and non-financial information on intangibles is value-relevant? A review of the evidence', *Accounting and Business Research*, vol. 38, no. 3, pp. 257–60.

18. Barton, A 2009, 'Book review: double accounting for goodwill: a problem redefined', *The Accounting Review*, vol. 84, no. 5, pp. 1695–7.

19. Wines, G, Dagwell, R & Windsor, C 2007, 'Implications of the IFRS goodwill accounting treatment', *Managerial Auditing Journal*, vol. 22, no. 9, pp. 862–80.

20. Skinner, DJ 2008, 'Accounting for intangibles — a critical review of policy recommendations', *Accounting and Business Research*, vol. 38, no. 3, pp. 191–204.

21. Lev, B 2008, 'A rejoinder to Douglas Skinner's "Accounting for intangibles — a critical review of policy recommendations"', *Accounting and Business Research*, vol. 38, no. 3, pp. 209–13.

22. Wyatt, A 2008, 'What financial and non-financial information on intangibles is value-relevant? A review of the evidence', *Accounting and Business Research*, vol. 38, no. 3, pp. 217–56.

23. ibid.

24. ibid.

25. ibid.

26. ibid.

27. Lev, B 2008, 'A rejoinder to Douglas Skinner's "Accounting for intangibles — a critical review of policy recommendations"', *Accounting and Business Research*, vol. 38, no. 3, pp. 209–13.

28. Skinner, DJ 2008, 'Accounting for intangibles — a critical review of policy recommendations', *Accounting and Business Research*, vol. 38, no. 3, pp. 191–204; Basu, S & Waymire, G 2008, 'Has the importance of intangibles really grown? And if so, why', *Accounting and Business Research*, vol. 38, no. 3, pp. 171–90.

29. Skinner, DJ 2008, 'Accounting for intangibles — a critical review of policy recommendations', *Accounting and Business Research*, vol. 38, no. 3, pp. 191–204.

30. Australian Accounting Standards Board (AASB) 2006, AASB comments on IPSASB consultation paper 'Accounting for heritage Assets under the accrual basis of accounting', AASB, viewed 10 November 2011, www.aasb.com.au.

31. ibid.

32. Deegan, C 2010, *Australian Financial Accounting*, 6th ed., McGraw Hill, North Ryde, p. 296.

33. Barton, AD 2000, 'Accounting for public heritage facilities — assets or liabilities of the government?', *Accounting, Auditing & Accountability Journal*, vol. 13, no. 2, pp. 219–35.

34. Mautz, RK 1988, 'Monuments, mistakes and opportunities', *Accounting Horizons*, June, pp. 123–8.

35. Barton, AD 2000, 'Accounting for public heritage facilities — assets or liabilities of the government?', *Accounting, Auditing & Accountability Journal*, vol. 13, no. 2, pp. 219–35.

36. Burritt, R & Gibson K 1993, 'Who Controls Heritage Listed Assets?', unpublished working paper, Australian National University, p. 20 in Deegan, C 2010, *Australian Financial Accounting*, 6th ed., McGraw Hill, North Ryde, p. 301.

37. Phillip, GJ & Stanton, PA 2004, 'Accounting for railway heritage assets: an evaluation of Australian reporting practice', *Accounting, Accountability & Performance*, vol. 10, no. 1, pp. 47–67.

38. Pallot, J 1990, 'The nature of public assets: a response to Mautz', *Accounting Horizons*, June, pp. 79–85.

39. Jones, R 2010, 'How do you value an asset like the Rosetta Stone?', *Third Sector*, London, April 13.

40. Glazer, AS & Jaenicke, HR 1991a, 'The conceptual framework, museum collections, and user-oriented financial statements', *Accounting Horizons*, vol. 5, no. 4, pp. 28–43; Glazer, AS & Jaenicke, HR 1991b, 'Accounting for contributions and collection items', *The CPA Journal*, vol. 61, no. 7, pp. 34–40; Jaenicke, HR & Glazer AS 1991, 'Auditing museum collections', *The CPA Journal*, vol. 61, no. 8, pp. 55–7; Jaenicke, HR & Glazer, AS 1992, 'Art and historical treasures: a solution to the museum collection controversy', *The CPA Journal*, vol. 62, no. 3, pp. 46–50.

41. Rowles, TR 1992, *Financial reporting of infrastructure and heritage assets by public sector entities*, discussion paper no.17, Australian Accounting Research Foundation, Caulfield.

42. Boreham, T 1994, 'Valuing heritage assets: is it worth the cost and trouble?', *Business Review Weekly*, vol. 16, no. 44, pp. 116–18; Carnegie, GD & Wolnizer, PW 1995, 'The financial value of cultural, heritage and scientific collections: an accounting fiction', *Australian Accounting Review*, vol. 5, no. 1, pp. 31–47; Carnegie, GD & Wolnizer, PW 1996, 'Enabling accountability in museums', *Accounting, Auditing & Accountability Journal*, vol. 9, no. 5, pp. 84–99; Carnegie, GD & Wolnizer, PW 1997, 'The financial reporting of publicly-owned collections: whither financial (market) values and contingent valuation estimates?', *Australian Accounting Review*, vol. 7, no. 1, pp. 44–50.

43. Carnegie, GD & Wolnizer, PW 1999, 'Unravelling the rhetoric about the financial reporting of public collections as assets: a response to Micallef and Peirson', *Australian Accounting Review*, vol. 9, no. 1, pp. 16–21.

44. Rentschler, R & Potter, B 1996, 'Accountability versus artistic development: the case for non-profit museums and performing arts organizations', *Accounting, Auditing & Accountability Journal*, vol. 9, no. 5, pp. 100–13.

45. Barton, AD 2005, 'The conceptual arguments concerning accounting for public heritage assets: a note',

Accounting, Auditing & Accountability Journal, vol. 18, no. 3, pp. 434–40; Hooper, K, Kearins, K & Green, R 2005, 'Knowing "the price of everything and the value of nothing": accounting for heritage assets', *Accounting, Auditing & Accountability Journal*, vol. 18, no. 3, pp. 410–33.

46. Micallef, F & Peirson, G 1997, 'Financial reporting of cultural, heritage, scientific and community collections', *Australian Accounting Review*, vol. 7, no. 1, pp. 31–7; Hone, P 1997, 'The financial value of cultural, heritage and scientific collections: a public management necessity', *Australian Accounting Review*, vol. 7, no. 1, pp. 38–43.

47. Boreham, T 1994, 'Valuing heritage assets: is it worth the cost and trouble?', *Business Review Weekly*, vol. 16, no. 44, pp. 116–18.

48. Rowles, TR 1992, *Financial reporting of infrastructure and heritage assets by public sector entities*, discussion paper no.17, Australian Accounting Research Foundation, Caulfield; Carnegie, GD & Wolnizer, PW 1995, 'The financial value of cultural, heritage and scientific collections: an accounting fiction', *Australian Accounting Review*, vol. 5, no. 1,

pp. 31–47; Carnegie, GD & Wolnizer, PW 1997, 'The financial reporting of publicly-owned collections: whither financial (market) values and contingent valuation estimates?', *Australian Accounting Review*, vol. 7, no. 1, pp. 44–50.

49. Hone, P 1997, 'The financial value of cultural, heritage and scientific collections: a public management necessity', *Australian Accounting Review*, vol. 7, no. 1, pp. 38–43.

50. Laugesen, R 2002, The sum of us', *Sunday Star-Times*, Wellington, 22 September, p. C.3.

51. Lev, B, Sarath, B & Sougiannis, T 2005, 'R&D reporting biases and their consequences', *Contemporary Accounting Research*, vol. 22, no. 4, pp. 981–1018.

52. ibid.

53. Peterson, J 2010, 'Re-Branding at PricewaterhouseCoopers — OMG, it's like totally awesome!', 16 September, viewed 10 November 2011, www.jamesrpeterson.com.

54. Beattie, V & Thomson, S 2005, 'Intangibles and the OFR', *Financial Management*, vol. 3, June, pp. 29–38.

55. Laugesen, R 2002, The sum of us', *Sunday Star-Times*, Wellington, 22 September, p. C.3.

56. ibid.

57. ibid.

58. Interbrand 2010, 'Interbrand's Methodology Becomes the World's First ISO Certified Approach for Valuing Brands', *Business Wire*, 1 December, viewed 10 November 2011, www.businesswire.com.

59. Holland, J 2006, 'Fund management, intellectual capital, intangibles and private disclosure', *Managerial Finance*, vol. 32, no. 4, pp. 313–14.

60. ABC News 2010, 'Green group wants end to Kakadu uranium mining', *ABC News*, 30 May; Aplin, G 2004, 'Kakadu National Park World Heritage Site: deconstructing the debate, 1997–2003', *Australian Geographical Studies*, vol. 42, no. 2, pp. 153–74; Carson, RT, Wilks, L & Imber, D 1994, 'Valuing the preservation of Australia's Kakadu conservation zone', *Oxford Economic Papers*, vol. 46, supplement, pp. 727–49; Fitzgerald, B 2011, 'Jabiluka still on, says ERA', *The Sydney Morning Herald*, 14 April; Statham, L 2011, 'Kakadu owners want stop to uranium mining', *The Sydney Morning Herald*, 7 April.

LIST OF KEY TERMS

A

accountability: the responsibility to provide information to enable users to make informed judgements about the performance, financial position, financing and investing, and compliance of the reporting entity (pp. 32, 399)

accounting conceptual framework: a coherent system of concepts that underlie financial reporting (p. 26)

accounting decisions: the decisions made by accountants relating to financial statement elements including measurement, estimation, recognition, presentation and disclosure (p. 147)

accounting for carbon emissions: the process of measuring, recording, summarising and reporting carbon emissions (p. 331)

accounting standards: authoritative statements that guide the preparation of financial statements (p. 65)

accounting theory: either a description, explanation or prediction of accounting practice or a set of principles on which to evaluate or guide practice (p. 6)

accrual accounting: recording transactions when revenue is earned or where expenses are incurred, regardless of whether cash has been affected (p. 259)

active market: a market in which transactions for the asset or liability take place with sufficient frequency and volume to provide pricing information on an ongoing basis (pp. 167, 293, 391)

adverse selection: a situation in which sellers have relevant information that buyers lack (or vice versa) about some aspect of product quality (p. 141)

agency relationship: a relationship where one party (the principal) employs another (the agent) to perform some activity on their behalf. In doing so the principal delegates the decision-making authority to the agent (pp. 135, 190)

agency theory: a theory concerning the relationship between a principal and an agent of the principal (p. 135)

asset: a resource controlled by the entity as a result of past events and from which future economic benefits are expected to flow to the entity (pp. 38, 387)

asset bubble: occurs when the price of an asset goes far beyond its underlying value (p. 373)

asset substitution: a problem that arises when an entity invests in assets or projects at a higher risk level than that agreed with lenders, thus transferring value from the entity's debtholders to its shareholders (p. 140)

association: a suggestion of a relationship between two or more sets of numbers when regressed (p. 227)

association study: a research method that looks for correlation between an accounting performance measure and share returns (p. 229)

B

bankruptcy: can refer to a company being insolvent and being wound up in the United States or a natural person becoming insolvent in Australia (p. 365)

big bath accounting: an earning management strategy used in accounting whereby a large losses are written off against income in an accounting period with the intent of demonstrating improved results in future accounting periods (p. 261)

big bath write-off: a situation where large losses are reported against income as a result of a significant restructure of operations (p. 261)

bonding costs: the restrictions placed on an agent's actions deriving from linking the agent's interest to that of the principal (p. 136)

C

capitalisation: the process of recognising an asset on the balance sheet of an entity (p. 386)

carbon disclosure project (CDP): an independent not-for-profit organisation holding the largest database of primary corporate climate change information in the world. Thousands of organisations globally measure and disclose their greenhouse gas emissions and climate change strategies through CDP (p. 327)

carbon emissions: the amounts of carbon dioxide released into the atmosphere by coal-fired power generators, transport, forest burning, slash-and-burn agriculture, etc. (p. 329)

claim dilution: a decline in the probability that a lender will be fully repaid, usually as a result of an entity taking on a higher priority debt (p. 140)

climate change: a significant change in the usual climatic conditions persisting for an extended period, especially those thought to be caused by global warming (p. 326)

comparability: the quality of the information that allows users to identify and understand similarities in, and differences among, items (p. 37)

conceptual framework: a set of broad principles that provide the basis for guiding actions or decisions (p. 25)

conservatism: a preference may exist for a cautious approach to measurement so as to cope with the uncertainty of future events, as opposed to being optimistic and taking risks (p. 347)

contingency theory: the theory that organisations are all affected by a range of factors that differ across organisations. Organisations need to adapt their structure to take into account a range of factors if the organisation is going to perform well (p. 147) contracting theory: a theory that organisations are characterised as a 'legal nexus of contracts', with contracting parties having rights and responsibilities under these contracts (p. 135)

convergence: the process of moving towards the adoption of one set of standards across the globe. This is also referred to as 'standardisation' or 'adoption' (p. 349)

corporate governance: the system by which corporations are directed and controlled. It includes the rights and responsibilities of different participants in the organisation, and the rules and procedures for decision making (p. 188)

corporate social responsibility: a term referring to management's choosing to voluntarily disclose non-compulsory information in annual reports (p. 175)

cost approach: a valuation technique that reflects the amount that would be required currently to replace the service capacity of an asset (p. 290)

current cost: the amount of cash or cash equivalents that would have to be paid if the same or an equivalent asset was acquired currently (p. 94)

D

decision usefulness: financial information about the reporting entity is useful to existing and potential investors, lenders and other creditors in making decisions about providing resources to the entity (pp. 32, 92)

deduction: the process of reaching a conclusion about particular instances from general principles (p. 8)

deprival value: the extent to which the entity is better off because it holds an asset (p. 96)

dividend retention problem: the reduced incentive of managers to pay dividends or take on optimal levels of debt (p. 137)

E

earnings: net income or profit, often called the 'bottom line'. It is a measure of firm performance (p. 257)

earnings management: a manager's use of accounting discretion through accounting policy choices to portray a desired level of earnings in a particular reporting period (pp. 164, 257)

earnings quality: relates to how closely current earnings are aligned with future earnings (p. 262)

eco-efficiency: a focus on the efficient use of resources to minimise their impact on the environment (p. 315)

eco-justice: a focus on intergenerational and intra-generational equity, and considers social justice (p. 315)

efficient market hypothesis: a market in which all share prices reflect fully all the available information, so that investors cannot make excessive returns by exploiting information (p. 231)

emissions trading scheme (ETS): a system used to trade emissions permits which is used to control and reduce greenhouse gas emissions (p. 329)

empirical research: research based on observation or experience (p. 12)

entry price: the price paid to acquire an asset or received to assume a liability in an exchange transaction (p. 303)

environmental accounting: the process of accounting for environmental costs of business (p. 315)

environmental management systems (EMSs): systems that organisations implement to measure, record and manage their environmental performance (p. 328)

equity: the residual interest in the assets of the entity after deducting all its liabilities (p. 38)

ethics: the standards of conduct that indicate how one should behave based on moral duties and virtues (p. 207)

ethical investment: environmentally and socially responsible investment (p. 327)

event study: a research method that examines the changes in level or variability of share prices or trading volume around the time new information is released (p. 229)

excessive dividend payments: the overpayment of dividends which may lead to a reduction in the asset base securing a debt or leave insufficient funds within an entity to service a debt (p. 139)

existing and potential investors: primary users to whom general purpose financial reports are directed according to the *Conceptual Framework* (p. 112)

exit price: the price that would be received to sell an asset or paid to transfer a liability (p. 280)

expenses: decreases in economic benefits during the accounting period in the form of outflows or depletions of assets or incurrences of liabilities that result in decreases in equity, other than those relating to distributions to equity participants (p. 38)

F

fair value: the price that would be received to sell an asset or paid to transfer a liability in an orderly transaction between market participants at the measurement date (pp. 95, 280)

faithful representation: the quality of information when it is complete, neutral and free from error and can be depended upon by users to represent faithfully that which it either purports to represent or could reasonably be expected to represent (p. 36)

falsification: the method of testing theories by attempting to find observations that conflict with the conclusions or predictions of the theory (p. 11)

financial accounting: the regular reporting of the financial position and performance of an entity through financial statements issued to external users (p. 3)

G

general purpose financial reports: the reports intended to meet the needs of users who are not in a position to require an entity to prepare reports tailored to their particular information needs (p. 31) goodwill: an asset representing the future economic benefits arising from other assets acquired in a business combination that are not individually identified and separately recognised (p. 392)

going concern basis: where the financial statements are normally prepared on the assumption that an enterprise will continue in operation (p. 35)

greenhouse gas (GHG): a gas within the earth's atmosphere that absorbs and emits radiation, thus affecting the earth's temperature. The most common GHGs in the earth's atmosphere are water vapour, carbon dioxide, methane, nitrous oxide and ozone. The burning of fossil fuels such as coal since the commencement of the industrial revolution has contributed to the increase in carbon dioxide levels in the atmosphere (p. 325)

H

harmonisation: the reconciliation of different points of view and reducing diversity, while allowing countries to have different sets of accounting standards (p. 78); also the adoption of the content and wording of IASB standards, except where there is a need to change words to accommodate Australia's legislative requirements (p. 349)

heritage assets: assets that have a cultural, environmental, historical, natural, scientific, technological or artistic significance and are held indefinitely for the benefit of present and future generations (p. 394)

heuristics: rules of thumb derived from past experience that are used in decision making (p. 241)

highest and best use: the use of a non-financial asset by market participants that would maximise the value of the asset or the group of assets and liabilities (e.g. a business) within which the asset would be used (p. 285)

historical cost: a measurement basis according to which assets are recorded at the amount of cash or cash equivalents paid or the fair value of the consideration given to acquire them at the time of their acquisition and liabilities are recorded at the amount of proceeds received in exchange for the obligation, or in some circumstances (e.g. income taxes), at the amounts of cash or cash equivalents expected to be paid to satisfy the liability in the normal course of business (p. 93)

horizon problem: the differing time horizons between the owners of an entity who are interested in the long-term growth and value of an entity and managers of an entity who are interested in short-term profitability (p. 136)

hypothesis: a tentative assumption or prediction of a theory (p. 8)

I

income: increases in economic benefits during the accounting period in the form of inflows or improvements of assets or decreases of liabilities that result in increases in equity, other than those relating to contributions from equity participants (p. 38)

income approach: a valuation technique that converts future amounts (e.g. cash flows or income and expenses) to a single current (i.e. discounted) amount (p. 290)

income smoothing: an accounting technique managers use to moderate year-to-year fluctuations in income (p. 260)

individualism: a preference for a loosely knit social framework where individuals take care of themselves and their immediate family (p. 346)

induction: the process of inferring general principles from particular instances (p. 8)

information asymmetry: the impact of managers having an advantage over investors and other interested parties as they have more information about the current and future prospects of the firm, and can choose when and how to disseminate this information (pp. 141, 392)

inputs: the assumptions that market participants would use when pricing an asset or liability, including assumptions about risk, such as the risk inherent in a particular valuation technique used to measure fair value and the risk inherent in the inputs to the valuation technique (p. 292)

insolvency: the inability of an entity to meet financial commitments as they fall due (p. 365)

institutional theory: a theory used to understand the influences on organisational structure and considers how rules, norms and routines become established as authoritative guidelines, and considers how these elements are created, adopted and adapted over time (p. 141)

intangible assets: identifiable non-monetary assets without physical substance (pp. 167, 388)

intellectual capital: an umbrella term encompassing capital created by employees (such as patents), relationships with customers and suppliers (such as brands, trademarks) and capital invested in employees (such as in training or education) (p. 168)

intergenerational equity: a long-term focus that recognises that consumption of resources should not affect the quality of life of future generations (p. 315)

integrated reporting: a proposed framework for accounting for sustainability. The framework is anticipated to bring together financial, environmental, social and governance information in a clear, concise, consistent and comparable format (p. 319)

interim financial reports: reports issued between annual reports (p. 163) intermediaries: financial analysts, auditors, managers and others who examine primary data and send a message about that data to investors (p. 233)

international accounting: encompasses both a description or comparison of accounting in different countries; and the accounting dimensions of international transactions (p. 343)

intragenerational equity: the ability to meet the needs of all current inhabitants (p. 315)

K

Kyoto Protocol: an agreement that commits signatories to achieve greenhouse gas emissions reduction by meeting pre-specified targets (p. 329)

L

legitimacy: the process by which organisations demonstrate they are operating within a value system consistent with society's expectations (p. 143)

legitimacy theory: a positive theory used to understand corporate action and activities, particularly relating to social and environmental issues (p. 142)

lenders and other creditors: a group of stakeholders who receive general purpose financial reports to assist them in making decisions about providing resources to the entity (p. 112).

Level 1 inputs: in relation to measuring fair value refers to quoted prices in active markets for identical assets or liabilities that do not need any adjustment (p. 293)

Level 2 inputs: in relation to measuring fair value refers to inputs other than quoted prices included in Level 1 that are observable for the asset or liability, either directly or indirectly (p. 293)

Level 3 inputs: in relation to measuring fair value are based on unobservable inputs that require estimation and inference by the entity (p. 294)

liability: a present obligation of the entity arising from past events, the settlement of which is expected to result in an outflow from the entity of resources embodying economic benefits (p. 38)

M

managerial branch of stakeholder theory: the aspect of stakeholder theory that relates to the influence stakeholders have on organisational actions (p. 145)

manipulation: the use of management's discretion to make accounting choices or to design transactions to affect the possibilities of wealth transfer between the company and society (political costs), funds providers (cost of capital) or managers (compensation plans) (p. 164)

market approach: a valuation technique that uses prices and other relevant information generated by market transactions involving identical or comparable (i.e. similar) assets, liabilities or a group of assets and liabilities, such as a business (p. 290)

market efficiency: the efficiency with which capital markets handle information (p. 227)

market participants: buyers and sellers in the principal (or most advantageous) market for an asset or liability who are independent of each other, knowledgeable, able and willing to enter into a transaction (p. 283)

materiality: the quality of information if its omission or misstatement could influence the economic decision of users taken on the basis of the financial statements (p. 36)

measurement: the act, process or system of measuring (p. 91)

mixed measurement model: an approach that uses different measurement bases to different degrees and in varying combinations during the preparation of financial statements (p. 98)

monitoring costs: costs incurred by principals to measure, observe and control the agent's behaviour (p. 135)

moral hazard: the risk that an agent might undertake actions that are detrimental to a principal (p. 135)

most advantageous market: the market that maximises the amount that would be received to sell the asset or minimises the amount that would be paid to transfer the liability, after taking into account transaction costs and transport costs (p. 283)

multinational enterprises: operate simultaneously in a number of different countries, and tend to be larger with more complex business operations than domestic entities (p. 355)

N

non-performance risk: the risk that an entity will not fulfil an obligation. Non-performance risk includes, but may not be limited to, the entity's own credit risk (p. 288)

normative branch of stakeholder theory: the aspect of stakeholder theory that relates to the ethical or moral treatment of organisational stakeholders (p. 145)

normative theory: a theory which prescribes what *should* happen (pp. 10, 134)

O

observable inputs: values that can be obtained independently from available market data which would be used by market participants when valuing an asset or liability (p. 292)

orderly transaction: a transaction that assumes exposure to the market for a period before the measurement date to allow for marketing activities that are usual and customary for transactions involving such assets or liabilities; it is not a forced transaction (e.g. a forced liquidation or distress sale) (p. 280)

P

positive accounting theory: a positive theory used to explain and predict accounting practice (p. 134)

positive theory: a theory which describes, explains or predicts what is happening in the world (such as describing, explaining or predicting current accounting practice) (pp. 8, 134)

post-earnings announcement drift: the finding that prices adjust gradually to new information (p. 231)

power distance: the extent to which members of society view power in organisations as distributed unequally (p. 346)

present value: a current estimate of the present discounted value of the future net cash flows in the normal course of business (p. 95)

prices lead earnings: the finding that earnings lag prices because prices contain information about future earnings (p. 230)

principal market: the market with the greatest volume and level of activity for the asset or liability (p. 283)

principles-based standards: standards that contain a substantive accounting principle that focuses on achieving the accounting objective of the standard. The principle is based on the objective of accounting in the conceptual framework (pp. 66, 354)

pro-forma results: financial statements for a period prepared before the end of the period, which therefore contain estimates (p. 165)

prospect theory: the theory that suggests that the pain associated with a given amount of loss is greater than the pleasure associated with an equivalent gain (p. 239)

R

real activities management: a process which occurs when managers make operating decisions that affect earnings (p. 260)

realisable value: the amount of cash or cash equivalents that could currently be obtained by selling an asset in an orderly disposal (p. 95)

recognition: the process of incorporating an item in the financial statements. It involves depiction of the item in words and by a monetary amount and the inclusion of that amount in the financial statement totals (pp. 39, 387)

regulation: the policing, according to a rule, of a subject's choice of activity, by an entity not directly party to or involved in the activity (p. 70)

relevance: the quality of information when it is capable of influencing the decisions of users by helping them evaluate past, present or future events or confirming, or correcting, their past evaluations (p. 35)

replacement cost: the cost the entity would incur to acquire an asset at the end of the reporting period (p. 94)

research: diligent, systematic enquiry into a subject to discover facts or principles (p. 12)

residual loss: the reduction in wealth of principals caused by their agent's non-optimal behaviour (p. 136)

risk aversion: the behaviour of an investor who prefers less risk to more risk, all else being equal (p. 137)

rules-based standards: standards that contain specific details and mandatory definitions that attempt to meet as many potential contingencies and situations as possible (pp. 66, 354)

S

scientific method: the process in which a theory is derived from observations and then makes predictions. Further observations are then made to test these predictions (p. 8)

social contract: the explicit and implicit expectations society has about how entities should act to ensure they survive into the future (pp. 142, 319)

stakeholders: those individuals or groups existing in society that an organisation impacts, and/or that have an influence on an organisation (pp. 145, 326)

stakeholder engagement: the process by which an entity involves people or organisations that may be affected by the decisions it makes or who may influence its decisions (p. 325)

stakeholder theory: a theory that incorporates the interests of a broader range of stakeholders in an entity, not just the shareholders (p. 145)

stewardship: requires that managers provide a report to the providers of resources to explain how well they have managed them (p. 32)

subprime lending: lending to people who may have difficulty making the payment schedule (p. 373)

sustainable development: development that meets the needs of the present without compromising the ability of future generations to meet their own needs (p. 315)

sustainability: the capacity for development that can be sustained into the future without destroying the environment in the process (p. 315)

T

technical default: a company violates a condition of a debt agreement (p. 366)

timeliness: the quality of the information that means having the information available to users in time to be capable of influencing their decisions (p. 37)

transaction costs: the costs to sell an asset or transfer a liability in the principal (or most advantageous) market for the asset or liability that are directly attributable to the disposal of the asset or the transfer of the liability (p. 303)

transfer pricing: the pricing of goods and services that are transferred between members of a corporate family (p. 356)

transport costs: the costs that would be incurred to transport an asset from its current location to its principal (or most advantageous) market (p. 303) triple bottom line reporting (also referred to as sustainability reporting): reporting about the economic, environmental and social performance of an organisation (pp. 317, 318)

U

uncertainty avoidance: the degree to which members of society are comfortable with uncertainty and ambiguity (p. 346)

underinvestment: an agency problem whereby managers have incentives not to undertake positive net present value projects which would lead to increased funds being available to lenders (p. 139)

understandability: the quality of the information that means it is readily understandable by users (p. 37)

unobservable inputs: inputs that are based on information that is not available to the market but must be inferred or estimated based on the best information available (p. 292)

V

value relevance: an item of accounting information that makes a difference to the decisions made by users of financial statements (p. 233)

verifiability: the quality of the information that provides assurance to users that the information is faithfully represented (p. 37)

INDEX